The JLC Guide to
Decks and Porches

Best Practice for Outdoor Spaces

From the Editors of
The Journal of Light Construction

A Journal of Light Construction Book

www.jlconline.com

hanley▲wood

Cover design: Colleen Kuerth
Cover photo: Theresa Coleman

Project Editor: Steven Bliss
Editorial Direction: Sal Alfano, Don Jackson
Managing Editor: Emily Stetson

Graphic Designer: Terence Fallon
Illustrators: Tim Healey, Chuck Lockhart
Production Director: Theresa Emerson

International Standard Book Number:
    ISBN 10: 1-928580-42-4
    ISBN 13: 978-1-928580-42-3
Library of Congress Control Number: 2009943014

Printed in the United States of America

A Journal of Light Construction Book
The Journal of Light Construction is a trade name of Hanley Wood, LLC.

The Journal of Light Construction
186 Allen Brook Lane
Williston, VT 05495

Acknowledgments

We wish to thank the many authors of *The Journal of Light Construction* and *Professional Deck Builder* who contributed to this book. These builders, remodelers, designers, code officials, and engineers are among the best in their fields, and we appreciate their generosity in sharing their hard-won knowledge with others in the field. Special thanks goes to long-time deck safety advocate Frank Woeste, PE, professor emeritus of wood engineering at Virginia Tech University, for his contributions to *JLC* and to this book on deck structural safety. We also wish to thank the Forest Products Society for allowing us to excerpt material from their valuable work on deck safety, *Manual for the Inspection of Residential Wood Decks and Balconies*, and to *Building Safety Journal* for allowing us to reprint building code information.

For their contributions as authors of this book, we wish to thank the following: Everett Abrams, Dustin Albright, Cheryl Anderson, Rob Arnold, David Baud, Brent Benner, Jennifer Benner, James Benney, Bill Bolton, Eric Borden, Joseph Bublick, Thomas Buckborough, Ricky Caudill, Mark Clement, Rob Corbo, Jim Craig, Dave Crosby, Ted Cushman, Christopher DeBlois, Greg DiBernardo, Laurie Elden, Andy Engel, Bill Feist, Paul Fisette, Jamie Fisher, Robert Gerloff, Scott Gibson, Mike Guertin, Cameron Habel, Cheri B. Hainer, Ron Hamilton, Robert Hatch, Katie Hill, Dave Holbrook, Katie Hutchison, Andrew Hutton, Georgie Kajer, Kim Katwijk, Linda Katwijk, Gary Katz, Mark Knaebe, Elaine Laney, John Leeke, Larry Lewis, Joseph Loferski, Paul Mantoni, Glenn Mathewson, Gary Mayk, Harrison McCampbell, Jim McKenna, Tim Meehan, Jay Meunier, Rosanne Minerva, Michael Morse, Paul Nichter, Maureen Nicolazzi, Peter Nicolazzi, Bobby Parks, Terry Platt, Cliff Popejoy, Jim Reicherts, Ron Sansone, Reid Shalvoy, Mike Sloggatt, Angus Smith, Quintin Smith, Scott Smith, Henry Spies, Sheldon Swartzentruber, John Sylvestre, Brian Trimble, Scott Uriu, Robert Viviano, Charles Wardell, Frank Woeste, and Bruce Zaretsky.

Our apologies to anyone we inadvertently left off the list.

Contents

Introduction

Many homeowners will tell you that their favorite space at home isn't actually in the house at all, but rather outdoors on an exterior deck or porch. These versatile spaces are ideal for casual living and entertaining, and in warmer climates they're being used more as prime living space, complete with sophisticated outdoor kitchens and year-round furnishings.

Building spaces for carefree outdoor living, however, presents numerous challenges to the home builder. For example, many customers want to use natural materials that last for years, never age, are easy to clean, and require little or no maintenance. But most wood materials, left to the elements, are prone to splinter, check, and decay, and require regular maintenance. Manufacturers have introduced a host of synthetic and composite materials that promise extreme durability and no- or low-maintenance, but figuring out which materials live up to their promises and how best to install them remains a challenge.

Homeowners also want decks that feel sturdy under foot (and maybe hold a hot tub), with railings strong enough to support a leaning crowd during a party, and which have an overall sense of integrity — all without a lot of heavy-duty hardware showing or bulky structural elements in plain view. On a deck, however, nearly all of the structural work also serves as finish work. And with little lateral bracing and relatively few structural posts, building a rock-solid deck takes some real ingenuity.

The challenge of finding structural details that work got a lot more complicated when manufacturers starting phasing out CCA-treated lumber in 2004, an old standby that had some 60 years of field data to support its durability. Builders must now sort through a wide range of new treatment formulations, each claiming to outperform the other, although often without enough field data to back their claims. Some of the new lumber treatments pose the risk of increased corrosion of metal fasteners and hardware, leading to potential failures of critical connections. Others are too new to have fully established their long-term resistance to insects and decay.

And while structural failures of decks are relatively rare, they are a real and pressing concern and have led to a number of recent code changes. In fact, every year, dozens of residential decks collapse around the country, often causing personal injury. According to Frank Woeste, PE, professor emeritus of wood engineering at Virginia Tech and a long-time advocate of deck safety, "Except for hurricanes and tornadoes, more injuries and deaths may be connected to deck failures than to all other structural failures stemming from typical residential code loads, including seismic and snow loads." (*JLC*, 11/06)

In this volume, Woeste and a number of other building experts share their insights into proven ways to build safe and sturdy structures. You'll learn how to select the right type of treated lumber for the job and how to avoid potential corrosion problems with metal fasteners. On-the-job reports will show you what you can and can't expect from synthetic decking products and how to install them for best performance. And many of the nation's finest professional deck builders, contributors to *The Journal of Light Construction* and *Professional Deck Builder*, share the techniques they've learned on the job site to efficiently build attractive, durable outdoor structures. We hope with this knowledge under your belt, the outdoor living spaces you build will offer carefree living to your customers and a profitable niche for your company.

Steven Bliss
Project Editor

Chapter 1: Design

Connecting Indoor and Outdoor Living Spaces

by Georgie Kajer and Scott Uriu

Thanks to Southern California's mild, dry climate, outdoor living and entertaining have always been popular here. In the past, those sorts of activities often took place on a simple backyard patio. But in recent years, there's been a trend toward more elaborate, better-designed outdoor living spaces.

In part, this may stem from a corresponding trend toward smaller building lots. Homeowners want their houses to "live larger" than they are, and one way to achieve that is to replace underused, undifferentiated yard space with areas that have been specifically designed for sitting, eating, and socializing. Depending on the situation, this can involve anything from tweaking an existing deck or patio by providing shade and improved access to the house to using reinforced concrete to create a multilevel terrace on a steep slope. But the same basic design considerations apply to all outdoor living spaces, no matter how simple or elaborate they may be.

Developing a Master Plan

We find that many of our outdoor living space design projects are spin-offs of an indoor project of some sort. As part of the design process that goes into developing a new kitchen or master suite, we encourage clients to take a step back and consider the bigger picture of easing the connection between

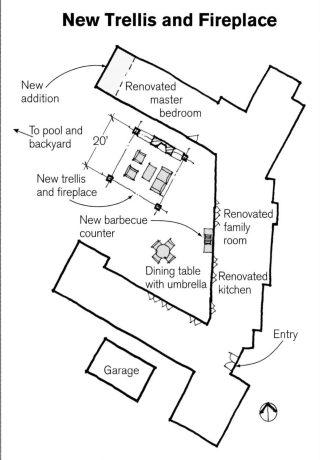

Figure 1. A plan view of the trellis project shows the relationship between the outdoor space and the renovated interior rooms. The small addition at upper left contains an indoor bathroom for the master suite and a smaller outdoor bathroom that's conveniently near the pool and sitting area.

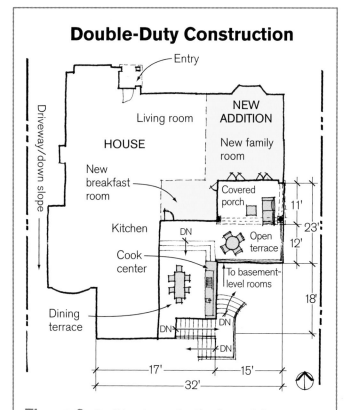

Figure 2. On this steep site, the floor of the upper terrace and porch also serves as the roof of the new basement-level family room/game room below. The floor system consists of I-joists covered with plywood, a waterproof membrane, and brick in thinset cement. The curved lower stairs lead to the family room, while the straight stairs lead to the backyard and driveway.

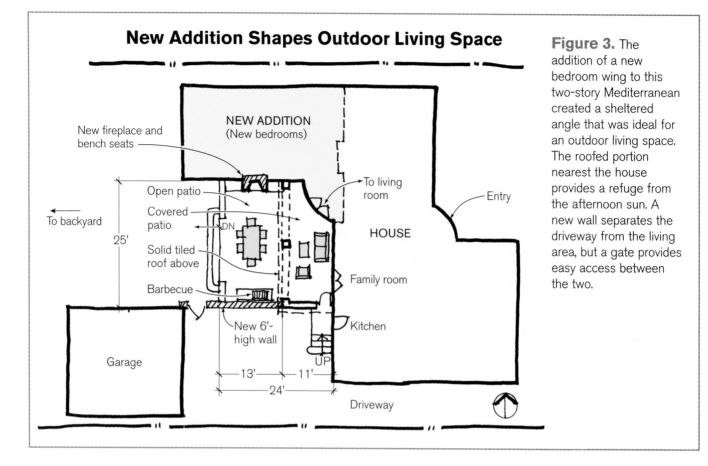

New Addition Shapes Outdoor Living Space

NEW ADDITION
(New bedrooms)

New fireplace and
bench seats

Open patio

Covered
patio

DN

Solid tiled
roof above

Barbecue

To backyard

25'

Garage

New 6'-
high wall

13'   11'

24'

To living
room

Entry

HOUSE

Family room

Kitchen

UP

Driveway

Figure 3. The addition of a new bedroom wing to this two-story Mediterranean created a sheltered angle that was ideal for an outdoor living space. The roofed portion nearest the house provides a refuge from the afternoon sun. A new wall separates the driveway from the living area, but a gate provides easy access between the two.

indoors and out. The response is almost always enthusiastic, even if it hasn't been a specific goal of the work (**Figure 1**).

In many cases, there's no way to stretch the project budget enough to do the outdoor work right away. But that's why this sort of master planning is such a good idea: It allows you to do preliminary work that will save the customer a lot of time and money later on.

For example, even if there's no money to install that set of French doors leading to the future patio, it may make sense to frame the door opening, document its location with a photograph, and run the wall finish over it. The plumbing, gas, and electrical connections to an outdoor barbecue area can be roughed into the outside wall so they'll be there when needed.

Access and Traffic Flow

Usually, the connection between the house and the outdoor living space should take place through a semipublic area. This can be a challenge in a home from the 1920s or '30s, in which the door to the backyard is ordinarily reached through the utility room. Today's homeowners don't want to escort their cocktail party guests past the washer and dryer. More contemporary homes generally have some orientation toward the outdoors to begin with, which

may make it possible to work around an existing patio door from the living or dining room.

If there are children in the house, it's best to avoid routing traffic through a formal living room. Locating the door in the family room is a good compromise. Like a family room, most outdoor living areas are fairly relaxed, informal spaces, so the two flow naturally into one another (**Figure 2**).

A Sense of Enclosure

It's convenient to think of outdoor living spaces as outdoor rooms or series of rooms. And like all rooms, they have walls, ceilings, and floors.

Walls. The exterior wall of the house often forms one wall of an outdoor living space (**Figure 3**). To create a comfortable sense of enclosure, consider adding one or more walls of wood, masonry, or even ornamental plantings. On elevated decks, railing systems may perform this function. In general, wall heights should be kept fairly low to avoid blocking sight lines. From a practical standpoint, outdoor walls can also serve to block the wind, screen traffic noise, and provide shade.

Ceilings. Outdoor living spaces are often left open to the sky, but spaces that face west or south may call for a solid roof, or at least a partial one, for protection from the sun. If the orientation of the space makes a solid roof unnecessary, some sort of trellis roof can help provide a cozy feel (**Figure 4**). A trellis roof and its supports also make it easier to provide overhead lighting.

Floors. Just as indoor flooring doesn't have to be the same throughout a house, patio surfacing can be varied to create the feel of different outdoor "rooms." Stone, brick, and concrete are all popular patio surfaces. We like poured concrete with score lines and a water-wash finish because it's inexpensive (about $7 per square foot in our area) and can be tinted almost any color. Another option is washed gravel, placed over landscape fabric to prevent weeds from taking root. On wooden decks, naturally decay-resistant species, as well as composite materials, work well.

Outdoor Conveniences

All outdoor living spaces have to provide at least one comfortable seating area. If space permits, it's best to distinguish casual conversation areas from dining areas. Dining tables are typically tied to the location of the barbecue and kitchen.

Cooking. Outdoor barbecue areas can be plain or elaborate. With a simple barbecue counter, easy access to the kitchen is important. A barbecue area that includes sink, refrigerator, and other conveniences may become almost a kitchen in its own right and can be farther away. The barbecue should be convenient to use, but avoid making it part of the view from the living room.

Keeping warm. A growing trend here, completely in the spirit of outdoor gathering spaces in this climate, is the outdoor wood- or gas-fired fireplace. The gentle heat it provides makes it possible to linger

Figure 4. A trellis "ceiling" over this outdoor sitting space gives the area around the outdoor fireplace the feel of an open-air room. The trellis was assembled from unpainted steel tubing to eliminate the need for intermediate supports; corner supports are reinforced concrete block faced with stucco.

outside for several hours longer than would otherwise be possible, and it is unmatched as a conversational focal point.

Georgie Kajer, AIA, and Scott Uriu, AIA, are architects in Pasadena, Calif.

A Solid Look for Spindly Posts

by Elaine Laney

In the North Carolina mountains where I have my design practice, there's practically no such thing as a flat building lot. Many sites drop 20 feet or more along the side of the house, and it's not uncommon to find basements with sweeping views of distant mountains.

Those sorts of slopes are a challenge in any number of ways, including one that I see again and again — how to design a good-looking back or side deck in a setting where the support posts are much more prominent than the deck itself. For a deck that will be reached from an upper level, that can be an issue even on a level site.

Perception vs. Reality

Because outdoor decks are subject to very heavy live loads, building codes require them to be solidly built. The problem is that even a deck that's perfectly adequate structurally often looks insecure if it's elevated well above the ground.

Under my local code, for example — in an area unaffected by seismic concerns — unbraced 4x4 posts have a maximum allowable height of 8 feet, while 6x6s can extend for up to 20 feet. In either case, though, the resulting deck will look frail and insubstantial, like a granddaddy longlegs spider.

Adding Braces

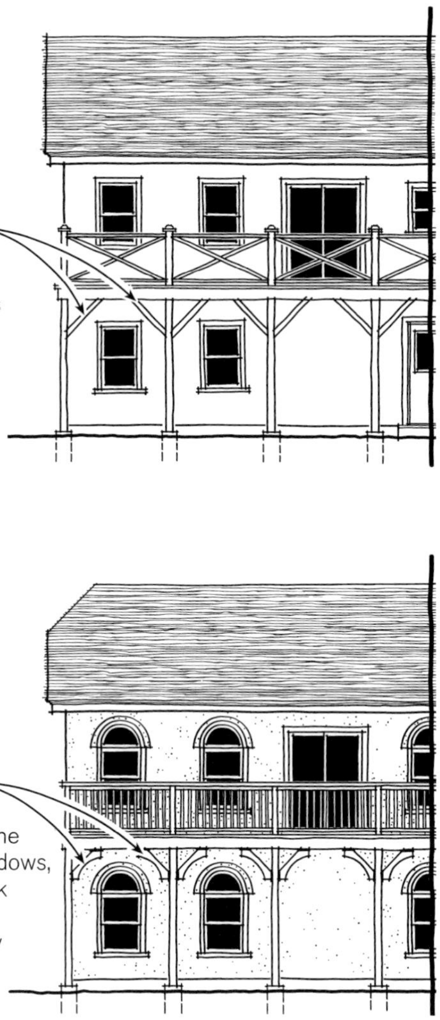

Diagonal bracing visually strengthens deck posts

Curved bracing, repeating the arched windows, makes deck posts look less spindly

Figure 5. Diagonal knee braces, even though structurally unnecessary, give otherwise spindly-looking posts a more substantial look. These can be simple angled braces (top), or repeat a design element found elsewhere on the house (above).

Braces and Bases

Beefing up the posts to a larger size than the code requires will help a little, but there are other ways to firm up the appearance of an elevated deck.

One simple approach is to add diagonal bracing between posts and girders, even though it may be unnecessary structurally (**Figure 5**). Their presence shortens the apparent height of the posts and seems to spread the load, both of which help tie the deck to the site. Bracing alone is usually adequate for posts up to about 8 feet in overall length.

Longer posts will look much better if they stand on substantial-looking raised piers, or are boxed in to look as if they do (**Figure 6**). If a house is sided with

Support Pedestals

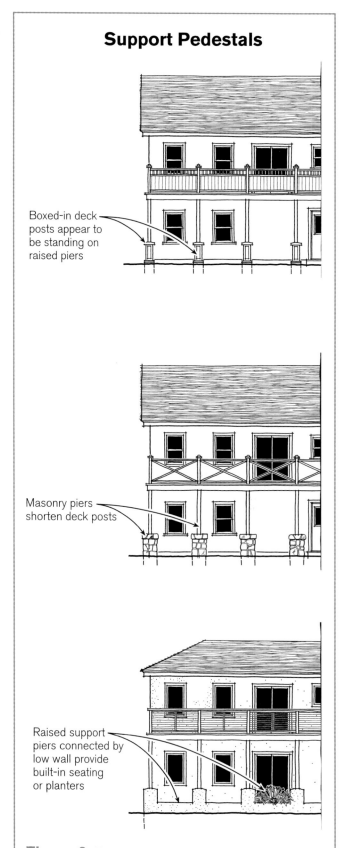

Boxed-in deck posts appear to be standing on raised piers

Masonry piers shorten deck posts

Raised support piers connected by low wall provide built-in seating or planters

Figure 6. Boxing in the lower third of a 6x6 post creates a pedestal effect (top), while masonry support piers permit the use of shorter posts (middle). A low wall with built-in seating strengthens the effect (above).

brick or stone veneer, you might consider mounting the deck posts on masonry piers faced with the same material. In most cases, a fairly utilitarian approach will do just fine — this is a back deck, not an elaborately finished front porch.

United We Stand

Isolated post bases work well, but look even better when linked with a low wall or planter, which need not be more than 18 to 24 inches high. The wall — which can double as a seat at the edge of a lower-level terrace — carries the viewer's eye horizontally and helps counteract the unrelieved vertical lines of the posts themselves. You can further link the paired or grouped posts visually with a railing, some trellis or latticework, or a design detail elsewhere on the house repeated to give continuity to the whole.

Another way to add interest and an appearance of solidity is to group three posts at the corners of a deck with individual intermediate posts as needed (**Figure 7**). That's illogical structurally, since the posts near the center of the span actually carry most of the load. But because the eye is initially drawn to the edges of things to define their shapes, adding support at the corners is more effective visually.

Elaine Laney is a designer in Hendersonville, N.C.

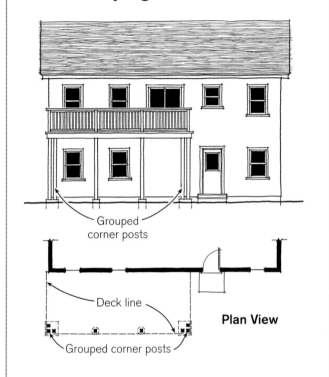

Grouping Corner Posts

Grouped corner posts

Deck line

Plan View

Grouped corner posts

Figure 7. Grouped corner posts have much of the visual mass of solid columns but are more appropriate to the casual nature of a deck.

Creative Guardrails

by Katie Hutchison

An exterior guardrail presents an opportunity to explore a house's design themes in detail. All too often, designers and builders opt for an ill-considered stock railing that technically performs the guardrail function but neglects the spirit of the building it serves. A well-designed guardrail should reflect a home's architectural context.

The following examples provide a range of exterior-railing options for a variety of house types.

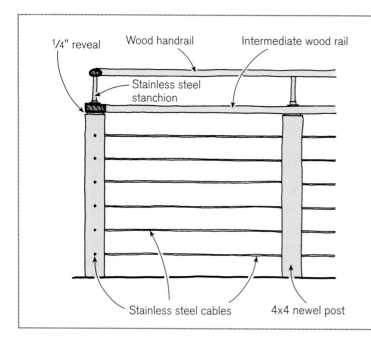

1/4" reveal   Wood handrail   Intermediate wood rail

Stainless steel stanchion

Stainless steel cables   4x4 newel post

Contemporary Cable Rail

This contemporary system uses 1/8-inch stainless steel cables that run through holes drilled into intermediate newel posts (as spans allow). They terminate at surface-mounted fittings with turnbuckles. The continuous top rail – designed to transition into a handrail at the deck stairs – contributes to the assembly's streamlined appearance, which recalls familiar boat railings.

When priorities dictate an unobstructed view, a contemporary design, and a feeling of openness, this largely transparent guardrail is a good choice.

3'-0"

Traditional Turned Balusters

Turned wood balusters are typical of traditional 18th- and 19th-century porches, balconies, and widow's walks. Originally, these railings tended to be stout, measuring about 2 feet tall. Today, however, residential building codes generally require 3-foot-high guardrails, which can result in the elongated turned balusters shown here. Unless the homeowner is doing a period-specific renovation or reproduction, I don't usually recommend this type of guardrail.

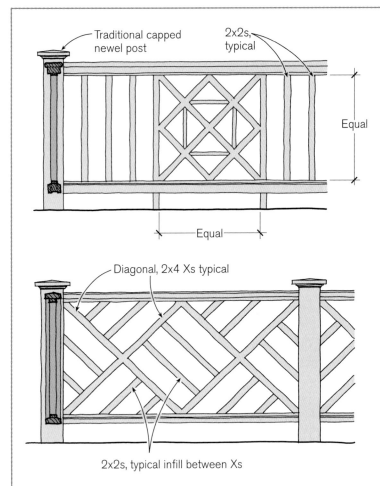

- Traditional capped newel post
- 2x2s, typical
- Equal
- Equal
- Diagonal, 2x4 Xs typical
- 2x2s, typical infill between Xs

Transitional Linear Guardrails

Creating a unique design in the center of a guardrail can subtly enliven a long and otherwise monotonous run of vertical wood 2x2 balusters. The pattern can incorporate the same components used in the rest of the structure.

The railing shown at top left has crisp, clean lines; the heavy top and bottom rails create strong horizontal boundaries for the pattern in between. Its formal feel derives from its symmetry and static geometry. It's a "transitional" design because it bridges the gap between traditional and more contemporary guardrails.

Composed of 2x4s and 2x2s, the second example of a transitional linear rail, shown at left, is more graphic in nature. The 2x4s establish primary diagonal Xs and the 2x2s fill in, completing the pattern.

A busy railing like this is a nice foil to a simple house form. The top and bottom rails are not as heavy as in the previous example, which helps to lighten the overall look. A continuous top rail – rather than one interrupted by newel posts – would make it less traditional.

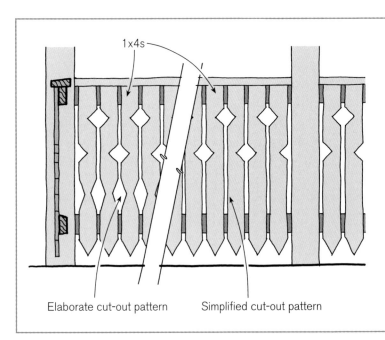

- 1x4s
- Elaborate cut-out pattern
- Simplified cut-out pattern

Carved Plank Rail

Of all the guardrail examples, this playful rendition is the most enclosing. The cutouts alleviate the opacity; the more there are, the lacier the effect, as seen to the left of the break lines in this drawing.

The placement of the top and bottom rails suggests a fence more than it does a guardrail, adding to the structure's informal feel. It also means that each side of the railing looks different.

Such a whimsical design might complement a small cottage or modest camp.

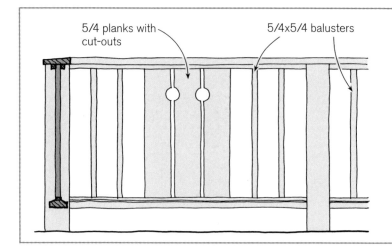

5/4 planks with cut-outs

5/4x5/4 balusters

Eclectic Carved Plank Rail

While still informal, this is a more sophisticated pairing of cut-out planking and linear balusters. Here, the pattern alternates between opacity and transparency. A continuous top rail helps keep the arrangement simple and more contemporary.

Unlike the previous example, this railing looks the same from both sides. It suits a variety of home designs, from older cottages to new custom homes that highlight wood craftsmanship.

Katie Hutchison is an architect and the owner of Earthlight Design in Salem, Mass.

Deck Design Case Studies

Case Study 1:
A Natural Extension of the House

by Rosanne Minerva

Decks are a mainstay of American residential architecture, especially since the introduction of pressure-treated lumber. Unfortunately, decks are often added as an afterthought and many of them end up looking like a tacked-on appendage. Even though the deck is usually behind the house, protected from street view, the design goal should still be to create a natural-looking, integrated extension of the house — essentially an outdoor room (see illustrations, next page).

Location, Location, Location

An appealing setting for a deck is important, whether you choose the location for sun, shade, quiet, privacy, or a lovely view. The deck should also relate to a room (or rooms) where it makes practical sense and will be used — off a kitchen, breakfast area, or family room. Adding a deck off of a bedroom is less practical. For one thing, privacy is an issue, and the deck will get used less frequently and by fewer people.

Size and Shape

The size and shape of the house should help dictate the form of the deck. The scale should be in keeping with the size and massing of the house — a small Cape should not have an enormous deck. On the other hand, a tiny deck will look odd on a large home.

When sizing a deck, consider the purpose of the deck and the furniture that it may be required to accommodate. Will it be used for entertaining and dining? Or is it just a balcony for taking in a view or quiet reading?

A deck should relate and align with elements of the house in both plan and elevation. Study the lines of the house before placing the deck. Make sure the transition lines in the deck (a corner or a change in level) fall where they relate to the lines of the house — corners, chimneys, and so forth.

If designing an upper level deck, consider how it works with the floor below. If posts and steps obscure windows and doors below, or do not relate to patios and planting areas, the design is unsuccessful.

Style

If you choose to echo a strong design shape from the plan of the house (like a curve or a bay) in your deck shape, make sure it makes sense in elevation as well

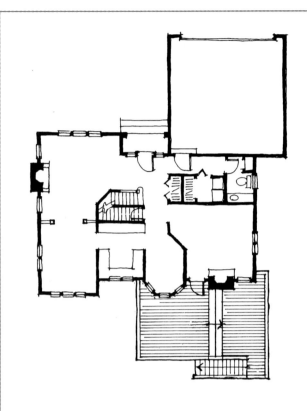

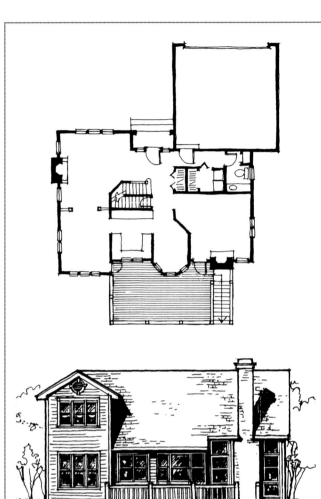

Deck as Afterthought

This deck seems tacked on to the house. Its location on the house seems arbitrary, and its level changes serve no real purpose. The posts and railings don't relate well to doors and windows or even to one another.

Design flaws
• Deck does not relate well to house
• Horizontal 1x6 rails look clumsy
• Posts too spindly for height of deck
• Steps obscure views from beneath

Integrated Deck

This simple deck feels anchored to the house and site in plan and elevation as it tucks neatly between two corners (offsets at the chimney and dining room). The size and symmetrical location balance the house design and make the deck easily accessible from both the family room and dining room. Note how the posts relate to doors and windows above and below: While not perfectly centered between openings, the post locations make design sense by not landing arbitrarily in the middle of an opening.

Design improvements
• Railing detail complements house
• Posts trimmed to look heftier
• Stairs relate visually to chimney, don't block views below
• Addition of planters creates shady patio below, in contrast to sunny deck above

as in plan. Often, keeping the lines of the deck square and simple is a better choice, and can help unify more complex forms on the existing house.

If the house is formal and symmetrical, then the deck should fit into that scheme.

Choose an appropriate deck style, taking design cues for railings, posts, and finishes from the rest of the house — perhaps from a porch or entry. Locate deck posts and railing segments to create "local symmetry" with doors and windows. For example, centering the deck's rail posts between door and window openings will help make the deck look like an integral part of the house.

Rosanne Minerva is an architectural illustrator and designer in Boston.

Case Study 2: Connecting to the Landscape

by Jamie Fisher

While a deck affords some of homeownership's simple pleasures, designing a deck is not always a simple matter. This is no wonder, for while you are creating a new living space, you are also trying to join house to landscape without compromising either one.

This deck I designed illustrates some of the issues and considerations that typically come into play. The house, a nondescript one-story with a midlevel entry and a full daylight basement, sits on a large, steep, heavily wooded, south-facing rural lot overlooking

Proposed Deck

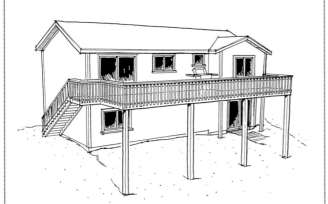

Figure 8. The original deck design for this house overlooking Puget Sound not only failed to connect the house to the surrounding landscape, but it also obscured views from the house and blocked light from the walkout basement.

Puget Sound. The owner, wanting a large deck to take advantage of this dramatic setting, came to me with a design calling for a single large platform (**Figure 8**). The proposed deck ran the entire length of the house to allow access from both the dining room and the master bedroom. To keep the square footage reasonable, the depth would be about 12 feet. A stair at the west end led to grade.

While straightforward and relatively economical to build, this design presented several serious problems. First, while a long, narrow deck works okay on a cruise ship, it's pretty worthless on a house, for by the time you accommodate tables, chairs, umbrellas, the hot tub, the barbecue, and other typical deck items, there isn't much room for people to move around.

Second, the sloping terrain of this lot put the deck's front edge about 14 feet off the ground. This would have created a very unbecoming appearance from below, blocked light from reaching the basement windows, and made the deck itself feel dislocated from the landscape.

Third, running the deck in front of the master bedroom would have meant that anybody could walk up to the bedroom door and stare in. This possibility would make the room feel less private, probably necessitating drapes or blinds.

Finally, and most serious, this deck would have spoiled the view it was designed to enjoy. Think of standing at the kitchen sink or lying in bed in the master bedroom. Without the deck, you can look out the window at the Pacific Northwest forest in the foreground with the water beyond. Once the deck is built, however, the foreground is dominated by the deck and its attendant clutter, and even the more distant view of the Sound must be glimpsed over and through the guardrail. Why locate a deck where it diminishes a view in the process of capturing it?

A Step-Down Does the Job

Now consider the revised deck shown in **Figure 9**, next page. Here, only a small 10x10 landing remains at the main-floor level, just outside the dining room door, where it provides room for a small table and a couple of chairs. The main deck is down seven risers, at a level between the main floor and the daylight basement. The master bedroom accesses the deck from its own small stair and landing.

This scheme offers several important advantages. It retains a convenient outdoor eating area adjacent to and level with the kitchen. But lowering the main deck 4$^1/_2$ feet not only allows the main deck a more squarish design, making it more flexible in supporting all manner of social interaction, it also opens the view from the kitchen window. And putting the deck itself closer to the ground reinforces its connection to the landscape, making it a more inviting place to hang out. Holding the deck back from the east end of the house preserves the master bedroom's unobstructed view, as well as its privacy. A secondary but significant benefit is that the basement workshop windows again receive light.

In short, this redesign better meets the deck's original purpose — tying the house to the outdoors and providing a way to enjoy the landscape — without compromising the views from the house. It will also look much better — far less monolithic and obtrusive — from outside.

Think Landscape

This example illustrates well the importance of thinking of a deck as landscaping. I think of the deck as an extension of the ground plane rather than as simply another room or as a platform for viewing nature.

I try to keep a deck as low as possible, preferably within 30 inches of the adjacent grade — the height above which a code-complying guardrail will be required. Below that height you can do what you want for edge protection, including planters, benches, or nothing at all, which is a much more interesting range of options than a 36-inch-tall, 4-inch-spaced balustrade.

Deck Aesthetics

Decks are about structure. They are honest, straightforward expressions of simple construction. Houses, on the other hand, put on airs and make claims to style. Successful designs accept this distinction, while those that try to bridge the inherent differences risk diminishing both the house and the deck.

Decks, being casual, belong in the backyard. If your view and solar orientation suggest a deck in your front yard, resist the temptation. Build a porch, a patio, a terrace, or even a veranda, but build a deck only if you have a rustic cabin or if you can keep the deck well away from the main entrance.

Jamie Fisher is an architect in Seattle, Wash.

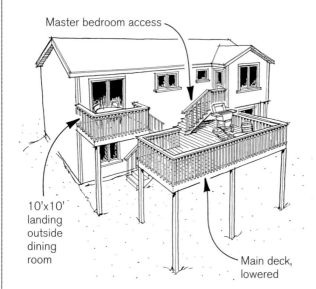

Redesigned Deck

Master bedroom access

10'x10' landing outside dining room

Main deck, lowered

Figure 9. The redesigned deck retains the most essential feature of the original — convenient access to an outdoor eating area — while connecting the main part of the deck more closely to the landscape below. Dropping the deck's center portion also opens views from the house, preserves the master bedroom's privacy, and allows some sunlight into the basement.

Front Porches That Work

by Robert Gerloff

I'm tapping out these words on my laptop while sitting on my front porch and watching the world go by. I love our front porch; time spent hanging out here is a mini-vacation from the stresses and worries of life — not to mention a welcome break from the damn telephone.

But not all front porches work as well as they could. I'm lucky to live in an older neighborhood full of wonderful front porches, but many new houses have porches that seem to have been built purely for their marketing value. As long as the real estate agent or sales department can point out that the house has a porch, the reasoning seems to go, it doesn't much

matter whether the porch is a living, functioning part of the house or just a useless ornament (**Figure 10**). Here are some important points to keep in mind when building or remodeling a front porch.

Depth and Height

A good front porch should be at least 8 feet deep. A porch much narrower than that can't support a decent "sitting circle" — the loose ring of chairs that allows friends and family to face each other while talking. Conversely, a porch more than 12 feet deep or so is too spacious to provide the sense of intimacy that a porch should and places the windows too far into the shade.

Figure 10. A well-thought-out porch is designed with occupant convenience and comfort in mind (left). The tacked-on, poorly dimensioned version, at right, on the other hand, is less a true porch than an oversized covered entryway.

Ideally, the porch floor should be between 24 inches and 36 inches above grade. The lower end of this range places the eye level of someone sitting on the porch higher than the eye level of someone walking by on the sidewalk, putting the sitter in a position of strength and safety (**Figure 11**). This gives someone sitting on the porch the power to decide whether to greet or ignore someone passing by on the sidewalk. To be lower than someone walking by on the sidewalk is to feel exposed, vulnerable, and unsafe. On the other hand, a porch that's too high provides too much separation between those on the porch and those passing below and makes desired conversation awkward.

A good front porch should be on the same level as the main floor of the house (**Figure 12**). A step from porch to front door that is higher than the 1½ inches or so necessary for the storm door to clear a welcome mat will isolate the front porch from the rest of the house. The more the front porch feels like an extension of the main house, the more likely it is to be used.

Steps and Railings

Steep, narrow steps isolate the front porch from the outdoors. Wide, shallow ones — say from a minimum of 6 feet wide to the width of the entire house, with risers no higher than 6 inches — invite the outdoors in. Wide, shallow steps are also a great place to set potted plants, take family photos, and relax from mowing the lawn when you don't feel like stepping all the way up to the porch itself.

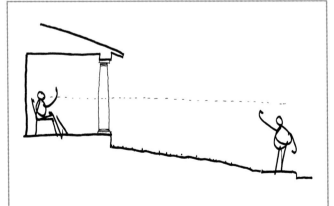

Figure 11. Placing a porch floor between 24 and 36 inches above grade raises the eye level of someone sitting on the porch above that of people passing by. That allows for some conversation between porch and sidewalk but puts the sitter in a comfortable, secure position.

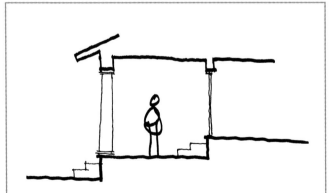

Figure 12. A porch that's isolated from the house will get less use than it otherwise might. Plan the grade so there's no need for more than one very low step — ideally, no more than an inch or two — between the porch floor and the indoor living space.

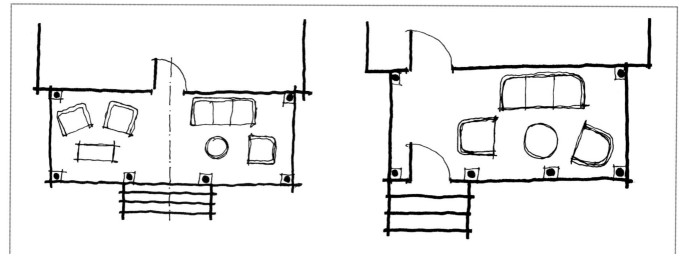

Figure 13. Stairs that are centered on the main entrance tend to split the porch in half, making it seem smaller and making conversation awkward for more than a very small group (left). Moving the stairs to the side makes the space much more comfortable and inviting (right).

The position of the steps is another important consideration. If possible, a porch should be entered at its edge, not near the middle. Centered front steps look wonderful from the street and play to many designers' love of symmetry, but they invariably cut the sitting area into two disconnected sections (**Figure 13**). Steps near an edge, on the other hand, allow for a big, welcoming sitting circle in the center of the porch.

Enclosing a porch with a light, airy railing, rather than a solid parapet, offers a better view of the outside world, especially if the railing is low enough to see over easily (**Figure 14**). But things can get tricky when the local code requires a guardrail: The stan-

dard 36-inch guardrail will obstruct the view of someone lounging in a wicker chair, and standard 2x2 balusters at 4 inches on-center are difficult to see through. (The International Residential Code requires a code guardrail only when the porch is 30 inches or more above grade.)

One possible solution is to push the guardrail down to 30 inches and run a continuous handrail at the required 36-inch level. Another is to use inconspicuous cable rails, if stylistically appropriate. If no guardrail is required, consider building a flat-surfaced railing at a height of 24 inches — just the right level to sit on or set down a glass of iced tea.

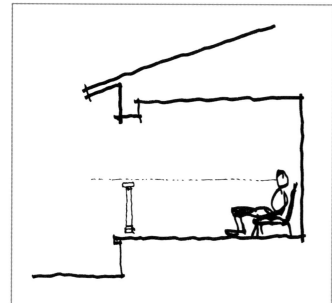

Figure 14. A standard 36-inch guardrail, required by code under some conditions, will obstruct the sight line of someone sitting on the porch, making it difficult or impossible to see what's happening at ground level.

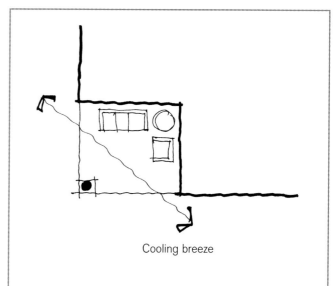

Cooling breeze

Figure 15. A built-in porch with only two exposed sides feels more like a room than a true porch. Because seating tends to be concentrated against the house walls, those sitting there miss out on the cooling effect of the evening breeze.

Orientation and Exposure

A front porch should be oriented to the street and human activity. Most Americans are inherently social creatures. We love to know what the neighbors are up to, who's walking by on the sidewalk, who's dating the younger Olson girl. Unlike private indoor living areas, a good front porch should be seen as a semi-public room that allows for some give and take with the outside world. It can't fulfill that purpose unless it's open and visible.

To retain the feel of an open outdoor room, a porch should be exposed on three sides. A two-sided porch that's tucked into a corner of the house seldom works well. It feels enclosed, making it too much like the inside of the house. And from a purely practical standpoint, it doesn't enjoy the total airflow of a porch that's open on three sides (**Figure 15**). For the same reason, porches should be open to the elements or, at most, screened to keep out mosquitoes.

In theory, a storm-window-enclosed "three-season porch" can be used earlier in spring and later into autumn, but the reality is that adding any glass — no matter how much or how wide the windows open — is the kiss of death. The wonderful feeling of sitting outside is lost, and in the summer, when the porch should be most heavily used, the glass traps heat and makes it unbearably hot. The sad reality is that most three-season porches just get used for storage.

Robert Gerloff is an architect in Minneapolis, Minn.

Enclosing a Front Porch
by Katie Hutchison

It used to be that on warm afternoons folks would sit out on the front porch to catch some air and chat with passersby strolling down the sidewalk. Nowadays, more and more of those porches face busy streets crammed with vehicles rather than pedestrians. Such porches may be prime candidates for enclosing, to create spaces where the sun can be enjoyed three seasons of the year without bothersome street noise, weather, or insects.

Here, we'll review several approaches to enclosing a porch on a small bungalow. The more successful designs balance the context of the main house with an enclosure that recalls the open porch that preceded it.

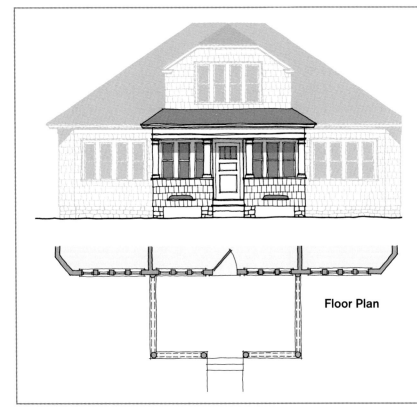

Floor Plan

Original Porch

This New England bungalow displays the style's trademark open front porch, composed of a shingle half wall on fieldstone piers with stout, square posts supporting the roof. The hipped roof and closed eaves are somewhat unusual for a bungalow and suggest the influence of the Prairie style. Because the open porch is rarely used, enclosing it to create a three-season room will add valuable space and daylight to the interior.

Enclosure With Double-Hungs

To enclose the porch, windows and trim are added above the half wall and in between the posts, while the existing exterior door is moved forward to give access to the new enclosure. Reusing the door helps maintain the building's street-front character. An interior French door with narrow lights is an ideal replacement for the now-relocated exterior door. It's wise to recess the front door and trim from the front of the posts to allow more of the post depth to be visible from the front, as in this example.

The shingled half wall that provided privacy to the open porch serves the same function in the enclosed porch. The windows let in plenty of daylight while keeping out wind and rain.

In this treatment, mulled double-hung windows with proportions similar to those of existing windows flank the door; four double-hungs of a slightly wider dimension fill in between the posts on the sides of the porch. The head and sill heights of the porch windows differ slightly from those of the house windows due to the existing porch frieze and rail heights.

Though this window choice seems logical, it creates a somewhat monotonous repetition of narrow double-hung windows, and it doesn't acknowledge that the porch is an intrinsically different type of space than the rest of the house and should be treated accordingly.

Enclosure With Casements

Here, two casement windows that are approximately one and a half times the width of the existing narrow double-hung windows flank the door, while three casements of the same size as those on the front are used on the porch sides.

The choice of wider casement windows helps define the enclosed porch as an entity distinct from the rest of the house. The muntins further differentiate the space. The narrow window lights recall the narrow proportions of the existing windows — without literally reproducing those units.

Having fewer windows allows for a more open, porchlike feel. Since casement windows operate by swinging clear of the wall plane, they are typically less enclosing than double-hung windows, which operate within the plane of the wall. This scheme communicates that the enclosure was once an open porch and thus more clearly conveys the building's evolution. Such an approach respects the original building while celebrating the new adaptation.

What If the Original Porch Had Full-Height Columns?

For the sake of discussion, suppose that instead of the more traditional half wall, the porch had full-height columns linked with a simple square-stock balustrade. If full-height columns were used here, they would most likely be square and tapered, though it's possible they'd be round. Enclosing this type of porch — rather than the typical bungalow half-wall open porch — poses a different set of challenges. Assuming we don't wish to preserve the balustrade, we will have more flexibility in selecting a sill height for the infill windows.

Double-Hung Windows and Panels

In this example, the porch windowsills align with the existing windowsills to increase the overall porch window height and better relate to the main house. As in an earlier example, multiple narrow double-hung windows are mulled together to infill between the columns and scribed trim.

Yet despite the lower sills, this window configuration is no more successful than the similar configuration was in the half-wall porch example. The MDO panels below the sills, which relate to the window sash sizes, are also fairly unsuccessful. For one thing, their formal appearance is out of keeping with a bungalow's characteristically unadorned informality. Further, the paneling's horizontal orientation conflicts with the vertical orientation of the existing and new windows.

Though not a glaringly bad solution, this approach leaves plenty of room for improvement.

Casements Work Better

In this case, too, the porch windowsills align with the existing sills. The casement windows are the same width as those in the earlier casement example. The row of narrow lights across the top of the sashes recalls the narrow proportions of the existing double-hung windows while allowing for more unobstructed glazing below. This type of light division is not uncommon on Craftsman-style houses. Vertical V-groove trim below the sills is appropriately informal and properly oriented.

This overall treatment is pleasantly porchlike and well-suited to its three-season function, and it captures the spirit of the main building.

Vertically Mulled Windows, Low Sills

Here, to maximize daylight, the sills have been dropped to 9 inches above the porch floor; this distance provides a measure of kick protection, though the glazing will still have to be tempered. In addition, the entrance door has been changed to a glazed door with narrow top lights that echo the muntin pattern in the original door.

The front elevation incorporates one large picture window with three narrow casements above on each side of the entrance; the sides contain two picture units mulled together with a band of four casements above. The casements provide visual differentiation as well as ventilation. Their narrow proportions reflect those of the existing double-hung windows, but the horizontal and vertical dividing mullions seem too heavy and distracting, especially if the goal of this scheme is to create a more open enclosure.

Full-Height Windows

In this solution, the large picture window is topped with a row of narrow lights. For cross ventilation, the side elevations have two mulled double-hung windows that match the height of the front units, including upper-sash lights of the same proportion as the picture-unit lights.

While the use of fewer, larger windows helps to achieve a more open feel, all of this glazing increases the porch's potential solar heat gain. It also makes the space much less private than the examples with the half wall. Certainly for a porch facing the street, this window arrangement could result in a fishbowl effect; for a porch overlooking a private yard, an exquisite water view, or a welcoming landscape, however, it could work well.

Katie Hutchison is an architect and the owner of Earthlight Design in Salem, Mass.

Posts, Columns, and Piers That Fit the Porch

by Katie Hutchison

There's no question that a porch looks and feels best when all of its components relate to the rest of the house's design. Here, we'll talk about ways that porch columns, posts, and piers can complement a home. Proportion and scale in particular are important when choosing vertical supports.

Full- and Partial-Height Columns

The terms "column" and "post" are often used interchangeably, but it helps to differentiate between the two. For the sake of this piece, we'll define a column as a vertical support, usually circular (but occasionally square) in plan, inspired by classical architecture, with a base, shaft, and capital. And we'll define a post as a timberlike vertical support that is generally square or rectangular in plan.

Column examples **A**, **B**, and **C** are roughly based on the Doric classical order. They are more formal and traditional than post examples **D**, **E**, and **F** (see next page).

Column **A** is fairly massive and supports an appropriately massive entablature. A column of this scale and detail is most appropriate on a large-scale, authentic classical reproduction; it would likely look overinflated and silly on most anything else.

As is typical of classical columns, the bottom third of the shaft extends straight up from the base diameter and the upper two-thirds of the shaft tapers, with a convex profile. This tapering is called entasis.

Column **B** is a square-plan version of Column **A**. It's a tad less formal but equally robust.

Column **C** is of a more moderate scale. Sitting the 9-inch-diameter column atop a pedestal allows it to occupy the same overall height as full-height columns **A** and **B** without the girth. The entablature at **C** is scaled down to accommodate the smaller column.

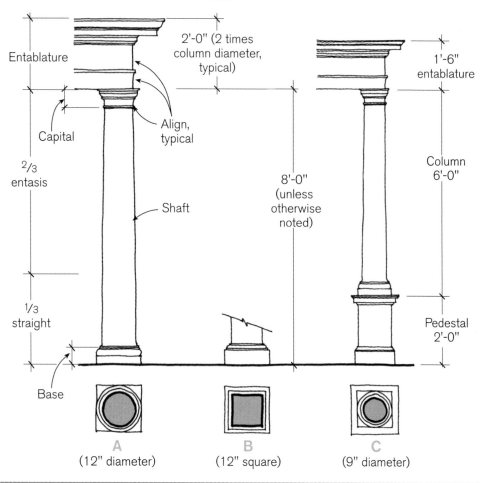

Entablature

2'-0" (2 times column diameter, typical)

1'-6" entablature

Capital

Align, typical

²/₃ entasis

Column 6'-0"

Shaft

8'-0" (unless otherwise noted)

¹/₃ straight

Base

Pedestal 2'-0"

A (12" diameter)   B (12" square)   C (9" diameter)

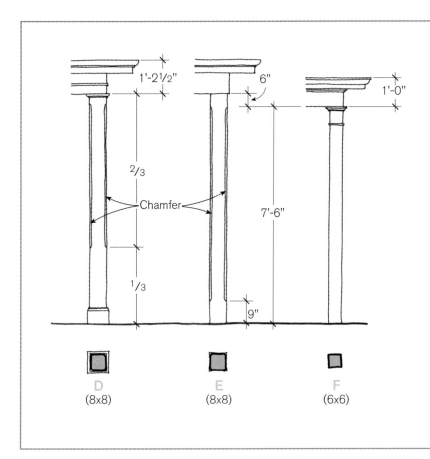

D
(8x8)

E
(8x8)

F
(6x6)

Full-Height Posts

Posts **D**, **E**, and **F** suit a wide variety of more eclectic homes.

Posts **D** and **E** are somewhat chunky and recall Arts and Crafts detailing. Post **D** is the dressier of the two; it's trimmed with modest base and crown moldings that are pared-down reminders of classical elements. It also features chamfered corners located to recall the division of classical columns into one-third and two-thirds portions.

Post **E** discards the base and trim moldings and instead uses the start and stop points of the chamfer to suggest a base and cap. The entablatures on both **D** and **E** have been downsized in proportion to the post dimensions, and simplified in relation to the post types.

Post **F** is the slenderest and thus has been made shorter. If it were any taller, the 6x6 might appear overly skinny. Its entablature is scaled back accordingly. Simple crown and necking trim highlight the cap with minimal fanfare.

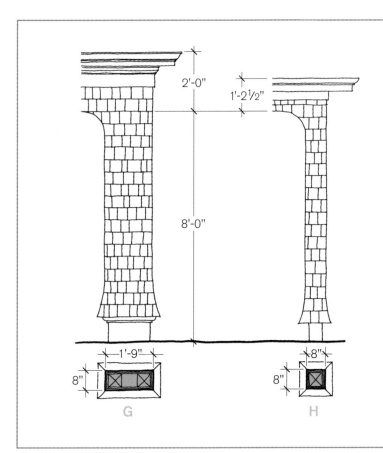

G

H

Piers

A pier differs from a column or a post in that it is usually more substantial and wall-like. Example **G** is a shingled pier featuring a flared shingle base with a bed molding. This pier supports a horizontal band of two full shingle courses, frieze trim, and a cornice, which together equal a quarter of the pier height. Pier **G** is comfortably proportioned for a generous porch or veranda.

Example **H**, however, is an unconvincing pier. Its slender dimension is more postlike. The narrow horizontal band of two partial shingle courses, frieze trim, and cornice is undersized. In general, **H** is too anemic for a pier.

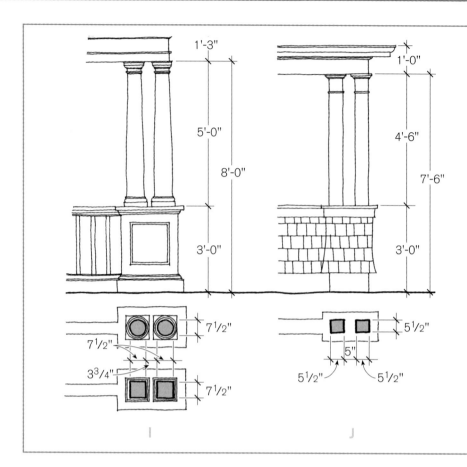

I

J

Paired Partial-Height Columns and Posts

On a porch that includes a typical 3-foot-tall guardrail, pairing posts atop a 3-foot pedestal creates a lighter look than a hefty full-height pier or massive full-height column would. The paired traditional columns in example **I** sit on a fittingly formal paneled pedestal.

The more informal smaller-scale posts in example **J** are better suited to the simple shingled guardrail and shingled pier-style pedestal. The porch with the **J** posts is decidedly more casual than the one with the **I** columns.

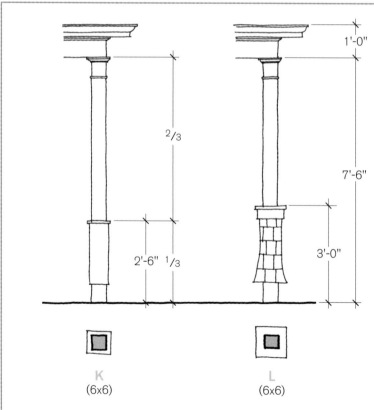

K
(6x6)

L
(6x6)

Modest Partial-Height Posts

If the slender full-height post **F** is too thin for your taste, it may make sense to trim out the lower third, as seen in example **K**. This simple treatment dresses up the post slightly while evoking the one-third-point dimensional shift of a classical column.

Example **L**, on the other hand, just doesn't work. The shingled lower section isn't chunky enough to pull off a pier-style shingle pedestal treatment. Also, the 3-foot height of the shingled section feels too tall for a single post with this overall support height; the post appears to be clad in a gawky tube sock.

For a partial shingle treatment to work, it needs to be scaled more like the shingled, pier-style pedestal in example **J**.

Katie Hutchison is an architect and the owner of Earthlight Design in Salem, Mass.

Front Porch Transforms Home

by John Sylvestre

One of the rewards of being a design/builder is making a house that is otherwise plain or unattractive into something lively, something that reflects the personalities of its owners. When my company designed and built a new front porch on a 1920s Craftsman-style home in St. Paul, Minn., the transformation was so dramatic that, looking at the before and after pictures, it's hard to believe it's the same house (**Figure 16**).

Unlike typical houses of that era, which have many fine exterior trim details, this house was nondescript. The existing porch was dark and unappealing. Instead of opening the house up to the outdoors, the porch prevented light from entering the rest of the house. It was a claustrophobic space that you wanted to pass through quickly, despite the beautiful views of a nearby lake. It was also in bad shape, with a leaky roof, rotten floor, and deteriorated substructure.

Our job was to come up with a porch design that suited the style of the house and gave it some character. With an ample budget, we set out to build a porch with durable, natural materials that would require minimal maintenance from the homeowners. We also wanted to create an open porch space that provided room for seating while letting plenty of light into the house.

Letting in Light

A front porch will make the front rooms darker unless it is thoughtfully designed. Raising the roof usually allows light into adjoining rooms but, in this case, it would have blocked the two front bedroom windows. Instead we added a steep gable at the center of the porch. The gable gives the porch a feeling of spaciousness and adds character to the house.

The gable takes off at a 45-degree angle from the lower roof, which is pitched at 5:12. The ceiling is 8 feet high on either side of the gable and 11 feet high at its peak. The gable also juts forward approximately 12 inches to cover a bow at the center of the porch. This bow softens the front edge of the porch and provides a little extra space for planters and furniture.

Figure 16. A well-designed front porch should complement the house and not darken the front rooms. The original porch (left) on this house was drab and dark. The steep-pitched center gable on the new porch (right) gives a feeling of spaciousness and lets light into the front rooms. The decorative cross brace also serves as a collar tie.

Figure 17. The author's crew built scrap-plywood boxes to protect expensive redwood structural elements during construction.

Decorative Details

In keeping with the spirit of the Craftsman style, we tried to make the structure of the porch an aesthetic element. Instead of using a few pressure-treated 4x4s as columns, and then going back and wrapping them with a finish wood, we used groups of 4x4 redwood posts. Designing the porch this way made it more difficult to build since there was no chance of roughing in the structure and then later covering any mistakes with finish trim.

We used redwood for all of the porch's exposed structural members. (Because of the style of the porch, this was almost all of them.) In Minnesota we go through wide temperature changes, so we knew we couldn't afford the cracks and checks that form as pressure-treated wood dries and shrinks. Clear redwood is not only stable and naturally rot-resistant, it provides a good surface for paint.

Redwood is also about five times more expensive than pressure-treated lumber, which forced us to be very careful with the material. During construction, we temporarily boxed in all the framing members with plywood so they wouldn't be nicked and dented (**Figure 17**). This created an extra step in the construction process but, as most of us know, it's easy to walk around a corner with a 2x4 over your shoulder and accidentally catch an edge on a pristine piece of redwood.

While all of the finish details are simple, we got creative with the cross brace at the gable's peak. The

detail, which is mirrored at the back of the gable where the roof meets the stucco siding, is a take-off on the trim piece at the front peak of the house. The brace is functional in that it serves as a tension member, but it was also a good opportunity for our lead carpenter to show off his woodworking skills.

The brick piers are a nice contrast in color and texture to the wood framing. They also match the new chimney (the owners had recently added a fireplace) and the retaining wall that wraps around one side of the house. Making brick piers look finished on top is a design quandary. You can make a brick cap, but it looks clumsy with all those joints. It's also not as weathertight as other materials, and the end bricks have a tendency to loosen and tumble off. Wood caps work all right as long as they are well protected from the weather.

For this porch, we had caps made from a native Minnesota limestone. The stone is maintenance-free and will probably outlast the other porch materials. We faxed our sketches to the quarry owner, who designed caps that overhang the brick on all sides by 1 inch. There is a slight taper (to provide drainage) up to a flat 12-by-12-inch surface at the top.

To attach the columns, we first used a hammer drill with a masonry bit to drill 1/2-inch-wide holes in the stone. We inserted 5-inch lag bolts and epoxied these in place, and then drilled pilot holes in the columns and screwed them onto the lag bolts. The pins prevent any lateral movement and the weight of the roof holds the columns down. We also inserted 1/8-inch metal spacers and caulked between the columns and the stone. This provides a sealant and keeps the posts from direct contact with the stone, thus inhibiting rot.

Latticework

Once the old porch was demolished, we made sure the ground beneath sloped away from the house wall so water wouldn't collect. We later went back and installed a layer of plastic sheeting. In some cases, you can cover this with 2 inches of gravel and place perforated PVC pipe 2 feet from the porch perimeter to lead water away from the porch. We also advise the homeowners to keep plantings a foot or two away.

The porch apron is a standard cedar lattice. This is not the most creative apron material, but it allows for plenty of airflow beneath the porch. It also does a good job of keeping the raccoons out. If the homeowners are worried about smaller critters getting in, you can put some screen behind it.

To keep the lattice securely in place, and to keep it from looking flimsy, we stiffened it at the top and bottom with 5/4-by-3-inch redwood. Since the area we covered was fairly large, we stabilized the lattice by securing the bottom framework to the ground with 2x2 pressure-treated stakes (**Figure 18**, next page). Because the porch apron is often in direct con-

Lattice Framework

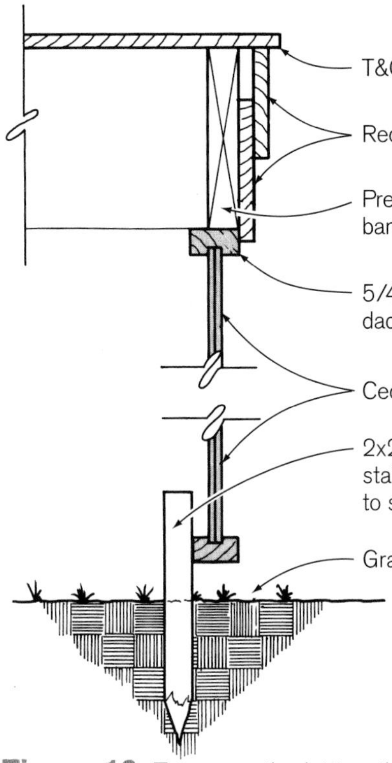

T&G decking

Redwood fascia

Pressure-treated band joist

5/4x3" redwood frame, dadoed to accept lattice

Cedar lattice

2x2 pressure-treated stakes, 4' on-center, to stabilize lattice frame

Grade

Figure 18. To secure the lattice, the author constructed a dadoed frame of 5/4-by-3-inch redwood. The top of the frame is secured to the porch band joist. The bottom frame stops about 2 inches above grade and is nailed to 2x2 pressure-treated stakes spaced 4 feet apart.

tact with the ground, it should be dipped in a wood preservative and covered with at least two coats of paint. It should also be nailed in place since staples tend to rust.

Painting

During the design process, the homeowners asked us to "do something" about the drab, beige stucco exterior. Since we had to patch the stucco in several spots anyway, we suggested redashing the entire house. We tinted the bond coat off-white — just a shade darker than the color the homeowners selected for the porch and the trim. We also used a deep green for an accent color on the shutters, window frames, and doors.

The off-white porch ceiling and floors helped bring more light into the front rooms. The bright exterior made the house seem larger and livelier. Once the homeowners added some new plantings around the front, the once tired-looking house became something of a showplace.

Hanging the swing. Our last step, when the painting was done, was to hang the porch swing for our clients. One of their prerequisites before we started construction was that there be plenty of room for this. So we planned ahead and added an extra ceiling joist so the swing could be securely screwed into a structural member.

John Sylvestre is the owner of Sylvestre Construction, a design/build firm based in Minneapolis, Minn.

Chapter 2: Codes & Safety

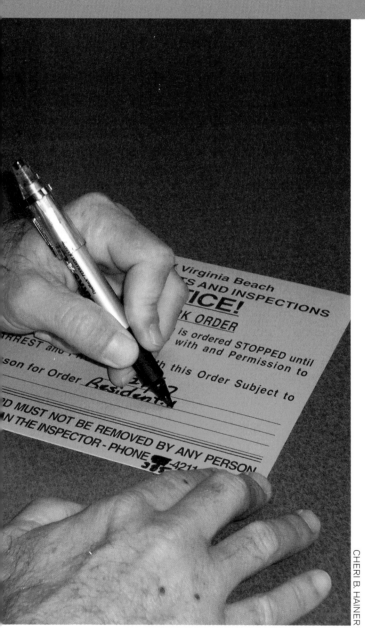

CHERI B. HAINER

Code Requirements for Residential Decks

by Larry Lewis and Frank E. Woeste

The International Residential Code (IRC) currently provides only limited prescriptive design requirements for decks, prompting many jurisdictions to develop their own set of design criteria and inspection procedures. The purpose of this report is to assist those who wish to revise their jurisdiction's deck safety program.

Note that the selection of cited code sections (from the 2003 edition of the IRC) and associated commentary is not intended to represent an official ICC interpretation, but rather to provide background into practical field issues.

Live Loads

R301.5 Live load. The minimum uniformly distributed live load shall be as provided in Table R301.5.

Table R301.5 of the 2003 IRC requires decks to accommodate a uniformly distributed live load of 40 pounds per square foot. Typical deck ledger-to-house band joist connections were recently tested at Virginia Tech University and Washington State University, and the results were reported in the *Building Safety Journal* (12/05) and are summarized in "Load-Tested Deck Ledger Connections," on page 86 in this book. The southern pine deck ledger-to-house band joist connection test data are now part of the Georgia, Indiana, and Virginia state residential codes.

Table R301.5 requires guardrails and handrails to safely resist a single 200-pound concentrated load applied in any direction at any point along the top of the rail and handrail, respectively. It also requires the rail infill to safely resist a horizontally applied load of 50 pounds on an area equal to 1 square foot.

Inspectors often field-test the 200-pound concentrated load resistance requirement by how stiff the guardrail "feels" when a relatively low load is applied at the top of the rail. In addition to being potentially dangerous for the person conducting the test, this test is not a reliable predictor of a guardrail's ability to safely resist 200 pounds of force. For example, a seemingly "stiff" guardrail when loaded to 50 pounds outward force may collapse the next week when loaded by 55 pounds (**Figure 1**). Consider that in research conducted at Virginia Tech University, not one guardrail post-to-deck band joist assembly using only ½-inch bolts or lag screws successfully passed the test based on the 2.5 safety factor given in the International Building Code (as reported in "Strong Rail-Post Connections for Wooden Decks," page 45).

The simplest solution for deck designers and contractors is to use a single stress-rated and notch-free post that serves as both the deck support column and guardrail post. In many cases, however, the contractor or designer chooses a guardrail post spacing that does not match the spacing of the columns that support the overall deck structure. Highly unsafe deck connections can result, so inspectors should watch for deficient details — especially if the connection of the guardrail post to the deck is hidden by a covering (**Figure 2**).

Stairways

R311.5.1 Width. Stairways shall not be less than 36 inches (914 mm) in clear width at all points above the permitted handrail height and below the required headroom height. [. . .]

R311.5.2 Headroom. The minimum headroom in all parts of the stairway shall not be less than 6 feet 8 inches (2036 mm). [. . .]

Bear in mind that minimum headroom can be an issue when perimeter stairs turn at a landing to terminate under the deck.

R311.5.3.1 Riser height. The maximum riser height shall be 7¾ inches (196 mm). [. . .] The greatest riser height within any flight of stairs shall not exceed the smallest by more than ⅜ inch (9.5 mm).

Poorly cut stringers often exceed the allowable height variance, and stairs that are built prior to patios being poured or landings being built frequently have considerably shorter first risers, which

Figure 1. The aftermath of an incident in which a young man died after falling through a guardrail that was nailed only to joists on the end of the deck.

Figure 2. The 4x4 guardrail post connection shown was completely covered by a wood-plastic sleeve and "skirt." An outward force on the top of the post or rail caused the toenails to be loaded in withdrawal: a failure mode that is typically sudden and without warning.

can lead to stumbling or falls when stepping off of the riser after descending the stairs.

R311.5.3.2 Tread depth. The minimum tread depth shall be 10 inches (254 mm). [. . .] The greatest tread depth within any flight of stairs shall not exceed the smallest by more than 3/8 inch (9.5 mm). [. . .]
R311.5.3.3 Profile. The radius of curvature at the leading edge of the tread shall be not greater than 9/16 inch (14.3 mm). A nosing not less than 3/4 inch (19 mm) but not more than 1 1/4 inch (32 mm) shall be provided on stairways with solid risers. The greatest nosing projection shall not exceed the smallest nosing projection by more than 3/8 inch (9.5 mm) between two stories, including the nosing at the level of floors and landings. [. . .] Open risers are permitted, provided that the opening between treads does not permit the passage of a 4-inch diameter (102 mm) sphere.

Open risers are common with decks, and the lack of infill is a common code violation. The main purpose of the 4-inch-diameter sphere provision is to prevent a small child from crawling through the opening and falling. Entrapment and possible strangulation is also a concern.

R311.5.4 Landings for stairways. There shall be a floor or landing at the top and bottom of each stairway. [. . .] The width of each landing shall not be less than the stairway served. Every landing shall have a minimum dimension of 36 inches (944 mm) measured in the direction of travel.

Landings are frequently concrete pads placed after the deck and stairs are built. The required 36-inch dimension in the direction of travel is measured from the nose of the lowest tread.

R311.5.6 Handrails. Handrails shall be provided on at least one side of each continuous run of treads or flight with four or more risers.
R311.5.6.1 Height. Handrail height, measured vertically from the sloped plane adjoining the tread nosing, or finish surface of ramp slope, shall be not less than 34 inches (864 mm) and not more than 38 inches (65 mm).
R311.5.6.2 Continuity. Handrails for stairways shall be continuous for the full length of the flight, from a point directly above the top riser of the flight to a point directly above the lowest riser of the flight. Handrail ends shall be returned or shall terminate in newel posts or safety terminals. [. . .]
R311.5.6.3 Handrail grip size. All required handrails shall be one of the following types or provide equivalent graspability.
1. Type I. Handrails with a circular cross section shall have an outside diameter of at least 1 1/4 inches (32 mm) and not greater than 2 inches (51 mm). If the handrail is not circular it shall have a perimeter dimension of at least 4 inches (102 mm) and not greater than 6 1/4 inches (160 mm) with a maximum cross section dimension of 2 1/4 inches (57 mm).
2. Type II. Handrails with a perimeter greater than 6 1/4 inches (160 mm) shall provide a graspable finger recess area on both sides of the profile. [. . .]

The graspability of the typical "handrail" on decks is an important issue: regardless of how they are installed, 2x4s and 2x6s do not meet the code criteria. It is also critical that handrails for stairs begin and end as prescribed by the code. The nerves in a person's hand signal his or her mind that stairs have ended when the handrail terminates. If steps remain beyond the handrail, trips and falls are likely.

R311.5.7 Illumination. All stairs shall be provided with illumination in accordance with Section R303.6.

The type and location of the stair illumination should be specified in the deck plans and inspected accordingly.

Guards

R312.1 Guards required. Porches, balconies or raised floor surfaces located more than 30 inches (762 mm) above the floor or grade below shall have guards not less than 36 inches (914 mm) in height. Open sides of stairs with a total rise of more than 30 inches (762 mm) above the floor or grade below shall have guards not less than 34 inches (864 mm) in height measured vertically from the nosing of the treads. [. . .]
R312.2 Guard opening limitations. Required guards on open sides of stairways, raised floor areas, balconies and porches shall have intermediate rails or ornamental closures which do not allow passage of a sphere 4 inches (102 mm) or more in diameter.

Exceptions:
1. The triangular openings formed by the riser, tread and bottom rail of a guard at the open side of a stairway are permitted to be of such a size that a sphere 6 inches (152 mm) cannot pass through.
2. Openings for required guards on the sides of stair treads shall not allow a sphere 4 3/8 inches (107 mm) to pass through.

Lower decks are frequently found to be in violation of railing requirements. Benches are often installed to define the perimeter of a deck when rails are required or built next to the rails. In either case, a bench with a 36-inch back measured from the deck surface and a 19-inch seat is actually a 17-inch barrier.

The deck/bench subject is not currently addressed in the IRC and deserves careful study by local jurisdictions.

Protection Against Decay

R319.1 Location required. In areas subject to decay damage as established by Table R301.2(1), the following locations shall require the use of an approved species and grade of lumber, pressure-treated [. . .], or decay-resistant heartwood of redwood, black locust, or cedars. [. . .]

The operative word above regarding decay-resistant species is "heartwood." Only the heartwood — the center portion of the log — of redwood, black locust or cedars is decay-resistant. Therefore, when a local jurisdiction establishes the need for protection against decay and a decay-resistant species is offered as a code-conforming product, inspectors should verify that deck materials are in fact heartwood.

Wood posts, poles, and columns embedded in concrete that is in contact with the ground or exposed to weather must be pressure-preservative treated for ground contact. The inspector should verify by inspection of end tags or otherwise that all materials in contact with soil are treated to the ground contact level defined by American Wood Preservers' Association (AWPA) standards.

R319.3 Fasteners. Fasteners for pressure-preservative and fire-retardant-treated wood shall be of hot-dipped galvanized steel, stainless steel, silicon bronze, or copper.
Exception: One-half-inch (12.7 mm) diameter or greater steel bolts.

Deck and Balcony Code Summary

Table 1 from the *Manual for the Inspection of Residential Wood Decks and Balconies* provides a summary of several model building code requirements for balconies and decks. Localities may modify these requirements. It is important to determine the code of jurisdiction for the structure since code requirements may have changed.

Requirement	CABO OTFDC 1995	ASCE 7 1998	Fairfax County 1998	ICC OTFDC 1998	IRC and IBC 2003
Deck live load (psf)	40	40	40	40	40
Balcony live load (psf)		60 psf, area ≤ 100 ft.²			60 psf, area ≤ 100 ft.² 100 psf, area > 100 ft.²
Dead load (psf)*			10		
Railing load in any direction (plf)		20	50		
Concentrated load for railing in any direction (lb)	200	200	200	200	200
Infill load, over 1ft.² area (lb)		50			50
Max. opening, railing**	4"		4"	4"	4"
Max. opening, triangle at stairway**	6"		6"	6"	6"
Height above grade at which guards are required	30"			30"	30"
Min. height of guards at railing	36"		36"	36"	36"
Min. rise of stairs required for guard	30"			30"	30"
Min. height of guards at stairway***	34"		36"	34"	36"

* *Dead load is generally the weight of the materials themselves.*
** *Maximum Opening: Will not allow a sphere of this diameter to pass through, shown in Figures B and C, pages 39 and 40.*
*** *If the top rail also serves as a handrail (R-2: apartments, two-dwelling units and R-3: permanent) the height must be ≥ 34 in. and ≤ 38 in. vertically from the nose of the leading tread.*

Reprinted with permission from the *Manual for the Inspection of Residential Wood Decks and Balconies*, by Cheryl Anderson, Frank Woeste, PE, and Joseph Loferski. © 2003 Forest Products Society.

Traditionally, the treated wood industry has recommended hot-dipped and stainless steel fasteners and connectors. Even with treatment formulations of alkaline copper quat (ACQ) and copper azole (CA) now available, hot-dipped and stainless steel fasteners and connectors are still strongly recommended. The higher copper contents in the newer formulations increase the likelihood of galvanic corrosion in exterior applications. Also note that we have not found an exception for larger bolts in our survey of fastener manufacturers' literature.

Deck fasteners exposed to ocean spray are currently not addressed by the IRC, but pending the findings of a study committee on Virginia code proposal RB122–06/07, we believe common sense dictates that elevated deck fasteners and connectors subject to salt spray be made of stainless steel grade 304 or 316.

Protection Against Termites

R320.3.1 Field treatment. *Field-cut ends, notches, and drilled holes of pressure preservatively treated wood shall be retreated in the field in accordance with AWPA M4.*

IRC Section R320.3.1 establishes the need for protection against termites in areas where damage is probable. AWPA Standard M4 recommends treating any cut, bored, drilled, or adzed surfaces of treated wood with a preservative solution.

Wood Floor Framing

R502.8.1 Drilling and notching in sawn lumber. *Notches in solid lumber joists, rafters and beams shall not exceed one-sixth of the depth of the member, shall not be longer than one-third of the depth of the member and shall not be located in the middle one-third of the span. Notches at the ends of the member shall not exceed one-fourth the depth of the member. [. . .] The diameter of holes bored or cut into members shall not exceed one-third the depth of the member. Holes shall not be closer than 2 inches (51 mm) to the top or bottom of the member, or to any hole located in the member. Where the member is also notched, the hole shall not be closer than 2 inches (51 mm) to the notch.*

Many of today's decks incorporate sinks, lights, cooking appliances, and other items that may require the routing of mechanical and electrical lines through structural framing. Due to moisture cycles in the lumber from outdoor exposure, notching may be more detrimental than for the inside "dry case." Alterations beyond the provisions of R502.8.1 should be evaluated by a design professional and repaired as necessary (see "Drilling and Notching Joists," at right).

R502.2.1 Decks. *Where supported by attachment to an exterior wall, decks shall be positively anchored to the primary structure and designed for both vertical and lateral loads as applicable. Such attachment shall not be accomplished by the use of toenails or nails subject to withdrawal. Where positive connection to the primary building structure cannot be verified during inspection, decks shall be self-supporting. For decks with cantilevered framing members, connections to exterior walls or other framing members shall be designed and constructed to resist uplift resulting from the full live load specified in Table R301.5 acting on the cantilevered portion of the deck.*

Based on our analysis, this code section disallows the use of 2x2 ledger strips attached to ledger boards because 2x2s tend to rotate under load, thereby subjecting the nails to withdrawal loads. Fastening joists to the ledger with connectors (joist hangers) appears to meet the intent of this provision, but it should be noted that the code requires the design professional to account for "lateral loads" not defined in the code or other literature. In any event, the connectors must be suitable for use with the new lumber pressure treatments. (See "New Rules for Deck Ledgers and Lateral Attachment," page 41.)

Drilling and Notching Joists

Notching and drilling of deck joists may be more of a problem than with indoor "dry" lumber because of the higher moisture cycles in lumber exposed to the outdoors. IRC limits for notching and drilling solid-lumber joists are shown below. Alterations beyond these limits should be evaluated by a design professional.

Joist Size	Maximum Hole	Maximum Notch Depth	Maximum End Notch
2x4	None	None	None
2x6	1 1/2"	7/8"	1 3/8"
2x8	2 3/8"	1 1/4"	1 7/8"
2x10	3"	1 1/2"	2 3/8"
2x12	3 3/4"	1 7/8"	2 7/8"

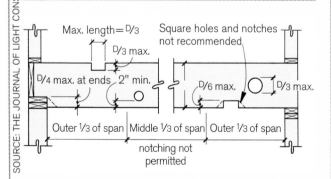

SOURCE: THE JOURNAL OF LIGHT CONSTRUCTION

With dimensional lumber, do not notch a span's middle third where bending forces are greatest. For all calculations, use actual, not nominal, dimensions.

Columns

R407.1 Wood column protection. Wood columns shall be protected against decay as set forth in Section R319.

R407.2 Steel column protection. All surfaces (inside and outside) of steel columns shall be given a shop coat of rust-inhibitive paint, except for corrosion-resistant steel and steel treated with coatings to provide corrosion resistance.

R407.3 Structural requirements. The columns shall be restrained to prevent lateral displacement at the bottom end. Wood columns shall not be less in nominal size than 4 inches by 4 inches (102 mm by 102 mm) and steel columns shall not be less than 3-inch-diameter (76 mm) standard pipe or approved equivalent.

Adequately securing columns or posts can be a challenge in the field when manufactured post connectors are not used. Useful illustrations for restraining columns can be found in the *2003 International Residential Code Commentary Volume 1*. In addition, precast concrete footings typically found at building stores do not prevent displacement unless they are secured to the supporting footing.

Footings

R403.1.1 Minimum size. [. . .] The size of footings supporting piers and columns shall be based on the tributary load and allowable soil pressure in accordance with Table R401.4.1. [. . .]

R403.1.4 Minimum depth. All footings shall be placed at least 12 inches (305 mm) below the undisturbed ground surface. Where applicable, the depth of footings shall also conform to Sections R403.1.4.1 through R403.1.4.2.

IRC Section R403.1.4.1 deals with footings and foundation systems extending below the frost line. In areas where frost line is not an issue, the footing is still required to be a minimum of 12 inches below undisturbed ground.

Girders and Beams

Per IRC Table R602.3(1), each layer of built-up girders and beams of 2-inch lumber layers must be nailed using 10d nails 32 inches on center at top and bottom and staggered, with two nails at the ends and at each splice. (See Section R319.3 for protection of nails.)

The quantity of nails is not a typical problem in the field, but improper placement of fasteners and unsupported splices are common.

Exterior Covering

R703.8 Flashing. Approved corrosion-resistive flashing shall be provided in the exterior wall envelope in such a manner as to prevent entry of water into the wall cavity or penetration of water to the building structural fram-

Figure 3. Severe water damage to the house framing can result from the lack of adequate flashing at the deck ledger-to-house band joist connection.

ing components. The flashing shall extend to the surface of the exterior wall finish and shall be installed to prevent water from reentering the exterior wall envelope. Approved corrosion-resistant flashings shall be installed [. . . w]here exterior porches, decks, or stairs attach to a wall or floor assembly of wood-frame construction.

As mentioned earlier, changes in the chemical makeup of the preservatives used for pressure-treated wood have increased the likelihood of galvanic corrosion between fasteners, connectors, and flashing. It is also worth noting that aluminum has never been recommended for use as flashing by the treated wood industry.

That said, the authority having jurisdiction should determine what materials and methods are suitable for flashing the deck connection to the house. (For some ideas on deck flashing, see Deck Ledgers, pages 85–107. Also visit www.fairfaxcounty.gov/decks/. Then click on "Fairfax County Typical Deck Details" and view "Siding and Flashing" on Sheet 8.)

The importance of effective flashing of the deck ledger to house band area cannot be overstated. The integrity of the ledger-to-house band joist connection comes down to sound wood, and inadequate flashing can also cause interior water damage (**Figure 3**). The issue of flashing thereby provides strong encouragement for requiring "self-supporting" decks.

Summary

Residential deck safety is a serious safety issue, and it is hoped that the preceding overview will provide a good starting point for discussions about the appropriate code requirements for a particular jurisdiction. The prescriptive deck design and inspection requirements developed by Fairfax County, Virginia, offer additional insight and direction, and are freely accessible online at www.fairfaxcounty.gov/decks/.

Larry Lewis is president of Homewise, Inc., a residential inspection company based in Alpharetta, Georgia. Frank E. Woeste, PhD, PE, is professor emeritus at Virginia Tech University, Blacksburg, and a wood construction and engineering consultant. This article was reprinted with permission from Building Safety Journal © 2007 International Code Council.

Prescriptive Guide Simplifies Deck Design

by Glenn Mathewson

When it comes to structural provisions for decks, the International Residential Code falls rather short. The IRC treats much of what we see in deck construction as an "alternative." Alternative designs and methods are those that are not prescribed in the code — they fall outside of the cookie-cutter construction recipe. It is within the authority of the building official to approve alternative materials, designs, and methods, as long as they are at least equivalent to what's provided in the code and are based on accepted engineering practice.

The local jurisdiction may also approve alternative provisions that are published by government agencies and reputable organizations. One such organization, the American Forest & Paper Association (AF&PA), has recently published the *Prescriptive Residential Wood Deck Construction Guide*, which is available as a free download from the American Wood Council Web site. (Click on publication DCA 6 at www.awc.org/codes/dcaindex.html.)

The AF&PA is also the publisher of the *National Design Specification* (a cornerstone of wood-frame engineering) and the *Wood Frame Construction Manual*, a standard that is specifically referenced by the IRC. Considering the AF&PA's involvement in code standards for wood construction, it would be reasonable to submit deck plans to your local inspector based on compliance with AF&PA provisions.

The *Prescriptive Residential Wood Deck Construction Guide* is not a building code in itself, however. It's intended to provide one alternative method to satisfy the code, but not represent the code specifically. In many ways it goes beyond code and in other ways it may be questionable. In general, however, it's very conservative. Following are some highlights of the differences between the AF&PA deck guide and the IRC.

Joists and Beams

The IRC contains span tables that are often used for sizing deck joists, but these tables include only a few wood species, and they don't account for wet-service conditions or incised materials, both of which may slightly reduce the materials' structural capacity.

The *Deck Construction Guide* provides a simple joist span table that accounts for all these reduction factors and includes values for redwood and western cedars — species absent from the IRC's span tables (**Table 1**). Span tables are also provided for multi-ply beams, from doubled 2x6s to tripled 2x12s (**Table 2**). These tables are incredibly useful, and I imagine most jurisdictions would approve the spans with little question.

Cantilevers

As mentioned previously, the IRC specifically allows designs that are in accordance with the *Wood Frame Construction Manual* (R301.1.1). In that book, the cantilever allowance for joists is L/4 — one-fourth the total span — which is identical to the allowance in the *Deck Construction Guide* (**Figure 4**, next page). Using this design provision shouldn't be a problem, as it's essentially allowed by the IRC.

On the other hand, the allowable cantilever for beams (also L/4) provided in the *Deck Construction Guide* is not found or referenced in the IRC (**Figure 5**, page 33). While beam cantilevers may be scrutinized by the building official, the acceptance of the guide's provisions would certainly add design flexibility.

Post Size

The *Deck Construction Guide* specifies a minimum 6x6 post and cites section R407 of the IRC. Strangely, this

Table 1. Maximum Joist Spans[1]

Species	Size	Joist Spacing (o.c.)		
		12"	16"	24"
Southern Pine	2x8	10'-6"	10'-6"	10'-2"
	2x10	15'-2"	15'-2"	13'-1"
	2x12	18'-0"	18'-0"	15'-5"
Douglas Fir-Larch, Hem-Fir, SPF[2]	2x8	9'-3"	9'-3"	9'-1"
	2x10	13'-4"	13'-4"	11'-1"
	2x12	17'-10"	15'-9"	12'-10"
Redwood, Western Cedars	2x8	8'-4"	8'-4"	8'-4"
	2x10	12'-0"	12'-0"	11'-3"
	2x12	16'-1"	16'-0"	13'-0"

1. Assumes 40 psf live load, 10 psf dead load, L/180 cantilever deflection with 230 lb point load, No. 2 grade, and wet service conditions. See span calculator at www.awc.org for simple span conditions without cantilevers.
2. Incising factor used for refractory species including Douglas fir-larch, hem-fir, and spruce-pine-fir.

Note: Based on Table 2 of the *Prescriptive Residential Wood Deck Construction Guide*. The joist span table in the guide includes common species not given in the IRC.

Table 2. Deck Beam Spans[1]

Species	Size	Joist Spans (ft) Less Than or Equal to:						
		6	8	10	12	14	16	18
Southern Pine	2-2x6	7'-1"	6'-2"	5'-6"	5'-0"	4'-8"	4'-4"	4'-1"
	2-2x8	9'-2"	7'-11"	7'-1"	6'-6"	6'-0"	5'-7"	5'-3"
	2-2x10	11'-10"	10'-3"	9'-2"	8'-5"	7'-9"	7'-3"	6'-10"
	2-2x12	13'-11"	12'-0"	10'-9"	9'-10"	9'-1"	8'-6"	8'-0"
	3-2x6	8'-7"	7'-8"	6'-11"	6'-3"	5'-10"	5'-5"	5'-2"
	3-2x8	11'-4"	9'-11"	8'-11"	8'-1"	7'-6"	7'-0"	6'-7"
	3-2x10	14'-5"	12'-10"	11'-6"	10'-6"	9'-9"	9'-1"	8'-7"
	3-2x12	17'-5"	15'-1"	13'-6"	12'-4"	11'-5"	10'-8"	10'-1"
Douglas Fir-Larch[2], Hem-Fir, SPF[2], Redwood, Western Cedars	3x6 or 2-2x6	5'-8"	4'-11"	4'-4"	4'-0"	3'-8"	3'-5"	3'-0"
	3x8 or 2-2x8	7'-2"	6'-2"	5'-6"	5'-0"	4'-8"	4'-4"	4'-0"
	3x10 or 2-2x10	8'-9"	7'-7"	6'-9"	6'-2"	5'-8"	5'-4"	5'-0"
	3x12 or 2-2x12	10'-1"	8'-9"	7'-10"	7'-2"	6'-7"	6'-2"	5'-10"
	4x6	6'-8"	5'-9"	5'-2"	4'-9"	4'-4"	4'-1"	3'-10"
	4x8	8'-9"	7'-7"	6'-10"	6'-3"	5'-9"	5'-5"	5'-1"
	4x10	10'-9"	9'-4"	8'-4"	7'-7"	7'-1"	6'-7"	6'-3"
	4x12	12'-6"	10'-10"	9'-8"	8'-10"	8'-2"	7'-8"	7'-3"
	3-2x6	7'-4"	6'-8"	6'-2"	5'-9"	5'-4"	5'-0"	4'-8"
	3-2x8	9'-8"	8'-9"	7'-11"	7'-3"	6'-9"	6'-3"	5'-11"
	3-2x10	12'-4"	10'-10"	9'-8"	8'-10"	8'-2"	7'-8"	7'-3"
	3-2x12	14'-6"	12'-7"	11'-3"	10'-3"	9'-6"	8'-11"	8'-5"

1. Assumes 40 psf live load, 10 psf dead load, L/360 simple span beam deflection limit, L/180 cantilever deflection limit, No. 2 grade, and wet service conditions.
2. Incising factor used for refractory species including Douglas fir-larch, hem-fir, and spruce-pine-fir.

Note: Based on Table 3 of the *Prescriptive Residential Wood Deck Construction Guide.* Spans for beams from a variety of species and configurations are provided by the guide.

IRC section requires a minimum 4x4 post. The larger cross section required by the AF&PA may be a result of diagonal bracing provisions in the *Deck Construction Guide* that are not in the IRC (**Figure 6**). This bracing places forces perpendicular to the posts, which increases bending stresses on them. The load path to the supporting soil requires all the components of the structural system to work together, so the system must be designed as a whole. By specifying braces for lateral support, the post size must be reconsidered. With these thoughts in mind, a jurisdiction might require the *Deck Construction Guide* to be used in its entirety, as a system design.

Cantilevered Joist Spans

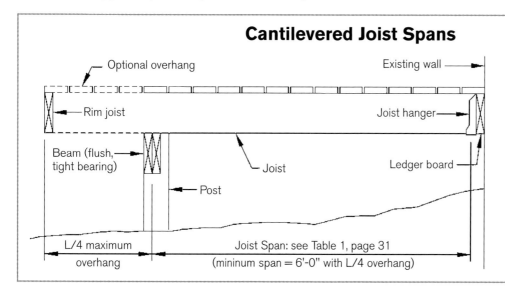

Optional overhang — Existing wall —
Rim joist —
Joist hanger —
Beam (flush, tight bearing) —
Joist —
Post —
Ledger board —
L/4 maximum overhang
Joist Span: see Table 1, page 31
(minimum span = 6'-0" with L/4 overhang)

Figure 4. Maximum joist cantilevers are spelled out in the *Prescriptive Residential Wood Deck Construction Guide* as one-quarter of the entire span.

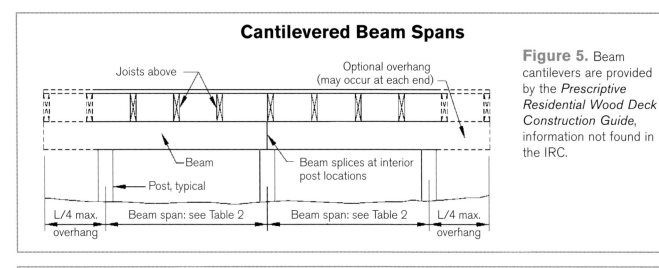

Cantilevered Beam Spans

Joists above

Optional overhang (may occur at each end)

Beam

Beam splices at interior post locations

Post, typical

L/4 max. overhang

Beam span: see Table 2

Beam span: see Table 2

L/4 max. overhang

Figure 5. Beam cantilevers are provided by the *Prescriptive Residential Wood Deck Construction Guide*, information not found in the IRC.

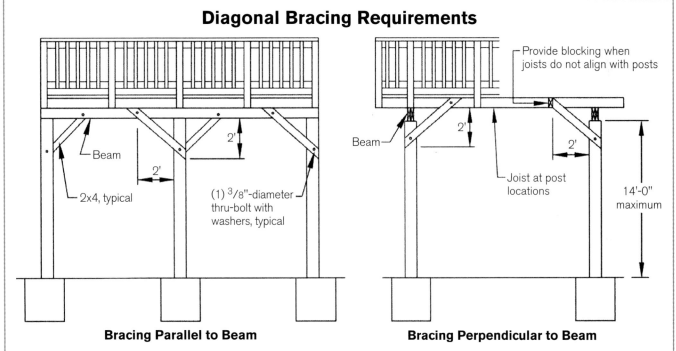

Diagonal Bracing Requirements

Beam

2x4, typical

2'

2'

(1) ³⁄₈"-diameter thru-bolt with washers, typical

Provide blocking when joists do not align with posts

Beam

2'

2'

Joist at post locations

14'-0" maximum

Bracing Parallel to Beam

Bracing Perpendicular to Beam

Figure 6. The *Prescriptive Residential Wood Deck Construction Guide* differs from the IRC on post size. The guide requires minimum 6x6 posts with diagonal bracing both parallel and perpendicular to the main carrying beams for decks greater than 2 feet above grade. The IRC specifies minimum 4x4 posts with no diagonal bracing.

Lateral Bracing

Not all forces on a structure act vertically. Lateral forces, often imposed on decks by the movement of people, act in a horizontal direction. Live loads account for the weight of people, but not the horizontal forces generated by their movement. Decks are notoriously places of high occupant loads and high occupant movement. Couple that with a lack of lateral bracing and a big party on the deck could cause it to pull away from the house.

The difficulty that may arise from trying to use the *Deck Construction Guide* methods for lateral bracing of decks is that many building departments also consult the newer supplemental codes for guidance

in approving alternatives. The IRC requires some sort of lateral bracing and the 2007 supplement to the IRC provides one possible method (**Figure 7**, next page). I think it's conservative — and impractical for existing structures.

While this particular connection is not required by the IRC, it does establish a minimum standard. By setting the bar for lateral restraint so high, the 2007 supplement to the IRC makes the *Deck Construction Guide* methods a questionable "equivalency."

Ledger Details

The ledger fastening table in the *Deck Construction Guide* is nearly the same as that in the 2007 IRC

Deck Attachment for Lateral Loads

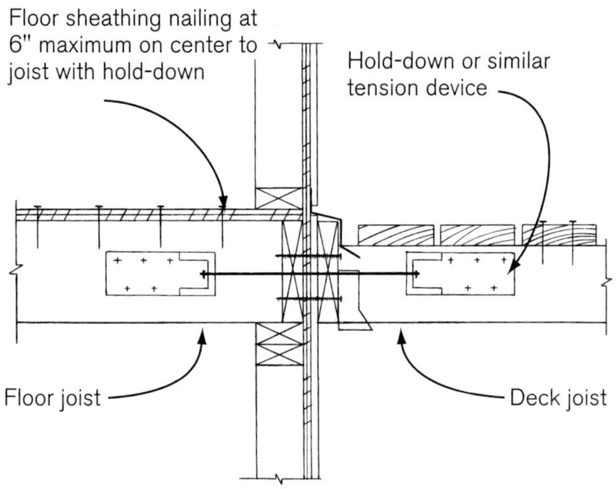

Floor sheathing nailing at 6" maximum on center to joist with hold-down

Hold-down or similar tension device

Floor joist

Deck joist

Figure 7. This illustration from the IRC suggests a more specific lateral attachment than does the *Prescriptive Residential Wood Deck Construction Guide*.

supplement. However, the two differ significantly in one way. While the *Deck Construction Guide* provides a detail for hanging a girder from a ledger (**Figure 8**), the 2007 IRC supplement states: "Girders supporting deck joists shall not be supported on deck ledgers or band joists." What this means is the standard practice of hanging a double beam from the ledger to carry other joists will no longer be allowed. This fact may make a building official wary of approving an almost identical table that then allows beams to bear at the ledger.

Also, the *Deck Construction Guide* includes fastener spacings for attaching deck ledgers to engineered wood (EWP) rim boards (**Table 3**). The IRC contains spacings only for dimensional lumber band joists. Pay close attention to the footnotes before using the table.

Stairs

To my knowledge the *Deck Construction Guide* is the first "reputable" document to provide structural details for typical deck stairs. While this is great, I also think that as written, it's both conservative and

Table 3. Fastener Spacing for Deck Ledgers
(Deck Live Load = 40 psf. Deck Dead Load = 10 psf)[3,6]

Joist Span	Rim Board or Band Joist	6'-0" and less	6'-1" to 8'-0"	8'-1" to 10'-0"	10'-1" to 12'-0"	12'-1" to 14'-0"	14'-1" to 16'-0"	16'-1" to 18'-0"
Connection Details		On-Center Spacing of Fasteners[4,5]						
½"-diameter lag screw with 15/32" maximum sheathing[1]	1" EWP[6]	24"	18"	14"	12"	10"	9"	8"
	1⅛" EWP[6]	28"	21"	16"	14"	12"	10"	9"
	1½" Lumber[7,9]	30"	23"	18"	15"	13"	11"	10"
½"-diameter bolt with 15/32" maximum sheathing	1" EWP[6]	24"	18"	14"	12"	10"	9"	8"
	1⅛" EWP[6]	28"	21"	16"	14"	12"	10"	9"
	1½" Lumber[7,9]	36"	36"	34"	29"	24"	21"	19"
½"-diameter bolt with 15/32" maximum sheathing and ½" stacked washers[2,8]	1" EWP[6]	24"	18"	14"	12"	10"	9"	8"
	1⅛" EWP[6]	28"	21"	16"	14"	12"	10"	9"
	1½" Lumber[7,9]	36"	36"	29"	24"	21"	18"	16"

1 The tip of the lag screw shall fully extend beyond the inside face of the band joist.
2 The maximum gap between the face of the ledger board and face of the wall sheathing shall be ½".
3 Ledgers shall be flashed or caulked to prevent water from contacting the house band joist.
4 Lag screws and bolts shall be staggered.
5 Deck ledgers shall be minimum 2x8 pressure-preservative-treated No. 2 grade lumber or other approved materials as established by standard engineering practice.
6 When solid-sawn pressure-preservative-treated deck ledgers are attached to engineered wood products (oriented strand board or structural composite lumber, including laminated veneer lumber), the ledger attachment shall be designed in accordance with accepted engineering practice. Tabulated values based on 300 lb. and 350 lb. for 1" and 1⅛" EWP rim board, respectively.
7 A minimum 1"x9½" Douglas fir-larch laminated veneer lumber rim board shall be permitted in lieu of the 2" nominal band joist.
8 Wood structural panel sheathing, gypsum board sheathing, or foam sheathing not exceeding one inch thickness shall be permitted. The maximum distance between the face of the ledger board and the face of the band joist shall be one inch.
9 Fastener spacing also applies to southern pine, Douglas fir-larch, and hem-fir band joists.

Note: Based on Table 5 in the *Prescriptive Residential Wood Deck Construction Guide*. The fastener spacing table in the guide includes data for fastening ledgers to engineered wood (EWP) rim joists. The IRC covers only dimensional lumber band joists. Pay close attention to all footnotes before using the table.

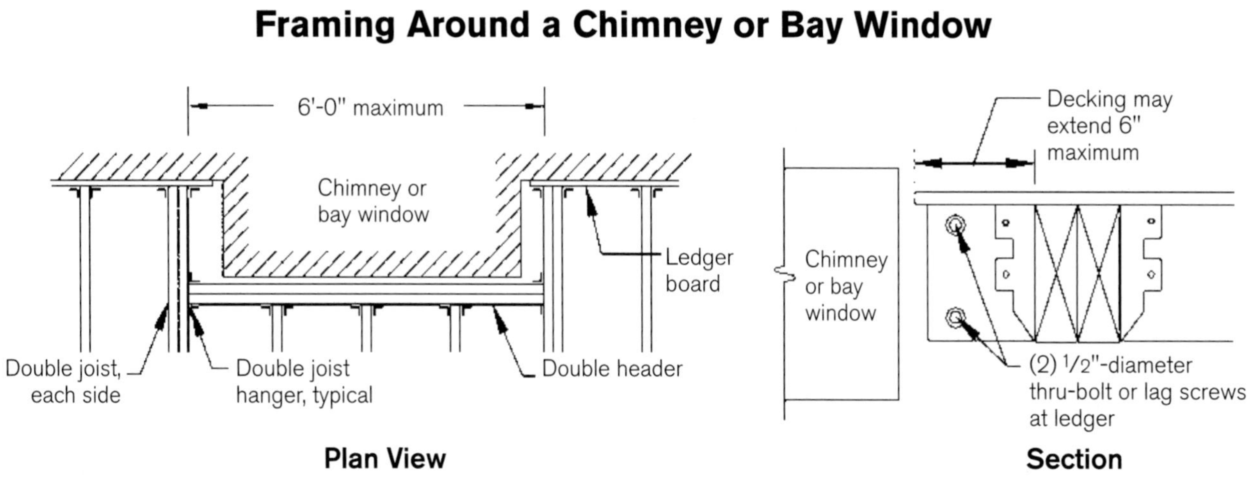

Framing Around a Chimney or Bay Window

6'-0" maximum

Chimney or
bay window

Ledger
board

Double joist,
each side

Double joist
hanger, typical

Double header

Plan View

Chimney
or bay
window

Decking may
extend 6"
maximum

(2) 1/2"-diameter
thru-bolt or lag screws
at ledger

Section

Figure 8. The *Prescriptive Residential Wood Deck Construction Guide* details a method for hanging girders from ledgers; the 2007 IRC supplement forbids this detail. The decision lies with the local inspector.

misleading. On the conservative side, notched stair stringers are limited to a horizontal span of 7 feet with southern pine, and 6 feet for other species. This may be a shock to deck professionals who are accustomed to longer spans. I assume that the use of a beam, posts, and footings set at midspan of the stairs would be an acceptable alternative that would allow longer flights with notched stringers.

What I find misleading about the section on stairs is that it allows stringers to be spaced at 36 inches and allows either a 2-by or 5/4 board to span this distance (**Figure 9**). Stringer spacing should be based on the maximum span of the tread material: Some synthetic decking materials can span only 8 inches when used as stair treads. I think the stair portion of the *Deck Construction Guide* should be used and approved with caution.

The *Deck Construction Guide* is not, nor is it intended to be, an all-inclusive code document. While it provides many useful specifications that aren't in the code, it also leaves some out. For example, opening limitations and minimum heights for stair guards are not mentioned, nor is the use of type II graspable handrails (those with a perimeter greater than 6 1/4 inches). But the value in the *Deck Construction Guide* is that it fills some holes in the

Figure 9. The *Prescriptive Residential Wood Deck Construction Guide* allows 3-foot spans between the stringers; the IRC bases these spans on the strength of the tread material.

IRC and provides a good framework for generally acceptable deck design.

Glenn Mathewson is a building inspector in Westminster, Colo., and a former deck builder.

Common Code Violations

by Cheri B. Hainer

A s a building inspector, I see a lot of decks that aren't built to code — despite the plan review process, the purpose of which is to identify any code issues before construction commences. But field changes are common, so an inspector is likely to find a different deck constructed at the site than what was detailed on the permit.

Only a few provisions in the International Residential Code specifically relate to building a deck. (The International Code Council is currently forming a committee to develop an appendix to the IRC that addresses deck construction.) For many specifications, like those for spans and guardrails, you have to apply general code requirements.

Consequently, a deck contractor may not be aware that certain changes could result in a code violation. Below are five common reasons decks fail inspection.

No Protection Against Decay

IRC Section 319 requires all structural elements exposed to weathering to be protected against decay, which usually means using preservative-treated lumber (requirements can be found in IRC Section R502.1.1).

It's a simple issue, usually noted on the plans and reiterated by the permit staff, but inspectors often find a completed deck built of standard-grade lumber. The contractor or owner must then apply an approved on-site treatment (per IRC 319.1.1) to the open and exposed ends and paint the rest to bring the deck into compliance (**Figure 10**).

Some are more obvious than others, but all are dangerous and can easily be avoided.

CHERI B. HAINER

Too Few or Inadequate Fasteners

In recent years, insufficient attachment — which includes the use of non-weather-resistant fasteners — to the existing structure has caused several decks to collapse. Fastener specifications aren't usually called out on the construction plans, and inspectors often

Figure 10. Untreated lumber, or above-ground-certified lumber used in ground contact, can trigger a failed inspection. Always check for appropriate treatment levels.

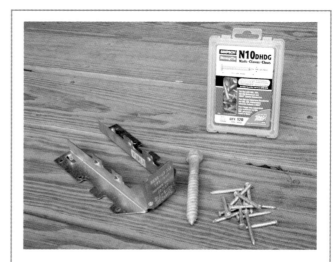

Figure 11. Corrosion-resistant hardware is a code requirement. It's doubly important when in contact with ACQ treated lumber.

Figure 12. Solid lumber such as a 4x4 or a 4x6 can no longer be used as a beam. Most beams must be built up from layers of 2-by material.

Figure 13. Frost footings do more than support the deck's downward load; they also anchor it against wind uplift. A positive hardware connection between the footing and the deck is needed.

find undersized nails, or untreated nails that will be nothing but rust in a year.

To resist corrosion, all fasteners used in deck construction must be hot-dipped zinc-coated galvanized steel, stainless steel, silicon bronze, or copper. Joist hangers and anchoring straps are subject to the same requirements as fasteners. IRC Table R602.3 (1), "Fastener Schedule for Structural Members," specifies the correct type, size, and number of fasteners required in common construction elements (**Figure 11**).

IRC Section R502.2.2 requires positive anchoring of non-freestanding decks to the primary structure and prohibits toenailing or using nails to make this connection. In the 2007 IRC Supplement, Section R502.2.2.1 was adopted to clarify this provision. It specifies the use of lag screws, or bolts and washers when attaching the deck ledger to the primary structure. The fastener schedule, based on research done at the Virginia Tech and Washington State University, is provided in IRC Table R502.2.2.1 (see page 44).

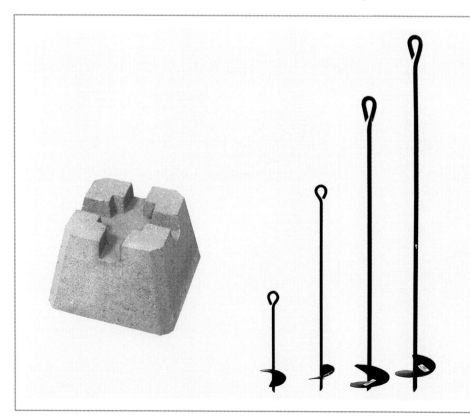

Figure 14. Ready-made footings such as the Dek-Block (CCI Industries, www. cci-industries.com) speed up the construction of freestanding decks, but don't provide uplift resistance. Easily engineered auger and cable tie-downs can answer that need.

Figure 15. Railings need be no higher behind a bench than anywhere else, but a bench alone cannot serve as a guardrail.

CLEMENS JELLEMA

Inadequate or Non-approved Structure

The IRC [Section and Table R502.5 (1)] no longer allows 4x4s or 6x6s to be used as girders (**Figure 12**, previous page). All structural beams and girders must be constructed with multiple 2x4s to 2x12s, with the depth and the number of layers of the members determined by the span and spacing.

Composite decking materials are becoming very popular, but many have been tested and approved for installation on joists spaced 12 inches on center, not 16 inches or 24 inches. You will need to check with the individual manufacturer's specifications.

Cantilevers

Deck joists often cantilever beyond the outer girder. The old-school rule of thumb was that as much as one-third of the length of the joists could cantilever beyond the beam. But about 10 years ago, the building codes reduced the allowable spans for most softwood lumber because of declining material quality, and now cantilevers shouldn't extend more than 24 inches beyond the beam, unless by specific engineered design.

Insufficient Support and Anchoring

Whether attached to the existing structure or freestanding, all decks are required to be anchored against uplift and braced laterally to prevent racking and to prevent the deck from becoming a projectile in high winds or an earthquake.

Deck footings or piers and their posts not only support normal loads, they also help provide the needed uplift resistance. Concrete footings, at or below the locality's frost line, can be as basic as a pad in the bottom to support the column, with stone backfilled around it, or a solid-concrete pile with an anchor bolt installed on top to hold the column in place (**Figure 13**, previous page).

Precast footings are a recent innovation (**Figure 14**, previous page). No holes need to be dug for footings, as the precast blocks are set on grade, and the posts or beams fit in pockets cast in the concrete block. To meet the uplift anchoring requirements, straps or augers are also required. If using precast footings, be sure to determine what additional equipment or devices are needed.

Missing or Noncompliant Guardrails and Handrails

Many owners don't want a guardrail to affect the view from their deck. They want something not too tall and often ask for benches or planters to act as guards.

IRC Section R312 requires a guardrail for porches, balconies, or other raised floor areas where the floor surface is more than 30 inches above the adjoining grade. Required guardrails cannot be less than 36 inches in height. The guards are to be constructed with infill rails or balusters no more than 4 inches apart. A bench can be installed against a guard, but if the deck is more than 30 inches above grade, a flat bench cannot be the guard (**Figure 15**).

Porches and decks enclosed with insect screening, if 30 inches or more above grade, must also have guards.

Handrails are not guardrails, although the terms are often thought of at the same time (see "Guardrails vs. Handrails," page 39). Per section R311.5.6, a handrail is required when there are four or more risers in the stair run. When the stair is more than 30 inches above grade or above the floor below, a guard is also required. A compliant handrail is either circular with a minimum 1¼-inch and maximum 2-inch diameter or 1½ inches square (conveniently the size of a dressed 2x2).

Cheri B. Hainer is the permits and inspections administrator for the city of Virginia Beach, Va.

Guardrails vs. Handrails

by Glenn Mathewson

The 2006 International Residential Code defines a *guard* as "a building component or a system of building components located near the open sides of elevated walking surfaces that minimizes the possibility of a fall from the walking surface to the lower level"; and a *handrail* as "a horizontal or sloping rail intended for grasping by the hand for guidance or support."

Note there is no requirement for a "guardrail," but simply for a guard – which can be any building component that provides the required level of protection, such as a wall, a half-wall, a planter box, a bench, or more typically, a railing.

A handrail, however, is specifically defined as a "rail." Its purpose is to give you something to hold; the purpose of the guard, on the other hand, is to keep you from falling over the edge. Thus, the IRC requirements relating to them are different.

Guards are referred to in Section R312.1 in the 2006 IRC: "Open sides of stairs with a total rise of more than 30 inches above the floor or grade below shall have guards not less than 34 inches in height measured verti-

cally from the nosing of the treads." It's important to highlight that this requirement is based on the height of a fall, not the number of rises in the stairs. For example, a set of stairs with four rises – each 7.75 inches high for a total rise of 31 inches – would require a guard on both sides. On the other hand, a set of stairs with 10 rises, each 3 inches high for a total rise of 30 inches, would not require a guard (**Figure A**).

Infill – balusters, pickets, solid wall, and the like – between the 34-inch minimum height and the nose of the stairs is considered part of the guard assembly, and is required only when guards are required (**Figure B**). Remember that guards on level areas such as decks, when required, must be a minimum of 36 inches high (**Figure C**).

Unlike the requirement for guards, the one for handrails (Section R311.5.6 of the 2006 IRC) considers the number of rises: "Handrails shall be provided on at least one side of each continuous run of treads or flight with four or more rises." This is because the need for handrails is based solely on the movement of the human body, not on the height of the stairs. The more times you

(continued on page 40)

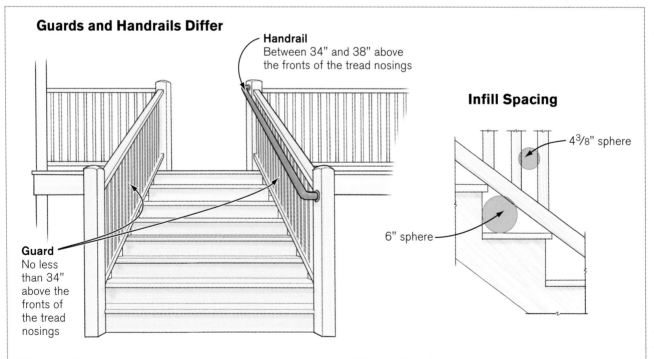

Guards and Handrails Differ

Handrail
Between 34" and 38" above the fronts of the tread nosings

Infill Spacing

$4^3/8$" sphere

6" sphere

Guard
No less than 34" above the fronts of the tread nosings

Figure A. *A guard is required when a stair rises more than 30 inches above the underlying surface. A handrail is required on stairs of four or more rises.*

Figure B. *On stair guards, the infill must not allow passage of a $4^3/8$-inch sphere. In the triangular space below a shoe rail, a 6-inch sphere may not pass.*

Guardrails vs. Handrails (continued from page 39)

must lift your legs and place your feet squarely on a tread, without an intervening landing, the more likely you are to trip or become tired. Also note that unlike guards, a handrail is required on only one side of the stairs.

Consider the two examples given earlier: The stair with four rises of 7.75 inches would require guards on both sides because the overall rise exceeds 30 inches, and it would require a handrail on one side because it has four rises.

Although the second stair, with ten 3-inch rises, wouldn't require guards (total rise doesn't exceed 30 inches), it would need a handrail on one side because of the number of rises. And since guards aren't required, there's no requirement for infill beneath the handrail.

Where both guards and handrails are required, as in the first stair, the top of the guard can be constructed to also function as the handrail. The three subsections of section R311.5.6 detail the height, continuity, and grip size that regulates the construction of handrails. The Stairway Manufacturers' Association provides excellent details and visual examples of these sections in its *Visual Interpretation of the International Residential Code*, available at www.stairways.org.

As always, consult the building department in the juris-

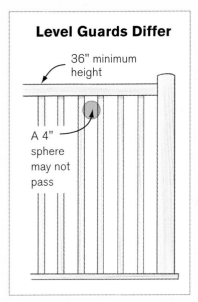

Level Guards Differ

36" minimum height

A 4" sphere may not pass

Figure C.
On decks more than 30 inches above grade, guards are required.

diction where the work is being performed. Some jurisdictions have adopted amended versions of the IRC or published their own code, or they may interpret these sections differently.

Glenn Mathewson is a building inspector in Westminster, Colo., and a former deck builder.

New Rules for Deck Ledgers and Lateral Attachment

by Cheri B. Hainer

Ledger-board attachment is a key element in deck failures. To address this problem, new prescriptive requirements for the attachment of deck ledgers were adopted at the International Code Council (ICC) conference in Rochester, N.Y., and are included in the 2007 International Residential Code Supplement.

An event underlining the need for this code change occurred in Virginia Beach, Va., on October 28, 2005. At a wedding reception, a third-floor deck holding 40 guests collapsed (**Figure 16**), and 28 people required medical treatment. The residence was located on a beach along the Atlantic Ocean; investigators found that the joist hangers and the nails used to attach the joists to the ledger board had rusted through. Also, because the ledger board wasn't bolted onto the house, it separated from the house as the deck collapsed.

The following month — though not in response to the Virginia Beach accident — the Virginia Uniform Statewide Building Code adopted provisions similar to those just adopted by the ICC.

Although the code-development community tries to be proactive, most current codes are reactions to events. For example, new wind-resistant construction requirements were adopted in response to construction failures during Hurricanes Andrew, Isabelle, Katrina, and Ernesto. And recent deck collapses (like the one mentioned above, and others in Atlanta; Kalamazoo, Mich.; St. Louis; Chicago; and on the New Jersey shore) led to the new ledger-attachment code provisions.

Most of the aforementioned decks were based on approved engineering designs. The failures occurred where the deck was attached to the primary structure; in many cases, the deck ledger had been attached to the house with nails rather than bolts, a method that was code compliant in many areas at the time the decks were built. Rust and decay of the nails also apparently accelerated the separation of the ledger board from the structure, which eventually caused the decks to collapse.

Ledger Connections Studied

Researchers at Virginia Tech University and Washington State University tested simulated deck ledger–to–house band joist connections. The testing included a practical range of pressure-preservative-treated (PPT) deck-ledger lumber (incised hem-fir and southern pine) attached to a simulated spruce-pine-fir band joist by $\frac{1}{2}$-inch lag screws or bolts with washers. The deck ledger was separated from the band joist by a piece of $\frac{15}{32}$-inch wall sheathing. In a separate test for bolts only, a $\frac{1}{2}$-inch stack of washers was inserted between the ledger and the sheathing to produce a drainage plane.

Figure 16. This third-floor deck collapse at Virginia Beach was one of several high-profile collapses that led to new code provisions for deck-to-house connections.

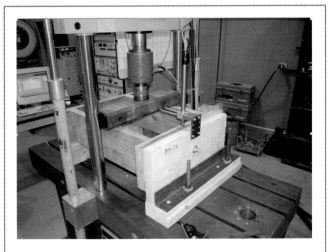

Figure 17. Researchers at Virginia Tech used this hydraulic apparatus to test the strength of various ledger-to-house connections.

The specimens were tested to failure (**Figure 17**); average test results were divided by a factor of 3.0 — intended to provide an adequate in-service safety factor — and further divided by 1.6 to convert from a "test duration" to a "normal duration" of 10 years, which is recognized by the International Building Code as the proper duration for occupancy live load. The findings, published in "Load-Tested Deck Ledger Connections" in *JLC* (November 2005), were the basis for the recently approved code change.

New Ledger Rules

Below is the resulting code provision approved at the ICC Final Action Hearings in Rochester in May 2007:

> **R502.2.2.1 Deck ledger connection to band joist.** *For decks supporting a total design load of 50 psf (40 psf live load and 10 psf dead load), the connection between a deck ledger of pressure-preservative treated*

Why Do Decks Need Lateral Anchors?

by Michael Morse

Prior to 2007, the IRC required only that decks be designed to safely transfer all anticipated live and dead floor loads to the foundation. What the code did not do is define how the lateral loads (away from the main structure) were to be transferred to the foundation. In some cases, the lack of a secure lateral connection has had devastating results.

Most deck collapses are due to failures at the deck-to-house connection. This includes the deck joists, the ledger board, the house rim joist, and the house floor joists. Decks detach from houses due to failure of the critical connections to keep the two structures together.

The IRC has now recognized the deck-to-house connection to be the weak link. A deck ledger board that is through-bolted to the rimboard still relies on the nails connecting the rimboard to the joists for the connection to the house foundation. The house rimboard and its connection to the house joists was never designed to support additional living space or to resist a lateral force trying to pull it out of the building. It was designed to resist racking of the house and its floor joists.

Lag bolts or through-bolts join the rim board and the ledger board to create a laminated beam that carries the vertical load imposed on a deck to the house foundation. Lateral anchors, on the other hand, are designed to resist horizontal or lateral loads. They keep the rim joist-ledger board beam from pulling away from the house (**Figure A**). Each type of connector performs a separate job, and both are necessary.

We recommend using a lateral anchor for a lateral attachment.

Lateral anchors are specifically engineered to maximize the performance of the deck-to-house connection. They are designed to work with the floor joists, to flex and distort to preserve the holding power of the assembly, and to resist ripping through the 2-by floor joist.

The lateral load connection shown in the IRC is a sim-

DEKLOK BRACKET SYSTEMS

Figure A. *Even with a solid connection of ledger to band joist, a deck can collapse if the band joist pulls away from the floor joists.*

Southern Pine, incised pressure-preservative treated Hem-Fir, or approved decay-resistant species, and a 2-inch nominal band joist bearing on a sill plate or wall plate shall be constructed with 1/2-inch lag screws or bolts with washers per Table R502.2.2.1. Lag screws, bolts, and washers shall be hot-dipped galvanized or stainless steel.

The proposed on-center spacing is the more conservative number that was found to be adequate in testing by the two universities for the two cases of deck-ledger lumber studied.

Because of limited information on the performance of composite-type rimboards and the possibility of new products entering the market of a lower quality than those tested, engineered rimboards are not included in the scope of the fastener spacing table (see IRC Table R502.2.2.1, page 44). Instead, as referenced in Footnote 6 of the table, the contractor or building official needs to refer to the manufacturer of the rimboard product.

Also, the researchers tested specimens with a 1x9½-inch LVL rimboard, so Footnote 7 allows LVL to be substituted for the 2x8 band joist. Most important, Footnote 8 allows the use of other types of sheathing, up to 1 inch in thickness, as long as the distance between the face of the band joist and the face of ledger is not greater than 1 inch. This allows the ledger table to be used for decks attached to houses sheathed with those alternative materials.

The following two additional sections have been included in the provision to allow the installer flexibility in locating the lag screw or bolt so that it does not interfere with installation of the structural connector; to clarify requirements for an engineered design; and to prohibit deck attachments to masonry veneer:

R502.2.2.1.1 Placement of lag screws or bolts in deck ledgers. The lag screws or bolts shall be placed two inches in from the bottom or top of the deck ledgers and between two and five inches in from the

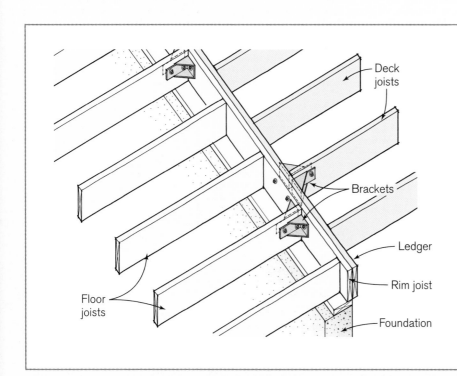

Deck joists

Brackets

Ledger

Rim joist

Foundation

Floor joists

Figure B. *The 2007 IRC requires a strong connection between deck joists and the house's floor framing. The DeckLok Bracket, shown here, is one option.*

plistic example in which the house floor joists and deck joists align both laterally and horizontally. Deck builders will not usually be so lucky, but the connection can still be made. Where house joists and deck joists do not align, one option is to anchor the ledger board to the house floor joists and, with a separate bolt and anchor, tie the deck joists to the rim board (**Figure B**).

The concept is the same no matter which way the joists run. The deck must be tied into the structure of the house. In cases when the deck ledger runs parallel to the house's floor joists, install blocking between the outer two floor joists and bolt lateral anchors to each of those joists. This will create a structural connection between the deck ledger board and the house floor system.

Michael Morse is president of DeckLok Bracket Systems, which manufactures steel framing connectors for deck construction.

Deck Attachment for Lateral Loads

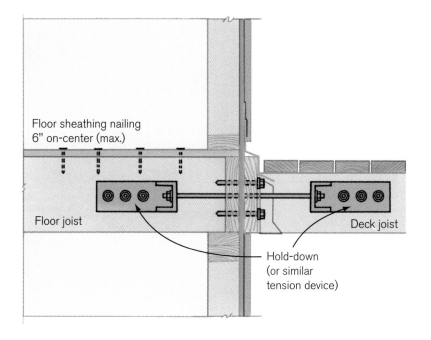

Floor sheathing nailing
6" on-center (max.)

Floor joist

Deck joist

Hold-down
(or similar
tension device)

Figure 18. The lateral load connection required by section R502.2.2 of the 2007 IRC requires hold-down tension devices like those shown here. This type of connector is required in at least two locations per deck, and each device must be designed for an allowable stress capacity of at least 1,500 pounds.

IRC Table R502.2.2.1

**Fastener Spacing for a Southern Pine or Hem-Fir Deck Ledger and
a 2-Inch Nominal Solid-Sawn Spruce-Pine-Fir Band Joist
Deck Live Load = 40 psf, Deck Dead Load = 10 psf[3,6,7]**

Joist Span	6' and less	6'-1" to 8'	8'-1" to 10'	10'-1" to 12'	12'-1" to 14'	14'-1" to 16'	16'-1" to 18'
Connection Details	On-Center Spacing of Fasteners[4,5]						
$1/2$" diameter lag screw with $15/32$" maximum sheathing	30"	23"	18"	15"	13"	11"	10"
$1/2$" diameter bolt with $15/32$" maximum sheathing	36"	36"	34"	29"	24"	21"	19"
$1/2$" diameter bolt with $15/32$" maximum sheathing and $1/2$" stacked washers[2,8]	36"	36"	29"	24"	21"	18"	16"

1 The tip of the lag screw shall fully extend beyond the inside face of the band joist.
2 The maximum gap between the face of the ledger board and face of the wall sheathing shall be $1/2$".
3 Ledgers shall be flashed to prevent water from contacting the house band joist.
4 Lag screws and bolts shall be staggered per R502.2.2.1.1.
5 Deck ledger shall be minimum 2x8 pressure-preservative-treated No. 2 grade lumber or other approved materials as established by standard engineering practice.
6 When solid-sawn pressure-preservative-treated deck ledgers are attached to engineered wood products (structural composite lumber rimboard or laminated veneer lumber), the ledger attachment shall be designed in accordance with accepted engineering practices.
7 A minimum 1x9$1/2$ Douglas Fir laminated veneer rimboard shall be permitted in lieu of the 2-inch nominal band joist.
8 Wood structural panel sheathing, gypsum board sheathing, or foam sheathing not exceeding one inch in thickness shall be permitted. The maximum distance between the face of the ledger board and the band of the joist shall be one inch.

ends. The lag screws or bolts shall be staggered from the top to the bottom along the horizontal run of the deck ledger.

R502.2.2.2 Alternate deck ledger connections. *Deck ledger connections not conforming to Table R502.2.2.1 shall be designed in accordance with accepted engineering practice. Girders supporting deck joists shall not be supported on deck ledgers or band joists. Deck ledgers shall not be supported on stone or masonry veneer.*

New Lateral Anchor Rules

Finally, to address concerns in high-wind zones and ensure that the rimboard is adequately anchored into the floor system (**Figure 18**), Section R502.2.2.3

requires positive anchorage of the deck joists to the floor framing. This provision is similar to a FEMA construction requirement (see "Why Do Decks Need Lateral Anchors?" page 42):

> **R502.2.2.3 Deck lateral load connection.** *The lateral load connection required by Section R502.2.2 shall be permitted to be in accordance with Figure R502.2.2. Hold-down tension devices shall be provided in not less than two locations per deck, and each device shall have an allowable stress design capacity of not less than 1500 lb.*

Cheri B. Hainer is the permits and inspections administrator for the city of Virginia Beach, Va.

Strong Rail-Post Connections for Wooden Decks

by Joseph Loferski and Frank Woeste, with Dustin Albright and Ricky Caudill

During the last several years, wood science researchers at Virginia Tech have scrutinized the structural connections commonly found in residential wood decks. Here, we turned our attention to residential deck railings — the guardrails intended to prevent people from accidentally falling off the edge. When decks rise more than a couple of feet off the ground, such accidents can be serious and even deadly, as news reports have corroborated. With many decks standing 8 feet or higher above grade, this is not an issue a builder can afford to ignore.

The point was brought home to us when engineer Frank Woeste was asked to inspect the railing on a friend's deck and found the rail posts toenailed into the decking (**Figure 19**, next page), an unacceptably flimsy connection. Looking around our area of Virginia, we spotted other railing connections that made it clear that some deck builders, at least, aren't aware of code requirements for deck railings.

What Code Says

The 2003 International Residential Code (IRC Table R301.5) specifies a minimum concentrated live load of 200 pounds for both guardrails and handrails (see "Guardrails vs. Handrails," page 39). Footnote "d" in the table defines the application of the 200-pound load as "a single concentrated load applied in any direction at any point along the top." Judging by what we were observing in the field, it seemed obvi-

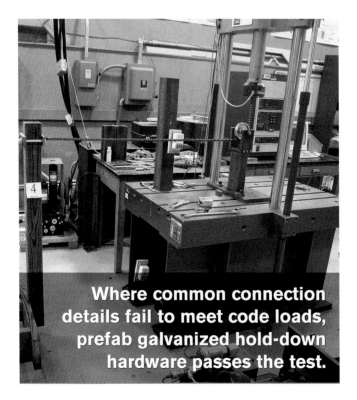

Where common connection details fail to meet code loads, prefab galvanized hold-down hardware passes the test.

ous that many deck railings would not pass this loading requirement.

A guardrail is really a system of components connected together and fastened to the deck, including posts, railings, and pickets (or balusters). Rather than look at the entire guardrail system, we decided to

Figure 19. Researchers at Virginia Tech applied measured loads to deck posts to see which connections could meet code. The tests were spawned in part by one author's observations of dangerously weak details on existing decks, as in the two examples above, where railing posts were simply toenailed into the decking. The post in the photo at right was covered by a decorative plastic cover, which concealed the flimsy connection.

Why Not Notch?

Several of the 4x4 posts we tested were notched around the band joist — a common detail in the field. While you might expect the notch to be the weak point in the connection, in fact none of the test posts failed at the notch. Even so, notching should be avoided, because it does substantially reduce the strength of the post. Here's why: Many years of observation have proved that moisture cycles will typically cause cracks to develop and propagate, parallel to the grain, from the corner of the notch. This may not be apparent when the post is first installed, but it happens gradually over time.

According to the grading rules for lumber, a piece of 4x4 No. 2 southern pine can have a "slope of grain" of up to 1:8 (or 1 inch in 8 inches). If a 4x4 with a slope of grain of 1:8 is notched 1.75 inches deep, a crack propagated along the grain will reduce the 1.75-inch-thick section at the notch to only $3/4$ inch at 8 inches above the corner of the notch — not something you'd want to bet your life on.

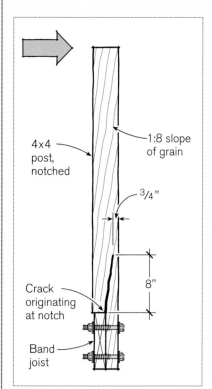

4x4 post, notched

1:8 slope of grain

$3/4$"

8"

Crack originating at notch

Band joist

Cracks will typically develop from the corner of a notch (photo, right). As a crack develops, a steep "slope of grain" can critically reduce the section of the post, as the drawing shows.

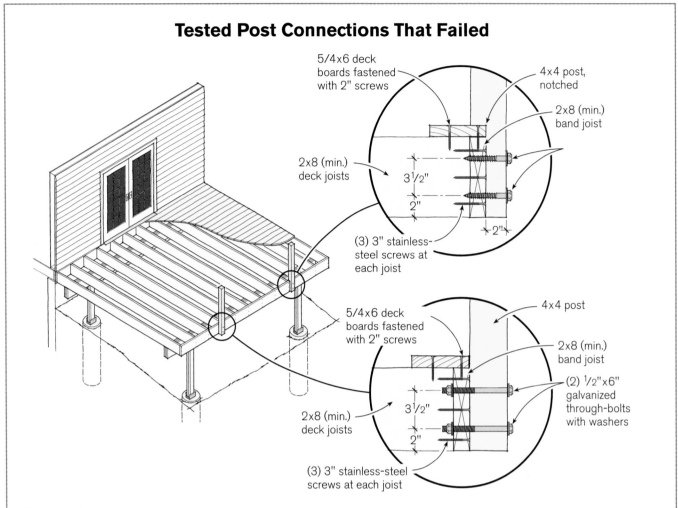

Tested Post Connections That Failed

5/4x6 deck boards fastened with 2" screws

4x4 post, notched

2x8 (min.) band joist

2x8 (min.) deck joists

$3\frac{1}{2}$"

2"

2"

(3) 3" stainless-steel screws at each joist

5/4x6 deck boards fastened with 2" screws

4x4 post

2x8 (min.) band joist

(2) $\frac{1}{2}$"x6" galvanized through-bolts with washers

2x8 (min.) deck joists

$3\frac{1}{2}$"

2"

(3) 3" stainless-steel screws at each joist

Figure 20. The authors first tested two post connections found commonly in their area, one where the 4x4 pressure-treated post is notched and lag-screwed to the band joist (top detail), and a second where the post is through-bolted to the deck band joist (bottom detail). Code requires that a rail post be able to withstand a 200-pound force applied in any direction. The researchers tested the worst-case scenario only, by pulling outward at the top of the post; they applied a 2.5-times safety factor, according to code-accepted test protocol.

narrow our testing to post connections. There are many ways to attach deck posts, so for practical reasons we decided to limit the possibilities to methods frequently used by carpenters in our geographic area.

What's being built. By far the most common details we found locally were the cases shown in **Figure 20**, where the post attaches to a "band joist" at the outer edge of the deck structure. These posts are typically notched (see "Why Not Notch?"), but not always, so we decided to test the connections both ways.

While many of the post connections we observed were obviously loose and allowed us to shake the railing, some of the posts seemed strong. But the question we wanted to answer was whether these connections would stand up to a code-protocol test load.

Setting Up the Test

A load "applied in any direction" includes people leaning against the railing or sitting on top of it. But it also means that the railing should be able to resist a load applied from the outside — for instance, a tree that falls against it. We decided to limit our testing to the worst-case scenario — that of a 200-pound load applied from the deck side perpendicular to the very top of the post. Making a connection to resist this force at the base of the post is harder than you might think, because of the lever-arm effect (force x distance): The magnification of this 200-pound horizontal force produces a couple of thousand pounds of load at the base of the post (see "Forces in a Typical Guardrail Post," page 50).

We assumed that the top of the railing was 36 inches above the deck surface (the minimum height allowed by the IRC) and that the deck boards in an actual application are at most 1.5 inches thick. Thus, the horizontal test load was applied to the post 37.5 inches above the top of the simulated deck joists.

Our test machine applied a measured force, using a roller chain and pulley to redirect its vertical

Test Results: Lag Screws and Bolts

Post-to-Deck Connection Assembly	Average Test Load (lb.)	Range of Test Loads (lb.)	Average Deflection at 200 lb. (in.)	Average Test Load as Percentage of 500 lb.*
¹/₂-inch Lag Screws	178	146 to 211	NA	35%
¹/₂-inch Bolts	237	217 to 248	4.4	47%

*Must be greater than 100 percent to be considered code-conforming

Figure 21. Although the bolted and lagged connections appeared sturdy, neither type could come close to meeting the target 500-pound test load, as the table shows. The authors tested five samples of each connection, applying a horizontal force at the top of the post until the post detached from the joist structure or the band joist itself came off. A piece of 5/4 decking nailed to the simulated joists and band joist did little to prevent failure.

Figure 22. After testing the bolted and lagged connections, the authors tried reinforcing the post with blocking in a variety of configurations. Each configuration they tried failed when the blocking split along the grain.

motion to a horizontal force at the top of the post. The post was attached to a simulated deck framing system that included two joists and a band joist with the post attached to the band joist with bolts or lag screws, just as in a real deck. We secured the deck joists to the concrete floor of the lab, and attached a transducer to the joist near the post location to verify that the test assembly didn't move. We also attached a transducer to the post 37.5 inches above the joist to measure how much it deflected during the test.

Safety factor. The code requirement says that the post must be able to withstand a 200-pound load. But when a structural assembly is tested in a lab, the load gets multiplied by an appropriate safety factor, which is intended to allow for the uncertainties of field installation and the fact that the connections may degrade in service from repeated loading and weathering (but not rot).

We used a safety factor of 2.5, a number that has been in the model codes for decades for testing structural assemblies. So, for our testing, we needed to apply a 500-pound load to determine whether the post

Post Connections That Passed

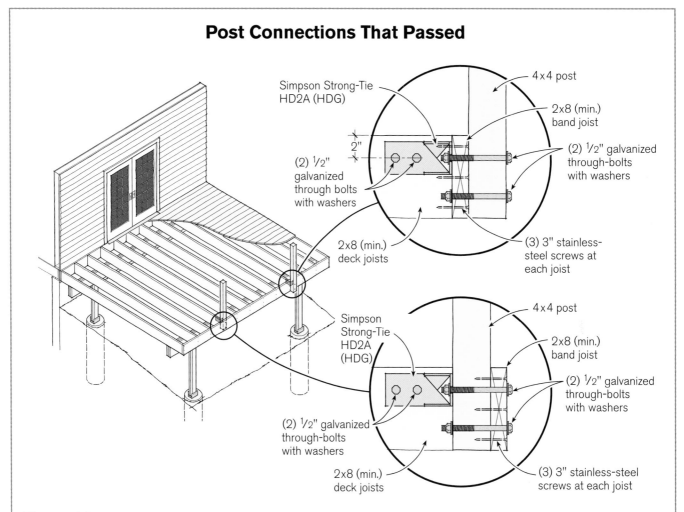

Figure 23. A Simpson Strong-Tie HD2A, installed sideways on a joist, proved able to resist the torque at the base of the post. This connection detail requires that the post be installed at a deck joist. The recently introduced Simpson Connector DTT2Z, designed specifically for this application, is a more cost-effective option.

connection could be considered "code-conforming."

Lumber grade and species. Because we were imitating local carpentry details, we used pressure-treated (ACQ or CA-B) 2x8 southern pine to simulate the joists and No. 2 southern pine 4x4 posts. Some of the tests included a PPT 5/4x6 radius-edge deck board attached to the joists and band joist. We bought the lumber in "wet" condition (moisture content greater than 19 percent) and kept it that way before the test so that we wouldn't have to apply an adjustment factor for "wet use" to our test data.

Test Results

We tested five samples each of the bolted and lag-screwed post connections shown in Figure 20 (page 47). What became obvious is that these standard details don't come close to meeting the code load requirement (**Figure 21**).

The lag-screwed connection failed at less than 200 pounds when the lags pulled out of the band joist. The bolted connections failed at an average load of

237 pounds — barely surpassing the code design load but with almost no safety factor for the service life of the deck. The bolted samples typically failed when the band joist peeled away from the deck joists, as the screws attaching the band to the joists pulled out. The screws holding the 5/4 deck board to the joists and band joist failed early in the tests.

Once it was clear these two common details were inadequate, we tried various ways of blocking around the post, attempting to distribute the load over many lag screws to reach the 500-pound test load. These attempts typically failed when the lumber split under perpendicular-to-grain loading — the kind of load exerted when you split wood with an axe (**Figure 22**).

A Different Approach

As the testing progressed, we realized that the high forces at the base of the post were not going to be resisted by fasteners loaded in withdrawal or by blocking loaded perpendicular to the grain. What we needed was a way to arrange the bolts so that the

Forces in a Typical Guardrail Post

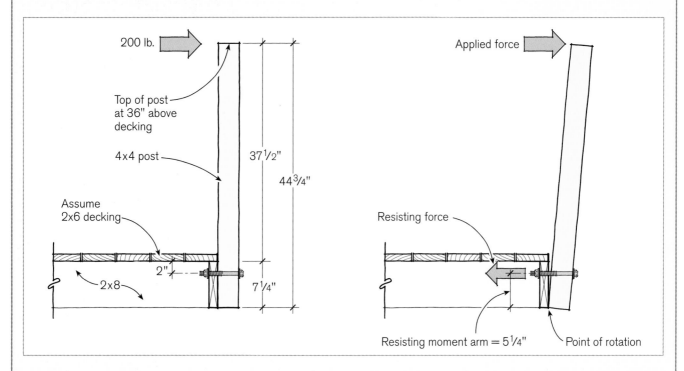

Moment = force x distance

Applied moment = resisting moment

Applied moment = 200 lb. x 44.75 in.
= 8,950 inch-pounds at base of post

Resisting moment = ? lb. x 5.25 in.

(5.25 in. is the distance from bottom of
joist to bolt centerline)

Resisting force = 8,950 inch-pounds / 5.25 in.
= 1,705 lb.

A guardrail post can behave like a lever: The force applied at the top gets multiplied by the length of the post – the lever arm – to produce a large moment, expressed in inch-pounds, at the base. The resisting force at the base, here represented by a single bolt, is also multiplied, but by a much shorter lever arm – $5\frac{1}{4}$ inches in this example. In the case shown here, representing a typical residential deck rail post 36 inches high, the bolt would have to provide nearly 2,000 pounds of resisting force. While the steel itself might be up to the task, the wood fibers under the washers would not be strong enough, as the authors' tests indicated.

load from the post to the joist would be transferred in shear (lateral loading), because bolted connections are very strong when handling lateral, or shearing, loads.

We turned to a commercial steel connector — a Simpson Strong-Tie HD2A — which is designed to resist wind and earthquake loads in shear walls. By orienting the connector sideways along the joist, we were able to use it to secure the post (**Figure 23**, previous page). We installed the HD2A with three 1/2-inch-diameter bolts: The two bolts in the joist are loaded in shear, while the third bolt, passing through the post, the band, and the connector itself, is loaded in tension. As part of the tested design, we also installed another 1/2-inch bolt in the lower part of the post and the band joist. We applied at least 650 pounds to the top of the post; every specimen successfully resisted the load.

We tested the connection two ways — with the post located inside the band and on the outside. We observed different types of failure for the two cases as the load increased up to the maximum of about 650 pounds (**Figure 24**).

When the post was mounted inside the band, the washers under the bolt head embedded into the wide face of the 2x8 band joist. When the post was located outside the band, the bolt head and washer pulled well into the 4x4 post, crushing the wood fibers beneath the washer.

We used only one Simpson HD2A per post, placing the centerline of the connector 2 inches below the top edge of the 2x8 joist. If you use this detail in the field, it's important to maintain this centerline distance, because it helps to limit the forces involved in the con-

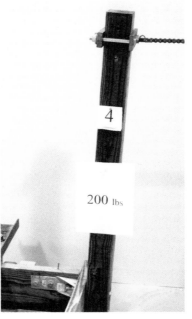
200 lbs

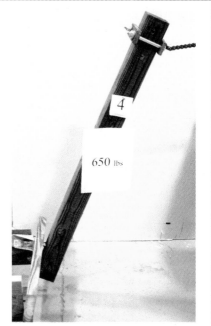
650 lbs

Test Results: HD2A Anchors

Post-to-Deck Connection Assembly	Average Test Load (lb.)	Range of Test Loads (lb.)	Average Deflection at 200 lb. (in.)	Average Test Load as Percentage of 500 lb.*
HD2A Anchor (4x4 post inside band)	645	593 to 687**	2	129%
HD2A Anchor (4x4 post outside band)	686	653 to 713**	1.9	137%

*Must be greater than 100 percent to be considered code-conforming
**Tests stopped to protect test equipment

Figure 24. The authors tested the HD2A connection with the post installed both inside and outside the band joist; both configurations withstood the full test load. At 200 pounds, the sample post shown above deflected but the connection held. At 650 pounds, with the post still holding, the test was ended so as not to damage the test machine.

nection. If you place the HD2A lower, you're reducing the resisting lever arm, which extends from the bottom of the band joist to the centerline of the connector. Losing even an inch of this resisting lever arm would greatly increase the forces in the connector.

We used a hot-dipped galvanized (HDG) HD2A connector for our tests. Because of the corrosive nature of the new lumber treatments, this is the version that should be used in practice. The 1/2-inch bolts, washers, and nuts should also be hot-dipped galvanized.

Note: In 2009, Simpson Strong-Tie introduced the DTT2Z connector, specifically designed to attach deck rail posts to deck framing. These are more cost-effective for deck builders than the HD2A holddowns we tested, which were designed for use in shear walls.

Limitations of Test Results

We didn't test the HD2A connector post-to-deck assembly in the inward loading mode — that of the tree falling against the railing. In our judgment, the assembly as tested would not carry a 500-pound inward force. However, we believe that the assembly would carry 500 pounds in either direction if you were to install two HD2A connectors per post, one 2 inches from the bottom of the 2x8 band joist and one 2 inches from the top.

Our test also applies only to the grade and species of lumber that we used. Keep in mind that southern pine is denser than most other common framing species (specific gravity [SG] = 0.55), which affects its ability to hold fasteners. Pressure-treated hem-fir is commonly available in the Western states, but because hem-fir is less dense (SG = 0.43) than southern pine, the same connections made with hem-fir lumber would probably fail at a lower load.

Joseph Loferski is a professor in the Department of Wood Science and Forest Products at Virginia Tech University, Blacksburg. Frank Woeste, PE, is professor emeritus at Virginia Tech. Dustin Albright is a graduate research assistant and Ricky Caudill is a lab technician.

Safety Glazing for Safer Decks

by Glenn Mathewson

The completed deck is beautiful and your client loves it. It just needs to pass inspection, then you can move on to the next job. No worries — it's a simple deck and there shouldn't be any problems. But when the inspector does the final inspection, he tells you it looks great — except you must "safety glaze" a window on the house.

What? You didn't do anything to that window, so how are you responsible? I can tell you that you're not the only deck builder to be surprised by this code requirement. As an inspector, I often see designs that don't account for the locations of the existing windows.

Windows are typically made from glass, or what the building codes call "glazing," which is dangerous when broken. Thus, Section R308 of the 2006 International Residential Code calls for safety glazing in locations it deems hazardous.

The safety glazing must display a manufacturer's designation, commonly called a "tempering bug," that specifies who applied the designation, what type of glazing was used, and which safety standard was met. Further, the tempering bug must be acid- or laser-etched, sandblasted, ceramic-fired, embossed, or otherwise applied so it can't be removed without being destroyed in the process; and it must be visible at final inspection.

The most common safety glazing is tempered glass, like that used in the side and rear windows of your truck. It shatters into small pieces, which are much less likely to cause injury than a big pane of broken glass.

Section R308.4 of the 2006 IRC specifies 11 different "hazardous locations" where safety glass is required; relevant to deck building are glazed areas near walking surfaces, stairways, doors, and hot tubs.

In all these locations, each individual pane of glazing is considered separately. The area, dimensions, and location of each pane are considered exclusive of the window frame or sash, and of the sum of the areas of the other panes in the same window assembly. It's not uncommon to have a single window assembly of multiple panes in which only select panes are required to be safety glazed.

Walking Surfaces

A glazing location may be considered hazardous by the IRC if it is within 36 inches, measured horizontally, of a walking surface. A deck is exactly that — a walking surface — and if it adjoins the house, it's likely to be within 36 inches of a window or glazing. When that glazing meets all the criteria in **Figure 25**, below, it must be safety glazed.

There are a couple of exceptions that allow regular glazing. The first is for "decorative glass," defined by the 2006 IRC as: *"A carved, leaded or Dalle glass or glazing material whose purpose is decorative or artistic, not functional; whose coloring, texture or other design qualities or components cannot be removed without destroying the glazing material; and whose surface, or assembly into which it is incorporated, is divided into segments."* In short, "stained glass."

The other exception applies if a protective bar, a minimum of 1½ inches thick, is installed on the

---

Adding a Deck Might Require Changing the Windows

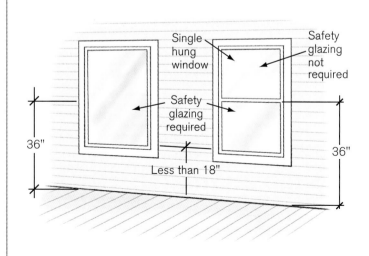

Figure 25. The 2006 IRC requires safety glazing when all four of these criteria are met:

1. Exposed area of an individual pane larger than 9 square feet.

2. Bottom edge less than 18 inches above the floor.

3. Top edge more than 36 inches above the floor.

4. One or more walking surfaces within 36 inches horizontally of the glazing.

Each pane is considered individually, so it's possible that the bottom pane of a single- or double-hung window would need to be safety glazed, while the top would not.

Safety Glazing Required Near Stairs

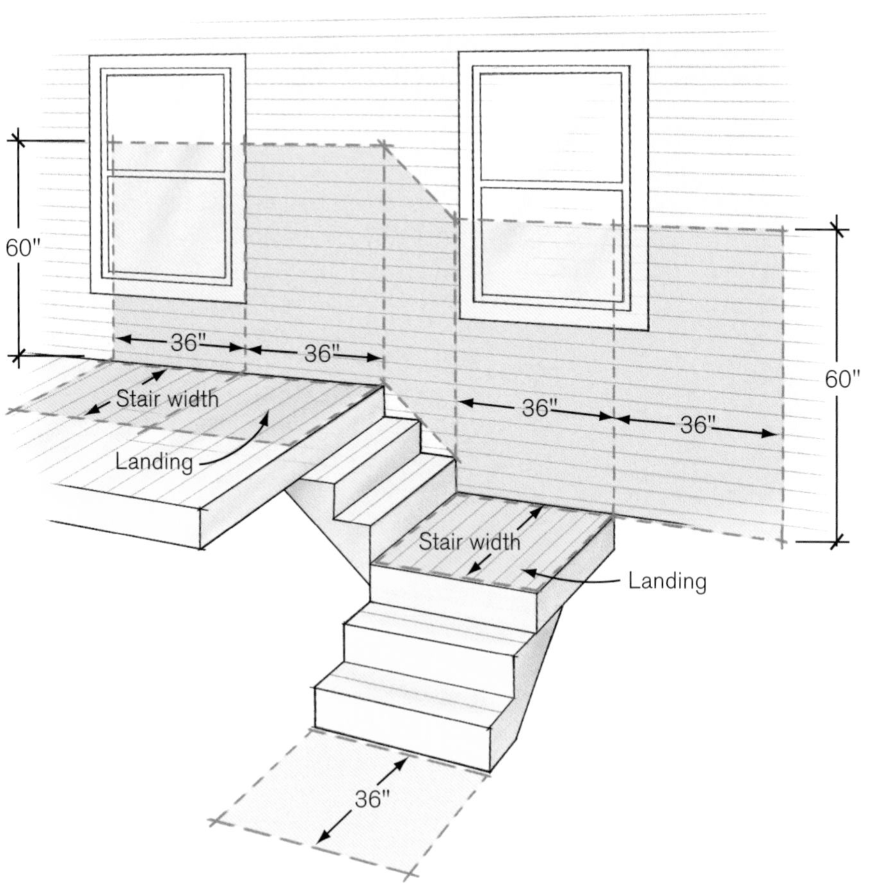

Figure 26. The 2006 IRC calls for safety glazing when glazing is "adjacent to stairways, landings and ramps within 36 inches horizontally of a walking surface when the exposed surface of the glass is less than 60 inches above the plane of the adjacent walking surface."

While we think of landings as being in the middle of a run of stairs, the IRC requires a landing at the top and bottom of each stair, even if it's a portion of the deck or the lawn. Such landings must extend at least 36 inches beyond the stair. The code further requires that glazing be safety glazing if it is within 36 inches of the landing, measured horizontally, and within 60 inches measured vertically. Effectively, that means windows within 6 feet (36 inches + 36 inches) of the top of a stair might need safety glazing.

accessible side of the glazing. The bar must be at a height between 34 inches and 38 inches above the walking surface and cannot contact the glass when a 50-pound per linear-foot horizontal load is applied.

Before relying on any code exception, always consult the governing building department, as exceptions can be subjectively interpreted.

Stairways

Stairs are inherently dangerous; people slip and fall on them. Because of this, safety glazing must be used when the glazing is adjacent to a stairway.

The IRC defines stairways as any elevation change of one or more risers, and includes landings in its definition. All stairways, even those consisting of a single step, require top and bottom landings that are the width of the stairs and extend at least 36 inches in the direction of travel.

The landing does not have to be a separate component; it may be a portion of a larger walking surface. If the stairs ascend directly to the main area of the deck, the portion of the deck that is the width of the stairs and runs 36 inches beyond the top nosing,

measured in the direction of travel, is considered the "landing" (**Figure 26**).

Another hazardous location with regard to glazing near stairs is the area within 60 inches of the bottom of the stairway (**Figure 27**, next page).

There are exceptions to these rules, also. As in areas adjacent to walkways, protective bars can be used to protect glazing within 36 inches of stairs and landings, unless the glazing is within 60 inches, measured horizontally, of the bottom tread.

Additionally, another exception implies that safety glazing is not required if the glazing is more than 18 inches beyond a guard (a wall or railing at least 36 inches high, with balusters or infill spaced at most 4 inches apart, all of which must resist a 200-pound load from any direction). This exception can be applied to both hazardous stairway locations, but it isn't clearly presented, and I recommend you check the local building department's interpretation of it before using it in your design.

Glazing used in all guardrails — both level and on stairs — must also be safety glazing.

Bottoms of Stairs Have Their Own Requirements

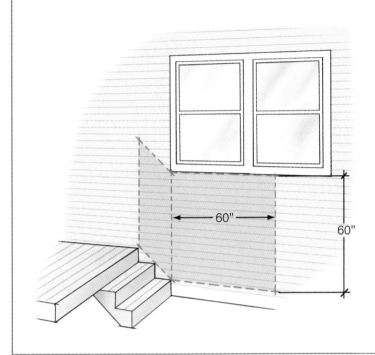

Figure 27. The 2006 IRC calls for safety glazing when glazing is "adjacent to stairways within 60 inches horizontally of the bottom tread of a stairway in any direction when the exposed surface of the glass is less than 60 inches above the nose of the tread."

There are two important aspects of this section to pay attention to. First, it clearly states "any direction." The literal words of the code are the requirements and could be enforced as such. Despite how irrational, even glazing within 60 inches horizontally behind and below the stair would fall into this area.

Second, the 60-inch height is measured above the nose of the tread, so you must include the height of the first rise when measuring off the floor or landing at the base of the stairway. For example, consider steps with 7-inch rises: If you measure horizontally 60 inches from the nose of the last step, as specified by the code, you actually need to measure 67 inches vertically from the landing below to determine the need for safety glazing.

Doors

Homeowners may wish to have a door installed leading to their new deck, often a simple matter of reframing an existing window opening. You may not even have to change any structural components of the wall, like the header or trimmer-king studs. Easy, right? By now, it should come as no surprise that there are other things to consider, one of them

being glazing near the future door.

Glazing that is within a 24-inch arc of a door jamb and whose lowest point is less than 60 inches above the walking surface must be safety glazing. **Figure 28**, below, shows how the arcs are measured. The exception for decorative glass, as previously defined for areas adjacent to walkways, can also be used to exempt glazing within the 24-inch arcs of the door jambs.

Adding a Door? Check Nearby Windows

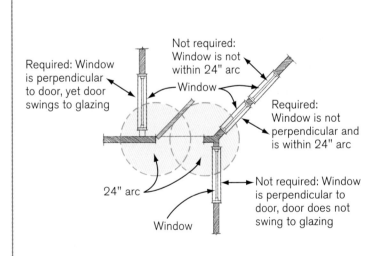

Figure 28. The 2006 IRC calls for safety glazing when glazing "is in an individual fixed or operable panel adjacent to a door where the nearest vertical edge is within a 24-inch arc of the door in a closed position and whose bottom edge is less than 60 inches above the floor or walking surface."

This section is not easily understood. Imagine attaching one end of a 24-inch-long string to the corner of the door jamb, then pulling the free end in a horizontal arc. Any glass less than 60 inches above the floor and within the reach of the string would need to be safety glazed.

Arcs are measured from both door jambs, on the inside and outside — four places. In the case of a sliding glass door, the whole assembly is considered the "door": You would not measure from the edges of only the operable panel, but from the edge of the inoperable panel as well — in other words, the edge of the door assembly.

Pools, Hot Tubs, and Spas Need Safe Glass

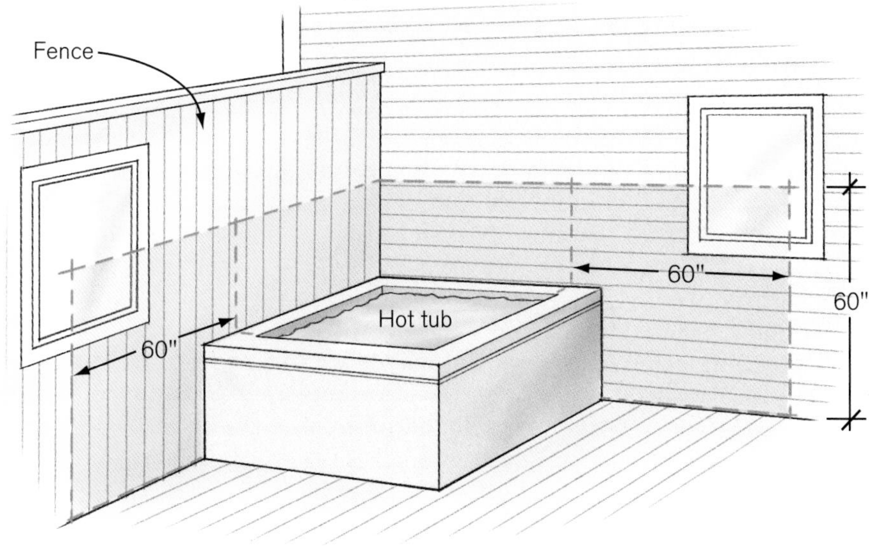

Fence

60"

Hot tub

60"

60"

Figure 29. The 2006 IRC calls for safety glazing when glazing is "in walls and fences enclosing indoor and outdoor swimming pools, hot tubs and spas where the bottom edge of the glazing is less than 60 inches above a walking surface and within 60 inches horizontally of the water's edge. This shall apply to single glazing and all panes in multiple glazing."

This is probably the simplest section. There are no exceptions — glass near wet areas must be safety glazing.

Pools, Hot Tubs, and Spas

It's no secret that water makes floors and decks slippery, and that the floor around pools and hot tubs is usually wet. Any glazing within 5 feet, measured horizontally, of the water's edge and less than 5 feet above an adjacent walking surface is required to be safety glazed — there are no exceptions to this requirement (**Figure 29**).

When designing for a hot-tub or spa location, always remember the "rule of 5," five items that, in general, must be at least 5 feet away: glazing, lighting, receptacles, switches, and unbonded-metal objects subject to becoming inadvertently energized (such as guardrails or barbecues).

Also remember that hot tubs and spas generally require an approved safety cover or security barrier to protect small children from injury (see "Hot-Tub Safety: Covers vs. Security Barriers," page 56).

Code sections are not always easy to understand, which often causes inconsistency in enforcement among jurisdictions. I encourage you to include the location of all glazing on the construction documents you submit for a permit. This gives the plan reviewers a chance to redline any glazing that may be subject to safety glazing. You will then be able to incorporate these requirements into your construction process or alter your design, rather than learning about them when your job is complete.

Glenn Mathewson is a building inspector in Westminster, Colo., and a former deck builder.

Hot-Tub Safety: Covers vs. Security Barriers

by Glenn Mathewson

Are security barriers required for hot tubs, as they are for swimming pools? The simple answer to this question is yes. Hot tubs and spas provide the same fundamental drowning danger to small children that swimming pools do, and this danger is real. According to the U.S. Consumer Product Safety Commission, pool drowning is the second leading cause of death in children younger than five; approximately 280 die each year. An additional nine die each year in hot-tub drowning accidents. Sadly, hot tubs and above-ground pools are often installed without a permit and without proper safety provisions.

At first glance, it would appear as though the 2006 IRC doesn't contain any provisions for pool security — you've got to look in the appendices at the end of the book. Standards in the appendices can be evaluated and modified by local jurisdictions separately from the body of the code and are not enforceable unless specifically adopted by the local jurisdiction. Additionally, many jurisdictions have their own codes and policies in place for pool security enforcement, so you should read this answer for comprehension of the general standard and for awareness of the issue only. Before installing a security barrier for a hot tub, consult the local authority with jurisdiction.

Appendix G in the 2006 IRC requires security barriers for swimming pools, defined as *any structure intended for swimming or recreational bathing that con-* *tains water over 24 inches deep.* This includes in-ground, above-ground, and on-ground swimming pools, hot tubs, and spas. It's clear in the definition that only structures "intended for swimming and recreational bathing" are required to have security barriers. Ponds and water features are exempted.

There are noticeable differences between security barriers and guards (the railing required around decks that are more than 30 inches above the surface below). Guards are required in situations where an unintentional fall is likely to result in injury, whereas pool barriers are there to stop intentional entry into the water.

Before discussing the detailed barrier requirements, I am going to cheat and take you straight to the exception reserved exclusively for spas and hot tubs; trust me, this is the easiest way to compliance. Section AG105.5 exempts hot tubs and spas from all the provisions of the appendix, provided they have been installed with a safety cover complying with ASTM F 1346.

Unfortunately, many hot-tub covers don't meet this standard. To comply, covers must be able to be locked or otherwise held securely in place by a means that will prohibit small children from entry, be labeled with a message about the dangers of drowning, and be capable of supporting 275 pounds (the presumed weight of an adult and one child).

Those are some of the specific provisions contained

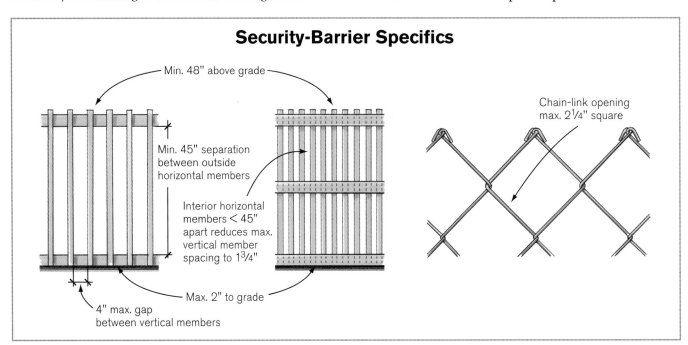

Security-Barrier Specifics

Min. 48" above grade

Min. 45" separation between outside horizontal members

Interior horizontal members < 45" apart reduces max. vertical member spacing to 1³⁄₄"

Max. 2" to grade

4" max. gap between vertical members

Chain-link opening max. 2¹⁄₄" square

in the standard, but all you need to see is that the cover complies with the standard. You can find this out from the manufacturer and have the cover approved by the building department.

While that's the simple approach to hot-tub-barrier compliance, a standard pool barrier can also be used. There are 10 specific requirements for construction of pool barriers, and after reviewing them you will see why I strongly suggest the use of the approved cover. Detailing the requirements is very involved and outside the scope of this answer; the following brief summary should be enough to convince you of this (see also "Security-Barrier Specifics"):

• The minimum barrier height is 48 inches above grade, as measured on the side of the barrier that faces away from the pool (outside the pool area).
• Maximum clearance under the barrier to grade is 2 inches.
• The barrier cannot be climbable.
• Solid barriers, such as masonry or stone, cannot have "indentations or protrusions other than for normal construction."
• Maximum mesh size is 2¼ inches square for chain link, unless filled with slats reducing the opening to a maximum of 1¾ inches.
• For diagonal members (lattice), the maximum opening is 1¾ inches.
• Horizontal members not on the pool side must be at least 45 inches apart.
• When horizontal members are on the pool side and less than 45 inches apart, the opening between or within vertical members must be less than 1¾ inches.
• Gates must comply with barrier requirements and have a locking device.
• Gates must swing away from the pool and be self-closing and self-latching.
• If the gate latch release is less than 54 inches from the bottom of the gate it must be located on the pool side at least 3 inches from the top of the gate, and the gate and barrier can't have an opening greater than ½ inch within 18 inches of the release mechanism.
• If the dwelling acts as part of the barrier, the doors to that area must be provided with an alarm system (full of specific details), or provided with self-closing and self-latching doors that are approved by the building department and provide the same level of protection as the alarm.

For deck construction including a hot tub, don't disregard the requirements for a safe installation. Glass, lights, receptacles, switches, unbonded metal objects, dead load — and especially children — must all be considered.

Also, keep in mind that even the inexpensive, vinyl above-ground pools that can be purchased at most big discount stores are often 24 inches or more in depth and must comply with these regulations. There's no question about the danger and legal liability of these "attractive nuisances."

Glenn Mathewson is a building inspector in Westminster, Colo., and a former deck builder.

Deciphering the Code for Fire-Resistant Decks

by Bill Bolton

As a deck designer and builder on the West Coast, I occasionally build decks in what's called the "wildland-urban interface." The geography here is a little different from, say, the woodlands of New England. Winter rains on the California coast support plentiful vegetation, which then dries out in the summer to become a tinderbox (**Figure 30**, next page). This large fuel source, coupled with high winds in the surrounding mountains and canyons, creates an environment ripe for the wildfires you see on the evening news.

Despite the danger, people continue to build homes in these fire-prone areas. Fortunately for them, a growing awareness of wildfire risk has led the International Code Council (ICC) to develop the International Wildland-Urban Interface Code. The IWUIC provides criteria for rating an area's fire potential as moderate, high, or extreme, and spells out prescriptive measures for building within those zones. Local jurisdictions often use this code or adopt something similar. Before building a deck in a zone requiring fire-resistant construction — before you even begin to price out the job — it's important to talk with the local building department.

The main goal of the IWUIC requirements is to prevent a deck from catching fire and — acting as kindling — igniting the house. Thus, freestanding decks built 50 feet or more away from the house are

Figure 30. Dried by the summer sun, wildland vegetation becomes the perfect fuel. Add a windy slope or canyon, and you've got the makings of a devastating fire.

generally exempt from the IWUIC, because fires on those decks are less likely to spread to the residence.

Igniting a Deck

Normally, decks catch fire one of two ways. A burning brand (piece of wood) landing on the surface of the deck is all that's required, particularly if the decking is dry or has wide gaps between the boards, which can permit airflow and harbor embers (**Figure 31**). Similarly, space between the first deck board and the house can provide airflow and catch embers, increasing the risk that the siding will ignite.

The other common cause of deck fires is flames from unmaintained vegetation igniting the deck from below, or a burning brand igniting debris below the deck. Again, dry or widely spaced deck boards will speed the spread of fire.

Once the deck ignites, it may in turn set the house on fire. Heat from the deck fire, for example, may break the glass in a sliding door, permitting flames to enter the house's interior. Or, combustible siding or soffits can ignite, carrying the fire to the house. The end result is the same. And even if the house itself doesn't ignite, the deck can lose structural integrity and become hazardous to anyone walking on it.

Codes

In any regulated area, building codes specify a particular class of construction depending on several conditions. In the 2006 IWUIC (Table 503.1), these include the fire classification of the area (moderate, high, or extreme), access to adequate water, and what's called "defensible space" — an area cleared of excessive vegetation and other fuel for a specified distance from the house (**Figure 32**).

Not much can be done to modify the first two conditions, but a property owner can control the defensible space. Wildland fires travel fast — in just five or six minutes, the majority of the flame front moves through — and minimizing the amount of nearby fuel reduces the chance that a fire will ignite a structure.

The distance the defensible space must extend from the house varies with the fire classification. Deadwood, dried leaves, and so forth should be removed from the defensible space, but fire-resistant vegetation is allowed, as are isolated islands of more flammable greenery and ornamental ground covers such as green grass and ivy — that is, assuming they don't provide a means to transmit fire from the native vegetation to the structure.

Once the fire classification of the property is determined, Chapter 5 of the 2006 IWUIC defines Class 1, 2, and 3 Ignition Resistant Construction. For decks, the requirements for Class 1 and Class 2 construction are identical. The IWUIC has no prescriptive requirements for decks in Class 3 construction.

The essential Class 1 and 2 requirements, as written in the 2006 IWUIC, are the following:

- *… decks shall be a minimum of 1-hour fire-resistance-rated construction, heavy timber construction, or constructed of approved noncombustible materials or fire-retardant-treated wood identified for exterior use and meeting the requirements of Section 2303.2 of the International Building Code.*

- *When … any portion of [the deck] projects over a descending slope surface greater than 10 percent, the*

Figure 31. Burning brands (pieces of wood) blown by a flame front or dropped by overhead trees are a common source of ignition. One test designed to determine the flammability of decking replicates that scenario in a controlled environment.

Defensible Space

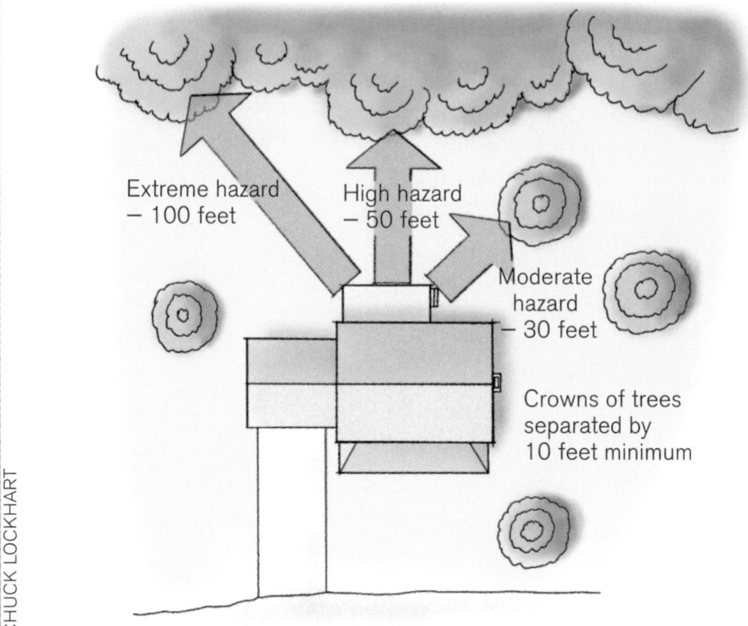

Extreme hazard
— 100 feet

High hazard
— 50 feet

Moderate
hazard
— 30 feet

Crowns of trees
separated by
10 feet minimum

CHUCK LOCKHART

Figure 32. Providing defensible space — the area surrounding a structure where vegetation is managed to minimize the spread of fire — is an IWUIC requirement for new construction in the wildland-urban interface. Depending on the overall fire-hazard classification of the area, as determined by the building department or fire marshal, the required space must extend 30, 50, or 100 feet from the house.

All "non-fire-resistive vegetation" must be removed from this space, as well as deadwood and litter. The crowns of trees that remain must be separated from structures, power lines, other trees, and unmodified fuel by at least 10 feet, and their branches must be at least 6 feet above the ground. Ornamental vegetation is allowed, provided it does not "form a means of transmitting fire from the native growth to any structure."

area below the structure shall have all underfloor areas enclosed to within 6 inches of the ground, with exterior wall construction in accordance with ... [see next].

- *Exterior walls ... shall be constructed with materials approved for a minimum of 1-hour fire-resistance-rated construction on the exterior side or constructed with approved noncombustible materials.*

One-Hour Fire Resistance

The first option above, building a 1-hour fire-resistive deck, isn't simple. Brian Thompson, an engineer with Aegis Engineering in Seattle, says, "[That's] in part because most decks are of combustible wood construction supported in part by the exterior wall of a structure that is not 1-hour rated." In other words, a strict reading of the code suggests that building a 1-hour fire-resistive deck simply isn't possible if it's

IWUIC Table 503.1
Ignition-Resistant Construction

	Fire Hazard Severity					
	Moderate Hazard **Water Supply**[b]		**High Hazard** **Water Supply**[b]		**Extreme Hazard** **Water Supply**[b]	
Defensible Space[c]	Conforming[d]	Nonconforming[a]	Conforming[d]	Nonconforming[e]	Conforming[d]	Nonconforming[e]
Nonconforming	IR 2	IR 1	IR 1	IR 1 N.C.	IR 1 N.C.	Not Permitted
Conforming	IR 3	IR 2	IR 2	IR 1	IR 1	IR 1 N.C.
1.5 x Conforming	Not required	IR 3	IR 3	IR 2	IR 2	IR 1

a. Access shall be in accordance with Section 402.
b. Subdivisions shall have a conforming water supply in accordance with Section 402.1.
   IR 1 = Ignition-resistant construction in accordance with Section 504.
   IR 2 = Ignition-resistant construction in accordance with Section 505.
   IR 3 = Ignition-resistant construction in accordance with Section 506.
   N.C. = Exterior walls shall have a fire-resistance rating of not less than 1-hour and the
   exterior surfaces of such walls shall be noncombustible. Usage of log wall construction is allowed.
c. Conformance based on section 603.
d. Conformance based on section 603.
e. Conformance based on section 603.

COURTESY INTERNATIONAL WILDLAND-URBAN INTERFACE CODE

Figure 33. Building a deck that meets the IWUIC's 1-hour fire-resistive construction requirement is a challenge. Wrapping the structure with a Type X gypsum sheathing is one approach; additional cladding will be needed to protect the gypsum board from the elements.

attached to a house that's not built in a like manner.

Even if that problem is surmounted, achieving a 1-hour fire rating is difficult. Neither the IWUIC nor the IRC provides much in the way of details for decks, so code in most jurisdictions reverts to the more commercial-construction–oriented International Building Code.

The IBC offers a plethora of ways to build a 1-hour fire-resistive structure. Most of these approaches, however, involve masonry, or they call for multiple layers of fire-rated gypsum board, which generally isn't meant to be used outside and must be protected from the elements (**Figure 33**).

Framing

The other two methods of complying with the code — using heavy timber and using noncombustible or fire-retardant–treated materials — are easier to apply. According to Glenn Mathewson, a building inspector

in Westminster, Colo., it may even be possible to combine the two to build a code-compliant deck.

Heavy timber is specified because it has a larger ratio of mass to surface area than smaller dimensions of lumber have; in other words, bigger is better (**Figure 34**). Even if the surface of a bigger timber catches fire, burning through the member takes considerably more time and contributes less intense heat. Think of starting a fire in a fireplace — the big logs take a long time to get going.

For heavy-timber construction, the IWUIC again references the IBC: Posts must be at least nominal 8x8s, beams at least nominal 6x10s, and joists at least nominal 4x6s on at most 16-inch centers; 2-by lumber isn't permitted. That's not so bad — a little expensive, maybe, but at least the materials are familiar.

The last option — fire-retardant–treated framing lumber — is perhaps the easiest. It's available in standard dimensions, and 2-by lumber may be used. However,

Figure 34. Heavy timber is one way to frame a fire-resistant deck. The larger the lumber, the harder it is to ignite, and the less intense the heat it contributes. National codes specify a minimum of 4x6 joists, 6x10 beams, and 8x8 posts.

Figure 35. Standard sizes of dimensional lumber can satisfy code requirements if they've been factory treated with a fire retardant. The stamp on the member must identify it as having been so treated and as being suitable for exterior use.

you may need to search for it. Hoover Treated Wood Products (www.frtw.com) makes a variety of fire-retardant–treated lumber products. Arch Wood Protection (www.frxwood.com) distributes an exterior fire retardant to a number of treaters nationally. A phone call to either should help to find local distribution.

Fire-retardant–treated lumber must be marked as such and carry an additional mark that shows it's intended for exterior use (**Figure 35**). Note that this lumber usually loses some strength in the treating process, so regular span tables don't apply. Follow the appropriate span tables from the manufacturer for the products you use.

Decking

Heavy-timber flooring would clearly be problematic on decks. The IBC calls for a minimum of nominal 3-inch tongue-and-groove or splined decking, covered with a second layer of at least 1-inch-nominal tongue-and-groove flooring, laid perpendicular to or diagonally across the subfloor. If that's not a recipe for rot outdoors, I don't know what is.

Fortunately, the county where I do most of my work offers other acceptable choices. We can use 2-by T&G planks, 1⅛-inch T&G plywood, 3-by lumber set on edge with no more than ⅛-inch space between members, or noncombustible decking with a Flame Spread Index not to exceed 80 and Smoke Developed Index not to exceed 285.

Several brands of composite lumber may satisfy the latter requirement, but confusion remains regarding this material's suitability in the wildland-urban interface. One attempt to clear this up can be found in a recent change to the IRC that includes the adoption of a uniform ASTM standard for composite lumber's performance in fires. This change will be part of the

Figure 36. It's hard to figure out the code requirements for decking in the wildland-urban interface. For heavy-timber construction, the IBC prescribes a layer of T&G 3-inch-nominal decking topped by a layer of 1-inch-nominal T&G flooring run perpendicular — not a very practical application. Aluminum, tile (above), or precast concrete decking products, on the other hand, are inherently noncombustible.

2007 supplement to the IRC, and will be fully embodied in the 2009 IRC.

Currently, though, requirements vary among jurisdictions. Local building departments are likely to want to know the Flame Spread and Smoke Developed Index of a particular composite decking before allowing its use in the wildland-urban interface. Most manufacturers post this information on their Web sites.

There are some inherently noncombustible decking options that would satisfy most codes, as well (**Figure 36**). Ceramic tile, precast concrete, and aluminum are a few examples (see "Sources of Noncombustible

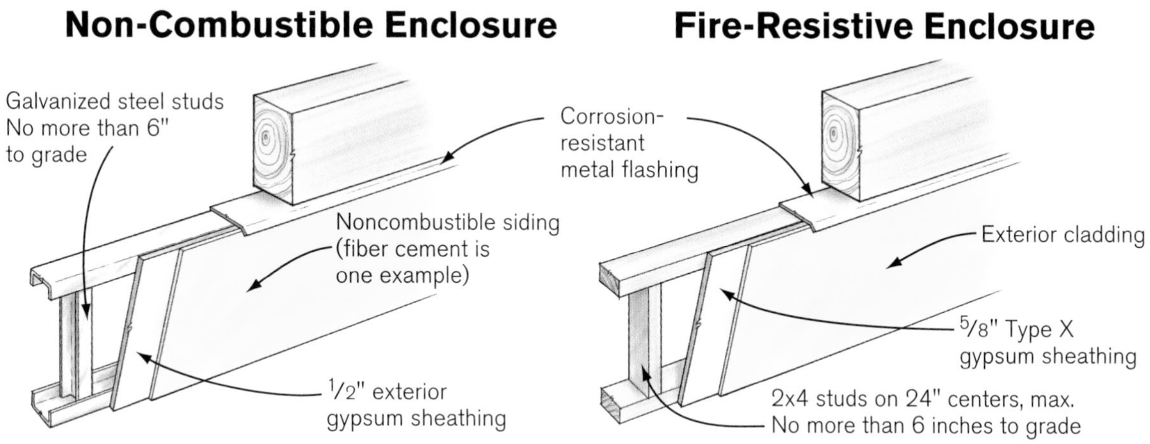

Non-Combustible Enclosure

Galvanized steel studs No more than 6" to grade

Noncombustible siding (fiber cement is one example)

½" exterior gypsum sheathing

Fire-Resistive Enclosure

Corrosion-resistant metal flashing

Exterior cladding

⅝" Type X gypsum sheathing

2x4 studs on 24" centers, max. No more than 6 inches to grade

Figure 37. Decks requiring Class 1 and 2 construction that are built over a slope of 10 percent or more must be enclosed to within 6 inches of the ground with a 1-hour fire wall or a wall of approved noncombustible materials. The International Building Code, which the IWUIC refers to, describes many such assemblies. Other options are offered by the Gypsum Association; the two above may satisfy local building departments.

Figure 38. Code requirements for railing combustibility are sketchy and subject to interpretation. One sure approach is a noncombustible system made from metal.

Decking," below). Also, ipe carries a Class A fire rating and may satisfy your local building department.

Finally, there's the option of building a beefed-up frame and pouring a concrete slab on top of it.

Slopes

Because of induced drafts, wildfires burn hottest and fastest going up a slope. The IWUIC requires any deck that has even a small portion over a slope of 10 percent (that's a 1-foot rise over 10 feet of run) or greater to be enclosed to within 6 inches of the ground with a 1-hour fire-resistive wall (**Figure 37**, previous page).

A strict interpretation of the code, according to Mathewson, requires that "you use an assembly such as described in the IBC, or tested by the Gypsum Association, UL, or some other ICC-recognized organization. Your installation must match the assem-

bly." Such a description from the Gypsum Association (www.gypsum.org) follows:

Two-by-four wood studs at 16 inches with double top plates, single bottom plate; interior and exterior sides covered with 5/8-inch Type X gypsum wall board and sheathing, respectively, 4 feet wide, applied horizontally or vertically with vertical joints over studs, and fastened with 2 1/4-inch Type S drywall screws, spaced 12 inches on center. Cavity to be filled with 3 1/2-inch mineral wool insulation.

Mathewson goes on to say, "Most inspectors would probably be fine with simply covering the studs with 5/8-inch rock for an installation on a below-the-deck wall. They probably would not ask for the assembly." That's one inspector's view; it's important that you verify the details of your own projects with your local authority.

One problem with any gypsum product, even one such as Georgia-Pacific's (www.gp.com) DensGlass Gold exterior sheathing (which comes in a 5/8-inch Type X configuration for fire resistance), is that it's not intended to be exposed to the elements for longer than a few months. It's easy enough to protect the face with a noncombustible product such as fiber-cement siding, but you need to weatherproof the top, as well. Use a noncombustible flashing — some sort of metal — that is corrosion resistant.

Such flashing will have to be compatible with any preservatives or metals used in the framing. For example, if you're using heavy timber treated with ACQ for rot resistance, you're pretty much limited to copper. If you use steel studs, though, to build the enclosure wall, copper won't work unless it's isolated from the steel by, say, a layer of gypsum. Make sure the building inspector approves.

Railings

Railings aren't specifically addressed in the IWUIC. Mathewson reads exception 2 in the 2006 IBC, Section 1406.3, to mean that railings limited to 42 inches in height don't have to be noncombustible. Nonetheless,

---

Sources of Noncombustible Decking

The companies below manufacture inherently noncombustible products that may be good choices for use in high-fire-risk zones, subject to approval by the local building department. This is by no means a complete list.

Aluminum Decking
AridDek; www.ariddek.com
FSI LockDry; www.lockdry.com
Last Deck; www.lastdeck.com
Veltech Corp; www.veltechcorp.com

Tile and Precast Concrete Systems
North American Tile Tool Co.; www.nattco.com
Stepstone; www.dekstone.com
Stone Deck; www.stonedeck.biz

that interpretation should be confirmed locally.

There are many ways that a fire-resistive or non-combustible railing system could be built. Metal rails, cable rails, glass, fire-retardant lumber, heavy timber, or a combination of these systems could all qualify (**Figure 38**). According to the 2006 IBC, composite or plastic railing systems with a self-ignition temperature greater than 650°F and a Smoke Developed Index not greater than 450 should also fly.

Requirements for decks built in high-fire-risk areas are an evolving part of the codes and confuse even building officials. Add to that the fact that codes differ throughout the country, and it's obvious that this information is only a starting point. When faced with building a deck in these zones, it's critical that you understand your local building department's requirements.

Bill Bolton is a deck builder in Santa Barbara, Calif.

Code Requirements for Commercial Decks

by Glenn Mathewson

Building a deck on a restaurant or other commercial establishment can be a great way to expand your business, but if you are a contractor accustomed to residential work there are significant code differences to be aware of. The movement and expectations of people as they interact with buildings play a tremendous part in the planning and design of public places. It can be surprising how many variables exist that limit the overall design of a deck at locations such as a restaurant, a day care, or an apartment complex.

Most districts regulate residential construction with some version of the International Residential Code, whereas for other classes of construction, they use the International Building Code. Though the IRC is based on the IBC, many differences exist (see **Table 4**, next page).

Buildings and structures are categorized by occupancy type: Assembly, residential, business, and educational are some examples. Throughout all building codes, requirements vary by occupancy. At a restaurant, which is an assembly occupancy, the basic design of a deck will be regulated in a much more specific manner than it would be at a home.

One of the driving forces behind the more specific regulations for commercial establishments is the need to provide safe egress for all the expected occupants.

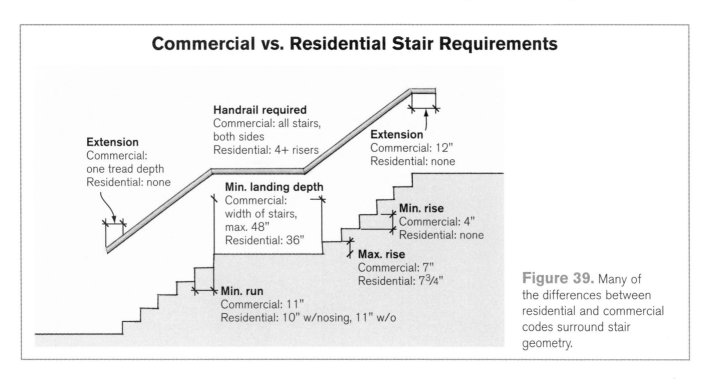

Commercial vs. Residential Stair Requirements

Extension
Commercial: one tread depth
Residential: none

Handrail required
Commercial: all stairs, both sides
Residential: 4+ risers

Extension
Commercial: 12"
Residential: none

Min. landing depth
Commercial: width of stairs, max. 48"
Residential: 36"

Min. rise
Commercial: 4"
Residential: none

Max. rise
Commercial: 7"
Residential: 7³/₄"

Min. run
Commercial: 11"
Residential: 10" w/nosing, 11" w/o

Figure 39. Many of the differences between residential and commercial codes surround stair geometry.

Table 4. Residential vs. Commercial Code

Component	2006 IRC	IRC Section	2006 IBC	IBC Section
Maximum rise (straight stairs)	7.75"	R311.5.3.1	7"	1009.3
Minimum rise (straight stairs)	no minimum	n/a	4"	1009.3
Minimum run (straight stairs)	10" w/nosing, 11" w/o	R311.5.3.2	11"	1009.3
Solid riser	not required	R311.5.3.3	depends on use	1009.3.3
Minimum stair width	36"	R311.5.1	depends on occupancy	1009.1
Landing depth (direction of travel)	36"	R311.5.4	width of stairs, max. 48"	1009.4
Landing width	width of stairs served	R311.5.4	at least stair width	1009.4
Minimum guard height	36"	R312.1	42"	1013.2
Guard opening limitations	0" to 36", 4" sphere	R312.2	0" to 34", 4" sphere 34" to 42", 8" sphere	1013.3
Handrail adjacent abrasive elements	permitted	n/a	not permitted	1012.6
Handrail extensions	not required	n/a	required	1012.5
Handrail interruptions at newel posts	interruption permitted	R311.5.6.2	interruption not permitted	1012.4
Stair handrail, when required	four or more riser stairs	R311.5.6	all stairs	1009.10
Stair handrail location	one side	R311.5.6	both sides, intermediate	1009.10
Step at doors	permitted	R311.4.3	depends on occupancy	1008.1.4
Live load on deck	40 psf	Table R301.5	depends of occupancy	Table 1607.1
Live load on stairway	40 psf	Table R301.5	100 psf	Table 1607.1
Exception to foundation frost depth	when self-supported	R403.1.4.1	no exception	1805.2.1
Elevation changes in walking surface	not regulated	n/a	regulated	1003.5

In codes for single-family homes, there is little to no consideration made for the size of the building or the expected occupant load (the number of people that may be inside).

In a commercial establishment such as a restaurant, however, the nature of the building's occupancy is highly scrutinized. The size of the building dictates the maximum allowable occupant load, which then determines the minimum width of all the exit components. A restaurant deck may be part of the exit, the exit discharge, or the exit access; all three of these components have differing requirements.

In general, the basic design of a deck at any commercial establishment, including apartments, is most appropriately the job of a registered design professional, or at least needs the helpful review of the jurisdiction's plans examiner. Requirements can be difficult to determine, so don't take this information as anything more than a general overview.

Foundations

For the foundation or piers supporting the deck, there is a convenient exception to depth below frost in the IRC: In residential applications, if the deck is not supported by the dwelling, such as with a ledger, then the foundation is not required to extend below the frost depth; this exception does not exist in the IBC.

Stairways

One aspect of deck construction that varies considerably is the geometrical limitations of stairs and stairways. When considering stairway requirements, keep in mind that a single change in elevation is considered a stair and requires a top and bottom landing; a stairway consists of all stairs and landings required to traverse from one floor level to another.

The general rule for commercial-use stair runs is a minimum 11-inch run, measured from tread nosing to tread nosing (**Figure 39**, previous page). Width of a commercial stairway is based on total occupancy and whether the stairs are part of the accessible means of egress. Residentially, a simple 36-inch minimum width is required.

Landing depth is measured in the direction of travel, generally perpendicular to the last tread. In commercial applications the depth must be at least equal to the

Figure 40. Even small public decks such as this view platform must have at least one accessible egress path.

stairway width, but need not be greater than 48 inches.

Guards in commercial settings are required to be 42 inches high. The "4-inch-sphere rule" for the maximum size of an opening applies only up to the height of 34 inches. For the top 8 inches of the guard, between 34 and 42 inches above the deck, the maximum size of an opening is larger — it can't allow passage of an 8-inch sphere.

If the stairway handrail is mounted on or adjacent to a brick or stucco exterior or any other "abrasive surface" it may be considered a violation of the IBC.

The IBC requires handrail extensions at the top and bottom of stairs when the handrail doesn't connect to the handrail of a lower or upper set of stairs. The top extension must extend horizontally for a minimum of 12 inches beyond the top rise and the bottom extension must extend sloped beyond the last tread for a horizontal distance equal to the tread depth.

In addition to the requirement for handrails on both sides of commercial stairways, there are times when an intermediate or center handrail may be required. Based on the minimum required width of a commercial stairway, as dictated by occupant load, no portion of that width can be more than 30 inches from a handrail. This means that if the minimum width for a stairway is 61 inches, an intermediate handrail is required.

In most commercial jobs, including restaurants, stairway minimum live loads are 100 pounds per square foot, more than 100 percent greater than the minimum load of 40 psf for residential decks.

Means of Egress

A priority in commercial deck design is making sure people can exit a building, particularly in an emergency. Chapter 10 of the 2006 IBC defines "means of egress" as "a continuous and unobstructed path of vertical and horizontal egress travel from any occupied portion of a building or structure to a public

way. A means of egress consists of three separate and distinct parts: the exit access, the exit, and the exit discharge." When a deck is added to a structure, the existing means of egress must not be compromised.

Every place in a building or on a structure outside a building is considered part of the means of egress (**Figure 40**), including enclosed areas such as decks and exterior exit stairways or ramps, where flames, airborne debris, or collapsing structures can still threaten occupants' safety and their ability to reach a public way. Travel can't be inhibited by security fences, gates, trip hazards, or excessively uneven or sloping surfaces.

Another limitation is found in IBC Section 1003.4, which generically states: "Walking surfaces of the means of egress shall have a slip-resistant surface and be securely attached." While it's obvious you don't want people slipping on a deck, and you certainly don't want the decking to move under their feet, there is no test standard or accepted criteria referenced by the IBC for determining whether a surface is slip-resistant. And stairways and approaches to stairways on the exterior of a building — in addition to being slip-resistant — must also be designed so that water won't accumulate on the walking surface (IBC 1009.5.2).

Elevation Changes

It's common at private residences to see decks with multiple levels separated by just one or two steps. Though that's a nice way to distinguish different areas of a deck for backyard entertaining, it might not be allowed on a public deck. Generally, if the elevation change is less than 12 inches, you can't put in steps — you must slope the surface so it's accessible to people with disabilities (**Figure 41**, next page).

There is an exception to that rule. While all paths are part of a means of egress, only some are required to be accessible. When just one exit is required, it must be accessible, and when two are required, both

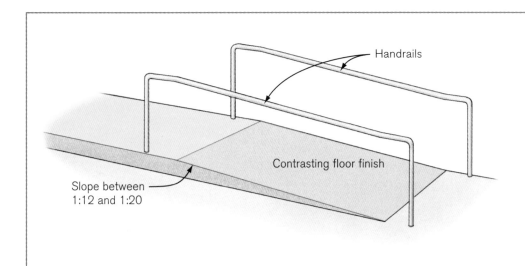

Figure 41. On public decks, elevation changes often must be made with a slope — between 1:12 and 1:20 — rather than steps. Small changes are difficult to see, so when the elevation change is 6 inches or less, the sloped surface must be distinguished with a contrasting floor finish or handrails must be installed.

Handrails

Contrasting floor finish

Slope between 1:12 and 1:20

must be accessible. However, when three or more exits are required, no more than two have to be accessible. So, when the elevation change is not part of an accessible means of egress, a change in elevation of less than 12 inches can be made by either one or two risers (7 inches, maximum) and a tread (13 inches, minimum), as long as no point of the normal path of egress travel is farther than 30 inches from a handrail. But unless you have the help of a design professional, avoid small elevation changes.

Elevation changes at doorways are also regulated by the IBC. In regions where it snows, many homeowners prefer a step down from the exit door to the deck to keep snow from piling against the door. You can't do that in commercial applications. The floor surfaces on both sides of a public doorway must be at the same elevation, no more than 1/2 inch below the door threshold (IBC 1008.1.4). Thresholds of sliding glass doors in the living and sleeping areas of apartments and hotels are an exception and can be as much as 3/4 inch above the floor.

Lighting

As a rule, all components of the means of egress must be illuminated (IBC 1006) to at least 1 foot-candle at the walking surface, as measured by a light meter at night. If you don't have a light meter, don't worry: Chances are pretty good your inspector won't have one either; nor is the inspection likely to be at night. A logical approach is best: Make sure the deck is significantly illuminated. In some instances, the lighting may be required to be connected to an emergency electrical backup system.

Type of Construction

The IBC categorizes construction into five types according to the combustibility of the building material and the fire-resistivity of the assemblies. All except type IV (heavy timber) have A and B subtypes,

with A requiring more fire-resistivity in the building assemblies than B. The maximum allowable height and area of a building are primarily determined by the type of construction. The more fire-resistant the building type, the larger and higher the structure is allowed to be.

In types I and II, both A and B, almost all the building components must be noncombustible. However, decks, porches, and exterior stairways not functioning as required exits can be constructed of fire-retardant-treated wood; and their handrails and guard components can be made of untreated wood. Neither exception allows the use of plastics or plastic-wood composites, but those could be approved by the local authority as an alternative for untreated-wood handrails and guards.

In types III, IV, and V, decks and exterior stairways can be built from combustible materials, yet the assembly may still be required to be fire-resistive. You would probably need to consult a design professional for the details of such construction.

Some site conditions, such as open yards around the building for fire-vehicle access, or a fire-sprinkler system, may allow for increases to the height and area of the building. These are important to identify because the design for any addition or modification to an existing building must take into account how its original height and area were determined. A large deck built on the back of a church, for example, may not be allowed to encroach into an open yard that was intended for fire access in the original design.

In all types of construction, the aggregate length of a deck along a building's exterior can't exceed 50 percent of the building's perimeter for each floor level. However, the presence of fire sprinklers at the deck can allow for exceptions to the maximum total length and fire-resistance requirements (IBC 1406.3). These are aspects of the code for which you definitely need the help of a design professional.

Occupancy Type and Occupant Load

After construction type, the next criteria to consider are the occupancy type, or intended use; and the occupant load, or maximum number of people that may legally occupy the building. The occupancy of a building has a dramatic effect on its design and construction and is a starting point for almost all the design provisions of the IBC — particularly the number of required exits.

Most deck construction occurs at Assembly (A), Mercantile (M), Business (B), and Residential (R) occupancies. Once the occupancy type has been properly identified, the current and new occupant loads must be considered. Occupant load is based on the "anticipated function of the space" and the amount of area thereby required for each person. IBC Table 1004.1.1, titled "maximum floor area allowances per occupant," provides 38 different functions

that a designer or plan reviewer will use to categorize building spaces.

In the case of a deck addition, the size and function of the spaces in the existing building and on the new deck combine to dictate the building's total occupant load (**Figure 42**). Each individual space must also be considered separately, as the required number of exits from each space is dictated by the occupant load of that space; and further, any accessory space that exits through another primary space must have its occupant load added to the load of the primary space it exits through. It is these final occupant loads, based on how the occupants travel to a public way, that determine how many exits are required.

Not only does the number of required exits vary based on the occupant load and occupancy type, but so does the total width of the exits (IBC 1005). When

Occupant Loads and Egress

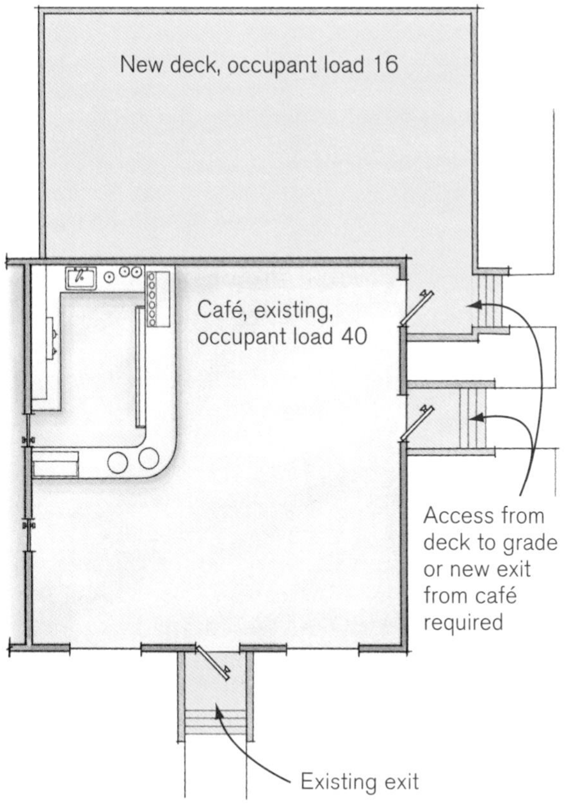

New deck, occupant load 16

Café, existing, occupant load 40

Access from deck to grade or new exit from café required

Existing exit

Figure 42. A new deck (above) is high above grade and surrounded by guards. If egress for the deck's 16 occupants were only through the café, the occupant load of the café would be increased to 56 (40 + 16). Spaces with a load of 50 or more usually require two exits, so a second exit door from the café would have to be added. However, if egress from the deck were provided directly to grade, the deck occupants wouldn't need to exit through the café and the additional door wouldn't be necessary.

Distance Between Exits

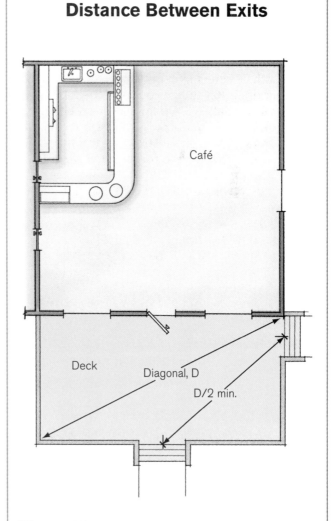

Café

Deck

Diagonal, D

D/2 min.

Figure 43. When two exits are required, they cannot be closer to each other — as measured in a straight line from the center of one to the center of the other — than half of the overall maximum diagonal distance across the area in question.

more than one exit is required from a space, the total width of the required exits must be properly distributed among all the exit openings, and the locations of the exits must be spaced according to provisions in the code (**Figure 43**, previous page). Each arrangement requires a specific evaluation and could result in dramatically different requirements. It's all about how people must move through the spaces.

Related to occupant load is the design live load. In commercial structures, the 40 psf live load typically required for residential structures is no longer the rule. The live load that a structure is required to resist varies and is based on similar criteria as the occupant load (Table 1607.1). For example, a restaurant deck without fixed seats must be designed to resist 100 psf, while a deck serving an office must resist 50 psf.

Occupant Load of 50 or More

As shown in Figure 42, the creation of a deck sometimes requires the addition of an exit. That prompts even more requirements. A space requiring two exits, for instance, must have illuminated exit signs above both exits (**Figure 44**).

In the example in Figure 43, where the deck itself requires two exits, exit signs would need to be provided at the exits from the deck, but not from inside the café. However, an exception in the IBC does allow the building official to approve the omission of exit signs when the exits are "obviously and clearly identifiable as exits." Of course, this is specific to an individual project.

When a door serves a space with an occupant load of 50 or more, the door must swing in the direction of egress travel. In the example shown in Figure 42, if the back deck were larger (750 square

Figure 44. When public decks have an occupant load of more than 50 and serve as a means of egress, illuminated exit signs may be required.

feet) and had access only through the café, the door would have to swing in.

The presence of an automatic fire-sprinkler system in an existing building can affect how codes apply to a deck addition, potentially allowing greater design flexibility in the new project. However, the presence of an existing fire-sprinkler system may also require newly constructed spaces, even decks, to be included within the protecting boundaries of the system. The details of this requirement are outside the scope of this book, but you should know that designing a deck on a building with fire sprinklers requires additional considerations.

Glenn Mathewson is a building official in Westminster, Colo., and a former deck builder.

Chapter 3:
Footings & Piers

KIM KATWIJK

- Designing and Building Pier Footings
- Job-Site Strategies for Faster Footings
- Footings & Piers Q&A

Designing and Building Pier Footings

by Robert Hatch

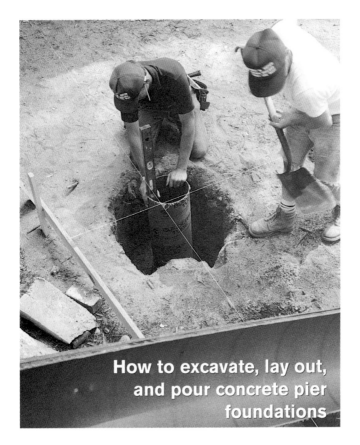

How to excavate, lay out, and pour concrete pier foundations

I've built lots of masonry pier foundations. I used to either stack concrete blocks or pour concrete into site-made wooden forms. Then, a few decades ago, the job got a lot easier with the invention of the Sonotube pier form, which is now an industry standard. Here, I'll give some basic tips for working with tubes, along with some unusual ways of using them that I've learned over the years.

Some Rules of Thumb

Before laying out a run of piers, I determine the required diameter, the size and depth of the footing, and the spacing between the piers. After fixing several sagging decks, I've developed a few rules of thumb, based on an old piece of Yankee logic — when in doubt, bigger is better.

Pier diameter. My rule of thumb for pier diameter is "1 inch per foot of span." Thus, a deck that spans 8 feet will stand comfortably on 8-inch-diameter piers, while a deck that spans 10 feet requires 10-inch-diameter piers. For spans longer than 12 feet, I always add a second row of piers and a second girder at the center of the joist span. (I use No. 2 or No. 3 grade pressure-treated lumber, so I don't trust it for spans longer than 12 feet.) Reducing the span

also cuts material costs by letting me use 2x8 joists rather than 2x12s.

Footings. A lot of builders install piers without footings. But I've found that footings help keep the structure from settling; to leave them out risks having a railing or rim joist that looks like a roller coaster. As a rule of thumb, a pier footing should be as thick as the pier's diameter, with sides that measure twice that much. So an 8-inch pier should rest on a footing that's 8 inches thick and 16 inches square, while a 12-inch pier should rest on a footing that's 12 inches thick and 24 inches square. When in doubt about footing size, it's best to calculate the load on each footing, and then determine the footing size based on the soil's bearing capacity (see "Sizing the Footing," page 72). If soil bearing capacity is at least 1,500 psf, you can find the required footing size on Table 1 (below) from the *Prescriptive Residential Wood Deck Construction Guide* (you can learn more about this guide starting on page 31).

The key factor in determining how deep to place the

Table 1. Footing Sizes[2]

Beam Span, L_B	Joist Span, L_J	Round[1] Footing Diameter	Footing Thickness[3]
6'	≤ 10	15"	6"
	≤ 14	17"	6"
	≤ 18	20"	7"
8'	≤ 10	17"	6"
	≤ 14	20"	8"
	≤ 18	23"	9"
10'	≤ 10	19"	7"
	≤ 14	22"	9"
	≤ 18	25"	10"
12'	≤ 10	21"	8"
	≤ 14	24"	10"
	≤ 18	28"	11"
14'	≤ 10	22"	9"
	≤ 14	26"	11"
	≤ 18	30"	12"
16'	≤ 10	24"	9"
	≤ 14	28"	12"
	≤ 18	32"	13"
18'	≤ 10	24"	10"
	≤ 14	30"	12"
	≤ 18	34"	14"

1. Square footings are permitted to have widths 2" less than the given diameter of round footings.
2. Assumes 1,500 psf soil bearing capacity.
3. Assumes 2,500 psi compressive strength of concrete. Coordinate footing thickness with post base and anchor requirements.

SOURCE: TABLE 4 FROM THE 2008 *PRESCRIPTIVE RESIDENTIAL WOOD DECK CONSTRUCTION GUIDE.* AVAILABLE AS FREE DOWNLOAD FROM WWW.AFANDPA.ORG OR WWW.AWC.ORG.

footing is the local frostline. Here in the White Mountains of New Hampshire, we typically set the top of the footing 4 feet deep. For critical applications, however, we go down to 8 feet. These include structures that will support a lot of weight, and piers that are close to a plowed driveway (where the lack of an insulating blanket of snow means a deeper frostline).

To ensure that you're on undisturbed soil, it's also wise to go deep when setting piers near an existing building. The backfill of an existing building might just contain a 6x6 wood scrap that's below your footing depth. When the 6x6 later decomposes, the resulting void will collapse under the weight of the tube.

Spacing. How closely we space our piers depends on the load they will carry, and the number and size of the girders. On a simple deck with a built-up triple-2x8 girder, an 8-foot spacing is fine. This spacing also works for most single-story additions. If the piers will have to support a two-story addition or a cantilevered deck with a hot tub, the spacing will have to be closer. When in doubt, it's best to call an engineer.

Digging the Holes

I hear that power augers can make quick work of soft soil. However, I know too many guys who hit a rock with a power auger and then went flying across the yard. We avoid power augers, opting instead for either a backhoe or a pick and shovel, depending on the number of tubes and the access to the work site. We dig by hand when there are only a few tubes to set, or at well-landscaped homes, where we don't

want a backhoe tearing up the yard. When working on existing homes, we spread the excavated dirt over the inside perimeter of the deck. We also set aside all the sod and some of the topsoil so that we can use it to dress up the perimeter when we're done. This is more work than just digging holes, but it makes for a cleaner job and puts a feather in our cap with the owners.

Regardless of the digging method, the footings should rest on good, undisturbed soil. Every good foundation specification requires the soil under foundation footings to be compacted, and pier footings are no different. You can't get a compactor down into the hole, but running a garden hose into it for three or four minutes will help the earth settle (**Figure 1**).

Setting the Forms

We make square footing forms from scrap one-bys and cap them with a plywood lid (**Figure 2**). The lid has a hole cut into it that's ½ inch smaller in diameter than the tube. We lower this form into the hole with a hoe, then plumb up to the dry line to center it. We don't add rebar to the footings unless it's specified by an architect.

The most accurate way to align a row of tubes is to stretch a line across where their outside edges will be, rather than across their centers (photo, previous page). This is also easier than centering the string — you just set the tubes against the string, rather than having to measure from their centers. On level lots,

continued on page 74

Figure 1. Saturating the pier hole with a garden hose helps compact the soil at the base to keep it from settling later.

Figure 2. The author makes pier footing forms from scrap lumber and plywood, and lowers them into the hole with a hoe.

Sizing the Footing

by Andy Engel

Deck footings can be called upon to support thousands of pounds each, even without considering the hot tub that may one day be added. The International Residential Code has specific requirements for pier footings, which most decks rest on. The size of a footing depends on two conditions: load and soil bearing capacity.

Calculating Load

Load is calculated by multiplying the tributary area on each footing by the deck's design load.

The tributary area is the section of the deck that bears on the footing. To calculate area, you need to find length and width. So, first identify the beam that's supported by the footing. Then measure halfway to the next beam on each side, and add the two distances together (**A**). If there's no intermediate beam, measure halfway to the ledger on the house. And if there's a cantilever to one side of the footing, add in its length (**B**). Call the resulting figure the width.

Calculating the length is similar to finding the width, only this measurement is made perpendicular to the first. Measure halfway to the nearest pier on one side of the footing and halfway to the pier on the other side, and add these two distances together (**C**). Then, multiply this number (length) by the width to get the tributary area.

Multiply the tributary area by the deck's design load to find the load the footing must be able to support. A common design load is 50 pounds per square foot (40 psf live load plus 10 psf dead load), although some jurisdictions require 70 psf (60 psf live load with 10 psf dead load). Snow loading can be even higher, so be sure to check locally.

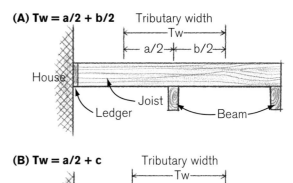
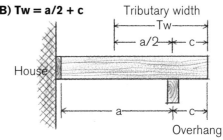

The first factor in calculating the tributary area is the length of joist that bears on the beam that's in turn supported by the pier. Tributary width extends halfway to the next beam or ledger, plus any cantilever.

Establishing Soil Bearing Capacity

The next factor you must consider is soil bearing strength. It's difficult to identify soils precisely in the field. In some cases, an engineering soil report will be required. However, a preliminary soil investigation may give enough information to go on. Some rough information about soils can be learned from these simple on-site tests (adapted from the *JLC Field Guide, Vol. 1*):

- **Dirt-ball test:** To assess soil cohesiveness, squeeze a

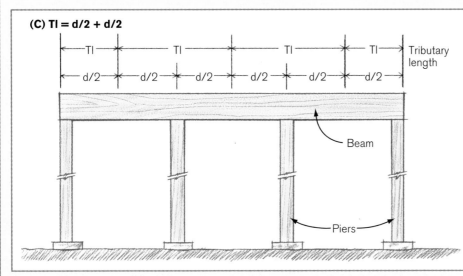

The second factor in tributary area is the length of beam that's supported by the pier. This extends halfway to the next pier on either side. On an end pier, tributary length extends halfway to just one pier.

A Footing Can Be Too Wide

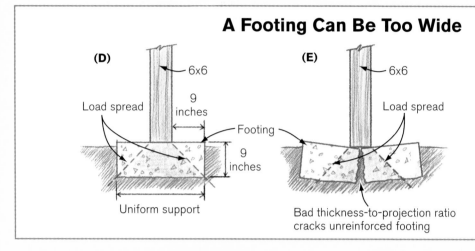

(D)
6x6
Load spread
9 inches
Footing
9 inches
Uniform support

(E)
6x6
Load spread
Bad thickness-to-projection ratio cracks unreinforced footing

Loads from a pier spread through a footing at a 45-degree angle. If an unreinforced footing is too wide for a pier, the footing will be subject to cracking due to shear loading. According to the ICC, the footing must extend beyond the pier by at least 2 inches, but by no more than the thickness of the footing.

moist double handful of soil into a ball, then drop it from a height of about 1 foot. If the soil will not form a ball or if the ball readily fragments when dropped, the soil is relatively non-cohesive and granular, with a low proportion of fine clay. However, if the soil forms a ball that holds together when dropped, it likely contains a high percentage of cohesive clay.

- **Water suspension test:** Drop a scoop of soil into a large jar of water. Gravel and sand will settle to the bottom of the jar almost immediately. Finer silt particles will take fifteen minutes to an hour to settle.

Clay particles will remain suspended in water for a day or longer. So, if the water remains very cloudy for a long time, the soil probably contains a high percentage of clay.

- **Noodle test:** Roll a small quantity of soil into a thin noodle or string shape between your palms. If the soil can be rolled as thin as 1 inch without breaking apart, it is probably a cohesive soil with a substantial percentage of clay.

Putting Them Together

As an example, consider a deck that spans 14 feet from the ledger to the main beam, with a 2-foot cantilever beyond. Half of 14 feet is 7 feet, to which is added the 2-foot cantilever: 7 feet + 2 feet = 9 feet. Assume the piers are spaced 10 feet apart. The tributary area on the corner piers would be only 5 feet x 9 feet, or 45 square feet. On center piers, it's 10 feet x 9 feet, or 90 square feet. Let's figure a center pier's design loading: 90 square feet x 50 psf load = 4,500 pounds.

On clay soils, the footing for that pier would have to be at least 3 square feet (4,500 pounds/1,500 psf). If the footing is square, that's 21 inches across. If round, the diameter is about 2 feet.

The IRC specifies that spread footings must be at least 6 inches thick and project at least 2 inches beyond the loaded surface. In addition, the projection must not exceed the thickness. So, if the pier is a 12-inch concrete column and the footing is 24 inches in diameter and 6 inches thick, you've met code. The footing projects 6 inches around the pier, exceeding the minimum 2-inch projection, and just meeting the maximum projection-to-thickness ratio.

You could also land a wooden column directly on a concrete footing. Let's use a nominal 6x6. It measures 5½ inches square, so the footing would project 9¼ inches beyond the 6x6. The projection exceeds the minimum 6-inch footing thickness, so to satisfy the IRC, this footing would have to be at least 9¼ inches thick. The reason is that loads spread through a footing at 45 degrees in a cone shape (**D**). Concrete supported by the soil outside of this cone imposes a shear load on the footing, and such an unreinforced footing is likely to crack down the middle (**E**).

Andy Engel is editor of Professional Deck Builder.

Soil Bearing Capacities

Material	Loadbearing Value (pounds per sq. ft.)
Crystalline bedrock	12,000 psf
Sedimentary rock	4,000 psf
Sandy gravel or gravel	3,000 psf
Sand, silty sand, clayey sand, silty gravel, and clayey gravel	2,000 psf
Clay, sandy clay, silty clay, and clayey silt	1,500 psf

Loadbearing values indicate the amount of force that undistributed, native soils can support.

2000 INTERNATIONAL RESIDENTIAL CODE

Figure 3. When mixing concrete by hand, a tube ripped in half with a circular saw makes a convenient chute.

Figure 4. Rebar goes in when the tube is partially full of concrete. The bend at the end of the rebar ties the pier to the footing.

we set the line a couple of inches above grade, then cut the tubes off just below the line. This is just a personal preference, as I don't like to see a lot of concrete sticking out of the ground. (On a slope, where the grade falls away from the line, we place a level against the outside of each form and level up to the reference line.)

If the piers must protrude above grade to directly support a rim joist, we install the tubes high, then cut them all at once. There are two easy ways to do this. One is to use a story pole and a transit to mark the elevation on each tube; the other is to level out from the house to the two end tubes, then snap a

chalk line from these two points across the remaining tubes. There is no need to cut the tubes at exactly this elevation. Once they're marked, we cut off the tubes a little high, poke a nail through the side at the reference mark, then pour concrete to the nail.

We tie our reference lines to stakes or batter boards driven outside the perimeter of the layout. We temporarily remove these lines while digging, and reset them after the holes have been roughed in. We then carefully backfill around the footing form by hand, and tamp it to keep it in place. One person then centers the tube on the hole in the form's lid while another backfills with a shovel.

Setting Tubes in Frozen Soil

Setting Sonotubes in midwinter is difficult at best. When the frost is set hard in the ground, it's tempting to load the truck with a pickax, a crowbar, a flamethrower, and some dynamite. Luckily, there's an easier way.

We remove any snow from the excavation area, and put an empty gallon-sized metal paint can everywhere there will be a pier. We start a good kindling fire in each can, and keep these fires going throughout the day. Every couple of hours we lift the cans, scrape away any willing soil from the excavation, and reset the cans into the holes. We use the excavated dirt to build a berm around the cans, which helps hold in the heat.

This goes slow at first – it can take five or six hours to get the cans set to their rims, but after that, the process gets easier. Before we leave for the day, we put a good

bed of coals and a perforated lid on each can. We also place a rock or a brick on top of each one; the heat tends to draw water out of the frost, so unweighted cans are apt to float up in the hole. We keep the rim of the can above grade so that any melted snow or ice will drain away rather than submerging the can and putting out the coals.

We can drive 3 feet of frost out of the ground overnight with this method. A paint can will typically melt a 12-inch-diameter cylinder of soil, which is easily dug out by hand. And though we can't get a box footing into the frozen ground, we take a spade and "bell" the bottom of the hole to act as a footing. Even stony hardpan is easier to dig after using this method. – *R.H.*

Figure 5. Tamping throughout the pour gets rid of voids in the pier. The nail in the side of the tube marks the finish concrete elevation.

Figuring Concrete for Tubes

You can quickly figure the amount of concrete needed to fill a tube by multiplying the following factors by the height of the tube in feet:

- 8-inch pier: .013 cu. yd. (0.6 80-pound bags of concrete mix per lin. ft.)
- 10-inch pier: .02 cu. yd. (0.9 bags per lin. ft.)
- 12-inch pier: .03 cu. yd. (1.3 bags per lin. ft.)

For rectangular footings, use these amounts per footing:

- 8x16x16-inch footing: .044 cu. yd. (2 bags each)
- 10x20x20-inch footing: .086 cu. yd. (3.8 bags each)
- 12x24x24-inch footing: .15 cu. yd. (6.75 bags each)

As an example, say you have four tubes that are 8 inches in diameter and 4 feet deep. With a total lineal footage of 16 feet, the tubes will require 9.6 bags of concrete mix (0.6 bags per foot). The four 8x16x16-inch footings will require a total of 8 bags (2 bags per footing). So you'll need 18 bags to complete the job. – *R.H.*

Pouring the Concrete

Redi-mix isn't cost-effective for small jobs, so when setting fewer than a dozen piers, we mix the concrete by hand. If we have to haul the concrete any distance from the mixer to the forms, we use a wheelbarrow, then shovel the concrete into the tubes. On steep grades, we make a handy cement chute by using a circular saw to slice a tube lengthwise into a pair of half-cylinders (**Figure 3**).

To eliminate voids and make sure the concrete fills the entire footing, we place the concrete slowly and tamp it vigorously with a stick or a paddle as we go. When the tube is half-full of concrete, we insert a length or two of rebar into the center, making sure the bend in the rebar extends well into the footing (**Figure 4**). We then continue pouring and tamping until the concrete reaches the reference nail we use to mark the finished elevation (**Figure 5**). Before the concrete sets up, we install whatever strap ties, anchor bolts, or stirrups the job requires. A dry line stretched across the row of tubes makes a good centering reference for the anchors.

Robert Hatch is owner of Robert Hatch Design-Build Construction in Freedom, N.H.

Job-Site Strategies for Faster Footings

by Andy Engel

Installation tips for supporting decks from across the U.S.

KIM KATWIJK

A decade or so ago when I still made my living as a carpenter and deck builder, I dreaded footings. The frost depth where I worked in northern New Jersey was 36 inches, and my home county was where the last glacier had stopped, depositing most of the rocks it had collected on its way down from Canada.

I tried all sorts of strategies to avoid digging footing holes. I'd cut my price if the homeowner dug them.

That didn't work so well, because homeowners rarely appreciated the importance of digging the holes exactly where I laid them out.

Once, I pulled $100 out of my wallet to entice a guy running a backhoe next door to drive on over. That didn't work so well either, because the machine's overdig was so large that I spent nearly as much time backfilling by hand as neatly digging the holes with a shovel would have taken in the first place. And I had to fill in the tire tracks in the lawn, and reseed the damaged areas.

Footings continue to be a fact of life for deck builders. Here are the best tricks from builders across the country. Geography makes a big difference in how footings are built, but a lot of techniques apply across broad areas — I wish I'd known about some of them in my deck-building days.

Fast and Accurate Layout

Rather than laying out footings the typical way — measuring out from the house, driving stakes, and stretching a string — Paul Mantoni, a deck builder in Terryville, Conn., came up with a different method: "I put the ledger on the house, and attach the two side joists and the rim joist, propping them up level; I check for square by measuring the diagonals. I usually build decks with the joists cantilevered a foot or two past the main beam. I stretch a string between the side joists where the beam will

Figure 6. Footings incorporating a Simpson EPB44T post base can be adjusted up to 2½ inches in height by turning the nut below the post base.

KIM KATWIJK

Nut & washer for adjustability

Washer shall directly bear on concrete

3"

3⁹⁄₁₆"

2"

Pilot hole (typ.)

2½"

Figure 7. Washington's damp climate ensures that dry concrete mix placed below and around a footing pier has sufficient moisture to set up within one day.

KIM KATWIJK

KIM KATWIJK

Figure 8. Framing lumber holds a footing-form tube above the bottom of the hole, allowing for a thickened spread footing. Backfilling is done after placing the concrete.

go, and lay out the footings from that. Because of the cantilever, there's plenty of room to work digging the holes."

"Our frost depth is 42 inches," says Mantoni, "but I usually go down to 48 inches. It doesn't take a lot longer, and it makes the building inspector happy. I charge about $200 per footing, more where I know the ground is rocky."

Like most other Connecticut builders, Mantoni doesn't enlarge the base of the footing beyond the size of a 12-inch-diameter Sonotube, which provides suitable bearing for the loads involved. He slides the Sonotube into the hole, and has a helper hold it plumb while he carefully backfills. After filling the form with concrete mix, Mantoni uses galvanized column bases and 6x6 posts to support the beam.

Dial 811 Before You Dig

Even though excavation for deck footings isn't heavy-duty earthwork, every state requires contractors to call their local utility-locating service before undertaking any excavation. It's free, whereas the penalties for damaging an underground utility range from the cost of repair, to fines, to injury or death from, for example,

Know what's **below.**
Call before you dig.

driving a rock bar through a power or gas line. Make the call at least two days before digging. If you dial 811 from anywhere in the country, you should be connected to your "call before you dig" center.

Simple Precast Piers

Compared with those of us in the Northeast, Jack Hanson of Boise, Idaho, has it pretty easy with footings. Because it's so dry in Boise, the frost line is only 12 inches deep despite the cold winters.

For low-level decks, Hanson uses precast concrete piers he buys locally. To level them easily, Hanson fills the bottom of the footing hole with 2 to 3 inches of pea gravel.

One big advantage of the piers that Hanson uses is the integral Simpson EPB44T post base (**Figure 6**), which can be adjusted in height over a range of $2^1/2$ inches. On very low decks, it's possible to skip the posts entirely by resting the beam directly in the saddles of these post bases.

Wet Climates, Steep Slopes

Like Hanson, Kim Katwijk of Olympia, Wash., uses precast piers, but he sets them on several inches of dry concrete mix, and then backfills around the pier with more dry concrete mix (**Figure 7**). "The soil is so consistently wet in coastal Washington," he explains, "that the concrete has usually set by the next day."

A less desirable consequence of Washington's wetness is an accelerated rate of wood decay, particularly where fastener penetration invites water into the untreated center of framing lumber. To combat this problem, Katwijk uses a turkey baster to inject wood preservative into the holes he drills for the lags that hold the hardware to the post.

Katwijk does occasionally need to dig deep footings — for example, when he's building on a steep slope (see "7-Foot Rule," paage 80). Washington's clay soils tend to creep downhill, and some engineered designs require footings and piers that extend 3 feet below where the pier hits the slope on the low side, and extend at least 6 inches above grade on the high side. In these cases, Katwijk reinforces the spread footing at the bottom with a mat of #4 rebar, and places vertical #4 bars in the pier to within 2 inches of its top (**Figure 8**, previous page).

Where there's a problem in the placement of the footings, Katwijk uses another strategy that allows him to shift the supporting beam and footings over a few feet. He points out that deck joists can usually cantilever farther past their support beam than the tables in code books prescribe, because those tables apply to houses — where the cantilever picks up dead loads from walls, ceilings, and roofs that just aren't a factor with decks.

Of course, varying from the code necessitates engineering, so Katwijk keeps on his Palm Pilot a spreadsheet his engineer created to show allowable

Alternative Engineered Footings

Most deck builders use fairly conventional concrete footings, whether poured in place or precast, but some other options are worth taking a look at, as well.

Diamond Pier. One engineered solution that works anywhere that's not terribly rocky, and might be a good choice for problem soils, is the Diamond Pier (Pin Foundations, www.pinfoundations.com). The piers are stabilized by pins – made from galvanized-iron pipe – that are driven into the ground with a demolition hammer. The pins go through guide holes in the reinforced concrete piers (**Figure A**). To determine the size and length of pipe, a soil report is necessary.

Because no excavation is needed, Diamond Piers are a good choice for environmentally sensitive areas.

According to the manufacturer, Diamond Piers will in most cases resist uplift from both frost and expansive clay soils.

Magnum Piering System. Another option for problem soils is the Magnum Piering system (www.magnumpiering.com), which consists of a 6-foot-long galvanized pipe with auger blades attached to the bottom (**Figure B**). It's driven by a skid steer, excavator, or tractor with an auger drive. As with the Diamond Pier, one advantage is there's no excavation, so there's minimal disturbance to the ground. If you use a tracked skid steer, the weight of the machine is distributed over a broad area, limiting any damage to landscaping.

Redi-Footing. This combination base and cap (www.redifooting.com) works with schedule 40 PVC pipe to form a footing (**Figure C**). If your back is anything like

Figure A. *Pin footings are an alternative to conventional footings in most soils, and can sometimes provide a solution in problem soils or environmentally sensitive areas. Determining the pin sizes requires a knowledge of the underlying soil.*

Figure B. *Like pin footings, helical footings are made from galvanized steel. No significant excavation is required for their installation, which can be done with a variety of machines with auger-driving capability.*

cantilevers for various joist materials and deck configurations. Having this information to hand allows for field adjustments to the location of beams and their supporting footings.

Power Auger to the Rescue

When contractor John Wilder moved from Minnesota to Jacksonville, Fla., I assumed he had also escaped the curse of digging deep footings. Not so, he says. "Florida's soils can be shifty sand, and I often have to dig down 3 feet to find good, solid ground."

Digging 3 feet down in sand could be pretty tedious, but Wilder doesn't do it by hand. He rents a walk-behind skid steer with a 2-foot-diameter auger (**Figure 9**, page 82).

continued on page 82

Figure C.
Combined with a length of schedule 40 4-inch PVC pipe, plastic Redi-Footings are lightweight alternatives to conventional footings and can support over 5 tons each, according the manufacturer's specs.

Figure D. *Bigfoot footing forms attach to round form tubes to create a spread footing that can be backfilled and inspected prior to placing concrete.*

mine, the light weight alone might tempt you to try it. According to the manufacturer, each Redi-Footing can support 10,500 pounds, when used with suitable soils. An ICC Evaluation Service report is still pending, but the Redi-Footing is accepted in some jurisdictions.

Plastic footing forms. Finally, there are a couple of plastic forming systems – the Square Foot (Sound Footings, www.sqfoot.com) and the Bigfoot (Bigfoot Systems, www.bigfootsystems.com) – that affix to the bottom of a Sonotube to create a larger footing base (**Figure D**). The advantage of these is that once the tube is attached, the entire assembly can be backfilled and inspected. A similar product, the Footing Tube (www.foottube.com) is designed for northern climates where frost heaves can wreak havoc on pier foundations (**Figure E**). The high-density plastic form combines footing and pier in a single form that also acts as a sleeve to prevent frost from attaching to and lifting the pier. The tapered shape of the pier also helps it resist frost action. – *A.E.*

Figure E. *The tapered shape and plastic sleeve of the Footing Tube are designed to prevent frost action from lifting the piers. Just set the form in place, backfill, and trim the top to the desired height before placing the concrete.*

7-Foot Rule

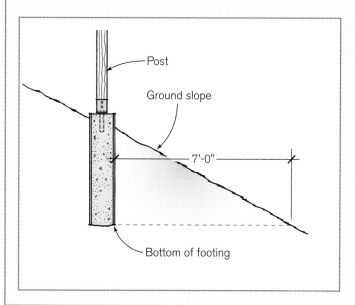

Post

Ground slope

7'-0"

Bottom of footing

On steep sites, the slope of the ground around the footings could affect the footing stability and should be noted. As a rule of thumb for steep slopes, at least 7 ft. of soil, measured horizontally from the footing, must be between the bottom of the footing and daylight as shown at left.

ADAPTED FROM THE *MANUAL FOR THE INSPECTION OF RESIDENTIAL WOOD DECKS AND BALCONIES*, BY CHERYL ANDERSON, FRANK WOESTE, AND JOE LOFERSKI.

In-Ground Posts Support Pergola

by Ron Hamilton

While deck posts should generally be set on top of concrete piers extending above grade, for structural reasons, freestanding pergolas should have posts that are deeply buried. In order to help resist wind uplift, pergola posts should be embedded in concrete, rather than in holes backfilled with dirt. But if the holes are backfilled with concrete, the concrete conforms to the irregular shape of the hole, allowing frost to grip the concrete in cold climates and heave the post. I prefer to insert the buried section of the post into a Sonotube.

Check with your local building officials for information regarding the frost depth in your area. Your post holes should be dug to the frost depth plus 6 inches. Each hole should receive 6 inches of crushed stone for drainage (see illustration). Drainage is important, since frost heaving is more likely in wet soil than dry soil.

The Sonotubes should extend from the crushed stone base to slightly above grade. After backfilling around the Sonotube with compacted dirt, insert the pressure-treated posts inside the Sonotube, holding the bottom of the posts about 6 inches above the crushed stone to provide a space where concrete can flow under the posts. Then plumb and brace the posts and fill the Sonotubes with concrete for solid post that will resist both wind and frost action.

Ron Hamilton is owner of Hamilton General Contracting, in Saylorsburg, Pa.

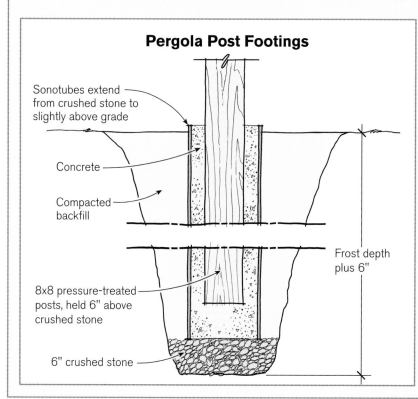

Pergola Post Footings

Sonotubes extend from crushed stone to slightly above grade

Concrete

Compacted backfill

8x8 pressure-treated posts, held 6" above crushed stone

6" crushed stone

Frost depth plus 6"

Simple Forms for Tapered Footings

by Bill Bolton

For the past eight years I've been shaping the tops of my footings into a sort of truncated pyramid to decrease their visible footprint (**Figure A**).

To do this, I use homemade reusable forms. They're wider at the bottom, which makes them simple to lift right off the set concrete. They're also easy to level, and since I place the forms after the footing holes are dug, aligning them under where the beams will go is a snap.

Each form is made from just four pieces of 1x4 or 2x4: two 24-inch-long pieces and two 7-inch-long cross members (**Figure B**). I use Douglas fir because it can withstand being repeatedly screwed to the stakes that hold the form in place. I've made forms from composite decking, but they haven't held up as well to repeated use.

Before cutting the 2x4 into four pieces, I rip one face at a 5-degree bevel. When the form is assembled, the bevel will face inward to create the pyramidal shape of the pier. I cut the ends of the two cross members at 5 degrees to fit to the bevel on the long pieces; then I fasten the cross pieces to the long members 7 inches apart.

I use a string line as a guide to dig the footing holes and then to locate the centers of my homemade forms. I drive four stakes into the ground to suspend each form so that the top of the concrete will end up above finished grade to protect the posts from moisture damage. Once I make sure the form is level, I drive screws through the stakes into the form itself to hold it in position.

Typically, a builder would place a cardboard form in each footing hole, fill the form with concrete, and backfill the hole with loose soil. The problem with this approach, however, is the backfill can take years to settle, during

Figure B. *The form for the top of the footing is made from 1x4s fastened together at a slight angle. Four stakes support it and keep it level above the footing hole.*

Figure C. *A string aligns the placement of a post base in wet concrete. Once the concrete has set, it will be easy to remove the form.*

which time the concrete footing can easily shift in the loose soil. Instead, I shovel the concrete directly into the hole, without the cardboard tube. That way, the concrete conforms exactly to the shape of the hole. Because undisturbed soil supports the footing on all sides, it will be stable as soon as the concrete has set.

I tamp the concrete thoroughly and screed it flat at the top of the form. Before the concrete begins to set up, I insert the appropriate post or column base connector or hot-dipped galvanized J-bolt, again using the string as a guide (**Figure C**). The next day, I'll remove the fasteners holding the form to the stakes and lift the form straight off the concrete, ready for reuse.

Bill Bolton is a deck builder in Santa Barbara, Calif.

Figure A.
Using this easily built reusable form, the author shapes and tapers the tops of his footings to make them less visible.

Figure 9. A walk-behind skid steer with an auger attachment makes quick work of footing holes, and can be rented on a daily basis.

and lighter framing — 4x6 beams and 2x6 joists in most cases.

The most common problem Bolton encounters is having to place footings close to the house. The first floor of many Santa Barbara houses consists of a slab — a troublesome place to hang a deck ledger — so Bolton frequently ends up building a freestanding deck with a line of footings near the house. To avoid placing piers near drainage systems or on questionable soils next to the foundation, he installs a beam and cantilevers the joists the last couple of feet to the house.

Engineered for Steep Slopes, Poor Soils

Bobby Parks runs an Archadeck franchise in metro Atlanta, where he faces challenges not from the frost depth or rocks, but rather from slopes and poor soils.

On slopes, Parks digs the footings to the depths and widths specified by his geotechnical engineer. Then he takes the extra step to dig out a keyway along the uphill side of the footing. Perhaps 6 inches wide and deep, once filled with concrete the key helps the footing to resist forces pushing downhill.

Other times, Parks finds poorly compacted soils with a limited bearing capacity. One solution would be to engineer a wide, steel-reinforced footing to spread out the loads. But bringing yard after yard of concrete into the backyard of most subdivision homes is a logistical nightmare.

Parks' geotechnical engineer, John Stanhope, has an easier solution. He has Parks dig the hole substantially wider and deeper than normal, and fill it with ASTM 57 crushed stone, a blend ranging from $1^1/2$ inches down to $1/4$ inch. Poured concrete footings rest on the crushed stone.

Andy Engel is editor of Professional Deck Builder.

Now, 2 feet may seem kind of large, but that's the diameter of the spread footings that Wilder uses. He fills the bottom of the hole with concrete, and wet-sets a Sonotube in that. After backfilling around the Sonotube, Wilder fills it with concrete.

Piers for Freestanding Deck

Bill Bolton starts with an on-site review before bidding any job — a practice that can be applied anywhere in the country.

As in Florida, frost isn't an issue in Santa Barbara, Calif. Bolton's footings, which he pours in place, are shallow and easily dug. Hence, he uses more of them

Footings & Piers Q&A

Locating Utilities Before Digging

Q. *Considering the minimal depth of deck piers, is it really necessary to schedule an underground utilities locator service?*

A. *Glenn Mathewson, a building inspector in Westminster, Colo., responds:* Yes! In many U.S. locations, winter temperatures require foundation piers for decks and other structures to extend below the frost line, which can be 48 inches or more deep. This well exceeds the minimum depth required for

some underground utility cables and pipes. Even in areas with warm winters and no frost depth, the International Residential Code requires footings to be at least 12 inches deep in undisturbed soil. Digging just those 12 inches could cause an unpleasant and unplanned encounter with the site utilities (see Table, facing page).

Not only do damaged underground utilities present an obvious safety hazard, they usually can't be repaired legally by the average deck builder. Most states require licensed electricians or plumbers to perform that work, and not many deck companies

Utility Depths in the 2006 IRC

Electrical service cable	18 inches
120-volt branch cable	12 inches
Gas supply pipe (usually plastic)	12 inches
Gas pipe for grills, lights	8 inches
Water supply	12 inches (in cold areas, 6 inches below frost depth)

have these on their payroll.

Excavating to repair a gas or water leak or an exposed live electrical conductor can make quite a mess of your client's yard — not a great way to start a project. Even if the utility is not damaged, you may need to relocate it or the pier, which may require modifications to the deck design and will certainly delay your schedule.

Calling to have utilities located is easier than ever. Dialing 811 from anywhere in the United States, including Alaska and Hawaii, reaches your local utility notification office, where you request the locator service. Make this call as early as possible, as the location of utilities can limit the deck design; you can't safely put a pier where there's a utility.

When I was a deck builder, I would sometimes ask serious clients if they'd mind if I had the utilities located before our first design meeting. That helped insure the design my clients fell in love with could actually be built. The forethought cost nothing, yet separated me from other contractors by demonstrating my competence and attention to detail.

Underground landscape sprinkler pipe, to my knowledge, is the only underground construction material that a common locator service doesn't detect.

Sonotube Reinforcement

Q. To support a beam for a residential deck, does a Sonotube pier need rebar?

A. Jay Meunier, contracting specialist at S.T. Griswold and Co., a ready-mixed concrete supplier in Williston, Vt., responds: First, check with your local building authorities to find out what local codes apply. I have never seen architectural or structural drawings that did not indicate some amount of reinforcing for concrete piers.

We usually recommend that a minimum of two pieces of #4 rebar be placed vertically in an 8-inch-diameter concrete pier supporting a structure. A larger-diameter pier should have four or more pieces of vertical rebar. The rebar provides the tensile strength needed to resist lateral stresses that can be applied to a concrete pier by ground movement, freeze cycles, and wind loads.

Posts Sunk in the Ground

Q. Can 6x6 pressure-treated deck posts be sunk into the ground or should they be supported on concrete piers?

A. Henry Spies, a building consultant formerly with the Small Homes Council/Building Research Council of the University of Illinois, responds: Theoretically, posts that have been pressure-treated for ground contact can be sunk into the ground. However, it is unlikely that the treatment has penetrated fully through a 6x6. So I would opt for the concrete piers with the posts supported on metal post anchors.

If the posts are sunk directly into the ground, the bottom of the post must not be cut. I have seen a number of posts with the center rotted out because the treatment chemicals did not penetrate completely, and water was wicked up through the untreated center. Post tops should be beveled to shed water, or have a metal post cap added. Any cut ends of pressure-treated material that are left exposed to the weather should be dipped in or painted with a copper napthenate solution.

New Piers Near an Existing Foundation

Q. Plans for a freestanding deck call for new piers about 2 feet from the house foundation. Is it necessary to dig down to the bottom of the house's footing to reach undisturbed soil, or would the soil around the foundation of a 60-year-old house be compacted enough to be considered undisturbed — in which case we could simply dig to below the frost line, per code?

A. Dave Crosby, an excavation contractor in Santa Fe, N.M., responds: Because undisturbed soil is usually more reliable than backfill, I typically make the extra effort to dig down to it, especially if the backfill contains soft soil (anything I can easily dig without a pick or bar). However, if the undisturbed soil is a long way below the frost line or has a lot of silt and clay — and I'm confident that I have good, compacted fill — I may dig only to the frost line. In either case, whether the soil is disturbed or undisturbed, what I'm looking for is adequate load-bearing capacity.

Bearing strength is a function of the soil's composition and density. Dense (because it's either undisturbed or has been compacted), well-graded soil that is properly drained and has little or no expansive potential should easily support a deck with properly sized footings. The age of the house and the surrounding soil is irrelevant, because no matter how long soil sits there, it won't compact itself. So be sure to address the soil's composition and density in the design of your footings and piers, and test the soil whenever you're in doubt.

You also have to be careful about lateral loads caused by placing your deck footings too near the foundation. Loads spread out through the soil underneath a footing at about a 45-degree angle, so that at a depth of 2 feet under a 2-foot-by-2-foot footing, the zone of influence is about 4 feet by 4 feet, or 16 square feet. Depending on the elevation of the bottom of your piers, deck loads could create lateral pressure on the foundation wall.

Side loading isn't a problem in my area (Seismic Zone 2), because we're required to build strong foundations. If your foundation wall is reinforced cast concrete and the floor joists run perpendicular to the deck footings, it shouldn't be an issue for you, either. But if the foundation is unreinforced concrete block or fieldstone set in lime mortar, you'll need to be careful about those lateral loads.

Use an Existing Slab for Footings?

Q. *I'm considering building a deck over an existing concrete slab. The slab is at least 20 years old and has no major cracks. Can I set the deck posts right on the slab?*

A. *Andy Engel, editor of* Professional Deck Builder, *responds:* No. Even though the slab is in good shape, it's likely that the point loads from the deck posts would crack it.

Loads spread out through a footing (the slab would act as a footing) in the shape of a cone whose sides slope at about 45 degrees. This distributes the load over an area of soil that should be large enough to carry the expected weight. Thicker footings spread loads over larger areas, and most footings are at least 12 inches thick and 2 feet square. Slabs typically are only 4 inches thick, which won't create a wide enough cone to distribute the loads over a very large area of soil. If the added weight from the deck compresses the soil under these points, the slab would crack and probably subside.

Also, the IRC requires that footings be a minimum of 12 inches below grade, even where frost is not an issue. Unless it's a very thick slab, this portion of the code isn't satisfied.

One solution is to cut away the slab to allow for full-size footings. They can be made level with the slab so that there's no elevation difference, but there should be no concrete-to-concrete contact. The slab has to be able to move around the new footings to accommodate thermal expansion and contraction, or else it will crack. To allow for this movement, line the edges of the saw cuts in the slab with foam sill sealer. Use mastic to hold it in place during the pour. Once the concrete sets up, tear out the topmost half inch or so of the sill sealer, and fill the joint with polyurethane caulk to keep out water.

Chapter 4:
Deck Ledgers

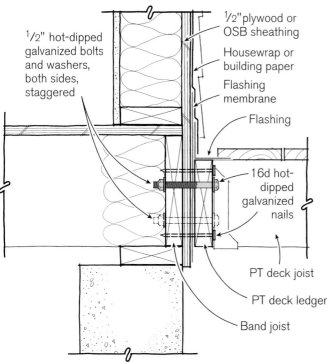

½" hot-dipped galvanized bolts and washers, both sides, staggered

½"plywood or OSB sheathing

Housewrap or building paper

Flashing membrane

Flashing

16d hot-dipped galvanized nails

PT deck joist

PT deck ledger

Band joist

Load-Tested Deck Ledger Connections

by Joe Loferski, Frank Woeste, Ricky Caudill, Terry Platt, and Quintin Smith

Beginning in 2001, members of the staff at Virginia Tech's Engineering and Wood Science Departments launched a project to develop and publish an inspection manual for residential decks and balconies. (The resulting *Manual for the Inspection of Wood Decks and Balconies* is now available from the Forest Products Society, www.forestprod.org.)

To our surprise, we found that problems with deck attachment are quite common and that the issues are more complex than we had thought. Here, we'll focus on the forces at work between the deck ledger and the band joist, and offer connection details that will safely carry the typical loads.

In addition to using the right fasteners in sufficient numbers, an important factor in designing ledger attachments is preventing moisture damage — rot — from weakening the ledger and band joist. Field observations of existing decks by Roger Robertson of the Chesterfield County, Va., Building Department revealed decay in untreated band joists where deck ledgers were attached. In some cases, the decay had spread into the interior floor joists.

Flashing between the ledger and the band joist is important for keeping water out of the interior framing. In his field studies, Robertson observed that aluminum flashing in contact with CCA-treated lumber had corroded within five years of construction. Our details show a flashing layer, but if you use flashing next to pressure-treated lumber, make sure you use an approved, corrosion-resistant material suitable for contact with today's more corrosive wood treatments (see "Treated Wood: New Formulations, New Fasteners," page 110).

Ledger Calculations vs. Load-Testing

In the article "Attaching Deck Ledgers," published in the August 2003 issue of *The Journal of Light Construction*, the authors used a procedure from the *National Design Specification for Wood Construction* (*NDS-2001*) to calculate the required on-center spacing of lag screws and bolts for deck-ledger-to-band-joist connec-

Note: The results of the tests described in this report have been incorporated into the building code as part of the 2007 IRC Supplement. For more information about the code changes, see "New Rules for Deck Ledgers and Lateral Attachment," on page 41.

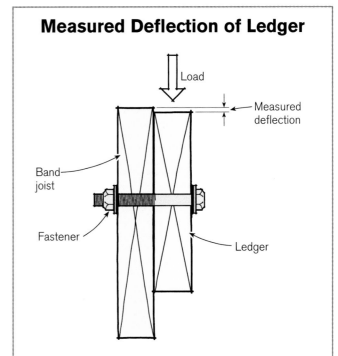

Figure 1. The testers measured the displacement of the ledger relative to the band joist for every specimen. The range of displacement for each connection detail is listed with the fastener schedule.

tions for various deck widths. Although the calculated spacings were "to code," they were too tight to be practical. The reason is that the *NDS* limits the allowable load for lag screws and bolt connections based on a very small "deformation" at the design load — a deformation limit intended to prevent undesirable movement of a wood-framed structure and to prevent finishes such as tile and drywall from cracking.

The purpose of this report is to provide the results of load tests conducted on four connection details that could be used to connect a residential deck ledger board to the house band joist. Using this test approach, which is recognized by the code, we found that the "allowable" loads for lag screws, for example, are two to three times higher than the values obtained using the *NDS-2001* equations. Bolts proved to be even stronger compared with *NDS*-designed connections.

The deflection of the ledger relative to the band joist (**Figure 1**) was measured at full design load. The range of deflections for the 15 samples of each detail tested is noted, so that the deck designer can judge whether the expected displacement is acceptable.

Code Allowance for Load Testing

The International Building Code (IBC, 2000 and 2003 editions), as well as previous codes, allows for load testing when "a construction is not capable of being designed by approved engineering analysis" or "does not comply with applicable material design standards."

In the case of deck ledger connections to the main structure, the minimum required fastener penetration of a lag screw into the house band joist is four times the fastener diameter (4D). This requirement cannot be met when you use 1/2-inch-diameter lag screws to attach the ledger to the band joist, because a typical band joist is only 1 1/2 inches thick (3D), not the required 2 inches thick (4D). Even if the band were 2 inches thick, the 1/2-inch lag screw values in the *NDS-2001* tables must be reduced by half because they are based on lag screw penetration into the main member (the band joist) of eight diameters (8D), or 4 inches.

Similarly, there are no available tables for designing a bolted ledger employing drainage spacers, or even for a ledger attached on top of structural sheathing (the *NDS* assumes the connected members are in direct contact).

Therefore, we tested simulated ledger-to-band connections and calculated allowable on-center spacings based on the *ultimate capacity* of the connection, applying a safety factor and an adjustment for load duration. The test load duration was about five minutes, whereas the assumed duration for an occupancy live load (40 psf for a residential deck) is ten years.

Code Language on Decks

Note that the International Residential Code (IRC 2003, R502.2.1 Decks) states: *"Where supported by attachment to an exterior wall, decks shall be positively anchored to the primary structure and designed for both vertical and lateral loads as applicable. Such attachment shall not be accomplished by the use of toenails or nails subject to withdrawal...."*

This section means that nails alone cannot be used to connect a ledger to a band joist when no other lateral bracing is in place to positively anchor the deck to the building against lateral loads. Thus, in the absence of adequate lateral bracing, lag screws, bolts, or some other positive connection will be required to design and build a code-compliant deck.

Test Setup

For the test, we fabricated specimens from 2x10 No. 2 spruce-pine-fir (SPF) lumber to simulate the band joist of the house. These were attached to a 2x8 No. 2 CCA-pressure-treated southern pine (SP) ledger board sample. We used either 1/2-inch-diameter lag screws or 1/2-inch-diameter bolts for all tests. Some specimens included 15/32-inch APA-rated plywood to simulate the gap produced by conventional wall sheathing between the ledger and band joist. One test case

included a 1/2-inch stack of washers between the ledger board and the plywood to replicate the drainage space sometimes incorporated into the connection, a practice shown in some deck design books.

The 2-by band joist was supported on the testing machine base to simulate direct bearing on the foundation sill plate (**Figure 2**, next page). The CCA-pressure-treated sample deck components consisted of two 2x8 joists attached to a 2x8 ledger with joist hangers. We used extra fasteners to attach the joist hangers to the ledger to ensure that failure would occur in the lag screw or bolt connection. The far end of the deck joists were supported on solid spacers on the base of the testing machine.

We realize that CCA-treated lumber is now restricted in residential applications, but at the time of the testing, we needed to include an unseasoned (wet) ledger as part of the test, and CCA was locally available. After testing, we verified that the ledger material was "green" — that is, having a moisture content well above 19 percent. By using unseasoned ledgers in our tests, we had no need to apply an adjustment to our test results for "wet service use."

On the specimens that included sheathing, the plywood was trimmed so it was 2 inches shorter than the width of the ledger board to prevent it from accidentally bearing on the test platform and artificially inflating our tested lag or bolt connection.

A universal hydraulic testing machine applied the load, at a constant rate of 1/2 inch of deflection per minute. The deflection was measured by an electronic transducer attached to the ledger board in such a way that it measured the vertical displacement of the ledger board relative to the band joist. During testing, the load and displacement data were continuously recorded by a computer.

The load was applied to the specimen at the center of the joist, and the load measured by the testing machine was divided by two to account for the reaction at the opposite end of the joist. In other words, half the load was applied to the connection itself, and half the load was applied to the foundation at the opposite end of the joists, just as in a real deck. The load was applied until the connection failed to carry any additional load.

Lag Screw and Bolt Installation

We followed the rules prescribed in *NDS-2001* for fastener installation as they relate to clearance, lead-hole diameters, and use of washers. For lag screws, two hole diameters are specified, a slightly larger clearance hole to allow the nonthreaded portion to penetrate the side member (ledger) without splitting and a smaller lead hole in the main member (band joist) to fully engage the threads.

We purchased 1/2-inch-diameter lag screws from a local building supply store and measured the root

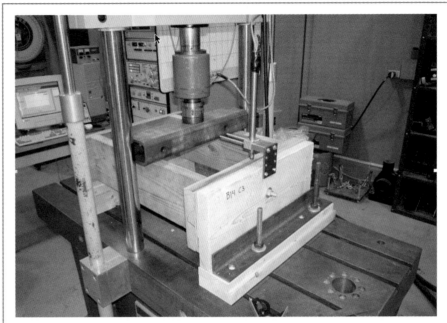

Figure 2. The hydraulic test machine put pressure on a pair of joists attached by hangers to the sample ledger (left). Extra fasteners in the hangers ensured that failure would occur not at the hanger but in the lag screw or bolt attaching the sample ledger to the sample band joist. A transducer measured displacement of the ledger (bottom left), while a computer continuously recorded measurement and load data. The load was applied until the connection failed (bottom right).

diameter of the threaded portion of the screws. The root diameter was 0.39 inch, so we used a $^3/_8$-inch lead hole, which is slightly smaller than the root diameter, to accommodate the threads of the lag screw in the band joist. We used a $^1/_2$-inch clearance hole in the CCA-treated ledger board to accommodate the nonthreaded portion of the shank. We tightened the connections normally, by hand with a wrench. In general, when installing lag screws, you should feel significant turning resistance; otherwise, the lead hole may be too large. Washers were not used under the lag screw heads because *NDS* does not require them. However, we believe that a washer on a lag screw will improve the connection, and we would use them on our own projects for added safety.

For the bolted connections, the *NDS-2001* requires the holes to be a minimum of $^1/_{32}$ inch to a maximum of $^1/_{16}$ inch larger than the bolt diameter. Therefore, we drilled $^9/_{16}$-inch holes in both the ledger board and the band joist to accommodate the $^1/_2$-inch bolts. We added washers on both sides of the bolt connections as specified by *NDS*: one between the head and the lumber, and the other between the nut and the lumber.

Four Cases Tested

We tested four different cases to represent common construction practices. Fifteen replications of each case were tested. **Case 1** included a 2x8 SP ledger attached to a 2x10 SPF band joist with a $3^1/_2$-inch-long by $^1/_2$-inch-diameter lag screw. Note that we used a $3^1/_2$-inch screw, because the tip of a lag screw is not effective in load transfer. **Case 2** incorporated the 2x10 SPF band joist and 2x8 SP ledger with a $^{15}/_{32}$-inch plywood spacer to simulate the wall sheathing commonly sandwiched between the ledger board and the band joist. We connected the ledger to

continued on page 94

Case 1: ¹/₂-Inch Lag Screw With Ledger Attached Directly to Band Joist

Tested Connection

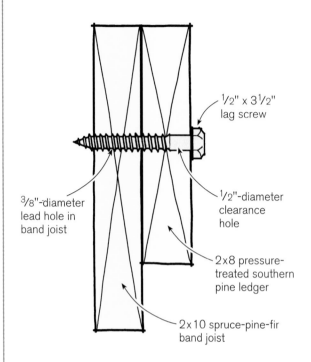

¹/₂" x 3¹/₂" lag screw

³/₈"-diameter lead hole in band joist

¹/₂"-diameter clearance hole

2x8 pressure-treated southern pine ledger

2x10 spruce-pine-fir band joist

Typical Detail

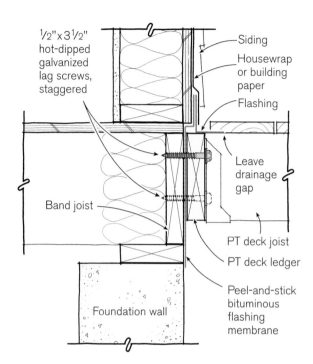

¹/₂"x 3¹/₂" hot-dipped galvanized lag screws, staggered

Siding

Housewrap or building paper

Flashing

Band joist

Leave drainage gap

PT deck joist

PT deck ledger

Foundation wall

Peel-and-stick bituminous flashing membrane

Joist span (ft.)	6	8	10	12	14	16	18
Fastener spacing (in.)	34	25	20	17	15	13	11

The tested deflection of the ledger relative to the band joist at design load (50 psf) ranged from 0.03 in. to 0.17 in.

Limitations

Lumber size. This schedule is valid only for 2x8 or larger ledgers with a specific gravity, G, of 0.55 or greater (G for southern pine = 0.55) and 2-by band joists with G of 0.42 or greater (G for SPF = 0.42).

Lumber type. Tabulated fastener spacings are based on virgin lumber with no decay. Flashing must be properly applied to keep water from penetrating the joint and wetting the untreated band joist. The deck ledger must be pressure treated with an approved chemical and retention. In the case of new home construction, a pressure-treated house band in the deck area is recommended.

Loads. The tabulated spacings apply to residential decks (40-psf live load, 10-psf dead load) and do not apply to residential balconies (60-psf live load) or other applications having design loads greater than 40-psf live load plus 10-psf dead load.

Lag screw installation. The results apply only to ¹/₂-inch-diameter lag screws long enough to fully

penetrate the band joist, not counting the tapered lag screw point. Lead holes in the band joist for lag screws must be drilled slightly smaller than the root diameter of the threads, so that the threads fully engage the main member. The clearance hole in the deck ledger must be drilled to the same diameter as the nonthreaded shank. Lag screws should be staggered to guard against splitting.

Joist configuration. The tabulated spacings apply to deck construction where the joists are laid out 24 inches on-center or less and run perpendicular to the ledger. The spacings do not apply to deck construction where the deck joists are parallel to the ledger and joist loads are transferred to the ledger using widely spaced girders. That produces a large concentrated load on the ledger; in that case, design by a professional is required.

Inspection. Deck framing and connections should be inspected annually to detect possible deterioration.

Case 2: ¹/₂ x 4-Inch Lag Screw With ¹⁵/₃₂-Inch Plywood Sheathing

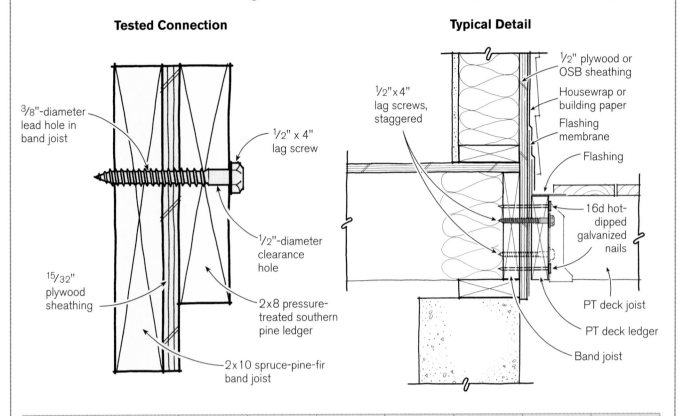

Tested Connection

- ³/₈"-diameter lead hole in band joist
- ¹/₂" x 4" lag screw
- ¹/₂"-diameter clearance hole
- ¹⁵/₃₂" plywood sheathing
- 2x8 pressure-treated southern pine ledger
- 2x10 spruce-pine-fir band joist

Typical Detail

- ¹/₂" plywood or OSB sheathing
- Housewrap or building paper
- Flashing membrane
- Flashing
- ¹/₂"x4" lag screws, staggered
- 16d hot-dipped galvanized nails
- PT deck joist
- PT deck ledger
- Band joist

Joist span (ft.)	6	8	10	12	14	16	18
Fastener spacing (in.)	30	23	18	15	13	11	10

The tested deflection of the ledger relative to the band joist at design load (50 psf) ranged from 0.08 in. to 0.24 in.

Limitations

Lumber size. This schedule is valid only for 2x8 or larger ledgers with a specific gravity, G, of 0.55 or greater (G for southern pine = 0.55) and 2-by band joists with G of 0.42 or greater (G for SPF = 0.42).

Lumber type. Tabulated fastener spacings are based on virgin lumber with no decay. Flashing must be properly applied to keep water from penetrating the joint and wetting the untreated band joist. The deck ledger must be pressure treated with an approved chemical and retention. In the case of new home construction, a pressure-treated house band in the deck area is recommended.

Loads. The tabulated spacings apply to residential decks (40-psf live load, 10-psf dead load) and do not apply to residential balconies (60-psf LL) or other applications having design loads greater than 40-psf live load plus 10-psf dead load.

Lag screw installation. The results apply only to ¹/₂-inch-diameter lag screws long enough to fully penetrate the band joist, not counting the tapered lag screw

point. Lead holes in the band joist for lag screws must be drilled slightly smaller than the root diameter of the threads, so that the threads fully engage the main member. The clearance hole in the deck ledger must be drilled to the same diameter as the nonthreaded shank. Lag screws should be staggered to guard against splitting.

Sheathing. The test results apply to wall sheathing thicknesses of ¹⁵/₃₂ inch or less.

Joist configuration. The tabulated spacings apply to deck construction where the joists are laid out 24 inches on-center or less and run perpendicular to the ledger. The spacings do not apply to deck construction where the deck joists are parallel to the ledger and joist loads are transferred to the ledger using widely spaced girders. That produces a large concentrated load on the ledger; in that case, design by a professional is required.

Inspection. Deck framing and connections should be inspected annually to detect possible deterioration.

Case 3: ¹/₂-Inch Bolt With ¹⁵/₃₂-Inch Plywood Sheathing

Tested Connection   **Typical Detail**

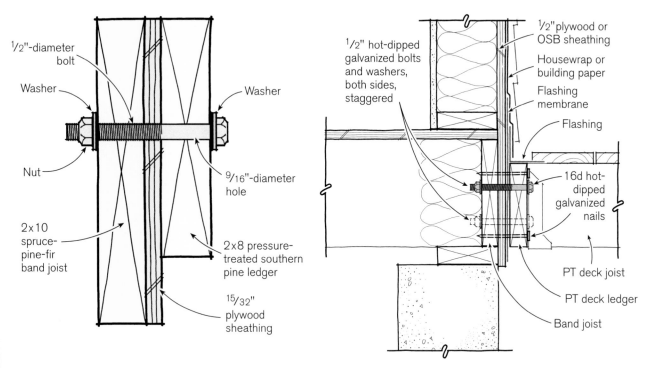

Joist span (ft.)	6	8	10	12	14	16	18
Fastener spacing (in.)	36*	36*	34	29	24	21	19

The tested deflection of the ledger relative to the band joist at design load (50 psf) ranged from 0.11 in. to 0.35 in.

*These spacings have been reduced from the allowable value determined by testing in consideration of the ledger's bending strength between bolts.

Limitations

Lumber size. This schedule is valid only for 2x8 or larger ledgers with a specific gravity, G, of 0.55 or greater (G for southern pine = 0.55) and 2-by band joists with G of 0.42 or greater (G for SPF = 0.42).

Lumber type. Tabulated fastener spacings are based on virgin lumber with no decay. Flashing must be properly applied to keep water from penetrating the joint and wetting the untreated band joist. The deck ledger must be pressure treated with an approved chemical and retention. In the case of new home construction, a pressure-treated house band in the deck area is recommended.

Bolt installation. The results apply only to ¹/₂-inch-diameter bolts of sufficient length to allow for a washer under the head and a washer under the nut. Holes for bolts must be drilled ¹/₃₂ to ¹/₁₆ inch larger than the bolt diameter. Bolts should be staggered to guard against splitting.

Sheathing. The test results apply to wall sheathing thicknesses of ¹⁵/₃₂ inch or less.

Joist configuration. The tabulated spacings apply to deck construction where the joists are laid out 24 inches on-center or less and run perpendicular to the ledger. The spacings do not apply to deck construction where the deck joists are parallel to the ledger and joist loads are transferred to the ledger using widely spaced girders. That produces a large concentrated load on the ledger; in that case, design by a professional is required.

Inspection. Deck framing and connections should be inspected annually to detect possible deterioration.

Case 4: ¹/₂ x 4-Inch Bolt With ¹⁵/₃₂-Inch Plywood Sheathing and ¹/₂-Inch Drainage Space

Tested Connection

Typical Detail

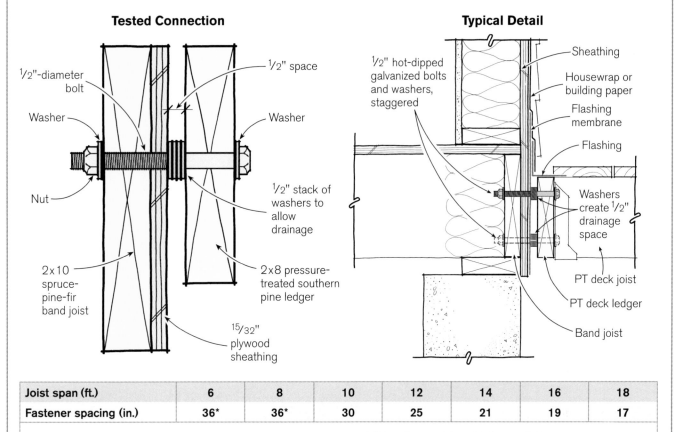

¹/₂"-diameter bolt

Washer

Nut

2x10 spruce-pine-fir band joist

¹/₂" space

Washer

¹/₂" stack of washers to allow drainage

2x8 pressure-treated southern pine ledger

¹⁵/₃₂" plywood sheathing

¹/₂" hot-dipped galvanized bolts and washers, staggered

Sheathing

Housewrap or building paper

Flashing membrane

Flashing

Washers create ¹/₂" drainage space

PT deck joist

PT deck ledger

Band joist

Joist span (ft.)	6	8	10	12	14	16	18
Fastener spacing (in.)	36*	36*	30	25	21	19	17

The tested deflection of the ledger relative to the band joist at design load (50 psf) ranged from 0.25 in. to 0.42 in.

*These spacings have been reduced from the allowable value determined by testing in consideration of the ledger's bending strength between bolts.

Limitations

Lumber size. This schedule is valid only for 2x8 or larger ledgers with a specific gravity, G, of 0.55 or greater (G for southern pine = 0.55) and 2-by band joists with G of 0.42 or greater (G for SPF = 0.42).

Lumber type. Tabulated fastener spacings are based on virgin lumber with no decay. Flashing must be properly applied to keep water from penetrating the joint and wetting the untreated band joist. The deck ledger must be pressure treated with an approved chemical and retention. In the case of new home construction, a pressure-treated house band in the deck area is recommended.

Loads. The tabulated spacings apply to residential decks (40-psf live load, 10-psf dead load) and do not apply to residential balconies (60-psf LL) or other applications having design loads greater than 40-psf live load plus 10-psf dead load.

Bolt Installation. The results apply only to ¹/₂-inch-diameter bolts of sufficient length to allow for a washer under

the head and a washer under the nut. Holes for bolts must be drilled ¹/₃₂ to ¹/₁₆ inch larger than the bolt diameter. Bolts should be staggered to guard against splitting.

Sheathing. The test results apply to wall sheathing thicknesses of ¹⁵/₃₂ inch or less.

Spacers. Where spacers are used for drainage, the gap between the ledger and the wall sheathing created by the spacers must be ¹/₂ inch or less.

Joist configuration. The tabulated spacings apply to deck construction where the joists are laid out 24 inches on-center or less and run perpendicular to the ledger. The spacings do not apply to deck construction where the deck joists are parallel to the ledger and joist loads are transferred to the ledger using widely spaced girders. That produces a large concentrated load on the ledger; in that case, design by a professional is required.

Inspection. Deck framing and connections should be inspected annually to detect possible deterioration.

Why Don't More Ledgers Fail?

by Cheryl Anderson, Frank Woeste, and Joe Loferski

At first glance, the lag and bolt spacings shown in the details in this article may appear to be overly conservative. Builders frequently attach deck ledgers only with nails, and when they use lag screws, it wouldn't be surprising to find that the screw spacings are far greater than those shown in Case 2 (page 90), for example.

So, the question is, why don't residential deck-to-house connections fail on a routine basis? There are a few possible reasons.

Loads Not Uniform

The fastener schedules here assume that the deck will be uniformly loaded, so that approximately half of the load will need to be supported by the ledger. But large groups of people don't normally sit right next to the house. Instead, more people tend to gather near the outer edges of the deck, so that live loads are typically greater on the outer supports compared with the house side (illustration below).

Decks Not Often Fully Loaded

Code design loads require residential decks to be able to support a 40-psf live load plus a 10-psf dead load. Assuming a 12x18-foot deck, 40 psf would be roughly equivalent to a gathering of 58 people, based on an average weight of 150 pounds per person. In reality, however, that many people are unlikely to gather at one time on a 12x18-foot deck during its entire service life.

Connector Safety Factors

The allowable shear values for lag screws are based on code-approved engineering standards. Laboratory tests of lag screws indicate that the safety factor on the allowable design values can be as high as 5. Thus, a properly installed $1/2$-inch lag screw in a band joist ledger application will typically carry a lot more than 180 pounds of load before the connection ruptures. (Nevertheless, the safety factor should not be encroached upon: Its purpose is to account for any uncertainties of design, construction, and service conditions that may crop up. For example, a carpenter might drill too large a lead hole for the lag threads, which weakens the connection. Or a carpenter might align the lag screws in two or more rows in the wet ledger, which will increase the likelihood that the lumber will split as it dries.)

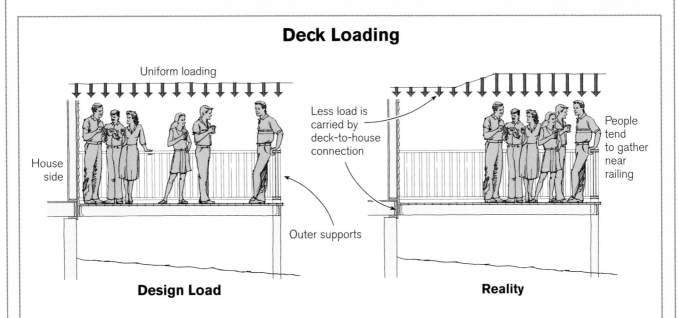

Deck Loading

Uniform loading

Less load is carried by deck-to-house connection

People tend to gather near railing

House side

Outer supports

Design Load

Reality

Decks are designed for uniform loading (left). In reality, people tend to gather near the railings rather than next to the house, taking some of the load off the ledger (right).

continued from page 88
the band with 4-inch-long by $^1/_2$-inch-diameter lag screws. **Case 3** included the 2x10 SPF band joist, 2x8 SP ledger, and the $^{15}/_{32}$-inch plywood layer, connected with a $^1/_2$-inch-diameter bolt with washers. **Case 4** was similar to **Case 3**, except that we added a $^1/_2$-inch stack of washers — the drainage space — between the plywood and ledger to simulate a nearly 1-inch gap (including the plywood) between the ledger and the band joist.

Safety factor applied. To determine allowable fastener spacings, we calculated the maximum average load for each case and reduced the results by factors to account for safety and the fact that the laboratory tests were of short duration.

The IBC requires that failure loads from tests of structural assemblies be divided by a safety factor of 2.5. For the purpose of decks, we used an even larger safety factor, of 3.0, to further account for possible variations in field installation of lag screws and bolts.

The average maximum load was further reduced by a load duration factor of 1.6 to account for the difference in performance between short-term laboratory testing (about five minutes) and ten-year continuous loading as defined for occupancy live load in the *NDS*.

Wet-use factor not needed. The *NDS* requires a "wet-use" reduction factor (C_m) to be applied to connection design values for situations where the wood is expected to be above 19% moisture content. For those tests, we used wet CCA-treated southern pine ledger boards, with an average moisture content of 44%. Because we expect the moisture content of deck lumber to remain above 19% during periods of wet weather, we applied no reduction in the calculated design strength; the effect of using wet lumber is included in the test.

Deck loads. After applying these reduction factors, the resulting values were used to calculate the required spacing between fasteners for various joist spans based on a design loading of 40-psf live load and 10-psf dead load, as specified in the IRC for residential decks. However, because residential balconies have a higher design load than residential decks, these spacing results do not apply to balconies.

Failures of Lag Screws vs. Bolts

The fastener spacings for the bolted connections (**Cases 3** and **4**) are considerably larger than for those of the lag screws (**Cases 1** and **2**). At high test loads, the washers under the head and nut keep the bolt from withdrawing completely from the connection; thus the ultimate loads for the bolted specimens were generally greater. For lag screw specimens, failure often occurred when the threaded shank withdrew from the band joist or when the head of the lag screw embedded itself into the ledger. Also, due to the threads, lag screws have a reduced diameter in the band joist, and thus the screw rotates more easily under load than a bolt of the same nominal size.

Expected deformations. The tables include the measured range of vertical deformation between the band and the ledger for each case. These numbers provide an estimate of the expected range of deformation at full design load for a short period of time. If the live load on a deck is sustained — for instance, from heavy planters — this expected deflection of the ledger relative to the band joist may be double the stated figure, or even greater. Judgment is needed in using this data for particular cases of significant sustained live loads. Occupant loading on a deck is not considered sustained.

Limitations of Results

The strength of mechanical connectors used in wood construction depends partly on the specific gravity, G, of the lumber. Southern pine, the ledger material we used, has a G of 0.55; SPF, the sample band joist, has a G of 0.42.

The main disadvantage of this test-based approach is that the allowable values cannot be extrapolated downward for materials having a lower strength. For example, we cannot use the test data to predict the strength of a lag screw connection made with a pressure-treated hem-fir ledger (G = 0.43). It would be acceptable to use the schedules with a hem-fir band joist, however, as long as the ledger was southern pine.

Joe Loferski and Frank Woeste, PE, are professor and professor emeritus, respectively, at Virginia Tech University, Blacksburg. Ricky Caudill is a lab technician, Terry Platt is a research scientist, and Quintin Smith is a former intern. Cheryl Anderson is a former graduate research assistant.

Supporting a Freestanding Deck

by Cheryl Anderson, Frank Woeste, and Joe Loferski

Attaching the ledger to the band joist may be common, but it makes it somewhat difficult for the builder — as well as the inspector — to be certain that the connection is safe and durable. In addition to the gravity loads, deck ledgers are subject to lateral, or sideways, loads, which are not addressed by the fastener schedules in the cases shown in "Load-Tested Deck Ledger Connections," page 86.

We recommend a different approach: supporting the deck with pressure-treated posts, as shown below.

This approach has several advantages:

• It eliminates the need to penetrate the house siding, sheathing, and band joist, thus eliminating the potential for decay.
• It relies on more efficient structural connections because the ledger rests directly on the end grain of the wood post. Connections that use lag screws, bolts, or nails loaded in shear require far more attention, in both design and construction, than a simple beam-to-post connection.
• It has structural redundancy, meaning that the pos-

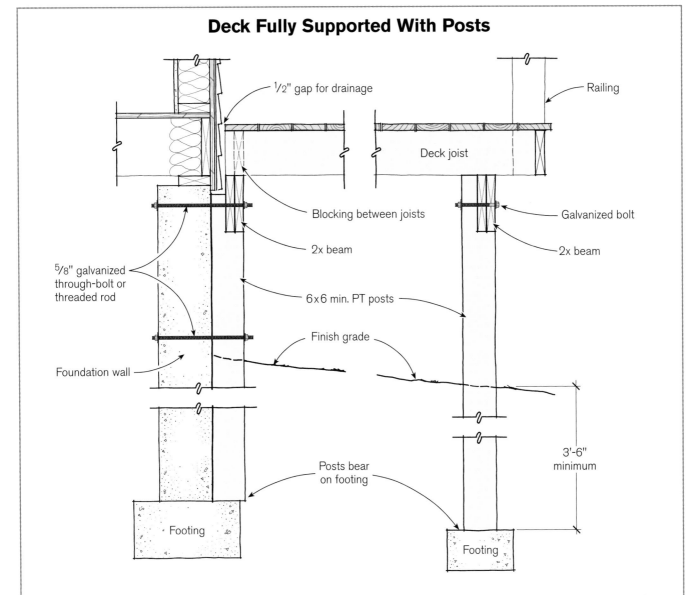

Deck Fully Supported With Posts

1/2" gap for drainage

Railing

Deck joist

Blocking between joists

Galvanized bolt

2x beam

2x beam

5/8" galvanized through-bolt or threaded rod

6x6 min. PT posts

Finish grade

Foundation wall

3'-6" minimum

Posts bear on footing

Footing

Footing

The authors strongly recommend avoiding mechanical shear connections (such as a deck ledger bolted to the house). Instead, they recommend supporting residential decks with PT posts, as shown here. For greatest durability of the in-ground posts, use treated lumber rated for use in permanent wood foundations and structural building poles.

sible failure of one element will not automatically produce or permit collapse of the entire structure. In this detail, the through-bolt prevents sideways movement of the deck, which might occur if the outside posts were not deeply embedded in the ground. In the unlikely event that the through-bolts should fail from corrosion or any other reason, the embedded 6x6 posts at the foundation wall would still prevent a lateral collapse of the entire deck.

• From an inspection point of view, it's easier to verify that a self-supporting deck is sound, because all the elements (except the footers) are exposed.

While the 6x6 posts commonly sold in retail building supply centers are treated for "ground contact," we recommend using posts treated to higher retention levels and rated for use in Permanent Wood Foundations and structural poles. The ends of the posts placed in the ground should not be cut, as that exposes untreated heartwood. Southern pine heartwood, as well as the heartwood of other softwood species, does not accept the penetration of the chemical treatment; thus, only the end surface contains the chemical.

The posts are located next to the house and notched to receive the ledger. The deck joists are then supported on the built-up beams, which further minimizes reliance on mechanical connections (joist hangers). The through-rods address lateral support, which, while not quantitatively addressed by the building codes, is extremely important.

Keep trash, vegetation, and construction debris out of the backfill around the post, as it would compromise the lateral resistance of the embedded post section. We also suggest that the post be backfilled around its base with an 80-pound bag of concrete mix, followed by 8 inches of well-compacted native soil or a sand and gravel mixture. The concrete above the footing pad will stabilize the bottom of the post in the unlikely event that the footing pad should rotate in service. The size of the post footing pad and the depth of the post embedment for a design should be determined by the deck designer and depends on local frost depth and soil strength, as well as local building codes.

Cheryl Anderson is a former graduate research assistant, Frank Woeste, PE, is professor emeritus, and Joseph Loferski is a professor at Virginia Tech in Blacksburg.

Ledgers on Challenging Walls

by Andy Engel

Readers of this book likely know how to safely secure a deck ledger to most houses. But what about the oddball situations? Can you attach a ledger to a concrete wall? What about to masonry veneer, stucco, EIFS, logs, SIPs, I-joists, or cantilevered floor framing? The answer is often nuanced, but sometimes it's a flat-out "No."

And it's not just the mechanical attachment that makes for a safe, durable deck. "Flashing is as critical as the original design," notes Frank Woeste, PE, PhD, professor emeritus at Virginia Tech. Poorly detailed flashing or flashing (such as aluminum) that corrodes in short order when in contact with ACQ preservatives lets in water that rots the house framing. It doesn't matter how many bolts you use to attach the ledger if the house framing it's attached to rots away.

The advent of engineered floor systems also brought about some unanticipated (by carpenters, anyway) structural issues. For example, some early engineered floors used only 3/4-inch OSB as a rim board. Compound that with poor flashing, and you've got a recipe for collapse (see "Siding Hides Warnings of Deck Collapse," facing page).

The details shown here are intended as guidelines; other solutions, good and bad, exist. And if you have any doubt at all, it's never a bad idea to pay for an engineer's expertise.

Masonry walls? It depends.

Direct attachment to solid masonry — poured concrete or grout-filled block — and concrete block is fairly simple. Details for doing so are widely available; the ones shown here (**Figure 3**) are from Virginia's state building code. For solid masonry, steel expansion

Ledger Fastener Spacing for Masonry Walls		
Joist span	1/2" bolts and expansion anchors	1/2" bolts and approved adhesive anchors
0 to 6'-0"	36"	32"
6'-1" to 8'-0"	36"	32"
8'-1" to 10'-0"	34"	32"
10'-1" to 12'-0"	29"	24"
12'-1" to 14'-0"	24"	24"
14'-1" to 16'-0"	21"	16"
16'-1" to 18'-0"	19"	16"

SOURCE: *PROFESSIONAL DECK BUILDER*

Attaching to Concrete or Hollow Masonry

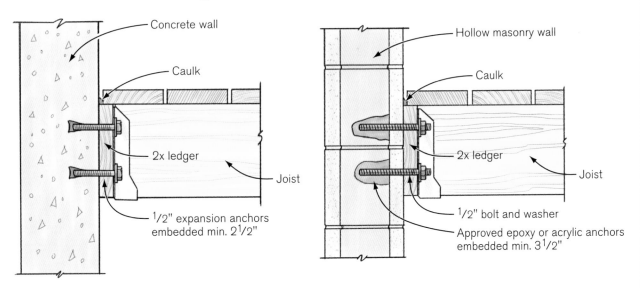

Figure 3. In most cases, deck ledgers can be bolted directly to poured concrete or concrete block walls. Expansion anchors — never lead shields — are used in solid masonry or filled block, and approved epoxy or acrylic anchors and bolts are used in hollow masonry.

anchors whose bolts are a minimum of $1/2$ inch in diameter and penetrate the masonry by at least $2^{1}/_2$ inches can take the place of lag bolts. The recommended anchor spacing is shown at left in the table "Ledger Fastener Spacing for Masonry Walls."

Note that this type of connection is only suitable for structural masonry, and never for masonry veneer. Attachment to masonry veneer is usually a bad idea for reasons discussed in "Bolting a Ledger Through Brick Veneer," page 103.

Siding Hides Warnings of Deck Collapse

by Laurie Elden

In May, 2007, a group of people went outside on a second-story landing to see what was going on. They had heard an ambulance only to end up needing an ambulance themselves when 4x7-foot landing pulled away from a residence in Normal, Ill. As a result of the collapse, six women were taken to the local hospital with non-life-threatening injuries.

Ironically, May was "Deck Safety Month," but the cause of this collapse wouldn't have been visible in a routine inspection, according to Greg Troemel, director of inspections for Normal. The landing and the stairs were intact when they separated from the building, and the building itself seemed to be in good condition.

Once the vinyl siding and sheathing were removed, however, the reasons behind the collapse became clear. When the structure had been built 18 years earlier, an I-joist floor system was used, with a $3/4$-inch OSB rim joist rather than solid dimensional lumber — without extra blocking. Since

the rim joist was the primary fastening point for the landing, the lags had only $3/4$ inch of material to attach to.

Compounding the problem was inadequate flashing of the connection. Water had intruded over the years, deteriorating not only the rim joist but also the header above the first-floor door under the landing and eight to 10 studs on either side of it.

To repair the damage, dimensional lumber was sistered to the second-floor joists, the rim joist was replaced with treated lumber, blocking was added between joists — giving the lags 3 inches to attach to — and the deteriorated first-floor header and studs were replaced.

A Bloomington, Ill., newspaper, the *Pantagraph*, reported that SAMI, the company that owns the now-repaired rental property, would be removing the siding from other properties built in the same time period in order to check for concealed damage on those buildings.

Laurie Elden is managing editor of Professional Deck Builder *magazine.*

Figure 4. Plan ahead to attach to ICFs. A plastic anchor tunnel screws into a hole drilled in the ICF. The tunnel holds an anchor bolt square to the wall, and the concrete is poured around it. Tunnels are installed in a staggered line to minimize forces that might split the ledger.

Flashing With Traditional Stucco

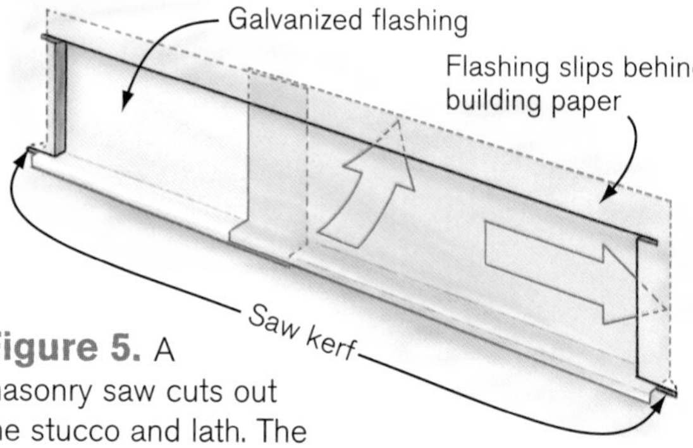

Galvanized flashing

Flashing slips behind building paper

Saw kerf

Figure 5. A masonry saw cuts out the stucco and lath. The bottom cut extends about 3 inches to the sides so that flashing can be extended beyond the ledger.

There is a potential problem with attaching a ledger to concrete, which Woeste says should trigger a building department to require an engineer's design: "Although the strength of some expansion anchor bolts is rated, the strength of the concrete into which they're placed is probably not known in practice."

When attaching a ledger to hollow masonry block, use adhesive anchors, such as the Epcon A7 from ITW Red Head (www.itw-redhead.com) or the Hilti HIT-HY 20 system (www.us.hilti.com). The threaded rod used with the anchors must be at least 1/2 inch in diameter and must penetrate the block by at least 3 1/2 inches.

The anchors used for this application are pouches made from plastic or stainless steel screen. They're filled with a special adhesive, inserted into a hole drilled (without using the impact feature of a hammer drill) in the block, and held in place with a tab. The threaded rod is inserted in the adhesive, which is allowed to set up according to the manufacturer's instructions before the ledger is installed. Be aware that these adhesive anchors are costly — over $40 per hole.

While there's no flashing called for when joining a ledger to masonry, it's recommended that the top of the ledger be caulked to the wall to keep out water. Buy a high-quality, premium caulk. It's all that's keeping water off the fasteners holding the deck up, and this is the only chance anyone will ever have to seal this joint.

Finally, when you're going to attach the joist hangers to a ledger installed on masonry, remember to order the 1 1/2-inch hanger nails.

Insulating concrete forms? Probably.

Forethought pays off when dealing with ICFs. To attach a ledger to an ICF wall, the IRC calls for direct concrete-to-wood contact, which is usually accomplished with "anchor tunnels." These plastic inserts thread into 6-inch-diameter holes drilled in the foam forms (**Figure 4**). Each tunnel holds an anchor bolt in its center, keeping it square to the wall as the con-

crete fills the tunnel during the pouring of the wall. Anchor tunnels are installed at a code-prescribed spacing, which varies with the floor loading and span, and they're staggered above and below the centerline of the ledger so as not to create a line that's likely to split the ledger.

But what do you do when the deck is an afterthought? Jim Eggert, a design-build contractor in Branford, Conn., specializes in ICF construction. He has supported ledgers on 5/8-inch or 3/4-inch stainless steel threaded rod that's epoxied into holes drilled in the ICFs. These thicker rods can offer a bending moment that is sufficient to bridge the thickness of the foam in an ICF wall, according to Eggert. Most jurisdictions would require an engineer's stamp of approval on such an assembly, however.

Traditional stucco? Sure, but flashing can be tough.

In theory, attaching a ledger to a traditional stucco wall is pretty straightforward. But while it might be tempting to simply bolt the ledger through the stucco, such an attachment won't meet the requirements in the 2007 IRC Supplement (see "New Rules for Deck Ledgers and Lateral Attachment," page 41). The ledger must be bolted to the framing because the stucco isn't structural and you'd be imposing shear loads on the bolts that aren't accounted for in the code tables.

To attach the ledger, you have to cut the stucco back to the framing with a masonry saw, which should be set deep enough to sever any wire lath underlying the stucco. This is easy enough to do if the stucco contractor achieved a uniform thickness. The next trick is to slip a piece of flashing (galvanized steel would be the best choice, to be compatible with the steel wire lath) about 3 inches up under the building paper that should underlie the stucco. If you're very lucky, there won't be any nails holding the lath in place for those 3 inches.

Most likely you will need to spend some time cutting nails with a hacksaw blade or with a long metal cutting blade in a recip saw. I would recommend double-flashing such a ledger, as well as extending the bottom cut in the stucco an additional 3 inches to allow for flashing to extend beyond the edge of the ledger (**Figure 5**).

Engineered floors? Maybe.

By engineered floors, I'm referring to either I-joists and open-web joists. The considerations are different for the two.

Whether or not a deck can be attached to an I-joist floor depends on the material used for the rim board. If it's an I-joist or plywood, it's best to forget the ledger and go with a freestanding deck — unless you can find an engineer to design and sign off on a suitable ledger detail. But if the rim is 1$\frac{1}{8}$-inch LSL or 1$\frac{1}{4}$-inch LVL, and the manufacturer lists that as appropriate for attaching a deck, then installation is pretty straightforward (see "Attaching Ledgers to Engineered Rim Joists," next page). On an existing house, it's important to field-verify the rim-board material before bidding the job.

Watch out, too, when you turn the corner. It's pretty common for the rim board running perpendicular to the joists to be LVL or LSL, while the end joist that parallels the other joists is just another I-joist. If that's the case, your engineer would need to detail the ledger attachment to that side of the house — or that portion of the deck would have to be freestanding.

Where attaching to engineered lumber is allowed, you can find recommended bolt spacings in Table 5 of the 2008 *Prescriptive Residential Wood Deck Construction Guide*, published by the American Forest & Paper Association. (The table can be found as Table 3 on page 34 of this book.)

Open-web floor trusses are another question. Codes in some areas outright forbid attaching a ledger to open-web floor trusses. Such floor systems are engineered, and adding a load outside of the design parameters can have unexpected consequences. While many truss manufacturers allow ledgers to be bolted to floor truss systems under certain conditions, you must check with them first and check with the building department before proceeding.

Log walls? Yes, with consideration.

If you've ever worked on a log home, you know that it brings some interesting challenges to the table. The walls aren't flat, for one, and you can count on them shrinking in height by as much as a foot, if green logs were used. Even so veteran deck builder Kim Katwijk, in Olympia, Wash., says, "Logs are pretty easy."

Katwijk explains that how you attach a ledger depends on the size and design of the logs: "West Coast logs tend to be big, say 18 inches in diameter, and there's a large trough between them." When the ledger needs to go in this space, Katwijk bridges the gap to create a reasonably flat surface with a horizontal 2x6 (**Figure 6**) or by custom-tapering a 4x6 for very long logs, which can vary in width. The ledger is then attached to the face of this horizontal shim.

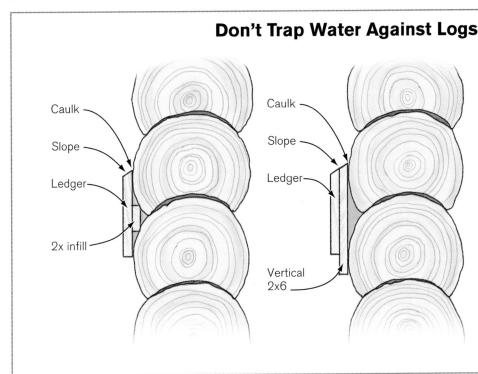

Don't Trap Water Against Logs

Caulk

Slope

Ledger

2x infill

Caulk

Slope

Ledger

Vertical 2x6

Figure 6. Logs aren't flat and can't be effectively flashed. Bridging the space between the logs with either a horizontal 2-by member or vertical 2x6 standoffs makes a flat surface. Engineering might be required, as these attachments aren't described in the code.

Attaching Ledgers to Engineered Rim Joists

by Christopher DeBlois

Lag bolts don't get the same purchase in a 1¼-inch-thick engineered LSL (laminated strand lumber) rim joist as they do in 1½-inch-thick framing lumber. If a lag bolt is properly installed, with its tip well through the rim joist and only the threads engaged in the band, its capacity relative to pull-out forces depends on the thickness of the band and the density of the wood. Because LSL rim joists are typically built up of the same wood species used for framing material (and thus have the same approximate density), the big variable is the thickness. A 1¼-inch-thick LSL is five-sixths as thick as 1½-inch-thick 2-by stock, and thus has 16 percent less holding capacity. To provide the same total pull-out strength, you'd need to provide six-fifths the number of bolts, an increase of 20 percent.

Although there may be other variables, the end result for shear and pull-out strength to carry the weight of a deck or porch will be similar — 20 percent more bolts in a 16 percent thinner band will provide about the same capacity. (See **Table 3**, page 34, for recommended fastener spacings for engineered lumber rim joists.)

Instead of using more lag bolts, an alternate approach (if you can plan ahead) would be to use 1¾-inch LVL material for bands or rim joists wherever you will be bolting a deck or porch to the house. That's the method I used for my own house, and the small increase in materials cost was well worth it when I added the deck a few years later.

To me, a bigger concern than pull-out strength is the strength of the connection between the band and the joists and subfloor when an LSL rim joist is used with wood I-joist floor framing. Because I-joist webs are so thin, the connection between each joist to the LSL band is weak; therefore, you must rely on the connection of the subfloor to the top of the band to keep from pulling the rim joist off the house. But since this band is thinner than 2-by material, it's a little bit easier for screws or nails from the subfloor to miss the band entirely, or to catch very little solid material. I've seen a deck literally collapse away from a house, taking the LSL rim joist with it. And if the rim joist is at the end of a cantilever or overhang with no wall below, the potential for this type of failure increases dramatically.

To ensure that the rim joist itself is well secured to the floor framing (at least where joists bear on the outside wall), I recommend reinforcing the connection from the joists to the band. In new construction, this can be done by adding plywood web stiffeners on both sides of each joist at their outer end so that they finish flush with the I-joist chords, and by nailing from one side through the OSB web into the stiffener on the opposite face (clinching over any nails that poke all the way through). Then install joist hangers upside-down over the top of the end of each joist before you set the subfloor, nailing the hanger off to both the I-joist and the rim joist to complete the connection (illustration, below).

For existing framing, install light-gauge framing angles (such as Simpson's L70s) to connect the web of each I-joist to the rim joist.

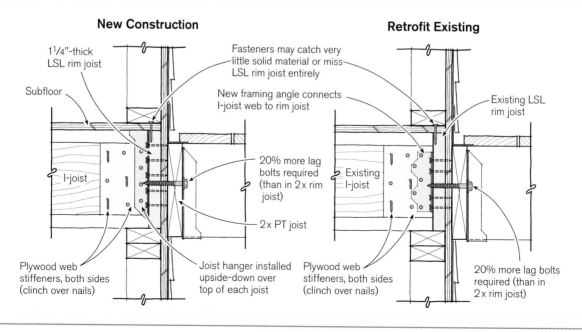

New Construction

1¼"-thick LSL rim joist

Subfloor

Fasteners may catch very little solid material or miss LSL rim joist entirely

New framing angle connects I-joist web to rim joist

I-joist

20% more lag bolts required (than in 2x rim joist)

2x PT joist

Plywood web stiffeners, both sides (clinch over nails)

Joist hanger installed upside-down over top of each joist

Retrofit Existing

Existing LSL rim joist

Existing I-joist

Plywood web stiffeners, both sides (clinch over nails)

20% more lag bolts required (than in 2x rim joist)

It's pretty much impossible to flash a ledger to a log home. You could cut a reglet (a slot meant to receive flashing) into the log above the ledger, but Katwijk believes capillary action is as likely to draw water in as the flashing is to keep it out. Instead, he tapers the top of the ledger, so water will drain away from the logs, and carefully installs the ledger so that no debris- and water-trapping pockets are created. He caulks the top of the ledger to the logs using a tri-polymer caulk, inserting backer rod where needed.

Another challenge is that logs settle as they shrink. New homes built from standing dead timber shrink the least, according to Katwijk, but they can still shrink several inches. The worst situation is a second-floor deck on a new home made from green logs. You can expect the supporting wall to shrink as much as a foot. In both these cases, the posts holding up the outside of a deck attached to a log home have to be made adjustable. Special hardware (**Figure 7**) takes care of such shrinkage, and you'll need to have it engineered. The log home supplier should be able to provide an estimate of the amount of shrinkage to allow for.

One relatively simple approach to hanging a ledger on a log house is to use a metal standoff (**Figure 8**). For example, the Maine Deck Bracket (www. deckbracket.com) is an aluminum standoff that's bolted to the house at intervals determined by the joist span. A double 2-by bolts to the brackets, and acts as a flush beam to support the joists at the house. This leaves a generous drainage space between the house and the deck, reducing the likelihood of rot.

Cantilevered floors? No (but sometimes they can be framed around).

Attaching a ledger to cantilevered floor framing is generally forbidden by code — for good reason. Often, a cantilevered floor is pushed to its maximum load-bearing capacity just by supporting the existing loads. You can't know this without an engineer's evaluation. And even if the joists have some unused bearing capacity, it's likely that the band joist on the cantilever, to which the deck ledger would be attached, is just nailed into the end grain of the joists. That connection isn't adequate to support a deck. The band joist to which you typically attach a deck is supported directly by the house foundation.

It's possible, but a lot of work, to pull the band joist off the cantilever, and slide the deck joists under the cantilevered floor to where they can bear on the house's top wall plate or mudsill. The span design of these joists must take into account not only the typical loads from the deck, but also the load now imposed by the house floor, wall, and roof. And it's practically impossible to prevent water from following the deck joists into the house and causing decay.

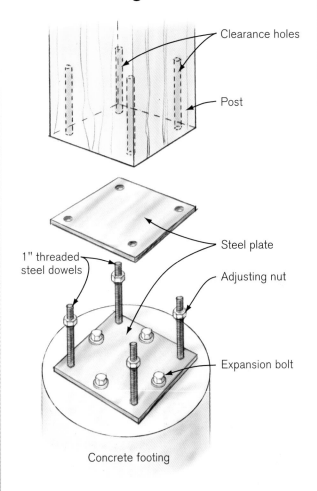

Post Bases for Decks on Log Homes

Clearance holes

Post

Steel plate

1" threaded steel dowels

Adjusting nut

Expansion bolt

Concrete footing

Figure 7. Logs shrink; vertical posts don't. Decks attached to new log homes have to accommodate the expected shrinkage in the logs. Fabricated engineered post bases that allow adjustment as the logs settle solve the problem.

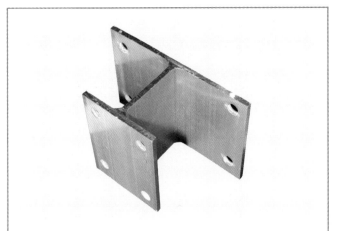

Figure 8. The Maine Deck Bracket is an option that works well on log homes.

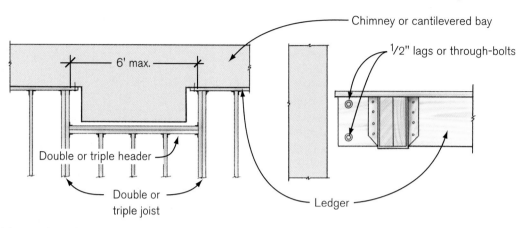

Getting Around a Chimney or a Cantilevered Bay

Chimney or cantilevered bay

1/2" lags or through-bolts

6' max.

Double or triple header

Double or triple joist

Ledger

Figure 9. It's a code violation to attach a ledger to either a chimney or a cantilever. Box framing around it is the solution, up to about 6 feet. A larger box-out may be permissible with engineering.

In fact, the first deck job I ever did was replacing such a deck, as well as a good portion of the house's walls and interior flooring. There were literally bushels of carpenter ants at work on that house because of the moisture damage caused by the deck. I'd avoid this approach at all costs.

If it's just a small cantilevered bay, then framing around it isn't very hard. Doubled or tripled joists on either side of the bay can carry a header, which in turn carries the framing beyond the cantilever (**Figure 9**).

Don't even think about it.

Clearly, there are more ways of attaching a deck ledger to a wall than are addressed even in the new ledger attachment section of the 2007 IRC Supplement. Nonetheless, there are situations where attaching a ledger just isn't appropriate.

For example, attaching a deck ledger to masonry veneer — where the brick or stone is applied over a framed wall — is a code violation nearly everywhere. Masonry veneer is not designed to transfer the loads imposed by a deck; the deck pulling away from the house could also pull the masonry veneer away. In some cases, however, you may be able to bolt through the brick veneer into the underlying house framing (see "Bolting a Ledger Through Brick Veneer").

Structural insulated panels (SIPs) also present prob-

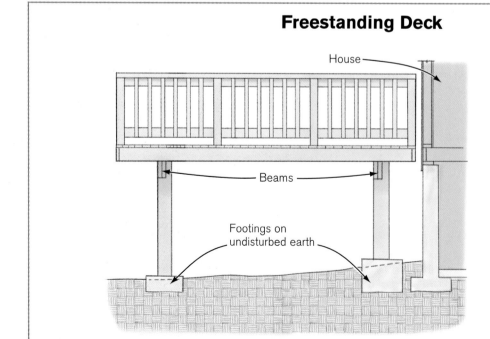

Freestanding Deck

House

Beams

Footings on undisturbed earth

Figure 10. Adding a beam near the house avoids the need for a ledger attachment. The biggest issue is finding undisturbed earth to support the footings close to the house.

lems for deck-ledger attachment. SIPs are a sandwich of OSB and rigid foam. Typically, there will be a 2x6 member at each panel edge, and there may or may not be more 2x6 studs running up the center portion of the panel. Although SIPs can be used for stand-alone structures, they are also often used to sheathe and insulate timber-framed homes.

While the 2x6s in the SIPS might seem to provide a good anchor for lag bolts, the foam and OSB don't. Without engineering, the IRC has no provision for attaching to SIPs. If the SIP wall rests on a conventional floor system, however, you can attach to that floor as you normally would.

EIFS, or synthetic stucco systems, are questionable for supporting a deck. Although the new drainable systems are a dramatic improvement over the older systems — which engendered a flurry of class-action lawsuits in the 1990s — flashing and sealing EIFS is a job for a specialist.

Unless the deck ledger is in place when the stucco is applied, it's best to avoid attaching a ledger to a building clad in synthetic stucco. Penetrations to the stucco cladding are notorious for allowing leaks, which the synthetic stucco doesn't allow to dry out. The result will be rot and mold.

So, what's a deck builder to do?

Few of us want to turn down a job. Luckily, it's rarely necessary to do so. On most houses where attaching a ledger is a problem, there's probably a solution. "Almost all jurisdictions accept the sealed design of a registered professional engineer in situations that aren't described in the IRC," says Woeste. "An engineered solution is a professional approach for the contractor, and most important, it protects the client from an accident." Additionally, from a contractor's

---

Bolting a Ledger Through Brick Veneer

by Christopher DeBlois

I generally recommend against bolting a deck ledger board through brick veneer whenever there is a design alternative. I prefer to provide independent support adjacent to the house, usually with posts and beams. In many cases, however, that is impractical or undesirable so the deck gets bolted to the house.

The brick veneer on a house typically supports its own weight and nothing else. The International Residential Code states, "Masonry veneer shall not support any vertical loads other than the dead load of the veneer above." When the deck is supported independently adjacent to the house, standard practice is to bolt through the brick and the house's band joist to provide lateral stability for the deck. That way the brick veneer is not forced to carry the weight of the deck, so there is no violation of the building code.

Although I'm against bolting the deck ledger through the brick veneer, I recognize that it's not an uncommon detail and that building officials often approve it. With that in mind, here are some thoughts if you choose such an approach:

I have heard people justify the direct bolting of a deck ledger through the brick veneer and into the house framing by arguing that because the bolts extend to the band joist, the band will carry the deck weight. I disagree. With a separation of several inches between the back of the deck ledger and the face of the house framing, the bolts will bend or rotate before the weight is carried by the house framing. As soon as that starts to happen, the bolts will bear on the brick, and the veneer will be carrying the load. The good news is that in most cases the brick has substantial extra capacity. In fact, the capacity of the bolt-to-brick component of this connection will generally exceed the capacity of the bolt to the deck ledger itself. As a result, the required size and spacing of bolts are no different than for typical wood-to-wood connections. You must bolt all the way through the house band joist to properly transfer forces pulling the deck away from the house into the framing instead of into the brick. Also, no lag bolts are allowed. And pay careful attention to sealing bolt holes and flashing against the house.

Regardless of what local building officials allow, in some situations it is a bad idea to require brick veneer to support the weight of a deck. Do not bolt the deck ledger through the brick veneer if you suspect that there are no brick ties (all too common on older houses), if the condition of the brick and mortar is questionable, or if the brick ledge or footing supporting the brick veneer is not sound and stable.

Finally, a number of circumstances may warrant contacting a structural engineer for guidance. If there are large openings in the brick (for a series of full-height windows, for example), stresses in the brick at the sides of these openings may be too high to permit support of deck loads. Similarly, if you need to support the end of a beam instead of just a continuous, uniformly loaded band, special support will be necessary.

Christopher DeBlois, PE, is an engineer with Palmer Engineering in Tucker, Ga.

Lateral Bracing for Freestanding Decks

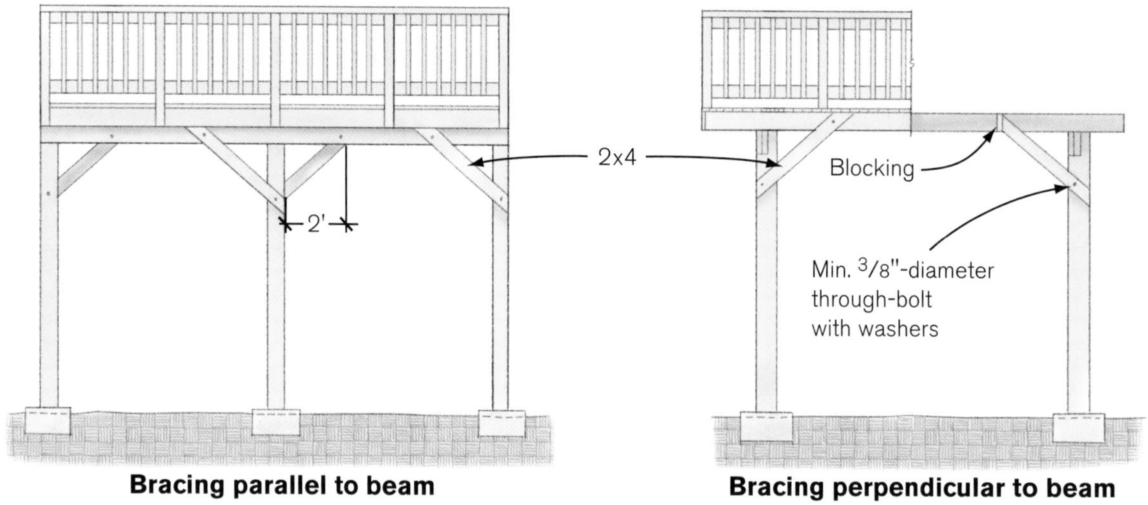

Bracing parallel to beam

2' ⊢

2x4

Bracing perpendicular to beam

Blocking

Min. 3/8"-diameter through-bolt with washers

Figure 11. Freestanding decks require lateral bracing. Decks attached to the house with a ledger gain much of their lateral stability from that attachment. Diagonal bracing must provide this stability on a freestanding deck.

point of view, an engineered design is a little like buying an insurance policy. While you're still liable for the construction of the deck, the engineer becomes responsible for problems with the overall design.

And, of course, there's a simple solution to problematic ledger-attachment situations: Don't use a ledger. Instead, build a freestanding deck (see **Figure 10**, page 102, and, "Supporting a Freestanding Deck," page 95), which uses a carrying beam, posts, and footings in place of the ledger. It's a good practice to set this beam 2 or 3 feet away from the house so the deck piers steer clear of the main foundation and footing drains (see "New Piers Near an Existing Foundation," page 83). Then cantilever the deck the remaining distance.

Both Woeste and Katwijk advocate this approach, and Rhode Island contractor Mike Guertin points out: "One of the main advantages to building self-supporting decks is the little-used IRC provision that exempts them from frost-depth footings."

In the 2006 IRC, R403.1.4.1 exception 3 states: *Decks not supported by a dwelling need not be provided with footings that extend below the frost line.* So the only provision for footings that applies to freestanding decks is in R403.1: *Footings shall be supported on undisturbed natural soils or engineered fill.*

Finding undisturbed soil to support deck footings in the backfilled area close to a new house can be

challenging. However, many building departments consider backfilled soil to be undisturbed after five years. Also, the worst thing likely to happen is that the deck might settle, an annoying but slowly occurring problem. Woeste notes, "To my knowledge, no one ever died from deck settlement." The same cannot be said of improperly fastened attached decks.

When properly constructed and attached, however, a ledger does help with lateral stability in addition to carrying part of the deck's load. When building a freestanding deck, that lack of stability must be taken into account. Katwijk will often tie a freestanding deck to the house for this purpose, but Woeste cautions against doing so in the case of masonry veneer, explaining, "Using masonry veneer to resist any load is a building code violation."

A less controversial option is to diagonally brace the support posts (**Figure 11**). Most deck builders brace the outer beam on taller decks anyway, so the method is familiar. The main differences are that you've got two beams to brace on a freestanding deck, and that bracing must be run both parallel and perpendicular to the beams. On a deck that attaches to the house with a ledger, the ledger provides the lateral stability perpendicular to the beam.

Andy Engel is the editor of Professional Deck Builder.

Deck Ledgers Q&A

Attaching Ledgers to I-Joist Cantilevers

Q. *Is there any safe way to attach a deck ledger to an engineered rim joist where the I-joists are cantilevered?*

A. *Frank Woeste, PE, professor emeritus at Virginia Tech in Blacksburg, responds:* While most I-joist manufacturers publish details for attaching a deck to engineered rim boards, to my knowledge, no I-joist manufacturer has a detail for connecting a deck to an I-joist cantilever. Although such a connection is possible, it requires the work of a registered design professional with knowledge of I-joist design and residential deck design (such as flashing, fastener and flashing corrosion issues, etc.). All design loads from the entire structure and from the deck that load the cantilever must be accounted for in the design of the I-joists, bearing capacity of the I-joist at the bearing wall, and connections between the deck and floor framing system.

In the photo (below) of a single-family residence under construction, what you see from lower left to top right is a brick veneer wall, the bottom flange of an I-joist with short 2x blocks above the flange, an engineered wood product (EWP) used as a rim joist and cantilever closure (yellow), and a lag screw connecting the PT deck ledger to a 2x block that has been split by the lag screw. This block ensures that under substantial load, it will tear off the bottom flange of the I-joist and cause the remaining I-joist section to fail.

Attaching a deck to a cantilevered I-joist floor requires an engineered solution. This ledger connection is woefully inadequate and could fail under substantial load.

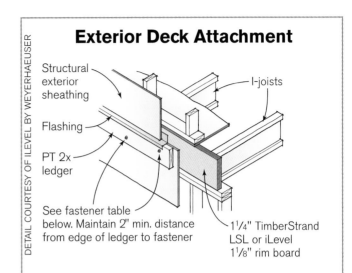

Exterior Deck Attachment

DETAIL COURTESY OF ILEVEL BY WEYERHAEUSER

Structural exterior sheathing

Flashing

PT 2x ledger

See fastener table below. Maintain 2" min. distance from edge of ledger to fastener

I-joists

1¼" TimberStrand LSL or iLevel 1⅛" rim board

Most I-joist manufacturers publish details for attaching a deck ledger to their floor systems. But the solutions are specific to the manufacturer's products and do not apply to cantilevers.

Fasteners	Allowable Load[1] (lbs)	
	1¼" TimberStrand® LSL Rim Board	iLevel® 1⅛" Rim Board
⅜" lag bolt	400	N.A.
½" lag bolt	475	400

(1) Allowable load determined in accordance with AC 124.
• Corrosion-resistant fasteners required for wet-service applications.

The yellow EWP rim joist in the picture does not bear directly on a sill plate or double top plate of the wall and therefore deck loads that that are intended to be carried by it are strictly limited to the capacity of the fasteners connecting the EWP rim joist to the ends of the I-joists. Blocking as shown and end grain nailing into an I-joist are woefully inadequate methods to transfer deck design loads.

Where engineered "rim board products" as tested and defined by AC124 (www.icc-es.org/criteria/pdf_files/ac124.pdf) project beyond the sill or wall top plate by any amount, it is a cantilever condition and thus the deck tributary load at the house plus the design load carried in the wall above must be transferred to the house foundation wall by passing through the I-joist. I-joist companies publish fastener schedules and details for attaching deck ledgers to a code-approved "rim board" bearing solidly on a sill or double-top plate (illustration, above). The use of a code-approved rim board coupled with a ledger fastener schedule from the rim-board manufacturer form the basis for your local building code official to approve the connection detail.

However, what contractors can miss in the detail is that the schedule is only valid for code-approved rim boards that are continuously supported and bear directly on a sill plate. Even if the I-joists are not cantilevered, it is very important for deck safety for contractors to:

A. use a code-approved rim board and a ledger fastener schedule published by the rim-board manufacturer

B. have approved deck plans showing the selected rim board, flashing, and a ledger fastener schedule, and

C. maintain evidence of the approved plans and final inspection by the local building department.

Of course, the same problem occurs when attaching decks to dimension lumber cantilevers, which is why the *Prescriptive Residential Wood Deck Construction Guide* (see page 31) does not permit attachment of decks to dimension lumber cantilevers. As with code-approved rim board, an engineered solution would be required for a safe deck connection.

Watch Out for Vents When Installing a Ledger

Q. *Should I be concerned about covering a foundation vent with a deck ledger?*

A. *Glenn Mathewson, a building inspector in Westminster, Colo., responds:* The short answer is yes. It's wise to assume that every element of a structure has a purpose and therefore design your work so as not to inhibit that purpose.

Vents, for instance, may be vital to controlling moisture in a crawlspace. Even if they are sealed shut from years of painting and poor maintenance, they shouldn't be covered by new construction unless alternative moisture-control methods are used.

Historically, building codes have required that crawlspaces be vented to the exterior to prevent water vapor from the soil below from building up and fostering rot or mold. If you've ever tarped your tools or lumber for the night, you may have found the tarp's underside dripping with water in the morning — that moisture was condensation, which came from water vapor that evaporated out of the earth. You don't want a building to act like that tarp, so vents are installed to move outside air through the space to remove the moisture-laden air.

How effective crawlspace vents are depends on the climate. What works in Seattle (cold and humid) may not work as well in Denver (cold and arid) or in Houston (hot and humid), so the 2006 International

Residential Code (iccsafe.org) provides for a crawlspace moisture-control method that doesn't require outside ventilation (2006 IRC R408.3). Though this provision may eliminate the need for vents in new construction, it doesn't help much in older crawlspaces — unless the client is willing to pay for remediation.

Foundation vents are not meant to work singly; there must be multiple vents on opposite sides of the crawlspace for air to cycle through the area. The 2006 IRC specifies the minimum size of openings based on the total area of the crawlspace and requires an opening within 3 feet of each corner to facilitate the movement of the air (2006 IRCC R408.1). Blocking just one vent can reduce air flow and trap moisture in the crawlspace, which could cause fingers to point your way if there were ever a mold, mildew, or moisture issue.

Blocking vents could also asphyxiate the building occupants. Many fuel-burning appliances get their combustion air [2006 IRC M1703.5, Figure M1703.2(4)] from vented crawlspaces (illustration, below).

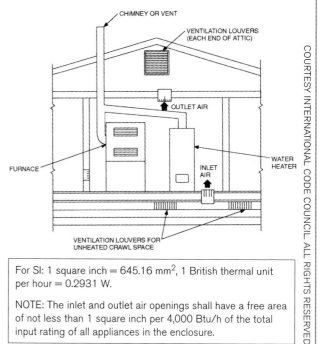

Figure M1703.2(4)
Appliances Located in Confined Spaces—
Inlet Air Taken From Ventilated Crawl Space and Outlet Air to Ventilated Attic

For SI: 1 square inch = 645.16 mm², 1 British thermal unit per hour = 0.2931 W.

NOTE: The inlet and outlet air openings shall have a free area of not less than 1 square inch per 4,000 Btu/h of the total input rating of all appliances in the enclosure.

Vents do more than flush moisture from crawlspaces: Sometimes they provide makeup air needed for furnaces and water heaters, as shown in this illustration from the 2006 International Residential Code. Closing them off could starve these appliances — and your clients — of air.

An outdoor source for combustion air performs a number of important functions: It balances the pressure differential created by removing the exhaust gas from the building; provides oxygen for combustion without taking it from the building occupants; provides air to start and maintain a natural draft in gravity flues; ventilates to cool the equipment; and acts as a backup exhaust vent.

Combustion air is not something you want to inhibit. The alternative to vents is to have the hvac system professionally evaluated to ensure there's sufficient combustion air.

If you know that combustion air is not a concern, you could modify the crawlspace to make it compliant with the new provisions for unvented crawlspaces. Details of this modification are outside the scope of this answer and likely would not be cost-effective or practical if your only goal is to install a deck ledger.

Another option is relocating the vents — and this may be a good idea anyway. Air movement may be limited to even wide-open vents when they are located under a deck at grade level or under decks skirted to grade at the perimeter. But if you move the vents, you need to make sure there is still one opening within 3 feet of each crawlspace corner, and that the total area of openings is no less than previously existed.

It's good practice to inspect the inside of the rim for any plumbing or wiring that you don't want to dissect when cutting in the vent. As was stated earlier, assume everything has a purpose. For example, that seemingly misplaced piece of blocking against the inside of the rim could be transferring an untold load from an unknown post in the wall down to the foundation — not something you want to cut out for a vent opening.

Code-Approved Flashing

Q. *I've been told that I have to use metal flashing at deck ledgers, but recently at DeckExpo, I noticed many other flashing materials being displayed. What gives? Can I use products other than metal?*

A. *Glenn Mathewson responds:* Requirements for deck ledger flashing can be found in the 2006 International Residential Code (IRC), section R703.8 Flashing:

"Approved corrosion-resistant flashing shall be applied shingle-fashion in such a manner to prevent entry of water into the wall cavity or penetration of water to the building structural framing components. The flashing shall extend to the surface of the exterior wall finish. Approved corrosion-resistant flashings shall be installed at all of the following locations ..."

This section then lists seven locations where flashing would be required — one of them being deck ledgers. The only descriptive terms provided for the flashing material are "approved" and "corrosion-resistant"; there lies the answer to your question.

So, can you use products other than metal? Yes ... and no. There is no single answer. When the IRC uses the term "approved," it means "acceptable to the building official" — that is, the building official of wherever you happen to be working. In the Denver metro area, for example, there are over 30 jurisdictions, and they don't all approve the same thing.

The approval of the building official should be based on the "intent" and "purpose" of the code. The remaining sentences in R703.8 explain the purpose of flashing and provide limited guidance for its installation. It must be installed in "shingle fashion," which basically means layers placed over layers below in such a way that gravity and physics will naturally shed the water to the surface of the exterior wall finish. The use of caulk or sealants would not be considered "shingle fashion." Other than this, the flashing must "prevent the entry of water into the building cavity."

When it is left up to the local jurisdiction, aluminum, galvanized steel, copper, vinyl, or self-adhering polymer-modified bitumen sheets (ice and water membrane) may be either allowed or disallowed. Even products with an International Code Council Evaluation Service Report don't have to be accepted by the building official. This refusal isn't common, but it does occur.

Flashing material must also be "corrosion-resistant," a term meant to define the flashing. However, the material the flashing is placed against also must be considered. Aluminum and galvanized steel are both considered "corrosion-resistant," but not when placed in contact with copper-treated lumber (ACQ, copper azole, perhaps MCQ). Then the only metal flashing that's corrosion resistant is copper, an expensive choice; materials such as vinyl may provide greater service and affordability than metal flashing.

Bottom line: Don't guess — ask the local inspector.

Chapter 5:
Deck Framing

Treated Wood: New Preservatives, New Fasteners

by Ted Cushman

For more than half a century, pressure-treated wood was a simple material to understand and purchase. Almost all the treated wood used in residential work was treated with chromated copper arsenate, or CCA. The rest was mostly ammoniacal copper zinc arsenate, or ACZA. Different suppliers used different brand names, but all the wood, CCA or ACZA, looked, handled, and performed just about the same. And the performance was good: While treated lumber might check, splinter, or warp from the effects of weathering, it generally would not rot or get eaten by termites. This has been confirmed by decades of field experience as well as testing by manufacturers and the USDA Forest Products Laboratory (**Figure 1**).

In both ACZA and CCA, the main preservative is copper — which, in high enough concentrations, will suppress or kill most kinds of fungi and insects, but doesn't hurt people or pets. The arsenic in both formulas serves as a "co-biocide" — controlling a few copper-tolerant fungi that would otherwise attack the wood, and putting the final nail in the coffin of termites and other wood-eating bugs. The chromium in CCA and the zinc in ACZA are mostly there as binders — they help lock the copper and arsenic into the wood by "fixation," forming chemical bonds between the biocides and the wood fibers. The big difference between ACZA and CCA is the carrier —

The latest generation of treated wood promises good protection with less corrosion, but the jury is out on long-term performance. With current formulas, some builders use an isolation membrane to protect metal hardware.

CCA uses mostly water, whereas ACZA includes an ammonia solution to help it better penetrate some hard-to-treat western softwoods such as Douglas fir.

Up through the 1990s, treated wood was treated wood. But a few years ago, all of that changed. For years, chemical companies that supply lumber

Figure 1. Continuous in-ground stake testing of traditional CCA lumber goes back 70 years. Newer formulas are holding up under similar testing, but some have only a four- to ten-year track record so far.

Table 1.
Treated Wood: What's on the Menu?

Compared to the good old days of the 1980s and 1990s, when treated wood was treated wood, today's marketplace offers a wide, and sometimes confusing, array of choices. Here's a short list of the products generally available today.

Arsenic-Containing Formulas
Contractors can still get old-style arsenic-based treated wood for certain uses. Here's what you might see:

Acronym	Generic Name	Trade name	Manufacturer	Website
CCA	chromated copper arsenate	Wolmanized® Heavy Duty™	Arch Wood Protection	WolmanizedWoodHD.com
		SupaTimber®	Viance	TreatedWood.com
		CCA	Osmose, Inc.	OsmoseWood.com
		CCA	Hoover Treated Wood	FRTW.com
ACZA	ammoniacal copper zinc arsenate	Chemonite®	Arch Wood Protection	Chemonite.com

Dissolved Copper-Based Formulas
These first-generation CCA replacements have dissolved copper as their primary preservative ingredient.

Acronym	Generic Name	Trade name	Manufacturer	Website
ACQ-A or ACQ-B	ammoniacal copper quaternary	NatureWood®	Osmose, Inc	OsmoseWood.com
		Preserve®	Viance	TreatedWood.com
ACQ-C or ACQ-D	alkaline copper quaternary	NatureWood®	Osmose, Inc	OsmoseWood.com
		Preserve®	Viance	TreatedWood.com
		DURA-GUARD®	Hoover Treated Wood	FRTW.com
CA-B or CA-C	copper azole	Wolmanized® Residential Outdoor®	Arch Treatment Technologies	WolmanizedWood.com

Copper Suspension-Based Formulas
Called "micronized" by one vendor and "dispersed" by another, these are the newer formulas based on finely ground copper particles suspended in water, instead of (or in combination with) dissolved copper.

Acronym	Generic Name	Trade name	Manufacturer	Website
μCA-C	dispersed copper azole	Wolmanized Residential Outdoor	Arch Treatment Technologies	WolmanizedWood.com
MCA	micronized copper azole	SustainWood®	PhibroWood	PhibroWood.com
		LifeWood	Osmose, Inc	OsmoseWood.com
MCQ	micronized copper quaternary	MicroPro	Osmose, Inc.	OsmoseWood.com

Carbon-Based Formulas
These systems contain no copper or other metals, but rely on combinations of insecticides and fungicides already approved for use in agriculture. So far, no carbon-based systems are yet listed for use in ground contact.

Acronym	Generic Name	Trade name	Manufacturer	Website
EL2	dcoi & imidacloprid	Ecolife™	Viance	TreatedWood.com
PTI	propiconazole-tebuconazole-imidacloprid	Wolmanized® L³	Arch Treatment Technologies	WolmanizedWoodL3.com

treatments had faced negative publicity about their products, particularly regarding the potential exposure of children to arsenic from backyard structures and playground equipment. While no public health threat from pressure-treated wood has ever been clearly established, arsenic is listed as a known human carcinogen by the EPA and by the International Agency for Research on Cancer (IARC) — and the resulting bad press and threat of lawsuits was hard for wood treaters to overcome. In 2003, the leading chemical suppliers for the wood treating industry decided to compromise, and entered into a voluntary agreement with the U.S. Environmental Protection Agency: in 2004 they would stop selling preservatives containing arsenic and chromium for treating residential lumber products, and switch to new formulas.

This new policy set the stage for the ongoing parade of new treated wood products and formulas (**Table 1**). First up was ACQ — ammonium copper quaternary or (depending on the carrier used) alkaline copper quaternary. This formula keeps the relatively benign copper, and replaced the arsenic and chromium "co-biocides" with a quaternary compound, or "quat." Compared with arsenic, quat is pretty mild stuff: it's basically a sanitizing soap based on ammonia. Quats are a universal ingredient in shampoo, for example. And the typical quat used in ACQ, known as "DDAC," for didecyl dimethyl ammonium chloride, is also an active ingredient in household products like Mr. Clean sanitary wipes and Febreze antimicrobial fabric freshener.

The other early entry was copper azole, or CA — which, like ACQ, has copper as the primary fungicide and insecticide, but uses carbon-based "azole" compounds called tebuconazole and propiconazole to do the job of arsenic. The azoles are pesticides, widely used in agriculture to control insects and fungi. Unlike arsenic, azoles are approved by the EPA for use on food crops. Seed treating is a common use for azoles; in California, the biggest users of tebuconazole are grape growers who spray it on their plants.

Beyond Copper: The Next Generation

Copper is a highly effective wood preservative, without the severe toxicity issues of arsenic and chromium. But copper may not be the last word in wood preservation. It's not completely free from environmental issues – in fact, three countries in Europe have already outlawed copper-based wood preservatives because of issues relating to copper's toxic effect on some aquatic life.

So U.S. companies are already looking beyond micronized copper formulas, and working on new formulas that contain no copper, or any other metal either. On the one hand there are the carbon-based or "organic" formulas, made up of combinations of commercially available fungicides and insecticides originally developed for agriculture, and already approved by the EPA for use by farmers. Then there are the borate-based formulas, mostly designed for use in dry indoor locations, but also including one system approved for outdoor use above ground.

Carbon-based formulas. When they first hit the market, the carbon-based wood preservatives were called "organics." Fair enough – complex carbon polymers are known in chemistry as "organic molecules," and the science of making them is called "organic chemistry." But confusion arose about the other, completely opposite, meaning of "organic" in the marketplace – the one that refers to natural farming without the sort of chemical pesticides used in these formulations. So the EPA told wood treaters to find another term – and the marketers came

Figure A. *"Carbon-based" treated wood such as Viance's Ecolife and Arch's L³ (shown above) use agricultural pesticides containing no metals. The copper-free wood is more suitable for painting and staining, and some consumers prefer the product's more natural wood appearance, without the green tinge of copper oxide.*

up with the less controversial "carbon-based."

So far, there are two carbon-based brands on the market: Ecolife, from Viance (www.treatedwood.com), and Wolmanized L³, from Arch Treatment Technologies (www.wolmanizedwoodL3.com). Ecolife uses the insecticide imidacloprid, paired with the fungicide DCOI, commonly called isothiazolone. L³, pronounced "L-cubed," also contains imidacloprid, but with the same "triazole" fungicides used in Arch's copper azole product: tebuconazole and

No question about it: ACQ and CA have fewer scary ingredients than CCA. But in use, they turned out to have a few significant drawbacks. The new treated boards and timbers had significantly higher copper content than the older CCA-treated wood, and tended to leach a lot of copper. The heavy leaching of copper, along with the surfactant action of the quat components and the "amine" carrier (ammonia or alkaline), has been blamed for leaving greenish stains on painted surfaces — for example, where water runoff from a deck flows onto trim or siding.

In addition, says wood scientist and consultant Mike Freeman (www.wooddoc.org), the amine carrier used to dissolve the copper in ACQ and copper azole turned out to be an excellent mold food. "The plants that converted over in 2002 and 2003 had a huge mold crisis," says Freeman. "Millions of dollars worth of wood almost had to be destroyed, or at least rewashed or retreated with moldicide. The levels of moldicide that were used with CCA just did not work well on the amine-based formulations."

The most significant problem, however, was the effect of ACQ and CCA on metal. The high levels of free copper that remain in the wood had a strong tendency to corrode fasteners, hardware, and flashing.

Corrosion Concerns

No sooner did ACQ hit the market in 2004 than complaints started to pour in. According to Mike Freeman, building code officials got 6,000 complaints about fastener or hardware corrosion in the first year after CCA was withdrawn. Some of those complaints may just reflect closer scrutiny, remarks Quentin Smith, Oregon Department of Transportation engineer and chair of an ASTM committee on fastener corrosion standards: "It's possible that people are just paying more attention then they used to, and that it's not actually any worse than [CCA] was."

But objectively, there's no disputing that ACQ and CA are more destructive of metal than CCA is. In comprehensive testing using methods standardized by the American Wood Preservers Association,

propiconazole (**Figure A**). So far, neither carbon-based brand is listed for ground-contact applications, although at least one vendor is reportedly working on getting that listing.

Carbon-based preservatives are generally much less corrosive than copper-based products. However, the carrier used to dissolve the chemicals might still be corrosive, cautions scientist and industry consultant Mike Freeman. Another big advantage to the carbon-based products is appearance. They start out the color of natural wood, and they're easy to paint or stain. But that hasn't proved as popular as the vendors had hoped. "I thought people would jump at the chance to have a carbon-based preservative in their wood, and sales have been okay; but it hasn't been as great as I expected," says Arch executive Huck DeVenzio. "I do think it's the wave of the future," he adds.

Ironically, some customers seem to miss the green tint they associate with traditional treated lumber. "Some customers wanted the wood to have some color so they could tell the difference between treated wood and untreated wood," says Freeman. "They want that green shade. And guess what the treaters are using to tint the wood? Copper." On the other hand, for uses where paintability is key, the neutral color is a plus. "People making molding and trim love it," notes DeVenzio. "People who make outdoor furniture, or storage sheds – they really like the natural look too."

Borate-based formulas. The other new entry into the field is preservatives based on boron, a mineral that effec-

tively controls both insects and fungi, and is widely considered a very benign substance to humans and other mammals. Experts say borate is no more toxic than ordinary table salt to humans; homeowners can buy nearly 100% pure boric acid off hardware store shelves in the form of roach-control products such as Roach Prufe.

All three of the big players in wood treating have borate-based products for aboveground applications protected from the weather: There's SillBor from Arch (www.sillbor.com), AdvancedGuard from Osmose (www.OsmoseWood.com), and TimberSaver from Viance (www.treatedwood.com). But because borates are very water-soluble and readily leach out of wood, none of those products are effective for outdoor use. One season in the rain, and preservative levels would be too low to protect the lumber.

More interesting for deck builders is a product called ES+Wood, from Wood Treatment Products, Inc. (www.ESWoodTreatment.com). This treatment uses Disodium Octaborate Tetrahydrate (DOT), a water-soluble borate compound, plus a penetrating polymer binder that seals the borate into the wood and keeps it from leaching out. ES+Wood is not code approved for ground contact, but it's available for use as deck framing, decking, railings, and trim, as well as playground and recreational equipment. ES+Wood carries a 40-year transferable warranty (limited to materials only) against damage by termites or fungal decay.

New Zealand researcher Gareth Kear and his colleagues found: "ACQ-treated timbers are more corrosive towards mild steel and hot-dipped galvanized steel than any other type of treated timber." ACQ wood corroded mild steel about five times as fast as CCA did, and corroded hot-dipped galvanized steel anywhere from 5 to 19 times as fast as CCA did. Galvanized steel lasted longer than mild steel, but only stainless steel held up without significant damage: "The 316 stainless steel performed very well in terms of corrosion resistance within all of the preservative treatments examined." (Kear's full 281-page report is available as a PDF download from the Building Research Association of New Zealand [Branz] at www.branz.co.nz/cms_show_download.php?id=225.)

In response to the increased corrosion and other problems associated with ACQ and CCA, within just four years of their introduction, these second-generation formulations had been largely replaced by a newer generation of "micronized" or "dispersed" formulas (**Figure 2**) with names like micronized copper azole (MCA), micronized copper quat (MCQ), and dispersed copper azole (μCA-C). As of 2008, says Mike Freeman, MCQ, MCA, and μCA-C accounted for 80 percent of the residential market, with ACQ and CA squeezed down to 20 percent or less.

These new third-generation formulas contain their copper in the form of very finely ground particles, rather than in dissolved form. They don't need the nitrogen-rich amine carrier — and because they are less prone to leaching, they can be treated with less total copper and still maintain adequate long-term concentrations. Suppliers also claim that these formulas are less corrosive to fasteners. Osmose, for example says that its SmartSense treated wood with MicroPro, a micronized copper quaternary formula, "exhibits corrosion rates on metal products similar to CCA pressure-treated wood and untreated wood."

Figure 2. The large incised beams in this photo are ACQ-treated western hem-fir, and have a dark green color. The double 2x ledger board, with a lighter golden hue, is hem-fir treated with a newer micronized-copper.

Peter Laks, a professor in the School of Forest Resources and Environmental Sciences at Michigan Tech, confirms that there is a lot of test data to support this claim. "It also just makes sense from the chemistry," he says. Dissolved-copper systems leave lots of free copper ions in the wood that act to corrode other metals like steel, zinc, or aluminum, he explains. In addition, the amine carrier (ethanolamine) that is used to help dissolve the copper "is inherently quite a corrosive material," he explains.

The micronized approach, says Laks, uses a "very different kind of protection mechanism" that avoids the corrosive effects of ethanolamine. The active ingredient, finely ground particles of copper carbonate, he explains, has a low level of water solubility. "Those particles penetrate through the micro-pore structure of the wood, and then just reside within the wood structure ... so that when the wood gets wet, a tiny little bit of that copper carbonate particle dissolves, and diffuses into the cell wall of the wood and protects it."

Other Approaches

Not sure which way the preserved wood market will evolve, chemical companies are hedging their bets with a variety of innovative approaches to wood treatment. Already, they have introduced formulas that don't use any copper at all (see "Beyond Copper: The Next Generation," page 112). As of 2009, none of the copper-free products had code approvals for use in contact with the ground. But as early as 2010, says Mike Freeman, we'll probably see copper-free treated wood that's code-listed for ground contact.

Despite the array of new products, Freeman expects

Code Requirements for Fasteners

With regard to nails, screws, and bolts, the 2006 International Residential Code (IRC) says, "Fasteners for pressure-preservative and fire-retardant-treated wood shall be of hot-dipped zinc-coated galvanized steel, stainless steel, silicon bronze or copper. The coating weights for zinc-coated fasteners shall be in accordance with ASTM A153. Exceptions: 1. One-half inch (12.7mm) diameter or greater steel bolts.
2. Fasteners other than nails and timber rivets shall be permitted to be of mechanically deposited zinc-coated steel with coating weights in accordance with ASTM B695, Class 55, minimum."

the industry to stabilize, at least for a while. "I foresee it settling down," he says, "when most of the market is probably going to convert over to a few very similar micronized copper azole formulas." As with CCA, he predicts, companies will again compete more on price than on who has the better technology.

Product Labels

New lumber treatments have to run a tough gauntlet in order to be accepted by the code and the marketplace. There are two pathways to gaining code acceptance. One is to get "standardized" by the American Wood Preservers Association (AWPA); the other is to gain an Evaluation Report, or ER, from the International Code Council Evaluation Service (ICC-ES). Either process takes many years and costs hundreds of thousands of dollars.

Once the product has an ICC ER or an AWPA listing, it has to undergo a continual verification process. Inspectors from an accredited agency such as the Southern Pine Inspection Bureau (www.spib.org) make surprise visits to the treating plant to check that treaters are following their standard procedures, and to test randomly selected product samples for the proper concentration (or "retention") of treating chemicals.

The AWPA or ICC listing, plus the continual inspections, qualify the product to carry an identifying plastic end-tag, stapled to the end of the board, with information contractors can use to choose their lumber. In addition to the inspector's logo, the tag lists an AWPA "use category" and an ICC "exposure category" that tell the builder where the material is safe to use (see "Read the Label," next page).

Long-Term Performance

Not everyone is convinced that the new micronized products are an improvement over the older solubulized versions. Their chief critic is ACQ manufacturer Viance, which has charged that MCQ-treated posts buried in the ground suffered extensive decay in testing funded by Viance. Manufacturers of micronized products counter that Viance's studies are biased and not representative of the MCQ products they are selling.

But with formulas changing, can contractors rely on the labeling to ensure that the wood is going to survive as well as the old CCA lumber? Yes — and no, say the experts. Stan Lebow, the USDA Forest Products Laboratory's top expert on treated wood, says, "There's just no way we can have as much confidence in the newer formulations, until they've been in service for many decades [like CCA]. This doesn't mean they're not as effective, it just means there's no substitute for real-time, in-service experience."

What we can do, says Lebow, is look at factors we know are relevant to the lumber's performance — for example, the lab-established potency of the treating chemical against bugs and rot. "All of the new formulations have shown efficacy in these tests, and concentrations used [to treat lumber in the market] are above those thresholds. Unfortunately, it is impractical to make these determinations for all types of wood-attacking organisms, so these tests are typically run against a subset of the most common organisms."

Leaching of preservatives is another factor that's hard to assess, Lebow points out. "All of the newer formulations do have some mechanism of stabilizing the preservative in the wood, although it's a different

PHOTOS: MAC MACDONALD

Figure 3. Especially in hard-to-treat western species, lumber treatments may not penetrate to the center of a large timber (top left), or even to the center of a 2x framing member (bottom left). Experts recommend field-treating all cuts (left) with a copper-based penetrating wood preservative such as Jasco Termin-8 (www.homaxproducts.com) or Wolman's CopperCoat (www.wolman.com).

mechanism than for CCA." As with decay and insect testing, he says, "we are not yet able to confidently apply the results of our laboratory leaching tests to predict leaching in real-world exposures."

Varying exposure conditions in the real world also complicate performance. "We know that the same piece of treated wood will last much longer in Montana than Florida, and much longer above-ground than in ground contact," says Lebow. "But we don't know exactly how much longer." Throw in rain, snow, sun, leaf and plant litter, or salt air, and the long-run performance of a piece of wood is hard to predict.

And keep in mind, says Lebow, that treating chemicals, whether CCA, ACQ, or the newer types, may not penetrate to the heartwood of large timbers, especially in hard-to-treat western species (**Figure 3**, previous page). So when you cut posts or beams in the field, especially in a structurally important role, you should field-apply a preservative to the cut end. Copper naphthenate (with at least a 1 percent concentration of copper) is the most common formula for that, says Lebow.

Corrosion and Hardware

At this point, the International Residential Code (IRC) allows only four fastener materials for use with any copper-based preservative-treated wood: copper, silicon bronze, stainless steel, or hot-dipped galvanized treated according to ASTM Standard A-153.

Read the Label

Like everything else about treated wood, the plastic labels stapled to the end of each board have been changing. Until recently, the end tags carried information about the "retention level" of the treating chemical in the wood. That practice started back in the days of CCA, when most wood in the lumberyard was rated for ground contact, and treated to a retention of .40 lbs/cu ft. Now, however, retention levels vary from one chemical treatment to another, and vary by lumber dimension as well. Due to the higher cost of the new treatments, manufacturers typically use less chemical, for example, in decking boards or 2x lumber than in 4x4s, which are more likely to be used in ground contact.

Accordingly most suppliers now leave retention levels off the tag (**Figure A**), preferring instead just to tell you the bottom line: where the piece of wood is recommended to be used. (You can still find out the retention level by contacting the treatment company directly, or by downloading the product's Evaluation Service Report, or ESR, from the company's website or the ICC website: www.icc-es.org/reports. ESR numbers are supplied on the lumber end tags.)

Retentions aside, even the usage labeling can be a little confusing. There are actually two systems for listing the allowable use conditions for treated wood. The American Wood Preservers Association (AWPA) has a system of "Use Category" designations. Lumber stamped UC3A, UC3B, and UC3C, for instance, are above-ground applications, while UC4A and UC4B are ground-contact applications. The International Code Council, by contrast, has chosen to go with basic descriptive words: "Decking Use," "Ground Contact," and "Above Ground" are the labels applied to almost all lumber you'll see stocked at a

Figure A. *Treated wood end tags no longer specify chemical retention levels. Instead, they specify the wood's allowable uses and provide an Evaluation Service Report number (which can be looked up online for treatment details at www.icc-es.org). Large-dimension timbers (far left) are typically rated for ground contact, while 2x stock (left) is usually rated for only above-ground use.*

Bolts ½ inch or larger in diameter are excluded (see "Code Requirements for Fasteners," page 114).

Of these four materials, only stainless steel and galvanized steel are widely available. But effective in 2009, the International Code Council Evaluation Service, ICC-ES, has published an updated "Acceptance Criteria," AC-257, which will allow other fasteners to earn Evaluation Reports (ERs) qualifying them as alternatives to the accepted fasteners. The AC-257 standard involves driving the nails to be tested into pieces of treated lumber alongside hot-dipped galvanized nails, placing the test pieces into a salt-water spray chamber, and then comparing the results, both visually and by weighing.

There are already hundreds of fasteners on the market, with a variety of ceramic, phospatephosphate, polymer, or mechanically plated or electro-plated zinc or other metal coatings, that are advertised as "approved for" or "compatible with" treated lumber. At this time, it's up to the buyer to ask what testing was done and what approvals are in hand. Now that AC-257 is in effect, however, many of these products are likely to gain their building code Evaluation Service listings starting around 2010.

Even before the development of AC-257 test, however, some fastener suppliers were working hard to demonstrate that their fasteners were compatible with ACQ lumber. One example is the popular "LedgerLok" structural screw from FastenMaster (www.fastenmaster.com), used to attach deck ledgers

---

lumberyard, often along with the AWPA designation. Lumber with heavy treatment retentions can be labeled "Foundation Use" or "Marine Grade."

For deck builders, the new system can cause problems. Jim Finlay, who operates an Archadeck franchise in suburban Boston, explains: "Pretty much all CCA lumber used to be certified for ground contact. But with ACQ, only the large timbers – the 4x dimension lumber and larger – is certified for ground contact." That's fine in most applications, says Finlay, but sometimes he needs to build a ground-level deck that requires a support beam placed at or below existing grade. In that situation, he says, "we dig out a slot in the ground, fill it with crushed stone and put our beam on top of a concrete footer (**Figure B**)."

To get 2x lumber for a built-up beam that's rated for ground contact, says Finlay, he has to special-order the pieces. "I have yet to find a lumberyard where I can walk in and buy a 2x8 or 2x10 rated for ground contact," he says. On the other hand, he says, for that application, he is still able to special-order CCA-treated 2x stock.

Ground contact, says wood scientist Freeman, is by far the toughest exposure. "The wood is much wetter," he explains, "and there are also increased fungal populations in the ground." The few inches of soil right at the ground line, richly supplied with both oxygen and water, is a particularly rough environment: lignin-destroying fungi and cellulose-destroying fungi both thrive in this "live soil" zone, along with insects that eat wood. Says Freeman, "The ground line is the number one area where utility poles fail in the United States, and that's the same for deck posts." So contractors need to be sure they're using the wood in

MAC MACDONALD

Figure B. *For a beam on grade like this, deck builder Jim Finlay says he has to specially order 2x8 material rated for ground contact, because lumberyards rarely stock it.*

accordance with its labeled exposure category – and be especially sure that they're not putting wood labeled for above-ground use in contact with the earth.

On the other hand, notes treated wood expert Peter Laks, you don't want to use more heavily treated wood than required – at least not the copper-based products like ACQ or copper azole. Wood rated for ground contact has more copper in it than wood rated for above-ground use, so in addition to being more expensive, it is more likely to corrode steel or aluminum, and more likely to interfere with paint and stain.

Figure 4. LedgerLok screws have the structural capacity of a larger lag bolt, but are easy to drive without predrilling. The manufacturer, FastenMaster, is currently working to get IRC code approval for use with pressure-treated wood under the newly adopted AC 257 Acceptance Criteria. For now, builders must rely on manufacturer assurances for any fasteners made of materials other than stainless steel, double hot-dipped galvanized, copper, or silicon bronze.

and make structural connections (**Figure 4**). LedgerLok is made of heat-treated carbon steel with a zinc plating plus an epoxy and Teflon surface coating. LedgerLok does carry an ICC Evaluation Report, ESR-1078, which you can download from the company's website or from the ICC site, www.iccsafe.org. But that report only addresses the screw's structural strength — it specifically states, "This evaluation report does not address fastener corrosion when the fastener is installed in chemically treated wood."

But FastenMaster itself does endorse the use of the LedgerLok screw with ACQ lumber or any other treated wood, except for coastal locations within 1,000 meters of the ocean. That recommendation, says FastenMaster Technical Manager Mark Guthrie, is based on an older accepted test method for corrosion in metal fasteners and hardware, AWPA Standard E-12. LedgerLoks and other FastenMaster coated screws were tested according to the E-12 protocol in a lab at Michigan Tech. As the test calls for, ten fasteners were screwed into untreated lumber, CCA wood, and two types of ACQ wood, then exposed to salt solution and heat in a corrosion acceleration chamber. Compared to galvanized lag bolts and galvanized nails, the LedgerLok screws showed no visual deterioration in the coating, and lost less than half a percent of their original weight. And according to Mark Guthrie, who handles callbacks for FastenMaster, field results bear the testing out: he has never seen a LedgerLok screw with significant corrosion in any kind of treated lum-

ber in actual use conditions. Guthrie says that FastenMaster is pursuing the process of getting the LedgerLok tested under the new ICC standard AC 257. But he says it may take a while: "There are very few labs currently that are set up for it."

By 2010 or 2111, however, contractors should have a reasonably wide selection of approved fasteners to choose from, backed by ICC Evaluation Reports. But will those fasteners hold up in service on your deck? According to John Kurtz, executive vice president of the International Staple, Nail, and Tool Association (ISANTA), who has been working for years with committees trying to develop testing standards for fastener corrosion in treated wood, "Corrosion is a very complex subject, and there are many variables. No one has figured it out well enough to be able to say, this behavior in a test will translate into 3 years or 12 years or 100 years of performance in a particular exposure in a particular part of the country or climate. It's a best effort, but there is no guarantee."

The best rule for anyone willing to pay the price of caution is probably this: When in doubt, use stainless steel. All the research testing shows that Type 304 and Type 316 stainless steel are practically immune to corrosion by any kind of copper-treated wood.

Simpson Strong-Tie, for example, advises stainless steel for any coastal exposure, or any situation where there might be an unusual chemical stress (such as next to swimming pools, where chlorine may be a factor).

Simpson's Ed Sutt looks at the judgment call this way: "You need to weigh, where is it important to get the job done, and where is it important to do the best job? So, for instance, if you're in a harsh environment and you don't want to spend the money for stainless on the whole job, maybe that critical ledger connection is where you should consider using stainless, to reduce the risk. Or attaching handrails — not the place where you want to save money. But when you are attaching the deck boards down, maybe that is the place where you want to save money — because that is not necessarily as critical."

Hangers and Connectors

AC 257 is the ICC test standard for nails and screws in contact with treated lumber. So far, there's no comparable test for hardware connector straps, joist hangers, or post bases, and no way for hardware suppliers to get specific code listings that apply to using their product with treated wood. For now, contractors have to rely on the recommendations of the wood treaters and the hardware suppliers. Connector manufacturer Simpson's advice, based on extensive testing, is posted online at www.strongtie.com/productuse/selection-guide.html. For USP's guidance, see www.uspconnectors.com/corrosion.shtml#guidelines.

In essence, the manufacturers call for increasing corrosion protection as exposure conditions grow more harsh. In protected dry locations, they recommend G-90 galvanized hardware (with a coating of .90 ounces of zinc per square foot of surface area). For wet exterior locations, this gets bumped up to a G-185 galvanized product (with 1.85 ounces of zinc per square foot), such as Simpson's ZMAX product line or USP's Triple Zinc line. But in severe exposures (including, says Simpson, "exposure to ocean salt air, large bodies of water, fumes, fertilizers, soil, some preservative treated woods, industrial zones, acid rain, and other corrosive elements"), the recommendation is for Type 303, 304, 305, or 316 stainless steel connectors and fasteners.

Simpson's "high exposure" category, it's worth noting, includes some types of treated wood — such as formulas containing a lot of ammonia, or wood that has been treated to unusually high retentions. Quality control is an important factor in the corrosiveness of treated lumber — if a given batch has more chemical than usual, or has not dried fully, for instance, then it could be rougher on fasteners. There may not be any easy way to determine this, unfortunately — so if you're thinking conservatively, you may want to go ahead and spend the money for stainless steel.

The Barrier Method

Another strategy, promoted by manufacturers of flashing membranes such as Grace Construction Products, is to place a long-lasting physical barrier, such a bituminous membrane, between the metal connector and the treated wood (**Figure 5**). In theory, the membrane prevents direct contact between the wood and metal and thereby reduces the electrochemical reaction. The electrochemical reaction, which requires moisture, is what causes corrosion.

In promotional literature for its self-adhesive "Vycor Deck Protector," Grace recommends flashing deck ledgers with the membrane before attaching joist hangers, and also wrapping joist ends before setting the joists. Grace says the method "significantly reduces corrosion rates of galvanized connectors to the levels of CCA wood" and "extends the useful life of ACQ, CA-B, and ACZA pressure-treated decks."

Simpson Strong-Tie has examined Grace's test data, and also ran its own corrosion tests. Simpson's endorsement is cautious, however, only stating that the membrane method "in some cases … allows you to use a connector with less zinc — such as Simpson's standard G90 galvanized connectors" — but only for dry indoor applications, not for deck framing. As to prolonging the life of a deck, Simpson states, "Due to the many variables involved in actual field applications, Simpson cannot provide estimates

MIKE GUERTIN

Figure 5. Installing a flashing membrane between the treated wood and the connector hardware seems to hold corrosion at bay. But it's a time-consuming step that, including labor, can be as expensive as using stainless-steel hardware and nails.

on service life of connectors, anchors or fasteners."

Attempts to apply this technique in the field have received mixed reviews from builders who describe it as labor-intensive, but possibly worth the effort in harsh environments. For example, Jim Finlay, of Archadeck of suburban Boston, says, "I used it a few times early on, before I was able to get the triple-coated zinc hangers."

In southern Rhode Island, builder Mike Guertin has used membranes this way for a couple of years and has found that it is economical if you use pneumatic nailers for the connectors, since until recently stainless steel hangers required labor-intensive hand nailing. If you ordinarily hand-nail, says Guertin, then stainless steel hardware is more attractive. (As manufacturers start to bring stainless-steel connector nails for nail guns onto the market, the balance is tipping further in favor of stainless steel.) Since he's found that the self-adhesive membranes do not stick well in cool weather or if the wood is damp, he sometimes prefers a simple non-adhesive plastic tape like YorkWrap (www.yorkmfg.com). In coastal areas, Guertin has noticed some corrosion on triple-zinc hangers with ACQ lumber, but none where a barrier material was used.

Ted Cushman reports on the building industry from Great Barrington, Mass.

Efficient Deck Framing

by Rob Arnold

My company specializes in building exteriors, both residential and commercial. We make most of our revenue from two specialties: residential decks and commercial framing.

That may seem like an odd blend, as the goal in commercial construction is to get it done fast, while with residential decks it's the quality that counts. They're not mutually exclusive, though. The key to speed isn't simply rushing through the job, it's becoming more efficient, and the systems I've developed to streamline the process have also yielded more consistent and higher-quality construction.

By applying the approach I use on commercial jobs, I've created a system for building decks that's both fast and accurate — and that keeps even fussy customers happy — while providing an excellent bottom line.

At the Desk

First and foremost is to think the entire job through so the crew knows exactly what to do from the moment it sets foot on the site. The first time I approached a job this way was when adding dormers to a house. We did all the figuring before we got to the site, then built the dormers on the ground and lifted them into place in a couple of easy pieces.

Compared with dormers, decks are a piece of cake. I start at my desk, where I make sure the plans contain every detail and upgrade that the homeowner desires (**Figure 6**). I make several copies of the final

Figure 7. Setting up a wheelbarrow or garbage can for scraps at the cutting station is an easy and fast way to keep the site cleaner.

Figure 6. Thorough planning in the office before starting the job keeps the crew moving the whole time the payroll clock is ticking.

plans to scribble on and to use for generating material take-offs and cut lists. Each step in the construction process — footings, framing, decking, railings, and extras — has a dedicated set of plans.

The plans for the footing layout are critical. Whether they're for an 8-foot-by-12-foot residential deck or 4,000 square feet of commercial deck, clear footing plans will save a tremendous amount of on-site head scratching and will jump-start the digging. I use my Construction Master (Calculated Industries, www.calculated.com) calculator to figure the locations of each footing in reference to the face of the ledger.

To locate each footing, I write down the perpendicular distance to its center from the ledger and calculate a hypotenuse from each corner of the ledger to each footing. The more information on the plans, the easier it will be for my crew to double-check that they're installing the footings correctly.

Still at the desk, I create a framing layout that includes the ledger, rim, joists, and beams. On this, I figure out the exact locations of guardrail posts, benches, planters, and blocking, including any needed to support a creative pattern in the decking. I calculate the lengths of all posts, beams, joists, blocking, and custom features and generate a cut list with

Figure 8. Houses aren't always straight, so the author checks the ledger with a string. Variations greater than ¼ inch mean that the joists will have to be custom cut.

six groups: beam, outer box, joists, guardrail posts, blocking, and upgrades like planters and benches.

To account for variations in material thickness, all blocking is specified to be cut shorter than the nominal dimensions of the lumber would dictate. For example, blocking between joists on 16-inch centers would in theory be 14½ inches long (16 inches – 1½ inches). But I specify it to be cut at 14⅜ inches because treated joists are usually thicker than 1½ inches and are often cupped; shorting the blocking by ⅛ inch allows for this.

On simpler projects, there won't be much figuring and the cut list will be short. On more complex projects with angled bump-outs and different levels, each section is separated into workable areas, and each area is grouped on the cut list as for a simpler deck.

I'll even set up a laser transit on site beforehand and figure out the overall rise of the stairs. With this information, I can decide at the comfort of my desk what size to cut the stringers.

The idea is to make the project into an easy puzzle. I'd like to think that I could give my list to anyone on the crew and he'd be able to finish the project with precision and speed, by following the steps.

Setting Up

With the planning done, we're ready to go on site. But before getting any tools out, I create a functional working environment. Locate the material pile or the main cutting station in the wrong place, and you end up working around them for the entire job. I take five minutes to lay out the cut stations, the material stacks, and the spot to eat lunch. Give yourself enough room to cut and install comfortably.

Another time-consuming part of building is

cleanup. It took a couple of years, but I learned to keep a barrel or wheelbarrow next to the cut station to take care of scraps as they come off the saw (**Figure 7**). Eliminating double handling of scraps can save 30 minutes a day. Taking the extra time to set up properly will have you moving quicker and easier, and installing more safely and efficiently.

Planning Pays Off

I install and flash the ledger before laying out the footings, ensuring the footings will be accurate to the

Figure 9. The person assigned to the cut station also assembles the beams, going so far as to lay them out and nail on the hurricane ties.

Figure 10. While one crew member starts cutting, others lay out the footings using a precalculated length for the diagonal measurement.

Figure 11. Using a laser level with an audible sensor, one man marks the footing forms with a nail through the cardboard, so all the concrete can be poured to the same height.

Figure 12. Precise placement of anchor bolts speeds locating the post bases.

plans created at my desk. I usually run a string line across the installed ledger to see if the wall is bowed out or in. If the ledger has more than a ¼-inch bow in it, I'll adjust the joist lengths accordingly (**Figure 8**, previous page). Once the ledger is done, I set one crew member up at the cut station and two on footings and layout.

Depending on the size of the crew and the size of the job, it may take a full day to lay out, dig, and pour all the footings, and cut, crown, and organize all the framing members. At the end of the day, though, the puzzle is ready to go together.

The person at the cut station doesn't only cut, he also crowns and organizes the pieces on the cut list — and he marks the joist locations on the beam and lays out the guardrail posts on the side and rim joists, using the detailed plans. If he gets ahead, he can nail the hurricane ties for the joists to the beam (**Figure 9**, previous page).

The other crew members use the detailed footing layout to locate the holes, starting with the outside corner footings and working toward the middle (**Figure 10**). Taking an extra minute to make sure the footings are set properly makes your work look much better. If all the measurements are followed, no posts should end up off-center on a footing.

Once the forms are in place, I use my laser transit to set the level I'll pour the concrete to (**Figure 11**). Placing all the concrete to the same level makes life much easier later because all the posts can be cut to the same size. If the grade around the deck varies too much, however, some of the footings will stick out of the ground like a sore thumb. In that case, I keep the

Figure 13. The right tool can be a big timesaver: The Big Foot Saw Adapter allows for a 10¼-inch blade in a standard Skilsaw and cuts 4-inch stock in one pass.

footings about the same distance out of the ground and cut the posts to length individually.

I set anchor bolts in the wet concrete, aligning them on a string line from the batter boards (**Figure 12**).

Cantilevered Joists

I prefer to support the outside of the deck with a beam, cantilevering the joists beyond it. Installing the beam is the first step. Assuming that the ledger is of the same material as the joists, the top of the beam must be level with the bottom of the ledger for the deck to be level.

To find the height difference between the tops of the post bases and the bottom side of the ledger, I use a laser. From that number, I subtract the width of the beam plus ³⁄₁₆ inch to allow for the thickness of the post-to-beam connectors. This calculation provides

the height of the posts that will carry the beam — one of the only measurements I can't predetermine at my desk. Variations in dimensional lumber and the height of the concrete are the determining factors.

I cut posts using a worm-drive saw with a 10¼-inch Big Foot Adapter (Big Foot Tools, www.bigfoottools.com). With one line and one cut the post is ready for installation (**Figure 13**).

The outer posts are attached to the pre-cut and laid-out beam, and the assembly is raised into place like an exterior wall. Once the beam is plumb, toe-nailing the outside joists secures and steadies it. Next, I infill the remaining posts, and the beam is ready to support the rest of the joists.

Cantilevering joists over a beam provides a level platform on one side of the deck to rest joists on, and means that one person alone can install a joist.

Figure 14. Resting the joists on the girder, one carpenter toenails them in place (far left). A second crew member follows behind, using a metal-connector nailer to fasten the joist hangers (left).

Figure 15. Before being attached to the beam, the joists are leveled with and nailed to the rim joist. Shims are added between the joists and the beam if needed; then the preinstalled hurricane ties are nailed to the joists.

To double the speed of joist installation, I use two carpenters, one at each end of the deck. At this stage, they just drive a couple of toenails into the ledger, and none in the outer beam (**Figure 14**, previous page). A crew member with a metal connector nailer will follow behind and install the joist hangers.

Once the joists are placed, the outside rim is ready to be fastened. When installing the rim, flush its top with the top of the joists (**Figure 15**). This will cause some joists to float above the beam due to the variations in dimensional lumber. Floating joists are shimmed and all are fastened to the beam.

Quick Guardrail-Post Installation

With the floor framing finished, it's time to install the guardrail posts, bench posts, and detail blocking for decking patterns. While one crew member is still installing hangers and hurricane clips, the other two

Figure 16. A nail placed in the side of the newel supports it while it's initially secured with LedgerLok screws. Later, the newel is shimmed plumb and secured with a DeckLok Bracket or a Simpson HD5.

Figure 17. The last step in framing is installing blocking for items such as benches, decking patterns, or planters.

split up the remaining blocking and post installation. All post locations have already been laid out by the cut guy, so all I have to do is install the posts.

On other crews, I often see two people installing posts — one holds a post while the other lags it into place. This should be a one-person job. I mark the location of the top of the joist on the bottom of the pre-cut posts, and set a 12d nail one-third of its length into the post. The nail supports the post on the joist while I drive a LedgerLok screw (FastenMaster, www.fastenmaster.com) to hold it temporarily in place (**Figure 16**). Many crews notch posts to set their heights; however, notching a 4x4 post doesn't leave enough meat to resist the code-required 200-lb. load for guardrails — and it's time consuming (see "Why Not Notch?," page 46).

After all the posts are set, I go back to plumb, bolt, and install a hold-down bracket on each one. When installing three or more posts on the same joist, I set and fasten the outer posts plumb and run a string line on the outside of the posts from one to the other. This saves time when installing the inner posts on the same rim. Instead of pulling out the level and checking each post, I set them to the string and fasten them properly.

Finally, all the odd blocking is installed (**Figure 17**). Decking patterns can dictate certain blocking locations. For example, I often run a picture frame of decking around the deck for a cleaner look. To support the ends of the deck boards and the perpendicular picture framing, 2x4 cleats are needed on the inside of the two end joists perpendicular to the house. Once guardrail posts, planter posts, and blocking are installed, the crew member that installed the joist hangers and hurricane clips uses the framing plan and the post-detail plan to double-check the installers' work before moving on to the next step.

The more you figure out at the comfort of your desk, the smoother the layout and installation will go. Every crew member always has a task, and often one is doing a task alone that other crews do with two workers. I also like to give crew members different responsibilities from one job to the next. It cross-trains the employees and prepares them for a job with a missing team member.

Rob Arnold is a contractor and deck builder from Hopkinton, R.I.

Rot-Resistant Details

by Kim and Linda Katwijk

Poor deck design and even some common building practices create what I call "collection zones" — places organic matter and moisture can accumulate — usually where two pieces of material meet. And not only does this organic matter itself provide a friendly environment for fungi, it also traps moisture, which encourages rot in the surrounding lumber.

Starting at 16 percent moisture content, wood is susceptible to rot. At 21 percent or higher, rot thrives, and in wet seasons this threshold is easily reached. We put a lot of faith in pressure-treated lumber, but when it gets wet, it swells; when it dries out, it shrinks. This process creates checking. All it takes is a check (which can be microscopic) that bypasses the treatment for rot to invade the wood beyond. Maximizing the drying potential of decks is the key to longevity.

Fascia Detail

A perfect collection zone is where the fascia board rims the deck. There's no airflow between the fascia and the framing, so the 21 percent moisture content required for rot can be maintained over long periods of time, and there's no way for debris to escape. But if you simply cantilever the deck boards one inch over the fascia you reduce the number of places dirt and moisture can get in.

Compare these construction details by looking at how many linear feet of collection zone each design creates (**Figure 18**, next page). On a 12-foot-by-16-foot deck with 6-inch decking, a fascia that is flush to the top will create 40 linear feet (12 + 16 + 12) of collection zone (the entire perimeter). But if the decking laps over the fascia, the collection zones are limited to the ¼-inch gaps between the deck boards, a cumulative 12½ inches. Using a belt and suspenders approach, you can also seal the top of the rim and fascia with peel-and-stick membrane, like Grace's Vycor Deck Protector (www.graceconstruction.com).

Built-up Beams

It's common practice to double- or triple-up 2-by material to form beams. Unfortunately, the space between the pieces creates a collection zone. A better practice is to use solid 4-by or 6-by beams to carry

Avoiding Collection Zones

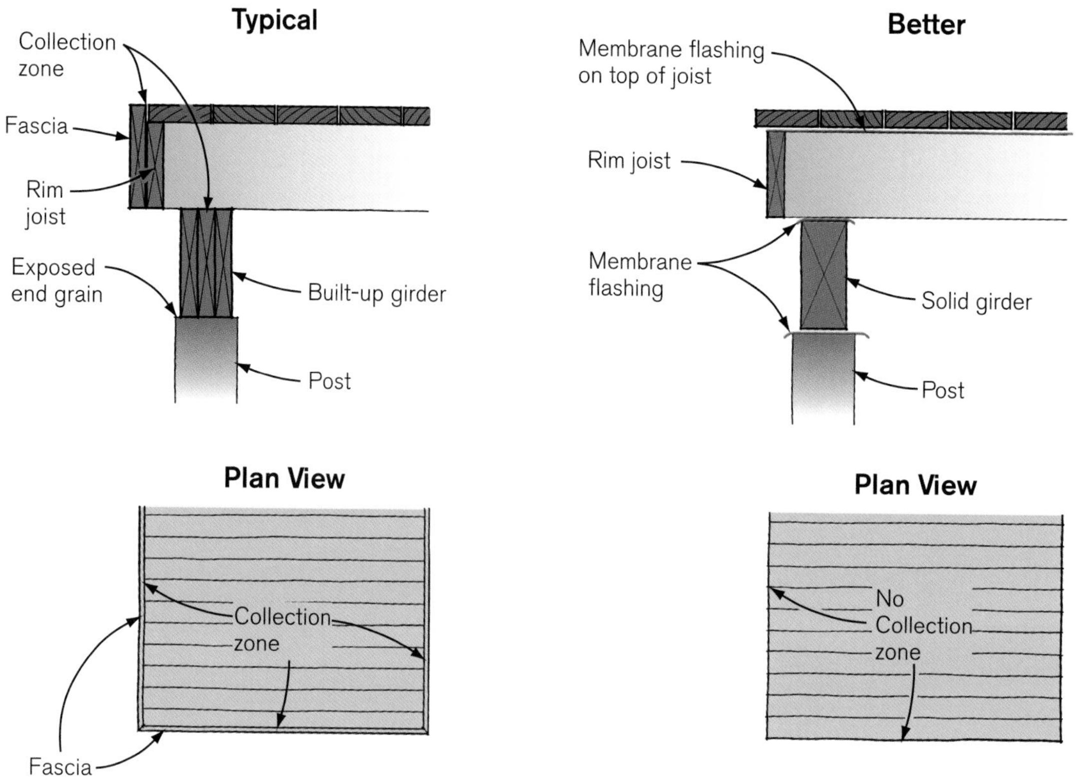

Typical

- Collection zone
- Fascia
- Rim joist
- Exposed end grain
- Built-up girder
- Post

Better

- Membrane flashing on top of joist
- Rim joist
- Membrane flashing
- Solid girder
- Post

Plan View

- Collection zone
- Fascia

Plan View

- No Collection zone

Figure 18. Wrapping a 12-foot-by-16-foot deck with fascia (left) creates 40 linear feet of potential collection zones, where rot-encouraging debris gathers at the rim joist. Running the deck boards parallel to the house and overhanging the fascia (right) will reduce the collection zones to a cumulative 12½ inches (¼ inch per gap x 50 gaps). While some water and debris will get in, the greatly reduced amount will be much less likely to cause rot.

loads. Still better is to cap the beam, whether it's solid or built-up, with copper or a membrane such as Vycor.

Attaching Ledgers

Another common building practice (and IRC requirement) is to use flashing to keep moisture from getting between the house and the ledger. Many contractors will install an L-shaped piece of metal here; the horizontal leg covers the top of the ledger, and the vertical leg goes up the wall and is lapped by the building paper above.

The problem is that rot can invade the deck board or the bottom of the siding when organic matter builds up in the space between the deck and the side of the house — especially on the wind-driven side of the house. The rain hits the siding and runs down into this collection zone, where organic matter creates a dam, preventing drainage. If the siding is not up off the deck, the water will soak into the backside of the siding, and from there can enter the house via capillary action.

One way to overcome this problem is to use a ledger that is larger than the joists. If you're using 2x8 joists,

you need a 2x10 ledger. Bevel the top of the ledger and install it 1½ inch higher than the joists (**Figure 19**). Install the first deck board ⅜ inch to ½ inch away from the ledger to allow the organic matter and water to drop through to the ground.

Deck Boards

Many carpenters use 16-penny nails to space deck boards. This creates a ⅛-inch-wide gap that forms a collection zone between boards and on top of every joist (**Figure 20**). It's nearly impossible to remove leaf litter from such a narrow gap. And once the organic matter is in there, it can induce rot in the deck boards and in the joists below.

My way around this problem is to install decking with a wider, ⅜-inch gap. Organic matter won't collect in this larger space, but will simply fall through. Some customers express concerns that such a wide gap will catch a woman's high heel. But I've found that once I explain the benefit — extending the longevity of the deck — they readily accept the gap. The larger space also allows air to circulate and dry out the decking and

continued on page 129

Debris-Free Ledgers

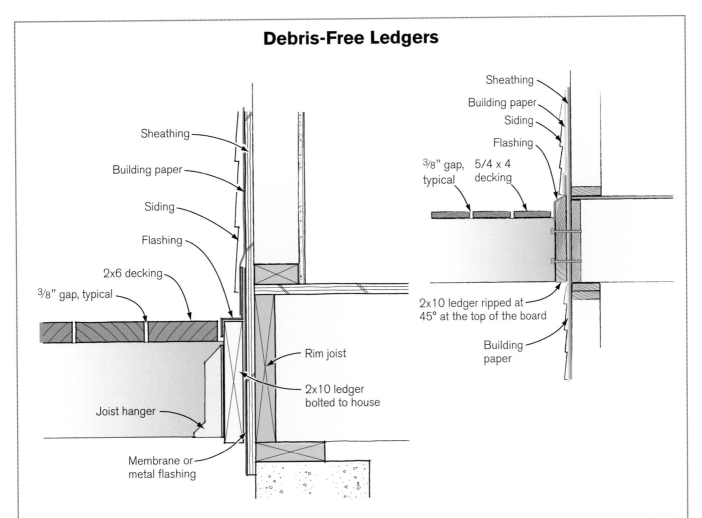

Figure 19. Keeping debris from collecting against the house is key to a long-lasting ledger connection. A sloped and flashed ledger (right) sheds water and debris. A properly flashed flat ledger that's flush with the decking (left) is another easily cleaned connection. Keep siding 2 inches above the ledger with this design.

Figure 20. Most carpenters space deck boards too tightly (left), leaving enough room for debris to get in but no way to clean it out. On this deck, organic matter collected at every gap and joint (center), as well as between a rim joist and blocking that landed under a gap in the deck boards (right).

Spacing Ledgers From the House

Another option for installing ledgers is to minimize their contact area with the house by using standoffs between the ledger and the house. However, changes to the 2007 IRC limit standoffs to being made from steel washers stacked no more than ½ inch deep, unless you have an engineering or ICC-recognized code report. Closer ledger bolt spacing is required when standoffs are used (see "New Rules for Deck Ledgers and Lateral Attachment," page 41).

For years I've made standoffs from scraps of composite decking. I used to run lag bolts right through these, but now I use 5-inch LedgerLoks, made by FastenMaster. FastenMaster had this connection tested by Washington State University. This testing showed that with 1-inch spacers as shown below, 5-inch LedgerLok screws performed as in the chart. Where two rows of fasteners are required, the fasteners should be at least 3½ inches apart to avoid splitting the ledger. (FastenMaster actually used 2x8 SPF spacers in their tests, so our 1-inch-thick spacers are more conservative). Your engineer can design similar connections for the decks you build. The test data for LedgerLoks can be obtained by contacting the manufacturer (www.fastenmaster.com).

Composite decking doesn't hold moisture, and leaves a gap of about 1 inch between the house and the ledger, allowing a generous space for airflow, and for leaf litter and rain to drop straight through. To assist with water runoff, I slant the top of the blocking 15 degrees from the center in both directions. I seal the top of the blocking by caulking it with Dap Sidewinder Polymer Sealant. − *K.T. and L.T.*

Live Load per Block	Number of LedgerLoks (inches)	Block Spacing SYP	Max Joist Span Hem Fir	Max Joist Span
40	2	16	14 ft 8 in	11 ft 2 in
40	4	20	23 ft 6 in	17 ft 11 in
40	4	36	13 ft	9 ft 11 in
40	4	48	9 ft 9 in	7 ft 5 in
50	2	16	12 ft 3 in	9 ft 4 in
50	4	20	19 ft 7 in	14 ft 11 in
50	4	36	10 ft 10 in	8 ft 3 in
50	4	48	8 ft 1 in	6 ft 2 in
60	2	16	10 ft 6 in	8 ft
60	4	20	16 ft 9 in	12 ft 9 in
60	4	36	9 ft 4 in	7 ft 1 in
60	4	48	7 ft	5 ft 4 in

Table A: Blocking and LedgerLok Spacing. Data is applicable only to LedgerLok fasteners.

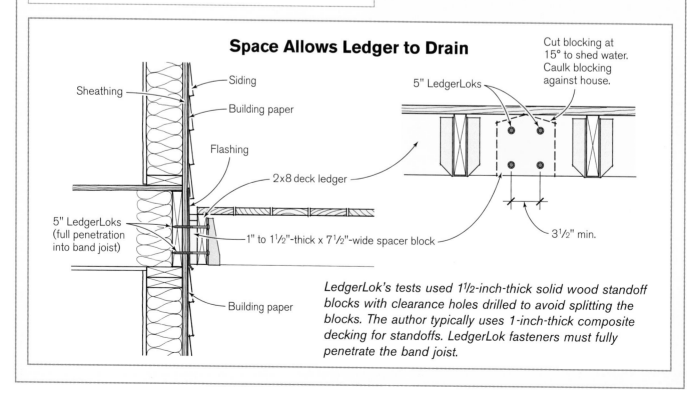

Space Allows Ledger to Drain

Sheathing

Siding

Building paper

Flashing

2x8 deck ledger

5" LedgerLoks (full penetration into band joist)

1" to 1½"-thick x 7½"-wide spacer block

Building paper

Cut blocking at 15° to shed water. Caulk blocking against house.

5" LedgerLoks

3½" min.

LedgerLok's tests used 1½-inch-thick solid wood standoff blocks with clearance holes drilled to avoid splitting the blocks. The author typically uses 1-inch-thick composite decking for standoffs. LedgerLok fasteners must fully penetrate the band joist.

Figure 21. Nailing balusters to the rim joist creates pockets that trap moisture and debris, which can cause rot.

joists. And on top of joists, where debris still collects, the space is wide enough to be raked clean with a screwdriver. The same rules apply to composite decking; even though captured organic matter may not affect the composites, it can still rot the framing below.

Screws or nails fastened from above should be driven flush with the deck surface, not recessed where they will hold water. This is especially critical for wood decks, as is sealing the wood deck boards after they're fastened.

Railings

Many carpenters nail 2x2 balusters to the fascia or rim joist, a poor practice because there are so many nails in the rim that it ends up looking like a pin-

cushion. The large number of fasteners can also split the rim and allow water to get inside (**Figure 21**). Any railing system that attaches to the top of the deck, on the other hand, is less likely to create a collection zone, especially if the bottom is caulked.

Some railing systems need to be attached through to the deck framing. If this is done inside the rim you create collection zones on two sides, if not all four sides, of the posts. If you attach your post to the outside of the rim you cut your collection zone by as much as 75 percent.

Kim Katwijk is a deck builder in Olympia, Wash., and a board member of NADRA (North American Deck and Railing Association). Linda Katwijk assisted with this article.

Coastal Deck Details

by Rob Arnold

I build decks in Rhode Island, the Ocean State, and I regularly work on the coast where high winds, constant humidity, and wind-driven rain take their toll on decks.

Always in the front of my mind is that as deck builders we are responsible for keeping people safe during evening cookouts, family gatherings, and even wild college parties that exceed design loads. In addition to the obvious joist, beam, and footing sizing, we need to make sure our decks are fastened and flashed to the house to withstand the extra demands of a northern coastal climate, and we need to use fas-

Coastal weather calls for added attention to flashing, fastening, and furnishing.

Figure 22. The constant winds common to coastal decks can blow lightweight outdoor furniture across the deck. This makes it easier to sell upgrades such as built-in seating.

Figure 23. Midday sun on the coast in the warmer months is intense. Shade structures such as pergolas are great upsells that in the long run will improve your clients' satisfaction.

teners that will hold up not only to wet conditions but to salt water, even though that sometimes means spending more money. Fortunately, the extra cost of using the right material isn't usually a problem with coastal decks as they're typically high-end jobs.

Figure 24. The first step in the ledger flashing sequence is to apply peel-and-stick membrane directly to the sheathing where the ledger will go, as shown above. The peel and stick is wide enough to extend above and below the ledger. After the siding is installed, the release film along the bottom will be removed so the peel and stick can be adhered to the face of the siding.

Design in Practical Extras

Wind whipping off the water is a constant, even when the sky is blue. During the design stage I try to sell the client on building as many seats and pieces of furniture into the deck as possible (**Figure 22**, next page). The built-in furniture may not be as comfortable, but it's much more convenient than chasing a wind-blown chair across the lawn or storing it out of the weather after each use.

I research the location before I meet the customer, as one area may get regular northeasterly winds while a few miles away another spot gets southwesterly winds. A decorative privacy panel may be enough to cut down the uncomfortable winds; a guard rail made from tempered glass also blocks wind — and maintains the beautiful coastal views as well. I note what time of day the clients believe they'll spend the most time on the deck. Along with the sailing furniture, umbrellas blow away with ease, so I offer built-in alternatives such as pergolas for shading the area (**Figure 23**).

Deck Protection

Often the homeowner won't see the evidence of a leak at the ledger. If left alone long enough, the leak will rot the framing to which the deck attaches, possibly leading to a catastrophic deck failure. Coastal decks experience a fair amount of sideways rainfall — and in Rhode Island, a considerable amount of snowfall as well — and rain and snow can find their way into some tight spots. Because of this, ledger flashing takes on even greater importance on the coast than at inland locations.

I always flash using Vycor peel-and-stick flashing

Figure 25. A second layer of peel and stick covers the installed ledger and laps up the wall. This layer protects the ledger fasteners from salt air, isolates the joist hangers from the corrosive effects of the pressure-treated ledger, and keeps water out of the joint between the top of the ledger and the wall.

products (W.R. Grace & Co., www.graceconstruction. com). My employees are familiar with them, they are easy to work with, and they come in different sizes for different applications. My first step in flashing the ledger is to install a layer of 12-inch Vycor on the surface I am attaching to (**Figure 24**). This layer will help to seal any penetrations into the house from the nails and ledger bolts.

I then install the ledger on top of the Vycor following the fastener-placement details in the 2007 Supplement to the IRC (see "New Rules for Deck Ledgers and Lateral Attachment," page 41).

The next step is to install Vycor 18-inch detail membrane over the ledger. This product was originally meant for roofing; however, it works perfectly in this application. I apply it to the face of the ledger, over its top, and up the wall (**Figure 25**). This leaves at least 5 inches of Vycor against the wall above a 2x12 ledger. The detail membrane protects the ledger bolts from the salt air, so I'm comfortable using hot dipped galvanized bolts rather than stainless steel. And the 18-inch membrane also helps to slow corrosion both by sealing the top of the ledger where it meets the house and by isolating the joist hangers from the treated ledger.

The house shown in the photos in this article had no building paper, as it is sheathed with Zip System sheathing (Huber Engineered Woods, www.huberwood. com), which has an integral weather barrier. But most houses do have building paper, and I'd ordinarily cut that out where the ledger was to be attached, before applying the Vycor. The first layer of Vycor would lap the building paper below, and the subsequent upper layer of Vycor would be lapped by the building paper above. I would seal any remaining slits where the

building paper joins the Vycor with strips of Vycor or housewrap tape.

After the second layer of Vycor is in place, I install a drip cap on top of it, at the top of the ledger (**Figure 26**). In the past, I've used either custom-bent copper or galvanized steel. Lately, however, I've been using a vinyl flashing such as DuraFlash (P&G Solutions, www.duraflash.net) or Pro-Trim DuroBend (Alum-A-Pole, www.alumapole.com). Vinyl flashing completely sidesteps the corrosion issue.

Once I install the drip cap, I apply a layer of 4-inch Vycor to the top of the flashing. If the house had

Figure 26. A corrosion-proof vinyl drip cap tops the ledger and is in turn capped by a third application of peel and stick. The sheathing used on this house has an integral weather barrier. On most houses, the building paper would lap these final waterproofing layers.

building paper, that would then lap over the Vycor and the flashing.

It's a good idea to explain this system to the homeowners on the sales call. They are usually aware of failing decks and are impressed to learn that I take pains with the flashing.

Avoiding Hardware Corrosion

Although salt air accelerates corrosion, it's not the only factor in play. By now we all know that some of the chemicals currently used to treat lumber corrode fasteners and hardware to a greater extent than the old CCA preservatives did. This corrosion occurs when the fastener or hardware contacts wet lumber. To separate the hardware from the lumber and thereby slow down the corrosion, I wrap the ends of the joists (**Figure 27**) and the posts with Grace Deck Protector.

Another spot where I use Deck Protector is on top of the joists (**Figure 28**). Not only does it help slow down the fastener corrosion by keeping the joists drier, but it also protects the joists from water intruding into splits (see "Membrane Deck Flashing," below). Because preservatives don't always penetrate into the core of a piece of lumber, any water reaching there can cause rot. Doubled joists are worse: It's easy for moisture to find its way between the two members and never completely dry out if they aren't protected. I apply Deck Protector over the tops of doubled joists to prevent water from collecting between them.

On decks that are right on the coast and subject to constant salt air, I use all stainless steel hardware and fasteners. Simpson Strong-Tie (www.strongtie.com) and USP Structural Connectors (www.usp

---

Membrane Deck Flashing

by Andrew Hutton

We always protect pressure-treated deck (**A**) and stair framing (**B**) by flashing edges where water might collect and cause rot. This is vital here in the West, because the preservatives don't penetrate very well into the hem-fir lumber used in this part of the country.

Several companies have recently released products designed for this purpose; probably the best known is Grace's Vycor Deck Protector. For 10 years, though, we've been using Polyken 626-35 Foilastic, an aluminum-foil–faced adhesive tape from Tyco Adhesives (www.tycoadhesives.com). Like other peel-and-stick membranes, it grabs well and self-seals around fasteners. It is also more resistant to UV rays than similar membranes (for up to a year in direct sun, according to the manufacturer) and can be painted.

We put it on the top edges of deck joists, where fasteners are concentrated and water tends to sit. We also put it on the vertical cuts of stair stringers (**C**), where the

notches go right to the untreated center of the material; merely painting the cuts with preservative can't provide the same level of protection. Foilastic comes in 50-foot rolls in widths as narrow as 2 inches and as wide as 36 inches.

Andrew Hutton is a site supervisor for Moroso Construction in Pacifica, Calif.

Figure 27. To isolate the framing hardware from corrosion-inducing wood preservatives, the author first wraps the wood with peel-and stick-membrane. Finish materials will cover the membrane, both for looks and to protect it from degrading in the sunlight.

connectors.com) both make stainless steel hardware in addition to their other corrosion-resistant offerings. I also use stainless framing nails as well as decking fasteners. Stainless steel isn't cheap, but neither is a lawsuit should a fastener corrode and someone get hurt as a result.

Winds, Floods, and Weathering

More so than inland decks, coastal decks may be subject to floating away in a flood or blowing away in a hurricane. A positive connection that resists uplift is always required between the footings and the posts; the posts and the beam; and the beam and the joists (**Figure 29**, next page). Often an architect or engineer will specify the proper connectors and hardware to meet the local requirements. If not, I take care of the calculations myself and reference Simpson Strong-Tie's Web site for proper connectors.

Seaside decks experience the most extreme weather, and more often than not they will be wet.

Figure 28. Even treated lumber is susceptible to rot and checking if water is allowed to accumulate or to enter cracks. Covering the tops of joists and beams with peel and stick avoids this problem.

Figure 29. Because of the potential for uplift from high winds and floods in coastal areas, joists, beams, and posts must all be connected to the footings through a chain of hold-downs.

Figure 30. The harsh sun and regular moisture take a big toll on decks built on the coast. Low-maintenance decking and railing are easy upsells in this environment.

Most customers don't have time to paint or stain their decks and don't want to pay a professional once a year to do it for them. I always recommend using low-maintenance decking and railing material, like PVC, or exotic hardwoods, like ipe (**Figure 30**).

Between the extra labor required to protect the joists and hardware, and the more costly materials, seaside decks can get very expensive. However, the builder is responsible for the safety of the deck. Not only are these extra precautions great selling points, but they can prevent an injury-causing deck collapse — and the lawsuits that follow.

Rob Arnold is a contractor and deck builder from Hopkinton, R.I.

Building Elevated Decks

by Bobby Parks

The company I work for in North Atlanta, Ga., recently built several elevated decks, two of which were 28 feet high. Because of the height involved, caution and planning are critical when building such decks.

The basic types are stacked multilevel decks (photo, facing page, top) and single upper-level decks (**Figure 31**). Loading and footings are more complex with stacked decks, but single decks can be more difficult to start building because their columns are frequently taller. Both are often built over sloping ground, which complicates footings.

Consulting both a geotechnical and a structural engineer is crucial. It's not cheap, but the more details you can provide the engineers for review, the less their charges will be. The alternative, risking a deck failure 20 feet in the air, could cost you everything.

Designing for Height

It's important to remember that an elevated deck isn't simply a regular deck on stilts; the large distance from the ground dictates a number of special design considerations.

For example, all decks need lateral stability, but the taller support posts on elevated decks increase the need for bracing. Generally speaking, if the width of

Engineering, slow work conditions, and safety issues add cost and complexity to tall decks.

a deck (across the house) is less than or equal to the depth (perpendicular to the house), bracing may be required. The wider a deck is compared with its depth, the easier it is to stabilize.

If the decking boards will be laid perpendicular or parallel to the house, the deck will need angle braces between the columns, along with bracing under the joists. I prefer diagonally installed decking because it significantly stabilizes the structure by tying all the floor joist structure back to the attachment to the house — and it looks clean and cosmetically appealing.

Stairs are an integral part of an elevated-deck design. If stairs will be connecting the upper and lower levels, I like to place them outside and at the

Figure 31. Elevated decks require more thought than ground-level decks. Difficulties of working at a height, safety concerns, increased footing loads, unfamiliar materials such as steel, and a greater need for lateral bracing all contribute to — and justify — significantly higher pricing.

Figure 32. Bringing stairs off the end of the deck saves floor space. Very high decks require landings between levels. Having the stairs reach the ground close to the house, where the grade is highest, keeps them as short as possible.

ends of the deck to conserve floor space. I find that constructing the stairs perpendicular to the deck out to a landing and then back to the lower deck often works best. To minimize the length of the stair, I try to land it near the house, where the ground should be at its highest grade. If there is no lower deck, you may need to work a series of landings into the design for the stairs to reach the ground (**Figure 32**).

The higher the deck, the more critical railing design is. I consider 42 inches (as opposed to the code minimum of 36 inches) to be a standard rail height for decks more than 12 feet high, because the extra 6 inches makes a significant safety difference. A 42-inch rail hits even tall people at a level that can make the difference between a fall and a recovery.

I also plan for what will be placed on the deck. We reinforce the structure where a heavy grill or other item will add a constant load; doubling or tripling the joists where the grill will be is usually adequate. Supporting a spa requires additional columns and beams that make a continuous load path down to the footings. We also double the joists under spas, and shorten the span between beams. Although these details aren't unique to elevated decks, the greater consequences of failure on a high deck underline their necessity.

But height isn't all about reinforcement and safety; sometimes a higher elevation offers additional design possibilities. On a stacked deck, for example, it's possible to create a porch on the lower level by building a watertight floor between the decks, and by framing and screening the walls. Extending the waterproofed upper deck beyond the lower deck will help to protect the porch from blowing rain.

Big Footings

The importance of consulting both a geotechnical and a structural engineer before beginning an elevated deck is worth repeating. The structural engineer details the plans, but the geotechnical engineer comes on site. Even though the local building inspector checks the footing holes, I ask the geotechnical engineer to determine the soil's bearing capability. With an elevated deck, the last thing you want to deal with is a settling footing. It's much better to spend the time and money up front to cover yourself.

It's likely that typical-size footings won't be adequate for a single elevated deck — and it's certain that they won't support a stacked deck. To handle the increased loads, the footings need to be wider

Figure 33. Piers rising above grade keep steel columns out of the dirt. Making them a larger diameter provides a larger target for locating the column, and helps to spread the load on the footing. Attaching columns with 1/2-inch bolts and wedge anchors adds stability and resists wind lift.

and deeper than usual, and reinforced with additional rebar.

Width and footing thickness should be engineered, and here's where the advice of a geotechnical engineer is invaluable. On sloping sites, the footing has to be deep enough to transfer loads, without having a tendency to slide or roll toward the outer slope. To prevent sliding on a slight slope, the bottom of the footing may need to be 2 to 3 feet below the downhill side of the pier; on a steep slope, that depth may be as much as 6 feet, or even more (see "7-Foot Rule," page 80).

To keep the base of the column from sitting in the dirt and corroding away, I make sure the top of the footing is raised above grade by extending it with 16-inch- or 18-inch-diameter piers that project 6 inches or so above grade (**Figure 33**). These large-diameter piers allow for a larger footing. They're also less prone to toppling or rotating under load than are more slender piers. I use #4 rebar to join the footings and the piers.

We dig the footings using shovels because moving digging equipment onto the site of an existing residence causes lawn and property damage. Where soil conditions dictate deep footings, say 6 feet, we'll dig down to 3 feet at twice the footing width. This creates a ledge we can stand on when digging the bottom 3 feet. We've been known to shorten shovel handles while working in a tight spot. It's awkward and difficult but often the only option we have.

On steep slopes, we key the footings into the ground (**Figure 34**) by digging the uphill half of the footing hole several inches deeper than the front to gain additional bite in the ground.

Figure 34. Footings for stacked decks need to be larger to support the increased loads. On sloping sites, special measures need to be taken to prevent the footing from sliding downhill; two such are digging a deeper footing, and digging the uphill side of the footing in deeper to provide a keyway.

Scaffolding

As the elevation increases, so does the overall level of difficulty of building decks. For one thing, scaffolding gets more extensive. And the higher the work zone, the more time it takes simply to move people, tools, and material.

On a deck just 12 feet up, for example, one carpenter standing on the ground can still hand lumber to another on the framing or a scaffold. As heights

Figure 35. Scaffolding is essential to provide a safe and efficient workplace at a height. Be sure to rent enough to scaffold the sides and the width of the deck, and have extra walk boards to facilitate material handling.

Figure 36. Multiple joists provide a continuous load path between upper-level and lower-level wood columns. Diagonally laid decking adds lateral stability.

approach 20 feet, however, the crew has to pass material from man to man on successive scaffold levels. Even lighter, smaller objects, like tools and hardware, take more time to move — usually with a rope and bucket.

I have found that multiple sections of pipe scaffolding with leg adapters, stabilizers, bracing, and walkboards work well on most sites (**Figure 35**, previous page). We start out with scaffolds along what will become the two sides of the deck; the sections can be relocated as needed during construction. Allow for extra walkboards on all levels to assist in transferring materials to the deck level. Scaffolding even helps with demolition of an existing deck, making the process faster and safer.

On sloped sites, you need to create a stable, level base for the low end of the scaffold; we use timber cribbing. Scaffolding always needs to be tied to the house and together. The crew fastens eyebolts to the house to secure the scaffold.

In most cases, the crews raise the columns and beams from the scaffolding. On a new construction site, cranes or forklifts may be used to handle steel columns and other materials. For existing residences, however, heavy equipment may not be an option because of tight lots, or risk of damage to the landscaping or driveway.

Stacking Decks on Wood Columns

For single-level decks up to 12 feet in height, I prefer to use 6x6s as columns. Beyond that elevation, my company uses steel columns, with some exceptions.

For multilevel decks, I prefer to stack the different levels using 6x6 posts in a continuous load path that incorporates the lower level's floor framing. This approach allows the crew to work its way up one level at a time, with no need for scaffolding: After the first level is framed and decked, the crew has a platform from which to build the next level.

Where one post stacks atop a lower level, we nail four or more floor joists together and run them directly over the lower column, and directly under where the upper column will land (**Figure 36**). This supports the upper deck structure and provides a solid-wood load path from column to column. We fit two thicknesses of solid bridging between the quadruple joist and the joists to either side, over the beam. Strapping ties the upper and lower columns together with the beam, creating a continuous tie to resist wind lift. At the house, fabricated steel brackets on both sides of the quad joist attach it to the ledger.

The size and number of decks that are being built

Figure 37. Using approved column bases takes on more importance on stacked decks. Be sure the ones used can handle the increased loads.

Figure 38. Notching 6x6 columns to receive a doubled 2-by beam provides a spot to positively anchor the beam to the column using bolts.

Figure 39. For decks elevated 13 or more feet, steel columns are needed to provide rigidity. Have the footings in place to determine column height before ordering.

and stacked determines the column layout. Tighter spacing of the columns can distribute loads over more footings and let you stack wood columns on wood floor framing without worrying about concentrated loads crushing the wood.

We anchor the 6x6 columns to the footings using brackets specified by the engineer (**Figure 37**). To attach the main beam, the crew notches the tops of 6x6s to fully receive the doubled 2x10 or 2x12 beam (**Figure 38**). That leaves a section of the post about 2½ inches thick that comes flush with the top of the beam. We double-bolt each post-and-beam connection with ½-inch galvanized bolts.

Another option for supporting upper decks is to use independent 6x6 columns (they can be up to 20 feet in height) that go through the lower deck's framing adjacent to the lower deck columns, distributing the upper-deck loads directly to the footings. You can stabilize the longer 6x6 by tying it into the first-floor framing and bolting it to the lower-level column. Steel columns can be used in this same fashion.

Using double columns from the footings to the first-level beam gives the structure a larger bearing base; and using twice the number of bolts where the beam bears on both columns assists with locking in the beam against beam roll.

Steel Columns

Many jurisdictions require steel columns for decks above a certain height. For decks higher than about 13 feet, it's advisable to use steel regardless, because of the added stiffness of the column and its connections (**Figure 39**). This should be engineered. Our structural engineer specs 4-inch or larger schedule 40 square tubing on high decks.

I keep the column count as low as possible on elevated single-level decks, while allowing for the loads,

because I want to handle as few steel columns and footings as possible. Those things are heavy — 16 pounds per foot for a 4-inch column, and 20 pounds per foot for a 5-inch column.

You need to factor in the lead time for steel-column orders, to minimize delays on the job. I like to establish the deck level on the house and pour footings before ordering the columns.

With the footings done and scaffolding erect, it's time to build. We usually get the beam to the top of

Safety, First and Last

Although in general I'm able to leave work at work, elevated decks make me lie in bed at night worrying about getting through the job with everyone on the crew intact.

Scaffolding and safety harnesses alone don't eliminate the possibility of serious injury. Management must stress safety and make sure that crew leaders buy in, too. Everyone involved has to understand the risks and difficulties of working at a height, and have a working knowledge of scaffolding safety and the proper use of a safety harness.

Equally important is communication. When undertaking a potentially dangerous task, such as raising a 300-pound column, every person on the job site has to know what he's expected to do and not do. Talk the process through before starting. Try to anticipate the difficult points and plan how to work through them. Encourage questions, and be particularly careful that any new people on the crew fully understand the entire process. – B.P.

Figure 40. Bracing the beams on steel columns is done first with temporary 2x4s tied to the ledger, then more permanently using joists.

the scaffold before raising the columns. It's best if the beam is built up of long 2x10s or 2x12s, which can be raised to the top of the scaffold and then assembled. That way, the columns don't get in the way of raising the beam, and the beam spanning the two scaffolds helps to brace them. It's possible to span greater distances using a treated glulam or steel I-beam, but those require the use of a crane.

To raise a column from scaffolding, the scaffolding has to be set up and secured to the house. We wrap the top of the column with a heavy-duty nylon strap, which is hooked to a ⅝-inch rope that runs to a block and tackle affixed to the scaffold's top. A slipknot keeps the strap from sliding past the saddle welded to the column's top.

Place the column perpendicular to the house, its top over the footing and its base closer to the house. Hoist slowly while two men on the ground move the base end of the column toward the footing. This relieves stress on the scaffolding. Raise the column until the base can be set on the footing.

When the column is correctly placed on the footing, we tie it off to the scaffold and drill into the pier for 4-inch-by-½-inch wedge anchors and bolts through the column's base plate. Then we bolt the column to the footing.

With both columns set, the crew drops the beam into the saddles on the columns, and braces it to the house — first with some 2x4s running to the ledger, and then with joists (**Figure 40**). Angled 2-by bracing fastened to stakes in the ground is also used as needed. Raising shorter columns in place may simply require a couple of men on the scaffolding with ropes or straps and a couple of men on the ground to help.

Using steel columns to stack decks can be a problem because code doesn't allow for steel columns to bear on wood. On two-level decks, however, it is possible to use square steel columns if you have brackets welded to receive the beam for the lower deck. The benefit of one continuous column is that you don't have to worry about beam roll or the crushing stress created by stacking structure on structure.

Bidding

When pricing elevated decks, you've got to allow for several items you don't encounter on most other decks. In addition to typical charges, I include the cost of a structural engineer and a geotechnical engineer; the cost of scaffold rental, as well as set up and teardown; and the extra cost of steel columns. And if you're stacking decks, don't forget the cost of the fabricated brackets to tie the quad joists to the ledger.

Footings can be surprisingly costly, particularly those on sloped sites. Of course, footing requirements vary geographically, but I allow as much as $500 per footing on some sites. I also include the cost of raising steel columns, which usually takes 4 to 5 man-hours per column.

Over and above these line items is an elevation charge. This is an attempt to cover the slowdown in production that occurs when crews work at high elevations, and to pay them a premium for doing such work. As a general rule, I add $2 per square foot at 12 feet in elevation, and another $2 per square foot for every 2 feet in elevation above that.

And sometimes, I walk away from a project. For example, if very large beams are required and there's no way to get in with a crane, it's just not worth the risk.

Bobby Parks owns Peachtree Decks and Porches in Atlanta, Ga.

Framing With Big Timbers

by Kim and Linda Katwijk

There's something awe inspiring about heavy timbers and huge logs, and when they're used in decks, they transform utilitarian posts and beams into a display of craftsmanship. Structurally, though the posts are logs and the beams are sawn timbers, these decks aren't much different from a regular deck. Posts and beams still support the loads, and hardware still connects the assembly to resist wind, seismic, and other loads.

However, challenges always exist when you're working outside the norm, and timber decks are no exception. To begin with, codes provide little design information; therefore, it's likely you'll need to have the structure engineered. The building department may require you to have the timbers graded, which means finding a certified lumber grader. You probably won't be able to find treated logs and timbers, so you'll have to pay close attention to assembly details to protect the wood from moisture. You may be able to find locally grown rot-resistant species — such as cedar, black locust, or white oak — but otherwise it will be necessary to apply some sort of preservative.

Buying Logs and Timbers

You're not going to find big logs and heavy timbers at your local box store, and even many lumberyards have trouble getting them. Local sawmills, though, are a good source for timbers, as is Wood-Mizer (www.woodmizer.com), a company that makes portable sawmills and maintains a list of customers who are commercial sawyers.

For logs, try the nearest log-home company. Other sources are pole yards (which supply telephone poles) and local tree services or loggers. There are two types of logs, milled and handcrafted. A milled log is perfectly round and the same diameter top to bottom, whereas a handcrafted log is tapered, just as the tree grew. The taper can vary dramatically from one species to another. Order logs longer than you need: Typically, 1 foot to 2 feet of extra length will be enough.

Logs can be finished products or raw material fresh from the forest. The latter will need to be debarked, which can be done with a draw knife or an adze. Logs fresh cut in the springtime when the sap is running can be debarked using a power washer at 3,500 psi or greater with a turbo nozzle. This method leaves the smooth cambium layer of the wood intact. You can also use an electric plane.

Footings

One reason for using big timbers is to span greater distances. Bigger spans call for bigger footings, though, which you may need to have engineered.

Regardless of the size of the footing where it bears on the ground, the top of the concrete — which I call a pedestal — needs to be 1 inch to 2 inches

Use chainsaw skills and engineered plans to produce handsome, sturdy timber decks.

Figure 41. Log posts are vulnerable to rot from water wicking up the end grain. Sizing the portion of the footing that's above grade to be 2 inches smaller than the post provides a drip-edge. Keep the post at least 6 inches above grade to minimize the effect of rain splashing upward.

smaller than the bottom of the log post. This provides a drip-edge around the bottom of the log, helping to keep water from running underneath the bottom of the posts. To prevent water splashing onto the base of the log or wicking up from the ground, the top of the pedestal should be at least 6 inches above grade (**Figure 41**).

With typical, smaller posts such as 4x4s or 6x6s, the post-base hardware allows for some adjustment. In the case of logs, where the log is larger than the pedestal and you want to maintain an even overhang, it's more important than usual to have accurately placed the footings.

To form a hold-down for the post, I embed a Simpson HD-10A about 10 inches into the pedestal, leaving 8 inches of the anchor protruding (see **Figure 44**, facing page). This will be fitted into a slot chain-sawn into the log, forming a blind connection that's more appealing to the eye than a hold-down mounted on the outside.

Preparing Log Posts

Determine the heights of the posts as you would for any deck. If you intend to seat the beam in pockets cut into the posts, then cut the posts to the elevation of the beam top. If the beams will sit on top of the posts and be connected with hardware, the posts should be cut to the elevation of the bottom of the beam, less 1/4 inch for the angle-iron hold-downs.

For either design, you need to cut the log ends square. To do this, first find the center of the log's end by measuring three ways: horizontally, vertically, and diagonally. For each measurement, mark the center. You'll usually end up with a triangle of dots; the center of this triangle is the point I use as the center point. Repeat at the log's other end.

With the log braced against rolling, use a level and a pencil to draw a plumb line up from the center point to the top edge of the log (**Figure 42**). Again,

Figure 42. All layout on logs springs from a centerline. To find it, a plumb line is drawn through the center of each end of the log (far left); the points where these lines intersect the face of the log are joined with a chalk line (left).

Figure 43. To mark the end of the log so it can be cut square to the centerline, a framing square is held to the layout line (left). It takes a little finesse to hold the pencil square to the framing square. After the cut, check for square (right), but remember to allow for any taper the log may have.

do this at both ends. Fill a chalk line with white or blue chalk (white and blue don't leave a permanent mark) and snap a line down the length of the log connecting the top points of the two plumb lines. This is the layout line.

Place the long side of a framing square against the layout line and draw a line square to the layout line 2 inches from one end of the log (**Figure 43**). Some

eyeballing will be required. Use a chainsaw with a sharp chain to cut the log. My favorite saw for this kind of work is Makita's model 5012B electric chainsaw, a little workhorse that generates a chain speed of 5,500 feet per minute — equivalent to a gas-powered saw, without the mess.

With the framing square, check from several points that you have cut the end square. Tapered logs will

Figure 44. The hold-down anchor (above left) will fit in a slot cut in the post's bottom. The odds are that the anchor is not centered exactly on the pedestal. Measure carefully to ensure that the anchor slot is cut so that the post will overhang the pedestal evenly.

Safe Plunge Cuts

Plunge cutting with a chainsaw must be done properly to be safe. If the top of the bar alone contacts anything while the chain is running, it will kick back at the operator, possibly resulting in injury. The author is an experienced hand with a chainsaw, and these photos show how he avoids this dangerous occurrence.

Start the cut with the bar at 45 degrees to the base of the log and the bottom of the bar tip contacting the wood.

While maintaining downward pressure to avoid kickback, slowly raise the saw as you push in.

Keep pushing down and inward, stopping the plunge when it's about 2 inches deeper than the length of the anchor strap.

The finished cut shouldn't be much higher than the width of the bar.

Figure 45. A propane-fired torch is used to heat torch-down roof membrane. Once heated, the membrane will be adhered to the bottom of the log post and trimmed to fit exactly. This membrane helps prevent water from wicking up the log and causing rot.

Figure 46. A torpedo level and a layout square are used to guide the drilling of holes for the bolts that will secure the log to the anchor.

Figure 47. Placing the post is a two-person operation. Be sure the log is oriented correctly, and not 180 degrees off.

require some approximation. Assuming a fairly uniform taper, find the difference between the diameter at the end of the log and that at the far end of the framing square. Half of this difference is the length of the gap you should have between the end of the square and the log. Once the bottom of the log post is squared, measure and cut the top to length.

Cutting the slot for the HD-10A requires you to lay out the bottom end again. Using the chalked layout line and a level, draw a vertical line on the log's end, then measure down the vertical line to find the center of the log. Next, measure where the HD-10A is in relation to the center of the pedestal and transfer that location to the base of the log, so the log will be centered on the pedestal (**Figure 44**, page 143).

Plunge cuts with a chainsaw take a little practice and a lot of caution. If you contact the log with the top of the chainsaw's bar, the saw will kick back at you. I typically start a plunge cut with the saw at a 45-degree angle to the bottom of the log and in line with its length (see "Safe Plunge Cuts," previous page). As I start to cut into the bottom of the log, I gradually raise the chainsaw bar to horizontal while applying downward pressure and pushing the bar forward into the log. If continuous downward pressure is not applied, the bar will jerk violently upward. You need to go in only about 2 inches deeper than the distance that the HD-10A protrudes from the pedestal.

Fitting Log to Pedestal

As protection against water wicking up from below, I seal the bottom end of the log with torch-down roofing. With a torch, heat a piece of roofing material that's slightly larger than the base of the log and —

while wearing gloves — adhere the hot roofing membrane to the bottom of the log (**Figure 45**). When it cools, trim it with a utility knife to match the bottom of the log and slit it at the plunge cut.

The log post will be attached to the HD-10A with through-bolts, and your next challenge is to drill the holes for them. Use a level to orient the log so that the plunge cut is horizontal.

Using the same technique as before, draw a plumb line from the center of the plunge cut to the upward face of the log as it lies on the sawhorses. Draw a matching line on the other end of the log and snap a new line down its length. The bolt holes will be on this line. Measure the height of each hole in the HD-10A from the top of the pedestal and transfer these measurements to the new chalkline.

The next step is a two-person operation. One person drills the hole, and the other guides the $^{11}/_{16}$-inch augur bit with a layout square and a torpedo level (**Figure 46**). With the holes drilled, slip the log over the HD-10A and see if they match up (**Figure 47**). Slide the $^5/_8$-inch bolts through the holes. The bolts should be about 1 inch longer than the diameter of the log so there's room for the nut and washer. Plumb the post and brace it from two directions.

Joining Post to Beam

Once all the posts are installed, you can lay out their tops for the beams. There are several ways the beams can meet the posts: The beam can sit on top, it can sit in a pocket cut for the beam to run through, or it can sit in a blind pocket, where the beam end is hidden in the post.

Pocket cuts require two parallel cuts for the sides and a plunge cut at the bottom. Working from scaf-

Figure 48. With the posts up and braced plumb, a string is used to establish the line of the beam. A carpenter uses a level to lay out the side cuts for the beam pocket.

folding for safety, run a string line from post to post down the length of the deck to represent one side of the beam. Mark that side on the tops of the posts, then measure over and mark the other side. From these lines, draw plumb lines down the sides of the posts; then mark the bottom at the proper elevation and chainsaw out the pocket (**Figure 48**).

Blind pockets are laid out and cut in much the same way, but the side cuts and the bottom plunge cut don't go all the way through (**Figure 49**). Also, you'll need to make a blind cut from above to end the pocket.

After test fitting the beam in the pocket, it's a good idea to bevel the remaining flat parts of the log's top to shed water (**Figure 50**). I fasten the beam to the pocket using FastenMaster's LedgerLok screws (www.fastenmaster.com). You could also use bolts or lags.

If the beams are to sit on top of the posts, I attach them using 4-inch-long pieces of 4-inch-by-1/4-inch powder-coated angle iron with two holes on each leg for lags. The angle brackets attach to the bottom side of the beam and to the side of the post to transfer lateral loads.

All these connections need to be engineered.

Figure 49. The pockets for beams also require plunge cutting with a chainsaw. The same safety rules apply, with the additional caveat that you should work from scaffolding for stability.

Figure 50. To shed water, the tops of the posts are beveled after the pockets for the beams are cut.

Figure 51. Before the beams are placed in their pockets, the wood is treated with a borate preservative. Note the torch-down roofing membrane applied to the beam and post tops in the background.

Preventing Rot

Because large timbers and logs are usually not pressure-treated, I use a three-prong approach to prevent rotting: preservative, sealing, and covering.

I prefer to use borate wood preservatives. Essentially nontoxic to humans, they're safe and simple to apply. Two that I've used are Timbor (Borax, www.borax.com) and Bora-Care (Nisus Corporation, www.nisuscorp.com).

Timbor comes in a powder and must be mixed with hot water. Bora-Care comes in a liquid form. To apply either, use a sprayer or brush.

In severe conditions, such as the windy side of a house in a moist climate, I also use Impel Rods (Wood Care Systems, www.ewoodcare.com). I insert them into holes — drilled in the log at vulnerable areas, such as the top and bottom where end grain can wick in moisture — and plug the holes.

The crystalline-borate rods, which come in $1/8$-inch to $1/2$-inch diameters, sit inside the wood until moisture dissolves them — then the dissolved borates move within the wood toward the highest concentration of moisture, inhibiting the growth of fungus or rot.

Because borate products are water-soluble, they need to be sealed into the wood. I use One Time (Bond Distributing, www.onetimewood.com), which is an acrylate resin that soaks deep into the wood and cures with sunlight. Over the past 12 years I have tested numerous stains and preservatives, and One Time is the best I've found. While its initial cost of about $75 a gallon may seem high, the manufacturer guarantees it to last seven years. This beats the annual or biannual reapplication required with most other sealers.

Finally, you need to provide a barrier to shed the water from the tops of the timbers and posts. I find that torch-down roofing gives the best results.

The application requires a handheld torch to melt the torch-down roofing to the top of the wood, both beams and posts (**Figure 51**). Torch-down roofing membrane comes in 18-inch-wide and 36-inch-wide rolls. Using a utility knife, I cut the membrane into long strips 2 inches wider than the beam. After adhering it to the top of the beam, I trim the membrane so that $1/2$ inch overhangs each edge of the beam to provide a drip-edge to direct the water away.

This three-pronged approach to preventing rot has satisfied every building department I've dealt with, although some have required an engineer's report. The engineer I use gladly provided the documentation.

Kim Katwijk is a deck builder in Olympia, Wash. Linda Katwijk assisted with this article.

Site-Built Under-Deck Drainage

by Scott Smith

As a deck builder in the Pacific Northwest, I often get requests to waterproof second-story decks to make the space below useful for leisure or storage. My standard approach used to be to build the deck with a slope, put plywood decking down, and apply a textured coating system over the plywood. Not only did this look bad and get dirty quickly, it puddled easily and leaked in a few short years. So I started looking for a long-lasting, problem-free product I could install easily and cover with good-looking decking, for any shape deck I dreamed up. I also wanted a good profit margin.

After doing some research, I found a geomembrane that was waterproof, inexpensive, and flexible, and rated to last 25 years in direct sun (**Figure 52**). I now use this membrane to create drainage troughs between the joists, and with some off-the-shelf aluminum or plastic gutter, I form the system I describe below. (See "Under-Deck Drainage Systems," page 154, for a description of underdeck drainage products.)

It works like a champ — and generally costs less than 50 cents per square foot for the membrane system and $5 per lineal foot for gutter and downspout. As added benefits, the membrane protects the joists from moisture, so the deck framing will last a lifetime; and the deck surface can be built level, because the slope for drainage is between the joists.

While I designed the system for new construction, it also works fine on pre-existing decks, with just a few alterations.

Overview

In brief, the process goes like this. After framing the deck but before installing the decking, I cut the membrane into pieces long enough to cover the length of the joists and lap over the ledger board and up the wall; and wide enough to droop down between the joists to create troughs.

The slope is created by increasing the amount of "droop" in the membrane from one end to the other. Lay the upper end of the membrane (usually next to the house wall) in place with only a small droop in the middle of the membrane. Droop the lower end of the membrane all the way to the bottom of the joist. A second installation of membrane starts at the outer rim joist, draining back over the support beam and into the first run of membrane.

The troughs drain into a gutter, which I place

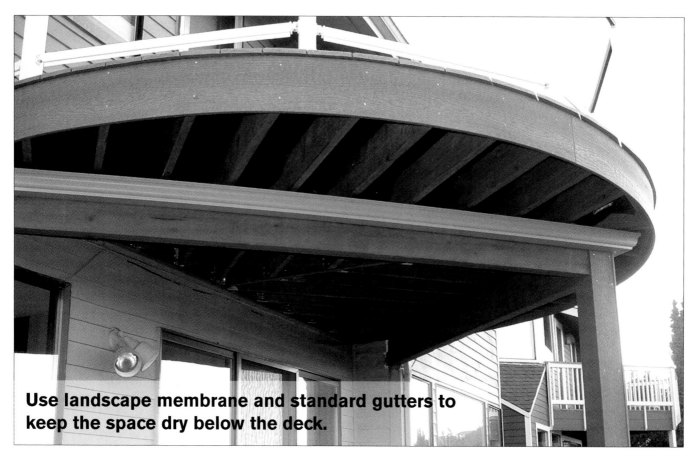

Use landscape membrane and standard gutters to keep the space dry below the deck.

Figure 52. Caulked and stapled to the joists, polypropylene geomembrane forms troughs that drain into a gutter.

against the outside edge of the support beam, tight against the bottom of the joists.

Cutting the Membrane

I use a 20-mil polypropylene membrane (Layfield Plastics, www.layfieldfabrics.com), which commonly comes in 10-foot-4-inch-wide rolls of just about any length you want. I chose this product because it's strong enough to span a 16-inch or 24-inch joist layout and it's durable. Readily available and inexpensive, it costs around 30 cents per square foot at a local landscape supplier.

To determine how much membrane you need, drape a string over two joists (**Figure 53**). At the low end of

the drainage system, the middle of the string should droop to the level of the bottom of the joists; at the high end of the system, the string should droop about an inch down from the tops of the joists. Overhang the ends of the string about 1 inch down the outside of each joist so you have a little extra to play with. Simply measure the strings to get the widths of the two ends of the membrane.

Find a flat, solid surface, such as a concrete slab, on which to lay out and cut the trapezoidal-shaped pieces of membrane. Then determine how many pieces you need and lay them out — alternating the wide and narrow ends — across the 10-foot-4-inch-wide sheets of membrane (**Figure 54**). I can usually get about five

Figure 53. Use a string to measure the span of the membrane. On the gutter end, it should droop almost to the bottom of the joists. On the house end, it should droop down only an inch or so.

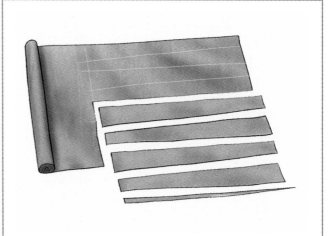

Figure 54. The string measurements are transferred to a layout, alternating wide and narrow ends across the width of the membrane. Cut lines are snapped with a chalk line.

Figure 55. After the polypropylene membrane is laid out on a concrete slab and scored with a utility knife, the membrane tears easily. It's best not to cut all the way through, to preserve the knife's sharpness.

Figure 56. Traditional aluminum or plastic gutter affixed to the main beam carries away the water from the membrane troughs.

pieces out of a roll. The length can be as long as you need, although 20 feet is the longest I've ever needed. Be sure to allow for enough excess membrane on one end to go up the house wall 3 inches, and on the other end to run to the center of the gutter.

I use a lumber crayon to mark the measurements on the membrane, and a chalk line to mark the cut lines. I score the membrane along the chalk lines using a utility knife; by not cutting all the way through, I save the point of my knife blade from being worn off by the concrete under the membrane. Once scored, the membrane easily rips along the score lines (**Figure 55**). I fold and roll my pieces

Waterproofing Existing Decks

To install this system under an existing deck, cut the membrane pieces with a shallower droop, no more than 4 inches, and staple the membrane to the underside of the joists, caulking each seam as described in the following pages. Screw 2x2s to the joists over the membrane as in the drawing below. –S.S.

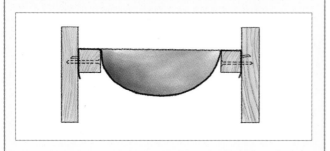

for easy handling and set different sizes into different piles.

Installing the Gutter

Before I install any membrane, I install the gutter; this sequence gives good access to the top of the gutter. If the gutter is short enough to be carried on my truck, I have it made to length at the gutter supplier's shop and install it myself. I also supply the shop with the location and measurement of the downspout, and have the hole for it punched. I usually have no problem matching the gutter to the ones already on the house, and this approach is much cheaper than having the gutter supplier come to the job site.

To make gutters and spouts less noticeable, I place the gutter against the outside edge of the support beam, tight against the bottom of the joists (**Figure 56**), and I run the downspouts down the support posts. If you build a deck with a flush beam that's on the same level as the joists, you may need to install a board under the beam to mount the gutter to, unless the beam is thicker than the joists.

Installing the Membrane

At the ends of troughs that are more than about 6 feet long, you'll need to install baffles to catch any water that may shoot out past the gutter. Baffles are simply scraps of membrane that span between the joists, running several inches higher than the trough, and lapping into the gutter. I attach the baffles to the joists using stainless steel staples.

One person can install the membrane, but it's

Figure 57. Polyurethane caulk seals the membrane to the joists.

much easier with two. Start the installation of the main troughs by running a bead of caulk along the top of the first joist (**Figure 57**). I usually use black Dap (Dap Products, www.dap.com) or Vulkem urethane caulk (Tremco, www.tremcosealants.com) to match the color of the membrane. Both brands are good quality, flow well in hot or cold, and are readily available. They adhere to polypropylene well enough to produce an effective seal.

With one person on each end of the joist bay to be covered, place the membrane over the caulk flush with the outside edge of the first joist. Leave enough excess membrane on the house end to go up the wall 3 inches (**Figure 58**), and to run to the center of the gutter on the outer end.

Staple the membrane along the first joist about

every 2 feet to hold the membrane in place until the decking is screwed down over it. I slide the stapler over the membrane on top of the caulk to flatten it out and get rid of any lumps (**Figure 59**). Tighten the membrane as needed to create a smooth trough for the water — make sure, though, there is adequate slack at the wall end to allow the membrane to lay flat over the ledger board — and staple the other side of the membrane to the top of the second joist.

The steeper the slope, the more easily rainwater can carry out any debris that falls through the gaps between the decking boards. Also, placing the low end of the membrane at the top of the gutter minimizes splashing.

Next, run a bead of caulk along the second joist on top of the membrane you just stapled in place.

Figure 58. The siding and tar paper on the wall of the house is peeled back to allow the membrane to be integrated into the ledger flashing system.

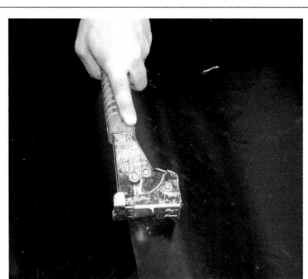

Figure 59. A stapler is used both to attach the membrane and to smooth out the caulk under the layers of membrane.

Figure 60. A bead of caulk atop the first piece of membrane seals the joint. Be sure to caulk over the staples to prevent leaks.

I always take care to cover the staples with caulk so there is no chance of a leak there (**Figure 60**). Put the next piece of membrane on top of the caulk, stretching it tight and placing it as before. Overlapping and caulking the pieces on top of each joist prevents leakage caused by wicking between the layers. Staple it in place, locating the staples over the caulk so it will fill the staple holes.

Stretch the membrane into a nice trough, paying

attention to the wall junction, and staple the other side of the membrane in position just as you did the first one. Repeat this procedure with all the remaining pieces.

The final touch is to cover each membrane seam over the joists with a self-sealing tape such as 4-inch Vycor Deck Protector (Grace Construction Products, www.graceconstruction.com). This tape seals around the decking screws to prevent leaks from occurring where the screws penetrate the membrane (**Figure 61**).

One important note is that this system may occasionally need maintenance in the form of debris removal. Usually, flushing the troughs with a garden hose is enough, but you need access — a strong argument for screwing down the decking. When the gutter needs to be cleaned out, access is easy from the underside of the deck. If you've installed soffit under your deck, it's wise to install the last board with screws, so it can be easily removed for gutter cleaning.

Return Troughs

A return trough is required from the support beam, whether the joists hang from it or are cantilevered beyond it (**Figure 62**). Typically, the main trough from the house drains to a gutter mounted on the outer edge of the beam. To drain the cantilevered portion of such decks, I install a shallower return trough from the outer edge of the deck to a point overlapping the main trough by about 6 inches (**Figure 63**). The water from the return trough will simply drop into the deeper trough and flow into the gutter.

The return trough is the secret to doing angled, round, and cantilevered decks. Return troughs can be as short as a few inches or as long as needed. Just be sure to leave at least a couple of inches of clearance

Figure 61. Vycor Deck Protector caps the joists and the polypropylene membrane, adding a layer of protection that self-seals around the decking screws. Note the Deck Protector continuing up the wall, lapping the joint between the pieces of membrane.

Putting Water in Its Place

Cantilever

Main trough

Baffle

Return trough

Baffle

No Cantilever

Figure 62. Main and return troughs work in tandem to drain the deck. The main return feeds directly into the gutter, aided by a baffle stapled to the main girder to prevent overshooting runoff from soaking the beam. The return trough passes over the main beam and drains to the main trough.

Figure 63. Just a slit between the troughs and the baffle shows water's path into the gutter below. Leave at least a couple of inches of clearance between the main trough and the return to prevent debris from hanging up and clogging.

between the return trough and the main trough so that debris in the main trough doesn't hang up on the return trough. Install the return trough the same way you did the main trough, with caulk, staples, and seam tape.

Joining to the House

The junction of the deck to the house wall is a delicate and important area. It's a common place for leaks to occur, and if the seal isn't tight, the house can suffer a lot of damage. You will have to get the mem-

Details Keep Framing Dry

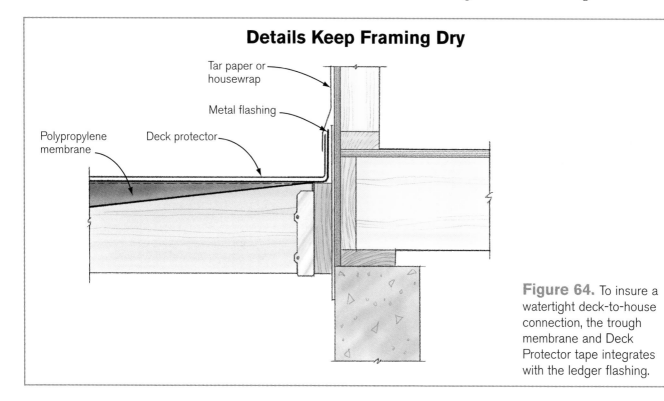

Tar paper or housewrap

Metal flashing

Deck protector

Polypropylene membrane

Figure 64. To insure a watertight deck-to-house connection, the trough membrane and Deck Protector tape integrates with the ledger flashing.

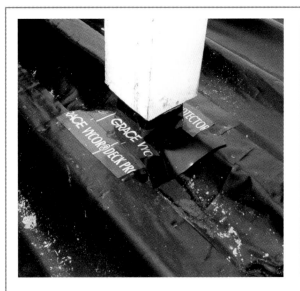

Figure 65. To waterproof around details such as posts (left) and steps (right), the author stacks the layers with the upper over the lower, just like roofing, and uses Deck Protector as flashing.

brane over the ledger and at least 3 inches up under the siding and housewrap or tarpaper to insure it will catch all the water blown against the wall in a driving rain. You may need to cut into the siding of the house to do this (**Figure 64**, previous page). I use Vycor Deck Protector seam tape to seal the membrane to the sheathing. Place a trim board or replace siding as appropriate after the membrane is run up the wall.

Deck Protector is also great for detailing around posts and steps (**Figure 65**). The final step is to screw the decking down to the joists over the membrane. It is harder to find the joists when they are covered with the tape and membrane, but to avoid leaks, care must be taken to be sure the deck screws hit the joists. If you miss, fill the screw hole you just made with a little caulk so a leak doesn't develop.

You can install soffit under the deck now, and even recessed lighting. If you install can lights, try to get the shorter versions and tell your customer to use only fluorescent bulbs, to keep the cans cool and not melt the membrane. I buy IC-rated lights, and place double foil-faced insulation over them to provide a heat barrier — in case someone forgets and puts a flood light in the fixture.

Scott Smith is a deck contractor in the Tacoma, Wash., area.

Under-Deck Drainage Systems

by Mark Clement

If a deck is far enough above the ground, beneath the prime living space above exists another, nearly accidental, outdoor living space. And while its creation may have been unintended, it can be valuable real estate if you trick it out.

The first step in upgrading this space is to shield it from rain and snow and divert the water into a gutter and downspout. All systems discussed here offer a warranty against leaks. Installation methods differ, however, and it's important to consider how they affect not just the underside of the deck but its entire design.

The systems can be divided into three basic catego-ries: waterproof sheets that fit over the joists before the decking goes down, systems that affix to furring strips below the joists, and between-joist systems.

Sheet Systems

Dek Drain and RainEscape are examples of sheet systems. The two products work on the same principle. After flashing against the house, you roll a membrane across the tops of two joists to create a long trough that's pitched to drain at the front of the deck into a gutter and downspout system. Adjacent rolls of membrane lap at the tops of the joists and are capped with more membrane or peel-and-stick tape.

Deck boards are screwed to the joists through the membrane, which self-seals around the fasteners.

Because sheet systems are typically only 4 inches or so in depth, you can run wire and junction boxes underneath the troughs. Then you can add a ceiling of your choosing — beadboard, for example. Another benefit to using this method is that the framing is protected from decay, as the systems keep everything below the deck boards dry.

Still, before selecting this type of drainage system, you should keep a few things in mind. Mid-span blocking has to be installed so that the troughs run above it. You can't use blind fasteners that install from the bottom of the deck. And deck boards can't be straightened by driving a chisel into the joist as a lever or by using a BoWrench.

Dek Drain

Dek Drain (www.dekdrain.com) is made from black rubber that remains stable during temperature changes and isn't affected by leaf acid, acid rain, or salt spray in coastal applications, according to the manufacturer (**Figure 66**). Direct sunlight (not that much will reach under the deck boards) is no problem.

Installation requires no caulk, a feature most deck builders will welcome. Post penetrations are flashed with peel-and-stick membrane or butyl tape. Dek Drain ships nationally and comes with a transferable, limited lifetime warranty.

RainEscape

RainEscape (www.rainescape.com) differs from Dek Drain in three main ways. For one, RainEscape is made from high-density polyethylene rather than rubber (**Figure 67**). Also, it's brown instead of black, making it less noticeable from below should there be no ceiling installed under the deck. And it drains into RainEscape's preformed scuppers that send the water straight down into a gutter.

Figure 66. Dek Drain is made from a chemical- and sunlight-resistant rubber; the system drains into standard K-style gutters.

Figure 67. RainEscape's brown polyethylene fabric drains into a proprietary gutter system.

While laps and caps can be sealed with caulk, RainEscape's butyl peel-and-stick tape is less messy and goes in faster. You can use it for wrapping posts or other penetrations (say there's a gas line plumbed through a joist bay for an outdoor kitchen assembly) so they drain into the troughs.

Ceiling Systems

The panels of ceiling systems hang from vinyl rails or 2-by sleepers that are attached to the bottom of the deck. They create a finished ceiling at the same time they waterproof the space underneath. It's a one-step process, but you have to like the look of the ceiling. Unlike sheet systems, ceiling systems don't keep the framing dry. This is something to consider if you want to add overhead electrical devices — say, lights or fans.

DrySnap

The key to DrySnap installation (www.drysnap.com) is properly laying out and installing the DrySnap joist brackets and pitch spacers on the underside of the deck joists. It takes a little bit of layout math to evenly space the joist brackets along the joists (**Figure 68**, next page). As you move out from the house, you create a pitch by adding spacers to the joist brackets. Once those are installed, you mount the ceiling panels on the bracket system. The result is a flat, slightly pitched vinyl ceiling with a beadboard appearance.

True to its name, the ceiling components pretty much snap together once the brackets are installed. The ceiling panel layout begins with a starter strip and finishes with an end cap. You need a rubber mallet to tap the panels into place and make sure they lock down, but that's the only tool you need that you don't already have in the truck.

DrySnap's installation instructions call for the

Figure 68. If a beadboard look is what you're after, DrySnap's vinyl panel system may be the solution.

ledgerboard flashing to extend 8 inches out from the house — easy if you're building a new deck. For retrofits, the company suggests using a peel-and-stick membrane detail on the ledger to direct water into the system and guard against back-splashing. Because vinyl is stiff when cold, DrySnap recommends storing the panels in a warm place prior to installation.

Airflow is good and the wood above the ceiling stays dry, according to DrySnap, because nothing actually touches the joists, so no spots are created that trap water.

While installation looks straightforward, the company offers regional classes and installation certifications for those who plan to install a lot of it.

American Dry Deck

The manufacturer describes American Dry Deck (www.americandrydeck.com) as a "watertight drop

ceiling." Made of vinyl, this snap-lock system is installed level below the joists on 2-by sleepers. It can be installed running in any direction, a trait unique to American Dry Deck (**Figure 69**). Unlike a typical drop ceiling, however, the panels run the length of the joists and are arched to direct water down into channels that in turn feed into a gutter and downspout.

Two gutters, one at the house and one at the front of the deck, collect water. Because the system is level, water moves by piling up in the channels until it reaches the ends where it drains into the gutters. Having two gutters provides good air flow, and since there's no water actually in contact with the deck, the framing dries, according to the company.

American Dry Deck is installed by attaching 2-by sleepers to the bottoms of the joists and then attaching stringers perpendicular to the sleepers. The arched ceiling panels are flexed and fitted into the sleepers; to finish up, the bottom locking cap is tapped into place with a dead-blow hammer.

Zip-Up UnderDeck

The Zip-Up system (www.zipupdeck.com) is a pitched, paintable PVC product that creates a flat, water-diverting surface under the joists (**Figure 70**). The ceiling hangs on furring-strip spacers installed under the joists at a 1/8-inch-per-foot slope. Zip-Up rails are screwed in place perpendicular to the sleepers.

The main structural element of the system is the rails. The only other parts are wall trim, seam trim, and the panels themselves. The whole thing is held together with screws and washers snugged just so to prevent deforming the PVC rails.

To lay it out, you begin by centering the field such that the left- and right-end pieces will be ripped to the same width, much like you would with a tile

Figure 69. The only drainage system to be installed level, American Dry Deck panels can be oriented in any direction.

Figure 70. Zip-Up UnderDeck uses paintable vinyl panels for the drainage plane and the finished ceiling.

Figure 71. DrySpace's V-shaped vinyl panels hang from ledgers that are fastened and taped to the sides of the joists.

Figure 72. UnderDeck's vinyl panels arch between the joists and drain to troughs that run the length of the joists into a gutter.

floor or a suspended ceiling. It requires a little line snapping. The company doesn't recommend installing its product in temperatures lower than 50 degrees. The panels are available in 8-, 12-, and 16-foot lengths and in white and black (with beige coming soon).

Between-Joist Systems

Between-joist systems use the edges of the deck joists themselves as a fastening point for the system's hardware. The hardware then guides the water into a V-panel (DrySpace) or into a below-joist gutter (UnderDeck). As with ceiling systems, the spaces between the joists are exposed to the elements, which your electrician needs to keep in mind.

TimberTech DrySpace

The anchor point to the deck frame for DrySpace's extruded vinyl under-deck system (www.timbertech.com) is a series of brackets (**Figure 71**). Ledger Brackets fasten to the ledger, and U-shaped Combo Brackets wrap the bottom of the joists. Both brackets are fastened like vinyl siding, with nails or screws driven loosely through slots in a nailing flange to allow the vinyl to expand and contract during temperature changes. The tops of the brackets are sealed to the framing with a butyl peel-and-stick tape. A V-shaped channel hangs from the brackets to collect and drain the water into a gutter.

For oddball joist spacing, you can combine the 12-inch and 14-inch DrySpace panels with 2-by filler strips to make the system work. TimberTech notes that this variation may leak a little.

The end joists have an odd trim detail. TimberTech says to cut the outside flange from a Combo Bracket with a utility knife. On high-end decks, you may want to add a trim board above that for a more finished appearance.

UnderDeck

Like DrySpace, UnderDeck (www.underdeck.com) uses the sides of the joists as the anchor point for brackets, which are called joist rails (**Figure 72**). But rather than draining to a trough in the joist bays, water drains into subjoist troughs from vinyl panels arched into place between the joists. These troughs clip to the joist rails, capping the bottoms of the joists and draining into a gutter at the front of the deck.

A water diverter, essentially a piece of vinyl flashing, is installed at the ledger in each joist bay prior to closing the system in with the arched panels. You can tuck the diverters (they look like little diving boards) up under the existing flashing, fastening and caulking them in place. The diverters drain into the troughs.

UnderDeck provides some helpful installation details. For oddball joist spacing, the company advises you to rip a panel to fit such that you can maintain a consistent arch on all the panels. And if the pieces oil-can or ripple due to joists running off layout, the company suggests running a pair of snips down the edge to trim the piece, like scribing a cabinet filler but much less exacting.

A sheet-metal brake would be a handy tool to have when installing this system, for two reasons. First, UnderDeck describes bending one of its diverter pieces to create an end cap, a nice detail that can easily be made with a brake. And while you can cut pieces to length and width with a utility knife, who has that kind of time or forearm strength? Snapping the vinyl panels into the jaws of a brake would speed things up.

Mark Clement is a remodeler and deck builder in Ambler, Pa.

Deck Framing Q&A

Rot in Pressure-Treated Wood

Q. *I've seen pressure-treated lumber rot only a couple of years after decks were built. How did this happen? I thought treatment was supposed to prevent that.*

A. *Andy Engel, editor of* Professional Deck Builder, *responds:* Several factors affect the life span of treated wood in outdoor use. To begin with, what's the preservative retention level of the lumber? That's expressed in pounds per cubic foot (pcf). Depending on the type of preservative (e.g., ACQ, CA-B, MCQ, CCA), a retention level of .20 pcf might earn a rating for aboveground use, whereas .40 pcf might earn approval for ground-contact use.

A certification tag on the end of the lumber will specify its approved use. In many areas of the country, particularly in the north, dimensional lumber treated for ground contact — other than post stock such as 4x4s and 6x6s — is difficult to find.

A disturbing article, "Brown-Rot Decay of ACQ and CA-B Treated Lumber," appeared in the June 2007 issue of *Forest Products Journal*. The authors describe the results of accelerated decay testing on CA-B- and ACQ-treated lumber, in which wood samples were inoculated with four common species of brown rot fungus and subjected to ideal heat and moisture conditions (see table below).

Both ground-contact- and aboveground-rated CA-B-treated southern yellow pine samples were tested. The aboveground samples performed only marginally better than the untreated control sample. The

ground-contact-rated sample fared better, but still lost about a third of its mass to two fungi and nearly half its mass to another.

The ACQ-treated samples included SYP treated for aboveground use, and Douglas fir treated for ground contact. Both generally fared better than the CA-B-treated samples, but the ground-contact-rated Douglas fir exhibited the best overall rot resistance.

According to the study's chief author, Barry Goodell, professor of biological science and wood science and technology at the University of Maine, Orono, "The decay testing represents many years of exposure in severe climates that would be conducive to decay." Also, the experiment was intended to test the durability of the samples under more severe conditions than the aboveground-rated samples were treated to endure. Nonetheless, given that many of the treated samples decayed, it would seem that there is reason to question the effectiveness of these preservatives.

Here's the final rub: Ground-contact conditions typically dictate that a relatively high constant moisture level is present in the wood, while also moderating temperature extremes that would discourage decay. It is entirely possible to create similar conditions above grade — between 2x10s sandwiched together as a beam, for example, or anywhere dirt and moisture have collected. And, it's rare for preservatives to fully penetrate thick lumber — if you cut through the middle of larger pieces of lumber, you will likely expose untreated wood.

All of which is a long-winded way for me to say,

Mass Loss (%)				
	Gloeophyllum trabeum	*Postia placenta*	*Serpula lacrymans*	*Meruliporia incrassata*
SYP untreated controls	58.6 (5.2)[a]	55.7 (8.7)	54.7 (6.6)	60.2 (2.1)
SYP CA-B (above ground)	29.5 (15.7)	47.3 (19.7)	56.0 (6.1)	53.1 (7.1)
SYP CA-B (ground contact)	3.9 (3.2)	33.0 (23.2)	47.4 (15.9)	34.0 (6.1)
SYP ACQ (above ground)	6.3 (4.9)	19.2 (15.3)	36.2 (14.7)	55.0 (3.2)
Douglas-fir ACQ (ground contact)	0.7 (0.9)	4.5 (3.0)	6.4 (9.3)	29.5 (16.5)

FOREST PRODUCTS JOURNAL

[a]Values in parentheses = standard deviations.

The figures above show the average percentage of mass lost to rot in treated-wood samples that were inoculated with four common decay fungi and kept in ideal conditions for 16 weeks. (Standard deviations closer to zero represent more consistent results in a group of samples.)

"Yup, no surprise that you're occasionally finding rotted treated wood." While the current crop of preservatives may be more environmentally acceptable than the old CCA, Dr. Goodell suggests "… they may not be as efficacious in all circumstances."

Best practice suggests that whenever you assemble two pieces of wood in a deck in ways that can trap moisture — built-up beams, post-to-beam connections, and even decking joined to joists — some sort of moisture-resistant membrane or flashing should be used to keep out water in the first place. And for cut ends of treated wood, of course, always dip or brush-flood the cut surface with a preservative solution.

Insects and Pressure-Treated Lumber

Q. *I've been noticing that cutting into 6x6 posts of treated southern yellow pine seems to reveal untreated wood in their centers. Can I still depend on this lumber, particularly regarding resistance to termites and carpenter ants?*

A. *Paul R. Fisette, wood technologist and professor of building materials and wood technology program at the University of Massachusetts in Amherst, responds:* Preservative treatments work by poisoning the destructive organism's food supply, which is wood. Using ACQ-treated wood can be an effective way to control termites and rot fungi infestation, but it is not as effective with carpenter ants. Unlike termites, carpenter ants do not eat and digest wood. Ants tunnel through and live in wood. Some borate treatments have demonstrated limited success with ants, but borate-treated wood is generally not used outdoors because the water-soluble borates leach out.

To be effective, the chemical treatment must fully penetrate the wood. Not all woods are receptive to chemical penetration. Southern yellow pine is a very receptive species, which is why it's commonly used for treated lumber east of the Rockies.

It is relatively easy to achieve full chemical penetration in wood up to 2 inches in thickness. As the cross section gets larger, however, it is more difficult for the chemical to penetrate the innermost part of the wood. Even with pressure treating, a 4x4 will not be fully penetrated. Another issue is the sapwood portion of the wood is more receptive to penetration than heartwood, and cores of larger timbers often contain heartwood.

Add all this up and you will find that the inner core of a 6x6 timber is typically partially or completely untreated. Once the timber checks or cracks, there is an unprotected pathway for water penetration. Insects and fungi can then attack the unprotected core. In very sensitive applications, you might consider using naturally decay-resistant wood or glue-laminate treated lumber to fabricate 6x6 posts.

Preventing Hanger Corrosion

Q. *I'm rebuilding a deck using ACQ framing. To combat any premature corrosion, I isolated all metal framing connectors from the treated framing with pieces of #15 felt. Each joist hanger needed two pieces, one applied to the ledger board or rim joist, and one strip a few inches wide wrapped around the three sides of the joist resting in the hanger. Is this necessary to avoid corrosion?*

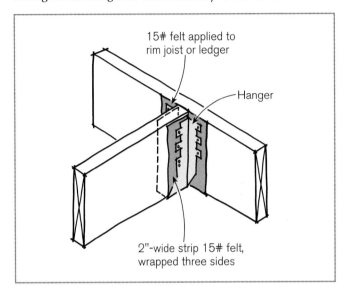

15# felt applied to rim joist or ledger

Hanger

2"-wide strip 15# felt, wrapped three sides

A. *The JLC editors respond:* Using a barrier such as heavy felt paper or Vycor Deck Protector to separate the connectors from the wood is a good idea, particularly with standard galvanized hardware. According to metal connector manufacturers, stainless-steel hardware and fasteners (Types 304 and 316) offer the best protection with ACQ and Copper Azole lumber. G185 galvanized hardware (1.85 ounces of zinc per square foot), such as Simpson's Z-MAX or USP's Triple Zinc is also recommended. At a minimum, use hot-dipped galvanized hardware and fasteners, but don't mix stainless fasteners with galvanized hardware (or vice versa).

Shrinking Joists

Q. *We have a problem with ACQ-treated southern pine joists shrinking unequally — sometimes with differences as great as 1/2 inch. The narrower joists then create a swale by pulling down the composite decking. We crown the joists before installation and check them to be sure they're in one plane before decking. Do you have any suggestions? What about steel joists?*

A. *Andy Engel, editor of* Professional Deck Builder, *responds:* In the 25 years that I've used southern pine joists, this problem has occurred more than once. Southern pine is strong and takes preservative treatment well, but in my experience its stability is hard to predict. I have several suggestions that might help.

First, movement in lumber is aggravated by unequal drying. If you close off the airflow below a deck, you can create a situation where the bottoms of the joists will stay wet while their tops bake in the sun. Try to build decks that allow air to circulate to encourage even drying.

In most cases, lumber will take its permanent shape upon its initial drying. So a simple solution would be to seek out joists that are dried after treatment, and stored under cover. You can spot these by the letters "KDAT" (Kiln Dried After Treatment) or "ADAT" (Air Dried After Treatment).

Dry lumber may be hard to find locally, and you may have to pester lumberyards to order it. You'll still find different widths in the same stack, but at least you can cull the oddballs while building the deck, and you'll have some assurance that the joists' relative sizes will be consistent.

Along the same lines, if you build a large volume of decks, you might find it worthwhile to buy joist material in bulk, and stack it somewhere it can dry for six months or longer. Don't stack it in direct sun, or the exposed wood will dry more quickly than the protected material, which will cause the exposed wood to warp. And don't expect any drying to happen outside in northern climates during the winter. You'd have to restack the lumber with stickers between the layers and with space between the edges of the lumber to allow for airflow.

Another strategy is to use shallower joists; a 2x8, for example, will shrink less than a 2x12, reducing the depth of any potential swale. You would have to decrease the joist spans, of course, by adding beams as needed.

Finally, yes, steel joists are an option. At least one company (Xccent, www.xccentdecking.com) makes steel joists for decks.

Stiffening a Bouncy Deck

Q. *I'm laying new decking on an old frame that is in good structural condition. The owners asked if I could do something to alleviate some of the bounciness in the deck. I checked the joist sizing and even though it meets the building code, there is a bit of deflection — any ideas?*

A. *Mike Guertin, a builder and remodeler in East Greenwich, R.I., responds:* I run into this all the time. Though the joists on an old deck meet the span requirements of the building code, the natural deflection can be unsettling, especially when groups gather on the deck. I use a few strategies to "stiffen up" a deck, depending on the circumstances and design.

Add a beam. My first choice is to add a beam at the center of the joist span to pick up the bounce. This works great for decks close to the ground without usable space beneath them that a beam and posts would interfere with.

Since the extra beam is not necessary to meet building code span requirements for the deck, I usually don't excavate to full frost depth for the footings. I just dig to suitable subsoil (usually 18 inches in my area) and place precast footings to support the posts. If there is a chance that the deck will be enclosed as living space or a three-season room, then size the footings and dig them to frost depth for the extra loads.

Add sister joists. Since you're removing the old deck boards anyway, another simple solution to take out the bounce is to add extra joists. You can sister every joist with a mate — but that may be overkill. I've often had good results just sistering every third or fourth joist to reduce the spring.

If the deck is high enough off the ground, try slipping a few sister joists into just one section of the deck to determine the optimal sister frequency before removing the old decking; then have your customers check the new feel of the test area. Add more sister joists until the customers are happy with the results. This is a great solution when there is usable space beneath the deck that you don't want to encumber with a beam or posts.

Solid blocking — under the right conditions. Solid-wood joist blocking will sometimes help reduce bounce, but the joists and the blocks need to be dry and the blocks must fit very tight. I purposely cut blocks a whisker too long and sledgehammer them into place. Nail them in a straight line, not staggered. You can add one, two, or three rows of blocking to help stiffen the floor.

I don't recommend this solution for areas with wide annual humidity swings. Even if you install blocking when everything is dry and tight, seasonal joist swelling can push blocking away and leave small gaps when the joists dry out again.

Chapter 6:
Decking Materials
& Installation

Choosing Wood Decking

by Mark Clement

A walk through any lumberyard or big-box store sends your head spinning to look at the seemingly endless material choices for building decks and guardrails. There's no shortage of wood — the tried and true treated southern pine and hem-fir, cedar, and a variety of tropical hardwood — as well as the veritable ocean of new composite and PVC products introduced to meet our customers' evolving preferences (see **Table 1**).

The decking market is expected to grow by about 20 percent annually to about 3.6-billion-lineal-feet of decking by 2011, according to Cleveland–based industrial-market research firm The Freedonia Group. That's enough decking to wrap around the Earth almost 27½ times.

As recently as 1992, wood made up about 98 percent of the decking market. While its domination has slipped a bit with the development of synthetic and composite alternatives, there's still a huge demand for tree-based material. If you think that "wood" means pressure-treated decking for the customers who'd rather save a few bucks, you're not entirely correct. Tropical hardwood is the fastest growing segment in the wood category, according to The Freedonia Group. Deck professionals we spoke with from California to Texas to New York support the numbers:

"Eighty percent of my decks are ipe, the Brazilian hardwood," says Al Terry of New York Decks in New York, N.Y.

"We're doing about a 75/25 split with natural wood over composites," notes Stephen Dillinger of Austex Fence & Deck in Austin, Texas. "Cedar is probably the most requested."

"Eighty to 90 percent of the decks that I build are ipe. Customers like the look," says Bill Bolton of DeckCreations in Santa Barbara, Calif. "They like that it's as low-maintenance as any of the composites. Many times they will call requesting a composite, but once they see and hear about ipe they usually go for it."

Ipe has earned its status as the bulldog of the wood decking world, withstanding serious wear and tear on the Atlantic City Boardwalk and on Treasure Island in Las Vegas. A dense hardwood, it is naturally resistant to rot and decay. In fact, it's so dense that it cuts slowly and deck builders must predrill for nails and screws, but many customers are willing to pay the upcharge for both the material and the labor to install it. There are hardwoods other than ipe as well, with similar performance and in some cases a lower price. Advantage Trim & Lumber Co. (www.advantagelumber.com) offers Tigerwood, for example, long familiar to woodworkers as goncalo alves (see "Alternative to Ipe," page 164).

Other tropical hardwoods offered by Advantage include the golden-colored garapa (**Figure 1**) and cumaru, also known as Brazilian teak. Other tropical hardwoods marketed for decking include cambara, which is less dense and lighter in color than ipe, and red meranti, which is related to lauan or Philippine

ADVANTAGE TRIM & LUMBER

Figure 1. Garapa, also know as Brazilian ash, is one of several lower-cost alternatives to ipe. The light yellow hardwood is naturally resistant to decay and insects and carries a 25-year warranty with no preservatives.

Table 1. Decking Options

Decking materials	Pros	Cons	Recommendations
Pressure-treated yellow pine	Inexpensive, strong, durable. Readily available in eastern states. Low toxicity preservatives.	Prone to check, crack, and splinter. Very corrosive to metal fasteners.	Economical solution for typical projects. Choose premium-grade, radius-edge decking (RED) for best performance. Use factory-sealed materials or seal soon after installation to prevent checking and cracking.
Pressure-treated hem-fir	Strong, durable. Readily available in western states. Low toxicity preservatives.	Cuts and drilled holes need treatment. Very corrosive to metal fasteners.	Economical solution for typical projects. Choose a visual grade intended for decking use. Treat all field cuts and drilled holes with copper-naphthenate solution. Treat wear surface with a water-repellent preservative.
Pressure-treated Douglas fir	Very strong, durable. Available in western states. Low toxicity preservatives.	Cuts and drilled holes need treatment. Very corrosive to metal fasteners.	For applications where high strength is required. Choose a visual grade intended for decking use. Treat all field cuts and drilled holes with copper-naphthenate solution. Treat wear surface with a water-repellent preservative.
Redwood	Heartwood is naturally decay-resistant. Attractive and easy to work with.	Splinters easily. Soft wear surface. Sapwood vulnerable to decay.	For high-end projects requiring natural materials. Use an all-heart grade, if available, which is increasingly difficult to locate away from the West Coast. Treat after installation with water-repellent preservative.
Cedar	Heartwood is naturally decay-resistant. Attractive, readily available.	Sapwood vulnerable to decay. Soft wear surface (western cedar).	For high-end projects requiring natural materials. Use an all-heart grade of western red, Port Orford, northern white, or Atlantic white cedar. Treat after installation with a water-repellent preservative.
Tropical hardwoods	Naturally decay-resistant. Hard, durable, and attractive. Tight grain resists water intrusion.	Availability varies. Environmental concerns. Must be predrilled.	High-end projects requiring natural materials. Ipe must be predrilled and should be treated upon installation with a UV-blocking sealer. For best performance, all tropical hardwoods should be treated periodically with a water-repellent preservative or penetrating oil finish. Contact supplier for specific recommendations.
Wood-plastic composites	Very durable, low-maintenance. Contains 50–100% post-consumer wood products and plastics. Looks and feels similar to wood.	Spans limited to 16 inches on some products.. Somewhat bouncy feel. Standard nails and screws leave pucker when set. Oil and grease can stain. Mildew potential. Surface gets hot under summer sun.	For any moderate budget project requiring low maintenance. Use as an alternative to treated lumber. Do not exceed recommended span for material.
Vinyl and other plastics	Durable and maintenance-free. Hidden fasteners. Systems designed for easy installation and may include integral railing.	Excessive thermal expansion. Vinyl may fade or crack over time. Few products effectively mimic wood.	Good for DIY projects where look of wood not required. Look for materials with skid-resistant surfaces and high-quality, UV-resistant plastics and finishes. Follow manufacturer's instructions.

mahogany (see "Tropical Hardwoods: Know What You're Buying"). Cost and availability of hardwood decking products vary depending on local distribution.

As for maintenance, premium tropical hardwoods such as ipe can be left unfinished, but weathering will occur along with some minor checking. For installations where a finished wood surface is desired, periodic treatment with a UV-blocking water repellent or penetrating oil finish is required. Meranti offers only moderate decay resistance and must be treated periodically with a water-repellent preservative, similar to decay-resistant softwoods such as cedar or redwood (see "Wood Decking Durability," page 166).

Environmental Concerns

Because ipe is a tropical hardwood, some question whether it and other tropical species can be considered "green" materials. "We are one of the leading ipe importers in North America," says Dan Ivancic of Advantage Trim & Lumber. "The company's owner makes frequent trips to Brazil to ensure responsible harvesting. That way we can maintain the rainforest and maintain a responsible supply of ipe and other fine hardwoods." This seems rational: One way to preserve forests is to through sustainable logging and other ways to give local people an economic incentive to preserve the forests. I've heard the same argument presented by such diverse sources as lumber

Figure 2. TimberSil is an innovative version of southern yellow pine that has been infused with microscopic layers of amorphous glass throughout the wood that protect against insects, decay, and fire. The specially treated wood is also nontoxic, noncorrosive, and harder and stronger than standard treated southern pine, according to manufacturer Timber Treatment Technologies.

Alternative to Ipe

by Scott Gibson

Ipe is a durable and attractive upgrade from the softwoods traditionally used for outdoor decking, but its growing popularity is affecting both price and availability. One good alternative is another highly durable Brazilian hardwood, long known to woodworkers as *Goncalo alves*.

Marketed as Tigerwood (www.tigerwooddecking.com), the decking is golden brown to reddish brown in color with black and brown stripes. According to the company, it's resistant to rot and insects, has a Class A fire rating, and doesn't splinter or crack. Tigerwood has a lifespan of more than 25 years, without the use of chemical preservatives.

The decking comes in two widths, 1x4 and 1x6, and can be ordered with a tongue-and-groove profile for porch floors or pre-grooved for use with hidden fasteners.

Tigerwood currently sells for about 20 percent less than ipe. The 1-by material has a net thickness of 3/4 inch and can span 16-inch on-center joists. Decking boards come in lengths up to 16 feet and larger dimen-

Goncalo alves *decking, also called "tigerwood," offers stripes for contrast.*

sional lumber may be available in the future. Although the wood is not certified by the Forest Stewardship Council, the supplier says it is "responsibly harvested" and not taken in clear cuts.

Scott Gibson is a writer in East Waterboro, Maine, who specializes in construction topics.

Tropical Hardwoods: Know What You're Buying

by *JLC* staff

Although pressure-treated softwoods are still the most commonly used decking materials, naturally rot-resistant tropical hardwoods are making headway as a substitute.

Name game. The variety of tropical hardwood species is bewildering. Mixed hardwoods that used to be grouped together under the single name "Philippine mahogany" are now often sold separately and marketed under less familiar names like meranti, cambara, batu, and pelawan. Subspecies add to the confusion: For example, the increasingly common dark red meranti is also available in the less common light red, white, and yellow varieties, which may have significantly different characteristics. Trade names add another layer of complexity. For instance, the wood widely marketed today as ipe (see photo), is also sold under the trade names pau lope, ironwood, and Brazilian walnut. In addition to its scientific name, *Tabebuia* spp., ipe is also known by more than 40 other names, including greenheart, amapa, and lapacho.

If you plan to use tropical hardwood decking, the first step is to find out what you're dealing with. One good source of information is a series of CD-ROMs called The Wood Explorer. Available in three versions (Pro, Standard, and Hobbyist), the Pro version covers more than 1,600 wood species, including common and scientific names, geographic origin, environmental status, physical properties, and working characteristics. Much of the information is also available free at the company's website: www.thewoodexplorer.com.

Installation and maintenance costs. The characteristics that make tropical hardwoods desirable as a decking material are their rich color, varied grain, high density, and natural decay resistance. These same characteristics also make them an expensive option. First, initial cost for the material is more than double or triple the cost of pressure-treated. And like any hardwood, these deck boards require more labor to install because they can't be nailed by hand without predrilling. On top of that, clients investing in premium hardwood often expect their exterior deck to be treated more like a piece of furniture. This typically means you'll have to spend additional time concealing fasteners and detailing posts and railings. And if the client is intent on preserving the natural beauty of the hardwood, plan to treat the wood right away with a water repellent and advise them to recoat the surface at least annually. Otherwise, it will weather to a gray, fuzzy surface much like other unfinished wood decking.

Environmental issues. While the hardwood alternatives eliminate the health and disposal concerns that surround pressure-treated lumber, the use of imported lumber has some environmentalists worried about depletion of the world's tropical forests. A number of organizations track the logging and marketing of tropical hardwoods and certify that they were harvested using sustainable logging practices. For more information, contact the Forest Stewardship Council (www.fscus.org) or the Smartwood program (www.smartwood.org).

PAU LOPE DECKING COURTESY OF GENERAL WOODCRAFT

Ipe, also known as pau lope, Brazilian walnut, and by various other names, is an extremely hard, dense wood with natural resistance to insects and decay. But installation is expensive and a water-repellent finish is required to maintain its good looks.

Wood Decking Durability

by Paul Fisette

Customers are very interested in the durability of wood decking. When pondering which type of wood lasts longer, there are several issues to consider. "Lasts longer" can mean both durable to foot traffic and durable to the weather, and finding the best balance is not a clear-cut decision. When selecting a deck wood, you also need to consider cost, availability, and environmental concerns. Here's a look at the choices:

Treated wood. The most popular decking is treated 5/4x6 southern yellow pine. Treated lumber is still the most affordable and readily available option and it won't rot for decades. Also, southern pine is a dense species, so it doesn't abrade under heavy foot traffic. A yearly maintenance coat of water repellent, such as Flood's CWF (www.flood.com), is required to reduce cupping and keep a bright surface. Some decking materials come pretreated with a water-repellent compound, but you'll still need to reapply a water repellent after a couple years.

Untreated woods. The most common untreated options include western red cedar, redwood, Port Orford cedar, and a South American wood called ipe.

Cedar (both western red and Port Orford) and redwood average a third to a half more expensive than treated wood decking, and are naturally decay resistant. Redwood and cedar look beautiful and weather well, but they are soft and do not wear as well as southern yellow pine in high traffic areas. Also, don't confuse decay resistance with maintenance-free. These woods must be treated with a water repellent every year to assure long-lasting dimensional stability and a good-looking deck. If you wish to use cedar or redwood, there are a number of sources of recycled and reclaimed wood of these species that I would encourage the use of whenever practical.

Other cedar species you might encounter include Alaskan, northern, and Atlantic, which are all similar in durability to Port Orford. Keep in mind that only the heartwood is resistant to decay. One difference with Alaskan yellow is that the heartwood color – yellow – makes it easier to distinguish the heartwood from the sapwood, which is pale yellow. With the other cedars, there is not a great difference between sapwood and heartwood colors, so it can be more difficult to tell if you have in fact purchased durable heartwood or nondurable sapwood.

Ipe is a South American wood that has been used to build docks. It is heavy and hard, and also very resistant to rot. Unfortunately, it is also expensive – about twice as much as southern pine. As an environmental concern, it's also worth asking for certification that the wood you buy is harvested from sustainably managed forests.

Heartwood only. When you select any untreated species, use only the heartwood. The tight-grained, slow-growth heartwood is rot-resistant. But the faster-growing, light-colored sapwood will rot! These days, all-heart redwood is hard to get, if not impossible. In my search recently, lumber dealers have told me that "select heart" is unavailable. If the grade you purchase has some sapwood mixed in, buy enough so you can cull the pieces that contain sapwood and use only the dark-colored heartwood.

Paul Fisette is a wood technologist and professor of building materials at the University of Massachusetts.

associations and the former leader of Greenpeace.

The Western Red Cedar Lumber Association (WRCLA) reports that interest in western red cedar has increased proportionally to the increased interest in green products. Like other woods, it is a renewable resource. Red cedar has a neutral carbon footprint, including the fossil fuels used to manufacture and transport the wood, according to the WRCLA.

Another type of wood, *Cunninghamia lanceolata*, commonly known as China fir, has found its way into at least big-box distribution. It's harvested in China and has an appearance and other characteristics that are similar to — but not the same as — western red cedar. The heartwood is classified as highly rot resistant, but as with all woods, the sapwood rots quickly. Anecdotal reports suggest that some of the China fir available in the U.S. consists primarily of sapwood. So it pays to be certain about what you buy.

The Southern Pine Council says that southern pine has always been a green building product, and that if you are choosing a product based on its track record, you can't beat 100 years of dependable use. The manufacture of plastic and composite decking requires up to eight times the energy needed to produce the same amount of pressure-treated southern pine lumber, according to the SPC. As for its environmental impact, the other side of the story is the preservatives used with southern pine and hem-fir. These have come a long way since 2004, when the

Figure 3. Using specially designed kilns, Bay Tree Technologies modifies wood into a state where it protects itself. Chemical changes the wood undergoes make it inedible to insects, fungus, and mold. The end product, PureWood, is chemical- and metal-free. It's also noncorrosive and nontoxic.

of fibers that comprise wood with layers of amorphous glass that are only a few molecules thick" says TimberSil's inventor Karen Slimak, an environmental toxicologist and CEO of TimberSil Products. The glass forms a barrier, making the wood fibers no longer available as a food source for bugs, fungi, and other microbial agents, according to the manufacturer. It also looks, feels, machines, and finishes like wood, is non-corrosive to fasteners, and carries a 40-year warranty (**Figure 2**, page 164).

An option under development is a preservative made from natural compounds found in trees. The Department of Forest Products at Mississippi State University claims it has created a preservative made from coniferous tree resin and an organic biocide that protects against fungi and termites.

Another approach, using Scandinavian-based technology, is marketed in the U.S. by Bay Tree Technologies under the brand name PureWood (**Figure 3**). Using specially designed kilns, Bay Tree Technologies heats the wood to high temperatures under controlled conditions that cause chemical changes in the wood sugars. The sugars are converted into a substance that resists insects and decay. The end product, shipped with a factory-applied sealant is chemical- and metal-free, noncorrosive and non-toxic, but retains the natural properties and beauty of the wood, according to the manufacturer (www. purewoodproducts.com).

Mark Clement is a remodeler and deck builder in Ambler, Pa.

use of arsenic-based preservatives for residential purposes was discontinued (see "Treated Wood: New Preservatives, New Fasteners," page 110).

While preservatives that protect natural wood from decay and termite abuse might not be the best medicine for a healthy planet, non-toxic alternatives are coming on line. One that's available now is TimberSil (www.timbersilwood.com), an innovative wood product that uses a proprietary process to fuse glassy layers into the cellular structure of wood. The wood is first infused with a water-based formula containing the relatively benign chemical sodium silicate. When the wood is then heated, "we surround the millions

Alternative Decking Options

by Scott Gibson

Dozens of manufacturers together churn out millions of board feet of wood-plastic composite decking a year. In addition, a growing number make all-plastic decking — and for those looking for maximum durability, there's powder-coated aluminum (see "An Aluminum Alternative," page 169).

With so many options, there's bound to be some trial and error when selecting and learning to work with a new material. One source of help is decking manufacturers, many of which provide detailed installation instructions on their Web sites (**Figure 4**, next page). A basic understanding of the material composition and characteristics can also help deck builders choose the right products.

Composite Soup

Wood-plastic composites are made from one of several polymers — polyethylene, polyvinyl chloride, and polypropylene are the three most common — plus finely ground wood flour and a variety of additives that stabilize the plastic and protect it from UV damage (see "Polymer Basics," page 171).

This medley of materials gives composites several advantages over most species of wood: Installed correctly, they're much less likely to check or crack, and there's no evidence that termites will attack it. Also, it doesn't have to be stained or treated with a preservative — that alone is enough to appeal to homeowners weary of trying to keep wood decking looking new.

Wood substitutes cost more but promise less maintenance.

Though having post-consumer plastic as an ingredient makes the decking more attractive from a green-building point of view, an obstacle is that recycled plastic may be a mixture of several types. As a consequence, its properties are less predictable than those of virgin plastics. Moreover, since some long-wearing types of plastics — polypropylene, for instance — are tough to get as a recycled product, manufacturers may be forced to use a blend of virgin and recycled polymers.

While they're all in the plastics family, these polymers have different characteristics. The strongest and stiffest of the three is PVC, according to Stark, followed by polypropylene, high-density polyethylene, and then low-density polyethylene.

All other things being equal, a plank made from PVC or polypropylene will be noticeably stiffer than one produced with low-density polyethylene. Decking made from polypropylene can span up to 24 inches while a polyethylene-based deck board will span only 16 inches.

The plastics weather differently, too. Polypropylene, for example, is more susceptible to weathering and surface oxidation than polyethylene, says Stark. PVC, though also susceptible to weathering, is easier to stabilize than either polypropylene or polyethylene.

The bottom line? The type of plastic used to make

Composite decking isn't bulletproof, however. The wood component can make these boards susceptible to mold, mildew, and under the right conditions, decay. And it still needs regular cleaning. "It's not a no-maintenance product but it's definitely low-maintenance," says Nicole Stark, a research chemical engineer at the Forest Products Laboratory in Madison, Wis.

How a particular brand of composite decking performs depends on a variety of factors, including what it's made of — the type of plastic, the kinds of additives and stabilizers, and the proportion of wood flour to plastic in the mix — and how it's manufactured and installed. However, since each manufacturer has its own proprietary recipe and method of production, it can be difficult to predict how different products will perform in the field over time. Some code jurisdictions may require proof that a product complies with the building code. In many cases, the manufacturer has proof in the form of an evaluation report from the ICC Evaluation Service (ICC-ES), a subsidiary of the International Code Council (see "Is the Decking Code-Approved?" page 173).

Plastic ingredients. As much as three-quarters of all wood-plastic composite decking is made with polyethylene (recycled or virgin), a soft plastic that's used for plastic bags and a variety of other products. A smaller number of manufacturers use polypropylene, which is a much harder plastic, or polyvinyl chloride (PVC).

Some manufacturers use only recycled plastics in their decking, but this is not universally the case.

Figure 4. For the most part, composites can be screwed down just like wood. However, tighter joist spacing may be required, special screws are recommended, and you generally need to consider the material's movement along its length, not its width. Most manufacturers have installation guidelines on their Web sites.

Figure 5.
Because composite decking contains wood, some brands may support mold growth. Depending on the proportion of wood flour to plastic resin and how the decking is manufactured, particles of mold-feeding wood may be exposed on the surface.

KIM KATWIJK

the decking is important, but it's not the whole story.

Wood flour. The amount of finely pulverized "wood flour" added to the composite mix is another important variable. The flour can come from either hardwood or softwood species, although some manufacturers avoid woods high in tannins, such as oak, because of the higher risk of staining. From a structural standpoint, the species of wood used probably doesn't make much difference.

Because wood flour doesn't add any strength — in fact, it makes the plastic a little weaker — the industry calls decking composites "filled plastics." Wood flour does make the material stiffer, however. If that seems counterintuitive, think of steel cable: It's very strong but quite flexible. Or glass: It's very stiff but relatively weak.

Wood flour decreases "creep," the tendency for materials to deflect over time under a load, and lowers the coefficient of expansion, meaning a composite board shrinks and expands less with changes in temperature than an all-plastic one does. Wood flour also gives the product a more woodlike appearance and feel. In some decking, wood flour is the only recycled content, with no use of recycled plastic.

Mold and Mildew

As many deck owners have discovered, wood-plastic composites can support the growth of mold and mildew — just like the wood they're designed to replace. That's part of the trade-off when using wood flour.

Generally speaking, wood needs a minimum of about 20 percent moisture content for attack by mold and fungal decay. "Solid wood absorbs water pretty readily. In wood-plastic composites, depending on how they're manufactured, the surface characteristics, and how much wood is in there, wood particles can themselves absorb moisture," says Stark.

She suggests taking a close look for wood particles at the surface of the composite. The more readily apparent they are, the more likely the board is to absorb water, thus increasing the risk of both mold growth and eventual decay (**Figure 5**).

Lower proportions of wood flour mean most of the particles will be encapsulated by plastic and safe from water. When the percentage of wood flour reaches 50 percent to 60 percent, some particles

An Aluminum Alternative

Manufacturers of most plastic decking and plastic-wood composites go to great lengths to make their products look just like wood. That's not the case with LockDry (FSI Home Products Division, www.lockdry.com), a powder-coated aluminum decking that looks just like, well, aluminum.

Like plastics and wood-plastic composites, LockDry doesn't have to be painted, stained, or waterproofed, and it won't splinter or crack. But unlike conventional deck planks, LockDry's interlocking pieces form a gap-less surface the company guarantees to be waterproof. That attribute makes LokDry an option for decks built over living spaces. Not only does the decking keeps water out but, according to the manufacturer, it's cheaper than installing sleepers and decking over a membrane roof.

The decking is available in four colors — none of them a wood tone — and in lengths up to 40 feet. It costs about $7 per square foot. Because installation is faster than for wood or composite decking, the installed cost is competitive with the rest of the market, according to the company.

LockDry stays cool under foot and can span 30 inches in residential construction (24 inches for commercial applications). It can be installed over wood, steel, or aluminum floor joists. – S.G.

inevitably will touch each other, making water absorption more likely.

Some manufacturers might not disclose the ratio of wood flour to plastic in their decking; in those cases, the best bet may be a close look at the surface of the decking. A large number of prominent wood particles on the surface doesn't mean the decking should be avoided, but it is an indication that the planks will be more likely to absorb water.

How a board is manufactured may also affect water absorption. Planks extruded under higher pressure tend to have a more polymer-rich surface, says Stark, which provides some protection from water. "Moisture really is the key to improved durability," she says. "You have to control moisture in wood-plastic composites. Any way you can improve that, you'll have improved durability, not only with decay and mold but also with weathering and color."

Regular cleaning can reduce the risk of mold. Contaminated surfaces may be brought back to life with a commercial deck cleaner and brightener, and some composites may even benefit from a water sealer and preservative or stain. "People think it's no-maintenance," says Clemens Jellema, a Washington, D.C.-area deck builder, who regularly uses composites. "But I tell them there's no such thing as no maintenance. You still have to clean it."

Fading

The other inherent problem with wood flour is that it fades in sunlight. Ultraviolet radiation attacks the lignin in wood; therefore wood-plastic composites made with a high proportion of wood flour will fade and weather much like solid wood planks. A number of stains specifically formulated for wood-plastic composites are available, and more are under development.

To combat fading, some manufacturers are using a "co-extrusion" process: An inner layer of wood-plastic composite is capped with a layer of plastic that keeps moisture out and reduces the risk of stains. Correct Building Products' CorrectDeck CX line (www.correctdeck.com), which incorporates an anti-microbial agent called Microban in the top layer, is manufactured this way.

According to the manufacturer, the polypropylene cap addresses three chief complaints consumers have about wood-plastic composites: color fade, mold and mildew growth, and the difficulty of removing stains. Adding a higher concentration of UV-blockers and

Keeping It Green

Synthetic decking cannot compete on price with pressure-treated lumber – but it can be appealing to homeowners who want sustainable-building and eco-friendly products. Decking made from recycled materials has kept millions of tons of discarded plastic and waste wood out of municipal landfills, turning low-value refuse into a useful and valuable end product.

However, not all synthetic products are equally green. While some synthetic decking is made from all, or nearly all, recycled material, that's not universally true. Moreover, some plastics are inherently more difficult to recycle at the end of their service life or are more hazardous to produce in the first place.

The Healthy Building Network is one source of information on this potentially perplexing topic. In its *Guide to Plastic Lumber*, it rates the environmental merits of 55 brands of plastic lumber from 44 different manufacturers and ranked them in five broad categories, from "most environmentally preferable" to "not environmentally preferable – avoid." Highest preference was given to products with a minimum of 50 percent post-consumer content and those made solely with high- and low-density polyethylene, an easy-to-recycle plastic.

FOTOLIA

The organization considered both the production and the afterlife of products in its review. It recommended limiting the use of wood-plastic composites, for instance, because the mix of synthetic and biological materials makes them difficult to recycle, and it put products manufactured from a mixture of post-consumer plastics in the same category because they are likely to contain contaminants.

PVC and polystyrene should be avoided altogether, it said, because of chemical hazards associated with their manufacture and disposal. A summary of all the findings and a product-by-product ranking is available on the Healthy Building Web site (www.healthybuilding.net).

– S.G.

Polymer Basics

by Reid Shalvoy

There are four basic polymers used in the composite and plastic decking market: polyethylene, polypropylene, polystyrene and polyvinyl chloride.

Polyethylene. Two types of polyethylene are used in decking. High density polyethylene – or HDPE – is a durable material used for plastic products that need to maintain a molded shape, like milk jugs. Low density polyethylene is the least stiff plastic available in the composite decking industry. LDPE is used to manufacture grocery bags, food wraps and other light, pliable plastic products. LDPE tends to experience more thermal expansion than the other plastics. Being petroleum based, both HDPE and LDPE are flammable.

Polypropylene – or PP – generally has the lowest density of all five plastics mentioned, though it is stiffer than HDPE and LDPE. PP is used for many different purposes, from clothing to automotive parts, due to its high resistance to chemicals and rugged durability. PP is prone to ultraviolet degradation and like PE, is flammable.

Polystyrene – or PS – is even denser than HDPE. It is the stiffest plastic used in the alternative decking market and also has the lowest thermal expansion coefficient. PS is used in a variety of different applications, including foam insulation and CD cases. To be safe for use, PS requires flame retardant additives. When untreated PS is ignited, it combusts rapidly and gives off very severe black smoke.

Polyvinyl chloride – or PVC – is significantly denser than the other plastics mentioned, though it is slightly less stiff than PS. PVC is used in a number of different products, including plumbing, siding, and credit cards. It typically has a slightly higher thermal expansion coefficient than PS. PVC is less flammable than the other plastics mentioned, though it is still dangerous when burned because it releases hydrochloride gas – a potentially deadly compound. PVC can be extruded to form hollow profiles like those used in vinyl windows and some decking products. PVC can also be modified to produce cellular foam PVC, with a density less than half that of regular PVC. After a "foaming extrusion" process that adds tiny bubbles to the foam, a hard waterproof skin forms. Cellular PVC is widely used for exterior trim in products such as Azek Trim, and more recently for decking.

Reid Shalvoy is a freelance writer based in Burlington, Vt.

---

anti-microbial agents to just the cap is more economical than adding them to the entire board. Even so, CX decking costs about 25 percent more than the company's standard line.

All-Plastic Decking

Manufacturers of all-plastic decking are quick to point out the downsides of wood-plastic composites: not only does the wood's porosity allow in water but it also makes the material readily soak up grease, sap, and other staining materials.

One all-plastic product, Bear Board (EPS Plastic Lumber, www.epsplasticlumber.com), is made from high-density polyethylene gathered mostly from post-industrial recycling. The all-plastic formulation 5/4 planks are stiff enough for 16-inch on-center framing in residential applications (12 inches on-center in commercial work), with none of the water or stain absorption problems of wood-plastic composites and virtually no color fade, according to the manufacturer.

All-plastic decking has its own downsides, however: Some has a shiny look that some customers dislike, and because there are no wood particles in the formulation, thermal expansion is a more pronounced problem. EPS's manufacturing process gives Bear Board more of a matte finish than some all-plastic planks, but little can be done to remedy plastic's thermal properties.

A 10-foot board can expand and contract more than ½ inch in a 100-degree temperature swing. That means even with careful installation it's inevitable that there will be some gaps between plank ends, at least at certain times of the year. Because high-density polyethylene moves around so much, Bear Board recommends using hidden fasteners and boards with grooved edges, rather than face-nailing or screwing, for lengths over 12 feet. Also, an intermediate cross-piece can be introduced on long runs to keep deck boards shorter (**Figure 6**, next page).

There are a number of other all-plastic deck options. Eon decking (CPI Plastics Group, www.eonoutdoor.com) is made from polystyrene. Deck Lok and Brock Deck (Royal Outdoor Produces, www.royaloutdoor.com) and Dream Deck (Thermal Industries; www.thermalindustires.com) are made

BEAR BOARD

Figure 6. One way to deal with the greater expansion and contraction of all-plastic decking is to avoid long lengths. Adding planks perpendicular to the main run not only adds interest, it allows for expansion joints.

Figure 7. TimberTech's XLM (extreme low maintenance) decking is made from cellular PVC. The boards are 40 percent lighter than the company's wood-plastic-composite planks and is available with a color-matched railing system.

from vinyl extrusions (PVC) similar in construction to vinyl window frames. A number of manufacturers have introduced cellular PVC decking, the type of plastic used in Azek's popular exterior trim boards. Cellular PVC decking products include Azek Deck (Azek Building Products, www.azek.com), TimberTech's XLM (www.timbertech.com — **Figure 7**), Sanctuary Decking (Fiber Composites, www.fiberondecking.com — **Figure 8**), and Vekadeck Pro (Veka Innovations, www.vekadeck.com — **Figure 9**, page 174).

Like high-density polyethylene, these plastics are less prone to staining than most wood-plastic composites, but also like polyethylene, they are more prone to thermal expansion. And while some brands have an embossed surface that realistically mimics wood grain, others have an unnatural surface sheen that doesn't look much like the wood it's trying to imitate.

Figure 8. Fiber Composites' Fiberon Sanctuary Decking (left) has no fiber fillers inside its cellular PVC board. The company claims its product eliminates all edge cracking, staining, and water absorption. The boards have an outer layer of PVC and ASA (acrylonitrile styrene acrylate), a material used to protect automobile bumpers and outside mirrors. The company's Tropics decking line (right) is designed to reproduce the look of tropical hardwoods.

PVC carries with it an added environmental burden: its manufacture produces some dangerous by-products, and it releases dangerous toxins when burned. That may not affect its in-service performance, but homeowners with strong eco-sensibilities may prefer to stay away from it, nonetheless (see "Keeping It Green," page 170).

Higher Costs vs. Improved Performance

Wood-plastic composites lag far behind wood in terms of installed square footage but are quickly gaining ground. Between 1997 and 2004, composites grew from 2 percent of the market to 15 percent

Is the Decking Code-Approved?

by Glenn Mathewson

You may be asked by a code official to provide an ICC-ES report for a plastic or composite decking product you are planning to install. An ICC-ES report is issued by the International Code Council Evaluation Service, a not-for-profit subsidiary of the ICC that provides technical evaluations of building products and methods. Reports describe the suitability of a product or method as an alternative to a prescriptive code requirement, or certify compliance with a specific code requirement.

ICC-ES reports are vital for the proper use and installation of many products, and in almost all cases supersede the manufacturer's specifications, requirements, and installation instructions. Unfortunately, I have seen cases where a manufacturer's published information conflicted with their product's ES report, leading the contractor into a code violation.

It is important to note that an ICC-ES report is not specifically required by the building code. The ICC Evaluation Service is merely a testing agency that is often recognized and approved by local building officials. It is up to the manufacturer to choose (and pay for) the lab that evaluates its product or method. Although many manufacturers use ICC-ES because of its national recognition, "evidence of compliance" can be provided by any agency that's approved by the building official, as stated in the 2006 IRC, Section R104.11.1.

While ES reports are important for the proper use and installation of many products – such as fasteners, hangers, decking anchors, manufactured guards and handrails, and pressure-treated lumber – they are especially informative when it comes to the installation of composite decking. Unlike wood, which is subject to an industry-wide grading system, composite decking can be produced with a variety of methods and compositions, and properties can vary widely between products.

Most composite decking is evaluated only for exterior use in residential occupancies, and almost all composite boards are required to span a minimum of three joists and be fastened with two fasteners per support. Other requirements, however, vary considerably. The distance that a deck board can span at angles to the joists, for example, is specific to the manufacturer.

Also, the distance a deck board can span when used as a stair tread will almost always be less than when the same material is used as decking. Stair treads are required by the IRC and IBC to resist not only the minimum uniformly distributed live load, but also a concentrated 300 lb. load on a 4-square-inch area in the middle of the tread span.

This concentrated load almost always requires the support spacing to be reduced. Some composite decking must be supported 8 inches on center when used as a stair tread. Correcting something like this after the fact would be a nightmare, pointing up the benefit to researching the ES report and product limitations before the project begins.

ES reports are free of charge and available to anyone at www.icc-es.org. When searching for an ES report, use specific spelling and keywords. Sometimes the search feature can be tricky, though. If at first the report you seek doesn't come up, try again with different words.

Another great Web site that may help you find an ES-report number for a composite-decking product is the Ten Thousand Lakes ICC-chapter Web site. This local ICC chapter has put together an excellent list of information on composite decking, including ES report numbers for those products that have one. The list is easily accessed by clicking the link "Composite Decking updated" at www.10klakes.org.

Glenn Mathewson is a former deck builder and an ICC-certified Master Code Professional, Combination Inspector for Westminster, Colo.

Figure 9. Vekadeck Pro is Veka Innovations' second-generation cellular PVC deck board. While the company's earlier version had a more characteristic PVC-style glossy finish, Vekadeck Pro has a satin finish and a deeply embossed wood-grain pattern it calls Traction Grip.

CORRECT BUILDING PRODUCTS

Figure 10. Depending on the product, composite decking may install more quickly than other options. Deck builders report that some hidden fastener systems, such as CorrectDeck's, actually speed installation, as well as provide a fastener-free look.

while wood dropped from 96 percent to 79 percent.

During that time, composite decking was on average about twice the price of 5/4 ACQ-treated decking. Because both pressure-treated and composite decking require the same structural framing, however, composite decking typically adds only 15 percent to 20 percent in material cost when compared with a deck made entirely from pressure-treated wood.

Contractors say that labor costs for plastic and composite decking are roughly the same as for wood or a little higher, although some composites with hidden fastening systems go down quickly, reducing labor costs (**Figure 10**). And because of lower maintenance requirements, the payback on composites for a homeowner could come in as little as two to five years.

Scott Gibson is a writer in East Waterboro, Maine, who specializes in construction topics.

Wood-Plastic Composites

by Reid Shalvoy

Manufacturers of composite decking are working hard to sell homeowners and builders on the long-term advantages of their products. Alternative decking products eliminate the expense of annual water sealing or staining. The composites don't check or split like solid lumber and promise to outlast even the most rot-resistant of solid-sawn species.

While the composites have several advantages, they have a few drawbacks, too. For example, many consumers have complained that they have a tendency to mildew, especially when installed in shady areas. Manufacturers respond that any decking product would mildew in those locations. While that may be true, the mildew has been a surprise to some homeowners, who felt they were promised a product that required no maintenance. The recommended solution to mildew is a semi-annual scrubbing with a deck wash that contains sodium hypochlorite and detergent. Keeping the spaces between boards free of debris also seems to help keep mildew at bay. Where composite decking has been left wet and poorly maintained for extended periods, fungal decay has also been reported with some wood-plastic composites (see "Composite Decking Durability," page 178).

Another complaint is that the surface of composite decks gets uncomfortably hot with summertime sun. While some manufacturers promise in their literature that their products are cooler to the touch than their competitors' products, no comparisons are made with solid wood decking.

Some consumers don't like the appearance of the composites they have seen. While that's a matter of opinion, the growing number colors and surface textures increases the likelihood that consumers can find something they like.

The Chemistry

Composite decking is made with wood fiber or another organic fiber combined with a weather-resistant polymer binder. Most composite decking is made with polyethylene (recycled or virgin), commonly used for plastic bags, bottles, and other consumer products. A smaller number of manufacturers use polypropylene, which is a much harder plastic, or polyvinyl chloride (PVC), more commonly known as vinyl (see "Polymer Basics," page 171). Many manufacturers use at least some recycled content in their products, and this is a selling point for some consumers.

While different plastics have different mechanical qualities, a decking product can't be judged solely by the polymer used, since the manufacturer can manipu-

These products promise durability and low maintenance – but they still require periodic cleaning and upkeep for best performance.

late the mechanical properties. But the type of plastic offers clues as to the product's performance. As Dr. Robert Tichy, Research Engineer at Washington State University, explains, "With the appropriate additives, you could make any polymer perform the way you want. It's just a question of cost."

Adding wood fiber to the composite offers several benefits. In addition to being cheaper than plastic, wood tends to outperform plastic in strength, rigidity and flammability tests. Wood experiences less thermal expansion than plastic and usually weighs less. The wood fiber also helps manufacturers more closely approximate the look of traditional wood decking. Of course, the use of organic fiber also makes the material more porous and vulnerable to stains, and introduces a risk of mold and decay problems.

Chemical additives, such as flame retardants and UV stabilizers, can be introduced to any construction plastic to enhance its performance. And with increasing concerns about mold and decay, a number of composite products are now treated with antimicrobial chemicals to protect against mold and insect infestation. Though with each additive, the production cost increases.

Solid Composites

Of all the composites on the market, solid composites like Trex, the original and best-known alternative decking, most closely resemble the size and thickness of solid sawn decking. Solid composites differ from wood decking in several ways. For one thing, they lack the stiffness of their sawn-lumber counterparts, typically requiring joist spacing no greater than 16 inches on-center. Diagonal and commercial applications are usually limited to a 12-inch spacing. The material's flexibility can also be an advantage in

some cases: because some composites can be bent more easily than traditional lumber, curves and round sections are easier to incorporate.

Because composites almost always fade when exposed to sunlight, customers should check weathered samples when choosing colors. Your supplier should have some. Weathering is usually complete in three to six months, depending on exposure (**Figure 11**).

Porch flooring. While most solid composites mimic square-edged deck boards, one exception is a solid tongue-and-groove porch flooring product called

---

Composites and Fire Safety

The fire safety of an exterior building product is an important issue, particularly in areas subject to wild fires, such as Southern California. Nearly all composite decking products have fire testing data available from the manufacturer. The most prevalent of these tests is the Flame Spread Index (ASTM E84).

Flame spread. The Flame Spread Index is on a numerical scale from 0 to 200, 0 being the best possible score. For a product to be eligible for a code listing, its Flame Spread Index must be less than 200. There is a class system, A (I) through C (III), which helps consumers and code officials better understand how well a product performs when exposed to fire. A (I), which is the best possible score, indicates a Flame Spread Index somewhere between 0 and 25, B (II) indicates a Flame Spread Index between 26 and 75 and C (III) indicates a Flame Spread Index of anywhere between 76 and 200.

Heat release rate. Another good measure of flammability in building products is Heat Release Rate, or HRR. HRR is best described as the driving force behind a fire. The higher the Heat Release Rate of a building product, the greater the intensity of fire it will produce if ignited; therefore, a higher HRR means a higher risk to human life. "Without copious amounts of flame retardants, construction plastics have heat release rates much higher than wood." Says Dr. Vytenis Babrauskas, author of the *Ignition Handbook*. "Though it is possible to add enough flame retardants so that this behavior is controlled, the majority of manufacturers do not do that."

Dr. Stephen Quarles, wood performance and durability Cooperative Extension advisor at UC Berkeley, headed up an experiment to see how plastic and WPC decking products perform when exposed to fire. Dr. Quarles designed this experiment to be as realistic as possible, using an 80kW flame and exposing the underside of each product for 3 minutes. Each test

was terminated after one of the following conditions was met:

• Combustion stopped
• Combustion accelerated rapidly
• Deck board collapsed
• 40 minutes elapsed

Of 15 products tested, two wood-plastic composites SmartDeck and WeatherBest (both HDPE-wood composites that are no longer available), Bedford Decking (made from FRP), and the solid redwood plank showed no degradation after 40 minutes. Two all plastic products – Eon (polystyrene) and MAXiTUF (HDPE) – required test termination in under 5 minutes due to uncontrollable combustion acceleration. (For more information visit http://firecenter.berkeley.edu/quarles/deck_kit-SQ.pdf)

California fire codes. As of January 1, 2008, the 2007 California Building Code requires all newly constructed decks to meet a more stringent fire-performance standard, called State Fire Marshal (SFM) standard 12-7A-4. The test is nearly identical to the one used by Steve Quarles, as mentioned above.

"To be code approved," according to Quarles, "the evidence of flaming or glowing must stop and the structure must still be intact after 40 minutes with the burner off. If the product has a Class C flame spread, then the walls must be covered with non-combustible materials like fiber cement or traditional three-coat stucco," Quarles says.

Manufacturers must submit test data to the California State Fire Marshal to be eligible code approval. You can find a list of products that pass 12-7A-4 on the California State Fire Marshal's Web site (http://osfm.fire.ca.gov/strucfireengineer/pdf/bml/wuiproducts.pdf). If a product that you want to use isn't listed, you must present the manufacturer's fire-performance documentation to the authority having jurisdiction for approval. – *R.S.*

Figure 11. It's best to show clients a weathered sample (left), of composite decking. These Fiberon samples demonstrate typical weathering that occurs in three to six months on virtually all composite decking. The unweathered sample is on the far left.

Correct Porch (formerly Tendura), made by Correct Deck (www.correctdeck.com). Other tongue-and-groove composites are hollow and designed with weep holes. Using a polypropylene-hardwood composite similar to the company's decking products, Correct Porch has a 3-inch coverage and the boards are butted like traditional solid-sawn porch flooring (**Figure 12**). The boards are predrilled 16 inches on-center and have a built-in spacer "bead" that creates a small gap between the planks. The spacer was added in response to thermal expansion issues some contractors faced with earlier versions of the product (a thermal expansion chart can be found on the product website). For warranty protection, the flooring must have a roof above, be pitched ¼ inch per

foot away from the house, and be well ventilated underneath to prevent heat buildup. The flooring can be left natural or painted over a primer recommended by the manufacturer.

Hollow Composites

Hollow composites are generally lighter than their solid counterparts. They are also engineered to be stiffer, which allows for wider on-center spacing — typically 20 to 24 inches for residential applications and 16 inches for commercial work. Hollow decking materials can't bend the way the solid composites can, however.

Hollow products typically require wood skirting or proprietary trim pieces to hide the cut ends of boards (**Figure 13**). Although hollow boards generally don't expand and contract as much as solid composites, most manufacturers still recommend end-gapping to allow for thermal expansion. Some hollow products are tongue-and-groove. In general, installers are supposed to gap these by about the thickness of a credit card to allow for expansion. Hollow T&G products

Figure 12. Correct Porch consists of solid T&G planks intended for use on covered porches with sloped floors. A built-in spacer "bead" creates a small gap between planks that allow for drainage and thermal expansion. The composite can be painted or left unfinished.

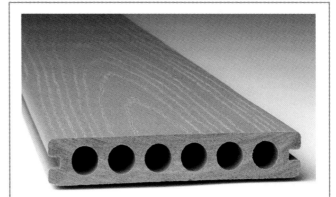

Figure 13. Hollow decking products tend to be lighter and stiffer than solid composites. For example, Cross Timbers' 5/4x6 radius-edge decking can span 24 inches in residential installations. Installers generally use skirting or trim pieces to hide the cut ends.

have weep holes, or fit loosely enough, to allow water to drain through the decking and prevent surface ponding. A sloped decking surface is also recommended or required. To maintain warranty protection, it's important to read and closely follow installation instructions.

The hollow profile also offers a convenient space for running wires and cables for lighting, electrical devices, and speakers. Like their solid counterparts, hollow composites fade as they weather, so customers should look at weathered samples.

The Cellular PVC Alternative

Cellular PVC decking has become the fastest growing segment in the alternative decking market, in response for consumer demand for a product that requires even less maintenance than wood-plastic composites. Industry leaders Azek, TimberTech, Trex, Fiberon, and Vecadeck have all recently added cellular PVC decking to their product lines. Touting its low-maintenance appeal, TimberTech named their product XLM for "extreme low maintenance" (**Figure 14**).

Cellular PVC, essentially the same material used in Azek's popular exterior trim boards and moldings, has a weight and workability similar to pine. As a decking material, cellular PVC has a number of advantages over wood-plastic composites, including better scratch and stain resistance, improved color retention, and greater resistance to weathering. With no wood content and a solid PVC or acrylic capstock, cellular PVC absorbs little moisture and does not support the growth of mold or decay. However, that doesn't mean that a pile of wet leaves left over the winter will not leave mildew stains on this or any other decking material.

While PVC decking typically has a higher rate of thermal expansion than wood-plastic composites, this is controlled by the use of inorganic fillers or additives (or, in the case of Azek Deck, a flax product made from agricultural waste). End-to-end spacing requirements are comparable to composites.

While cellular PVC does not have the strength and rigidity of most composites, it is generally rated for a 16-inch span under normal residential loads. Most

Composite Decking Durability

Mold growth, termite damage and material decomposition can be a concern for any exterior building product with organic fiber, especially in areas with high humidity. Wood-composite decking manufacturers tend to downplay the possibility of biodegradation and UV damage benefitting from consumer assumptions that it's a "plastic" product and can't decompose. However, in light of problems in the field, nearly all manufacturers recommend regular cleanings and others have added special coatings or compounds to help ward off UV-degradation, mold, and decay.

The Consumer Products Safety Commission (CPSC) reported that GeoDeck issued a recall on products sold between April 2002 and July 2005 for premature degradation. The CPSC warned that GeoDeck planks exposed to high temperatures and direct sunlight can prematurely

degrade, compromising structural integrity and posing a fall hazard to consumers (see above). Though 370 reports of degradation were filed, no one was ever reported as being hurt.

GeoDeck was sold to LDI in 2005 by its original owner, Kadant Composites. All affected boards were manufactured before LDI took over GeoDeck production, so they claim no responsibility. At first, Kadant Composites continued to honor warranty claims for this issue but has since gone out of business.

More recently, Louisiana-Pacific Corporation released a product advisory regarding WeatherBest, Veranda, and ABTCo decking and railing products. In the advisory, Louisiana-Pacific indicated that WeatherBest decking and railing products sold at building products dealers nation-

 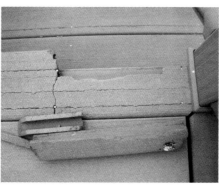

Exposure to high temperatures and direct sunlight caused early versions of GeoDeck composite decking to prematurely degrade (far left) and, in some cases, fail structurally (left), according to the Consumer Products Safety Commission.

products are installed in the same way as composites — either with decking screws from the top or with hidden fasteners in precut grooves.

Despite its mostly plastic content, some cellular PVC decking products have achieved a Class-A flame spread rating and some have been approved by the State of California and San Diego County for new construction use in Wildland-Urban Interface (WUI) fire zones

PVC's greatest advantage — it's lack of wood content — is also its biggest drawback when it comes to aesthetics. Wood-plastic composites still do a better job of realistically simulating wood. Manufacturers are seeking to address PVC's plastic look with a less shiny matte finish, more realistic wood colors and textures, and darker hues. For example, Fiber Composite's Sanctuary line and Timber Tech's XLM planks are both available in colors that mimic ipe and driftwood. Over time, manufacturers believe that the gap between the two will narrow.

With a price point up to 20 percent higher than

continued on page 182

Figure 14. Several leading manufacturers have introduced cellular PVC decking, promising consumers a product that requires even less maintenance than composites — and better resistance to fading, staining, and scratching. TimberTech XLM decking's "desert bronze" color does a respectable job of mimicking ipe.

wide and Veranda and ABTCo decking and railing products sold at Home Depots in the western United States have shown premature deterioration and breakage. Since Louisiana-Pacific is no longer manufacturing WeatherBest, Veranda, or ABTCo decking products, they claim that they will replace all affected decks with any product of equal or lesser value.

Mary Cohn, Louisiana-Pacific Corporate Affairs Manager, says, "It is important to note that in 2007, Louisiana-Pacific sold WeatherBest and Veranda to Fiber Composites. It is our understanding that Fiber Composites changed the (composite) formula and that no WeatherBest or Veranda products manufactured after November 2007 are showing signs of deterioration. This product advisory applies only to products manufactured by Louisiana-Pacific." More information on the product advisory is available at www.deckingnotice.com.

Trex, by a wide margin the overall market leader in alternative decking, was on the receiving end of a class-action lawsuit filed in 2000, which alleged mold-growth and rotting in boards still under warranty. The lawsuit was settled out of court, though Trex never admitted to any wrongdoing. Trex is of course not the only company experiencing mold growth. Many others have had to reformulate their composite mixtures in recent years to mitigate mold-related problems.

ChoiceDek composite decking, made by Advanced

Environmental Recycling Technologies, and distributed by Weyerhaeuser (and sold exclusively through Lowes) is also in the process of settling a class-action lawsuit over excessive mold spotting. The companies have tentatively agreed in a proposed settlement to have the decks professionally cleaned and treated with a mold inhibitor. If the mold returns within 18 months, they will do additional cleanings, replace the decking, or compensate the owners, depending on test results.

Kim Katwijk, president of Deck Builders Inc., has a great deal of experience installing composite decking and has seen product failure on many different levels. Katwijk says, "The worst issue I've ever had with mold growth was on Rhino Deck, After installing Rhino Deck on some projects a few years back, each one bloomed mold so badly that they had to be completely removed and replaced."

Anna Andvik from Rhino Deck explains that, "There were some reoccurring mold issues in products manufactured prior to 2003, but since then we've begun using a mold inhibitor and haven't seen any problems since."

A few different wood-composite manufacturers are now boasting the use of anti-microbial coatings or additives in their decking products. Aside from Rhino Deck, CorrectDeck coats its CX plank with Microban, an industrial anti-microbial additive that reportedly resists mold and other harmful microbes to reduce the possibility of premature degradation. – R.S.

What's New in Composite Decking?

MoistureShield

MoistureShield decking is made from 90 percent recycled material – using a 50/50 blend of wood fiber and polyethylene (low- and high-density) and meets the LEED environmental standard for residential decking. Using a manufactured process that completely encapsulates the

wood fibers, MoistureShield is designed to withstand high moisture conditions including ground contact. The decking is available in nominal 5/4x6 and 2x6 sizes with a ribbed bottom to provide extra rigidity and ventilation over the joists. The decking comes in seven colors, including tropical hardwoods, and has a deeply embossed wood grain finish. A full line of matching trim and railing components is available. Typical installation is with stainless steel trim-head screws, two at each end and one or two at each joist. Grooved edges for hidden fasteners are available by special order.

Manufacturer: Advanced Environmental Recycling Technologies, Inc. (AERT); (www.moistureshield.com)

CorrectDeck CX

CorrectDeck CX, the newest generation decking from Correct Building Products. CorrectDeck is made from 60 percent recovered hardwood fiber and 40 percent polypropylene (a mix of virgin and reclaimed). The polypropylene gives the product greater rigidity than other solid composites, according to the manufacturer. The surface is capped with a solid layer of polypropylene, about $3/16$ inch thick, which fully encases the exposed wood fibers on the top and sides of each board providing added resistance to color fade, staining, and water absorption. The

surface layer includes UV inhibitors an antimicrobial agent that resists mold and mildew growth. CorrectDeck has a wood-grain texture and is available in three wood tones

along with tan, sage, and gray. A matching railing system and trim boards are also available.

Also available is Correct Porch, a solid tongue-and-grove board intended for use in covered porches with sloped floors. The composite material is similar to CorrectDeck's, but formulated to better control thermal expansion. The product is predrilled for trim head screws and has built-in spacer to create a small gap between boards, designed to accommodate any expansion of the material without excessive movement or buckling. The decking has an embossed wood-grain and can be primed and painted or left unfinished.

Manufacturer: Correct Building Products (www.correctdeck.com)

Cross Timbers

CrossTimbers is a composite of polypropylene and non-wood organic material The planks have a hollow core, making a product that is about 30 percent lighter than solid composites. The hollow-core cross section is engi-

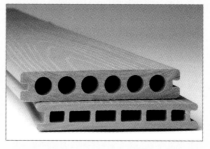

neered for stiffness, giving its 5/4x6-inch Professional line an allowable span of 24 inches. The lighter 1x4 Classic series spans 16 inches. The decking can be either predrilled and screwed or installed with hidden clips that lock into the grooved sides. Matching L-trim acts as an end cap and matching fascia and railings are available. The fire-resistant version of the Professional Grade decking meets the requirements of the California Wildland Urban Interface Building Code. The embossed surface is available in four wood tones.

Manufacturer: GAF-Elk (www.gaf.com)

Fiberon

Fiberon professional decking is an HDPE-wood composite made from about 80 percent recycled and reclaimed materials. Available in three wood tones and gray, the decking has an embossed wood grain on both sides and comes in a nominal 5/4x6 profile. Fiberon only needs one fastener at each joist (two at ends), speeding up installation, according to the manufacturer. Fiberon offers an attractive line of railings and accessories in matching composite materials.

In addition, Fiberon offers a complete line of lightweight cellular PVC decking and railing products. Fiberon's Sanctuary decking has an acrylonitrile styrene acrylate

(ASA) finish for better color retention and durability. This is the same material that is used to protect plastic car bumpers. The embossed wood grain finish mimics ipe or driftwood gray. Boards have grooved sides for easy installation with a hidden fastening system.

Manufacturer: Fiber Composites (www.fiberondecking.com)

GeoDeck

GeoDeck by LDI Composites is a strong and light-weight hollow composite made from partly recycled high-density polyethylene and a special formulation of wood fiber and minerals that reduces fading, according

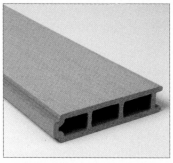

to the manufacture. Available in three profiles: 5/4x6 tongue-and-groove (for covered areas), 5/4x6 square-edge, and 2x8 heavy-duty plank, all products are available in cedar, mahogany, and driftwood colors. Square-edge decking is surface-nailed or screwed, while the tongue-and-groove decking installs with concealed trim-head screws or ring-shank siding nails. T&G decking must be gapped with a credit card or similar item for drainage and expansion, and should also be sloped for drainage and well-ventilated beneath. The manufacturer offers a matching line of end caps, fascia boards, risers, and railing systems.

Manufacturer: LDI Composites (www.geodeck.com)

RhinoDeck

RhinoDeck uses 100 percent recycled and reclaimed wood and plastic to make its wood-HDPE composite decking. Additives are now used in the composite to resist mold growth. The solid decking is available in nominal

5/4x6, 2x4, and 2x6 dimensions, and comes in five embossed wood-grain finishes including tropical hardwood, and weathered gray. The 5/4x6 decking is available square-edged or grooved with companion hidden fasteners. Matching fascia boards, bendable trim, and railing systems are also available.

Manufacturer: RhinoDeck (www.rhinodeck.com)

Tamko

Tamco makes two lines of composite decking using a mix of wood fiber and polyethylene (HDPE and LDPE). The Elements series uses 100 percent recycled materials and EverGrain up to 70 percent, according to the manufacturer. Elements planks are extruded with a wood-grain surface,

and the premium EverGrain series is compression-molded to create a deeply embossed wood texture in seven colors. Extruded skirting is also available in coordinating colors. Both lines are available in nominal 1x4, 1x6, 2x4, and 2x6 dimensions. Installation is by decking screws or with hidden fasteners (not supplied).

Manufacturer: Tamko (www.tamko.com)

TimberTech

Timber Tech uses reclaimed wood in its HDPE-wood composite decking products. The company offers a wide variety of profiles and finishes including a 1½x60-inch tongue-and-groove hollow profile (Floorizon), and 5/4x6 solid planks (Earthwood and TwinFinish) with optional grooved sides to accept hidden fasteners. The Earthwood series is available in tropical hardwood colors, and the TwinFinish planks has an embossed wood-grain on one

(continued on page 182)

wood-plastic composites, cellular PVC decking will appeal primarily to customers whose top priority is very low maintenance. Its also well suited to poolside, beachfront, and similar high-moisture environments.

Appearance

How realistically a synthetic product mimics wood decking is a key issue for many homeowners. Jack Hanson, president of Woodpile Construction in Meridian, Idaho, tells his clients, "There's nothing more beautiful than a wooden deck … for the first six months. Then it becomes a maintenance issue from there on out." He goes on to explain that composite products look better over a much longer period of time than traditional wood decking. Hanson concedes that occasionally a composite deck plank will fade differently than the rest of the batch, but it's a rare occurrence.

Exotic finishes that emulate the look of exotic hardwoods, and deeply embossed wood grains are the most popular with customers of George Drummond, owner of Casa Deck of Virginia Beach. But finding a deck board that will keep looking good for many years can be tricky, he says. "A lot of the exotic-style deck boards have a sheen on the surface that scratches really easily," explains Drummond. "We install them using drop cloths to protect the surface from our tools, but as soon as the homeowner drags a chair across the deck, there's a problem."

Kim Katwijk set up an experiment in which nearly 600 customers were asked to rate nine different products. He found a similar trend to what Drummond describes. The most popular boards were those with a deep, embossed wood-grain — products such as EverGrain (Tamco Building Products, www.evergrain.com), CrossTimbers (GAF-Elk, www.gaf.com), and TimberTech (www.timbertech. com), among others. These products have a rough-sawn appearance that closely approximates the look of a traditional wood plank.

This may be the one edge that composites hold over the new cellular PVC decking products. The cellular PVC planks perform very well but tend to look more like plastic.

What's New in Composite Decking? *(continued)*

side and a brushed finish on the other.

The tongue-and-groove planks are designed for concealed screws and have weep holes to improve drainage. The solid planks can be installed with surface fasteners or with a manufacturer-supplied concealed clip, using the grooved planks. Matching trim pieces, including end caps, fascias and risers, and complete matching railing systems are also available.

TimberTech's newest decking product, its XLM Plank, is a cellular-PVC solid plank with an embossed flat-grain finish on one side and a vertical-grain finish on the other. Planks are available grooved for use with hidden fasteners provided by Timber Tech. XLM has a Class A flame spread rating.

Manufacturer: TimberTech (www.timbertech.com)

Trex

Trex, the original recycled-content composite lumber, uses plastic that is about 50 percent recycled and reclaimed

(HDPE and LDPE). The wood content is 50 percent reclaimed from sources such as sawdust and wood pallets. In fact, seven out of 10 recycled grocery bags in the U.S. end up in Trex, according to the manufacturer. It has spawned a number of imitators, and many alternative decking options look similar. The product is now offered in a wide variety of colors and textures in 5/4x6 and 2x6 planks. Most planks are available grooved for the company's hidden fastener clips. New products include Trex Origins, a bendable plank for curved installations and Trex Accents Fire Defense, which has a Class B fire rating and exceeds California's fire regulations. Trex has also introduced a cellular PVC decking product called Trex Escapes. Most Trex decking products are available with matching trim boards, railings, and other accessories.

Manufacturer: Trex (www.trex.com)

Code Approval

There's more to consider here than just durability and good looks. Frank Woeste, a professor of wood science and forest products at Virginia Tech says, "It appears that less than half of all composite and plastic decking manufacturers have a code report."

Currently, for a plastic or composite decking product to be code approved, it must have an International Code Council Evaluation Service (ICC-ES) Legacy Report (ESR) listing. To obtain a code listing, a product must submit to a series of tests outlined in ICC-ES document AC 174, which is based directly on ASTM standard D 7032 (see "Is the Decking Code-Approved?" page 173).

ASTM D 7032 helps a manufacturer determine the proper on-center span for deck boards, as well as the modulus of rupture and modulus of elasticity, temperature and moisture effects, UV resistance, freeze/thaw resistance, fungal decay, termite resistance, and fire performance.

For now, you can find out if a product is code listed by asking the manufacturer or checking on the ICC-ES web site (www.icc-es.org). Another good source is www.10klakes.org, run by the Ten Thousand Lakes ICC-chapter. Click on "Composite Decking Updated."

Under a 2007 IRC update that adopts ASTM D 7032, all composite manufacturers must label their product packaging with their code listing. Once this version of the IRC is adopted by your local code, finding out whether or not a product is listed will be much easier. In areas, where wildfires are an issue, additional fire code regulations may apply (see "Composites and Fire Safety," page 176).

Installation

Composite decking weighs more and flexes more than traditional wood decking so moving it around the job site may be a two-person job. Also its allowable span may be less than for wood decking, requiring a tighter joist spacing. Even if the allowable span is the same, you may want to reduce the span by about 4 inches to provide a solid, non-bouncy feeling above. This means that tearing up an old, lumber deck and recovering it with composite or plastic planks may not work with some brands.

In addition, composites have greater thermal expansion and contraction than solid lumber, so the spacing between boards should be adjusted based on the temperature during installation. Correct spacing, both side-to-side and at end joints, is critical. Most manufacturers have a prescriptive spacing guide for between boards and at end joints — typically in the neighborhood of 3/16-inch when installing boards at cooler temperatures. As the temperature of the board increases, the amount of gapping required for ther-

mal expansion decreases. When deciding what size gap to use, you may want to measure the temperature of the boards before installation with an I.R. thermometer for accuracy.

Nails and screws. Composite manufacturers typically specify hot-dipped galvanized, stainless steel, or specially coated fasteners for their decking. It is important to remember that many pneumatic fasteners are zinc electroplate coated, not hot dipped, and therefore not recommended. When pneumatic nailers are used, they often drive the fastener slightly below the surface. The resulting "mushroom" around the nail head can then be hammered flat.

Trying to avoid mushrooming around screw heads can slow down an installation. In response, many installers now use special screws such as TrapEase Composite Deck Screws (www.fastenmaster.com) and Headcote Composite Screws (Starborn Industries, www.starbornindustries.com), which are designed to self-countersink without mushrooming. Even with decking screws, predrilling may be necessary at edges and ends of boards.

For a still cleaner look, free of fastener heads, some installers prefer breakaway screws such as the Counter-Snap Headless Deck Screw (O'Berry Industries, www.compositedeckscrew.com), which leaves a nearly invisible hole after the screw head snaps off with the help of a drilling jig.

The temperature during installation can also have an effect on screw installation. When a board cools significantly, it becomes denser and can make inserting screws very difficult, and in worse cases, can split the board. With some products it is necessary to predrill all fastener holes when the temperature drops to around freezing. Even at normal temperatures, it may be necessary to drill or even countersink end joints to avoid end splitting.

Hidden fasteners. In recent years, most composite and plastic decking companies have begun offering boards with grooved sides to accommodate hidden fasteners. Brands like CorrectDeck (www.correctdeck.com), Rhino Deck (www.rhinodeck.com), and Trex (www.trex.com), among others, offer their own proprietary clip-style fasteners, but for the manufacturers that don't, there are plenty of aftermarket options to choose from.

In selecting among the many hidden fasteners, consider the strength and durability of the fastener, along with the price, speed of application, and visibility of the clip from above. In addition to the widely used Eb-Ty fastener, TigerClaw, Ipe Clip, and Lumber Loc are a few of the many options on the market (for details on these fasteners, see "Hidden Deck Fasteners," page 187).

Reid Shalvoy is a freelance writer based in Burlington, Vt.

Bending Trex

by Mike Sloggatt

Clients, I've found, often make requests that force us to think outside the box. In the project shown on these pages, for example, a concrete deck surrounding the homeowners' in-ground pool had caused their barefoot grandchildren too many stubbed toes and skinned knees. To gain a friendlier walking surface, they wanted to extend their house deck — which had Trex fiber-composite decking — so that it completely surrounded the pool area. Curves would be a big part of the design.

I initially proposed pulling up the existing concrete, which had its share of cracks and other tripping hazards, and installing new footings, beams, and framing to support the new Trex deck. But the cost was impractical, so we elected to fasten PT sleepers to the existing concrete instead, and then attach the new decking to the sleepers.

That part of the job was pretty straightforward. To help get the new 2-by sleepers level, we used a laser level with a remote sensor, shimming where necessary in the low spots before screwing the sleepers down with long Tapcon screws. As we installed the decking with coated deck screws, we heated the mushrooms around the screws with a heat gun and tapped them down with a finish hammer to hide the face screws.

For Tight Curves, Just Add Heat

For both aesthetic and safety reasons, I wanted to avoid sharp miters on the outside corners of the pool

Special heating blankets were used to form the tight curves of this pool's retrofitted fiber-composite decking.

deck. While I was comfortable cutting curves in Trex decking, I wasn't exactly sure how to bend skirts made of this material around these tightly curved corners. But a recent project installing heat-radiused

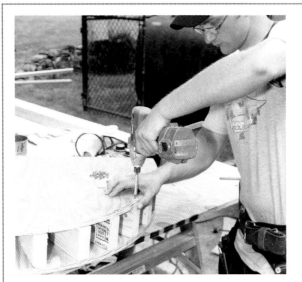

Figure 15. After laying out the 20-inch radius of the outside corners of the pool deck, a crew member built a form of plywood and framing lumber with the same radius (left); this form would be used to mold the outside skirtboard. For the inside corners, a tracing was made of the pool's coping, and then a plywood form was built to match (right).

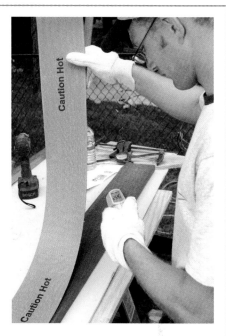

Figure 16. To heat the Trex enough to mold it to the shape of the forms, the author's crew used temperature-regulated Heatcon heating blankets (left). Sandwiching the Trex between sheets of scrap cement backerboard and fireproof Sheetrock helped minimize external heat loss and speed up the heating process (center). A few degrees makes a big difference in the workability of the board; the infrared thermometer included in the Heatcon kit allowed the crew to track the surface temperature accurately (right).

PVC trim gave me an idea.

To curve PVC trim, we use Heatcon's heat forming kit (www.heatcon.com), which consists of a pair of 6-foot-long by 6-inch-wide heating blankets with an electronic controller to regulate the temperature. In use, a trim board sandwiched between the two blankets is heated to a predetermined temperature, then bent into the desired shape.

Trex — which is composed of hardwood sawdust and recycled polyethylene — can be heat-formed, too; the company's Web site offers guidelines and a couple of different techniques. Even though the manufacturer doesn't mention heat blankets, I thought we could use them in the same way.

To test my theory, I put short decking cutoffs in the blankets and heated them up to see what would happen. I overcooked the first pieces, discovering that the boards expand like marshmallows and aren't very attractive when overheated. But I reduced the temperature, and after some trial and error determined that 260°F seemed ideal: The Trex became flexible without distorting or disfiguring.

Once I was satisfied I could successfully heat-bend the Trex, my crew and I laid out and installed sleepers for two of the deck's outside corners, giving them a comfortable 20-inch radius (the other two corners would be treated slightly differently). Then we built a plywood form with that same radius, which we would use to form the corner skirt boards (**Figure 15**).

Forming the Outside Corners

After ripping the outside Trex skirts to width, we placed a 6-foot-long board on one of the heat blankets and covered it with the other (**Figure 16**). We let each board simmer under the blankets for about 20 minutes or so, using this time to continue installing the straight sections of decking.

When we removed the blankets, lifted the board, and carried it over to the form, we used the special gloves supplied in the heat kit to protect our hands from the heat.

These outside skirt boards easily conformed to the shape of the form, but we also lightly clamped the ends as they cooled and assumed their new shape (**Figure 17**, next page). After they reached normal temperature, we fastened the curved corner skirts in place with stainless steel trim screws. Then we fastened the remaining sections of straight skirt, tightly butting them to the corners for a snap fit.

Forming the Inside Corners

I thought the inside curves for the pool corners should be formed to match the pool's existing coping, eliminating the miter joints that could plague me later on by opening up. To accurately match this shape, I traced the corner coping pattern onto a sheet of plywood, then used this template to build the plywood form.

Ripped to a narrower dimension than the outside

Figure 17. When placed on the radiused form, the heat-treated Trex board easily relaxed into shape (left). A crew member lightly clamped the board ends to coax them the last couple of inches into their final position (right), then allowed the board to cool.

Figure 18. Ripped to a thinner width to fit on top of the pool's coping, the inner skirts were extremely flexible after heating (top left) and conformed to the angular shape of the form with only hand pressure (above). The right temperature is critical when molding complex shapes: If it gets too hot, Trex deforms, but if it's not hot enough, it can tear (left).

Figure 19. As with the outside corners, the inside corner skirts were installed first, with stainless fasteners screwed into the sleepers, followed by the remaining sections of skirt (far left). In the completed project, the top of each skirt is flush with the surface of the decking (left).

corners to fit on top of the pool coping, these thinner pieces bent more easily when we heated them. In fact, it took two men to handle the hot boards, which felt like giant pieces of spaghetti but were easy to mold into shape by hand (**Figure 18**).

Again, we set these inside corner skirts first, attaching them to the sleepers with stainless trim screws (**Figure 19**). Then we were able to spring in the remaining straight sections of skirt for a nice tight fit. Because we fit the skirt first, each section of decking that butted into the skirt had to be scribed to fit,

a time-consuming process. But scribing each piece and chamfering the cut ends with a router produced a very nice edge detail.

And while creating all these curves was a little more labor-intensive than simply squaring off the ends of the deck with miters, the end result is much more appealing. My clients are pleased: In addition to really liking the finished look of the deck, they're hoping they'll recoup some of its cost in fewer Band-Aids.

Mike Sloggatt is a remodeling contractor in Levittown, N.Y.

Hidden Deck Fasteners

by Andy Engel

Who came up with the first hidden decking fastener is open to debate. Weston Leavens remembers first seeing them in a magazine sometime around the end of the Reagan administration. A screw or nail affixed the clip to the first board and to the joist, and the second board was driven onto a prong protruding from the first clip.

At the time, Leavens was the owner of one of the largest deck-building companies in San Diego. Intrigued, he ordered a box of the fasteners and used them to build a display deck for the annual home show. "The deck moved and squeaked," says Leavens.

"It was embarrassing. I thought we'd done something wrong, so I called the author and arranged a visit to see the deck. Well, it squeaked and moved, too, but the owners didn't seem to mind." That experience led Leavens to invent the Deckmaster, a track system that he began to use in his own business in about 1989.

That was a fertile time for the hidden-fastener industry. Sometime in the early '90s, Harry Eberle was working on a high-end house in Hunterdon County, N.J., and as seems common with busy builders, his mind was in two places at once. While he was using a biscuit joiner to put together the cabinets, he was also

Choose a system that's right for the decking material and consider cross-bracing the joists below.

noodling out the best way to fasten down the furniture-grade ipe for the deck. His solution was a special biscuit-type fastener, later called the Eb-Ty.

Concealed deck-board fasteners now come in a variety of flavors. It seems that the prong type was the first, followed by tracks, biscuit systems, and, recently, clips that either interlock or fit in grooves cut down the sides of the boards. The newest development is composite decking systems that come grooved for a proprietary clip from the manufacturer. Ipe and other hardwoods may be available locally with similar grooves milled in. As with nearly any product, some users get good results, and others don't. Below are a few things to consider, to make the most of hidden fasteners.

Exposure

All hidden fastener systems solve one obvious problem, which is that of being exposed. It's more than just an aesthetic issue. The movement of wood or composite decking that's been exposed to the rigors of the outdoors commonly results in nails or screws standing proud of the surface of the board. That's a trip hazard, as well as a minor annoyance to those inclined to take a snow shovel to their deck.

Movement

All deck boards move, but in different ways that depend on the material. Wood expands and contracts mostly because of changes in moisture content.

Composite decking, on the other hand, expands and contracts with changes in temperature. Deck builders ignore these facts at their own risk.

Wood decking should be installed at a moisture content that's appropriate for the climate. For example, if you install kiln-dried decking in, say, coastal Washington, it's going to expand. It can expand enough across the grain to buckle, no matter what type of fastener you use. Go to a drier area and install wet decking, and you can count on it shrinking. Anecdotally, that can be a particular problem with some biscuit and pronged types of fasteners. In some cases, boards have reportedly shrunk enough to disengage from the fasteners. Using lumber that has the correct moisture content for the climate should avoid such problems.

Composite decking that's installed at a high ambient temperature will shrink as the weather cools. Install it in the cold, and it will expand as the temperature rises. Pay attention to the manufacturer's instructions regarding installation in extreme temperatures.

Structure

Since we're talking about wood movement, we should also discuss deck movement. Several contractors I spoke with reported that decks built with a variety of concealed fasteners moved and creaked. A conversation with Frank Woeste, PE, professor emeritus at Virginia Tech University, confirmed one possible reason for this (see "Strength of Hidden Deck Fasteners," page 191).

Traditionally built decks, where 6-inch nominal decking is nailed or screwed with two fasteners to each joist, are stiffened against lateral movement by the diaphragm this construction creates. This is similar to how a house floor is stiffened by the plywood sheathing, and although the strength gain offered by 6-inch planks isn't what you get from 4x8 sheathing, it's still significant.

Concealed fasteners may not provide the same rigid fastening that creates the diaphragm effect in a traditionally built deck. In fact, due to plastic's high coefficient of expansion, many fasteners that are intended for use with composite decking are designed to allow the decking to expand along its length. Attaching decking in a way that allows movement, by definition, will lend less rigidity to the structure. It would appear that only systems that rigidly attach each deck board in two places to each joist could come close to replicating the diaphragm created with 6-inch decking and exposed fasteners.

Leavens says, "The tightest any deck will ever be is on the day you finish building it." It's indisputable that time and weather take their toll on outdoor structures. One method to give any deck — whether built with concealed fasteners or not — a shot at a long, safe, and creak-free life, is to build redundantly

Pronged-Clip Systems

Dec-Klip

The Dec-Klip is a toothed, galvanized clip that's nailed or screwed into place. One fastener enters the side of the deck board, and another is driven into the joist. An outward-facing prong penetrates the edge of the next board as

it's driven in with a sledgehammer. It's fully galvanized after stamping so that all edges are protected. The deck boards are raised slightly above the joists.

Manufacturer: BEN Manufacturing (ww.dec-klip.com)

Deck-Tie

Before installing a deck board, the galvanized Deck-Ties are nailed to its rear-facing edge so that they'll be an inch or two away from the joists. The front edge of the previous deck board is secured to the joists with toe-

nails or screws, and the Deck-Ties on the second board slide below the first board. Toenails or screws in the second board tighten up the system.

Manufacturer: Simpson Strong-Tie Company (www.strongtie.com)

Invisagrip

This T-shaped, stainless-steel fastener, a German-made system, has prongs on both sides. A couple of taps with a hammer and a block sets one prong of the Invisagrip into the first board; the Invisagrip is then screwed down to the

joist. A proprietary tool squeezes the next board onto the outer prongs of the first board's fasteners, and the process repeats. A set of two tools costs $600, but saves you from having to sledgehammer the boards onto the fasteners.

Manufacturer: Southland Fence Company (www.invisagrip.com)

Tiger Claw

Tiger Claw offers a variety of fasteners for softwoods, hardwoods, composites, and grooved boards, in stainless steel or powder-coated. Except on the grooved-board fastener (the TC-G), the dual-pronged clips work pretty

much the same on all the versions. A proprietary block is used to drive the fastener into the first board, the fastener is toe-screwed to the board and the joist, and the next board is driven onto the exposed prongs. The TC-G is not much different, except that instead of driving prongs into the edge of a deck board, the wings on the TC-G simply hook into pre-milled grooves in the boards.

Manufacturer: Tiger Claw Inc. (www.deckfastener.com)

Interlocking Clips

FastenMaster IQ

Working from above with the deck board upside down, you screw two polycarbonate IQ clips to the bottom of the board, centered approximately over each joist. You then flip the board over, and the inboard clip interlocks with the one on the previously installed board. The outboard clip is screwed to the top of the joist.

Manufacturer: FastenMaster (www.fastenmaster.com)

Invisi-Fast

Made from Lexan, a strong, clear plastic, Invisi-Fast clips screw to the side of the joists, minimizing water intrusion. The deck board is laid in place, and the clips are screwed to the joist and to the bottom of the decking. A spacer, avail-

able in several sizes, sticks up between the boards.

Manufacturer: M.M. Products (www.invisifast.com)

(continued on page 190)

(continued from previous page)

Interlocking Clips

Hidden Link

Hidden Link is a new product from Sure Drive. Working with the board upside down, you attach the inboard clip to the bottom of the deck board. The board is flipped over, and the inboard clip slips below

the previous deck board. The outboard clip is screwed to the side of the previous deck board and then to the top of the joist. It is currently available only in powder-coated steel; a stainless-steel version is in the works.

Manufacturer: Sure Drive USA (www.suredrive.com)

Biscuit Systems

Eb-Ty

Eb-Ty started out with one polypropylene fastener designed to fit in #20 biscuit slots cut in the sides of the deck boards. A screw down through the center of the

Eb-Ty affixed the board to the deck, and the next board would slide onto the Eb-Tys. The basic idea has changed little, but there are currently eight versions intended for a variety of composites and hardwoods, including for pre-grooved composites.

Manufacturer: Eb-Ty Hidden Deck Fasteners (www.ebty.com)

Ipe Clip

This is another biscuit-type clip. The manufacturer claims that its round shape offers more latitude during installation than the competing fasteners do. Made specifically with the idea of holding

down ipe, a tough, hardwood, the Ipe Clip is made from fiberglass. The Extreme version is reinforced with a stainless-steel washer. Some suppliers sell the clips along with pre-grooved ipe decking, greatly simplifying installation.

Manufacturer: The Ipe Clip Company (www.ipeclip.com)

Lumber Loc Exotic

A copolymer blend of polypropylene, the Lumber Loc Exotic is designed to withstand expansion and contraction along both the length and the width of the decking. It installs in either biscuit joiner slots or grooves milled in the boards, and screws to the top of the joists.

Manufacturer: KK Manufacturing (www.lumberloc.com)

Track Systems

Deckmaster

Available in a powder-coated version for most applications and a stainless-steel version for coastal use, the Deckmaster screws to the sides

of the joists and the bottom of the decking. It comes in 22$^1/_2$-inch lengths that accommodate four nominal 6-inch deck boards. Installation requires either access from below, or working upside down from above.

Manufacturer: Grabber Construction Products (www.deckmaster.com)

Shadoe Track

Shadoe Track is nailed or screwed to the tops of joists. Deck boards are attached with screws from below, and,

again, access from below or lots of bending at the waist is called for. It comes in 8-foot lengths in galvanized, powder-coated, and stainless-steel versions.

Manufacturer: Sure Drive USA (www.suredrive.com)

Strength of Hidden Deck Fasteners

Q. *I use the Eb-Ty fastener on 80 percent of the decks I build, and many are one or more stories high. I also live in a heavy snow area. The clips in that system hold the decking to the framing with pressure, not with mechanical fasteners, and I'm concerned that the detail may not be strong enough to brace the deck. I have been taking extra steps by letting cross bracing into the joist system. Is this type of bracing necessary?*

A. *Frank Woeste, PE, professor emeritus at Virginia Tech University in Blacksburg, responds:* You certainly are not wasting your time by being cautious in building a deck. Like roofs, decks don't experience their full design load (such as a heavy snowfall or a large party) every day or every year. But you must build them to handle that extreme design load when it does occur, because a failure can be catastrophic.

I don't know of any engineering numbers on the type of fasteners you're using, but they may not be designed to resist all the forces a deck can experience. And we haven't had 40 years of experience with the product to learn from, as we have with traditional 8d or 10d threaded nails that would typically be used with 5/4 decking boards. It's safest in this case to disregard any bracing effect of the decking and fasteners and build the structure to stand up without them.

However, the diagonal let-in bracing you mention, whether it's installed within the floor frame or between the posts and the deck framing, probably is not going to do the job. There are two important issues to consider: twisting of the deck joists and racking of the deck in plane. Even with the joists secured against any rotation at each end, they'll tend to twist within the span when a load is placed on top if they're not restrained somehow. Assuming no help from the decking, you'd be wise to install solid 2x PT blocking between the joists at 2 feet on-center. That probably sounds like a lot to most carpenters, but that spacing is borne out by experience with long-span truss chords that are held with 2x4 purlins at 2 feet on-center. If you wanted to space the blocking farther apart, you'd need engineering for the specific span and joist spacing, and lumber size, grade, and species.

As for racking, one solution when earthquake loads aren't involved is to firmly attach the deck to the house and to its carrying posts (which should be minimum 6x6 posts treated for a structural application in ground contact) and to embed the posts firmly into the earth at least 3½ feet deep. Then the supports can hold the deck in place without the need for racking resistance from the deck boards in the plane of the deck itself. However, diagonal bracing of the posts might be required to "stiffen" the system, depending on deck height, post size, and deck size.

with lateral bracing. Doing so becomes more important as decks increase in size, because larger decks and higher columns exacerbate any movement.

I would consider adding cross bracing below the joists, or beefing up the angled braces between the deck's support posts and its main beam, and I'd ask my structural engineer to consider this issue in his design. Additionally, some manufacturers recommend using an adhesive such as Liquid Nails or PL 400 with their hidden fasteners to improve the performance of the decking as a diaphragm, and to alleviate potential squeaking.

Water

One other potential issue is common to most hidden fasteners and to all exposed fasteners. In time, water can follow these fasteners down and into the heart of the joist, where the preservative often doesn't reach. It makes sense that this process would shorten the life of joists and decking. Leavens is certain of this, and claims one advantage of the Deckmaster to be that its screws are installed in the side of the joists, not the

top. Another response to this concern would be to use one of the self-sealing flashing tapes on the market.

Time

The final issue that's raised when talking about hidden fastening systems is labor. I don't think anyone in the industry would argue with the statement that it takes longer to install concealed fasteners than to use a nail gun or a collated screw gun to fasten decking from above. The solution is to sell hidden fastening systems as the upgrade they are.

Manufacturers are aware of the time concerns, as well. Some of the newer systems claim labor savings over earlier concealed fasteners. Initial reports regarding the labor savings offered by the pre-grooved composite lumber systems, for example, seem positive. Paul Mantoni, a Connecticut deck builder who's been using Tiger Claw fasteners for some time, says that their new TC-G fastener, privately labeled as Fiberon's Phantom, saves him a lot of time.

Andy Engel is the editor of Professional Deck Builder.

Installing Hidden Fasteners

by Dave Holbrook

Aside from the fact that many people don't like to see them, visible deck fasteners invite problems. Splitting at board ends, corrosion and rust-stains, and water penetration leading to rot can all be blamed on face-nailing. Plus, nail pops and loose boards create unsafe conditions. So what's the best way to fasten a deck surface without making a feature of the nails or screws?

Hidden deck fasteners reduce or eliminate the visual and physical defects of face nailing by fastening the decking boards at their edge or underside. Whether you're using an expensive tropical wood or ordinary pressure-treated pine, a nail-free surface simply makes a nicer-looking job. Keep in mind that the following systems, although they vary in method, all cost more and take more time to install than a conventionally fastened deck surface. A number of systems have come and gone over the past decade. Those covered here have all be available at least since 2000.

Starting and Finishing

Most hardware systems fasten the decking by its edges, though a couple of them work from the bottom. All concealed fasteners share a minor quandary: How do you start the first board, whether the deck abuts a building or is open-sided, without showing any fasteners? You don't, exactly. The easy answer, whether they work from the edge or from underneath, is to drive and set finish nails through the face of the starter board, then fill the holes with col-

---

Different Approaches

Eb-Ty

Clever in its simplicity, the Eb-Ty makes it possible to prepare the decking boards ahead of installation. Your main weapon is a biscuit joiner or slot-cutting router, used to cut a slot in both edges of the deck board at the specific

Originally designed to take advantage of the biscuit-joiner, the versatile Eb-Ty is easiest to install on pregrooved decking. Eight different versions are designed for use with softwood, hardwood, and composite lumber of any thickness. Construction adhesive is recommended to prevent squeaks.

joist spacing. Both composite and hardwood decking is now readily available pre-grooved, greatly simplifying installation.

The Eb-Ty connector is a UV-resistant polypropylene biscuit with a 3/32-inch-thick raised auto-spacing tab at its center and an elongated screw-hole in the middle. Because of its thin, low profile, you can use the Eb-Ty with 1x decking material. After inserting the connector in the slot, a #7 stainless-steel finishing screw, driven through the biscuit and board edge at a 45-degree angle, holds the decking in place. You may have to predrill hard lumber species before installing the screws. Each successive board, prepared with mating slots, is tapped into place over the exposed half of the biscuit connector, and the sequence is repeated.

Unlike some of the other connectors available, the Eb-Ty puts the deck board in direct contact with the joist. The manufacturer recommends the additional use of an exterior-grade flooring adhesive in conjunction with their fastener to offset the possibility of squeaks and rattles, a legitimate concern with edge fastening systems.

Butt joints. A single Eb-Ty connector can be installed across a butt joint by cutting the slot in place on the center of the joint. Common biscuits may also be used to align butt joints of slightly differing thickness before installing the Eb-Ty.

I like this system, because you're cutting, rather than punching, the edge slots, ensuring that the lumber won't

ored putty. Or, you can cut matching wood plugs to cap recessed screws.

You can't use a hidden fastener at the outer edge of the last decking board, either. A face-nail or screw must be used here as well. Another option is to toe-nail the outer edge of the decking to the frame and cap the deck's perimeter with a trim board.

Choosing the Right Fastener

Dimensional irregularities in lumber spell trouble with the self-spacing systems. It's not unusual, especially with treated yellow pine, to find discrepancies in board width as great as 1/4 inch. Depending on the surfacing material you plan to work with, you may want to choose a system that allows you to customize the board spacing.

Moisture in lumber can also be a problem, particularly with edge-fastening systems. Too-wet lumber, installed in a sunny location, can undergo a radical transformation in a matter of days. Warping and shrinkage may exceed the tolerances of some edge-clip systems. It's best to determine that the lumber you're using is at the ideal moisture content for your region, before installation. To minimize the likelihood of problems, avoid wet or unseasoned lumber when building a deck, regardless of the fastening system used. If you think warping or cupping problems are likely, a bottom-fastening system may be your best option.

Whichever system you choose, don't be misled by claims that there's no labor penalty involved. I'd set aside any benchmark deck installation numbers you have and think through the steps involved in the system of choice. New methods call for new numbers. And, the decision to conceal the fasteners indicates an intention to raise the quality, and thus the cost, of the deck job.

Dave Holbrook is a builder on Cape Cod, Mass.

surprise you later by splitting around the fastener. It also isn't limited for use with softer wood species and thicker profiles. But, unless you are using pre-grooved material, it requires the patient focus of a cabinetmaker to make sure that the slots are all properly aligned and cut. And because you have to prepare both edges, you're handling each piece of lumber a lot.

The Eb-Ty comes in eight different models for different types and thicknesses of material. In general, you'll need 2.75 fasteners per square foot on 3 1/2-inch-wide decking over 16-inch on-center framing. That works out to about $1 per square foot of installed decking for the Eb-Ty fasteners and included stainless steel screws.

Manufacturer: Eb-Ty Hidden Deck Fasteners (www.ebty.com)

Deckmaster

This bottom-fastening 22-inch-long, T-section bracket attaches to alternating sides of each joist with the provided #8x1-inch screws. The top flange flares out to catch the decking before doubling back to rest on the joist's edge, creating a small gap between decking and joist.

There are 23 joist and deck screws combined per track-length, which translates to 12.5 screws per linear foot of track installed. That's a lot of screwing and, when working with dense, hard decking material, probably pre-drilling, too. The included screws do have self-drilling tips.

The Deckmaster track is attached to alternating sides of each joist before fastening it to the decking. Unless there's good access from below, deck boards are connected by reaching underneath and screwing upward through the perforated flange.

The manufacturer suggests preparing the top of the track – which comes in galvanized- or stainless-steel – with black spray-paint to reduce its metallic glare between deck boards on sunny days.

To calculate the number of brackets needed, multiply the linear footage of the deck joists by 12 and divide by 22. On 16-inch joist spacing, you'll need 10 brackets per 25 square feet of deck surface. A case of 100 powder-

(continued on page 194)

coated brackets and all necessary screws costs $300; that works out to about $1.20 per square foot for 16-inch o.c. joists. Stainless steel brackets cost $685 per 100, or $2.74 per square foot. Because the track is fastened to the joists first, you'll want to plan the occurrence of butted decking seams ahead in order to provide fastening at both sides of the joint.

Manufacturer: Grabber Construction Products (www.deckmaster.com)

Shadoe Track

Another bottom fastener, the steel Shadoe Track employs a continuous-angle track that is first nailed along the top edge of each joist. The decking is then screwed to it from below. Shadoe Track's profile is relatively flat, with a small, 90-degree bend that registers against the joist's edge. The track fastens to the joist using galvanized spiral or annular-ring nails. Deck boards are installed one at a time and secured with screws by kneeling on the deck board and reaching underneath to drive the screws. If you've got one, a right-angle screwgun will provide an ergonomic advantage here.

It's said that once you acclimate to an upside-down position, the throbbing pressure in your head equalizes. Whether you can adjust to this work position, you'll find out for yourself after peering under the decking at your 3,000th screw. If you're lucky, you'll be able to work from below the deck, with the aid of a helper or a clamp to hold the board down.

The manufacturer calls for 9 nails and 52 screws per 8-foot length of track. Shadoe Track is available in 8-foot lengths of 20-gauge steel in three finishes: G-185 galvanized, beige powder-coat, and stainless-steel. Eight-foot lengths galvanized costs $8.60, powder-coat costs $11.80. and stainless steel costs $18.95. Galvanized is also available in 4-foot lengths. Drill-point screws and annular-ring nails are available at additional cost.

Manufacturer: Sure Drive USA (www.suredrive.com)

Tebo

Tebo's stainless-steel connector looks like an unused heavy-gauge staple, with a third leg projecting from the crown at a 45-degree angle. The Tebo has little in common with other edge-fastening systems. And it's the only system that's likely to challenge the speed of traditional nailing.

A $300 proprietary tool — essentially an upright, mallet-driven flooring nailer — is used to install the Tebo connector. The connectors aren't collated, which could make tool-loading tedious, but installation is fast and simple.

The shallow profile of the Shadoe Track registers against the edge of the joist. Annular-ring nails fasten the track to the top edge of each joist (left). A right-angle screw gun helps ease the pain of upside-down screwing (right). If you're lucky, you'll be able to work from below.

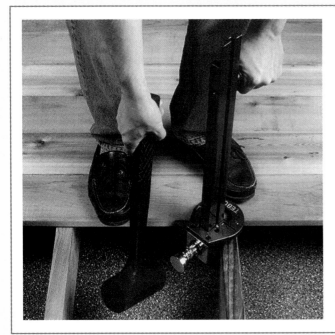

The oddly shaped Tebo connector stacks in a special driving tool for rapid-fire installation that rivals face-nailing for speed.

A mallet blow simultaneously drives the connector into the joist and the edge of the decking at a 45-degree angle. The third spur on the Tebo connector sticks out at 90 degrees to the edge, ready to spear the back edge of the next board in line. The installer drives the board onto these spurs, working down the length of the board with a heavy maul (using a beater-board to protect the decking edge from hammer dents). There's some body English involved, using the balls of your feet to hold the board down while you sledge it into position.

The Tebo fastener can be used as a self-gapping system – the shank is a skinny $1/8$ inch at its widest section – but with softer decking materials like redwood and cedar, you could have problems. The use of temporary gapping shims, such as tapered cedar shingles, is advised to maintain even spacing between boards. Because the connecting spur is only $9/16$ inch long, though, you have to be careful not to make the gap between the boards too wide.

The Tebo connector is designed on the assumption that most installers work from left to right. According to the manufacturer, installation is awkward but manageable for left-handed people.

To fasten deck boards at butt joints, Tebo connectors may be driven into either face of the joist into each respective butt end. However, a Tebo connector driven from the left side of the joist will have to have its spur manually bent over after installation in order to project at a 90-degree angle. Alternatively, that spur may be hammered over flat to get it out of the way.

The Tebo system can be used to install decking on the diagonal. But for installations where the right side of the joist-deck board intersection (with you standing on the decking, facing the joists) exceeds 90 degrees, you'll need to bend the prong back to 90 degrees to the decking edge after installation. This requires a proprietary tool that comes with the installation kit.

Dense hardwoods like ipe are also a challenge for the system. While the Tebo may work with wetter stock, the dry material more common today requires pre-drilling using a special drilling jig available from Tebo.

Also, pressure-treated lumber, if not kiln-dried after treatment, may be too wet for these connectors to be effective. Excessive shrinkage could allow the board to pull free of the connecting spur. The connectors come in boxes of 120 for $50, or about 42¢ each. For a 200 square foot deck using 6-inch boards you will spend about $120 for the Tebos.

Manufacturer: Spotnails (www.spotnails.com)

Deck Finishing Options

by Scott Gibson

Despite the growing use of wood-plastic composites and all-plastic or metal decking, most new residential decks are still made from wood. And while pressure-treated lumber and naturally decay-resistant species such as cedar and redwood can last a very long time outside, they aren't immune from the effects of weather. Thus, most homeowners and deck professionals will turn to a deck finish to slow the aging process and prolong the life of their decking.

The available finishes run the gamut from semisolids that hide wood grain to clear preservatives designed to keep wood looking lumberyard fresh — and the options continue to multiply. In addition to traditional finishes made from natural oils, there are finishes made from modified oils called "alkyds"; water-based acrylics; and coatings that combine acrylics and alkyds.

No finish does everything perfectly, especially in a grueling environment where heavy foot traffic, unrelenting sun, and exposure to rain and snow are the norm. Also, there's no such thing as a permanent, maintenance-free finish — all will need periodic cleaning and recoating.

That said, there are fundamental differences between families of finishes that affect performance, appearance, longevity, and (of course) price. And just as your painter will tell you, surface preparation is everything (see "Surface Prep Makes All the Difference," page 201).

The Basics: What Pigments Do

There are three basic flavors of deck finishes: clear, semitransparent, and semisolid. Formulations differ widely, but a key difference among them is the

Be prepared for regular maintenance no matter what finish you choose.

THE THOMPSON'S COMPANY

THE THOMPSON'S COMPANY

Figure 20. Clear sealers are the easiest to apply and they show the wood's figure. However, they're the least durable type of finish — with an expected life span of only a year or two — and many clear finishes offer little protection against UV degradation of the underlying wood.

amount of pigmentation they contain. Whether the finish is water-based or oil-based, finely ground pigments are the ingredients that prevent surface damage and natural graying due to ultraviolet radiation. Increasingly, coating manufacturers are exploring the use of extremely fine pigment particles to limit UV damage (see "Invisible UV Blockers," page 200).

Clear sealers last only about a year, or possibly two, before they need recoating, but they are relatively easy to apply and require the least amount of prep work before a reapplication (**Figure 20**). They may be either oil- or water-based, and may contain ingredients to absorb UV radiation to slow natural graying and a fungicide to retard the growth of mold. What makes clear finishes appealing is they allow the natural figure of the wood to show through — and if you've just spent a bucket of money on a deck of all-heart redwood, that argument can be persuasive.

For these reasons, a clear water repellent containing an agent to combat mold is the first choice of Sam Williams, a research chemist at the Forest Products Laboratory in Madison, Wis., when he finishes his own deck. Although he can count on reapplying the finish every couple of years, Williams can prep the

Figure 21. Tinted sealers offer a couple of years' durability and show off the grain of the wood. Also called "semitransparent," these finishes are fairly easy to apply. Their pigments change the wood's color while providing some defense against UV.

deck and reapply finish in an elapsed time of only about 60 minutes.

After clear finishes, next on this gradient of increasing opacity is a class of tinted sealers and stains, sometimes called toners or semitransparents, that contain some light-blocking pigments (**Figure 21**). Their advantage is that they offer some protection from UV damage while allowing some wood grain to show. Depending on weather, sun exposure, and foot traffic, you can count on two or possibly three years of service on a horizontal surface before recoating.

The most opaque finishes are the semisolid stains, which contain a lot of pigmentation — enough to offer the best long-term protection against sun and weather damage (**Figure 22**). They might not be the first choice for a deck of clear redwood or cedar, but semisolid stains come in a wide range of colors that can spruce up the uniformity of pressure-treated softwood. These stains last longer than the others — up to five years, according to one deck-restoration specialist.

There are a couple of downsides, however, to semisolid finishes. They are harder to apply evenly and may show brush marks where the surface doesn't dry evenly. The best advice is to apply the finish on just a couple of deck boards at a time, following them from one end to the other, and then move on to the next section of deck.

Semisolid stains will make wear patterns on the deck more obvious, and they require the most prep work before they can be recoated. The manufacturer may, in fact, recommend the surface be completely stripped and cleaned before any new finish is applied. Bottom line: Semisolid stains offer more protection for a longer period of time, but they're harder to apply evenly and require more work to prepare for recoating.

Avoid Film-Forming Finishes

Paint forms a tough film designed to block sun and water for long stretches of time. These attributes

make paint ideal for exterior trim and siding, but they're not advantages for a deck. Penetrating deck stains and sealers are designed to protect without forming a film.

As explained by lumber-industry veteran Ed Burke, who's a member of the coatings advisory committee at the Forest Products Laboratory, film-forming finishes are very good at protecting wood, but they inevitably develop hairline cracks — particularly on a deck. When they do, rainwater will get beneath the film. "And then these coatings are going to do an equally good job of keeping it there," Burke says. "The problem with that is that any time wood does not dry out between rainstorms, you have the potential for decay and rot."

Opaque deck stains can be paintlike in this respect when too much is applied. Homeowners sometimes take a look at the result and think the deck needs multiple coats. Yet when they try to make the surface of the deck look as uniform as a freshly painted ceiling by applying more finish, the stain morphs into a film-forming finish.

"The problem is," explains Burke, "there's so much pigment in this stuff that if you put it on too heavily or you put on two coats, bingo — you've got an oil-based paint. It doesn't matter what you put on the can. It's paint because it forms a paint film." Avoid the problem by following the recommendations of the manufacturer.

Oil- or Water-Based?

For a variety of reasons, acrylic latex paint is gradually replacing traditional oil-based formulations, and manufacturers are showing equal resolve in developing water-based deck finishes. There have been steady improvements in their durability: Some now perform as well as their oil-based counterparts

Figure 22. Semisolid stains show only a hint of the underlying wood grain. Their heavy pigments offer the best UV protection, and they can be expected to last as long as five years.

Figure 23. Water-based finishes can be as durable as oil-based. This clear finish looks milky during application but dries to a satin finish. Water-based finishes wear differently than oil-based, tending to eventually flake or peel away, rather than abrading with time. Refinishing may be more likely to require stripping the deck to bare wood than with oil-based finishes.

(**Figure 23**). "Three years ago I would have said don't ever use them," Williams says. "But some of the acrylics are starting to get a little better. It's a brand-by-brand situation. Some of the waterbornes seem to work as well as some of the old [oil] systems."

Water-based finishes, however, typically don't penetrate very deeply into wood decking (if they penetrate at all), so they wear differently — they're more likely to peel than gradually erode like oil-based products, according to the makers of Thompson's deck products. But they are lower in volatile organic compounds (VOCs), making them a natural choice where air-quality regulations are toughest. They also hold color well and can be cleaned up with soap and water — all decided advantages.

Everett Abrams, owner of Deck Restoration Plus in Shamong, N.J., calls water-based finishes the "enigma of the industry." He explains that while water-based finishes are durable, they also are harder to strip back when it's time to recoat. And if the surface isn't consistent when a new coat is applied, he notes, the finish can look blotchy. Abrams says strippers that effectively remove water-based finishes are becoming more widely available, but when faced with a deck that's been finished with a water-based product, he's still likely to sand before recoating.

Among oil-based finishes, linseed and soy oils have been traditional choices. They are easy to apply and they penetrate more deeply than water-based coatings. Another plus: They wear gradually by erosion.

On the other hand, natural oils have two big disadvantages: First, these finishes contain more solvents containing VOCs than water-based coatings do — and VOCs are falling under increasingly stringent government regulations, though rules vary around the country. In California, the South Coast Air Quality Management District regulates products sold in several counties in the Los Angeles area. In the Northeast, the Ozone Transport Commission has jurisdiction over a dozen states plus the District of Columbia. Manufacturers may sometimes adjust their formulations to meet these local or regional requirements.

Second, natural oil can be what Burke calls "mold fertilizer." Given the right moisture and temperature, mold colonies thrive as they feed on the organic compounds in oil as well as on the extractives in the wood decking itself (**Figure 24**). "When you load up a piece of redwood or western red cedar with linseed oil, the mildew just goes to town on it," Williams says. "In fact, you can turn a piece of redwood black in about a week under the right weather conditions. It's really a disaster."

Fungicides added to the mix by the manufacturer can control the problem. Beware of the anti-mildew additives sold at paint stores, however: They probably have limited usefulness.

Alkyds, which are modified oils, don't have the same potential for mold. Greg Portincasa, a technical and customer support supervisor for Sikkens Wood Finishes, says alkyds are more expensive than natural oils, but they cure faster and last longer.

Increasingly, manufacturers are finding ways of combining alkyds with acrylics for a finish that

Figure 24. Natural oil-based finishes soak in to seal out water but may bring other problems. Linseed oil is itself gourmet mold food. If you're planning to use such a product, be sure it's got a factory-blended fungicide.

Table 2. Finishes For Exterior Decks

Finish Type	Pros	Cons	Best Uses	Application	Service Life
Water repellents	Prevents water intrusion and resulting checking and warping. With UV blockers, also inhibits deterioration of wood surface. Easy application. No peeling of finish.	Needs frequent recoating. Limited UV protection.	Undercoating for paint or stain on pressure-treated (PT) wood or decay-resistant species. Final coating on decay-resistant species.	Surface of wood should be dry before application. Can be brushed, rolled, or applied with low-pressure sprayer. Dipping provides best coating.	1–2 years
Water repellent preservatives	Same as above, but also inhibits mildew growth and provides some above-grade protection against decay in cut ends of PT wood and sapwood of decay-resistant species.	Needs frequent recoating. Limited UV protection.	Undercoating for paint or stain on all species. Final coat on naturally decay-resistant species.	Same as above. Also make sure cut ends are treated before installation makes them inaccessible.	1–2 years
Semitransparent stains (oil-based)	Same as above, but offers increased protection against UV degradation of wood surface. Outlasts clear finishes. Provides redwood and cedar with some pigmentation while allowing wood grain to show through.	Limited abrasion resistance for decking. Note: For best results, choose products specially formulated for decking.	Finishing pressure-treated wood. Also can help preserve the original look of redwood and cedar decking.	Wood surface must be dry enough to absorb finish before application. Can be brushed, sprayed, or rolled and back-brushed. If applying over sealer or factory-sealed lumber, allow to weather until surface will absorb finish. Apply a second coat before first dries completely.	2–3 years (single coat on new decking); 3–6 years (recoating with two coats).
Paints and solid stains	Offers best protection against UV degradation and moderate resistance to abrasion. Longest-lasting finish with most color choices.	Prone to bubble, crack, and peel when applied to horizontal surfaces. Time-consuming to apply and difficult to recoat. Must be scraped and sanded.	For trim, railings, and other decorative surfaces not subjected to foot traffic or ponding of water. Wood must be dry at application. Primer required.	Wood should be fully dried or pressure treated before painting. Use over sealer for best finish. Seal and prime all end grain prior to installation. Generally not recommended for use on decking.	**Decking:** 2–3 years for paint; 1–2 years for solid stain. **Trim:** 3–6 years for paint; 3–4 for solid stain. (Assumes one primer coat and one top coat. Second top coat can double service life.)

Figure 25. Yes, you can finish composite decking. No manufacturer requires that composite decking be finished, but colors can be changed, and older decks can be made to look newer.

CABOT STAINS

Invisible UV Blockers

Nanotechnology is a word that's steadily creeping into our vocabulary. It comes from nanometer, or one billionth of a meter, and it means the manipulation of matter at an extremely small scale in order to change its physical properties or behavior. Scientists believe nanotechnology will have a profound effect on our lives in the decades ahead, making possible advances in medicine, agriculture, and dozens of other fields. When it comes to paints and finishes, the future may already be here.

Nanotechnology allows UV-blocking compounds that are normally opaque to become transparent, giving clear finishes the ability to protect against UV damage as effectively as a pigmented stain. Finish manufacturers are no doubt developing new formulations that take advantage of this phenomenon, but that's apparently nothing new. "Paint companies have been working on nanotechnology for 15 years," says Sam Williams of the Forest Products Laboratory, "except that they didn't call it that. They just said they had UV-resistant pigments in there."

When transoxides, a kind of pigment, are ground down into the nano range, Williams explains, they become opaque to UV light and transparent to visible light. "If you take a clear film and load it with these nano particles, you can see through it," he says, "but you'll never get a suntan through it." Improved performance from clear and semiclear finishes can be attributed to these precisely ground pigments that interact with UV radiation – even when you don't know they're there.

forms a shell of acrylic resin around a core of alkyd resin — what Thompson's describes as something like a Tootsie Pop. These finishes can be produced with lower VOCs, and they wear by erosion like other oil-based products.

Ipe and Wood-Plastic Composites

While most woods last longer and look better with a finish, caring for super-hard tropical hardwoods, such as ipe, and for the growing number of wood-plastic composites can be more complicated.

Ipe is a naturally decay-resistant wood that will last a long time in the weather, even if it turns gray in sunlight and the board ends show some minor cracking or checking. These characteristics might seem to make this family of South American hardwoods a good candidate for a clear UV protector, except that finishes have a tough time penetrating the surface. Some manufacturers have developed finishes that are specifically marketed for this purpose. But in the end, ipe, like other naturally durable woods, can be allowed to weather naturally if the homeowner doesn't find fading objectionable. A water-repellent preservative applied to the end grain can reduce checking.

Composites pose a different problem (**Figure 25**). There are now many brands on the market, each with its own formulation. But because these man-made planks contain significant amounts of wood fiber, they are susceptible to fading and mold growth — just like wood. The material itself is challenging, too. A mix of wood flour and recycled or virgin plastics, composite decking combines two materials with dramatically different characteristics. The finishing industry has been stymied at times as decking producers continue to modify their formulations.

Should some kind of finish be applied? It depends. Trex says its decking needs no stains or sealants, just regular cleaning. CorrectDeck, on the other hand, says clear or solid-color stains may be used. The

Forest Products Lab has found that composites with high wood content can be maintained with a clear penetrating finish after the boards weather for several years. Given the difference in composite content, however, it would be a good idea to check with the manufacturer to see which, if any, type of finish or stain is recommended. Regular cleaning will take care of any mold and dirt.

No Magic Answer

If you're looking for the single best deck finish, one that works on every decking material all the time, no matter where you are, you're going to be disappointed. There are just too many variables.

Keeping the pros and cons of various families of finishes in mind will help determine what finish to use, as will the particular requirements of the homeowner. Should, for example, the finish enhance the natural color and grain of the wood (clear preservative) or mask it (pigmented stain)? How much maintenance is the homeowner willing to accept — a minor cleaning before recoating or more extensive chemical stripping and sanding? How long does the finish have to last? What is the decking material?

Long-term third-party testing of finishes would be useful, but there's not much of that around. Consumer Reports magazine conducts multiyear weather tests for a variety of finishes, periodically reporting the results. Those surveys may provide clues about performance, as will asking around for what brands and types of finishes seem to work best locally.

Williams suggests trying a couple of brands to see

Surface Prep Makes All the Difference

Getting a durable, uniform finish on a wood deck depends on having a surface that's ready to accept a coating.

In some cases, timing is key as well. The longer new wood sits in the sun, the more damage UV radiation will do to the lignin, the essential binder of wood fiber. Lignin begins to break down immediately with exposure to sunlight in a process called "photochemical degradation," turning the surface gray and making it more porous. This increases the absorption of penetrating oil and alkyd finishes, but makes it difficult for an acrylic finish to bond well and can significantly shorten the life of a paint film.

If you've chosen an acrylic finish, it should be applied as soon as possible. Wood should not be allowed to weather. For penetrating oil finishes, a few weeks or even months of weathering won't make much difference and, in fact, will make the surface more porous so it absorbs more finish.

When it comes to applying maintenance coats, some deck finishes should be stripped back nearly to new wood before a new coat is applied. Read the manufacturer's directions carefully. A clear alkyd finish won't need as much attention as a heavily pigmented deck stain, because much of it will have worn away. More robust coatings may need chemical strippers or sanding to adequately prepare the surface.

Also, coatings can weather unevenly, depending on where they are applied. Surfaces protected by roof overhangs or shade trees will not show as much wear as areas in heavy traffic zones. Applying new finish to a deck that has weathered or worn unevenly invites a blotchy, unattractive job.

A variety of deck cleaners are available that are capable of removing dirt and mold, probably a better bet than brewed-at-home blends of bleach, water, and laundry soap. Power washers can be useful, but take care to control pressure so the surface isn't abraded or "pulped." Decks should dry out for a day or two after washing before a finish is applied.

WOLMAN WOOD CARE PRODUCTS

Finishing is all about preparation. New wood can (and should) be finished within a couple of weeks of installation to prevent UV damage. Older decks will likely require the use of a cleaning agent and a light, careful pressure washing before refinishing.

Figure 26. Sample boards help customers decide between finish options. There's no substitute for seeing the real thing.

which look best and then contacting the manufacturer's customer service department to ask specific questions about the formulation (**Figure 26**). Does the finish contain alkyds? Or is it made with a natural oil or with a polymer such as acrylic or vinyl acrylic? If it's a polymer base, don't expect much penetration. If it's made from a natural oil, expect a higher risk for mold.

Finally, take a close look at the surface of the wood after the finish has been applied. If it's shiny, it means the finish hasn't really penetrated the surface. What you're looking for is a dull surface, meaning the finish has soaked in.

Ultimately, Mother Nature is going to prevail. Finishes can help preserve color, at least temporarily, and a preservative applied every couple of years won't hurt.

"Does the wood need it?" asks Williams. "To a certain extent, yes, but not to the extent that you're out there every year for three or four hours finishing your deck. Most people finish their decks because they want a certain look. They want to maintain the natural look of the wood or match the color scheme of their home. If you have a redwood or cedar deck, it's really important to put a penetrating preservative on it every two or three years. Other than that, decks don't require much maintenance."

Scott Gibson is a writer in East Waterboro, Maine, who specializes in construction topics..

Decking Materials Q&A

Bark Side Up or Down?

Q. *Should you lay wood decking boards bark side up or bark side down?*

A. *Paul Fisette, wood technologist and professor of building materials at the University of Massachussets in Amherst, responds:* Depending on the wood type, moisture content, and exposure, deck boards can cup, twist, or decay. Theoretically, you can ensure that a board will cup downward to shed water, and thereby reduce deterioration, by exposing one face or the other. In fact, seldom does a week pass that I'm not involved in a discussion about whether to install deck boards either bark side up or bark side down. But such recommendations usually only account for one of a handful of factors that control cupping.

Original moisture content. The original moisture content of a piece of lumber controls a board's final shape. Wood is stable when its moisture content is above 30% (fiber saturation point). As wood dries below 30%, it shrinks. Wood shrinks and swells twice as much in the direction parallel to the growth rings as it does perpendicular to the growth rings. The combined effect of these different rates of movement causes lumber to deform.

Flat-sawn lumber, which is cut so its wide face is parallel to the growth rings, cups as it gains or loses moisture. A good way to visualize the typical distortion is to imagine that the growth rings straighten as wood dries. Therefore, wet lumber will tend to cup toward the bark side as it dries. Kiln-dried lumber, on the other hand, is usually surfaced after the lumber has been dried, and will tend to cup away from the bark side as it gains moisture.

Heartwood and sapwood. Heartwood is often more resistant to decay than sapwood of the same species. But heartwood is difficult to impregnate with wood-preserving chemicals, while sapwood is easy to treat. As a result, the most resistant face of treated wood is often the bark side.

Shelling. Growth rings have two parts — earlywood and latewood. The inner layers of each growth ring (closest to the center of each ring) are formed during the early part of the growing season. The outer layer grows later in the season. Repeated cycles of wetting and drying sometimes cause the layers of earlywood to separate from the layers of latewood. This separation, called shelling, occurs infrequently. When it does, it is associated with flat-sawn softwoods like Southern Yellow Pine and Douglas fir, that is laid bark-side down.

In-use conditions. No matter which face is up, the ultimate shape of a board will be influenced by its moisture content. If one side is wetter than the other, that side will expand and cup the board. Since the underside of a deck built close to the ground experiences higher relative humidity than the upper surface, which is exposed to wind and sun, the boards often cup upward. If this is the problem, increasing the under-deck ventilation or using a moisture barrier and gravel beneath the deck may help.

Pick the best face. When all is said and done, you needn't remember all these factors when trying to decide which face to install up. In truth, the answer is very simple: Pick the best looking face, selecting out the faces with the most knots and wane, and install your decking best face up. Secure fastening and an annual coating of water repellent will do the most for keeping the boards flat.

Oozing Knotholes in Decking

Q. *Is there anything that can be done, short of tearout and replacement, to prevent the knotholes in pressure-treated pine decking from oozing on hot days?*

A. *Paul Fisette responds:* The sap in the knotholes softens and begins to runs as it is heated by the sun. Sap is composed of liquid and solid materials. If it is heated to 160°F while it is being kiln-dried, the volatile liquid substances will flash off, leaving the solids behind in a hardened state. Once the sap has set, it will never run again. This doesn't help you now, however, since the wood in your deck was obviously not kiln-dried at a high enough temperature during production.

There are a couple of options. You can wait it out; sooner or later the sap will stop running out of the wood. In the meantime, you can clean it up with turpentine. Or you can try to set the sap in the knots using a heat gun. Just be careful not to start a fire or singe the wood.

Black Stains from Redwood

Q. *On elevated decks, the redwood decking often causes black streaks on the joists below. How can we prevent this?*

A. *Building consultant Henry Spies reponds:* Redwood contains tannins and extractives that are water-soluble. The extractives will wash down onto the wood below, leaving brown or black streaks. The best way to minimize this streaking is to treat the redwood with a water repellent. If the water does not penetrate the redwood, only a minimum amount of extractives will dissolve to wash down on the wood below.

According to work done by wood researcher Brian Buchanan of the Texas Forest Service, some of the best water repellents are clear or cedartone Amteco TWP Roof and Deck Sealant (www.amteco.com), ABR X-100 Natural Seal, (www.abrp.com), and WoodGuard (www.woodguard.com). For color maintenance, Amteco TWP tested best.

Painting PT Decking?

Q. *Some of my customers want their pressure-treated decks painted, but I've had trouble getting paint to adhere well to pressure-treated wood. What's the solution?*

A. *Mark Knaebe, research chemist at the USDA Forest Products Laboratory in Madison, Wis., responds:* Treated lumber is not the source of your deck painting difficulties. Clean, dry treated lumber is actually a better surface to paint than untreated wood of the same species. The real problem is that a paint's performance suffers on a horizontal surface that is exposed to the weather. To make matters worse, deck boards are usually flat-grained, high-density wood that doesn't hold paint as well as edge-grained, low-density wood.

For exterior decks, you're better off using a water-repellent preservative or a penetrating-type semi-transparent pigmented stain. Solid-color stains and film-forming paints aren't recommended for horizontal surfaces because they may fail early. Hard enamel paints lack the flexibility to accommodate the movement of exposed wood. Flexible latex paints are not tough enough to stand up to foot traffic.

In contrast to paint, which flakes and peels, stains "erode," or wear away gradually. Stains must be reapplied more often than paint, but it's an easier job because there is no need for extensive scraping and sanding. Also, weathering stain is less of an eyesore than failing paint.

Sheltered porches can be painted with porch and deck enamel. First, treat the deck with a water-repellent preservative (check the label to make sure the product contains a preservative and is paintable). Second, prime the wood with enamel diluted with paint thinner. Last, apply two topcoats of straight enamel. Railings, whether exposed or sheltered, can be painted with latex paints.

Remember, wood to be painted should be dry but not exposed to more than a few weeks of sunlight. The sun's ultraviolet rays damage wood fibers and weaken the wood's ability to hold paint.

Ipe's Fire Rating

Q. *I thought that ipe decking had a Class A fire rating, making it suitable for use in places such as the urban-wildland interface (areas prone to wildfire —*

typically a concern in the arid West) and on urban high-rise rooftop decks. However, I haven't been able to secure approval for its use in downtown Chicago. What's up?

A. *Andy Engel, editor of* Professional Deck Builder, *responds:* I had thought the same thing. Indeed, a Web search on the topic brings up pages with language such as "ipe is given a Class A fire rating under the UBC-uniform building code, the same rating given to concrete & steel" and "the NFPA test results have shown that ipe is ... naturally resistant to fire (and rated Class A by the NFPA or class 1 by the UBC)."

Despite this online information, which creates the impression that ipe is widely approved as a fire-resistant material, its acceptance in fire-sensitive construction is still an emerging issue. A scientist I called at USDA's Forest Products Laboratory (www.fpl.fs.fed.us), a respected source for information on all things wood said he'd recently received a lot of questions about ipe's fire rating, couldn't provide a definitive answer.

Next, I spoke with Carl Widder, residential deck product sales manager at Timber Holdings, a major ipe importer. Widder says that in 1989, Timber Holdings had ipe tested using the ASTM E-84 protocol, which is how materials are rated for fire resistance, and the ipe received a Class A rating.

So what's the problem? There are several. First, the test data above is owned by Timber Holdings. Because of quality control and liability — and because it paid for the testing — Timber Holdings provides documentation only for its own ipe. Other importers may provide testing documentation, but you will have to request it from your supplier.

Also, about two years ago, the ASTM E-84 test protocol changed. Timber Holdings hasn't yet tested ipe by the new procedure, and that's probably true of other importers as well. Your local inspector may be satisfied with the old E-84 data, but some inspectors may not.

To further complicate matters, California is currently developing new standards for construction materials used in the urban-wildland interface. A significant amount of real estate will be subject to the new rules, and the state's emerging standard is likely to affect how all decking — not just ipe — is rated for fire resistance.

Testing is expensive, and Widder says Timber Holdings isn't likely to retest its ipe until there's a consensus on a national standard. Unless the local authority accepts the old E-84 rating, ipe users may be scrambling for approval in fire-sensitive areas for a time. Widder did tell me that ipe is generally accepted (even in Chicago, a jurisdiction that historically takes fire protection seriously) as having a Class B fire rating, which means it's fine for use on most backyard decks. But if you're working where fire is of particular concern, don't assume the local inspector will allow the use of ipe just because the information you find online says it's a Class A material.

Chapter 7: Railings

- **Fast and Sturdy Guardrails**
- **Installing Cable Railings**
- **Site-Built Rod Railings**
- **Installing Hollow Aluminum Balusters**
- **Manufactured Railing Options**
- **Building Composite Curved Railings**
- **Deck Railings Q&A**

Fast and Sturdy Guardrails

by Mark Clement

No matter how you approach it, installing effective, good-looking guardrails takes time. Cutting, plumbing, shimming, and fastening the numerous individual parts is not full-speed framing. It's trim work, where you can (and should) show off your carpentry skills to customers.

That doesn't mean, however, that guardrails can't be built efficiently. The system I've developed over the years combines simple installation with crisp looks and bombproof structure. Two key aspects are integrating the post with the framing on the inside of the band joist, and assembling the 2x2 balusters and the top and bottom rails into panels that install between the posts. I can employ the same process equally well with composites or wood.

Blocking Anchors the Posts

The first step is to lay out the post locations on the band joists. For MoistureShield composite railing and decking (Advanced Environmental Recycling Technologies, www.moistureshield.com), which I used for some of the projects shown here, post spacing must not exceed 72 inches on-center. Measuring from the outside corners of the deck frame, I mark the locations of the posts as evenly as possible around the deck's perimeter. This is the time to make final decisions about openings in the guardrail — for stairs, gates, and upgrades such as planters and benches — that might affect post placement.

Sometimes layout drops a post right on a joist, but don't alter the post or the joist; just move the post to the side of the joist that's closest to the proper layout. If you can, move any posts that might be in line with it on the other side of the deck a similar distance. If you can't, spans are typically large enough that the difference won't be terribly obvious.

For added stability, I frame housings for the posts into the joists using blocking cut from joist stock (**Figure 1**). I cut the between-joist blocking 1/8 inch to 1/4 inch short because joists are never perfect and pounding in a block can easily deform a joist, especially one on a side of a deck. This, by the way, is when you'll thank yourself for setting up a slide compound miter saw. It saves untold amounts of time and energy (**Figure 2**).

I make the housings about 1/8 inch larger than the posts, which leaves wiggle room to slide the post into the housing. Later I'll shim as necessary. It's easiest to build the housings piece by piece in place, squaring them to the framing with a small square. I've tried making up blocking assemblies on the bench and then installing them, but I found it took more time.

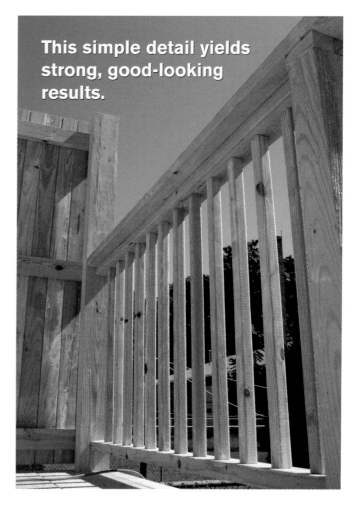

This simple detail yields strong, good-looking results.

You can use 3 1/2-inch screws or nails to assemble the housings. I drive a fastener into the top, middle, and bottom of the blocking at each nailing location. This fastening schedule not only makes a strong mechanical connection to the framing, it also leaves known areas clear of fasteners that could get in the way of drilling for bolts (**Figure 3**).

Install the Posts

Finished post and rail heights vary (within code) depending on design, but posts should always extend at least to the bottom of the joists.

The key to laying out a post is to make a story pole showing all the spaces, gaps, and assemblies. This approach avoids math and makes it easy to see if you've remembered everything: the decking, the toe space, the baluster assembly, any post extension above that, and a rail cap. Once you've mapped out the story pole, you can forget all the numbers except for the overall height and the distance from the top of the post to where the post meets the joists.

Figure 1. Housings assembled from joist stock and tied into the framing provide stout anchors for guardrail posts. Make the post openings a little big and cut the blocking a little short so it doesn't force the outer joist out of line.

Figure 2. It takes a little extra time in the morning to set up a miter saw, but it pays dividends of fast and accurate cuts all day long.

Figure 3. The post housings can be nailed or screwed into place. Locate fasteners where they won't be in the way later on when you drill for bolts.

After cutting the post to length on a miter saw, I measure down the post to where it will meet the top of the housing, square a line across, and partly drive two nails right on the line. Slide the post into the housing, and the nails will keep it at the proper elevation until it's fastened. This common trick, when used in combination with a housed post (compared with a face-mounted post), enables one worker to handle a post solo (**Figure 4**, next page).

For a rock-solid connection, whether I'm using composite or wood, I coat the interior of the housing with construction adhesive before inserting the post. With the post in place, I double-check that the bit won't hit nails in the blocking, then drill two holes through the framing using a 3/4-inch-diameter auger bit. The holes go through the band or side joist, the post, and the blocking behind the post. One hole is drilled about 2 inches down from the top of the joist and the other about 2 inches up from the bottom.

I then install and lightly snug two 1/2-inch-diame-

Figure 4. Nails driven partway into the post will support it at the correct height on the housing. This makes it easy for one person to plumb, shim, and bolt the post home.

Figure 5. A heavy-duty drill and an auger bit make quick work of the bolt holes. The author drills $3/4$-inch holes for $1/2$-inch bolts to provide flexibility for shimming the post plumb.

Figure 6. Use a cordless impact driver to quickly cinch down the bolts. LedgerLok screws are an alternative to bolts for wood posts, subject to local approval.

ter through-bolts. The oversize holes make it easier to place the bolts, and they allow some wiggle room to shim the post plumb before cinching the bolts tight (**Figure 5**).

Cedar shingles, naturally rot resistant, work nicely as shims. An alternative is to cut slivers from treated scrap for site-made shims. They work just as well, and you don't have to transport a bucket full of cedar shingles from job to job.

When I'm satisfied, I tighten the bolts (whenever possible I use my cordless impact driver for this), checking that the posts remain plumb. When the bolt heads crunch into the joist stock, I know they're tight enough (**Figure 6**).

While both composite and wood posts can certainly be installed using the method above, on wood posts the local inspectors allow me to use 6-inch-long LedgerLok screws (FastenMaster, www.fastenmaster. com) instead of through-bolts as fasteners. The glued-and-screwed connections I made this way a year ago are still rock solid.

Notch the Decking

Unfortunately, 6-inch deck boards have to be notched to fit around 4x4 composite posts. I use decking scraps as test pieces before cutting new deck boards. The extra time spent is paid back with dead accurate cuts in the full deck boards. MoistureShield recommends a $1/8$-inch expansion gap between the board and the post, but check with the manufacturer of the decking you're using, as that space may vary. I

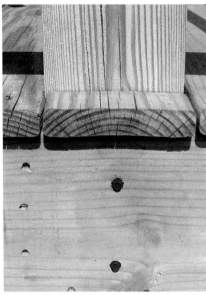

Figure 7. Using 4x6 wood posts eliminates the need to notch the ends of boards. Lay out the final location of the posts as you run the decking so that the boards and the posts are aligned. Construction adhesive and finish nails hold the outboard piece of decking in place.

begin by drilling the corners of the notch using a 1/2-inch spade bit, then I jigsaw the hole square.

On a wood deck, though, I can avoid notching the boards: I spec 4x6 posts rather than 4x4s and face the 6-inch side inward. I wait to install the posts that fall at the ends of the deck boards (usually the posts on the sides of the deck) until I'm installing the adjacent decking. By slightly tweaking the layout of the posts I can line them up with the deck boards, thereby eliminating the need for notching. I glue and finish-nail a short piece of decking on the outside of the post (**Figure 7**). The result is a clean look and faster installation, and without notches the deck boards will be less likely to split due to wood movement.

There's no way, however, to avoid notching the last board (**Figure 8**). If it overhangs the framing more than 2 inches, I rip it to width and rout a bullnose on the inside edge to match the other deck boards (**Figure 9**). Another method is to rip the next-to-last board installed so that the last board on the deck is full width.

Figure 8. The last board always requires notching. Drill the corners of the holes first, then use a jigsaw to cut out the notches.

Figure 9. Often, the last (or next-to-last board, if you want the last one to be full size) must be ripped to width. Run a roundover bit in a router along the ripped edge to blend it in.

Railing Rules

by *JLC* staff

Under the International Residential Code, guardrails ("guards" in the code) are required on any deck more than 30 inches above grade and along any stairs that rise more than 30 inches (see "Guardrails vs. Handrails," page 39). The guard must be at least 36 inches high at the deck and 34 inches high at a stairway, measured vertically from the leading edge of the nosing.

Guardrails and handrails must be able to resist a 200-pound point load applied in any direction to any point along the top of the rail. The balusters or other infill must be able to resist a horizontal load of 50 pounds applied to any one-square-foot area.

The guardrail can either be solid or an open railing with balusters or other infill. In a open railing system, a

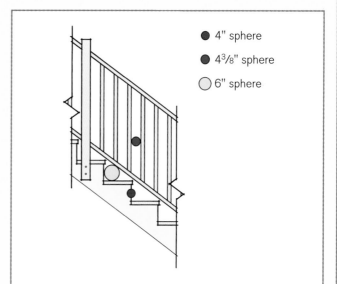

Figure B. *In stair railings, a 6-inch ball should not pass through the triangular openings along the bottom of the railing. Baluster spacing must be less than 4³⁄₈ inches and, if risers are open, the spaces between treads must not allow a 4-inch ball to pass through.*

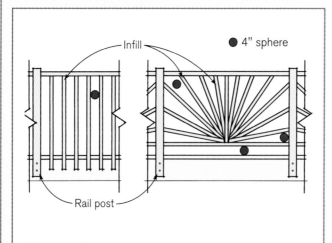

Figure A. *It's a code violation if a 4-inch ball can pass though the infill in a deck railing.*

4-inch diameter sphere should not be able to pass through any space between balusters or other decorative elements (**Figure A**).

For guardrails along a stairway, a 4³⁄₈-inch sphere should not pass through any space, except at the triangular spaces along the bottom of the railing, which must not allow a 6-inch sphere to pass through. Open risers are allowed, but for stairways over 30 inches high, the spaces between treads must not allow a 4-inch sphere to pass through (**Figure B**).

ILLUSTRATIONS REPRINTED WITH PERMISSION FROM *THE MANUAL FOR THE INSPECTION OF RESIDENTIAL WOOD DECKS AND BALCONIES*, BY CHERYL ANDERSON, FRANK WOESTE, AND JOSEPH LOFERSKI. © 2003 BY THE FOREST PRODUCTS SOCIETY.

Assemble Baluster Panels

Instead of laying out 2-by rails and installing the 2x2 balusters one at a time, I build panels and install the whole assembly between the posts. While this approach is typical for composite systems, it's fast and accurate for wood decks too.

I begin by measuring between the posts at the base. This determines the length of both the top and bottom rails. Unlike how I treated the blocking, I take precise measurements and cut the top and bottom pieces of composite railings to match.

If I'm using wood, to increase the strength of the post connections to the railings I'll cut the top rail longer than the space by the width of a 4x6. (The

bottom rail is cut to fit exactly between the posts, just like with composite railing.) I lay out the balusters so that half this extra length extends out on each end of the panel. The top rail is placed on the 4x6s, covering up half of each one and providing plenty of meat for screwing the rail to the top of the post.

The balusters are spaced 4 inches apart on the railing using a spacer block. Four inches is the maximum allowed by code (see "Railing Rules," above). I start the baluster layout in the center of the rail so that the distance between the last balusters and the posts ends up equal. There are two choices when beginning the layout — you can center a baluster, or you can center one of the spaces. It's worth looking to see which works better. Sometimes, to make the layout work just

Figure 10. MoistureShield's rails are L-shaped and the balusters are face-screwed in place.

Figure 11. Spreading out wood balusters on lengths of 1-inch-thick decking centers them perfectly on 2x4 rails. An impact driver makes quick work of the 3½-inch screws that join the parts.

right, I butt a baluster right to the post.

With the rails cut to length and spread out with the balusters on the deck, I'm ready to build the rail panels. In the case of the MoistureShield system, the rails are an L-shape that requires setting fasteners in the face of the 2x2 (**Figure 10**).

For wood decks, the top and bottom rails are 2x4s. I center 2x2 balusters on the rails using pieces of decking as a jig (**Figure 11**). One 3½-inch screw in the top and bottom of each baluster secures it to the railing. While screws are best, gun nails work too; just make sure to keep the tool's nose straight to prevent blowouts.

Install the Rail Assemblies

To keep the rail panel at the right height, I set it on blocks that are the same height as the toe space (2x4 scraps work great) then fasten the railing per the manufacturer's instructions (**Figure 12**). The cap rail,

Figure 12. With a 3½-inch toe space, you can rest the rail on 2x4 blocks for support while fastening it.

Figure 13. Pieces of 2x2 support the railing midspan. Composite-railing manufacturers generally require this, and it's a good idea with wood railings as well.

Railing Styles

by Rosanne Minerva

Railings serve an obvious and important utilitarian purpose. People lean against railings and children climb on them, so foremost they have to be strong and code-compliant. Understandably, this is often your first concern as the builder. But railings are also one of the more visible details on a house, so it pays to think about their aesthetic design as well.

Horizontal Tie

A railing creates a horizontal band that helps to visually organize and tie together a house design. Railings are a good way to break up the monotony and verticality of a tall elevation (much the way the balconies on old triple-decker homes do). Because of its horizontal lines, a railing that extends off the main house can also help

Three Railing Styles

Contemporary

Traditional

Rustic

Use a deck railing that matches the style and period of the house. The railings shown here can easily be built from stock lumber.

Historic Designs

When it works, borrow from the masters, and don't be afraid to depart from convention. Shown here are a railing from Monticello, designed by Thomas Jefferson (top), and a whimsical railing from Boston's Henderson Boathouse, designed by Graham Gund.

anchor a building to the surrounding landscape.

A nicely detailed railing can also enhance a house by:

• creating visual interest and a focal point on the exterior – often missing on the rear of a house
• providing an opportunity to add a touch of whimsy or "gingerbread" within the limits of the house style
• repeating a detail from somewhere else on the house – a front entry railing, for example – to give continuity.

Borrow From the Best

Look around at railing designs and try to figure out why the good ones are successful. It could be the materials, the scale, the rhythm created by the repeating pattern of railing sections, or how the railing relates to and adds to the overall house design. Don't be afraid to copy an idea that you like. There are many famous railing details, both traditional and contemporary, that can be adapted for your specific design.

As with any detail, use a style that is in keeping with the style and period of the building. Don't put a '70s-style horizontal board railing on a colonial or Victorian house.

Rosanne Minerva is an architectural illustrator and designer in Boston.

which installs quickly, is next; it isn't just decorative, as it also reinforces the railing attachment. With MoistureShield's composite system, the cap rail fits between the posts and covers the top rail. For wood, if your railing attaches to the top of the posts, you'll run the cap on top of, rather than between, the posts.

Without midspan support, most railings will sag, including those made of wood. The maker of MoistureShield requires this support, as do other synthetic-railing manufacturers. I use a piece of 2x2 (**Figure 13**, page 211).

Only a few details are left. If there's a gate, I assemble it as I would a rail panel. To prevent the gate from sagging, I install diagonal bracing. When there are post caps, I find that attaching them with adhesive is easier and faster than screwing them down. I use a bead of Phenoseal (Phenomenal Brands, www. phenoseal.com) on the top of each post (**Figure 14**), then set the cap into the bead. Before the adhesive sets, I eyeball the cap to make sure it's square to the rail.

Mark Clement is a remodeler and deck builder in Ambler, Pa.

Figure 14. Instead of screwing or nailing post caps in place, the author uses a bead of adhesive caulk. This holds the cap firmly in place — without fastener holes.

Installing Cable Railings

by Kim and Linda Katwijk

Stainless steel cable railing is low maintenance and long-lasting. It's also fairly easy to install: Horizontal cables are strung through holes drilled in railing posts and tightened with cable studs — fittings that grip the end of a cable run and allow it to be tensioned — until they "sing." With its open, airy design, cable railing virtually disappears, providing an unobstructed view and a clean, contemporary look.

My company specializes in building decks. Though cable railings don't make up a large percentage of our work, we have seen an increase in demand for them since they were approved in recent versions of the building codes. Many customers ask about cable railings but lose interest after learning that they cost almost twice as much per foot as wood ones.

I buy cable in bulk and have the fittings I need made in a local millwork shop. This substantially reduces my material costs compared with using an off-the-shelf cable-rail system. For convenience, however, you may want to consider one of the available packages if you're doing only one deck (see "Buying Components," page 218).

With just a couple of specialty tools, you can offer this sleek look on high-end projects.

Figure 15. Although wood is the most common material for posts, powder-coated steel and aluminum are clean-looking alternatives and can be engineered to withstand the forces involved with cable railing.

Cable and Posts

Cable comes in diameters of ⅛ inch to ½ inch, in 1/16-inch increments (see "Cable Configurations," below). The sizes most often used for residential applications are ⅛ inch, 3/16 inch, and ¼ inch. With very large posts — say, 10-inch-diameter logs — the larger ¼-inch to ½-inch cable should be used, to balance the look of the railing. For commercial applications, 3/16 inch is the smallest size allowed, but ¼ inch is recommended. In my area, 3/16-inch cable runs around 80 cents per foot when bought in 100-foot rolls.

Posts can be made of a variety of materials, such as wood, powder-coated steel, and powder-coated aluminum (**Figure 15**). Cables should be spaced no more than 3½ inches apart, so that a 4-inch sphere can't pass between them (code requirement). This means there are at least nine cables on a 36-inch-high residential railing, and since each cable exerts roughly 300 pounds of tension, the posts need to withstand a minimum of 2,700 pounds of pull. Posts require stout mounting plus a cap rail that spreads the load out from the anchor posts to the intermediate posts (**Figure 16**).

Cable Configurations

Different configurations of stainless steel cable vary in flexibility. For example, semi-flexible 7x7 cable has seven cords, each with seven individual wires; it's used for straight runs and corners where cable runs between multiple posts. The smooth cable preferred by most customers is 1x19 rope, made by twisting 18 wires around one center wire. Since it's semi-rigid, it's used for straight runs and gentle turns.

Stainless steel is an alloy of iron and carbon that contains between 12 percent and 30 percent chromium. The chromium forms an oxide film on the surface, which is what gives stainless its superior corrosion resistance. Still, the alloy can discolor or rust if it comes in contact with chloride salts or sulfides.

There are several grades of stainless steel. Type 303 contains sulfur to enhance machinability; typical applica-

1x19 cable   **7x7 cable**

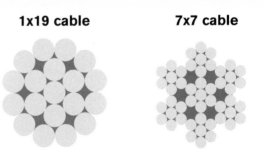

tions include bolts, bushings, nuts, and shafts. The most widely used stainless for aesthetic purposes is type 304, a low-carbon, general-purpose alloy. Type 316 is the most corrosion-resistant form commonly available; it contains extra nickel and molybdenum and is used in marine environments. It's also the type most often used for cable railings.

Basic Framework

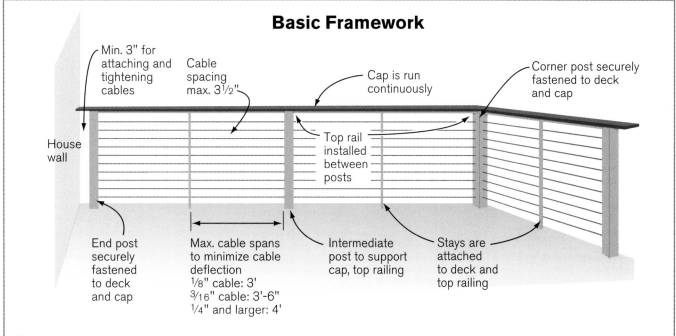

Min. 3" for attaching and tightening cables

Cable spacing max. 3½"

Cap is run continuously

Corner post securely fastened to deck and cap

House wall

Top rail installed between posts

End post securely fastened to deck and cap

Max. cable spans to minimize cable deflection
⅛" cable: 3'
3/16" cable: 3'-6"
¼" and larger: 4'

Intermediate post to support cap, top railing

Stays are attached to deck and top railing

Figure 16. Because the cables exert a tremendous amount of tension on the end posts, it's critical to mount the posts firmly to the framing, and brace between them with a subrail that's capable of withstanding the pressure.

Most wood 4x4 posts can withstand these pressures. Because cedar is so soft, though, you must use wider washers at cable terminations to prevent the cable from pulling through — and you should consider using larger posts, such as 4x6s or 6x6s.

Steel posts can be 1-inch-by-3-inch flat bar, 2-inch-by-2-inch-by-⅜-inch angle, schedule-80 pipe, or ¼-inch walled tubing. With all steel posts, you need to use sleeves of rubber, nylon, or stainless steel to separate the cable from the steel and prevent wear. Aluminum posts of the same dimensions can be used, but 2-inch-by-2-inch angle must be beefed up to ½-inch thickness.

Do not attempt cable railing with solid composite posts, as they will warp when the cables are tightened. Composite or plastic sleeves that fit over a wood post are fine.

Post Configuration

You can use single-posted (**Figure 17**) or double-posted (**Figure 18**, next page) corners. Post spacing should be determined according to the strength of the top rail, which — according to code — needs to withstand 200 pounds of pressure in any direction (see "Strong Rail-Post Connections for Wooden Decks," page 45). Plus, the top rail helps spread out the tension from the

Single Post

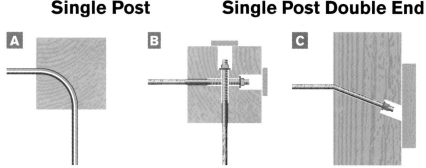

A

Single Post Double End

B

C

Figure 17. There are two ways to handle a single-post corner (left). One is to drill a curved hole through the post (A). Because there's a lot of tension on the inside corner of wood posts, a hardwood like ipe is recommended over soft cedar or pine for curved-hole corners. The second method is to terminate two cables at the post (B). For the cables to exit at about the same height, one of the stud holes must be drilled at an angle so it doesn't intersect the other hole (C).

Figure 18. For double-post corners, you can either set the posts within 4 inches of each other and terminate the cable at each post (far left) or run the cable through both posts (left).

Double Corner End Posts

Double Corner Posts With Pass-Through

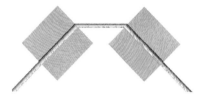

cables to the other posts. Most railing materials are limited to 6 feet or less, though with engineering, steel railings can exceed 6 feet.

In most cases, the rail can span a greater distance than the cables. The smaller the cable, the closer together the posts need to be — no more than 36 inches between posts for 1/8-inch cable, 42 inches for 3/16-inch cable, and 48 inches for 1/4-inch-diameter

and larger cables. If you want a more open look, you can avoid placing full-sized posts midspan by substituting "stays" — thinner pieces of steel, aluminum, fiberglass, or wood. The cables run through holes drilled in the stays.

Because long runs are harder to tension, I try to avoid straight runs of cable longer than 80 feet. For runs that have one or two 90-degree corners or up to four 45-degree corners, 40 feet or less is the rule of thumb. End posts need to be spaced away from the building (**Figure 19**) to allow for tightening the cable. When the face of an end post is exposed, the ends of the studs are covered with caps that can be removed for subsequent tightening (**Figure 20**, next page).

When using wood posts and rails, I order all the railing components before building the deck. If I'm using a welded steel or aluminum frame whose dimensions can't be easily changed, I order it after the deck is built. I like having the flexibility to make changes in the deck framing without worrying about the railing being exactly right.

Cable Connections

The machine shop I use makes the cable studs from 4-inch lengths of 1/4-inch 303 stainless rod. The shop drills a 1/8-inch hole down the center of one end to a depth of 1 1/4 inches, and threads the other end for 2 1/2 inches to take a 1/4x20 nut. The stud slides over the cable and is swaged, or crimped, with an H.K.

Figure 19. Space end posts away from the house to leave room for tightening the cables with a wrench.

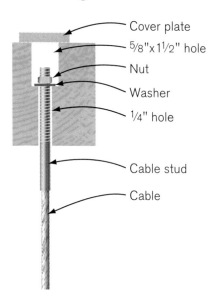

Single Post

Cover plate

5/8"x1 1/2" hole

Nut

Washer

1/4" hole

Cable stud

Cable

Figure 20. A removable cap protects people from the ends of the cable hardware while allowing for maintenance tightening.

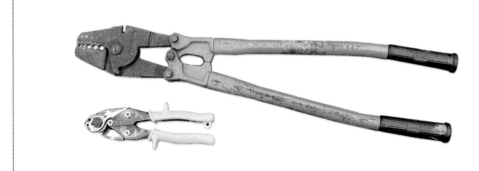

Figure 21. A swaging tool (top left) and a cable cutter (below left) are the only special tools required. A cable cutter cleanly snips multiple steel strands, and a swaging tool crimps connectors onto cables for a permanent connection.

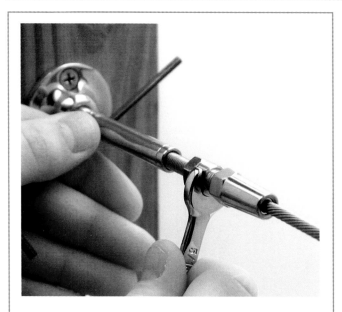

Figure 22. The author's favorite commercial cable stud is made by Atlantis Rail Systems. A cap nut and bushing eliminate the need for a swaging tool, and the flange mount allows the stud to work at a variety of angles.

Porter swaging tool (www.cooperhandtools.com). Swaging makes a strong, permanent connection (**Figure 21**).

Alternatively, the Atlantis Rail System uses a mechanical swaging that is an integral part of its universal turnbuckle (**Figure 22**). Its ball joint and flange mount allows it to be used for straight runs, turns, or stairs. Tightening a cap nut secures the cable — no swaging tool needed, just a wrench. The turnbuckle screws to the inside of the post, so it can be installed tight to the building. The screw attachment also saves time that would otherwise be spent drilling the end posts. Though it costs about $15, this is the only commercial stud I would use.

For short runs — straight runs up to 40 feet or runs of less than 20 feet that have one corner — studs aren't needed at both ends. Instead, one end (usually on the far side of the last post) is anchored with a swaged cable stop and washer (**Figure 23**, next page). Cable stops, which are available from any professional fastener supply shop, are simple 1/2-inch-by-1/2-inch aluminum tubes with a hole sized to fit the cable. For the stops, I drill a 3/4-inch-diameter hole

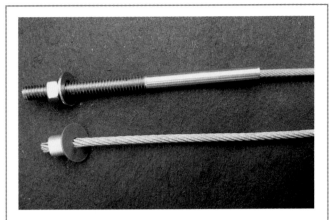

Figure 23. Studs and stops end the cable runs. Stops are simple aluminum rings that are swaged onto one end of the cable. Used with a washer, they resist the tension applied by the stud. The author has studs made locally from stainless steel rod; they're swaged to the cable and tightened with a nut.

Figure 24. Curving holes are made possible with Rover bits by Bad Dog Tools.

¾ inch deep, then continue through with a small hole sized for the cable. If the posts are ACQ-treated lumber, I make sure to use stainless steel stops.

Preparing Posts for Cable

The first step in installing a cable railing is locating the posts and making sure they're spaced to support both the upper railing and the cable. The post locations dictate how to drill the posts. For example, single-post corners get holes that curve, while double-posted corners are drilled straight through. Posts at stairs need angled holes.

I drill straight through most posts, using a bit that's ¹⁄₁₆ inch larger than the cable size. To drill accurately, I use a simple jig made from a piece of 1x4 the height of the posts, with guide holes where the cables are located. I use a Milwaukee Pathfinder bit to drill the curved holes in single-post corners; I start these holes from each side and join them in the middle. Milwaukee no longer makes Pathfinder bits, but Bad Dog Tools (www.baddogtools.com) has similar ones (**Figure 24**). Single posts on 45-degree

Figure 25. A two-step hole makes room for a socket wrench. The cable and stud enter the opposite side of the post through a smaller hole, and the nut used to tension the cable is buried inside a ⁵⁄₈-inch-diameter hole that also accommodates the socket.

Figure 26. A long level on the tread noses establishes the stair pitch, and a Speed Square, held level, measures the stair angle (left). Use the angle to make a simple guide block for drilling cable holes in stair posts and newels (right).

corners are mounted at 22.5 degrees and drilled straight through.

End posts need two-step holes to fit the cable stud, washer, and nut. I use a ⅝-inch Forstner bit to drill a hole about 2 inches deep for the washer and nut (**Figure 25**). I center a ¼-inch bit in the ⅝-inch hole and drill the rest of the way through for the cable stud. (The Forstner bit makes an indentation in the center so you can line up the ¼-inch bit.) It's important for the larger and smaller holes to line up, because there's little room for a 9/16-inch washer and the cable stud to align.

Figure 27.
To pretension the cable before final tightening, the author uses locking pliers to grip the cable, and wedges to stretch it. He does this at several spots along a run, particularly at corners.

To find the right angle for drilling the stair posts, I use a 6-foot level, a Speed Square, and a torpedo level (**Figure 26**). After cutting a small angle block for guiding the drill, I make a hole halfway through the post with a 6-inch-long drill bit; then I remove the guide and continue to drill through.

If the stair post is going to be used as an end post, it will also need a two-step hole to accommodate a cable stud or stop. This can be tricky to drill. I use the angle block and a Forstner bit with a drill stop mounted 2 inches back from the cutting head. I start drilling with the bit vertical, then carefully tip it back to meet the guide block and continue to drill until the hole is 1½ inches deep.

Capping and Cabling

Once all the posts have been installed, the top rail is fitted between them to resist the tension when the cables are tightened. The decorative cap is then installed continuously over the top rail and the posts.

Cable comes on a large spool, which I mount on a spindle so that it feeds easily from post to post. It's usually best to set up the spool so that it feeds straight into the end post — generally an end post that's not against the house. Before threading the cable, I wrap the end with tape to keep it from fraying on its journey through the holes. A HIT Tools 22WRC75 cable cutter (www.hittools.com) cuts the cable cleanly. Once the cable is fed through all the posts, I swage a cable stud or a stop to its end.

The next step is pretensioning, or stretching the cable tight before putting on the end stud (**Figure 27**). If you skip this step and rely only on the threaded studs for tightening, you may run out of thread before the cable is tight enough. Then you'll have to cut off that stud — now expensive scrap — and swage on another.

Pretensioning is done with locking pliers, scraps of wood or composite decking slit to fit over the cable, and wedges. Working back from the first end post, I pull the cable hand-taut and slip a piece of wood over it on the pull side of the post. With the locking pliers, I gently grip the cable right behind the block. Then I drive the wedges between the block and the post to tighten the cable. Next, leaving the pliers and wedges in place, I jump ahead three or four posts and repeat the process. I pretension at every corner and typically use four or five pairs of locking pliers in a run.

With the cable taut at the last post, I cut it to fit in the stud so that there's just enough thread left to engage the nut. I swage the cable stud, slip it into the end post, and tighten the washer and nut. I install the rest of the cables the same way.

Once all the cables have been pretensioned, it's time to fully tension each one. There is a correct sequence to this: Start with the center cable, then tighten the remaining cables by alternating above and below the center cable (**Figure 28**). All cables should be of uniform tension, with no sag. Each should sound the same note when plucked.

The final step is to cover the holes in the end posts. I rip a ¼-inch-thick by 1½-inch strip of the same material as the post, cutting it long enough to hide all the

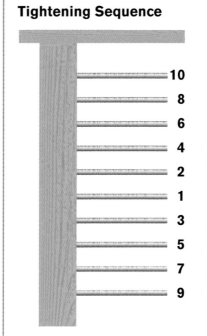

Tightening Sequence

10
8
6
4
2
1
3
5
7
9

Figure 28. Because the top and bottom of the posts are braced, tightening starts in the middle. Tighten the center cable enough to remove sags, then alternate between the cables that are directly above and below. When properly tensioned, all of the cables should sound the same note.

holes. This I attach with three stainless steel screws, for easy removal in case the cables need tightening.

Kim Katwijk is a deck builder in Olympia, Wash. Linda Katwijk assisted with this article.

Site-Built Rod Railings

by Kim and Linda Katwijk

Cable railing has a wonderful, inconspicuous look, but it also has a few drawbacks. For one, horizontal cables form a ladder that is dangerous for children to climb. And although vertical cables are safer, installation is more challenging: It's labor intensive, there are more cables to tighten, and it can be difficult to build rails that are stout enough to resist the tension.

After I installed vertical cable railing on two decks, I knew there had to be another option. My creative juices began to flow, resulting in the vertical-rod railing system described here.

Steel Rods

For the balusters, which are about the thickness of a pencil, I use ¼-inch-diameter rods made either of stainless steel or of plain steel that I have powder-coated locally. The standard powder-coat color is black; the rods can be custom colored, too, but the advantage to black rods is that they virtually disappear when you view a landscape through them. For water views, stainless steel rods have a similar effect, as their silver color blends with the silvery appearance of the water.

Obtaining the rods will take a little initial legwork — you can't just go to any lumberyard and pick them up off the shelf. You'll need to find yourself a good metal-fabricating shop or a steel supplier. For a 36-inch-high guardrail, I order ¼-inch-diameter cold-rolled steel cut to 30¾-inch lengths. The rods need to be clean-cut at both ends and straight; don't accept bent rods.

After being cut to length, the rods go to a powder-coating shop. My powder coater stands the rods in ¼-inch-diameter holes drilled in a piece of ¼-inch flat steel bar. This allows the entire rod to be powder-coated, except for ¼ inch of one end. I order them

With steel rods and stock rails, you can build a safe and nearly invisible balustrade.

1,000 at a time, and currently the cost of the rods with powder coating is $1.80 each. Stainless steel rods are more expensive at $2.34 each (2007 prices).

Composite Railing

Sometimes customers request wood, aluminum, or another composite as the framework for the rods, but mostly I build with EverGrain composites (Tamko Building Products, www.evergrain.com).

I use the company's Designer Universal Rail — which I call a "unirail" — for both the upper and lower rails. It comes in 12-foot lengths, and as long as the lower rail is supported every 3 feet, posts can be spaced as much as 6 feet apart. For a cap rail, I install a deck board over the tops of the posts, which gives the railing a clean line.

Assembling the Rods and Rails

I start building the railing after I've installed the 4x4 wood posts to extend 35 inches above the decking. I cover the posts with EverGrain post sleeves, and then cut the unirail to fit between the covered posts. To make a flat top on what will be the top rail, I use a Skilsaw to cut the ¼-inch-by-¼-inch ridge off the unirail (**Figure 29**).

Next, I lay out the rod spacing on the top of the bottom rail and on the bottom of the top rail. Assuming the rods will be installed on 4-inch centers, the space between the posts and the end rods may be

Figure 29. Stock pieces of EverGrain Designer Universal Rail form the frame for the author's vertical-rod railings. In order to use deck boards for the cap rail, he has removed the ridge from what will be the upper rail (right in photo), with a circular saw.

Figure 30. The author drills ⁹/₃₂-inch holes in the rail to accommodate ¼-inch steel-rod balusters. He drills completely through the top rail, but only halfway through the bottom rail. When the bit reaches the central hole in the bottom rail, visible in Figure 29, he knows he's drilled deeply enough.

Figure 31. After installing the top rail, rods precut to the correct length help determine the bottom rail's height. With the rod bottomed out in the lower rail, the author raises the rail until he feels the rod become flush with the top of the upper rail. That's when he screws home the lower rail's support bracket.

Figure 32. Holes in stair rails have to be drilled at the correct angle, which is easily measured using a level and a Speed Square (left). To make a drill guide (right) for the stair rails, the author drills through a scrap of decking and cuts it in half along the drill hole. He then cuts the bottom of the scrap to the angle he measured above.

less than 4 inches, but should be more than 2 inches.

Drill the holes in the unirail with a 9/32-inch drill bit (**Figure 30**), all the way through the top rail and halfway through the bottom rail. With unirail, it's easy to tell when you've drilled halfway, because there's a hole running lengthwise through the center of the rail.

Install the top rail first. Then put the bottom rail in place, and slide a rod into one of the two end holes. I use a piece of 4x4 to hold up the rail while I do this.

To set the bottom rail at the correct height, push it up until the rod goes through the corresponding hole in the upper rail and is flush with the top (**Figure 31**). Attach the bottom rail to the post on that end. Next, insert a rod at the opposite end of the rail and repeat the process. Remove the 4x4 block, and attach that end of the lower rail to its post.

After installing the rails to the posts, slide the remaining rods into the holes with the uncoated end up. The rods should fit tightly in the holes and not rattle. Install the deck-board cap rail with stainless steel trim-head screws.

Guardrails on stairs are done in a similar fashion, but in this case, I drill the holes at an angle that I measure in place using a rail, a torpedo level, and a Speed Square (**Figure 32**).

I've used this system now for more than two years. Though I offer several other options, the rod railing has consistently been the No. 1 choice among the majority of my clients. I love it because it's easier to install than vertical cable railing — which also makes it more economical for the client and more profitable for the contractor.

Kim Katwijk is a deck builder in Olympia, Wash. Linda Katwijk assisted with this article.

Installing Hollow Aluminum Balusters

by Bobby Parks

Aluminum balusters are affordable, visually appealing, and low maintenance. The ones I use most commonly are made by Deckorators (see "Baluster Manufacturers," next page); these hollow tubes slip over connectors that are screwed to the 2x4s that form the top and bottom rails (**Figure 33**).

My carpentry crews saw the advantages of these balusters, but laying out the bottom and top 2x4 rails, and then accurately screwing down each baluster connector was slow and awkward. Consequently, we came up with a jig to speed up the process.

Horizontal-Rail Jig

Start with some 1-inch screws, a 6-foot length of 1x4 cellular PVC (such as Azek), two 6-foot strips of 5/8-inch-by-3/4-inch PVC, and PVC glue (**Figure 34**, next page). I use PVC instead of wood; wood swells and shrinks as it gets wet or dries out, while PVC is more stable.

I draw a line down the center of the 1x4 and mark it every 4½ inches, which reflects my standard baluster layout. The 1x4 needs to be drilled at these marks to accept the baluster connectors. For Deckorators' 34 mm baluster connectors, I drill 35 mm diameter holes at each layout mark. A drill press is ideal for this task, but you can get by with using a hand-held drill if you're careful.

Then I attach the narrow PVC strips to the 1x4. When the jig is in use, these strips will locate and

Figure 33. Hollow aluminum balusters fit over connectors screwed to the upper and lower rails. A home-made jig speeds the accurate placement of the connectors.

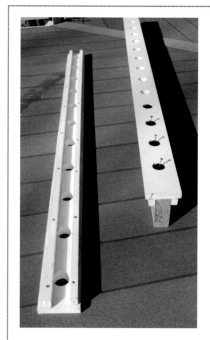

Figure 34. The jig is made from PVC sheet such as Azek, preferred over wood for its stability. Holes drilled on 4½-inch centers hold the baluster connectors as they're screwed home.

good idea to mark a centerline across the first three holes on each end of the jig and transfer them down the sides of the jig. When adjusting the placement of the jig, you can measure to the ends of the 2x4 from these lines instead of trying to measure to the center of the hole.

Install one baluster connector by dropping it in one of the predrilled holes and screwing it home (**Figure 35**). The jig is now held in place and the rest of the connectors can be installed through the layout holes. This method allows for consistent baluster spacing and saves a surprising amount of installation time.

Making the Stair Rail Jig

A jig can be made for the stair rail using a similar method. Although stair pitch can vary from job to job, most of the stairs my company builds are somewhere near a 10-inch run and a 7½-inch rise. I've found that one jig made for a 35-degree angle works on most of them, particularly because Deckorators makes an adjustable baluster connector for stair rails.

There are two main differences between this jig and the one for level rails: The holes are drilled at a 35-degree angle, and they're spaced at 5½ inches. Because this spacing is measured on the stair's rake angle, it results in a baluster spacing of just less than 4 inches.

A drill press is definitely preferred to make this jig, but if careful, you can get by with an angle guide and handheld drill. The stair jig works better if you can pre-mount a baluster connector on the rail section,

secure the 1x4 over the railing's 2x4s. I center the drilled 1x4 over the narrow edge of a straight 2x4 and screw baluster connectors to the 2x4 through the two end holes and the center hole in the 1x4.

Keeping the 1x4 on these connectors, I flip the assembly upside down. Next, I drill pilot holes through the PVC strips on the ¾-inch side on about 12-inch centers. With PVC glue brushed onto the exposed 1x4, I screw the PVC strips to the 1x4 against the 2x4, making a U-channel out of the PVC. The strips should be snug to the 2x4, but loose enough that the jig can slide on and off without a struggle.

Using the jig is very simple. Lay it on top of the 2x4 rail so that the distance from the last layout holes to each end of the 2x4 is equal and less than 4 inches from the end — to comply with code. It's a

Figure 35. Lines drawn square down the side of the jig ease its alignment with the ends of the 2x4 railing. Without the lines, placing the jig to provide even spacing of the end baluster connectors would require measuring to the center of the jig's holes. To use the jig, simply place it where you want on the rail, drop in a connector, and screw.

Baluster Manufacturers

BW Creative Wood Industries
www.bwcreativewood.com

Deck Solutions
www.decksolutionsllc.com

Dekor
www.de-kor.com

DECKorators
www.deckorators.com

Fortress Iron Railing & Fence Systems
www.fortressiron.com

which helps keep the jig from slipping downward. You could also drill a hole in the PVC to tap-screw it temporarily in place. Clamps work as well.

Threaded Rods for Stability

Another method I've adopted when using aluminum balusters doesn't save time, but I feel it improves the rail's stability. I install a ¼-inch galvanized threaded rod to draw together the top and bottom sections of rail to prevent sagging or bowing, which might cause the balusters to become loose or fall out (**Figure** 36). This approach works as an adjunct to the installation of short vertical legs between the deck and bottom of the rails to keep the rail from sagging.

Begin by dropping a baluster connector into a middle hole in the baluster jig, and drilling a 5/16-inch hole through it. Continue the hole completely through the 2x4 or rail-material sections. Do this to both the bottom and top rail sections.

Follow up by drilling a 7/8-inch-diameter hole about ½ inch deep through the top of the upper 2x4 and the bottom of the lower 2x4.

After the holes are drilled, feed the rod through the 2x4, the drilled-out connector, the baluster, and the other connector and rail section. Installing and tightening the nuts and washers clamps together the rail.

I like to double up on the nuts to prevent them from loosening over time. The long ends of the threaded rod are sawn off flush with the rail after the nuts are tightened. A reciprocating saw with a metal-cutting blade makes quick work of this.

The rail cap covers the top hole, but the hole in the bottom rail remains exposed. If you set the nuts

Figure 36. To firm up the assembly, the author drills a through hole at one of the central baluster connectors and runs a length of threaded rod between the upper and lower rails.

even with the end of the rod on this end prior to installation, you can recess them into the 2x4 far enough to allow a plug.

Bobby Parks owns Peachtree Decks and Porches in Atlanta, Ga.

Manufactured Railing Options

by Dave Holbrook

Railings add cost and complexity to any deck project. Preengineered railing systems and pre-assembled modules may take some of the head-scratching out of design issues as well as the pricing of materials and labor.

While wood has long ruled the roost in deck construction, its shortcomings are well known. A regular diet of scraping, sanding, and painting is required to keep a wooden railing looking good. Maintenance-free materials and finishes save everybody work, from the installer to the homeowner. Finding a system that looks like wood is a priority for some homeowners, while others are concerned only with durability and convenience. Price also

plays an important role; not surprisingly, the more it looks like "the real thing," the more it generally costs. While some products have come and gone from the marketplace, these systems have all been available at least since 2000.

PVC Systems

In spite of manufacturers' claims that vinyl provides the "classic look of wood" without the maintenance, smooth, glossy PVC (polyvinyl chloride) does little to impersonate the look and feel of the wood it replaces in a railing system, at least close up. From a distance, the illusion is more successful, because the component dimensions of vinyl railings mimic those of

THERMAL INDUSTRIES

Maintenance-free materials and ready-to-assemble components can simplify railing installations.

their wood counterparts, such as 4x4 newel posts and 2x2 or turned balusters. If the trend toward vinyl siding is any indication, many of your clients may care less about the "wood look" than about having a rail that requires no scraping, sanding, and repainting. What PVC lacks in strength and stiffness is compensated for with metal or wood inserts or an integral structural matrix.

Brock Deck

ROYAL CROWN

The more than 1/8-inch-thick walls of Brock Deck's extruded newel post enable it to stand alone, secured on a proprietary steel deck post mount. The railing, available in five styles including square balusters or decorative spindles, is part of an entire deck system. As an option, you can have the entire deck and railing factory cut, shipped, and installed by a local dis-

tributor. The benefits are said to include a firm quote; tight, accurate assembly; no waste; and warranted installation by others.

Color Guard

COLOR GUARD FENCE

With three railing styles to choose from, and a choice of a steel bracket or site-installed 4x4 newel support, Color Guard's system uses routed rail-to-post and baluster insert connections. Railings are secured with a capped retaining screw through the side of the post. The company boasts more than 20 years in the railing business and "near perfect shipping performance."

Dream Deck

THERMAL INDUSTRIES

Dream Deck's PVC post sleeve is made to clad a pressure-treated 4x4. The aluminum-reinforced contoured railings insert through precut openings in the post sleeve and are secured to a concealed bracket screwed to the site-rabbeted post core. The system is mostly self-explanatory, but there are certain techniques that have

been worked out to provide ease of assembly and eliminate "gotchas." For example, if you're going to use the one-piece trim collar at the base of the post to conceal a sloppy cutout through the deck, don't forget to slide it over the post before you install the railing assembly, or you'll be starting over.

EverNew

CERTAINTEED

At the heart of the EverNew post is a galvanized steel pipe, welded to a right-angle mounting flange. Blocking may have to be added to the deck frame at post locations lacking a usable corner. Spacers center the vinyl sleeve on the post support. Aluminum-reinforced railings install in precut openings through the post sleeve, and are held captive between posts, which eliminates the need for mechanical fasteners.

Gossen

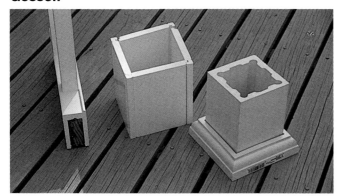

Gossen's cellular PVC balusters stand alone in the all-PVC field with the only non-tubular, solid-vinyl balusters, available in a square or in a lathe-turned profile. The vinyl railings are reinforced with Doug fir and interlocking panels provide cover for on-site pressure-treated 4x4 newels. Although one of the principal selling points of PVC is that it "never needs painting," this manufacturer suggests their railing components may actually require painting after a number of years, with acrylic latex- or alkyd-based paint. Check with individual manufacturers for their recommended painting procedure.

Kroy

Kroy offers four tubular PVC baluster profiles, including octagonal, rectangular, square, and decorative

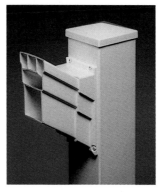

KROY

turning. Aluminum reinforcement adds strength to the railings, while steel beefs up the post sleeve. The company also makes a premium composite railing system with a vinyl capstock exterior.

Sheerline

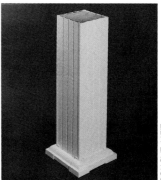

L.B. PLASTICS

The 3¼-inch-wide aluminum-reinforced Sheerline 3250 PVC railing is rated to span 10 feet, post to post. The System 4500 railing can span 10 feet without any metal reinforcement, due to the wider, 4½-inch structural cross section. Build your stairs to suit the system: Surface-mounted angle brackets define a standard 32.5-degree, 7:11 step incline. Step railings have elongated openings to receive balusters on the angle. Individual post panels interlock to wrap a 4x4 core.

Urethane Foam

High-density molded urethane foam is arguably the material most like wood in look, feel, and workability. Unlike wood, urethane is stable, lightweight, and impervious to moisture. Urethane will break down under UV exposure — it's sold primed and must be kept painted. Paint may perform more reliably on urethane than on wood, because the foam isn't subject to thermal expansion or the variations in moisture content found in wood.

There is a broader selection of railing forms and styles available in urethane than in any material other than wood. Elegant curved balustrades are a specialty niche of urethane systems. Urethane component balustrades require the most skill of the builder; baluster layout, fitting, and railing assembly, whether level or sloped, must be done on the job. Pre-assembling railing sections in a shop setting can eliminate some of the difficulties of field installation. Urethane systems are priced at the high end.

Fypon

Fypon's stately posts, railing segments, and balusters are structurally reinforced with galvanized steel tubing or heavy-duty vinyl pipe. If the job calls for a truly classy or classic railing, molded urethane, with a vast selection of profiles to choose from, is a good place to start.

Wood-Resin Composites

Composite lumber addresses the desire for a material that more closely resembles wood but without wood's natural defects and the need for frequent maintenance. Made from wood fiber and either virgin or recycled polymer resin, composite lumber can be worked much like solid wood. Wood-composite weathers to a uniform silver-gray color, but tends not to split, shrink, warp, absorb water, or decay like wood. Wood-composite can be extruded into tubular sections, giving it greater tensile strength than solid stock of the same material.

Fiberon

Fiberon system components are made of composite wood, extruded in tubular sections, and finished with an outer layer of solid-color PVC in four shades,

pre-empting the paint option. The "sprayed-on" texture of the finish gives it an attractive painted, rather than plastic, look. Fiberon railings ship in 4- and 6-foot preassembled sections, which automatically restricts the post spacing to a rated safe span. The proprietary universal post mounting flange can be simply converted to bolt either inside a framing corner or on the straightaway.

Trex

Perhaps the best-known composite lumber, Trex is available in decking, railing, post, and baluster profiles. A spokesperson for the company states that they prefer their product to be viewed not as a "kit," but as a substitute for solid wood with most of wood's creative potential. Trex will weather to a natural silver-gray just like solid wood, but without the attendant splits, checks, and decay. Wood-polymer lumber can be painted or stained, best done after four to six

months outdoors, when the surface has developed a little "tooth" from weathering.

Metal Railings

These railing systems take advantage of the high strength of aluminum or steel with component profiles that are much smaller than their wood and plastic counterparts. Metal railings may be appropriate when the view, and not the railing, is the desired focal point. Metal frames provide the strength and stiffness needed to replace ordinary balusters or pickets with clear-view tempered glass panels.

CableRail

FEENEY WIRE ROPE

Homeowners pay top dollar for real estate with a view, so the last thing they want to do is block the scenery with a bulky railing. CableRail's high-strength 1/8-inch-diameter stainless steel cable, strung horizontally and tensioned between posts, calls little attention to itself, leaving the vista relatively unobstructed. Proprietary fittings at end posts have one-way "jaws" that grip the cable and provide adjustable tensioning. For safety, it's recommended that the cables be run no more than 3 inches apart, and that vertical posts or spacers be provided every 3 feet. The system works with wood posts as well as square or round metal tubing.

As with any horizontally oriented railing system, codes may restrict or prohibit the use of horizontal railing members due to their ladder-like "climbability," so check with your local building department first.

DEC-K-ING

DEC-K-ING's all-aluminum railing system, combined with their rein-forced, welded-seam PVC roof membrane, offers a durable, attractive, and waterproof method to rehabili-

DEC-K-ING

tate an older deck. Posts mount flush on the surface via an integral flange. The railing can be finished with

aluminum pickets or tempered glass panels, using snap-in spacers between pickets or a fitted glass gasket. The aluminum railing sections can be cut to length using a carbide-tipped saw and joined using slide-on surface-mount couplings.

DECKorators

The unique, custom look of a DECKorators railing is a result of your woodworking and their solid 3/4-inch-diameter cylindrical aluminum balusters. The upper and lower railings are bored to receive the balusters, which are captured between them without adhesives or fasteners. Balusters are the most labor-intensive

DECKORATORS

part of a railing paint job, but these have a baked on maintenance-free finish with four color options. Available embellishments include decorative center-pieces and aluminum finials for the newel posts.

Durarail

Durarail's railing system accommo-dates glass, pickets, or even a combina-tion, in a convert-ible aluminum frame. Tempered glass panels are usually ordered separately from a local provider. A glass railing may eliminate the hori-zontal rail-climbing problem, but will require frequent cleaning to remain transparent.

DURADEK

Deck Railing Comparison

Product	Manufacturer	Material	Colors	Paint Required	Rail Span (feet)	Reinforcement
Armor-Rail	Shakespeare Composite Structures www.armor-rail.com	FRP	black, white, beige, green	no	12	integral
Avcon	Avcon www.avcon.com	Thermoplastic	black, white, brown, gray, special-order custom colors	no	no limit	steel
Brock Deck	Royal Outdoor Products www.royaloutdoor.com	PVC	white, tan, gray	no	6	steel
CableRail	Feeney Architectural Products www.feeneyarchitectural.com	Metal	mill	n/a	3	none
Carefree	Carefree Decks & Patio Covers www.carefreedecks.com	HDPE	white, tan, brown, gray, weathered wood	no	6	integral
Color Guard	Color Guard Inc. www.colorguardfence.com	PVC	white, tan, gray	no	8	steel
DEC-K-ING	Global DEC-K-ING Systems www.dec-k-ing.com	Metal	white	no	4 to 9	integral
DECKorators	DECKorators Inc. www.deckorators.com	Metal	black, white, pewter, green	no	n/a	n/a
Dream Deck	Thermal Industries www.thermalindustries.com	PVC	white	no	8	aluminum
Durarail	Duradek www.duradek.com	Metal	white	no	8	integral
EverNew	CertainTeed www.certainteed.com	PVC	white, tan, gray	no	8	aluminum
Fiberon	Fiber Composites www.fiberondecking.com	Wood-Resin	white	no	6	integral
Fypon	Fypon www.fypon.com	Polyurethane	primed	yes	8 to 10	integral
Gossen	Gossen Corp. www.gossencorp.com	PVC	white	no	8	wood
Kroy	Kroy Building Products www.kroybp.com	PVC	white, tan, gray, brown, green	no	8	alum/steel
PermaRail	HB&G www.hbgcolumns.com	PVC and polyurethane	primed	yes	8 to 10	wood/steel
Sheerline	L.B. Plastics www.lbplastics.com	Wood-Resin	white, beige, gray	no	10	aluminum
Trex	Trex Company www.trex.com	PVC	white, gray, tan	no	n/a	none

Fiberglass

Pultruding refers to the manufacturing process of drawing glass fibers through polyester- or epoxy-resin and a heated mold to produce high-strength FRP (fiber reinforced plastic, or fiberglass) components. This method is used to make everything from fishing rods and sailboat masts to deck railings.

Armor-Rail

Armor-Rail's FRP railing system takes advantage of the inherent strength of the material to produce smaller, thin-walled tubular sections with no need for additional reinforcement. A hollow, rectangular section of FRP with a 1/16-inch wall thickness safely spans

SHAKESPEARE COMPOSITES & ELECTRONICS

12 feet between posts, while providing all the stiffness necessary to meet code requirements, as well as the user's expectation of an unyielding barrier. The heavyweight newel post friction-fits over a glass-filled-polycarbonate flush mount. Along with their stock-in-trade post and picket design, the Armor-Rail system readily supports tempered glass panels.

Other Plastics

It's easier to stand out if you stand alone. A couple of manufacturers offer unique plastic formulations with outstanding performance characteristics.

With any plastic, it's recommended that you avoid dark colors in sunny locations, because of the material's tendency to fade under UV exposure. Dark colors also absorb, rather than reflect, the sun's infrared rays. Most plastics soften and expand when heated and may temporarily deform if the expanding plastic can't stretch out unrestricted.

Avcon

High-performance thermoplastic acrylonitrile styrene acrylate is used in Avcon's railing system. A monolithic, tubular system of consistent diameter, the contemporary-style railing can be formed into curved transitions, allowing it to "flow" from deck to step without termi-

AVCON

nations or sharp angles. The top guardrail is reinforced with a concealed steel insert for added stiffness. The acrylic composition qualifies the railing for use in demanding commercial, as well as residential, applica-

tions, and it can be tinted to nearly any color desired. Avcon's acrylic railing is produced on a custom basis in four standard colors, with special-order colors available.

Carefree

Carefree's HDPE deck railing is made of 90 percent recycled plastic milk and laundry detergent bottles, which makes it appealing to "green" builders. It also features a splinter-free surface and hefty, solid body extrusions that can be cut and conventionally  fastened like wood, preferably using stainless steel screws. Predrilling is unnecessary. The integral color eliminates painting; in fact, paint and most adhesives will not bond to HDPE. Maintenance is said to be limited to "soap and water."

Permarail

HB&G

The PermaRail system uses a variety of materials, defying easy categorization. Natural cedar forms the structural core of the expanded, or cellular, PVC railing. The square or decorative-turned "Perma Newel" has a full-length cedar core inside a cast polyurethane shell. The balusters are made of solid expanded PVC, available in square and turned profiles. Proprietary rail fasteners provide concealed connections.

Dave Holbrook is a builder on Cape Cod, Mass.

Building Composite Curved Railings

by Gary Katz

The new generation of composite and plastic materials works well for low-maintenance period trim.

Victorian homes, with all their elaborate details, are a challenge for the carpenter to trim and a bigger challenge for the home-owner to maintain. Queen Anne homes, a specific Victorian style, are also all about curves — radius porches and verandas, radius windows, radius gable-end decorations, and radius turrets. Here, I'll describe how we tackled the radius balustrade for a contemporary Queen Anne we trimmed out recently.

New-Tech Materials

When we met the architects on this project, they told us that the owners loved the Victorian style but hated maintenance — a tough contradiction for a finish contractor. To satisfy on both fronts, we used the latest generation of materials available for exterior trim work, products that won't warp, twist, cup, crack, or peel within two years, something impossible with even the best second-growth redwood.

For the molded radius pieces — all the balustrade railings — and any decorative turned elements, we used high-density rigid polyurethane moldings from Fypon (www.fypon.com). For all the flat trim, including the radius spindle railings, we used treated exterior

composite trim from Miratec (www.miratectrim.com). While I was comfortable with my knowledge of poly-urethane moldings and confident that Fypon would outlast wooden railings and balusters, I had reserva-tions about exterior composite trim. To quell my fears, I cut a 4-inch-square piece of the 1-inch trim, left the ends raw, and submerged it in a bucket of water for two weeks. When I removed the material, it was still exactly the same size and the water hadn't penetrated the raw ends: Shaving less than 1/16 inch off the raw ends revealed clean, dry trim. After that test, and after reading all the literature I could find on installing composite trim and polyurethane molding, I was ready to start work on the job.

Spindle Railing

Our installation began with the spindle railing — the short decorative balustrade that hangs from a Victorian porch beam — because we couldn't install the balus-trade below until the decking was finished. The top and bottom rails on the straight spindle runs were easy: We used 3-inch-wide material, ripping the top rail to 2 inches and the bottom rail to 2½ inches, then beaded the bottom rail with a roundover bit so water

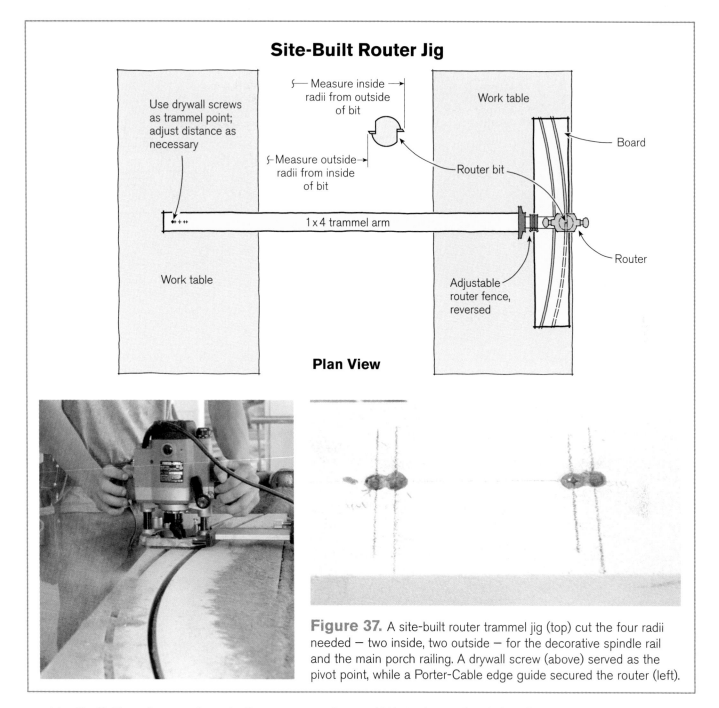

Site-Built Router Jig

Use drywall screws as trammel point; adjust distance as necessary

Measure inside radii from outside of bit

Work table

Board

Measure outside radii from inside of bit

Router bit

1 x 4 trammel arm

Work table

Router

Adjustable router fence, reversed

Plan View

Figure 37. A site-built router trammel jig (top) cut the four radii needed — two inside, two outside — for the decorative spindle rail and the main porch railing. A drywall screw (above) served as the pivot point, while a Porter-Cable edge guide secured the router (left).

would roll off. To make sure the spindles were spaced evenly, I used a Construction Master Pro calculator (see "Speedy Layout With a Calculator," page 235).

For the radius sections of railing that ran around the turrets, we ordered 4/4-by-12- and 5/4-by-12-inch Miratec boards. I first used the calculator to determine whether I'd be able to get every rail out of a single 11½-inch-wide board — I didn't want to laminate any of the bottom rails because they'd be spanning almost 9 feet. I'm no math wiz, but it didn't take me long to figure it out: I punched in the 9-foot span and hit RUN, then entered the 12-foot radius (you have to push the CONV key first, then the DIAG key). Finally, I hit RISE, and the result —

10½ inches — landed well within the width of my 11½-inch boards.

Cutting the Radius Rails

I used an inexpensive site-built trammel arm and plunge router to cut the radius rails. I screwed the railing material down to a sacrificial piece of scrap on top of my workbench. Porter-Cable manufactures a great adjustable fence for its plunge router, which can be easily adapted for standard routers. I reversed the fence, then attached a piece of 1x4 to extend the trammel arm. The radius at the outside rim of the deck was 12 feet (**Figure 37**). However, the railing was centered on the porch columns, 6 inches from the

Figure 38. Two extra pieces of railing served as an extendible template for laying out the radius rails (left). After scribing the ends to fit the posts, the carpenters stretched the two pieces apart until they were tight against the new posts, then fastened the pieces together with drywall screws. Tracing the template directly onto the railings guaranteed a tight fit (right).

edge of the deck, which made the center of the railing an 11-foot-6-inch radius. Since the bottom railing was 2½ inches and the top rail was 2 inches wide, I needed four radius center marks in the trammel arm.

I first marked the radius centers with a pencil, then punched them with my nail set (those holes had to be located perfectly) before attempting to drill pilot holes. I used a drywall screw as a trammel point. After all the setup, swinging the plunge router on the trammel arm was a breeze. I made several passes for each cut, burying the bit about 3/16 inch with each pass. Miratec cuts easily, but taking too deep a bite with the router bit will stress the trammel arm and throw off the smoothness of the cut.

Extendible Measuring Jig

I knew that measuring the exact length of each railing was going to be a problem and that getting a perfect cut on the end of the rail would be even more difficult. So I cut two extra ¾-by-2-inch spindle rails for each section, then sandwiched those two pieces to use as a template (**Figure 38**).

Working in place between the porch columns, we slid the pieces apart until both ends were tight against the posts. We then scribed both ends and trimmed them until the joints were snug. At that point, we screwed the two pieces together securely, then used that template to mark the top and bottom rails for that section.

Laying Out the Spindles

Laying out the spindles stumped me for a minute while I pondered how to use the Construction Master to calculate the spacing around the radius. Then I

decided on a much simpler but almost as precise method. I first laid out the centers of the two end spindles, 2 inches in from each end of the rail. Then I ripped a ¼-inch-thick strip of ¾-inch exterior trim, curved it around the radius, and marked the distance between the two end spindles (**Figure 39**). After that, I was able to use the calculator to find the centers of each spindle. I marked them, then bent the trim strip around the radius again to transfer the center marks onto the rail.

Figure 39. Instead of trying to lay out the spindle centers on the curve, the author used a thin strip of flexible material, marking it in a straight position then bending it to the radius to transfer the marks.

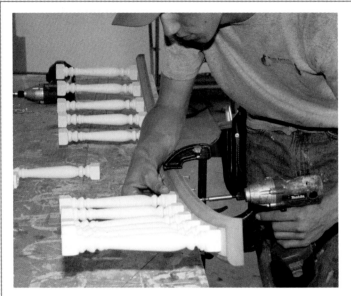

Figure 40. Holes for the galvanized screws were predrilled in both the rail and the spindles (left), but the Fypon adhesive provides the real strength for the spindle assemblies (right).

Assembly and Installation

Assembling the rails was definitely the easiest part of the job (**Figure 40**). First we drilled pilot holes with a tapered countersink so the painters could fill over the decking screws that secured the spindles. Before placing the spindles, we squeezed a good dab of Fypon adhesive on top of each hole. Once all the spindles were installed and the adhesive had dried, each ladderlike section was rigid and strong, even though the spindles themselves are lightweight unreinforced polyurethane.

Installation was almost as easy. Because we had used templates, each section fit perfectly the first time. We secured the top rail to the ceiling with galvanized finish nails, toenailed the bottom rails to the post capitals, then installed brackets beneath the railing with nails and more polyurethane adhesive.

The Balustrade Railing

The lower balustrade railing was a different story. It was too beefy to make with a router and a trammel arm.

Speedy Layout With a Calculator

I use a Construction Master Pro calculator (Calculated Industries, www.calculated.com) to lay out nearly *everything*, at least everything I can. It's the only way to ensure quick, precise layouts on the first try. For both the spindle railing and the lower balustrade, I first decided on the end spacing – the distance between the last baluster and the newel post. Those spaces appear best if they're about half the distance of the on-center spacing. So I chose 2 inches for the spindle railing (4 inches on-center) and $2^1/2$ inches for the lower balusters (5 inches on-center).

After marking off those measurements, I measured the intervening distance and divided that number by 4 inches for the spindle railing and 5 inches for the balustrade. Of course, the quotient always included a whole number and an odd fraction: For instance, a $102^3/8$-inch run divided by 4 inches equals $25^5/8$ inches. I rounded the fraction up if it was well above $1/2$ inch and down if it

was close to or below $1/2$ inch, then divided the distance by the resulting sum.

But a Construction Master calculator is even more useful when it comes to marking the layout for each spindle. Stretch a tape measure down the railing. First, divide the distance by the number of spindles and press the = button to arrive at the spacing between the center of the first spindle and the center of the second spindle. Then, simply press the + button once, then the = button again. That sum is the exact center of the third spindle. Now press the = sign again and the Construction Master Pro will calculate the exact center of the fourth spindle. And I mean exact: The calculator remembers all fractional sums less than $1/16$ inch (you can program the calculator to work in almost any fractional increment, but I prefer $1/16$), so it's always adding the fractional increment whenever it exceeds $1/16$.

Figure 41. Balusters for the main railing were laid out on 5-inch centers (left). A hole saw in a drill press made for fast, accurate boring in the PVC radius railings (right) as well as the steel-reinforced straight rails.

Instead, I ordered the rails pre-bent by the manufacturer to the radius required. The plans specified every radius on the house. Just as with the spindle railing above, all I had to do was subtract the distance from the edge of the deck to the center of the posts. I then used that center measurement to order all the rails.

Fypon manufactures straight balustrade railing embedded with a 3-inch-diameter steel pipe, so the typical 8-foot to 9-foot spans between my posts were stiff and rigid. But Fypon's bent railing is formed around 3-inch PVC pipe, obviously because PVC is easier to bend. I would have preferred steel pipe in the radius sections, but with the 1/4-inch steel cable supplied by the manufacturer, we were able to stoutly reinforce the long spans.

Layout and cutting. We were able to reuse the template we'd used for the spindle railing because the radius was exactly the same. After marking the top and bottom rails for each section, I used my miter saw to cut the PVC embedded railing.

Figure 42. When assembling the Fypon railings (far left), 2¹/₂-inch galvanized finish nails, four in each baluster, held the balusters in place until the polyurethane adhesive dried. Fitting the top rail (left) was tricky and required two sets of hands because of the varying lengths of the ³/₄-inch pipe projecting out the end of the balusters. This required finding and setting the longest dowels first.

Figure 43. The PVC radius railings rely on a tensioned steel cable for strength (left). A come-along provided the necessary pull (right). The 3-inch hole where the cable is cinched will be covered by a removable section of straight railing, should the cable ever need retensioning.

We laid out the balusters in the same manner, though the end balusters were centered 2½ inches in from the ends of the railing because the spacing was 5 inches on-center (**Figure 41**).

Drilling. Fypon balusters are formed around ¾-inch aluminum pipe, with the pipe extending from the baluster by 1 to 1½ inches. For drilling the ¾-inch holes in the railing, I experimented with several types of drill bits on both the PVC and the steel-embedded railings. I found that a ¾-inch hole saw worked best on both. I thought I'd have to stop the drill every three or four cuts to clear the hole saw, but luckily, after two or three holes, the compressed polyurethane inside the hole saw acted like a spring and pushed out the waste, which we then removed from the spinning hole saw with a small stick.

Assembling the Railings

Assembling the railings' lower baluster was a little trickier than assembling the spindle railings. We started at the bottom rail, applying a liberal amount of Fypon adhesive around each hole, then inserted the baluster (**Figure 42**). After squeezing each baluster tightly against the railing, we toenailed each one with 2½-inch galvanized nails.

Next we added the top railing, starting at one end and slowly working each of the balusters into its hole. Then we turned the section upside down and used 5-foot Bessy clamps to hold things together. The deep plastic jaws reached well over the railing and didn't mar the polyurethane. Once the entire section was snugly clamped, we toenailed the top balusters, too.

I learned the hard way that I had to let the adhesive dry before moving and installing the balustrade, because the mixture of nails and polyurethane wasn't strong enough to secure the joinery. Once the adhesive dried, the pieces were practically welded together.

Threading the Cable

Before starting the installation, we drilled a ½-inch hole through each of the porch posts, exactly at the center of the top railing, then passed a fish tape through each hole with a pull string attached. We did the same with each section of the radius railing, leaving a pull running through the hollow top rail.

Starting at one end of the railing, we pulled the ¼-inch steel cable through each post and railing section until the cable reached the opposite side of the last post. Then we installed all the railings on L-clips, first applying a generous amount of adhesive on each end.

After all the railings were mounted, we slipped several fender washers over the dead end of the cable, secured the loose end with a compression fitting, then pulled the cable tight with a come-along until it sang like a piano string (**Figure 43**). In fact, we had to release a little tension on the cable, because it began to flatten the radiuses.

Before starting the installation, I drilled a 3-inch-diameter hole into the last post so we'd have room to tighten the compression fittings. Once we were satisfied with the tension on the cable, we locked it down but didn't cut the cable. Instead, we left the end long and looped it inside the oversized hole. The next section was straight railing, which didn't need to be fastened with adhesive. The end of the straight rail would cover the hole, but if the cable ever loosened, I'd be able to access the cable to retighten it by removing that section of straight rail.

Gary Katz is a finish carpenter in Reseda, Calif., and author of Finish Carpentry, *a JLC book.*

Deck Railings Q&A

Why Build Posts for a 500-Pound Load?

Q. *I recently saw several demonstrations at a trade show, showing how to attach a 4x4 guardrail post to withstand a 500-pound side load, which was claimed to be the code requirement. But the 2006 IRC only calls out a 200-pound load from any direction. Why test the greater load?*

A. *Andy Engel, editor of* Professional Deck Builder, *responds:* If you have ever taken a physics class, you may remember that *force = mass x acceleration*. Get a 200-pound person moving, and he can develop dynamic loads well in excess of his weight. As some-one whose weight exceeds 200 pounds, and who has occasionally become, shall we say, clumsy while at a party on someone's deck, that 500-pound load requirement starts to seem meaningful.

So, while it's true that the IRC requires only that a guardrail withstand "a (200-pound) single concen-trated load applied in any direction at any point along the top," accepted engineering practice applies a safety factor — as is explained in the following passage from "Strong Rail-Post Connections for Wooden Decks," (which appears in this book starting on page 45):

… when a structural assembly is tested in a lab, the load gets multiplied by an appropriate safety factor, which is intended to allow for the uncertainties of field installation and the fact that the connections may degrade in service from repeated loading and weathering (but not rot). We used a safety factor of 2.5, a number that has been in the model codes for decades for testing structural assemblies. So, for our testing, we needed to apply a 500-pound load to determine whether the post connection could be considered "code conforming."

In essence, no standard bolted or blocked post con-nection was able to withstand the 500-pound force applied to the top of a 4x4 southern pine post 36 inches above the level of the deck. The only attach-ment that the authors found to work is shown in the illustration "Post Connections That Passed" on page 49.

The Simpson HD2A connector (www.strongtie.com) referenced in the drawing isn't the only connector that might fulfill this requirement. Simpson's new DTT2Z connector, specifically designed for this appli-cation, is a more cost-effective option. DeckLok brackets (www.deck-lok.com) and USP TDX2 connec-tors (www.uspconnectors.com) would also seem capable of providing the necessary strength, although they were not included in the test described.

Adding such a bracket, including the requisite two additional bolts, would increase the material cost per post by $10 to $15. The additional labor is minimal, and the necessary up-charge is the sort of value-added item that a deck builder can use to set himself apart from his competitors. Beyond that, what's the value of being able to sleep at night, knowing you've done your best to increase your customers' safety and reduce your liability?

Notching Posts

Q. *Construction experts advise against notching posts that support deck rails, but I see that done all the time. What's wrong with notching posts?*

A. *Andy Engel, editor of* Professional Deck Builder, *responds:* This, too, was addressed in "Strong Rail-Post Connections for Wooden Decks," starting on page 45.

In the tests described, several of the 4x4 posts were notched around the band joist, as is often done in the field. Even though none of the test posts failed at the notch, notching should be avoided, according to the researchers, "because it does substantially reduce the strength of the post." Here's why:

Based on many years of observation, the research-ers note that "moisture cycles will typically cause cracks to develop and propagate, parallel to the grain, from the corner of the notch. This may not be apparent when the post is first installed, but it happens gradu-ally over time."

If a crack devel-ops, and the post has a steep "slope of grain," the crack can criti-cally reduce the strength of the post, as shown in the drawing (right). Grading rules a No. 2 southern pine 4x4 allow a slope of grain of up to 1:8 (or 1 inch in 8 inches). If a crack followed such steep grain, the cross section of the post could

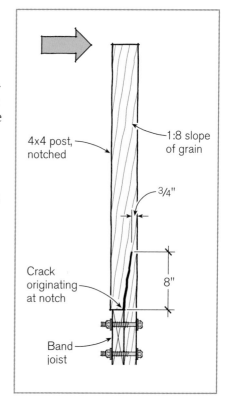

4x4 post, notched

1:8 slope of grain

3/4"

Crack originating at notch

8"

Band joist

be reduced to as little as 3/4 inch at 8 inches above the corner of the notch — not something you'd want to rely on for safety on a raised deck.

Painting Steel Railings

Q. *I build deck railings, awning frames, and other structures out of welded, galvanized steel tubing. I can't get paint to stick for very long. So far I have only tried Rustoleum after using a mild acid rinse. It lasted about two years before the paint started to peel. Is there a product or technique that will last longer?*

A. *James Benney, a painting contractor with Paintcraft Associates in Orinda, Calif., responds:* Yes! Following proper preparation and application of the right product under the right conditions, the paint should never peel, but should provide many years of service before it simply wears away or oxidizes enough to warrant redoing.

We wipe down all new galvanized metal with a rag or sponge saturated with pure white vinegar (that's your acid rinse), then we rinse thoroughly with clear, clean water and let it dry. This is to remove slick manufacturing residues that will prevent your paint product from adhering to the metal.

You have to treat all surfaces, because you will have problems with any areas you miss.

Under warm, dry conditions (this is important!), there are many paint products that can now be applied directly to the metal, including most high-end latex paints. Often on gutters and downspouts, we will use our latex or oil trim color as a first and second coat. On railings and awning frames we recommend Benjamin Moore's Iron Clad Low-Lustre Metal & Wood Enamel as both a primer and finish paint because of its unusual durability and its soft, low-luster finish. Whether brushing or spraying, make sure you cover it with a nice full coat on each application. You might be surprised by how long it lasts.

Chapter 8:
Decks Over Living Spaces

- Building a Wood Deck Over EPDM
- Rooftop Decks With Duradek
- Waterproof Fiberglass Decks
- Attaching a Deck to a Sloped Roof
- Rooftop Decks Q&A

Building a Wood Deck Over EPDM

by Thomas Buckborough

Sloped framing, a carefully installed membrane, and good flashing details are key to this watertight roof.

Building an outdoor deck on top of a finished room may not sound like the best proposition. But when a good past customer asked us to design a project that would do just that, we didn't hesitate. Adding to its complexity, the deck had an irregular shape because it was built to join two octagonal rooms of the house. We also had to control the water runoff from the house and direct it to a dry well to satisfy town conservation regulations. In addition to the deck, the design included another flat roof area, on a second level, that would have a decorative balustrade at its edge.

Many homeowners here in New England are concerned when I suggest a "flat" roof design. They worry that snow will be a problem, or that the roof will be more likely to leak. But a properly detailed EPDM (ethylene propylene diene terpolymer) membrane roof installed over a properly designed structure can actually be much tighter and less problematic than other roof types.

Of greater concern to me was the difficulty of venting a flat roof. Rather than get bogged down in devising a system for this project that would work well in theory, I relied on a carefully installed airtight vapor barrier and mechanical control of humidity in the heated space — in effect, a "hot roof" approach.

Railing Design

The first challenge was to design deck railings that would not only look good, but also allow roof drainage while being rugged enough to resist lateral movement. There were four 45-degree corners to wrap the railing around. These would be difficult to treat with conventional square posts and rails. After considering the details for several weeks while designing the rest of the project, I decided to build a combination railing, with rail-height solid walls at the corners connected by open baluster railing sections and a low retaining curb.

A membrane roof should always provide positive drainage — the roof may look flat, but it shouldn't be level. In this case, the roof deck would pitch to a curbless edge, where a gutter would capture the runoff.

To frame the main roof deck, we installed a series of four flush steel I-beams that spanned the room below, eliminating the need for intermediate posts or exposed beams. We pitched the beams 1/8 inch per foot to establish drainage (**Figure 1**). The framing crew in-filled 2x10 joists between the I-beams and sheathed the deck with a 3/4-inch T&G plywood subfloor. Our lead carpenter then framed the rail-height walls and curb sections. With the framing completed, we were ready to install the EPDM roof membrane.

Roof Deck Over Living Space

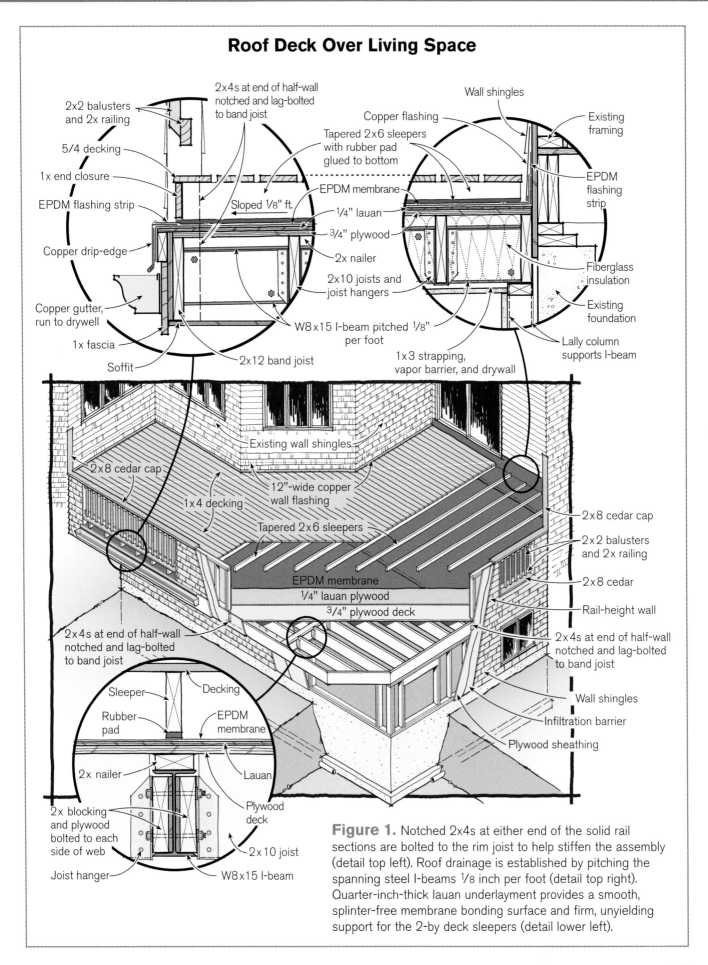

2x2 balusters and 2x railing

2x4s at end of half-wall notched and lag-bolted to band joist

Wall shingles

Copper flashing

Existing framing

5/4 decking

Tapered 2x6 sleepers with rubber pad glued to bottom

1x end closure

EPDM membrane

EPDM flashing strip

Sloped 1/8" ft.

1/4" lauan

EPDM flashing strip

3/4" plywood

Copper drip-edge

2x nailer

2x10 joists and joist hangers

Fiberglass insulation

Copper gutter, run to drywell

W8x15 I-beam pitched 1/8" per foot

Existing foundation

1x fascia

1x3 strapping, vapor barrier, and drywall

Lally column supports I-beam

Soffit

2x12 band joist

Existing wall shingles

2x8 cedar cap

12"-wide copper wall flashing

1x4 decking

2x8 cedar cap

Tapered 2x6 sleepers

2x2 balusters and 2x railing

EPDM membrane

1/4" lauan plywood

3/4" plywood deck

2x8 cedar

Rail-height wall

2x4s at end of half-wall notched and lag-bolted to band joist

2x4s at end of half-wall notched and lag-bolted to band joist

Wall shingles

Sleeper

Decking

Infiltration barrier

Rubber pad

EPDM membrane

Plywood sheathing

2x nailer

Lauan

2x blocking and plywood bolted to each side of web

Plywood deck

Joist hanger

2x10 joist

W8x15 I-beam

Figure 1. Notched 2x4s at either end of the solid rail sections are bolted to the rim joist to help stiffen the assembly (detail top left). Roof drainage is established by pitching the spanning steel I-beams 1/8 inch per foot (detail top right). Quarter-inch-thick lauan underlayment provides a smooth, splinter-free membrane bonding surface and firm, unyielding support for the 2-by deck sleepers (detail lower left).

EPDM Roofing

Our roofing contractor prepared the roof surface by installing an underlayment over the T&G deck ply. EPDM is typically installed over rigid insulation board or a proprietary soft fiberboard. However, concerned that the weight of the deck on top of the membrane would compress a soft underlayment and cause damage or premature wear to the EPDM, our roofer chose 1/4-inch lauan plywood.

Technically, you can bond an EPDM membrane directly to a plywood roof deck, but we wanted to start with a smooth, clean, nail- and splinter-free base. We fastened the lauan with 1 1/4-inch ring-barb copper nails, with the heads set flush and spaced 6 inches along the sheet edges and 12 inches in the field. The copper nails strongly resist pullout and won't rust.

The membrane we used, 60-mil Johns Manville UltraGard nonreinforced EPDM (www.jm.com), is available in several widths; we used 10-by-100-foot rolls. Some rolls come treated with a talc-like powder; our roofer orders it "clean," or talc free. He prefers to use Carlisle system adhesives and accessories (www.carlisle-syntec.com), although the company won't sell its EPDM membrane to uncertified installers and will certify only large-volume commercial roofers. However, EPDM is EPDM, essentially identical from one producer to the next, so the adhesives are completely compatible.

To install the membrane, you roll it out to length on the roof, cutting it long enough to allow the ends to transition up sidewall terminations by 9 to 12 inches and hang over outside edges by 3 to 6 inches. Snapped chalk lines on the plywood guide the alignment of the upper edge of the membrane.

Carlisle Sure-Seal 90-8-30A Bonding Adhesive, an extremely flammable, yellow synthetic rubber contact cement, is applied to both the membrane and the underlayment, using a 9-inch low-nap paint roller. It's then allowed to dry to the touch — from 5 to 50 minutes, depending on the temperature. You get about 60 square feet of coverage per gallon. To get a reliable bond, you don't want to install at temperatures lower than 40°F.

The easiest way to apply the adhesive is to fold the lower half of the membrane lengthwise and coat the exposed backside and underlayment, then carefully unfold it into position and bond it to the underlayment by brushing it down with a soft-bristle push broom. Repeat the process on the upper half. It takes a few hands and a coordinated effort to control a long sheet and prevent trapped air bubbles and misbonds (**Figure 2**).

Sealing seams. Obviously, tight seams between sheets are critical to leak-proof performance. Every sheet overlaps the previous one by 6 inches, and laps are given a special sealing treatment. The overlapping surfaces must be kept clear of adhesive. After all the sheets have been bonded to the roof, the installer folds each seam edge back and applies Carlisle Sure-Seal Primer to the bonding surfaces (**Figure 3**, next page). The primer prepares the surface for Carlisle Seam Tape, a 6-inch-wide, double-faced peel-and-stick seam sealer. The installer applies the tape, letting its edge stick out of the seam by about 1/4 inch to avoid pockets.

Any necessary joints in the membrane are treated in the same manner as the seams between courses — that is, prepared with primer on both surfaces, overlapped a minimum of 6 inches, and bonded with seam tape. To eliminate any doubt about the security of the seams, our roofing contractor goes one step beyond the prescriptive requirements. After brushing a 6-inch-wide stripe of primer down the center of

Figure 2. Four hands are better than two to prevent wrinkles and trapped air bubbles in the EPDM bonding process.

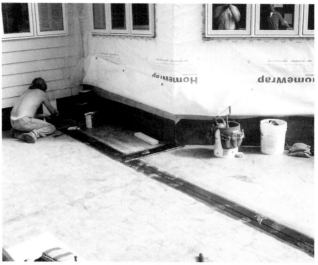

Figure 3. The overlapping seams in an EPDM membrane are treated separately from the main bonding operation. After brushing the seam with primer, the author applies a pressure-sensitive seam tape to secure and seal the edge (left). As a redundant fail-safe measure, the author applies a 6-inch-wide peel-and-stick rubber flashing strip over every seam in the membrane and seals the strip's edges with a lap sealant (right).

each seam, he applies a 6-inch-wide, pressure-sensitive peel-and-stick flashing strip (**Figure 3**, right photo). After bonding the flashing with a steel roller, he carefully seals all edges with a finishing bead of proprietary lap sealant, applied with a caulking gun.

Covering corners. Uncured rubber, although less resistant to UV degradation than the roof membrane, is far more pliable and is therefore used to treat corners and junctions with multiple angles. The uncured rubber comes in pressure-sensitive peel-and-stick sheets and can be stretched to conform to the shape of the corner, then glued and lap-sealed in the same manner as a common seam seal, after priming the bonding surface.

You don't cut the roof membrane to form an inside corner but fold it back on itself in a triangular flap, and glue the folds into place against the wall. The flap gets covered with an uncured patch, with its edges lap-sealed.

To seal an outside corner, where the membrane must be cut to fit, the roofer prepares two 9-by-13-inch strips of rubber membrane and glues them in a double layer over the corner, wrapping the first layer 3 inches on one side and 6 inches on the other, then reversing the overlap on the second strip. He covers the three-way bottom of the corner with a circular patch of pressure-sensitive uncured rubber and finishes all edges with a bead of lap sealant. All corners on the patches are rounded to resist snags and uplift.

Metal Flashing

All of the flashing on this job was copper, either uncoated red or lead-coated. We capped the sidewall membrane terminations with a 12-inch-wide strip of red copper, to shield the rubber against possible

puncture from feet or furniture. The wood shingle siding on this job begins just above the finished deck surface, leaving a narrow strip of flashing exposed.

Drip-edge. The perimeter drip-edge goes on after, and on top of, the membrane. A two-piece lead-coated custom drip-edge along the upper flat roof cleverly eliminates penetration of the membrane and any exposed fasteners (**Figure 4**). The roofer face-nails the first piece to the fascia board, covering the dangling edge of the roof membrane. The secondary piece caps

Figure 4. A custom-made two-piece lead-coated copper drip-edge conceals face-driven fasteners. The drip-edge will be sealed to the membrane with a 6-inch-wide rubber cover strip.

Figure 5. A soldered copper drip pan, nailed on top of the membrane, is sealed under a self-sticking rubber flashing strip. A pliable self-sticking uncured rubber patch seals the junction of the outside wall corner and deck (left). The drip pan directs runoff into a copper gutter (right).

the first and is crimped tight along its lower edge, which kicks out to shed water. The flashing gets sealed to the deck membrane in a manner similar to the seam treatment, with a 6-inch strip of pressure-sensitive flashing rubber centered on the primed joint, pressure-bonded, then edge-sealed with lap sealant.

Next, he soldered a custom red copper pan and drip-edge to direct roof runoff between the wall openings into a stock copper gutter (**Figure 5**). He ran a bed of lap sealant on the roof membrane, then nailed the copper in place on top. After soldering, the joints are cleaned with water to remove the excess flux, which could otherwise interfere with the roofing adhesive. If the copper requires further preparatory cleaning, he uses a clean rag soaked in tolu-

ene, which won't adversely affect the rubber. Avoid direct skin contact with this stuff, though — wear rubber gloves for protection — and work with plenty of ventilation.

Flashing penetrations. The balustrade posts that penetrate the membrane on the upper-level roof were tricky to flash. After the posts were secured in place, the roofer ran a bead of lap sealant around them, then bedded a snug-fitting custom-made copper post sleeve and flange into the sealant (**Figure 6**). The flanges were nailed to the deck, then sealed with 6-inch pressure-sensitive rubber flashing glued to the membrane and the copper. Again, all edges received the lap-sealant treatment.

Figure 6. The roofing contractor installed custom flanged copper sleeves over the railing posts and plumbing vent. The flange is bedded in sealant on top of the EPDM membrane, then tightly covered under peel-and-stick rubber flashing strips.

Finishing Up

We covered the half-wall railings with wood shingle siding. We fashioned the infill balusters and railings from standard 2x2 pressure-treated wood. A running cap of 2x8 red cedar protects the overall assembly and ties the rails and walls together visually.

The finished deck rests on pressure-treated 2x6 sleepers, taper-cut to compensate for the 1/8-inch slope and bring the surface back to level. To protect the membrane from wear, we glued 1 1/2-inch strips of rubber, cut from a product called Walkway roof pads (R.B. Fuller Products, www.rbrubber.com), to the bot-tom edge of the sleepers. These 2x2-foot pads have a pattern of rounded knobs molded into the underside to allow water to drain away in multiple directions. The sleepers are loose-laid on the deck on 16-inch centers. We screwed the 5/4x6 pressure-treated deck-ing to the sleepers with stainless-steel square-head deck screws. This permits pieces of the decking to be removed at a later date, in the unlikely event that the membrane requires servicing.

Thomas Buckborough is a general contractor and designer-builder in Concord, Mass. Jim McKenna was the roofing contractor on this project.

Rooftop Decks With Duradek

by Rob Corbo

Most of the single-story bump-out additions we build have pitched roofs, though under the right circumstances it's not hard to add a flat rooftop deck to the design. That was the case with the job shown here — a 6-foot-by-20-foot kitchen expansion with a master bedroom roof terrace above. In the past we'd used asphalt-based or single-ply rub-ber roofing membranes for flat-roof jobs, then covered the roofing with deck boards. But for this project, the architect specified Duradek, a PVC thermoplastic waterproof deck membrane (www.duradek.com).

What Is Duradek?

Originally developed in the 1960s as a slip-resistant flooring for small boats, Duradek was later intro-duced as a roofing material, first in Canada and then in the United States. In the manufacturing process, PVC is pressed through rollers into a thin film that is then laminated to a woven polyester fabric for stabil-ity and multidirectional strength. Because the mem-brane serves as both a walking surface and a roof covering, it's textured for slip resistance, and the vinyl formulation includes mildew and ultraviolet inhibitors and heat stabilizers for better long-term performance. Duradek comes with a 10-year manu-facturer's warranty (see "Weatherproof Sheet Flooring," page 252).

The 60-mil-thick vinyl traffic membrane — called Duradek Ultra — that was installed on this project is Class C fire-rated (Class A when installed over 5/16-inch HardieBacker or concrete) and approved for use over conditioned living space. (The membrane is also sold in 40- and 45-mil thicknesses for decking applications with no living space below.) Test results show that Duradek exceeds IBC requirements for resis-

This durable, slip-resistant deck surface also serves as the roofing membrane for the space below.

tance to wind uplift, even in special wind regions.

Our membrane was delivered in a 72-inch-wide roll (slightly narrower than our roof deck); 54-inch rolls are also available. According to Duradek, the product comes in two textures and 18 colors and patterns. While colors can vary slightly, production orders are tagged so that all the rolls for larger projects are shipped from the same production run.

Like other sheet goods, Duradek is subject to wear and tear. But punctures, cuts, and burn marks are relatively easy to repair with glued and welded patches, and won't compromise the membrane's watertightness.

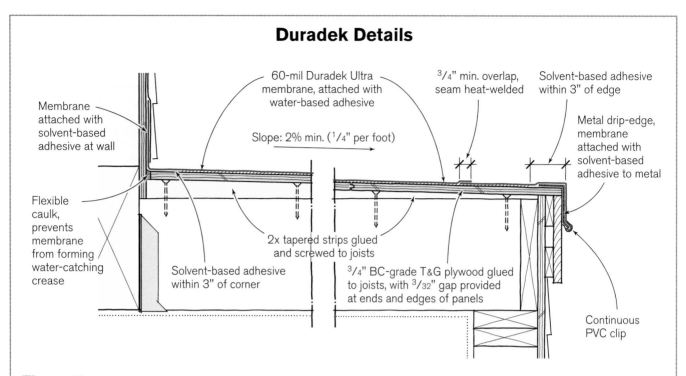

Duradek Details

Membrane attached with solvent-based adhesive at wall

Flexible caulk, prevents membrane from forming water-catching crease

Solvent-based adhesive within 3" of corner

60-mil Duradek Ultra membrane, attached with water-based adhesive

Slope: 2% min. (1/4" per foot)

2x tapered strips glued and screwed to joists

3/4" BC-grade T&G plywood glued to joists, with 3/32" gap provided at ends and edges of panels

3/4" min. overlap, seam heat-welded

Solvent-based adhesive within 3" of edge

Metal drip-edge, membrane attached with solvent-based adhesive to metal

Continuous PVC clip

Figure 7. Duradek Ultra is intended for use as both a roof covering and a traffic surface, making it a good choice for residential decks built above living spaces.

Figure 8. Tapered strips of framing lumber glued and screwed to the deck joists supply the necessary 2 percent slope for drainage (left). Four-by-four PT railing posts are bolted to the framing (below left) before the plywood deck sheathing is installed (below right).

Figure 9. After installing the metal perimeter drip-edge, the Duradek installers patch joints, nail heads, and voids in the plywood deck with a silica-based floor filler (left), then sand the deck smooth (top right). Sealant fills the joint between the deck and wall sheathing, preventing the membrane from forming a water-collecting crease (bottom right).

For cost information and a list of authorized installers, I went to the company's Web site, where I found the names of three local contractors. Two returned my calls and provided bids for the project. For 130 square feet of deck area with 22 linear feet of drip-edge flashing, 25 feet of wall flashing, and four rail posts, the bids came in at about $12 per square foot (in 2008). Although we'd never worked with Duradek before, the installation — which was done by factory-trained installers — was straightforward and quick. The installed cost was less than that of a conventional roof with protective deck boards, and we were able to start working on the railing immediately after the membrane was glued in place.

Flat Roof Framing

Although the PVC membrane itself can be installed only by an authorized Dura-dek dealer, we needed to construct the deck properly to receive it. For proper drainage, the manufacturer requires a deck slope of 2 percent, or 1/4 inch every 12 inches (**Figure 7**). For our 6-foot-wide deck, we pitched the roof 1 1/2 inches by ripping tapered wedges from framing lumber and gluing and nailing the wedges to the ceiling joists (**Figure 8**).

After bolting the 4x4 rail posts in place, we installed 3/4-inch T&G plywood, per the manufactur-

er's recommendations, gluing the plywood to the joists and leaving the proper gap at the ends and edges of panels. Because of compatibility problems between the PVC membrane and the compounds used with treated plywood and polymer-enhanced OSB underlayments like AdvanTech, those sheet goods aren't recommended.

We next installed the fascia boards, then covered the deck with 15-pound felt paper and installed temporary flashing at the deck-wall intersection to keep the plywood dry until the Duradek sub arrived approximately three weeks later. The manufacturer recommends that the decking be at no more than 12 percent to 14 percent moisture content at the time of installation. In hindsight, getting estimates earlier in the process would have tightened the schedule.

On the day of installation, we removed the felt and flashing and swept and vacuumed the deck. When the installers arrived, we made ourselves available, but stayed out of their way.

Prepping the Deck

The two installers started by nailing a galvanized metal drip-edge around the outside perimeter. Duradek offers several edge-finishing options; the one used here is designed so that the membrane laps over the metal and is secured with continuous PVC

Figure 10. After cutting the first section of membrane to length (left), the installation crew dry-fits it to the deck. Once it's in position, they roll back half the membrane lengthwise (below left) and apply adhesive to the exposed part of the deck before laying the membrane back in place (below right).

Figure 11. A crew member carefully marks and cuts openings for the rail posts (far left). Then, after gluing down the strip of membrane along the edge of the deck, he glues down the main section of membrane, overlapping the perimeter strip 1 inch (left).

Figure 12. Watertight joints are made by heating overlapping edges of the membrane with hot air from a heat gun and then applying pressure to the seam with a hand roller (left). The collars around the posts are also heat-welded to the deck membrane (right).

clips that slip over the metal's flared edge.

Next, the installers filled the plywood joints, voids, knots, and low areas with a patching compound they mixed up on site. Duradek — like vinyl — will telegraph even small imperfections in the deck sheathing, so they inspected carefully as they smoothed the compound with their sanders (**Figure 9**, page 249). After filling the joint where the terrace plywood deck meets the second floor walls with a flexible caulk, they carefully swept and vacuumed again.

Cutting the Membrane

To cut the membrane, the installers rolled it out on the ground and measured its length so that it would fold up the walls surrounding the deck by at least 6 inches (**Figure 10**).

Planning for seams. Because the deck was slightly wider than the membrane, there would have to be one seam; it fell under the railing where it was barely visible. The 9-inch-wide strip of membrane that finishes the deck is overlapped by the first piece and folds down over the drip-edge.

Duradek seams are heat-welded rather than glued together, and require a minimum 3/4-inch overlap. Making these seams properly is the most critical part of the installation: The weld will fail if any of the adhesive used to fasten the membrane to the deck contaminates the seam.

Installing the Membrane

After dry-fitting the full-width piece, the installers pulled the material back away from the wall and folded it in half lengthwise onto itself. They then spread the water-based Duradek adhesive on the exposed plywood and folded the first half of the membrane back into place, taking care to eliminate air pockets as they smoothed out the material and pressed it into the adhesive.

Once the first half of the Duradek was glued down, the installers carefully cut openings for the four railing posts (**Figure 11**), marked the position of the outside edge of the unglued half of the membrane, and then folded this half back over the glued section. Next, they glued down the narrow outside strip of membrane, then glued down the second half of the large piece. They used heat guns to heat the overlap, blowing hot air into the seam and then pressing the two halves together with a roller (**Figure 12**). Every few feet, they checked the seam strength.

Around the base of each post, the installers wrapped a 6-inch-wide PVC collar; L-shaped flaps cut at the bottom of the collar overlap the deck membrane and were heat-welded in place. To create a watertight joint, small corner patches were slipped behind each slit in the membrane before it was welded together. When the railing was assembled, boxed newels that slide down over each post would cover the PVC collars, making the joint completely waterproof.

At the parapet walls, the outside corners were treated in a similar way. At inside corners, the installers used a folded "pig's ear" detail to create a watertight joint.

At the new doorway into the master bedroom, the membrane wraps up and over the rough sill. To make this critical area watertight, all of the joints were welded. After the membrane was in place, we installed the new door, which sits on top of this waterproof pan.

Figure 13. Boxed newels slide down over each post, covering the collar at the bottom.

In other areas where the membrane folds up onto a wall, the installers used Duradek's solvent-based adhesive, which is applied like contact cement to both surfaces. Later, we patched in the housewrap and shingles, lapping them over the membrane.

Around the perimeter of the deck, the membrane folds down over the drip-edge. The installers heat-welded the corner seams and fused the overlapping membrane to the metal. After trimming the edge of the membrane flush with the bottom of the metal, they finished the bottom edge with continuous PVC clips.

Railing

As soon as the membrane was installed, we were able to get to work on the railing. This is when we really began to appreciate Duradek: Working on top of an asphalt-based membrane in the summer heat typically means scuffing and uncomfortable conditions, even if we plan our work schedule to avoid the hottest parts of the day. But the light-colored Duradek surface doesn't radiate heat to nearly the same extent as asphalt roofing, and we were able to finish the project comfortably and without damaging the roof.

We first wrapped the 4x4 posts with boxed newels,

Weatherproof Sheet Flooring

by Sheldon Swartzentruber

Duradek is a PVC-based material that can be installed over virtually any solid surface. Available in more than two dozen colors and patterns, the surface is textured for slip-resistance when wet, and the vinyl is treated with mildew inhibitors and ultraviolet stabilizers. To prevent premature fatigue, which has been known to occur in some vinyl roofing products, Duradek is backed with

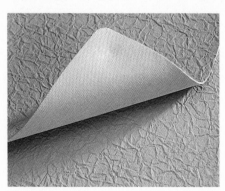

fiberglass reinforcement and treated with citrus-based plasticizers. Manufactured in rolls beginning at 30 mils in thickness, the heavier 60-mil Ultra series is ASTM tested and approved as a roofing material that can be used over conditioned living space.

Certified installers order material through local distributors, who typically require no more than a week's

lead time for delivery. When multiple rolls are ordered, the material is color matched by lot number at the factory to avoid any variation in color from one lot run to the next. Although Duradek should be installed at temperatures above freezing, the material remains flexible to -40°F.

The manufacturer also makes a lightweight, powder-coated aluminum railing system called Durarail. The interchangeable components are available in stock or custom colors, with a choice of rail profiles. Guard rail designs include "view-through" tempered glass, traditional picket, or a combination of the two.
For more information, visit www.duradek.com.

Sheldon Swartzentruber owns and operates Delmarva Roofing & Coating in Greenwood, Del.

Figure 14. A simple painted cedar railing finishes the deck (left). Balusters are attached with screws through a rail insert at the top (below left). A V-shaped notch at the base of each baluster (below right) matches the beveled top of the shoe rail.

treating the ends with a penetrating sealer and holding the newels up off the roofing membrane (**Figure 13**). At the inside corners, we lag-bolted short 4x4 PT posts to the wall, then wrapped these posts with three-sided newels.

We used stock cedar handrail and balusters and ripped the rail inserts — which hide the upper baluster fasteners — from clear 2x4 cedar. We gave the lower balustrade rail a water-shedding beveled profile and put a corresponding V-shaped notch cut into the bottom of each baluster (**Figure 14**).

At the sides of the deck, the railing follows the profile of the sloped roof. We gave the rail a paint finish and topped the posts with copper caps.

Rob Corbo is a building contractor in Elizabeth, N.J.

Waterproof Fiberglass Decks

by Eric Borden

We build along the Jersey shore, and whether a house fronts the ocean, the bay, or the river, our clients want to enjoy the view. To give them a good view from inside the house, we might have to go up three stories. But for the view from outside, we add a deck or two.

The project discussed here is typical of most of our jobs, because the decks serve double duty — as both outside living space, and as a weatherproof cover for rooms below. At the rear of the house, we added a deck off the second-floor kitchen that overlooks the pool and creates a covered patio underneath. At the front of the house, we removed an existing first-floor exterior porch to make room for an enlarged great room. We extended this deck to one side to cover the entrance to the garage and to provide an additional 12-by-20-foot covered carport with access from the dining room through a new slider. We also extended this deck 8 feet to the other side to create a covered entrance to the house.

Both of these decks had to protect the spaces below from water. We could have used EPDM single-ply rubber, which is easy to install, but has to be replaced eventually. And because EPDM can't be walked on directly, we would have had to install deck boards on top of it.

The option we prefer is fiberglass, which does not need any additional decking to protect it and, if re-

This site-mixed two-part resin provides a seamless, watertight deck surface over living space.

coated every 7 to 10 years, will last forever. A fiberglass deck covering is also relatively inexpensive and, in most cases, can be completed in two days. Costs in our area range from $6.50 to $8.00 per square foot, including the second layer of plywood and all labor (in 2000 dollars).

Sound Substrate

Polyester resin fiberglass has a solid track record — it's been in use since the 1950s in the boating industry — but it's messy and somewhat finicky to install. To avoid problems later, we spare no expense preparing a sound deck structure.

First, we step up one size on our joist sizing, because we rip a pitch (1/8 inch per foot, minimum) into the deck framing. You can also create a pitch by adding sleepers to the top of the joists, but I feel that this increases the odds that the finished deck will squeak.

Next, we sheathe the deck with 3/4-inch tongue-and-groove Douglas fir plywood, glued with construction adhesive and fastened with 8-penny ring-shank nails placed 8 inches on-center. If you use square-edge plywood, be sure to block all seams; any movement in the plywood substrate will stress the fiberglass. When the sheathing is complete, we through-bolt any railing posts to the framing at the

Figure 15. Fiberglass resin is mixed on site with a hardener (methyl ethyl ketone peroxide) in a ratio that can be varied to extend or shorten set time. The base coat is applied over plywood with reinforcing mesh at joints and penetrations, then finished with a gel coat.

Figure 16. On the day the fiberglass will be applied, a clean, dry layer of $1/2$-inch AC plywood is laid over the base layer of $3/4$-inch T&G plywood. Joints are staggered and the sheets are fastened with 8d ring-shank nails.

Figure 17. A 1x4 fastened to the rim joist will be wrapped with fiberglass to provide a clean termination at the deck perimeter. Fiberglass doesn't bond well at 90-degree corners, so the top outside edge of this trim piece is eased with a $1/2$-inch round-over router bit. A 20-degree ripped undercut serves as a drip-edge.

intersection of the joists and the inside of the rim board. We add blocking so that the posts are secured on three sides, because any movement could cause the fiberglass to crack and leak.

Applying the Resin

I leave the application of the fiberglass coating to the professionals. My installers are former boat builders who take great pride in their finished product and are knowledgeable about the quirks of fiberglass.

Polyester resin fiberglass is a two-part product. The general-purpose resin is mixed on site with a hardener (**Figure 15**). The mix ratio determines how long the resin remains workable, and may need to be adjusted for weather conditions and other variables. Humid weather will delay drying, so we increase the amount of hardener added; conversely, dry weather will cause the resin to set up too fast, so we use less hardener. Open time can also be affected by the surface area of the container used to make the mix; a larger container disperses the heat of the chemical reaction, delaying the chemical reaction and extending open time.

The resin is applied over a fiberglass mat, which acts as a binder and adds strength to the coating. Essentially, the mat serves the same function as wire mesh does in a concrete slab. Various other components, such as ground silica and microballoons (small glass beads) can be added to the resin for filleting or patching.

Double plywood layer. When the fiberglass installers show up on site, they bring with them the second layer of plywood for the deck. They use $1/2$-inch AC

fir plywood, which provides a smooth surface for the resin to adhere to (**Figure 16**). They prefer to provide the plywood because they can be sure of the moisture content of the wood. Moisture is probably the biggest problem at this stage of the game. The resin does not soak into the wood very well, so any moisture in the pores of the wood prevents the resin from penetrating and destroys the bond. The key is to never install more plywood than can be covered with fiberglass in a day's work: Two experienced workers can cover about 600 square feet in a day.

Joints in the second layer are staggered over those of the first. The two layers of plywood are not glued together; they're only nailed with 8-penny ring-shanks, 6 inches on-center at the joists and 4 inches on-center at the edges. This makes it easy to remove the top layer of plywood if there is a problem down the road.

Edge work. After the plywood is installed, a 1x4 pine drip-edge is fastened flat against the outside of the rim joist, flush with the deck (**Figure 17**). This trim piece is undercut at 20 degrees to create a drip-edge.

Where the deck meets the wall, a cant strip, made by ripping a kiln-dried fir 2x4 at a 45-degree angle, is installed against the sheathing (**Figure 18**, next page). Any species of lumber will do as long as it's dry, but we prefer fir because the better quality material gives us fewer problems. The cant strip keeps the glass, which extends approximately 6 inches up the wall, from pulling away from the corner. The cant strip also prevents water from ponding in the deck-wall joint. Wood strips are also installed at the sills of

Figure 18. A 45-degree cant strip keeps water from ponding in the corners and prevents cracking in the fiberglass where it turns up the wall (far left). At door sills, a narrow trim strip serves as a backstop for the fiberglass, which will create a seamless waterproof pan under the door (left).

Figure 19. Before applying the fiberglass mat flashing, all edges — including the bottoms of railing posts, the edges of door openings, and all plywood joints — are knocked down with a coarse-disc grinder.

any door openings to serve as the backstop for the fiberglass, which will create a seamless pan.

Once all the edge pieces and cant strips are nailed in place (again, glue is not necessary), the outside corners, including the drip-edge, are rounded using a ½-inch rounding-over bit in a router. Because fiberglass doesn't adhere well to a 90-degree corner, all edges must be knocked down. Joints in the plywood are lightly sanded with a coarse disc in a grinder, as are the bottom few inches of the posts where they meet the plywood and the edges of door openings (**Figure 19**).

While one person completes the sanding, the other mixes the "fairing" — a boat-building term for a compound used to smooth and level a curve. Made from resin, hardener, and finely ground silica, the fairing is spread on all joints and nail heads, and is also used to fill any voids around posts and deck-wall joints (**Figure 20**). The fairing compound takes about 30 minutes to dry, after which any lumps are hand-sanded.

Polyester resin is nasty stuff, so it's important to take safety precautions from the moment the fiber-

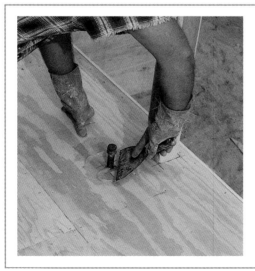

Figure 20. A site-mixed fiberglass and silica leveling compound is applied to all joints and nail heads, and is used to fill in gaps around posts and other penetrations (far left) and at cant strips and door sills (left). When dry, any lumps and high spots are hand-sanded.

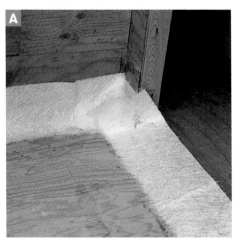

Figure 21. At cant strips, a band of fiberglass mat is pressed into a bedding coat of resin (A), then coated with more resin (B) and rolled with a small steel roller to force out any trapped air (C). Door sills get the same treatment (D).

Figure 22. At the railing posts and perimeter drip-edge, fiberglass mat flashing is bedded flush with the backcut bottom edge and wrapped up onto the deck surface, then coated and rolled.

glass is first mixed. Make sure the work area is well ventilated, and always wear gloves and goggles. A respirator is standard equipment during sanding as well.

Glass mat flashing. Next, a bedding coat of resin is applied at the cant strips, then a 9-inch strip of 2-ounce fiberglass mat is pressed into place (**Figure 21**). Then, more resin is used to "wet it out," and the whole thing is rolled with a small (1-inch-diameter)

grooved steel roller to force out any air trapped under the mat. Excess resin is cleaned off the roller periodically with acetone.

After all of the cant strips are treated, the same process is repeated at all of the railing post bottoms. Strips of glass mat are also wrapped over the 1x4 drip-edge at the rim joist (**Figure 22**). The edge of the mat strip is lined up with the backcut bottom edge of the

Figure 23. At the main deck, a bedding coat of fresh resin is applied in 4-foot bands using a short-nap paint roller, covered with a full-width sheet of fiberglass mat, then rolled again (far left). Clean sand is then spread over the still wet mat to provide a nonskid surface (left).

Figure 24. After the base coat has dried, sandpaper is used to knock down edges and rough up the whole surface to improve bonding with the finish coat (far left). Brooms and leaf blowers are used to remove excess particles from the surface before applying the gel coat finish (left).

Figure 25. Tinted gel coat is applied first at edges and penetrations (left), then on the main deck (middle), using short-nap paint rollers. The final product cures in about 30 hours and looks much like the surface of a fiberglass tub (right).

Figure 26. On this job, the wood railings were also flashed with fiberglass mat (far left), then finished with white gel coat to contrast with the deck color (left).

drip-edge, "wet out" with resin, and rolled over on top of the deck. Particular care is taken where the drip-edges meet the walls to prevent any voids from developing that might lead water into the structure. About 100 linear feet of edging can be flashed in 1½ hours.

Base Coating

When all the edges are complete, the main field areas of the deck can be coated (**Figure 23**). Using a new batch of resin and hardener, the deck is coated in 4-foot sections. First, resin is rolled onto the plywood using a paint roller with short-nap throwaway covers; then a 4-foot run of 2-ounce mat is laid, "wet out," and rolled to remove any air. The mat is precut to save time, and the edges are frayed to feather the joints and make them less visible. The mat is non-woven, so fibers can be pulled out by hand to thin or fray the edge. Before moving to the next 4-foot section, clean sand is broadcast by hand over the still-wet surface to create a nonslip texture. Work proceeds in 4-foot increments until this first coat is complete.

The fiberglass doesn't fully set up for about 8 hours (faster if it's in direct sunlight), so the surface should be protected from all traffic, including children, pets, and curious passersby. The resin will cure completely in several days.

Gel coat. The next day's work begins with more sanding (**Figure 24**). Using a 36-grit sanding disc on a grinder, all of the frayed seams at the drip-edges are sanded back to true the edges; the rest of the surface is sanded to remove any lumps and to rough up the base for good bonding. In final preparation for application of the gel coat, dust and residue from the sanding are cleaned off the deck using brooms and gas-powered leaf blowers.

The gel coat our installers used is formulated for exterior applications and contains UV inhibitors as well as additives to increase abrasion resistance (**Figure 25**). It is also available in several colors; on this job, we used beige for the decks and white for the continuous rail capping the 3-foot tall bulkhead walls that were used instead of posts (**Figure 26**).

Once the resin is mixed with hardener, application begins at the edges and proceeds to the field. As with the base coat, the gel coat is applied using throwaway paint rollers. The finished product looks similar to the surface of a fiberglass tub, except slightly rougher, because it picks up the texture of the glass mat below, and also because of the nonskid surface provided by the sand. We allow the gel coat to cure for 30 hours before we set the doors. We always work while standing on sheets of plywood placed on the deck, because at this point the gel coat is not fully cured. Even after the surface is cured, we always work off of the plywood to protect the surface. The gel coat will take a lot of abuse, but early on it's still tender. Nothing will ruin a day faster than dropping your hammer off of a 6-foot ladder and putting a chip in the new surface.

Details and Maintenance

Siding is installed as usual, with the building paper overlapping and taped to the fiberglass where it runs up the wall. At railings, we have had problems in the past with checking of the wood posts, which allows water past the fiberglass counterflashing and into the building envelope. Now we usually wrap our posts with 1x6s, holding the boards ½ inch off the surface of the deck to prevent wicking of moisture. In the search for the perfect railing, we have tried a few vinyl systems. The vinyl post covers that come with some of these systems work fine.

Routine maintenance of the fiberglass deck surface is the same as any fiberglass boat. The surface should be cleaned periodically with a non-abrasive cleaner, such as Spic 'N Span, and visually inspected every year for signs of excessive wear, especially at the deck-wall junction and around the posts. We have decks out there that are 10 years old and have needed nothing more than an additional application of gel coat.

Repairs are fairly easy. The affected area is removed, the edges of the fiberglass are ground back, and the plywood is reinforced to ensure a sound surface. Then the fiberglass is reapplied to make the patch. The gel coat blends almost perfectly.

Eric Borden owns ESB Contracting, a remodeling company in Forked River, N.J. Dan and Rick Winkle were the fiberglass installers on this project.

Attaching a Deck to a Sloped Roof

by Dave Holbrook

These simple stainless-steel hold-downs are easy to remove for reroofing.

I once designed and built a whole-house remodel that was located just a little too far back from the waterfront to enjoy an unobstructed ocean view. When I suggested a rooftop deck, to my pleasure, the owners jumped. I'd stuck my neck out a little, not having built a rooftop structure before — I knew there were a couple of unique problems to solve. I wasn't too worried about the structural issues; we'd retained only about 10% of the original building (to satisfy zoning requirements), so it was wide open for modifications. I figured a structural ridge beam and some ganged rafters would handle any point loads imposed on the roof by the deck and its occupants, and I had an engineer work out those details. My main concerns were how to tie the deck to the roof and how to make the connection leakproof. I expected the deck to outlast at least two generations of asphalt roof shingles, so the connector had to accommodate an eventual reroofing job.

Inspecting the site, I noted that plumbing vents poke through the roof in a nice, dry fashion, so I used a standard plumber's neoprene roof boot with an aluminum flange (**Figure 27**) as the jumping-off point for my deck post anchor design. If I could support the deck on small-diameter steel tubing, a roof boot would seal the connection. Because roof boots are typically replaced along with the roofing, I had to make sure the supporting connectors could be easily removed and set back into place, one at a time, by the eventual roofer. I drew a couple of plans of the connector, made a couple of templates to duplicate the two roof pitches I had to contend with, and headed for my local welder's shop.

The Design Is Simple

A rectangular, stainless-steel flange, 1/4 inch thick by 6 by 12 inches, forms the base of the connector. Its perimeter is drilled with six 1/2-inch-diameter holes for lag-bolting to quadruple 2-by rafters. The holes are staggered and placed so that they'll be close to the center of the rafter they land on, for maximum connector strength (**Figure 28**).

Next, a 6-inch length of 3-inch-outside-diameter stainless-steel tubing is welded to the center of the flange. The tubing is first cut at the appropriate angle to stand plumb on the roof, and this angled end receives the weld. A second, 11 1/2-inch length of smaller, 2 1/2-inch-O.D. tubing gets the same angle cut and slips inside the first piece. It's permanently welded to the base tube, sealing the joint completely. A third piece of 3-inch-O.D. tubing, 6 inches long, fits over the insert. At the bottom end of this third piece, I had the welder drill and tap a hole to receive a stainless-steel set screw. The set screw firmly clamps this tube to the inner sleeve. Welded to the top of this same tube is a U-shaped yoke, 3 inches wide by 6 inches high, with a

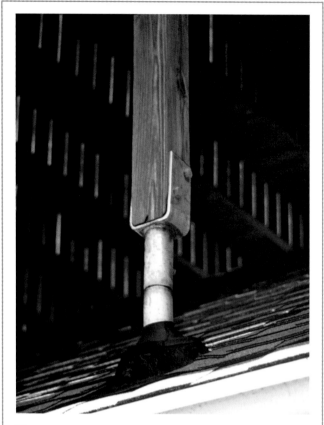

Figure 27. Making use of standard flashing components, the author designed this hold-down around a common plumbing vent roof boot.

Hold-Down Details

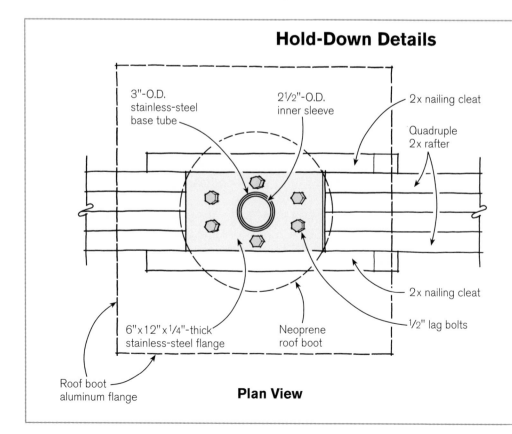

3"-O.D. stainless-steel base tube

2 1/2"-O.D. inner sleeve

2x nailing cleat

Quadruple 2x rafter

6"x12"x1/4"-thick stainless-steel flange

Neoprene roof boot

2x nailing cleat

1/2" lag bolts

Roof boot aluminum flange

Plan View

Figure 28. The roof framing was modified with a structural ridge beam and quadruple rafters to carry the point loads of the deck above. Flange bolt holes were oriented to center on the rafter for maximum thread hold.

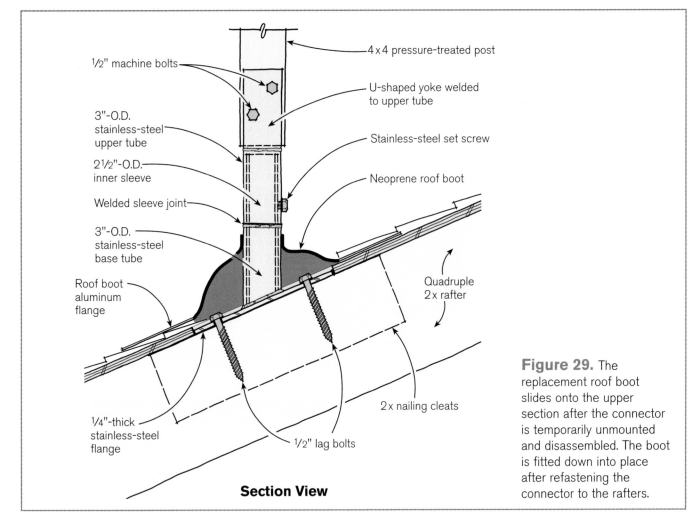

1/2" machine bolts

4 x 4 pressure-treated post

U-shaped yoke welded to upper tube

3"-O.D. stainless-steel upper tube

2 1/2"-O.D. inner sleeve

Stainless-steel set screw

Welded sleeve joint

Neoprene roof boot

3"-O.D. stainless-steel base tube

Roof boot aluminum flange

Quadruple 2x rafter

1/4"-thick stainless-steel flange

2x nailing cleats

1/2" lag bolts

Section View

Figure 29. The replacement roof boot slides onto the upper section after the connector is temporarily unmounted and disassembled. The boot is fitted down into place after refastening the connector to the rafters.

3 1/2-inch interior spread to receive a 4x4 pressure-treated wood post (**Figure 29**). The yoke is through-drilled for two 1/2-inch-diameter machine bolts to secure the post.

My welder charged me $100 per connector, less than I'd expected to pay for custom stainless brackets. So far, so good; but when we got them on the roof, I realized that the combined thickness of the flange and the lag-bolt heads was not going to allow the boot to lie down flush. I always use minimum 5/8-inch plywood to sheathe a roof, so I decided to let the brackets into pockets cut into the sheathing, atop the rafters. The plunge-cut pocket left a foot-long unsupported edge of plywood on either side of the ganged rafter, so I added 2-by nailing cleats along the underside of the cutout.

After almost ten years in use, the connectors have performed well. When it comes time to reshingle, the roofing contractor can unbolt the flange from the roof, remove the two post bolts, and remove the connectors (one at a time!) from the roof. After the set screw is loosened, the lower section of the connector can be slid off. The replacement roof boot is slid onto the upper section, the connector is bolted back into place, the boot slides down, and it's roofing as usual.

Dave Holbrook is a builder on Cape Cod, Mass.

Rooftop Decks Q&A

Attaching Posts Without Penetrating the Roof

Q. *How can I mount newel posts to a deck on a flat roof without cutting into the roof?*

A. *Paul Nichter, a contractor in Islesboro, Maine, responds:* I've been building wood decks with safe railings over flat EPDM roofs on the rainy coast of Maine for over 15 years without compromising the waterproofing. I avoid the traditional method of bolting a 4x4 post deep into the framing, as it penetrates roof surfaces and increases the possibility of a leak long before either the decking or the roof membrane is worn out from age. I take a two-pronged approach to keeping water out while achieving good resistance to lateral forces. My approach is based on the deck being built on sleepers above the roof.

First, I design rooftop decks with corners every 6 feet to 12 feet. Corners stabilize the railing, as lateral loads aren't borne by just one post; rather, the loads are shared with adjacent posts.

Second, I mount the posts with hardware that bolts to the top of the deck (**Figure 30**). Each post is a hollow box that fits over a vertical threaded rod. The rod threads into a 3/4-inch nut welded to the center of a 1/4-inch-thick steel plate. I secure the plate to the deck with four 2 1/2-inch RSS Structural Screws (GRK Fasteners, www.grkfasteners.com), but galvanized lags would work too. The screws or lags should be as long as possible without protruding from the bottom of the sleepers and putting holes in the roof membrane. It is essential to secure 2x12 blocking on the flat between the sleepers at post locations so the lags will have something solid to bite into.

Once the plate and rod are installed, I stand the post in place. Usually, some scribing and fitting are needed to make it stand plumb without wobble or lean. Then I run a bead of construction adhesive on the bottom of the post and seat it on the deck surface.

A second piece of 1/4-inch plate fits at the top of the post in a rabbet cut for that purpose. The threaded rod runs through a hole drilled in the plate, and the assembly is drawn tight with a nut. The nut tensions the threaded rod, compressing the post and creating a solid connection.

I've also used manufactured posts from Fypon (www.fypon.com) and WeatherBest (www.weatherbest.com). One advantage of using manufactured posts is that their makers have tested them for code compliance.

EPDM vs. Modified Bitumen Roofing: Which Is the Best Roofing Membrane?

Q. *Why is EPDM roofing so much more expensive than torch-applied modified bitumen? Is EPDM roofing that much better?*

A. *Architect and roofing consultant Harrison McCampbell responds:* For a variety of marketing reasons, the bids you receive on small jobs may not reflect national averages. Normally, the cost of a fully adhered EPDM roof should be fairly close to the cost of a modified bitumen roof.

EPDM is a butyl-based rubber treated to withstand UV and direct exposure to the sun. An EPDM roof will probably outlast a modified bitumen roof or any other asphalt-based membrane. Asphalt products contain oil, which evaporates, eventually rendering the carrier dry and brittle. Frequent wet-dry cycles will accelerate that process, especially if the wet periods are prolonged. Other factors that can affect the

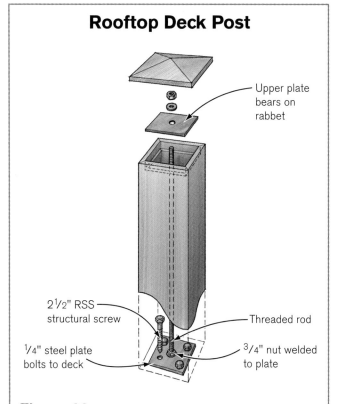

Rooftop Deck Post

Upper plate bears on rabbet

2 1/2" RSS structural screw

1/4" steel plate bolts to deck

Threaded rod

3/4" nut welded to plate

Figure 30. A threaded rod between one plate screwed to the framing and another plate at the top of the post firmly connects a hollow newel to a rooftop deck.

longevity of a roofing membrane include the specific details of insulation, fastening, flashing, lap treatment, and maintenance.

EPDM Substrates

Q. *Is it best to put EPDM roofing over polyisocyanurate insulation, or can it be installed directly over OSB? Are bubbles a concern with either substrate?*

A. *Roofer Joseph Bublick responds:* Although I prefer a base of polyisocyanurate, OSB or plywood will work fine under fully adhered EPDM. Install the OSB smooth side up. To ensure an even surface, I make sure the fasteners are flush, and install duct tape over the sheathing seams to soften any transitions that may occur if the sheathing begins to curl. There is no need to prime the OSB before installing the EPDM adhesive.

EPDM sticks more tenaciously to OSB or plywood than it does to polyisocyanurate. If you are used to being able to adjust the EPDM slightly as it's installed, this can be a disadvantage. Once the EPDM is cemented to OSB, you won't be able to pull it up for readjustment.

The most common cause of bubbles is the application of rubber to the deck or insulation board too soon, before the adhesive is dry enough. In some cases, a contributing factor can be high pressure in the roof system. If this is the problem, the solution is to install pressure-relief vents. Pressure-relief vents, which are one-way air vents typically measuring about 2 to 3 inches in diameter, are available from roofing manufacturers.

To repair bubbles, cut them out and repair the areas according to the roofing manufacturer's instructions.

Chapter 9:
Porch Construction

Efficient Custom Porches

by Jim Craig

My company specializes in decks and porches. We keep 10 two- to three-person crews in the field and build more than 90 screened porches every year. To compete against the many superb craftsmen in my area, we've had to develop methods and construction details that enable us to work efficiently but still produce a porch that says quality.

Premium Materials

For starters, I always use top-quality materials, for a couple of reasons. First, using premium materials reduces the risk of callbacks and warranty issues. Second, it tells my customers that I'm concerned about the quality and longevity of my product. And because the materials cost more, the markup yields a greater profit than more conventional materials would.

Kiln-dried PT. We use Madison Wood Preservers' (www.madwood.com) pressure-treated southern pine for all of the structural floor and enclosure framing, and for the newel posts and railing systems. Madison includes a water repellent in the treatment process to retard moisture absorption and to resist the effects of weathering.

Primed trim. We use pre-primed pine for all of our painted trim. This lumber is coated on all sides with an oil-based primer, and all minor defects and knots are filled and sealed with an exterior-grade filler to prevent sap streaking and bleeding. We apply two

With high-quality materials and standardized methods, you can create custom porches at a production pace.

topcoats of latex trim paint in the field.

Trex. We use this wood-plastic composite lumber for the deck surfaces outside our screened porches, as well as for rail caps. It's good looking, machines easily, and cuts down on maintenance chores. Trex decking (www.trex.com) is available in 5/4 and 2-by profiles; we prefer the more substantial look of the 2-by stock.

Figure 1. The author installs 2x6 pressure-treated T&G decking to prevent insects from entering between the floorboards of a screened porch. The decking is blind-nailed through the tongue to conceal the fasteners.

Figure 2. Two-by blocking, installed on the flat between joists (left), supports the transition between the diagonally installed porch and Trex sundeck surfaces (right).

Flooring to Keep Bugs Out

Many builders screen the underside of the porch deck or install a screened skirt panel around the porch perimeter to keep insects out. We prefer to use Madison's C-select 2x6 tongue-and-groove boards for a solid, gap-free porch floor (**Figure 1**). The product we use is kiln dried after treatment, which eliminates the warping, twisting, and splitting common with ordinary wet PT lumber.

The boards are reversible, with a square-edge finish on one side and a V-groove edge on the other. We typically install the boards diagonally across the joists, V-groove up, and blind-nail the boards through the tongue to conceal the fasteners.

There's a good reason I run my decking diagonally. Whenever you run decking perpendicular to the joists, you end up with scattered butt joints, which degrade the deck's appearance. By running the decking in opposing diagonals from a central point, you can cover a large surface with no end-butts. It's a clean, stylish look.

If a sundeck surrounds the porch, the two structures will share a common floor frame. I use gapped 2x6 Trex decking for the outside portion. To back the seam where the Trex meets the T&G decking, we install 2x6 PT blocking on the flat between joists, flush with the top edge (**Figure 2**).

Floor framing. Whether we're building a deck or a porch, we run the floor framing on 12-inch centers. Considering that we always use 2-by decking, that may seem like overkill when 16-inch, or even 24-inch, spacing would be acceptable. But 12-inch centers provide a stiffer platform to build the porch on, particularly if the porch structure is set in from the perimeter of the overall deck framing by several feet. I'd rather not have a cluttered-looking forest of posts and pilings below the deck to support the structure.

The added weight of the 2-by surface material — up to double the dead load of 1-by or 5/4 decking — also makes it advisable to beef up the framing. I run my Trex decking on the diagonal and screw it down at alternating edges to reduce the frequency and appearance of surface fasteners. The closer joist spacing keeps the screw pattern tight. Diagonal decking increases the distance that the board must span between joists, so, again, the closer spacing offsets this effect. And although 16-inch spacing may satisfy the code and my customers might not notice the difference, my floor systems are stiff and rugged — no one has ever complained to me about a springy-feeling deck.

Framing the Enclosure

We assemble the pressure-treated porch enclosure system on the deck, using 4x4 uprights to define the openings, a 2x4 bottom plate, and a 1x4 top plate. Our stock black aluminum screening comes in 5x100-foot rolls, so I design the porch with 5-foot-maximum spacing between the upright centerlines (see illustration, next page).

We have a standard 2-8 x 6-9 wooden screen door that we use on nearly every porch. To keep all of the openings at a uniform height around the enclosure, we cut all the uprights equal to the finished height of the door, plus swing clearance. Including the bottom plate, the resulting opening height is 6 feet 11 inches. A 2x4 stretcher at the head of the door opening compensates for the height gain of the bottom plate and provides a backer for the finish trim.

On top of the 1x4 top plate, we build a continuous box beam, using a pair of 2x6s flush with the outside

Figure 3. A box beam lintel consisting of 1x4 plates and 2x6 sides caps the 4x4 posts and runs the entire perimeter of the porch enclosure.

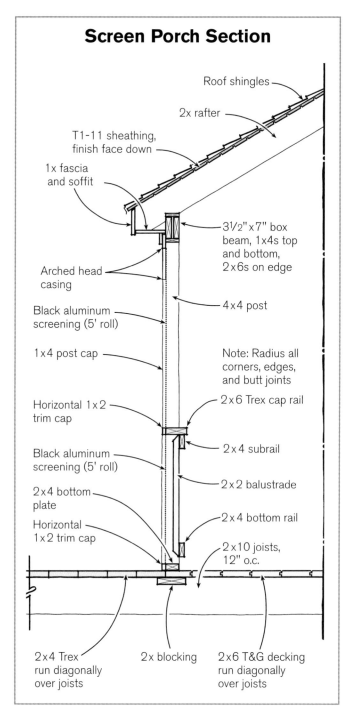

Screen Porch Section

Roof shingles

2x rafter

T1-11 sheathing, finish face down

1x fascia and soffit

3½" x 7" box beam, 1x4s top and bottom, 2x6s on edge

Arched head casing

4x4 post

Black aluminum screening (5' roll)

1x4 post cap

Note: Radius all corners, edges, and butt joints

Horizontal 1x2 trim cap

2x6 Trex cap rail

2x4 subrail

Black aluminum screening (5' roll)

2x2 balustrade

2x4 bottom plate

2x4 bottom rail

Horizontal 1x2 trim cap

2x10 joists, 12" o.c.

2x4 Trex run diagonally over joists

2x blocking

2x6 T&G decking run diagonally over joists

of the 3½-inch-wide plate and capped with another 1x4 (**Figure 3**). We shoot all of these components together in place with 12d galvanized nails. There tends to be some discrepancy between the width of a 4x4 and the width of a 1x4. Because the screening and trim boards will be applied to the exterior face, we're careful to keep all of the framing flush to this plane.

Building the Roof

The roof configuration depends on the porch design, which is keyed to the style of the home we're working on. One detail that we use on a straight gable roof has become something of a signature for us. We build what I call a flying gable, which, aside from being attractive, serves an important function (**Figure 4**). Water will penetrate only about a foot or so into the porch along the eaves during a rain, but it can penetrate much deeper through a high screened gable. The projecting "prow" of our flying gable provides a deep overhang that keeps the interior space drier.

We use treated lumber to frame the roof, too. The rafters rest directly on the 2x6 box beam. If the rafters are to remain exposed on the interior side, we use ⅝-inch T1-11 plywood channel siding, finish face down, to sheathe the roof. The siding provides a finished appearance inside and an adequate nail base for the roofing (it's thick enough to prevent ¾-inch roofing fasteners from penetrating through to the interior). For a more formal interior, we'll frame a flat ceiling and finish it with clear fir T&G edge-and-center-bead paneling. We give the fir three coats of clear urethane finish, or prime and paint it to match the trim of the existing home — either way, it makes a beautiful ceiling.

Roofing. We generally use asphalt shingles on the roof, though occasionally we hire a metal roof specialist to install a standing-seam prefinished metal roof.

Railings

Our typical porch railing system consists of a 2x4 sub- and top-rail with 2x2 square balusters. The balusters are beveled at each end and screwed to the wide face of the 2x4s on 4-inch centers. The 2x4 rails are nailed to the inside face of the 4x4 posts, mitered at inside corners. The balusters thus finish up 2 inches inside the outer face of the enclosure (**Figure 5**). We

Figure 4. The author's signature "flying gable" roof helps keep windblown rain out of the porch.

Figure 5. Surface-installed rails and balusters simplify construction and protect the screening from damage by children and pets. Because the screening doesn't contact the railing or balusters, they are barely visible from outside.

cap the subrail with a Trex 2x6, notching it fully around the 4x4 uprights. The outer edge of the rail cap ends up flush with the exterior post face. Wider than the 4x4 posts by 2 inches, the 2x6 cap rail overhangs the 2x4 subrail by ½ inch on the interior side of the enclosure.

An upgrade rail system consists of a colonial profile pressure-treated top- and shoe-rail, installed on-center between posts. The balusters fit into dadoed grooves in the rails.

Screened Openings

Many builders rely on removable screen panels to complete the porch enclosure. Custom wood frames, aluminum frames with vinyl splines, or a combination of the two will certainly do the job, but they also add a lot of labor and unnecessary cost to the job.

My system is much faster to install, completely effective, and equally good looking. Once the fram-

ing is complete, it doesn't take long to screen the openings. We unroll and cut a length of screening sufficient to cover the opening from top to bottom. A couple of ¾x1-inch-wide pneumatic roofing staples tack the screen at the top while we staple down one side, taking care not to pull and distort the screen (**Figure 6**, next page). Then we staple the opposite side. If the staples are widely spaced initially, the installer can tug at the screen between fasteners to remove ripples and sags. After the bottom and top edges are tacked and the screen is drumtight, infill stapling completes the job. Any excess screening is trimmed away with a utility knife.

The use of roofing staples may seem unusual, but the heavier wire penetrates the hard pine more effectively than lightweight screening staples. Pneumatic stapling is also quicker and much less tiring than squeezing off an equal number of conventional screening staples.

Figure 6. Asphalt roofing staples hold the screening tight, and are less tiring to install than conventional screen staples (far left). Sagging screen is pulled tight between staples and secured to ensure a drum-tight fabric installation (left).

Fast Arches

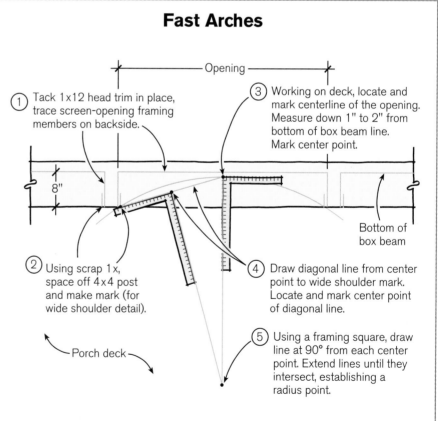

① Tack 1x12 head trim in place, trace screen-opening framing members on backside.

② Using scrap 1x, space off 4x4 post and make mark (for wide shoulder detail).

③ Working on deck, locate and mark centerline of the opening. Measure down 1" to 2" from bottom of box beam line. Mark center point.

④ Draw diagonal line from center point to wide shoulder mark. Locate and mark center point of diagonal line.

⑤ Using a framing square, draw line at 90° from each center point. Extend lines until they intersect, establishing a radius point.

Opening

Bottom of box beam

8"

Porch deck

Figure 7. The author uses a simple method for producing custom arches in the continuous, dropped headcasing that accents the individual screen openings. After establishing the radius point of the arch, he uses a site-made trammel stick to draw it directly on the 1x12 stock. The resulting arch, cut with a jigsaw, is perfectly matched to each opening.

Figure 8. Simple, router-rolled corners finish nearly every edge and joint in the system, giving an appearance of heightened detail while concealing small deviations in plane and material thickness.

Arched Trim

Most of our porches feature painted trim that matches the existing house trim. Before installation, we paint the edges and one face of all the primed stock with two coats of premium exterior latex. Whenever possible, instead of measuring, we tack-fit and mark all of the trim in place for speed and accuracy. The first trim board to be fitted is the arched head casing above the openings (**Figure 7**), which is made from a single 1x12 with its lower edge dropped 8 inches below the box beam. We trace all of the upright locations and the bottom edge of the box beam onto the backside of the head casing for layout and cutting. We hold a scrap of 1-by material alongside the top of the 4x4 posts to create a wide shoulder detail at the arches' spring lines.

Working on the deck, we use a quick layout method to establish the radius for the arches, then cut them out with a jig saw. We touch up the cut with a belt sander, then round over the edges with a 1/2-inch-radius router bit.

Fast dimensions. Before we take the head casing back down for cutouts, we map out the rest of the trim. We temporarily cap the bottom plate with a continuous 1x2 base molding. This makes it easy to mark all of the vertical 1x4 post trim in place by standing it on the base mold and marking it for cutting where it meets the head casing.

We cover the edge of the Trex rail cap with a piece of 1x2 horizontal trim. After dry fitting, we label all the pieces for location and take them down for cutting, edge routing, and painting. We prime all of the cuts with an oil-based primer, then coat the weather side of the trim with two coats of latex.

Fussy details. The routed rollover edge is another of our signature details (**Figure 8**). Every last finished edge, notch, and joint in my system receives the rollover treatment. The final appearance is not only attractive, but also subtly informs my customers that every piece of the porch has been "fussed over." Rolling the edges also eliminates the need to shim joints for precise alignment — joints where the boards may be slightly out of plane or of unequal thickness.

When the paint is mostly dry, we install the trim in the same sequence as it was originally laid out: head casing, base mold, post caps, and frieze board. The frieze board closes the gap between the top of the head casing and the roof soffit. We fasten all of the trim with flush-set, stainless, hex-head finish screws. They're easy to reverse if you forget a step or need to make an adjustment.

Finishing. Although the trim goes up primed and painted, there's always a need for touch-ups. With all of the jobs I have going, I can keep a subcontracted paint crew pretty busy. To reinforce the water repellent in the treated lumber and keep it looking good, we always apply a semi-transparent finish to the floor, American Building Restoration Products's (www.abrp.com) X-100 Natural Seal in Cedar Tone Gold shade. We use the same product in white for all of the railings and balusters. My customers receive a product brochure at the first sales call. I make sure that the supplier has stamped his business address and phone number on the brochure so they know where to get their materials when it's time to stain or touch up again.

In my experience, the first stain job lasts only about three years on pressure-treated lumber. I tell the homeowner to expect this, but that the follow-up stain job should perform for seven years or more.

Jim Craig is the owner of Craig Sundecks and Porches in Manassas, Va.

Fast, Low-Maintenance Porch Enclosures

by Paul Mantoni

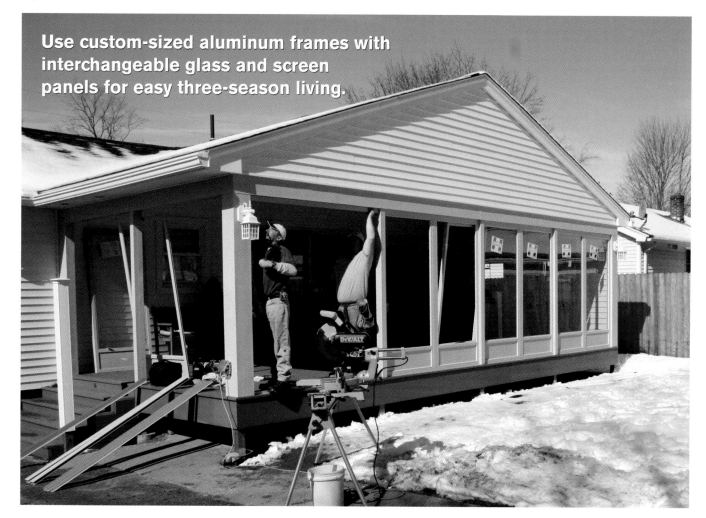

Use custom-sized aluminum frames with interchangeable glass and screen panels for easy three-season living.

Over 20 years ago, on a vinyl siding job, I screened in a deck that had a shed roof. I used wooden screen doors for the panels and framed out openings to fit them. Some years later, I went back to the same house to install some windows, and the vinyl siding looked great — but the screens didn't. The frames hadn't been painted in some time; what was left of the paint was peeling, and the frames had started to rot.

I see a lot of wood trim that's been neglected, just like the screen-door frames on that porch. Being a vinyl-siding contractor as well as a deck builder, I'm interested in low-maintenance alternatives, so now I use storm doors made of aluminum, instead of wood, for the panels. They last for decades with only seasonal cleaning, as the finish doesn't peel and the aluminum doesn't rot.

Aluminum storm-door panels aren't just durable, they're also versatile: The screens can be swapped for glass, extending the seasonal use of the porch considerably. Even in winter, the porch can be comfortable for parties and holidays, with a space heater.

I buy the panels in custom sizes that range in width from 6 inches to 42 inches. My supplier, Harvey Industries (www.harveyind.com), also sells everything needed to join the panels into a screen system: upper and lower track, F-channels to attach the panels to the support posts, and H-channels for joining the panels to each other. I can get them in three colors and four styles, along with matching coil stock for trimming the posts. There are probably similar products available in other parts of the country.

Installing the panels proceeds as shown in the photos on pages 273 and 274. Note that there are typically two panels between each pair of support posts.

Paul Mantoni owns Exteriors Plus in Terryville, Conn.

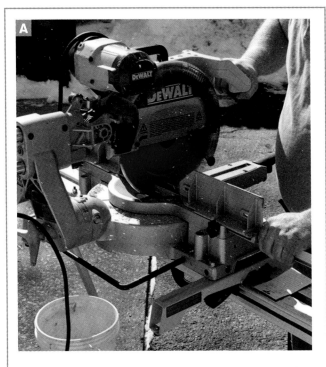

The F-channels, upper and lower tracks, and H-channels — used to join aluminum storm-door panels together and to framing — are supplied long. Cut them to length using a chop saw; a standard trim blade works well.

Bed the base track in caulk and screw it to the decking. Attach the top track, which is deeper than the bottom one, the same way. Drill weep holes in the base track 3 inches from the ends and 16 inches on-center.

Measure each side F-channel separately to fit plumb between the top and base tracks. Screw the channel to the posts between the tracks.

With the glass or screens removed to lighten the panels and reduce the risk of damage, join two panels with an H-channel that's cut to fit between the top and bottom tracks.

continued on page 247

Slide the pair of wall panels up into the deeper top track until they clear the bottom of the opening, then drop the panels into the base track.

Adjust both panels to fit evenly and securely in the H-channel and the F-channels.

Using the supplied screws, fasten the panels to the F-channels and the H-channel.

For the final step, install the glass or screens in the panels.

Restoring an Open Porch

by Katie Hill

Though it reduced floor space, converting a sunroom back to an open porch added value to this home.

Porches are often among the first architectural elements to be sacrificed on an old house — both because they require a lot of maintenance and because they are obvious candidates for conversion to year-round living space.

On a recent job, we went the opposite way: We were asked by the owners of a 1928 Colonial revival to convert a sunroom back to an open-air porch.

Design Meets Demo

During the design phase, we narrowed down the design options to two choices — a porch with custom posts and handrail or a porch with round columns atop the shingled half-wall that already existed as part of the sunroom. We estimated the cost of the first design at approximately 65% higher than the second.

The clients opted for the shingled-wall version — that is, until we discovered, during demolition, thousands of carpenter ants were swarming around the sills and the bottom of the half-wall framing, as well as substantial rot and fungus.

So much for the plan to keep the shingled half-wall. There had been no evidence of rot inside the sunroom, and not even a hint of mildew, but given the extent of the damage, it was clear that the roof would eventually collapse without structural repair.

The first orders of business were to call the exterminator and stabilize the structure, while we went back to the drawing board with the clients.

Mock Column Proves Handy

Once the rotted framing had been removed, the clients stepped out onto the porch and loved the open feeling and view across their large front lawn. At that point, we suggested that they retain that open feeling by simply regrading around the foundation to meet code and create a porch with no handrails. They agreed, but, based on our drawings, they couldn't decide between square chamfered columns and classical columns.

So we got out our Japanese saws and rasps and made mockups out of rigid foam insulation primed with white latex (**Figure 9**, next page). We made square pedestals and moldings, attaching the pieces with bamboo skewers (essentially oversized toothpicks). On top of the pedestals, we attached two-dimensional silhouettes of both the tapered posts and the round columns. The clients chose round columns, and we were easily able to easily modify the dimensions until we got a thumbs-up.

Finally, using stock moldings, plywood, and white paint, we mocked up a pedestal to help them decide between raised panels and flat panels with panel moldings; they chose the latter.

A Well-Proportioned Column

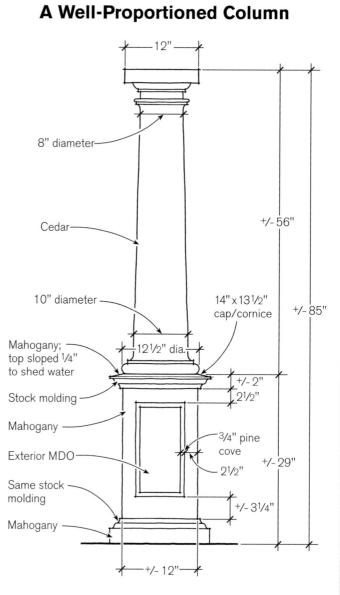

12"

8" diameter

+/- 56"

Cedar

+/- 85"

10" diameter

14" x 13½"
cap/cornice

12½" dia.

Mahogany;
top sloped ¼"
to shed water

+/- 2"

2½"

Stock molding

Mahogany

¾" pine
cove

Exterior MDO

2½"

+/- 29"

Same stock
molding

+/- 3¼"

Mahogany

+/- 12"

Figure 9. Sometimes scale drawings are not enough: A mock rigid-foam column helped the clients visualize what they were getting (left). In the final design (right), manufactured cedar columns sit atop a basic MDO box pedestal trimmed with Honduras mahogany stiles and rails and stock moldings to imitate true raised panels.

As fussy as this process may seem (it took a couple of days), it avoided the problem of the clients not liking the finished project because they thought it would look different.

New Support Beam

The original support beam had to be replaced with one that would center over the new columns. Working a section at a time, we installed a built-up beam of three 2x8s, reinforced by galvanized-steel framing anchors at the corners.

We added soffit and fascia to match those on the rest of the house, and installed new wooden gutters

to match the originals. We moved the downspouts so they wouldn't be in front of the new columns. All the trim (we used clear pine) was primed, back-primed, and end-primed with oil-based paint. We used stainless-steel fasteners for longevity.

Concrete Repair

The concrete floor of the porch had a rough-textured edge that projected a few inches over the exposed foundation. One corner had broken away and was badly in need of repair. Rather than try to match the texture with a finishing tool, we used a quick-setting two-part rubber molding compound, available at sculpture supply houses. You mix this to the consistency of pizza dough, then press it against the surface you want to make a mold of. It sets up in a few minutes.

We made a mold of the opposite porch corner, which was still in good shape. Then, lining the form with that mold, we poured a new corner, first drilling and epoxying 1/2x8-inch bolts into the broken edge to ensure a strong joint (**Figure 10**).

Installing the Columns

The porch roof is actually supported by 3-inch-diameter, adjustable steel jack posts — the kind with a welded base plate at the bottom and a screw plate at the top. The jacks run through the center of the wooden columns.

The paneled pedestals were built in three pieces: a top with a hole in it for the jack post to fit through and planed slightly toward the outer edges to shed water; a box with three sides; and a fourth side that could be screwed in place after installation.

To install the columns, we first slipped the cedar column and the top of the pedestal over the top of the jack post. Next, we put the jack in place and tightened the screw until it was snug against the beam. At this point, we lifted the cedar column and pedestal top — which had been fastened and caulked together — up to their final height (**Figure 11**). A two-piece bolt-on standpipe clamp held the column snug.

With the cedar column raised into position, we could now slide the three-sided box into place (**Figure 12**, next page). We used aluminum bar stock

Figure 10. To repair a missing corner of the textured concrete floor, the crew first made a latex mold of the opposite corner. The mold was then used to line the small form, to capture the edge texture. Galvanized bolts were epoxied in place to strengthen the new corner.

and angle to attach the box to the floor. This ensured that all the wood was out of contact with the concrete floor. Finally, we screwed the remaining panel into place.

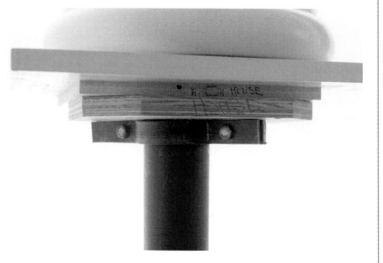

Figure 11. The first step in installing the columns was to slip the cedar column and the top of the pedestal over the screw jack post and position the jack (left). The cedar column was held in place with a clamp-on standpipe bracket, reinforced with a piece of marine plywood (above).

Figure 12. With the jacks and cedar column in position, the three-sided pedestal was slipped into place and fastened with shop-made aluminum hardware designed to stabilize the column while raising it off the floor to prevent moisture problems (left). After the fourth side was biscuited and screwed on, the base moldings were nailed off (right).

Preventing Rot

As restoration contractors, we see a lot of rotted wood. We knew our posts would be vulnerable and had considered three alternatives for the bases of the pedestals: a metal base, a base raised off the floor, and wooden moldings covering the gap between base and floor. For aesthetic reasons, we decided to use mahogany moldings, tapered to match the pitch of the floor. The bottoms were painted with wood consolidant before being primed and top-coated. Even with this care, we anticipate that these trim pieces will eventually deteriorate with the absorption of moisture from the concrete floor, but the pedestals themselves should be fine.

Katie Hill is a principal of Sands-Hill Restoration, LLC, in Torrington, Conn.

A Simple, Classic Entry

by Charles Wardell

Many homes are built with uncovered exterior doors that open onto the main living space. That's a shame. Not only does a sheltered entry provide a needed transition between inside and outside, but it's also a place to kick the mud or snow from your shoes and to stay dry while you're fumbling with the lockset in a rainstorm. One reason so few homes have good entries is the perceived cost. But as this entry that I built a few years back in Cambridge, Mass., shows, it's easy to build an attractive entry with stock materials from the local lumberyard.

The frame was a model of simplicity (**Figure 13**). The gable end rested on a pair of 4x4 pressure-treated posts that rested on sonotubes sunk 4 feet into the ground (the code-mandated depth for footings in this area). Against the house, I installed a pair of 2x4 pressure-treated pilasters right over the vinyl siding and lagged them to the house framing. A built-up beam made from three 2x4s linked the top of each post with the corresponding pilaster. I cased the frame with pine primed on both sides with two coats of oil-based primer. The roof was framed with 2x4s and sheathed with plywood. A 3/4-inch exterior-grade plywood arch beneath the rake matched the arches on the porches of the other Colonial homes in the neighborhood.

I trimmed the entry with stock moldings from the lumberyard. Most exterior structures rot from the ground up, but a gap beneath the plinth block at the base of the posts, and a concealed drainage space between the posts and the deck frame help to prevent this. The ceiling consisted of beaded-edge, tongue-and-groove pine. If I were doing the job today, though, I would use a new product called Ply-Bead (Georgia-Pacific, www.gp.com/build). It's an exterior-grade plywood panel with decorative beads routed into its face.

The pine was painted white and the ceiling a traditional light blue.

Charles Wardell writes on construction topics from Vineyard Haven, Mass.

Construction Details

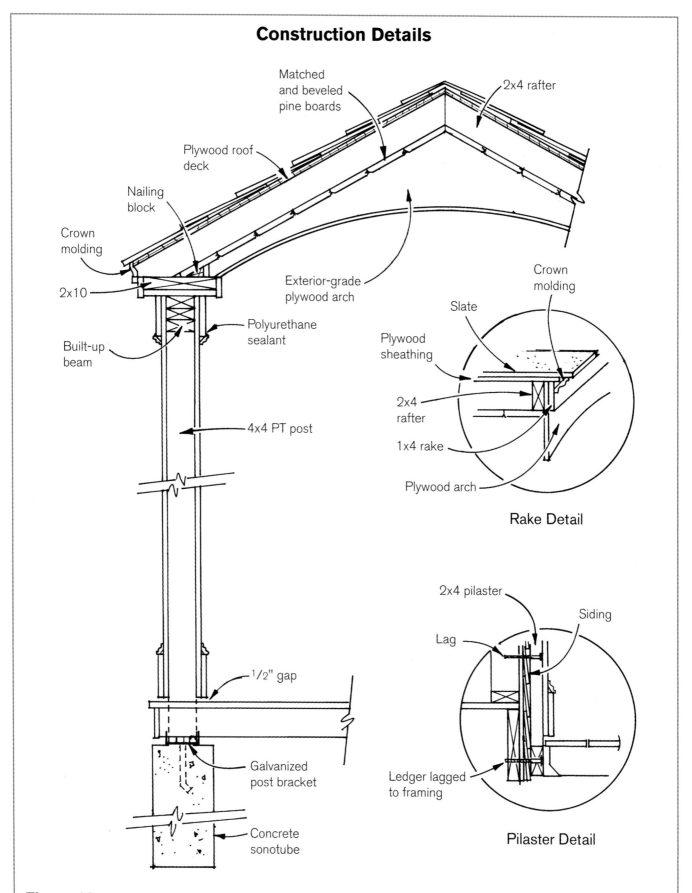

Matched and beveled pine boards

2x4 rafter

Plywood roof deck

Nailing block

Crown molding

2x10

Built-up beam

Polyurethane sealant

Exterior-grade plywood arch

4x4 PT post

1/2" gap

Galvanized post bracket

Concrete sonotube

Rake Detail

Crown molding

Slate

Plywood sheathing

2x4 rafter

1x4 rake

Plywood arch

Pilaster Detail

2x4 pilaster

Siding

Lag

Ledger lagged to framing

Figure 13. Borrowing from nearby houses, the author used off-the-shelf moldings and lumber to design and build this classic entryway. Pressure-treated lumber and watershedding details ensure a long life.

Curved Porch Framing

by Tim Meehan

Laminated beams and PVC trim round off this new porch for a historic building.

One of the oldest and most visible structures in Stowe, Vt., is the historic Stowe Inn, located near the center of the village. When its owner decided to expand the dining room by adding a large wraparound porch, I was glad to get a call to discuss such a highly visible project.

Because of the building's historic status, the town's historic preservation commission insisted that the porch look like it had been around for a long time. Accordingly, the architect designed a porch reminiscent of those from the late 1800s. Most notably, the design included a rounded outside corner, a signature Victorian element.

Deck Framing

Other than the curved corner and a barrel vault over the inn's front door, the porch design was conventional. We built a 2x10 pressure-treated floor system supported by 6x6 posts bearing on concrete piers spaced about 8 feet apart. To support the joists at the curved corner, we glued up a rounded girder from six layers of ½-inch pressure-treated plywood. The joists bear directly on this girder, and terminate in a curved band joist, which we laminated from three layers of ½-inch PT plywood. We also placed posts and girders

near the building, so that most of the loads from the deck — which would support 100-psf commercial loads — would be carried directly to the ground, not to a ledger attached to the building.

We spent a little extra time laying out a double

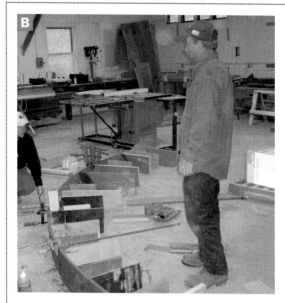

floor joist coming off the building's outside corner at 45 degrees — or as close to 45 degrees as we could make it, given that the old building was not perfectly square. Since we planned to lay out the roof framing above from the same diagonal reference, we wanted it to be accurate.

To support the porch roof, we attached a ledger to the solid brick building with a combination of 3/8-inch lags and lead shields and epoxied threaded rod (**A**). At the eaves, we used three-layer, built-up 2x8 beams for the straight runs and a laminated beam for the radius, all supported by fiber-reinforced synthetic columns.

Laminating a Curved Beam

While the crew worked on the straight sections of the roof, our lead carpenter made the curved beam, using the same method he'd used to make the curved girder for the floor (**B**). He first did the layout on the plywood floor of our shop, using a trammel arm,

then screwed 2x10 blocks to the floor, which provided the formwork for the six layers of 3/4-inch CDX plywood. Given the relatively large curve, we didn't think we needed to compensate for spring-back, so we simply used the 9-foot design radius, figuring we could persuade the beam ends into position with clamps.

We let the glue dry for a couple of days, then delivered the beam to the job site in our stake-body truck and had a crew of four lift it into position. A plumb bob helped us line it up with the curving band joist below. Once the beam was level, we clamped it in place and marked where it would tie into the straight beams (**C**). As expected, we had to do a little prying and clamping to get the beam in its final position.

We removed the beam and made stepped cuts on both ends using a circular saw, a recip saw, and a chisel (**D**); we also made corresponding cuts at the ends of the straight beams (**E**). We covered the

mating surfaces with a thick layer of polyurethane glue, then pulled everything together with clamps (**F**).

Round Roof Framing

The next day we removed the clamps and went to work on framing the roof. Our lead carpenter positioned the top end of the first rafter at the outside corner of the ledger (**G**), then used a plumb bob to line up the rafter tail with the diagonal floor joist below. This placed the first rafter in the center of the arc, where a supporting column would be located. For the rest of the rafters, he made long cheek cuts that tapered anywhere from ¾ inch down to zero.

We spaced the eaves ends of the rafters 20 inches on-center (**H**) so the segments of plywood sheathing (**I**) would be the same size and shape as the standing-seam panels that would ultimately cover the roof. Matching the sheathing and the steel panels minimizes oil canning, the distortion in standing-seam panels that can be made worse by uneven substrates.

Soffits and Trim

With the roof framed, we moved on to the soffit and fascia. For the curved sections of the soffit, we used segments of ¼-inch AC plywood, first scribing the joints in place to get a tight fit (**J**). We then used a simple site-made compass to mark a fair curve on the outside edge (**K**), and finished up by grinding and sanding to the line (**L**). We secured the soffit with polyurethane glue and finish nails.

We used cellular PVC boards for the curved fascia. We left the material in direct sunlight for a few hours, which increased its flexibility enough that we were able to make the bends (**M**).

We used similar methods to frame and trim the porch's curving half wall. We framed the 2x6 walls with plates laminated and routed from ¾-inch plywood. For the frame-and-panel treatment, we used ¼-inch MDO for the panels and primed pine for the frames. A panel molding hides the gaps between the frame and panel.

Tim Meehan owns Northern New England Homes in Stowe, Vt.

Framing a Grand-Scale Seaside Porch

by David Baud

M y company built a large oceanfront home on Narragansett Bay in Rhode Island. A sheltered porch spanned the 96-foot-long east elevation, with each end of the porch topped by a conical roof. Seventeen round Tuscan-style columns supported those porch roofs. My associate supervised fabrication of the more complicated porch roof components in our shop. These included large, composite carrying beams for the porch rafters, the two conical roofs, and parapet wall surrounds for three second-floor balconies inset in the porch roof. The standard rafters would all be cut to fit on site.

Establishing Accurate Layout

We had plenty of I-joists on hand, so we used them to set up a full-size layout grid at the shop. The plan was to set up the grid on site — like a giant story stick — and eliminate the need for batter boards and string layout. I'll describe them in more detail later.

Rather than laying out individual footing pads for the porch columns, we poured a continuous wide footing (**Figure 14**). After the concrete hardened, we shipped the I-joist grid to the site and assembled it, spacing it off the building with 2x8 spreaders. We

shimmed it dead straight to a laser line and propped it up level on 2x4 legs above the footings (**Figure 15**). The centerline of the I-joist determined the general

Figure 14. Rather than individual pads, a continuous footing permitted unlimited side-to-side adjustment for precisely placing the pier forms.

Laying Out Concrete Piers

108'-0"

55'-0"

Temporary I-joist layout grid supported on 2x legs and braced back to building

Continuous footing

Porch line

Concrete formwork

Bracing

Bracing

House footprint

Plan View

Figure 15. The author used I-joists instead of string for laying out the 17 porch columns, setting the bottom of the I-joists level with the top of the footings (left). This allowed the crew to accurately set the metal column anchors by tacking them to the I-joists. Spreaders, shimmed laser-straight off the building, set the center of the I-joist flange at the colonnade centerline. Two-by blocking tacked to both sides of the I-joist web at precise column locations established bull's-eye centers below which the pier forms could be set (right).

Figure 16. Engineered post anchors were tacked to spacer blocks on the I-joist grid (left). The anchors were set to within ⅛ inch before any concrete was poured. Circular nipple forms created a pier insert to help center the bottom of each column (right). The nipple was ½ inch smaller in diameter than the column interior to allow for leveling the base.

center of the columns in parallel to the building. The underside of the I-joist also established the top of the concrete formwork that would support the columns.

Resisting Wind Uplift

The hollow DuraCast fiberglass columns we worked with (Dixie-Pacific, www.dixie-pacific.com) are structural members with a stated load-bearing capacity of 22,000 pounds. On the other hand, wind uplift, especially under an open roof in an exposed location, is at least as great a concern as bearing capacity. Although the manufacturer suggests using small,

through-bolted L-brackets as column anchors, that wasn't suitable for this application. Instead, we used pressure-treated 4x4 posts, concealed inside the columns and connected to a concrete pier with Simpson CB44 post base hold-down anchors.

Anchoring to concrete. We nailed 2x4 blocking to both sides of the ½-inch I-joist web at each column's center location, providing a properly sized block to hold the Simpson anchors. With the anchors held in precise position, we were able to accurately place the pier forms below, on the footing. Each anchor was also encircled by a custom-made "nipple" form, made

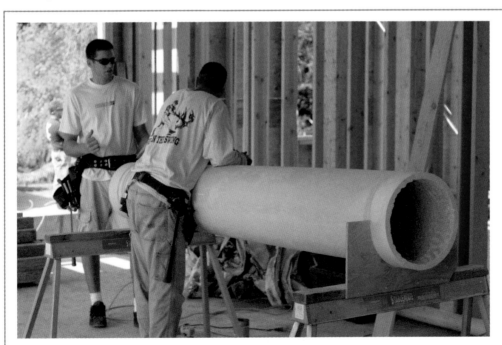

Figure 17. A simple plywood cradle held the columns at a comfortable height for cutting to length. The crew found that carbide-tipped blades dulled quickly, but that abrasive diamond blades worked well.

Figure 18. Instead of strap ties, the author used 4x4 posts running through the columns as hold-downs for the box beam on top. Square holes in the top and bottom flanges of the box beam allowed the beams to drop over the 4x4s (left). Square notches in the ends of the beams fit around the posts, allowing the sections to be fastened together. After the beam was fastened to the posts with bolts, the protruding tops (right) were cut off.

from bendable plywood (**Figure 16**). These were nailed directly to the underside of the I-joist flange. The resulting concrete nipple would fit inside the bottom of the fiberglass column and prevent lateral movement. Rebar, grouted into the footing inside each form, provided a positive mechanical connection for the pier.

We didn't leave any measuring for our concrete sub to do, so he was in and out in two days. We used a fairly stiff, 3,000-psi mix with 3/8-inch aggregate to fill the forms, and troweled the tops smooth.

After the concrete hardened and the inspector signed off on the work, we dismantled the layout grid and backfilled the area. We then installed the 4x4 posts using Simpson SDS screws in the base anchors. The 4x4s were 12 feet long, accounting for the combined heights of the column and the carrying beam, with some overage to be trimmed later. Setting the fiberglass columns followed immediately, so we didn't bother bracing the posts.

Columns 101

The classical formula for Tuscan column proportions states that the column's height must be equal to seven times its diameter, including the plinth and capital. So, technically speaking, a 16-inch-diameter column ought to stand 9 feet 4 inches overall. When designing with and specifying columns, this is a good rule of thumb to keep in mind to ensure a good appearance.

The column also features true "entasis," or an aesthetic tapering over its length. Ours measured 16 inches in diameter at the bottom and 13½ inches at the top. The tapering occurs in the upper two-thirds of the column's length, and any necessary shortening

is done at the bottom. These columns were 10 feet long in the rough and had to be cut to finished length before standing. We cut them about ¼ inch short to allow for shimming and leveling.

Cutting. There's a mineral component in the columns' fiberglass matrix that gives the material a stone-like appearance. You can effectively cut one or two columns with a carbide-tipped blade, but the teeth quickly dull. Instead, we used an abrasive diamond chip masonry blade in a circular saw, resting the columns in a basic cradle to hold them at a comfortable cutting height (**Figure 17**). One worker did the cutting while another slowly rotated the column.

Lifting and setting. A single column of this size weighs about 200 pounds. We looped a nylon choker strap around the top of each column in turn and used a Lull to lower them over the 4x4 posts. After each column was set, a worker slid the one-piece cast polyurethane plinths and capitals over the top. We set all 17 posts, including the 4x4s, in about six hours. Although we'd anticipated having to brace the columns after standing, that proved unnecessary. Thanks in no small part to careful cutting and pier preparation, as well as the columns' own mass, they stood nearly plumb all on their own.

Carrying Beams

The roof's straight carrying beams were a series of composite box beams, built in sections to bear on three or more columns each and butting over column centers (**Figure 18**).

A 3½-inch-square opening cut through the top and bottom plates of the beam on layout captured each

Column Installation

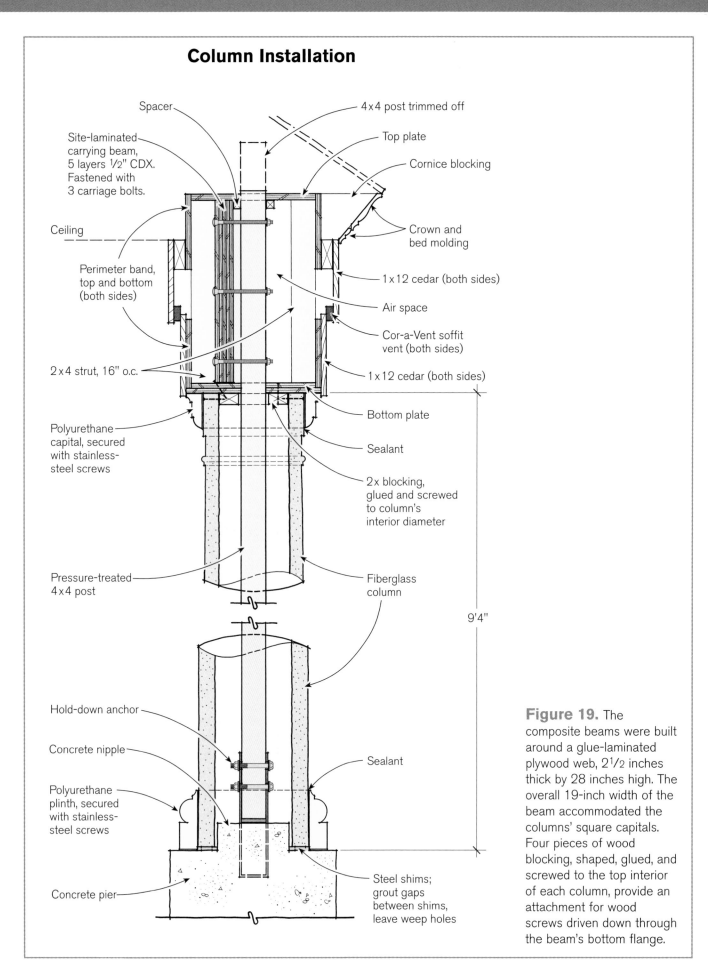

Spacer

Site-laminated carrying beam, 5 layers 1/2" CDX. Fastened with 3 carriage bolts.

Ceiling

Perimeter band, top and bottom (both sides)

2 x 4 strut, 16" o.c.

Polyurethane capital, secured with stainless-steel screws

Pressure-treated 4 x 4 post

Hold-down anchor

Concrete nipple

Polyurethane plinth, secured with stainless-steel screws

Concrete pier

4 x 4 post trimmed off

Top plate

Cornice blocking

Crown and bed molding

1 x 12 cedar (both sides)

Air space

Cor-a-Vent soffit vent (both sides)

1 x 12 cedar (both sides)

Bottom plate

Sealant

2x blocking, glued and screwed to column's interior diameter

Fiberglass column

9'4"

Sealant

Steel shims; grout gaps between shims, leave weep holes

Figure 19. The composite beams were built around a glue-laminated plywood web, 2^1/$_2$ inches thick by 28 inches high. The overall 19-inch width of the beam accommodated the columns' square capitals. Four pieces of wood blocking, shaped, glued, and screwed to the top interior of each column, provide an attachment for wood screws driven down through the beam's bottom flange.

Figure 20. A nonstructural frame under the circular roof (left) aligns with the box beam entablature. The circular roof loads are carried to the columns by a site-laminated round top plate. Note how the plinth and capitals are wedged safely out of the way during construction (right).

post. A worker on a ladder guided the 4x4s into their pockets as the crane operator lowered each beam into place.

For the two circular beams, we laminated two 4-inch-thick ring beams from 16 layers of 1/4-inch lauan plywood, bonded with West System epoxy. The rafters were set in pockets cut into the rings' inner face. Below the ring beams, we constructed an open framework of plywood plates and 2x4 struts to continue the 28-inch-wide entablature band around the circular porch sections.

Fastening the Columns

The beam rested directly on the fiberglass columns, which we'd modified at the tops with four pieces of 2x blocking, screwed and urethane-glued to the interior circumference (**Figure 19**). The blocks allowed us to screw directly down through the bottom plate of the beam into the tops of the columns, drawing them up tight to the beam. We used steel shims under the column on the concrete pier to raise the column and beam to final height, checking level with a dot laser.

Once the entire beam was leveled, we secured it with three 1/2-inch carriage bolts passed through the post and flange. To plumb the columns, we'd left about 1/2 inch of play between the concrete nipple and the columns' interior diameter. Using a stick level held against a straightedge equipped with standoff blocks to compensate for the column's taper, we nudged the bottom around until the column

stood plumb in all directions. Later, we grouted the shim gaps at the pier with cement mortar, leaving weep holes to allow any condensation inside the columns to drain.

Finishing Up

We left the cast plinths and capitals loose on the columns, wedged partway up the columns, out of the way of the framing and finish work (**Figure 20**). We framed the porch floor on independent supports, with the column piers buried below the framing line. The 1x4 tropical Ipe decking was fitted around the columns, then covered by lowering the plinth. The beam trim was cut around the tops of the columns; then the capitals were slid up into place. We secured the castings to the columns with Excel XPress polyurethane glue (AmBel, www.excelglue.com) and a couple of countersunk stainless-steel screws. The countersinks were capped with epoxy filler and sanded to disappear. The columns arrived with rough-ground molding seams that required top-dressing with thickened epoxy (using West's 401 filler additive), followed by sanding to produce a uniform smooth surface before painting. The completed assemblies were sprayed with latex primer, caulked, and finished with high-quality exterior-grade latex trim paint.

David Baud is president of Baud Builders in Narragansett, R.I. His associate Mike Rand supervised fabrication of the more complex roof components.

Porch Construction Q&A

Porch Floor Board Layout

Q. *I'm building a roofed porch with tongue-and-groove fir decking in New England. The boards will be primed and painted on all sides before installation. The joists run perpendicular to the building, and I'd like to install the flooring parallel to the long dimension of the porch. Does the orientation of the porch boards matter?*

A. *John Leeke, a preservation consultant from Portland, Maine, responds:* The deck will definitely drain better if the boards run from the house down the slope toward the edge of the porch. I usually slope my porch decks about 1/4 or 3/8 inch per foot. I've found that 1/8 inch per foot is not enough to get the water moving off the porch.

If you are concerned about end checks developing in the exposed end grain of the deck boards, I suggest treating the end grain of the boards with a penetrating epoxy consolidant before any other finish is applied. This seals the end grain, limiting the movement of water in and out and minimizing checks.

Choosing and Finishing Porch Boards

Q. *I am planning to replace the porch floor on a 120-year-old Victorian home. Since cedar and redwood seem too soft for a porch floor, I am choosing between tongue-and-groove yellow pine, vertical-grain fir, and mahogany. What are the advantages and disadvantages of these species when used for a porch floor?*

As for the finish, I'm considering a semitransparent oil stain, because deck paint is slippery to walk on and prone to peeling. Also the stain will allow the wood grain to show through. What is your advice?

A. *Bill Feist, a former wood finishes researcher with the Forest Products Laboratory in Madison, Wis., and co-author of* Finishes for Exterior Wood, *responds:* The National Park Service often specifies vertical-grained Douglas fir for its decks and porches. This wood has a good combination of hardness, moderate rot resistance, dimensional stability (resistance to warping), and cost. This may be a special-order item at your lumberyard.

A true mahogany would be the optimum choice for a deck because of its excellent durability, its rot resistance, its hardness and wear properties, and its very good dimensional stability. The only major drawbacks are its high cost and limited availability.

Tongue-and-groove yellow pine would probably be the last choice. This wood tends to be less dimensionally stable than Douglas fir or mahogany, and it can be difficult to nail. Untreated yellow pine would have

a high potential for rot problems. However, several commercial wood treaters offer 5/4 radial-edged yellow pine decking with dual treatment, combining a water-repellent with the preservative treatment. This lumber is marketed under brand names such as Viance Preserve-Plus, Georgia-Pacific Premium Southern Gold Plus Water Repellant, and Thompsonized Wood. These brands typically use a better grade of wood, with fewer knots or other defects, than is usually used for standard pressure-treated wood. The wood tends to have few warping problems.

I agree that paint is not a recommended finish for a deck or porch. Because the horizontal surfaces are exposed to the sun and collect moisture, and because the finish is subject to abrasive wear, a paint or a solid-color stain would be likely to crack, flake and peel. These film-forming finishes also tend to trap water, leading to a greater possibility of rot problems.

A penetrating water-repellent preservative, or a semitransparent penetrating oil or alkyd-based stain, may provide the best finishing solution. Special formulations specifically made for decks are available. These penetrating deck finishes are easily renewed and enhance the appearance and service life of both naturally rot-resistant wood species and pressure-treated wood.

Sealers for Porch Floors

Q. *We just installed a T&G fir floor on a covered porch that the customer plans to have painted in the spring. I would prefer to at least seal the wood against the weather until the painter has a chance to prime and top-coat the floor. Do you have any recommendations?*

A. *Wood finishes expert Bill Feist responds:* To protect the fir flooring over the winter, your best choice would be to use a paintable water-repellent preservative (WRP) like Wolman's Woodlife Classic Clear Wood Preservative (www.wolman.com), or Cuprinol Clear Deck & Wood Seal (www.cuprinol.com).

There are a variety of WRPs on the market. Many of them are formulated for use as natural finishes on decks and fences, but these are not paintable and could cause paint-adhesion problems like blistering or peeling later on. So it's very important that the treatment you choose be described by the manufacturer as paintable.

There are many advantages to using a paintable WRP on unpainted porch flooring before priming and painting (although painting is not my recommendation for a porch floor — see the question above). Besides inhibiting mildew growth and retarding decay in above-ground applications, the treatment reduces raised grain, checking, warping, and splitting. It also improves paint adhesion, which would be especially valuable on a difficult-to-paint wood like flat-grain fir.

It's always best to treat all sides (front, back, ends, and edges) of your flooring with the WRP before installation. But even when unfinished porch flooring has already been installed, it's helpful to back-treat with WRP as much as you can, assuming access under the porch is reasonable. Research has shown conclusively that solid wood products back-primed with a WRP retain paint better — and perform better overall — than those coated on one side only.

Durable Porch Ceilings

Q. *Patios with roofs are standard features of nearly every home built in the Phoenix area. Standard construction is wood frame with a drywall ceiling, taped, textured, and painted. Within ten years, the taping and texturing start to separate from the drywall. Retaping and texturing might make it last a few more years. Is there an economical alternative to drywall that would provide a more permanent and relatively maintenance-free ceiling?*

A. *Jim Reicherts, of United States Gypsum Company, responds:* Drywall, including moisture-resistant (MR) drywall, is not designed for exterior applications, even in low-moisture desert climates. Although it will cost more, the best solution for the carport is to use a water-resistant cement board (like USG's Durock) or gypsum fiber panel (like USG's Fiberock) instead of the drywall.

After attaching the cement board or gypsum fiber panels to the framing, cover the joints and the panel surface with a latex-modified thinset basecoat. You can then finish the surface with an aggregated acrylic textured finish to provide a stucco look. These basecoat and finish materials are available from manufacturers of exterior insulation and finish systems (EIFS), such as Dryvit, Senergy, Parex, and Sto.

Chapter 10:
Finishing Touches

Add Character With Curves

by Robert Viviano

In order to separate our company from deck builders who were pushing angles as the big option, we took the first steps toward becoming the "curved-deck specialist" of the greater Pittsburgh area.

We now have a track record of building thousands of curved decks from cedar, ipe, aluminum, vinyl, and composite materials.

The key to building a profitable curved deck is to keep the construction as basic as possible. We design our curved decks to be almost as simple to build as angled decks by keeping the framing straight and square — it's mostly the decking and railing that make up the curves. Here I explain the decking details.

Framing the Cantilever

The curved deck shown (photo, right) has a semicircular cantilever extending 5 feet from the main deck. It's framed with pressure-treated southern yellow pine, and the decking and railing are Trex.

No special treatment of the beam or its footings was required. The joists for the curving cantilever are simply longer versions of the common joists; they don't require a second carrying beam but just cantilever farther out than the commons. This deck supports a roof as well, and two of the roof columns originate where the semicircle meets the straight part of the deck.

For any deck, the last thing you want is a cantilever that bounces like a springboard. Because 5 feet is a pretty large cantilever, we had the entire deck design engineered: 2x10 joists are spaced 12 inches on-cen-

Smart framing and a few simple tricks can round out your deck business.

ter, and in the cantilevered portion every other joist is doubled. We don't cut cantilevered joists to length initially but rather let them run long. A mitered six-section band board assembly will close off the cantilevered joists (**Figure 1**).

We secure the joists to the house and the beam.

Figure 1. The mitered band board is pre-assembled and then installed as a unit. Blocks screwed to the bottom of the joists hold the band board in place while it's being installed. Note the doubling of every other joist.

Then we establish the center of the semicircle to provide a point of origin to lay out its arc. In this case, the center point is on the main part of the deck, set in from the edge by a distance equal to half the diameter of the porch columns and centered between them (illustration, below).

Usually blocking must be installed between the joists so we have a place — other than air — to mark this point. If the center point did fall on a joist, we'd still block between that joist and its neighbors, to prevent movement and ensure accurate measurements.

The next step is to account for the railing. On the curved section, it will start at the porch roof columns and incorporate two 8-inch-square newels, which

---

Calculating Sides and Angles

If you haven't thought about circles and trigonometric functions since high school, don't panic — these days you can use a calculator. Mine is a Texas Instruments TI-30Xa, which costs about $11. I have four of them, so there's always one at hand.

Since a circle contains 360 degrees, a semicircle — like this deck — contains half of that, or 180 degrees. A six-sided rim board works well with the substructure of a projection of this size (a 5-foot radius).

Dividing 180 degrees by six yields equal pie-shaped sections of 30 degrees each, as seen in the illustration below. Bisecting a 30-degree section provides two things: a right triangle (which enables use of the trig functions) and an angle (15 degrees) to plug into the formula. Toss in the radius (60 inches) and a calculator with trig functions, and you can quickly figure half the length of a side. Doubling that provides the total length, of course.

Start with the basic formula for calculating the sine of an angle from the lengths of the opposite side and the hypotenuse of a right triangle:

sin (A) = opposite ÷ hypotenuse

Rearrange the formula to solve for the length of the side that's opposite the inside angle:

sin (A) x hypotenuse = opposite

We know the angle is 15 degrees and the length of the hypotenuse is the same as the radius, which is 60 inches. Plugging those numbers into the calculator, we find that the opposite side measures 15.529 inches:

15 sin x 60 inches = 15.529 inches

However, we bisected this side to make our right triangle, so we have to double the result to get the full length of the side:

15.529 inches x 2 = 31.058 inches, or roughly 31¹⁄₁₆ inches

The miter angle is half of 30 degrees.

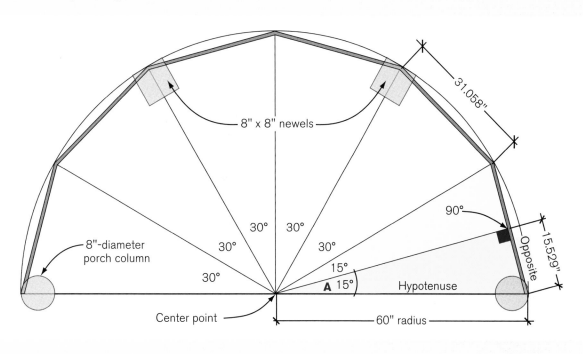

Figure 2. The lengths and miters of the band board's parts are figured on a calculator. To prevent the mitered band-board assembly from tweaking while it's being handled, 2x4 braces reinforce the desired shape.

Figure 3. Always double-check the band board's size. The distance from the points of the miters to the center point of the curved section should be equal to the radius.

will be installed symmetrically around the curve. The band board will join with miters at the points where the newels will go. This will require a little calculator work (see "Calculating Sides and Angles," page 295).

Once we figure out the miter angle (15 degrees), the number of boards (six), and the length of each board (31¹/₁₆ inches), we cut the members of the band board and screw them together into a unit (**Figure 2**). We confirm the numbers by making sure the two ends measure 10 feet apart and the projection measures 5 feet from the miter points to the center point (**Figure 3**).

We use the assembled band board to lay out the cuts on the cantilevered joists. Our process is straightforward: Temporarily tack down spreaders to keep the joists on their centers. Overlay the band board so that its ends align correctly on the main deck (**Figure 4**). Scribe the inside of the band board to the joists and then move it aside.

Next, extend those marks square down the joists and use a speed square to determine the angle of the saw cut for each joist (**Figure 5**). A couple of blocks screwed to the bottom of the joists support the band board during installation.

Figure 4. The cantilevered joists are purposely run long. The band board, aligned with the main deck, is placed atop the joists, which are then marked to be cut to length. Cleats nailed to the joists prevent them from moving and help to ensure accurate layout.

Figure 5. Mark the cut lines square down from the tops of the joists. The bevel angle for the saw is measured with a speed square from the marks atop the joists.

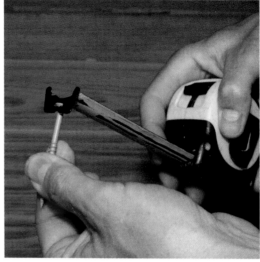

Figure 6. Curved shims are screwed to the band board to support a curved fascia (left). A tape measure hooked on the head of a screw (right) set at the center point is used to lay out the curve on one piece of 2-by, which is cut out carefully and used as a template for the rest.

We don't worry at this point about where the newels fall in relation to the cantilever joists. At worst, we'll have to header off a joist or two to fit the newels later.

Finishing the Curve

If you don't mind the look of the exposed band board, it can be considered completed at this point. If you want a curving fascia, however, you need to shim out the face of the band with curved 2-by material running horizontally at the top and bottom **(Figure 6)**.

To create the shims, we take a 2-by that's a little longer than the length of a side, hold it flat against the outside of one section of the band board, and scribe onto it an arc with a 5-foot radius. To scribe

an arc this big, we simply set a screw partway into the center point and hook the end of a tape measure to it. Then we hold a pencil at the tape's 5-foot mark and swing away.

Mark this first piece carefully and cut it out using a good jigsaw with a sharp blade: Since all the sides are the same length, this piece becomes the template for the rest of the shims. Trace its curve onto the other lengths of 2-by, cut them out, and then screw all the shims in place.

PVC trim board (Azek is one example) will easily wrap around an arc of this radius. In fact, we've used Azek on arcs with radii as tight as 2 feet without heating it or kerfing the back. Other materials might require kerfing — you'll probably have to experiment.

Figure 7. Notched to bend, an aluminum drip-edge is installed below the decking to prevent streaking of the fascia. Bituminous roofing membrane on the joists prevents direct corrosive contact, and more membrane atop the drip edge seals the notches.

Finding the length of the fascia board is a simple matter of measuring.

To protect the wooden fascia from streaking, we incorporate a standard aluminum drip edge between it and the decking (**Figure 7**, previous page). The back of the drip edge is notched with a series of Vs that allow it to curve. To seal the notches and to prevent the aluminum from contacting the corrosive pressure-treated frame, we install bituminous membrane or Grace Ice and Water Shield.

Fan Pattern

Any pattern of decking can be used on a curved deck. The trick is to let the boards run long and then cut them all off at one time. The decking here is cut into wedge shapes and fan-laid to radiate from the center point into the field decking (**Figure 8**). We add blocking where needed between the joists to support the decking and to allow the screws to run in concentric circles (**Figure 9**).

To figure out how many boards you'll need for a

Figure 9. Where decking in the fan shape runs parallel to the joists, the need for blocking to support it is obvious. Additional blocking allows the decking screws to be installed in concentric circles.

Figure 10. Cutting straight-edged wedges requires a jig. This is the sort of work where errors accumulate, so accuracy is called for from the start.

simple decking circle, first calculate its circumference: Multiply pi (3.1416) by the circle's diameter, including the distance that the decking overhangs the band board or fascia.

You want the deck boards to be as wide as possible at the outer edge of the circle, to minimize waste. The decking we use is 5½ inches wide, plus we allow a ¼-inch expansion gap, for a total of 5¾ inches. Using a calculator, we divide the circumference by this amount; for this deck the result was 68.02 — close enough to call it 68 pieces, each with an end width of 5½ inches. (When the quotient isn't a whole number, we round it up to the next whole number and divide the circumference by that number to find the end width for each piece.)

After we'd cut the wedges using these calculations, however, the customer asked for a change — to add even more visual interest. We came up with the cross pattern you see in the photos, which meant all the wedges needed to be recut to accommodate the cross.

Though adding it was extra work, the cross looks good and even offered up an installation advantage. It's easy to spiral out of alignment if the wedges or your layout is off by even a hair. By breaking the circle into quadrants, the cross made it a little easier to control loss or gain.

Instead of using the center point of the circle as the starting point for the wedge layout, we used the inside corner of the cross in each quadrant as a pivot point. The width of each wedge on the inside of the circle is simply a point, and the length is equal to the radius of the framing plus the overhang and minus the centerpiece.

Because it's important that the wedges be uniform and have straight edges, we use a jig to rip them (**Figure 10**). After cutting the wedges, we rout their sides with a round-over bit to match the factory edge.

To save material, we try to cut overlapping wedges from the decking. We cut the pieces a little long so we can adjust them while we are installing them — we trim them after they're installed. The pointy ends don't need to be perfectly cut at first either, because they'll be trimmed later to fit neatly around the centerpiece.

We use an installation jig to align the wedges radially (**Figure 11**). Essentially, it's a piece of wood with a hole at one end that's screwed to the center point on the deck. A "bulge" in the wood accommodates the screw, and the edge beyond the bulge is cut at an angle that mirrors that of the wedges.

The wedges are adjusted in and out slightly to keep

Figure 11. Another jig aligns the wedges radially. Cut to mirror the angle of the wedges, this second jig revolves on the center point.

the margins correct. Once a quadrant is laid out satisfactorily, we screw it down using markings on the edge of the installation jig to keep the screws in concentric circles: Nothing looks worse than a precise pattern with randomly placed screws.

To cut the ends to form a perfect circle, we affix a router to a long plywood arm, the bit at the correct distance from the center point. (Note that here I'm talking about the center point of the circle, not the corners of the cross.) The plywood arm is screwed to the center point, and the decking is cut off using a ¼-inch up-spiral bit, which removes the material upward and out of the groove.

Don't rush this part; it takes two to three passes, but it comes out dead-on. We cut inner and outer arcs by simply adjusting the pivot point on the plywood arm. After the edges are cut, we rout a round-over to match the factory edges.

The field decking is then laid to abut the circle. The ends are scribed with a compass, cut with a jigsaw, and rounded over with a router.

Robert Viviano owns Deck the Yards in Pittsburgh, Pa.

Housed-Stringer Exterior Stairs

by Andy Engel

I prefer to build stairs using housed stringers, which means that the ends of the treads and risers are wedged and glued into mortises routed into the stringers. While this approach sounds like a lot of work, it doesn't take much longer than crafting a decent set of notched-stringer stairs. What you get for the extra effort is a stronger stair, since you haven't notched away half the stringer, and one that's practically seamless.

While I first used this technique to build interior stairs, I particularly like it for exterior ones. The tight, glued joints at the stringer tend to keep out water, and I pitch the stairs about ⅛ inch per foot of run to prevent water from puddling. Stairs built this way stand up to the weather without the cupping and cracking common to most porch or deck stairs. And because each riser acts as a beam supporting the tread above, I've never felt the need for more than two stringers. I've built porch stairs that were 8 feet wide using just two housed stringers.

Preparing the Stock

You can use any rot-resistant material for exterior stairs. For the project shown on these pages, I chose relatively cheap pressure-treated 2x12s for the treads, since they would be painted to match my client's painted porch floor. The stringers (which would also be painted) are treated 2x10s; because they remain mostly intact, they're actually much stronger than notched 2x12s. I used 4/4 meranti — a fairly rot-resistant tropical hardwood that's readily available in my area — for the risers, in part because PT stock isn't available in the 1x8 or 1x10 sizes that I needed. In addition, meranti risers clear-finished with a Penofin penetrating oil finish (www.penofin.com) would nicely match the meranti porch railing that I'd already made for the deck.

When I'm building a set of stairs, I select the best stock I can, checking for knots, digs, and pitch pockets and cutting out as many defects as possible.

I pay close attention to the bows and crowns in all the stringer, riser, and tread stock. In every case, any crown faces up. Additionally, when I lay out the stringers, I make sure that the bows in them will face each other. That way, the bows more or less cancel each other out, resulting in a straight, square stair.

After cutting the treads and risers to length, I rip them to width. To straighten the edges, I like to rip both sides of the stock. These treads are 11 inches wide, which, with a 1¼-inch nosing, gives me a run of 9¾ inches. After ripping the treads, I bullnose

A simple site-built jig makes it easy to build an elegant outdoor staircase.

them with a ⅜-inch roundover bit. This bullnose perfectly matches the radius left at the front of the mortise by the ¾-inch-diameter bit I use to hog out the mortises. I rip the risers to the stair rise of 7½ inches, except for the bottom one, which has to be one tread thickness — 1½ inches — narrower.

Laying Out the Stringers

There are two main differences between laying out housed-stringer stairs and notched-stringer stairs. Unlike notched stringers, housed stringers are laid out from the bottom edge of the stringer. And instead of marking the bottom of the tread and the back of the riser, the layout marks you make for housed stringers represent the top of the tread and the front of the riser (**Figure 12**).

I set stair gauges on my framing square exactly as if I were going to notch the stringers, with one gauge on the 9¾-inch run and one on the 7½-inch rise. Working from the bottom, I lay the square on the stringer, mark the run line, then remove the gauges and shift the square forward along this line by about 2 inches. Holding the square exactly on this line, I reset

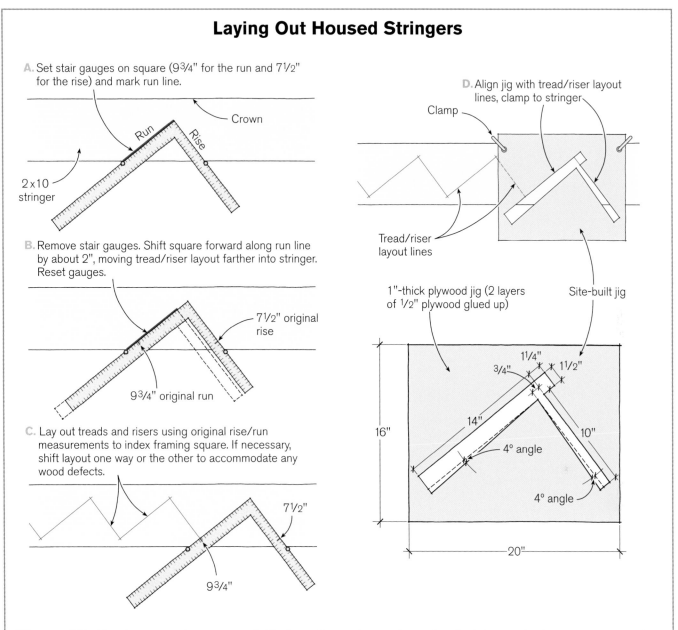

Laying Out Housed Stringers

A. Set stair gauges on square (9¾" for the run and 7½" for the rise) and mark run line.

Crown

Run — Rise

2x10 stringer

B. Remove stair gauges. Shift square forward along run line by about 2", moving tread/riser layout farther into stringer. Reset gauges.

7½" original rise

9¾" original run

C. Lay out treads and risers using original rise/run measurements to index framing square. If necessary, shift layout one way or the other to accommodate any wood defects.

7½"

9¾"

D. Align jig with tread/riser layout lines, clamp to stringer.

Clamp

Tread/riser layout lines

1"-thick plywood jig (2 layers of ½" plywood glued up)

Site-built jig

16"

1¼"

3/4"

1½"

14"

4° angle

10"

4° angle

20"

Figure 12. After laying out the stringers (left), the author makes a plywood jig (right) to guide the pattern routing bit he will use to cut the mortises for the treads and risers.

the gauges, then lay out the first riser and tread.

As I move the square down the stringer to lay out the rest of the treads and risers, I align the original 9¾-inch run length on the square with the riser line I've just marked; if I'm moving up the stringer, the original 7½-inch riser height on the square lines up with the tread I've just marked.

When all the treads and risers are laid out, I mark the top and bottom cuts. The top cut is one riser thickness behind the face of the top riser. I like to make the bottom plumb cut about half the thickness of the newel beyond the bottom tread nosing.

Starting at the back-of-the-tread/bottom-of-the-riser intersections, I use a square to transfer index marks

to the second stringer. When laying out the second stringer, be sure that those same tread and riser intersections align with the index marks. You may have to fudge one or two by as much as ⅛ inch, but as long as you stay within that tolerance, the stringers will be consistent and your stair will be square. Fudging the layout in this way may require you to plane some of the treads for an exact fit.

Because more than half the stringer will be visible to anyone walking up the stairs, I pay attention to knots and the like. Simply shifting the layout 6 inches one way or the other can place wood defects behind the treads and risers, making a piece of #2 material look like #1.

Figure 13. Because the site-built jig will guide the router, it's important to cut the template carefully. Here, a carpenter makes the first plunge cuts with a circular saw (far left) and then finishes up with a jigsaw (left).

Cutting the Mortises

You don't need a lot of specialized tools to build a set of housed-stringer stairs.

To cut tread and riser housings, I use my old 2½-hp Bosch plunge router (anything smaller would be straining) with a pattern routing bit (I use a CMT 811.690.11B) guided by a jig I make from plywood scraps. I use a Kreg pocket screw guide to help me fasten everything together (Kreg Tool Co.,

www.kregtool.com).

A simple jig. The key to housed-stringer stairs is the jig and a pattern routing bit. To match the 1-inch depth of the available pattern routing bits, I make my jig 1 inch thick by gluing up two 16-inch-by-20-inch thicknesses of void-free ½-inch plywood.

I mark the cutouts in the jig several inches longer than any stair layout I'll ever make, since they have to be long enough for the mortises to extend

Figure 14. Using a plunge router with a ¾-inch-diameter pattern routing bit, the carpenter cuts ½-inch-deep mortises in two passes. The jig is clamped to the stringer so that the top of the tread and the front of the riser align with the layout marks.

Figure 15. Cut from 9-inch-long scrap riser material, the wedges are beveled at 4 degrees, which is done by setting the saw to 2 degrees and flipping the stock end-for-end at each cut. The carpenter eyeballs the cuts so that the sharp ends of the wedges measure about 3/16 inch.

Figure 16. With the tread seated and the stringers bar-clamped together, the carpenter drives home a heavily glued wedge on each side.

through the bottom of the stringer, and any extra opening beyond the bottom of the stringer helps in clearing chips. It's okay to make the jig larger, but don't make it any smaller, or the clamps used to hold the jig in place will get in the way of the router.

When I cut out the opening, I plunge cut with a circular saw and finish up with either a jigsaw or hand saw (**Figure 13**). Since this jig will guide the

router bit, any flaws in the cuts will show up in the mortises, so I cut carefully.

Rout in a clockwise direction. I clamp the jig to the stringer so that the top of the tread and the front of the riser align with the layout marks. The tread nosing, of course, sticks out past the riser mark. Using a ¾-inch-diameter pattern routing bit, I cut ½-inch-deep mortises in two passes, making sure that the bit is lowered enough that the bearing rides on the jig. (If the bearing doesn't ride on the jig, the bit will cut into it.) To minimize any chance of nicking the jig, I lower the bit into the jig beyond the stringer before starting the router (**Figure 14**).

With such a large bit buried in a tough southern yellow pine stringer, feed direction is critical. I move the router clockwise so that I don't jam the router by climb cutting, and stop when necessary to clear chips. To avoid tear-out where the back of the tread meets the front of the riser, the routing passes are made working from the top to the bottom of the right stringer and in the opposite direction on the left stringer.

After cutting the mortises, I make the top and bottom cuts in each stringer with a circular saw.

Assembling the Stair

Before putting the stair together, I cut wedges from 9-inch-long scrap riser material with a miter saw. The wedges are beveled at 4 degrees, which is done by setting the chop saw to 2 degrees, then flipping the stock end-for-end at each cut. I eyeball the cuts so that the sharp ends of the wedges measure

Figure 17. To set a riser, the carpenter runs a bead of glue along its top, then seats it in its mortises so that it contacts the tread above and smears the glue around, which helps prevent drips (left). Then he runs a bead of glue along the back of the tread before driving home wedges on each side of the riser (right).

Figure 18. Using a Kreg jig, the carpenter drills three pocket screw holes into the top of the riser, then uses epoxy coated 1⅝-inch deck screws to pull the tread and riser together (far left). Next he predrills (left) before driving 2½-inch stainless steel screws through each riser into the back of the tread below.

about 3/16 inch, and cut two for each tread and riser (**Figure 15**, page 302). A word of caution: Don't cut too many wedges from each piece of stock; to keep your fingers intact, throw away at least 3 inches of each block.

Next I set the stringers upside down on horses and firmly seat the top and bottom treads in their mortises with their crowns facing up. Then I check that the back of each tread aligns with the riser cut above ("above" and "below" in this case refer to the orientation of the stair once it's installed). If the tread's too wide, I plane it down to fit. With the tread seated and the stringers bar-clamped together, I drive home a heavily glued wedge on each side, stopping when the end of the wedge starts to splinter (**Figure 16**, previous page). If the wedge has intruded into the riser mortise below, I chop off the intrusion with a chisel. For glue, I prefer to use Titebond III (Franklin International, www.titebond.com), which is rated for outdoor use, but PL 400 (OSI Sealants, www.stickwithpl.com) or a polyurethane glue would work, too.

After I've set the top and bottom treads, I check for square by measuring the stair's diagonals. If the treads are squarely cut, the stair should be dead on. If it's off a bit, I adjust the stringers to get the diagonals even. Then I set and wedge the rest of the treads, cutting back any wedges that extend beyond their tread with a handsaw.

Gluing sequence is important. When placing the risers, I make sure that any crown faces the tread above. First, I run a bead of glue along a riser top, then quickly seat it in its mortises so that it contacts the tread above. This smears the glue around, and helps prevent drips.

Then I pull the riser away from the tread below and run a bead of glue along the back of that tread before sliding the riser back into position (**Figure 17**, previous page). Finally, I liberally apply glue to a pair of wedges and smack home a wedge on each side of the riser, occasionally tapping the riser to keep it seated against the tread above.

Screws complete the assembly. Using a Kreg jig, I drill three pocket screw holes into the top of each riser. Epoxy-coated 1⅝-inch deck screws driven here pull the tread and riser snugly together, and help ensure a sound glue joint. Using the Kreg pocket screw bit (any countersink bit would work, but this one's handy), I then predrill for 2½-inch stainless steel screws into the back of the tread below (**Figure 18**). As soon as the last riser is in, I flip the stairs over so that I can scrape off any glue drips.

Setting the stairs is a piece of cake. Two or three guys can move them into position, and half a dozen screws into the top riser secures them.

Andy Engel is editor of Professional Deck Builder.

Building Pergolas and Arbors

by Kim Katwijk

Deck accessories like pergolas, trellises, privacy screens, and arbors offer many benefits. They can provide shade, define an outdoor room or an entry, screen an unpleasant view (or frame a pleasant one), create a style such as Japanese or Tuscan, provide a structure on which to hang a swing or support climbing plants, give height to the deck, or just plain add fun to a deck design. Once the purpose — shade, privacy, looks — has been decided, the design of the project begins.

Basic Structure

I believe in the KISS (keep it simple, stupid) principle when it comes to designing pergolas and arbors; most of mine spring from one simple design (**Figure 19**). My basic pergola usually runs along one side of a deck, appears T-shaped when viewed from the end, and is filled in with vertical lattice panels, which create a privacy screen. This last feature is very popular as it goes a long way toward distinguishing a deck while offering shade and privacy.

Adding a second basic pergola and bridging between the two with longer rafters creates a more elaborate structure. This approach works well with modular pricing, as it's simple enough to double the cost of one basic module and add in the cost of rafters.

My standard pergola is built from cedar, with four 4x4 posts four feet on center. When designing a pergola or privacy screen, care must be taken to provide a good foundation and lateral load support.

A privacy screen will have to resist about 10 pounds per square foot of lateral load in an 85-mile-an-hour wind, which is a typical design requirement in my area. A 12-foot-long privacy screen that's 6½ feet high, for instance, would generate 780 lb. of lateral load in those conditions.

On a second-story deck, I would typically build such a screen using four posts attached to the rim joists. Each center post has to resist a 260 lb. wind load, and each end post, a 130 lb. load.

To attach the posts to the rim joists, I block behind each post to transfer the load to two or more joists. These blocks are screwed in with a strap on the top

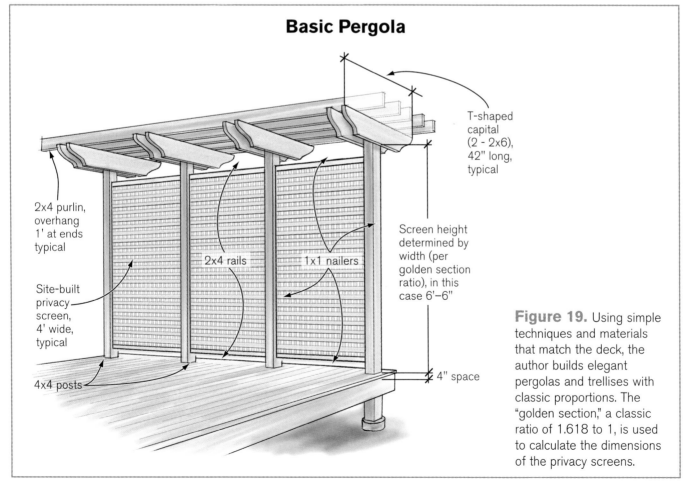

Basic Pergola

T-shaped capital (2 - 2x6), 42" long, typical

2x4 purlin, overhang 1' at ends typical

Site-built privacy screen, 4' wide, typical

2x4 rails

1x1 nailers

Screen height determined by width (per golden section ratio), in this case 6'-6"

4x4 posts

4" space

Figure 19. Using simple techniques and materials that match the deck, the author builds elegant pergolas and trellises with classic proportions. The "golden section," a classic ratio of 1.618 to 1, is used to calculate the dimensions of the privacy screens.

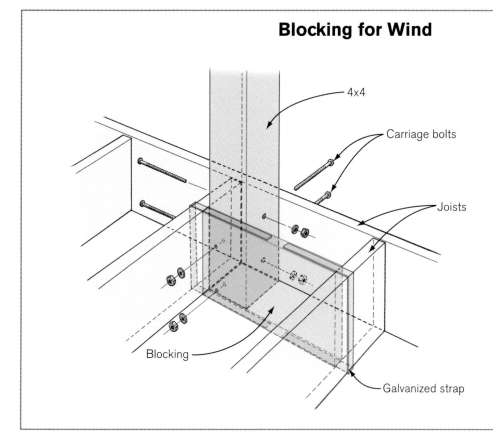

Blocking for Wind

4x4

Carriage bolts

Joists

Blocking

Galvanized strap

Figure 20. Privacy screens can experience considerable wind loading and must be stoutly anchored. On low decks, anchoring directly to the footings is recommended. On high decks, the author uses blocking to transfer wind loads to multiple joists.

and bottom (**Figure 20**). Turning the corner with the pergola and adding at least one 4-foot bay also helps to stiffen things.

On a lower deck, I can anchor the posts to the footings. I screw the posts to the rim joists to gain lateral support from the deck. When pergolas and privacy screens are stand-alone items, I use a Simpson CBSQ44 Standoff Base (Simpson Strong-Tie, www.strongtie.com) embedded into a concrete footing that has been dug down a minimum of 2 feet.

Superstructure

I make the capitals for the posts from two 2x6s, each about 42 inches long. I usually cut the bottom corners off the ends at a 45-degree angle (**Figure 21**).

To determine where to cut, I apply the golden section, a ratio of 1.618 to 1 that's been used for centuries to create rectangles with pleasing proportions. Dividing 5½ inches (the length of the end of the 2x6) by 1.618, I get 3⅜ inches. I start the 45-degree cut this distance from the bottom corner, and remove a right triangle with equal sides of 3⅜ inches.

Occasionally, I make decorative scroll cuts instead of 45-degree cuts on the ends of the capitals. Sixteen-penny stainless steel nails or 3½-inch stainless screws secure the capitals to the top of each post.

Five 2x4 purlins run the length of the pergola and overhang 1 foot on each end. One purlin is centered over the posts, and the outer purlins align with the

45-degree cuts at each end of the capital blocks. The remaining two purlins are evenly spaced between these three. All are secured with stainless screws that are toed into the capitals.

I install the privacy screen between the posts, starting with a 2x4 installed 4 inches above the decking.

Cutting a Capital

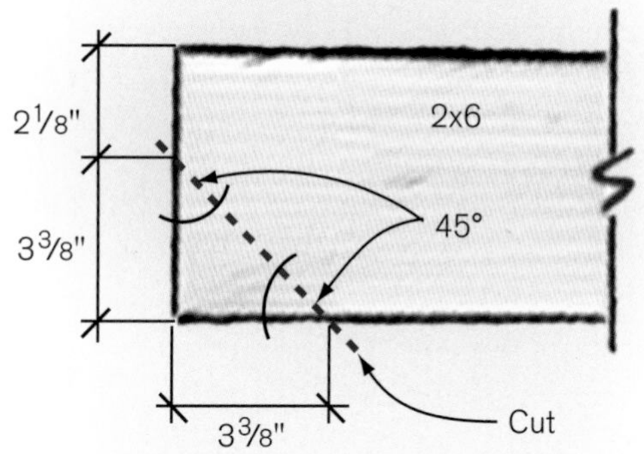

2⅛"

3⅜"

2x6

45°

3⅜"

Cut

Figure 21. The bottom corners of 42-inch-long 2x6s are cut off at a 45-degree angle to make the capitals.

Figure 22. Site-built privacy screens add a custom touch. They're made with the same material as the deck, and assembled with stainless steel staples.

The space allows clients to easily clean their deck off with a blower, hose, or broom.

The height of the top 2x4 is determined by applying the golden section: Multiplying the 4-foot width by 1.618 equals about 6 feet $5^{11}/_{16}$ inches, which rounds up to 6 feet 6 inches. So, I make the 4-foot-wide panels in the privacy screens 6½ feet high.

The space between the 2x4s is filled with a grid made from $^{7}/_{16}$-inch by 1½-inch strips of cedar, which I rip from D clear-grade 2x6s (**Figure 22**). It's important to use clear material not just for appearance, but because knots would weaken these thin strips too much. To create a nailer, a 1x1 is nailed into place on each of the horizontal 2x4s and to each post. I use a layout stick about 7 feet long with lines every 1½ inches on center to mark the locations for the upright grid pieces on the 2x4s.

After the vertical strips are cut to length, they are fastened to the nailer with 1-inch narrow-crown stainless steel staples. The layout stick is then temporarily nailed to one side of the opening for aligning the horizontal strips. I hold a torpedo level on each strip, line the strip up on the layout stick, and staple it to the nailers on the posts.

Once all the strips have been affixed to the nailers to make the grid, each overlapping piece is stapled from both sides with ¾-inch stainless steel staples. I shoot the staples to run with the grain of the strip, and their holes blend right in.

Some clients like the look of angled lattice instead of the up-and-down screens I usually make, but I never use store-bought lattice. I build my own in my shop so I can match the deck material, be it cedar, mahogany, cambarra, or redwood. First, I build a lattice jig (**Figure 23**), using a sheet of plywood as a base. Whatever you have lying around will work — mine is 1⅛-inch plywood, but ¾-inch ply would be fine.

It's tedious, but the next step is to lay out a 45-degree grid on the plywood with a straightedge and a pencil or a chalkline. I space the lines 3½ inches apart, then cut out a bunch of 2-inch square blocks. These are glued and stapled along the layout lines all the way around the outside edge, creating stop blocks for aligning the strips. The 2-inch blocks are 1½ inches apart, exactly fitting the lattice strips.

You can use the other side of the same piece of plywood to build a second lattice jig with larger spacing. You can also lay your strips out using every other block to get an even larger grid. When laying up lattice using a jig, hold the strips to one side of the spacing blocks, and check that the lattice looks evenly spaced along the lines before stapling the overlapping strips together.

Log Posts

Peeled-log posts supporting a pergola create a rustic look that's popular in the Northwest (**Figure 24**, next page). I usually use Douglas fir, but nearly any locally available species will do. Rot-resistant species are best, of course, but no matter what the wood is, it's important to detail the post to shed water and minimize the chance of rot.

I prefer to support logs on concrete footings, going

Figure 23. When a client wants a diagonal lattice, the author custom builds one using a jig made from plywood with guide blocks glued and stapled in place.

Figure 24. Pergolas can be built from a variety of materials including locally available logs.

Log Post–Footing Connection

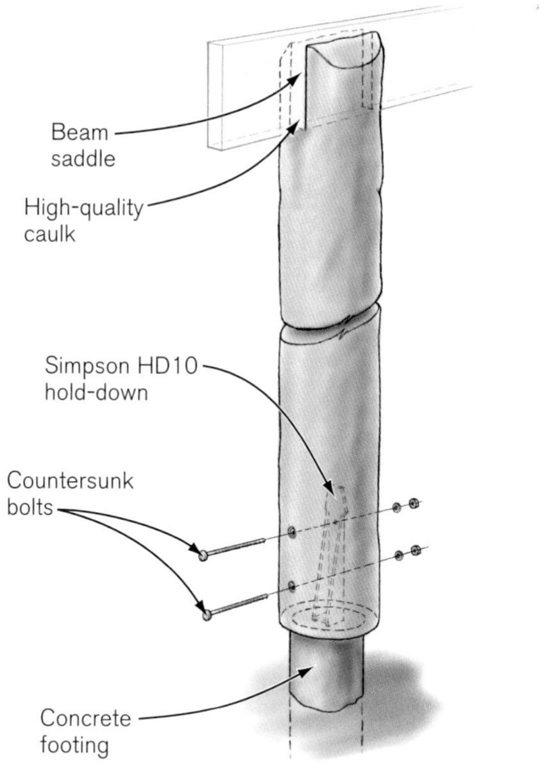

Beam saddle

High-quality caulk

Simpson HD10 hold-down

Countersunk bolts

Concrete footing

Figure 25. Log posts are supported on concrete footings that are slightly smaller than the post, encouraging water to drip. A hold-down anchor fits in a pocket that's chainsawn in the log, and countersunk bolts complete the connection. High-quality caulk helps seal moisture from the beam saddle, whose sides are chamfered to drain.

through the deck surface if necessary (**Figure 25**). I use Sonotubes to form footings that rise about 6 inches above grade. These are smaller than the base of the log, with the aim being for the log to overhang the concrete by about an inch on all sides.

I cast or epoxy a foundation bolt in place to secure a Simpson HD10 hold-down (Simpson Strong-Tie, www.strongtie.com). This hold-down will fit inside a slot cut into the base of the log with a chainsaw. Cutting the slot calls for caution, as there may be a tendency for the nose of the chainsaw bar to kick back when making the initial cut.

All of the cuts to the log are made with a chainsaw, and to align this inherently imprecise tool with the irregular surface of the log, layout lines are needed on the full length of the log. To make them, I first find the approximate center of each end of the log. Then, with the log horizontal and blocked to prevent rolling, I use a level to draw a plumb line and level line through each centerpoint. I snap lines down the length of the log between where these lines hit the face of the log. I use white chalk for this, as it doesn't leave permanent stains.

The reference lines are used to align a square so the log can be trimmed to height and square, top and bottom. You'll have to find the center points again after trimming, which can be done by reconnecting the reference lines across the cut ends of the log.

Mark the location of the hold-down slot on the bottom of the log, being very careful — there's no adjustment with this system. Make the plunge cut, lining up the bar of the saw with one of the refer-

ence lines so the cut will end up plumb.

Next, I cut the beam saddle atop the post, again using the layout lines. So water can drain, I chainsaw the sides of the saddle at about a 45-degree angle. When I set the beams in the saddles, I run a good bead of DAP Side Winder caulk (DAP, www.dap.com) all around the perimeter of the saddle to prevent water from reaching its end grain.

It can be challenging to raise a heavy log and place it accurately over the HD10, but with a couple of helpers it's not bad. Having measured the height of the bolt holes in the HD10 beforehand, and again using the reference lines as a guide, I drill holes for the bolts that will secure the log post to the hold down. Countersink these holes so the bolts don't protrude from the sides of the logs. Once the log posts are set, building the rest of the pergola proceeds pretty much like any other.

Material Options

Pergolas and arbors can be built from a variety of materials. Kits are available even in aluminum and

Figure 26. Fiberglass arbor and pergola kits are available to create a classical or Tuscan look. These hollow columns anchor to the deck framing using a length of all-thread.

fiberglass (**Figure 26**). I tried out an aluminum pergola once. The brand I used was made out of a very thin aluminum; it was difficult not to damage it during construction and my client wasn't happy after the first windstorm. Perhaps it's not fair to judge all aluminum arbors based on one bad experience, but I've avoided aluminum ever since.

I just installed my first fiberglass pergola, which came from Arbors Direct (www.arborsdirect.com). All the pieces were precut and finished to perfection. The assembly time was about six hours with a two-man crew, but after building one, I'm sure assembly time could be cut in half.

The columns anchor using an all-thread that runs through the center of the column to the deck's substructure. Once the columns were placed, the beams, purlins, and runners were easily installed. Angle brackets reinforce the joints. My client loves it, and I was impressed. The only caveat I have is that you need to allow a four- to six-week lead-time.

Another material I've used for pergolas is polyethylene-coated wood from Woodguard (www.wood-guard.com). The size of the materials — 2x6 and 4x6 are the largest sizes available — limits how far you can span between posts. Decorative caps are used to finish the ends. This product was easy to work with and my clients liked the end results.

Kim Katwijk is a deck builder in Olympia, Wash.

Benches Built for Comfort

by Kim and Linda Katwijk

I have to admit that coming up with the bench design I describe here was due more to luck than to skill. Several years ago, I was building a deck for a client who wanted a conversation area with benches for hosting political planning meetings. Pointing to a chair, she asked, "Can you build me a bench that's as comfortable as this?"

In response, I traced the shape of the chair's back onto a piece of plywood and reproduced it on the 4x10 stock I was using for the back posts. I framed the seat with 2x4s and installed 5/4-by-6-inch deck boards to form the seat and the back. The result was a curved-back bench that draws rave reviews from everyone who sits on it.

Patterns Ensure Consistency

The first step is to make a pattern on a piece of 1/2-inch plywood. You can either use the dimensions in the drawing (**Figure 27**, next page) or trace a comfortable chair. If you plan to build benches regularly, paint the plywood and seal its edges to make it last

A curved back, modeled after a comfortable chair, makes for relaxing seating.

longer.

Using the pattern, lay out the back posts on the 4x10s, alternating the orientation of the pattern to use the material most efficiently. I get four pieces out

of a 10-foot 4x10.

You'll need to make one post for every 4 feet of bench, plus one more — but don't cut the corner posts just yet. Use a circular saw with a 10-inch blade to cut all the way through the thick stock with one pass (**Figure 28**). Then finish the cuts with a reciprocating saw and smooth the saw marks with a handheld grinder equipped with a 24-grit abrasive disc (**Figure 29**).

After cutting the posts for the straight run, I turn to the corners. The deck shown here has a 45-degree corner, and the corner posts are notched to fit the angled rim joist (**Figure 30**). (If it were a 90-degree corner, the main difference would be in the angle of the notches.) The notches are made with blind cuts — that is, they stop before reaching the end of the workpiece — so one circular saw can't make both cuts. You'd have to start one side with a plunge cut or back the saw into the second cut — both dangerous maneuvers.

A better way is to use two circular saws: one that tilts left and one that tilts right. Set the saws at 22½ degrees and cut the notches. Remove the waste with a sharp chisel.

Cutting 4x10s can expose untreated wood — preservatives rarely reach the center of large timbers — so you'll need to treat the cuts with an end-cut preservative (**Figure 31**) such as Jasco Copper Brown Wood Preservative (The Homax Group, www.homaxproducts.com).

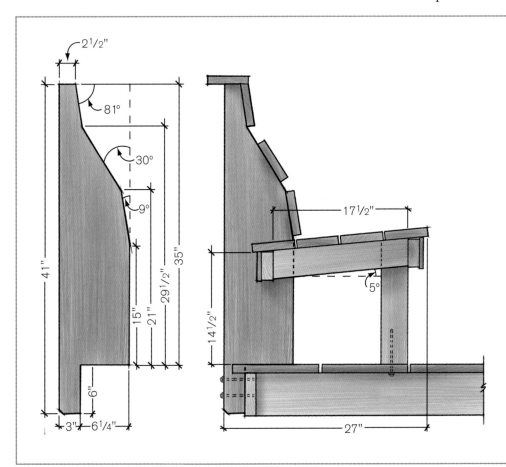

Figure 27. The secret to a comfortable bench is getting the height and the angles right. The author's design is based on that of a comfortable chair, the shape of which he traced onto a plywood template.

Figure 28. The back posts are laid out next to each other on 4x10 stock, minimizing waste. Cutting such thick material requires a 10-inch circular saw; the author will finish the cuts using a reciprocating saw.

Figure 29. It's nearly impossible to cut thick stock perfectly, but a coarse abrasive disc makes quick work of the glitches.

Frame the Seat With 2x4s

To support the seat boards, I attach two 2x4s to each back post (**Figure 32,** next page). For all the seat supports except those for the end and corner posts (discussed below), I cut the 2x4s 17$\frac{1}{2}$ inches long with a parallel 5-degree angle on each end. Then I mark the posts just below the first angled cut — which, when the posts are installed, will be 14$\frac{13}{16}$ inches from the deck surface — with lines slanting 5 degrees down to represent the top of the

2x4s. The 2x4s will extend 3 inches onto the back posts, leaving plenty of room for the long 2x4s that will eventually be fastened to the back of the seat supports, between the posts.

I preinstall the seat supports on the posts. To start with, I attach the 2x4s with construction adhesive and one nail (**Figure 33,** next page). Before locking them in place with a second nail, I set the 2x4s at 5 degrees to the bottom of the post, verifying the angle either with a layout square or with a framing square

Figure 30. Two circular saws — one right-tilting and one left-tilting — are used to notch the back posts to fit the angled rim joist. A chisel cleans out the waste.

Figure 31. Cutting timbers usually exposes an untreated core. For longevity, coating all cuts in pressure-treated wood with an end-cut preservative is crucial.

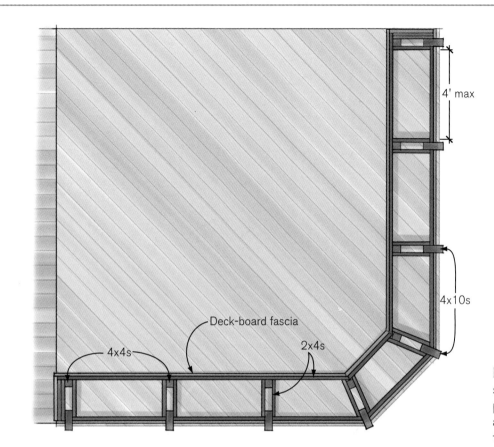

Deck-board fascia

4x4s

2x4s

4' max

4x10s

Figure 32. Seat posts shaped from 4x10s are placed no more than 4 feet apart to support the 2x4 framing of this bench.

set at a 1-in-12 pitch, which equals 5 degrees. When I'm certain of the angle, I drive a second nail to lock it in place. It's important to accurately place the 2x4 seat supports, as they must all line up when the assembly is installed on the deck.

Figure 33. The author uses a framing square to be sure the seat-support 2x4s are at the correct 5-degree angle — which is a 1-in-12 pitch — as he nails them to the 4x10 posts.

On the end posts, the inside 2x4 supports are preinstalled just like those described above; the supports on the outside, however, are a little different. They are also preinstalled, but they're longer, and there are two of them. I cut two 19-inch-long pieces for each end post and set them $4\frac{1}{2}$ inches, instead of 3 inches, onto the post. The extra $1\frac{1}{2}$ inches brings the back of these 2x4 supports even with the long 2x4s that will be installed to support the back of the seat. Doubling the outside supports provides better attachment for the short section of seat board that continues past the end of the last post.

Screw the Posts to the Rim

To install the back posts, I notch the decking as needed and fasten the lower part of the post to the deck's rim joists using two $5\frac{1}{2}$-inch FastenMaster LedgerLoks (www.fastenmaster.com). Once all the posts — except the corners — are in place, install the 2x4s that run the length of the front of the seat, allowing them to run long at any inside corners (so you can measure from them to size the seat supports).

Next I fasten the corner posts to the rim joists with $5\frac{1}{2}$-inch LedgerLoks, as I did with the other posts. Then to determine the angles and lengths of seat supports for the corner, I measure from the corner posts to the 2x4s that I let run long for this purpose

Figure 34. The author allowed the 2x4s that join the front of the bench to run long at inside corners. This made figuring the angles and lengths of the corner seat support 2x4s a matter of measurement, not complicated math.

Figure 35. Installing the seat and back is the easy part, although compound angle cuts are required at the inside corners.

(**Figure 34**). I cut 2x4s to my measurements and fasten them onto each side of the corner posts.

The 2x4s that will run along the back of the seat can now be cut to fit between the back posts and screwed to the seat supports. Install 4x4s for front posts by nailing through the front and side 2x4s. These 4x4s should be about 16¼ inches tall. To fasten them to the deck, I run a LedgerLok into them up through the decking. For a finished look, I attach the appropriate fascia material on the front, back, and sides of the seat frame.

Surface the Seat and the Back With Deck Boards

Once I'm done putting the fascia in place, I start installing the seat decking, using stainless steel trim-head deck screws. To avoid having to match up the mitered ends of the seat boards at the corners, I use a divider board. This is a piece of deck board ripped to about 4 inches wide, whose edges I round over with a router. I attach the board over the center of the corner 2x4 seat supports, and allow it to run long in the front. This leaves plenty of meat on the 2x4s for attaching the main seat boards.

I lay the seat boards, including those on the angled

corners, from back to front, and I gap them ⅜ inch. The front and ends should hang over the fascia by 1 inch. I trim the front ends of the corner divider boards even with the seat boards, and round over the ends with a router.

I start the back by installing the bottom board between the two corner posts. The joints between the corner backboards and the rest of the backboards will be compound miters. The bevel cuts will all be 22½ degrees (45 degrees if the corner is square), but the miter angles will vary depending on what part of the post the board is on. I lightly draw a line down the center of the posts, and mark where the top and bottom of each board will intersect it. Measuring between these lines at the top and bottom of each board gives me the board's length and the angle of the cut.

The cap board is installed last (**Figure 35**). Starting at the center between the two corner posts, line it up with the top backboard to make a smooth transition. Once this beauty is complete, sit down and relax your back for a moment. You deserve it!

Kim Katwijk is a deck builder in Olympia, Wash. Linda Katwijk coauthored this article.

Simple Curved Bench Details

by Scott Smith

Benches are popular upgrades, and building them in a shape other than the usual boxy rectangle immediately distinguishes you from your competitors. But of the three approaches to forming a curve, two present serious challenges. The most difficult method is to bend wood or composite into a shape it doesn't want to be. Whether you heat or steam the material, or laminate thin strips on a curved form, you need expensive equipment, a shop, and lots of time.

A second method is to cut curved pieces from wide boards. This works well if you can cut curves consistently and don't mind a lot of waste. However, longer benches must be built from segments, which will require joints in the surface of the bench. You will also have to sand and rout the edges of the curved pieces to make them look finished.

Most of the time, though, I use a far simpler method. I rip 1-inch wood or composite decking into slats about 2 inches wide. I stand the slats on edge, bend to the desired curve, and secure. Spacers allow for drainage, a particularly nice feature in a wet climate. To support the slats, I anchor 4x4 posts into the framing before installing the decking. In the project discussed here, the deck had already been built, so I had to remove decking for access.

Place slats on edge and flex them to create distinctive seats without steam bending or laminating.

Design With the Material in Mind

Most benches will be shorter than the longest available deck board, which normally runs about 20 feet. Placing a joint in the middle of a curve to make a longer bench is difficult at best, and usually leaves a flat spot on the curve.

You also need to know how far the material can be bent before it will break. I have bent composites to as tight a radius as 8 feet — but that's been in the summer, when I could pre-bend the slats by leaning them against a wall in the sun. You can make even tighter bends by heating or steaming the slats, but that complicates the process considerably.

The seat has to be supported in at least four places to define a curve (**Figure 36**). Using only three will give you a V-shape. I usually place a support post — made from a treated or composite 4x4 — about 1 foot in from each end of the curved bench and space the other posts evenly within the remaining span. Spans greater than 4 feet are likely to sag.

I like to build curved benches with EverGrain composite decking (Tamko Building Products, www.evergrain.com). I've also successfully bent Trex (Trex Company, www.trex.com) and cedar. Most of the other composite products I've tried haven't worked as well. If you build with wood, be sure to use clear material. Wood tends to break at the knots when it's bent.

Figure 36. The curved bench will need at least four points of support (three points results in a V-shaped bench). The author has spaced out the posts evenly across the deck to verify position before removing the decking to gain access to the framing.

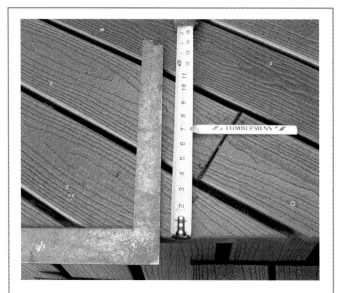

Figure 37. On an existing curved deck, the author locates the posts by measuring in from the deck's edge.

Figure 38. With the decking removed, each support post is nailed in place with blocking on all four sides. If the post lands partially on a joist, notch the post, not the joist.

Lay Out the Arc

Determining the curve of the bench can be done several ways. Most of the time, I'm building a bench to match the curve of the deck. When that's the case, I simply mark in from the edge of the deck half the width of the bench to locate the center of the support posts (**Figure 37**). I use thirteen rows of slats on most benches, making them a little more than 13 inches wide, so the center radius is about 7 inches in.

Block the Posts

Once the arc is marked, I affix all the support posts. Because most posts will land between the joists, I use blocking. It's necessary not only to support seated people, but also because the stress of bending the slats for the bench top will tend to move the posts if they are not fastened securely.

The blocking is cut to fit between the joists — square to the radius to keep the posts aligned properly. I find

Square Decks

When I build a curved bench on a square deck, I decide on a radius for the arc that defines the outer edge of the bench, say 10 feet. Then I locate the center point of the arc's circle, which is 10 feet from the outer edge of both ends of the bench. If this point lands between joists, I put a temporary wood block there.

Next, I build a simple compass with a 1x2 and a nail. For a 10-foot radius, I measure 10 feet minus half the width of the bench — about 9 feet 5 inches, total — from the end of the 1x2. I drive a nail at this point into the 1x2, through the center point on the deck. Holding a pencil at the other end of the 1x2, I swing it across the framing to mark the arc along which the support posts will be placed.

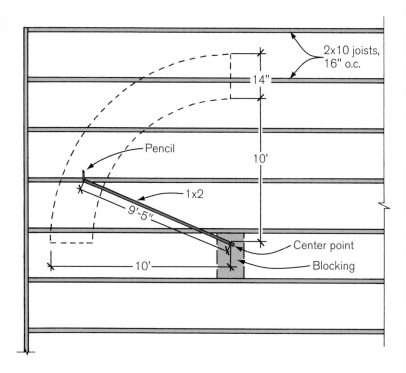

JOSEPH GRIFFITHS

Figure 39. Three screws hold each 2x4 bench support to its post. The inner ends of the 2x4s are run a little long, allowing them to be trimmed exactly after all the seat slats are installed.

the radius by using two framing squares back to back so that they look like a T. Place the squares so the same measurement on each, say 12 inches, aligns with the outer edge of the deck, and the line between their other legs runs through the center of the post location.

Next, I mount the posts to the framing. I secure all four sides of the 4x4 posts to the joists and blocking with plenty of 3½-inch nails (**Figure 38**, previous page).

If a post falls on a joist, notch the post — do not cut the joist. I set posts 17 inches above the tops of the joists. This will make the finished bench 18 inches high (add 2 inches for the thickness of the slats and deduct 1 inch for the decking), which is a comfortable sitting height for most people.

Frame Supports for the Slats

I glue and screw treated 2x4s on two sides of the posts, flush with the tops, to support the slats (**Figure 39**). To determine the length of the supports, I measure the width of however many layers of slats will make up the bench top, usually 11. Yes, I said 13 before, but that number includes the front and back fascias, which fasten to the ends of these 2x4s, not their tops.

I always cut the 2x4 supports an inch or so long. As the slats are bent into place, their actual combined width will vary depending on how tightly the bench boards fit together. Leaving the supports a little long allows them to be cut to the exact length after the slats are installed.

I center a 2x4 support on a 4x4 post, set it flush with the top of the post, and nail it once using a nail gun. Then I level the 2x4 and nail it again. I set the support on the other side of the post the same way and then run at least three 3-inch deck screws through each 2x4 into the 4x4. It's a good idea to apply glue between the post and the 2x4.

Fascia Board

Once the supports are all installed, I mount the outer fascia board (**Figure 40**). The fascia boards are full-width deck boards, usually 1 inch thick by 5½ inches wide. I use a tape measure to get an approximate

length, allowing for the fascia to extend about 1 foot past the end supports.

When I'm done, fascia will wrap the front, back, and ends of the bench. The joints between the fascia ends and the front and back fascia will be miters, so I bevel cut each end of the outer fascia at 45 degrees when I cut it to length. If the fascia board has a grain pattern on one side only, be consistent in which side shows.

Either blocking or a helper supports one end of the fascia while I work from the opposite end, bending and attaching it with two 3½-inch deck screws to each support 2x4. The bottom of the fascia should be flush with the bottom of the support 2x4s, and the ends of the fascia should extend equal distances from the support posts. If not, use a circular saw set at a 45-degree bevel to shorten the longest end. I also make sure the fascia board extends above the 2x4s by about 2 inches.

Figure 40. Allowed to run about 1 foot past each of the end supports, the outer fascia is cut to accept a mitered end piece, and screwed into the ends of the 2x4 supports. This fascia is set flush with the bottoms of the 2x4s, and its height above them will be the same as the dimension the slats are ripped to.

Figure 41. Spacers are screwed to the fascia board above the 2x4 supports, and the slats are bent into place.

Figure 42. In addition to being screwed to the block behind, each slat is toe-screwed to the 2x4 supports.

Install the Seat

I rip three deck boards down to 2 inches for the slats, preserving the factory-molded edges. This produces six long pieces, but only five will be needed for slats. The extra piece will be cut up for blocking between the slats at the 2x4 supports.

You may need to cut more pieces of blocking from deck scraps. Most of the time, I cut these blocking pieces so that they're about an inch longer than the combined width of the post and the 2x4 supports. This usually works out to be 7½ inches. Once installed, the slats and blocking will cover the support framing so it can't be seen from above.

Place one block, ripped edge down, over each set of supports next to the fascia (**Figure 41**). Drill and countersink one hole in the center of each block,

Figure 43. Cutting the spacers at varying angles and lengths results in a circular pattern. The 2x4 supports will be cut off flush with the final block.

and attach the blocks to the fascia using 1⅝-inch deck screws. The screws should exert enough force to curve the center of the block tight to the fascia, but you may need to encourage them with a clamp or additional screws, particularly in cold weather.

Lay the first slat next to the blocks, ripped edge down. Make sure the ends extend beyond or at least flush with the end of the fascia on each end. If the slats have a grain pattern on one side, your finished product will look better if you mount them all with the grain facing the same direction.

Drill and countersink holes near, but not exactly lined up with, the screws holding the blocks in place. Attach the slats with one 2½-inch screw through each block and into the fascia or previous slat. Then angle one 2½-inch or 3-inch screw through the slat into each support 2x4 (**Figure 42**). You may need to use a chisel to shave off the bump that the screw creates, or the bump will prevent the next piece of blocking from pulling tight to the slat.

Continue in this manner, lining up each block with the previous blocks. The twelfth row should consist of blocks. Once they're all attached, use a reciprocating saw to trim the 2x4 supports flush with the blocks.

On this particular deck, I added more interest to the bench by cutting the blocks so they'd look like a circle once installed. I drew a pattern of a circle whose diameter equaled the finished width of the bench. By laying the blocking stock on this circle, spaced one slat-width apart, I was able to mark each piece of blocking at the correct length and angle to create the circular shape in the bench (**Figure 43**).

Mitered Ends Finish the Bench

I use a framing square and pencil to mark both ends of the slats for cutting. I cut them flush with the inside of the miter cut on the existing outer fascia

Figure 44. The author screws the inner fascia home.

board, finishing the cut on the last one using a hand-saw or reciprocating saw.

Next, I select a full-width deck board for the inner fascia, and bevel one end of it 45 degrees. Line this end up so that the inside of the miter cut is flush with the slats and its top is flush with the top of the blocks. Attach it to the 2x4 supports as you did the outer fascia, working toward the outer end and carefully pushing the fascia into the curve as you go (**Figure 44**). Be patient and give the board time to adjust to the bend. Bar clamps may help.

After attaching the inner fascia to the last support, mark and bevel cut the remaining end at 45 degrees using a circular saw. Cut two fascia boards for the ends and screw them to the slats. I finish up by easing the mitered corners with a ¼-inch or ⅜-inch round-over bit in a router.

Scott Smith is a deck contractor in the Tacoma, Wash., area.

Easy, Durable Planter Boxes
by Brent and Jennifer Benner

Planters enhance the appearance and the function of a deck, making them popular add-ons. Plantings soften the rigid look of decking material and provide bursts of flower color that clients love. Large planters filled with tall plants like ornamental grasses or shrubs can be used to create privacy or conceal eyesores like utility boxes and storage areas. And a planter that puts a bounty of fresh herbs or tomatoes right at the chef's fingertips makes a perfect complement to an outdoor kitchen.

While planters are easy to build, they do require some thought beyond simply constructing boxes and filling them with dirt. For one, contained gardens can tack on a few hundred pounds — especially once they've been watered — and the deck must be able to handle the extra weight. It's a good idea to double the joists where the planters will sit.

Figure 45. A self-watering container like the one shown above can be easily dropped into a wood frame.

Build a basic pressure-treated frame around a store-bought plastic liner and dress it up to match the deck.

Water presents other challenges — and opportunities as well. Plants need it to grow and flourish, so you'll have to provide for drainage and shield the decking materials from moisture. You can also increase customer satisfaction by building in a watering system.

Liners

A liner keeps the wood of the planter box from directly contacting soil moisture, which might cause rot or insect problems. For clients who are planning on growing edibles, liners also prevent any worry about lumber treatments leaching into the soil.

One option for a liner is a rubber membrane, such as PondGard from Firestone (www.firestonesp.com). Drop-in metal liners made from copper or galvanized steel are another possibility, but they can be tricky to locate and often need to be custom ordered.

We prefer plastic containers that we can drop into a wood frame. They are quick, reliable, and — when you factor in the labor costs of other methods — relatively cheap. The self-watering EarthBoxes (www.earthbox.com) used in this project cost about $30 each (**Figure 45**).

Irrigation and Drainage

Container plantings tend to dry out quickly in the heat of the summer and sometimes need a drink almost daily. No one wants to drag a hose around all summer, though, so offer your clients a watering system.

Drip irrigation on a timer is a great way to simplify the chore of watering and get plants the water they need. Irrigation tubing can be run behind planters,

or for a planter that sits out in the open, it can be run underneath the decking and up through the bottom. Then, individual tubes with emitters are placed at the base of the plants to deliver water right where

Figure 46. The outer frame of the planter box is essentially a stud wall made from treated lumber.

Figure 47. A plywood face stiffens the planter's frame and provides nailing for finishes (far left). The author leaves out sections of plywood to fit the planters around the newels (left).

it's needed. Numerous sources, from home-and-garden centers to plumbing suppliers, sell kits. Two to consider are Netafim (www.netafimusa.com) and DripWorks (www.dripworksusa.com).

An excellent alternative to drip irrigation is a self-watering container. It comes with a reservoir, which needs only periodic replenishments of water. When the reservoir is full, the water slowly wicks through the soil, providing moisture to the plant roots. To make watering even simpler for your clients, you can set up an automated watering system to refill the reservoir.

While plants need water, they shouldn't be swim-

ming in it. Good drainage is a must for planter boxes. Be sure the liner and planter have adequate drainage holes. If you will be supplying the potting soil, choose what is called a soilless mix, which typically contains a blend of peat moss, composted pink bark, or coir; vermiculite; and sand or perlite. Regular

Figure 48. Keeping the plywood above the decking prevents it from wicking water, which could eventually cause delamination.

Figure 49. Once filled with dirt, the liners will be too heavy to hang from their rims. Risers ripped from 2-by stock support the bottom of the liners. When installing the risers, place them where they won't interfere with the liners' drains.

Figure 50. With the liner in place, the author drops a marking pen through its overflow to mark the location of a drain hole (far left). The hole is large — 2½ inches — to prevent clogging (left).

dirt from the backyard tends to have poor drainage and can be the kiss of death for plants in a container.

Building the Boxes

Because the dimensions of the planter assembly depended on the size of the liner, we purchased the liners first and used them as a guide. We also factored in the measurements of the decking materials that we were going to use for the fascia.

Making the frame was straightforward; we fastened pressure-treated 2-by stock together with stainless steel screws (**Figure 46**, page 319). We attached ¾-inch pressure-treated plywood to the outside of the frame — for stability as well as to provide a place to attach the decking fascia (**Figure 47**). Then we screwed the planters to the joists (**Figure 48**).

To support the weight of the soil-filled containers, we installed 2-by risers along the bottom of the planter boxes. These were ripped so that the container's lip would just barely rest on the top of the frame (**Figure 49**). Next, a container was placed in position, and a 2½-inch hole for drainage was marked and drilled (**Figure 50**).

The outside of the planter boxes is finished with TwinFinish composite decking (TimberTech, www.timbertech.com). Because it's generally less affected by water than is wood, composite decking is a great material for planters. To fasten the lowest row of decking to the planters, we used screws from the inside; we used hidden fasteners to attach the rest (**Figure 51**).

The tops were a little more work than the sides. We

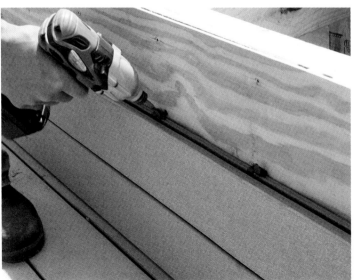

Figure 51. The lowest piece of the composite-decking facing is affixed to the planter from inside with screws (left). Subsequent pieces are attached with hidden fasteners (right).

Figure 52. The top of the planter is made from composite decking rabbeted to overlap the liner rims.

Figure 53. Screws hold down the surface facing, allowing it to be removed should the homeowners want to pull out the liners.

Figure 54. Trim pieces are nailed home.

wanted to cover up the lips of the EarthBoxes, yet allow them to be removed. So we ripped the decking to the right width and rabbeted the edges to fit over the EarthBoxes (**Figure 52**). To allow for removing the boxes, the tops are fastened down with screws, whose color matches the decking (**Figure 53**). A small piece of decking material finishes the corners (**Figure 54**).

After we built the planter, we installed a cable railing system to allow maximum light to reach the plants while still providing safety. Check with your local inspector about railing heights. Some inspectors measure from the decking, some measure from the top of permanent structures such as planters and benches.

Brent Benner is a carpenter, and Jennifer Benner is a horticulturist and writer. They live in Roxbury, Conn.

Wiring for Low-Voltage Lighting

by Cliff Popejoy

A great deck deserves great lighting, not just a couple of wall-mounted 100-watt floodlights that glare down on the deck — which is almost worse than no light at all.

There are two different types of deck lighting systems: One operates on household voltage (120 volts, also called "line voltage"), and the other runs on low voltage (12 volts). Each has pros and cons, but except for very large residential projects, low-voltage systems are usually a better choice.

Low-voltage systems are inherently safer. Because there's virtually no electrocution hazard, codes don't require exposed low-voltage cable to be run in conduit, and in most jurisdictions, no electrician's license is required to install low-voltage wiring (if you need to run an additional line-voltage circuit to feed the transformer, call an electrician). Additionally, there are a wide variety of low-voltage outdoor fixtures available.

Low-voltage systems do have a few downsides, though. The fixtures put out less light than line-voltage fixtures, and if the distance from the transformer to the farthest fixture is 100 feet or more, voltage drop can cause a dim, yellow light unless you use special installation techniques. You'll also need to find an unobtrusive place to install the transformer. And even though installation is faster because you don't need conduit, it does leave the cables exposed and vulnerable to damage.

For large-scale projects, line voltage is a good choice. A circuit can accommodate many fixtures and each one can put out a lot of light. No transformer is needed, which saves a few dollars, and adding dimmers to line-voltage systems is easier than

Make your decks great spaces after dark with low-voltage lighting. Beyond post caps, consider a wide variety of fixtures for general, decorative, accent, and safety lighting.

DE-KOR

adding them to low-voltage ones. And since you'd be running conduit for the cable anyway, it's simple to add outlets around the deck.

LED or Incandescent?

Some fixtures have a light-emitting diode (LED) instead of an incandescent lamp as the light source. An LED is a semiconductor device like a transistor; it will last virtually forever (typically 50,000 hours) and use a lot less energy than an incandescent bulb. Most solar-powered deck lighting uses LEDs.

Generally, though, a single LED produces much less light than a standard 5- or 7-watt lamp, and so-called white LEDs give off a cool, bluish light, noticeably different than an incandescent lamp. LED fixtures cost a lot more than similar ones that use incandescent lamps, and the variety of styles of fixtures with LED light sources is pretty limited at this time.

If long lamp life and energy savings are paramount and cost is not an issue, LEDs can be a good choice. First, though, I recommend demonstrating an LED and an incandescent fixture side by side, so the client knows what to expect from the LED.

Have both members of a couple there to see the LED; one may love the energy-saving aspect, while the other hates the way it looks. It's not good to find that out when the installation is complete. As it stands now, you can't just swap out LEDs and put in incandescent lamps; the fixtures are different.

KICHLER LIGHTING

KICHLER LIGHTING

Figure 55. Task lighting can be a small work light for checking to see if the steaks are medium rare (left), or a chandelier that lights a friendly game of poker (above).

However, the greater shock and electrocution hazards of line voltage, combined with fewer fixture choices, make me favor low-voltage systems for smaller projects.

Transformers and Voltage

The device that changes 120-volt electricity to 12-volt is called a transformer. Transformers are made with different capacities (rated in watts), and each one runs a single circuit. I strongly recommend using a transformer that has a UL 1838 listing, which means that its voltage output is limited to 15 volts and the wattage to 300.

Why would you want the option of 15 volts on a nominal 12-volt system? Because the greater the distance the electricity has to travel, the more voltage is lost to the resistance of the wire. The extra 3 volts can compensate for this voltage drop. If you feed the fixtures from a loop at the end of a long supply line

at 14 or 15 volts, then even the farthest fixtures will still provide light that's bright white.

Because of the danger of fire, it's safer to limit the power to any circuit (fed from one transformer) to 300 watts. An output of 300 watts at 12 volts means you have 25 amps of current available, which can feed a lot of fixtures. If there's a dead short with a UL 1838–listed transformer, the breaker protecting the secondary winding of the transformer will trip. However, if there's a moderate-resistance short circuit, or a short to ground, the breaker might not trip or might take a while to trip.

The current is converted into heat at the point of the short, at a weak connection, or where a cable is damaged. The higher the amperage, the greater the chance of a fire if something goes wrong. The risk increases, therefore, with larger wattage transformers; 12-volt 600-watt transformers have 50 amps of available current.

If you need more than 300 watts, install another

DE-KOR

Figure 56. Safety lighting helps to keep people on their feet going down stairs or walking around spas.

Figure 57. Accent lighting creates memorable grace notes by illuminating such features as flowers, trees, or murals.

DE-KOR

transformer. Also, there are products available with two separate transformers in a single housing, and the whole assembly is UL 1838 listed. Each transformer in such a combination has one set of output terminals rated at 300 watts.

Additionally, UL 1838–compliant transformers offer overcurrent protection (that circuit breaker I mentioned above, usually with a push-button reset) and a thermal cutoff switch, which cuts the power to an overheated transformer.

I usually plan for a load (the sum of the wattage of all the lights on the circuit) on any transformer of no more than 80 percent of the transformer rating (this is called *derating*). It's pretty easy to figure out the circuit load. Each lamp has a wattage rating, typically 5 or 7 watts. A 300-watt transformer derated to 240 watts can power up to 34 7-watt bulbs.

Derating does a couple of things. First, it allows for adding a fixture here or there. Second, a derated transformer will last longer, because a maxed-out transformer runs hot and heat breaks down the insu-

lation, eventually causing a short in the windings.

This is also why most transformers are listed for outdoor mounting only and the installation instructions state that the cooling louvers/vents on the housing have to be kept unobstructed.

Lighting for Tasks, Safety, and Decoration

You can use light several ways. Spotlights and hanging fixtures are ideal for task lighting that illuminates a specific area — say for grilling or for reading (**Figure 55**). Safety lighting is used on stairs, transitions, and spas (**Figure 56**) and may be required by code in some areas (see "Stair Lighting and the Code," page 327). Mini recessed lights that fit into holes drilled along stairs are another option (see "Recessed Stair Lighting," next page). Lighting these areas also accentuates them, but true accent lighting focuses on a feature, such as a tree or mural (**Figure 57**).

Decks are fun places, and decorative lighting that is

KICHLER LIGHTING

DE-KOR

Figure 58. Lighting can be whimsical (far left) or artistic (left).

Recessed Stair Lighting

People trip and fall on stairs, and in many cases, building codes require lighting to minimize this hazard. Poorly done stair lighting can be even more dangerous than none, as inconsistent shadow and light confuse the eye. Below are three reliable ways to illuminate stairs.

 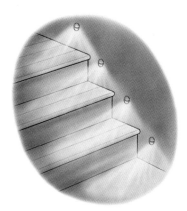 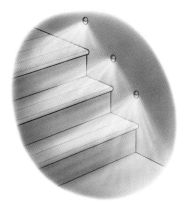

Perhaps the most obvious way to light stairs is with fixtures recessed into the risers. One downside of this approach can be that light shines right into the eyes of those climbing the stairs.

Lighting a stair from the side may be easier on the eyes of climbers. One recessed fixture placed low on the stringer and centered on each tread provides plenty of light.

Another way to light stairs is to mount the lights a little higher and slightly forward of each riser. This lights each tread and uses one less fixture per flight.

---

a feature in itself underscores this point (**Figure 58**, previous page). Post-top lights can serve as both decorative and general lighting (**Figure 59**).

No matter how you combine the lights, don't overdo it. You want enough light, but it's the contrast between darker and lighter areas that makes a space interesting.

I set up systems to allow for different levels of light, one for entertaining and one for private relaxing. To this end, it's a good idea to set up the fixtures on two or more circuits that can be switched independently. Put the general lighting and task lighting on one circuit and the decorative lighting on another.

Figure 59. Probably the most common deck lighting, post-cap fixtures provide general lighting and decoration at once.

For relaxing on the deck, it's nice to have the lights low. You could run just the decorative lights, but a more sophisticated approach is to use a dimmer. While there are dimmers designed for 12-volt systems, I find that it's less expensive to dim the 120-volt line going to the transformer. Make sure the dimmer is rated for the size (wattage) of the transformer and for an inductive load. This information should be available in the product literature.

Dimmer switches should be installed inside, though this complicates matters somewhat. While it's possible to install a regular switch outside in a weatherproof box with the right weatherproof cover, it's not a good idea with a dimmer switch because its electronics don't handle outdoor humidity, heat, and cold well.

You'll need to extend a circuit and add the dimmer switch and an outside GFI receptacle outlet for the transformer(s), or possibly run a new circuit with the dimmer switch and GFI receptacle.

Planning for Changes

I always talk to the clients about how they expect to use the deck, and offer thoughts on what other clients have done. Getting a client's input minimizes changes after the installation. Still, clients do sometimes request changes. I prepare for this when I design the system so any changes are easy to accommodate.

For example, when running the supply line, I put a short loop of cable at the midpoint between the fixtures. If you want to add another fixture later, having 4 inches to 6 inches of slack will make all the difference.

Stair Lighting and the Code

by Glenn Mathewson

The 2000 IRC introduced a requirement for illumination of all stairways in residential buildings. The main body of the code section detailing this requirement has remained relatively unchanged through the 2003 and 2006 IRCs. The code sections discussed here are from the 2006 IRC, which includes the following:

R303.6 Stairway Illumination. All interior and exterior stairways shall be provided with a means to illuminate the stairs, including the landings and treads. ... Exterior stairways shall be provided with an artificial light source located in the immediate vicinity of the top landing of the stairway.

The previous sentences are two of the sections of the code that refer to exterior stairways. The first sentence specifies which areas of interior and exterior stairways are to be lit; the second sentence specifies where the light for an exterior stairway must be located. As long as all the landings and treads are illuminated, the requirement in the first sentence is satisfied; theoretically, the light source could be a single floodlight on the corner of the house 30 feet away or multiple low-voltage lights mounted to the guardrail posts at the side of the stairway.

The second sentence provides additional criteria for where the light source must be located: "in the immediate vicinity of the top landing of the stairway." The phrase "immediate vicinity" is subjective, however – my idea of "immediate vicinity" may be different from yours or your inspector's. Nevertheless, according to this portion of the code section, the hypothetical floodlight 30 feet from the stairway would probably not satisfy the requirement; an additional light source would be required.

Many jurisdictions interpret the second sentence as a "specific requirement" and the first as a "general requirement." In IRC chapter one, "Administration," Section R102.1 states, "Where there is a conflict between a general requirement and a specific requirement, the specific requirement shall be applicable." In applying this section, many jurisdictions would require illumination only of the top landing of an exterior stairway, on the basis that that is the specific requirement.

I think that interpretation is wrong, however, as there is no conflict between the two requirements. One requires

"a means to illuminate" the stairs, and the other specifies the general location of "an artificial light source."

Another subjective part of the illumination requirement for exterior stairways is that no measurable unit of illumination is specified, which will ultimately lead to variations in enforcement by code officials. Assessing the level of artificial illumination in daylight hours, when most inspections are performed, is difficult, and without the requirement of a definitive, measurable quantity of illumination, there's little limitation of a code official's judgment as to what is "illuminated" and what is not.

There's more. The last sentence of Section R303.6.1, and the exception that follows, states:

R303.6.1 Light activation. ... The illumination of exterior stairways shall be controlled from inside the dwelling unit. Exception: Lights that are continuously illuminated or automatically controlled.

A common way of approaching this requirement is to replace the porch light outside the door leading to the deck with a floodlight aimed at the top landing of the stairway. For this to work, the light source must be "in the immediate vicinity of the top landing" and must illuminate all treads and other landings, as well. If this is not possible or desired, other light sources controlled from inside the home that would meet those requirements will need to be installed.

The exception allows for more flexibility in lighting options, such as the limited use of low-voltage lighting. A photocell, for example, illuminating for the full duration of dark hours, could be considered "continuous," and a motion sensor, activated when the deck is occupied, could be considered "automatic."

The use of a timer or photocell-timer combo would be questionable, because its automatic capabilities would depend on how the timer was set; that might not be considered sufficient to satisfy the light activation requirements.

As with all discussions about building codes, always double-check with the local authority that has jurisdiction.

Glenn Mathewson is a building inspector in Westminster, Colo.

Figure 60. Silicon-filled wire nuts twist on like regular wire nuts, but they keep out the water that corrodes connections.

KING INNOVATION

Figure 61. Clip-on connectors are a speedy way of splicing the fixture's wires to the main supply cable.

KICHLER LIGHTING

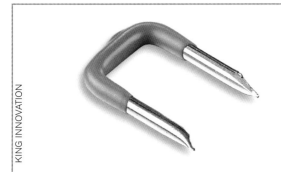

KING INNOVATION

Figure 62. Finding truly corrosion-resistant cable staples is nearly impossible. A plastic coating will help to protect the exposed portion of the staple, but avoid using staples in places where rust trailing down part of the deck will be objectionable.

Figure 63. Concealing wire runs to the fixtures takes ingenuity. Be careful not to place cable where it can be damaged by fasteners added later, and to avoid a short, be sure the power is off when working with low-voltage wiring.

DE-KOR

If the client wants to implement the design in stages, or has a track record of wanting changes, I load a transformer to 50 or 60 percent of its capacity, rather than 80 percent. Having the unused capacity means you can add fixtures and not overload the transformer. Sure, you could add another transformer later, but then you have to add more supply cable along the same path. It's a lot more efficient to plan ahead for change.

When you're designing the lighting layout, place the light fixtures symmetrically so if you add additional fixtures, it will still look good. For instance, place a fixture on every other post. If the client wants more light (and I usually encourage them to live with the layout for a week before we make changes), you can add fixtures so that every post has one.

When adding fixtures that require cutting an opening in a post or in the deck, I first mount a dummy block on the surface and run temporary wiring to give the client a preview. It gives the client a good idea of the effect of more fixtures and can be removed easily, leaving little damage.

Loops and Lollipops

The cable used for low-voltage deck lighting is the same two-wire cable used for landscape lighting, which is like lamp cord or zip cord, only heavier gauge, more

rugged, and able to handle sunlight exposure. As a rule of thumb, use 12-gauge cable for the supply lines unless the transformer is more than 50 feet from the first fixture; then use 10-gauge cable to minimize voltage drop.

If you're loading a circuit to the max, it's a good idea to run the supply cable in a loop that's fed from each end. Otherwise, the fixtures at the far end will be dim due to voltage drop.

Just be sure not to mix up the conductors of the supply line — opposite ends of each conductor have to attach to the same lug on the transformer (maintaining "polarity"). Mix them up and you'll short out the system, and the breaker will trip.

I've been called in to troubleshoot where the installer didn't understand polarity and had reset the breaker a dozen times. I guess he thought that one more reset would fix the problem. A circuit breaker generally is good for a few trips, but each trip stresses the mechanism. At some point, it just won't reset anymore.

Usually, one of the sides (conductors) in landscape cable has smooth insulation, and the other side has very fine longitudinal ribs in the plastic. This is one way to check polarity. Do not use the cable labeling for this purpose; the printing isn't always on the same side of the cable from spool to spool.

On decks requiring multiple circuits and transformers, using loops from the transformers to the more distant circuits can eat up a lot of cable. I often put just the closer fixtures on a loop circuit, as described above.

The more distant fixtures are also on a loop circuit, but the loop doesn't start and end at the transformer — it starts at and loops back to the fixture in that circuit closest to the transformer, and a single supply line then runs back to the transformer. Such circuits look like a lollipop. To minimize voltage drop, I get the power to the first fixture on a 10-gauge cable, and from there create a loop of 12-gauge cable in the area where the fixtures are located.

Lollipop circuits work great when the transformer is 75 feet to 100 feet from the first of a group of fixtures. This is also the right time for a transformer output greater than 12 volts.

Try the 13-volt tap first. Use a volt meter to measure the voltage at the farthest fixture. If it's between 11.5 volts and 12.5 volts, it's good. If it's lower than 11.5 volts, check it again using the 14-volt tap, and so on. If 15 volts at the transformer doesn't produce 11.5 volts at the distant fixture, have an electrician run a 120-volt line out closer to the group of fixtures and put a transformer there.

Connecting the Cable

You have to connect the supply cable to each fixture. The fixture wire or tap is usually 14- or 16-gauge wire. There are several ways to make these splices, but never use regular wire nuts. Corrosion will make the connection fail sooner rather than later.

The old-school way to make connections is to use silicone-filled wire connectors (**Figure 60**) designed for wet (direct burial) conditions (DryConn, King Innovation, www.kingsafety.com). These work fine, but you have to cut the supply cable at each tap, and you have to pay attention to polarity. Another approach is to use clip-on connectors (**Figure 61**) that pierce the insulation of the supply cable (Kichler Lighting, www.kichler.com).

Below the deck, the cable should be attached with electrical-cable staples (**Figure 62**). Above, it can be concealed inside holes drilled in the deck posts, run in molding, or hidden in routed grooves behind battens (**Figure 63**).

Cliff Popejoy is a licensed electrical contractor in Sacramento, Calif. He does both residential and commercial work on lighting and power, data communications, and photovoltaic systems.

Chapter 11: Maintenance & Repair

Maintenance and Restoration of Wood Decks

by Everett Abrams

With a small investment in equipment and some chemical know-how, you can breathe new life into aging decks, and expand your client base. The best customer, it's often said, is the one you already have. Build a relationship with a customer, and he'll have you back again and again. How can a deck specialist make that model work?

The answer is maintenance. When homeowners decide to add a deck to their home, they picture it freshly completed and looking brand new. But a deck is new only once. Every deck needs regular maintenance, and you should make a point of sharing this information with the homeowner.

Add deck cleaning and maintenance to your list of services, and a large number of those customers you've already established a relationship with are going to have you back annually to take care of what you've built (**Figure 1**). As a contractor, your investment in equipment will be minimal — a pressure washer (see "Choosing a Pressure Washer," page 337), a couple of garden sprayers, and some brushes.

You can also take on new customers who hire you to fix a poorly maintained deck. They might become your most loyal fans. That's because even the decks that have been cleaned and sealed regularly may look terrible if the work was done poorly. Some finishes actually feed mold and mildew, or attract dirt. Multiple layers of finish muddy the look of the

Breathe new life into old decks with a pressure washer and some basic chemical know-how.

wood. They've watched their deck go downhill despite their attempts at maintenance, and you do something no one else has done — make the deck look good again (**Figure 2**). That's what my company, Deck Restoration Plus, in Shamong, N.J., has been doing for more than 15 years.

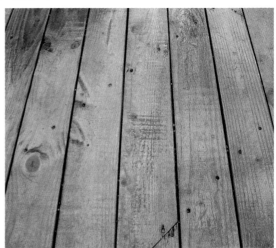

Figure 1. A few hours labor spread over two days restored this deck to nearly new condition (right). An initial rinse was followed with one application of stripper, and one of brightener. After a few trouble spots were sanded, the deck received a finish.

Figure 2. Cleaners make quick work of common finish problems such as the stains and mildew shown above. Items like potted plants, patio heaters, or grills leave stains. Mildew and fungi grow on damp wood, fed sometimes by linseed-oil–based finishes.

Poor Maintenance Is Nearly as Bad as None

The first and most costly mistake that many people make is to assume that all they need to do to clean a deck is grab a pressure washer and start blasting away. Pressurized water alone doesn't restore wood, it damages it. Too much pressure or unskilled use causes splintering, raised grain, lap marks, and severe etching (**Figure 3**). The remedies range from sanding the entire deck to replacing boards. If enough boards need replacing a complete "re-skin" may be in order (see "Rebuild the Deck or Just Re-Skin?" page 335).

A pressure washer has a role in deck cleaning, but it's not a solo performance. A good analogy is cleaning an oven. It would take forever and a day to scrub off the baked-on buildup with just water and elbow grease. But spray oven cleaner on the surface, give it time to work, and it's relatively easy to wipe off the surface to a like-new condition. This same principle applies to successful wood restoration. A cleaner lifts the buildup to make it easier to remove without damaging the surface underneath.

Getting the Grunge Off

Some wood decks simply need cleaning, but others need to be stripped of old finishes. If the existing finish is in good shape, and only a maintenance coat of finish is needed, use a deck cleaner and lightly wash. After the deck dries, apply the maintenance coat. Vertical surfaces might need this coat only every other time.

Figure 3. Be careful with the pressure washer. The cross-grain scars on this decking were caused by a pressure washer held too close to the wood.

Figure 4. If water beads up, there's an existing finish. If the finish is in bad shape, stripping is called for. If there's no surface finish — or the finish looks good — only a cleaning is needed.

Figure 5. Cleaning or stripping begins with wetting. For the chemicals to work, the deck must first be sprayed with water. In dry weather, it may be necessary to mist the deck several times while the stripper or cleaner is working.

Figure 6. Apply the chemicals with a garden sprayer. To verify correct application rates, compare the square footage of the deck, the amount of product you're using, and the manufacturer's suggested coverage.

Even if the existing finish looks bad, a wash might still be all that's needed. A "splash test" will tell you if there's an existing finish that needs to be stripped off. Throw some water on the wood's sur-face. If it soaks in, a cleaner is all that's needed. If the water beads up, you need to use a stripper (**Figure 4**, previous page).

My company uses cleaners containing either oxygenated bleach or sodium percarbonate. Chlorine-bleach cleaners can be effective, but they are harder to use properly. The wood stripper we use is sodium hydroxide based. A good professional stripper will melt off the existing coating or finish, making it easier to remove.

You use cleaners and strippers in the same way. Mix a concentrate with water in a pump-up garden sprayer. Remove loose material such as leaves from the deck, wet the deck down with a hose or a pressure washer (**Figure 5**), and spray on the cleaner or stripper (**Figure 6**). The manufacturers of strippers, cleaners, and for that matter, finishes, all provide coverage rates — how much product is needed for a given number of square feet. This is useful information when ordering the products, and it's also a way to tell if you're using enough. If the manufacturer says a gallon covers 400 sq. ft., but you just did that area with a half gallon, something's wrong.

Cleaners and strippers both need "dwell time" to work. The length of time varies with the temperature and humidity: longer in cold weather and shorter in hot weather. If it's too hot, however, the water evaporates and the chemical stops working. You may need

Deck Cleaning Safety

The chemicals used in deck cleaning can be strong enough to cause burns. Particularly when working with the concentrates, it's smart to wear eye protection and heavy-duty rubber gloves. Cleaners and strippers are slippery, and care should be exercised when walking on surfaces that are slick with them. Be sure the customer knows that they and their pets must stay off the deck when you're working.

Follow the manufacturer's directions for protecting plantings. Some recommend tarping plants and shrubs; you should at least wet them down with clean water before starting, and again after finishing.

Pressure washers present their own dangers. Water spraying from them can be at a high enough pressure to be injected under the skin. This is a medical emergency, and requires a visit to the ER. Never place any body part into the spray pattern of a pressure washer.

Rebuild the Deck or Just Re-Skin?

by Greg DiBernado

At least half of my deck projects are "re-skins," where worn-out wood decking, railings, and staircases are removed, but the existing joists are left intact to be used as a base for new (usually synthetic) decking and railing.

For obvious reasons, if the clients are willing to pay for a complete demo and rebuild, the deck will be better for it. But a re-skin can be a great lower-cost alternative, provided the existing framing is up to the task.

If the clients are satisfied with the design of their existing deck, a re-skin can get them a renewed look quickly. Plus, I'll often change the shape by clipping a corner, adding a new staircase, or extending the existing deck.

While I'm taking measurements on the sales appointment, I make a careful inspection, looking for obvious signs of rot, mildew, or decay on the deck surface. More often than not, if the deck boards have begun to rot, the framing beneath them is also rotted. Simple things like a leaky gutter or downspout in a shady corner of the deck can destroy an isolated section of an otherwise structurally sound deck.

If I can access the underside of the deck, I'll poke and prod to identify framing that needs to be replaced. I'll also note the cause of the rot and add the cost of remediating it to my proposal. If the root of the problem is not corrected, failure down the road is guaranteed

While I'm under there, I inspect the ledger to make sure it's flashed and fastened to the house properly; I make sure all joists have hangers and that any hangers present are in good condition; and I check for signs of rot between the layers of built-up girders. I also check built-up girders to ensure there's no separation between the 2x10s or 2x12s. If there is, I'll draw the layers together using TimberLok screws (FastenMaster, www.fastenmaster.com).

It's critical to have access under the deck to ascertain whether the framing is worth reusing. My rule of thumb is if the deck is too low for me to get underneath to inspect, the framing has to be demolished and rebuilt. Generally, the low-to-ground decks of yesteryear weren't built with airflow in mind. Most of such decks I've come across are examples of rot, mold, and decay. There's no point installing a modern synthetic decking product with

a 25-year warranty over a frame that's past its prime. Although my inspection is thorough, some issues may remain hidden until the decking and railings are removed. Therefore, I include a clause in my contract permitting me to replace framing members at a fixed cost as I deem necessary once I begin.

Another important consideration is how the existing decking is attached to the joists. If the decking is nailed down perpendicular to the joists, it can be pried up with little damage to the joists. Removing diagonally installed nailed decking is usually as harmless; it just takes a bit longer.

Screwed-down decking, though, can be difficult to remove – be warned. Unscrewing each fastener usually doesn't work because the heads strip. Prying up the boards may or may not be possible and usually damages the joists, anyway.

The fastest way to remove screwed down deck boards is to cut them on either side of the joists, letting the pieces of decking fall between the joists. The $1^{1}/_{2}$-inch-long pieces of decking remaining on the joists can be removed with a prybar, leaving the screws in place. The fastest way to remove the screws themselves is to cut them with a grinder equipped with a cut-off disk.

Most of the time, if a deck has screwed-down decking, I demo the entire deck. I cut the decking with a chainsaw run in between the joists; then I cut the joists, now with short pieces of decking attached to them, into manageable pieces to cart to the trash bin.

I always tear off existing staircases and rebuild them to my spec. I have never encountered a staircase I couldn't build stronger and safer. Besides the safety issues a wobbly or rotted staircase presents, most of the staircases I come across do not have the proper tread width to accommodate typical $5^{1}/_{2}$-inch synthetic deck boards, with a $^{1}/_{2}$-inch-thick riser and a 1-inch nosing.

I also make sure the old stairs landed on a solid surface such as a concrete slab or pavers. If the existing stairs land on the ground, I include the cost for installing a 4-inch-thick concrete pad for my new staircase to sit on.

Greg DiBernardo is a deck builder in Waldwick, N.J.

Figure 7. You can see that a stripper has begun to penetrate the old finish when the initial beads spread out to a sheen.

Figure 8. After the old finish has softened and lifted so it easily scrapes away (don't scrape caustic stripper with a fingernail!), a pressure washer sluices off the grime.

to mist down the area to keep the chemical active.

Strippers need a longer dwell time than cleaners to work effectively. You can tell when they've done their work in a couple of ways: Water no longer beads on the surface, and a very light test scrape will pull off the film (**Figure 7**).

Cleaning or stripping should leave a consistent look, with the deck being generally lighter in color. Dark spots could mean that some existing finish remains, and you may want to re-apply and wash again.

Solid body stains, which are more permanent and film-forming, may require several applications of stripper, and what remains will need to be sanded. They don't have to be recoated as often, but when they do, there's more work involved.

Figure 9. Use the right tip. The first two numbers on a pressure washer tip indicate the width of the spray fan. This one is 40 degrees, right for washing decks. The next three numbers are the flow, in this case 4.5 gpm. To avoid damaging the machine, always use tips with a greater flow capacity than the machine can provide.

Washing and Brightening

Once the stripper or cleaner has finished working, you need to rinse it — and the grime it has lifted — from the deck. If you've used the correct cleaner or stripper and dwell time, most wood can be rinsed using a garden hose. However, pressure washers will save a lot of time if used correctly — several hours on an average deck (**Figure 8**). A two-man crew might save four hours a day by using a pressure washer, enabling them to complete an extra deck each day.

A range of 300 to 1,000 pounds per square inch on a pressure washer is often all that is needed for wood surfaces. Use lower psi settings when working with softwoods like cedar, and slightly higher settings when working with hardwoods like mahogany. The idea is to avoid scarring the wood with the water pressure. Always use a wide fan spray. One way to reduce the pressure at the tip, while still maintaining a sufficient flow of water, is to use a tip with a higher flow rate. I use a tip that produces a 40-degree spray fan, and whose maximum flow exceeds that of the pressure washer (**Figure 9**).

If you encounter a difficult area, it's better to leave it to be sanded rather than increase pressure or get too close with the wand — either of these can scar or splinter the wood, and then you will need to sand anyway.

I use a pendulum or golf-stroke motion that allows the water to continually flow. Stopping and starting

Figure 10. After cleaning or stripping, the author always uses a deck brightener. Oxalic-acid based, it neutralizes the alkaline cleaner or stripper, lightens the wood, and removes metal stains. No rinse is required after the brightener, just 48 hours of drying.

the water flow on the wood will cause lap marks and etch the surfaces. Always work with the grain of the wood when cleaning, and keep the wand 6 inches or more away from the surface, depending on the psi rating. The wand needs to be only close enough to remove what the cleaner or stripper has lifted. Getting closer increases the likelihood of damage and will not get the project done any sooner. I don't adjust the psi at the machine, but rather move the wand farther or closer from the deck, as needed. Starting farther away and moving closer, rather than starting close and moving away, reduces the chance of damage.

After all the wood surfaces are clean comes another important step that is often skipped. This is surface neutralization or "brightening" of the wood (**Figure 10**). Cleaners and strippers are alkaline, or bases, and darken the wood. To make the wood appear as "like new" as possible, apply a brightener. The active ingredient in brighteners, oxalic acid, neutralizes the alkaline cleaner or stripper — important if you want the finish to adhere properly later, because alkalines remaining on the deck can react with the oil in finishes and saponify, or form soap, which prevents adhesion.

The brightener reacts with tannins in the wood to lighten it close to its natural tone. Oxalic-acid–based brighteners work quickly, so you can see any missed

areas right away. They also remove iron or metal stains caused by nail bleeds and such. After the brightener has been applied, it's allowed to dry for approximately 48 hours before coating, if needed. The brightener leaves the surfaces chemically neutral and rinsing is not necessary.

Before leaving the deck to dry, check for dark spots that need a second application of brightener. The better it looks prior to coating, the better it will look when complete. While this sounds like a lot of work, it goes quickly. A two-person crew can wash two to four decks on an average day, depending on the sizes of the decks. At about $1.25 per sq. ft. for a basic washing, there's good opportunity for income here.

Finishing Up

The more preparation you do, the better the deck will look when the finish is applied. It is important now to perform any sanding or address problem areas before applying a coating. Take a few minutes to inspect for areas that might need sanding. Look for any remaining stain or sealer, or any area with an inconsistent look. I have never done a deck that did not need some sanding, even if it was just a light touch-up on the handrails. In the very worst cases, you'll need to use a floor sander on the entire deck.

To avoid a blotchy look, it's important not to change the wood's surface characteristics much or close the pores in the wood. I sand with 80-grit sandpaper, and feather in around a sanded area so that

Choosing a Pressure Washer

For a deck builder adding deck maintenance to his services, I recommend a pressure washer that delivers at least 4 gallons per minute.

A 4-gpm machine works well with available attachments and that volume will get the job done in an efficient amount of time.

I don't recommend a particular brand as much as I recommend a belt-drive machine. These outlast direct-drive pressure washers.

Figure 11. Sanding is unavoidable. On a well-maintained deck, a light sanding prepares the rails for finish. Most decks will also have some flooring that requires sanding. To avoid creating spots that will become blotchy with the finish, feather the sanding around the trouble spot.

Figure 12. The slowest way is best. Most finishes can be sprayed, but the author gets the best results from China bristle brushes. For speed and a healthy back, get brushes with handles that can be removed and replaced with a broomstick.

any change in the way the wood absorbs the coating is gradual (**Figure 11**).

When the wood is fully prepared, it's time to apply a finish. Choosing one is a big decision, complicated by the range of products available. Some products are easier to maintain, while others last longer. There is no one best coating for all circumstances. You have to ask a lot of questions. Who is going to perform future maintenance? Does the owner want a color stain or clear coating? Will a water-based or an oil-based product be better? Where is the deck located?

Matching products to the answers to these questions is beyond the scope of this article. Talking to manufacturers and knowledgeable paint-store employees is a good starting place. Very generally, for hardwoods I recommend a parafinic or mineral-oil–based penetrating oil that is easy to maintain. Ready Seal (www.readyseal.com) is a good choice. I avoid film-forming oils on hardwoods, as they are prone to peeling because of the density and oil content of these woods.

Many products work well on soft woods like cedar and pressure-treated pine. You have to balance appearance and maintenance. Penetrating oil finishes tend to be easier to maintain and recoat, while film-

forming finishes tend to crack and peel, and are harder to maintain and recoat. Cabot (www.cabotstain.com) is a mainstay that's been rated very well by Consumer Reports magazine for many years. Another good product is Flood's Supreme Performance (www.flood.com).

You can apply all these products by sprayer, roller, lamb's wool mitts and pads, and brushes. In my experience, the most effective method is using a Bestt Stainer China bristle brush (www.besttliebco.com). It's soft and holds more product, so it's easier to apply stains and sealers (**Figure 12**). One worker should have no problem sealing or staining 100 square feet of decking an hour by brush and quicker if using a sprayer. I carry several sizes of them for doing deck boards and railings.

Most coatings will need approximately 24 hours to completely dry, and your customer has to commit to staying off the deck for the period.

Everett Abrams is president of Deck Restoration Plus, which offers both deck-cleaning services and franchises. He is also an instructor for the Power Washers of North America (www.pwna.org), and sits on the USDA Forest Products Laboratory's Joint Coatings/Forest Products Committee.

Repairing Cantilevered Balconies

by Angus Smith

My company specializes in condominium maintenance and repairs. In California, homeowners have up to 10 years to bring suit against the original builder for faulty workmanship. Condo associations are often awarded settlements for remedial projects that can run into the millions of dollars — work that is usually undertaken by companies much larger than mine.

We're most often hired by associations that have already passed the 10-year limit, which means that the work must be paid for out of a maintenance budget. Our most common job involves repairing water-damaged framing, especially in the cantilevered balconies that are so popular in multifamily buildings here. The jobs we tackle are awarded in quantities from 1 to 50 balconies at a time.

Anatomy of a Balcony

The typical condo balcony we encounter is framed with cantilevered joists that project about 6 feet from the face of the building, or from one-fourth to one-third of their overall length. The remainder of the joist is buried inside, an integral component of the interior floor system. A fractured or delaminated balcony surface (typically plywood, covered by one of several possible waterproofing systems) is usually the first tip-off to greater problems; all too often, the unseen damage is extensive and poses a hazard to the occupants (**Figure 13**). Stucco, a common exterior finish in this part of the world, can also conceal a multitude of problems. Although the surface sel-

dom reveals underlying rot, staining and discoloration should raise suspicions.

Water, water everywhere. We rarely encounter cantilevered joists with a deliberate, taper-sawn slope to drain water away from the structure, despite the minimum 1/4-inch-per-foot slope requirement specified by most waterproofing manufacturers. These flat decks permit water to pond on the surface, leading to premature failure of the waterproofing membrane. In addition, we often find poorly detailed or missing flashing at the balcony perimeter, which allows wind-driven water to enter the framing.

Railing systems are usually solid half walls rather than open assemblies, which makes for easy construction and provides privacy for the residents. It also prevents runoff from a balcony from dripping directly onto one below, but at a cost: The rainwater that falls onto each balcony must be collected and directed outside. This is usually handled by a floor drain or an open, floor-level scupper draining to a gutter. Either drainage method can lead to rot unless the spout that passes through the framing is properly installed and sealed (**Figure 14**, next page).

Inadequate flashing and finishing at railing post penetrations often allow water to run down into the framing cavity, making those common points of failure as well. We frequently find railings that are attached to the building without proper flashing, allowing water to become trapped against the wall. As the framing decays and the fasteners corrode, the railing provides little support, and the condition is often dangerously invisible.

Joist Repair

Repairing rotten joists is particularly difficult because we can't go inside to tear up the floor or open the ceiling over the occupant below. We've had to devise effective techniques for repairing damage and preventing future problems while working almost entirely outside.

Bolted sisters. The first order of business is to expose the bare joists by tearing off the railing, the plywood deck, and any soffit paneling underneath. In most cases, we find enough sound wood to permit repairing the joists, rather than replacing them. Rot is often concentrated in the outermost 6 inches of the joists and along the upper edges, where nail penetrations have allowed water in. We cut the damaged ends back to healthy wood and sister new, 6-foot-long joists of equal dimension alongside, using two carriage bolts at the center and two at each end to tie the joists solidly together. To make a neater-looking repair and provide

Figure 13. Surface cracks in a balcony's waterproofing are often the first sign of hidden structural damage. Cracks typically appear above joints in the plywood deck sheathing.

Figure 14. Improperly flashed scuppers (left) and floor drains (right) often allow water into the framing, leading to hidden rot.

Figure 15. To eliminate puddling, the author rips a ¼-inch-per-foot taper from the top edge of the cantilevered joists, creating a positive drainage slope. A power planer cleans up the cut.

Figure 16. Joists that are too far gone to repair must be replaced between the wall plate and the new double rim joist (far left). The rim hangs at the ends of the intact cantilevered joists on upside-down joist hangers. The replaced "cripple joists" are hung conventionally (left).

full nailing for the deck sheathing and trim, we fill in the end cuts with blocks of lumber.

Any top-edge rot gets ripped away to undamaged wood and replaced with a new ripping, which we simply gun-nail into place. We treat all cuts with a termite and rot repellent, Jasco Termin-8 (Jasco Chemical Corp, www.jasco-help.com), a green, oil-based copper-naphthenate solution that helps prevent future infestation. If the original joists didn't incorporate a drainage slope, we'll rip a full-length, 1/4-inch-per-foot taper on the top edge, cleaning up the cuts afterward with a power plane (**Figure 15**).

Shifting the load. Joists that are too far gone to repair must be replaced. With no practical way to insert a new cantilever, this can pose a real problem if the rot is extensive. Fortunately, we usually find that only one or two of the original joists are rotted to the point of being unusable. In such cases, we rely on the remaining members for structural support by installing a new, double rim joist at the outboard edge and tying it to each solid joist with an upside-down joist hanger (**Figure 16**).

This beefed-up rim hangs from the sound joists, providing outboard support to the few joists that must be completely replaced. The inboard ends of the replaced joists rest on the wall plate, while the outboard ends are supported by conventionally installed joist hangers at the rim — an approach that shifts the load from these replaced "cripple joists" to the repaired and sistered joists through the rim.

I gleaned this detail from a structural engineer many years ago, and it has proved to be reliable in practice. But obviously, it demands common sense and good judgment. If more than two in ten joists must be replaced, I'll consult an engineer. That also applies to another situation we sometimes encounter, where the damaged cantilever framing consists of a heavy beam at either end of the balcony with perpendicular infill joists running between them. In either case, it will usually be necessary to tear up the floor inside or post the balcony to the ground, but that's another story.

Buttoning Up

Once the joists are repaired, we apply a 3/4-inch T&G plywood deck, glued and screwed to the joists, to help create a strong, unified structure. It's important to observe the prescribed 1/8-inch spacing between plywood sheets; otherwise, this is the area where a waterproofing membrane will first show signs of stress.

In replicating the original closed or open railing system, we pay strict attention to the sequence and detailing of the flashing. (Incredibly, we often find that the original flashing was mindlessly installed to trap rather than shed water.) Where the railing abuts the building, we break back the stucco or siding and weave Moistop flashing (Fortifiber, www.fortifiber.com) a polyethylene-fiberglass composite membrane, behind the existing building paper to protect all framing transitions from water penetration. The top of the railing gets a sheet-metal cap flashing, followed by Moistop, woven behind the existing building paper.

California condo framing typically has no sheathing over the wall studs, except where a shear panel is required. Instead, stucco lath is applied directly to the studs over 60-minute building paper. To make sure that the transition from deck to side wall is watertight, we break the stucco (or other siding) back about 6 inches up the wall and run a 9-inch-wide Moistop strip over the side-wall framing, behind the original building paper and over the flange of the 26-gauge bonderized, galvanized sheet-metal (C&J Metal Products, www.cjmetals.com) transition flashing that runs onto the deck surface (**Figure 17**).

Figure 17. Flexible membrane flashing, tucked behind existing building paper and overlapping a sheet-metal skirt flashing, provides positive wall drainage onto the new balcony surface.

Figure 18. Galvanized expanded metal lath, thoroughly stapled to the plywood deck, reinforces the cementitious waterproofing membrane. Plywood expansion joints are isolated and protected from filling by a proprietary seam tape.

Figure 19. Stucco siding repairs follow the original three-layer process of scratch coat, brown coat, and color coat. A narrow strip of the sheet-metal flashing is left exposed to allow crack-free movement between wall and deck.

Waterproofing

To prevent future problems in the repaired balcony, proper waterproofing is essential. I rely on Life Deck AL (Life Deck Specialty Coatings, www.lifedeck.com), a reinforced three-coat cementitious product made for exterior plywood walking surfaces. We handle the installation ourselves, paying close attention to the manufacturer's specifications.

First, we install bonderized sheet-metal wall flashing and drip-edge, nailing it directly to the plywood and sealing overlaps with an approved polyurethane caulk. To prevent the expansion joints between plywood sheets from filling up, we cover them with self-adhesive, 40-mil-thick Life Deck Seam Tape. Then we install a layer of galvanized expanded metal lath over the plywood and flashing and thoroughly fasten it with a pneumatic stapler, using at least 16 staples per square foot (**Figure 18**). The base coat — a thick, soupy mix of cement and acrylic polymer — is poured on and troweled into the lath. After the base coat cures, we trowel on a similar, slurry layer to build up the membrane and fill any voids. The third, texture-coat layer is splattered

Figure 20. A final, acrylic color coat seals and protects the multilayered deck system from water absorption.

on using a hopper-fed texture gun, at about a 70% coverage rate, and knocked down with a steel trowel while wet.

Once the texture coat can be walked on, we complete the patching of the stucco siding, following the original steps of 60-minute building paper, stucco lath (wire), scratch coat, brown coat, and a color and texture coat (**Figure 19**). Usually, we're patching small areas, so we use a quick-drying mortar mix to help expedite the job. We take the stucco down over the apron flashing but not all the way to the deck,

leaving a narrow band of metal exposed. This allows for some necessary structural movement and eliminates cracking at the junctions.

A proprietary acrylic color coat seals and completes the deck surface treatment (**Figure 20**). The deck can be walked on within about 4 hours, but it's best to wait 24 hours before putting the surface to regular use.

Angus Smith owns Angus Smith Construction in Aliso Viejo, Calif.

Porch Repair From the Bottom Up

by Peter and Maureen Nicolazzi

The porch looked well-maintained, spruced up with yearly paint jobs. The owners just wanted us to check out a minor problem — a broken decorative bracket. We soon discovered, however, that everything above eye level was held up mostly by the trim, and everything below our feet was on the verge of collapsing.

Naively, the owners had hired people to do a yearly camouflage job to cover up water stains on the porch ceiling and floor. They also hired a guy to come out every six months and jack the porch roof back up. No one had told them the porch had major problems. On a large porch like this, you can't repair just one or two places. You have to work on it "from the bottom up."

Where to Start

The first thing we did on this job was to inspect the entire porch — footings and piers, posts, beams, joists, flooring, railings and columns, cornice, and roof. We sketched out the areas that needed attention, a step we feel is absolutely essential in repair work.

In this type of work, you learn to recognize little clues. For instance, if we see a brown stained area on the porch ceiling, we know water penetration may have damaged the structure. If we see little pellets trapped in spider webs under the porch floor, we're clued in to the possibility of termite damage. Above all, this first inspection has got to be thorough. You don't want to miss termite damage, carpenter ants, structural weakness, nonexistent footings, rotten wood, gutters pitched the wrong way, mortar failure, or a host of other problems — especially if you're bidding the job at a fixed price.

Start by digging down to the footings. Make sure all the footings lie below frost line. Examine the foot-

ings and piers with an awl or pocket knife. If concrete, are they solid? If they're crumbling or severely cracked, they'll need to be replaced (**Figure 21**). On this job we found every kind of footing imaginable. The most common footing was, simply, six unmortared bricks, stacked criss-cross, a foot below ground. We also found cinderblock props, crumbling concrete, and wood blocks.

Next, you inspect posts and beams to see if they're structurally sound. Check for sagging, cracked, or rotten timbers. When you walk on the porch does the floor feel springy beneath your feet? Measure the size and spacing of framing materials. Are they adequate for the span? Older buildings sometimes used smaller-dimension lumber with a greater spacing than the code allows today. If you have to repair the substructure anyway, you might as well replace it

Figure 21. Dig down and you'll often find surprises at footing level. This concrete footing, cracked apart, is resting on the original hunk of limestone.

Figure 22.
Columns wrapped in 1x stock can conceal hidden damage. Take the columns apart very carefully because much of the material can be reused.

top. The minimum recommended pitch for a porch floor is ¼ inch per foot. We checked the porch with a level; in some places the porch dropped 2 inches per foot in the proper direction; in others, it sloped the other way, with water running onto the porch.

Inspect the columns and balustrade. With solid columns, you'll have to make sure the lumber is structurally sound by poking the column base with a scratch awl. We had boxed columns, so we opened them up to check the internal structural member (**Figure 22**). These were supposed to be supporting the roof structure. Instead we found that the built-in gutters above had rusted through, turning the top of each column into a funnel. Water had funneled from the roof into the entire lower structure and caused extensive damage.

We also made another appalling discovery. When we took apart the columns of the original porch (the front section), we looked up into the chamber at the top of the columns expecting to find a beam. There wasn't one. We could see 2x4 rafters, 24 inches on-center, with a 17-foot span. The rafters were toe-nailed to the wall. They'd been nailed with 20-pennies, but the nails had pulled all the way out. Sitting on top of this flimsy platform was a scabbed-on roof. We had planned to take the roof down anyway, but the discovery of the undersized rafters and the missing structural member caused us to approach demolition with extra caution.

Our first indication of the roof's structural damage

with framing that meets code. Otherwise, if the substructure is generally sound, you can divide the load by placing a new beam in the middle of the span.

Where rain or snow hit the edge of the porch flooring, you'll often find water damage, especially if the water doesn't drain off quickly. On this job we found extensive damage in a 2-foot ring around each column. This was our first clue that water damage was related to column construction. The porch floor looked worse from the underside than it did from the

Patching With Epoxy

Epoxy is expensive, so it's best to use it sparingly. And, you may not be able to find the material in your local hardware store. This means you have to figure out about how much epoxy you'll need, and order in plenty of time for mail-order delivery.

Epoxy repairs are done in two stages. First, we use a very liquid epoxy, called a consolidant. Drill tiny holes through the rotten wood. Mix two parts of the consolidant epoxy according to manufacturers' instructions. Mix very small batches. We use a foam coffee cup for mixing and to apply the stuff. When you put the two parts together, the epoxy generates a lot of heat. (Watch out for coffee cup melt-down, which can occur if you try to mix too much at one time.) Squeeze the coffee cup and dribble the epoxy into the tiny holes.

An empty, squeezable mustard bottle with a tapered top will work too. Load the epoxy from the mixing cup into the squeeze bottle; then inject the epoxy into the holes. Make sure you have epoxy solvent on the job. (Get this from the manufacturer when you order your supply.)

Otherwise, the bottle clogs up quickly and you won't be able to use it more than once. The consolidant hardens as it dries, turning the wood into essentially "petrified wood." The wood absolutely will not absorb moisture once it has been consolidated. This works great for solid column bottoms, normally made of end-grain wood, which soaks up water like a sponge.

The next step is to fill the wood with epoxy filler. Usually the manufacturer gives you a waiting period for this step — between 6 and 24 hours. We normally use Abatron epoxies because they're close to our location in the Midwest and we're used to working with their materials (Abatron, www.abatron.com). Abatron also has distributors around the country and sells online as well.

You mix up an epoxy filler that looks like wood dough and apply the filler to the rotten areas you've just consolidated. The filler bonds to the consolidant. When the filler dries, sand it with ordinary sandpaper. If some areas still need to be filled, you can build up a thick coat of this filler and shape it with a rasp. — *P.N. and M.N.*

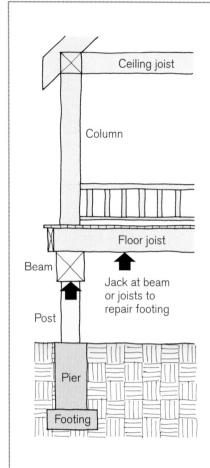

Figure 23. Arrange jacks on either side of posts or columns to carry the loads during repair. Note the relationship between the beam atop the column, the column, and the beam below the column. This is the straight path the loads will follow.

Figure 24. Jacks support the floor joists while a beam is being repaired. Make sure the jacks sit on a solid base (inset).

had been peeling paint around the tops of the columns. Peeling paint indicates the presence of moisture, especially when the wood beneath the paint is stained and discolored. Left unchecked, the moisture promotes rot. If the roof is leaking, spread tarps over the roof and allow the wood to dry before you start repairs on either the substructure or the roof. A lot more becomes evident when wood dries. You can thump dry wood and tell if it's damaged. Sometimes a piece will surprise you. It may look water stained, but when it dries out, it's fine.

Start at the Bottom

After the initial assessment, we plan how to repair each of the problems we've identified. We always start at the lowest point of deterioration.

Footings and piers. You can't do structural work until you have good footings beneath the structure. Brick or block footings and piers can be repaired by repointing if the masonry is in good shape. If the piers are exposed and an important design element of the porch, find a mason who can mix mortar to match the old. Wide Brixment joints will spoil the appearance of a repair job. If you need to replace piers, concrete footings and piers (if historically acceptable) would be our first choice. Replacement

requires jacking and temporary supports. If the beam above the posts is solid, you can set jacks under the beam (**Figure 23**). If the beam is not solid, jack under the floor joists (**Figure 24**). Jacking under the floor joists will also let you replace the beams as needed.

We used 22-ton hydraulic jacks because we didn't have much working room under the porch. (The long handle of a screw jack won't work in tight spaces.) Hydraulic jacks are easy to move around, but you can't trust them completely, so we always shore with a solid post to solid blocking. We use 4x4, 6x6, or 8x8 jack posts with a ¼-inch steel plate (the same size as the post) on top of the jack. The steel keeps the jack from driving into the end grain. We place the jacks on cribbing so we don't drive them into the ground. Before raising the structure, we take benchmark measurements at the points we are jacking. We measure the distance from the floor to the ceiling and the floor to the soffit, because we want to see if the whole thing is moving up as we jack. If the column and header are crushing as we're jacking, we stop and rearrange the set-up. Sometimes we need to go out to the yard and jack the roof. In that case we build an A-frame brace to support the roof load. We may jack against 4x4s placed against the rafter seats.

After we've made sure the jacking setup is working, we jack the beams or joists just slightly — enough to

Figure 25. New posts are in place. The post-anchors will reduce future water damage.

Figure 26. The thermos jug marks the spot where new tongue-and-groove porch flooring begins. Douglas fir flooring to match the old is still available.

relieve weights from the posts. Then we remove the existing posts, which are often rotten. If we can salvage them, we mark their position for re-use. If more than one jack is being used, we jack equally to distribute the load evenly among the jacks.

Once we have the posts out and the structure supported, we dig below frost line and pour new footings and piers to 8 inches above grade. Anchor bolts should be centered in piers to accept metal post brackets centered on the piers. On this job we eventually dug 32 new footings by hand and poured concrete with buckets. We only had 2 to 4 feet of head room, so this part of the job was literally a pain in the neck. The structural work below the porch floor would eventually be hidden by a lattice screen.

Posts and beams. We take out any beams that need to be replaced while the structure is jacked. When we put in the new beams, we cut the spans from 20 feet to 10 feet by adding extra beams. I prefer to use Douglas fir instead of pressure-treated lumber. Even though this porch is outside, it is protected by the roof, and the substructure will be protected by the painted porch floor. Rot shouldn't be a problem because the space is so well ventilated.

Once we're ready to set new posts, we lower the jacks until the porch has the proper pitch. Next, we measure the distance between the beam and the pier or post-bracket and cut the post to size. We install it

by raising the jack enough to slip in the post. After we plumb the post, we remove the jack (**Figure 25**).

Floor joists. We sistered all broken, stressed, or inadequate floor joists, and replaced all those that had rot or termite damage. We also had to add joists in between the existing 2x6s to beef up the structure. The owners use this as an outdoor room all summer long, so it needed to support a full load of people.

Floor. We replaced sections of the tongue-and-groove flooring with Douglas fir porch flooring (**Figure 26**). We prime the new floor boards before they go in — edges too.

Columns and railings. The columns are both structural and ornamental. They are generally worth repairing due to the high cost of replacement. We repair with epoxy or with wood patches to avoid the headache of duplicating the original pieces.

We didn't need to on this job, but occasionally we remove the columns for repair. To do this, you need to jack against the roof beam. It's best to remove any finish material and jack directly against the beam.

You don't need to raise the roof structure a lot; 1/8 inch will do. If the substructure is completed, you can jack from it. Make sure you support the roof load securely on braces before you remove the columns. Use a jigsaw or hacksaw blade to cut through the nails at the top and bottom of the columns.

There are three ways to repair columns. First, if the

column is not solid (the middle may be made of 2xs nailed together), simply replace the core with new pressure-treated lumber. You may need to rip down 2x6s or 2x8s to get the same nominal dimension as the original columns. Make up new column interiors by nailing this lumber together. Then repair the column casing with wood patches or epoxy as described below. When you reinstall the column interiors, it's best to seat them in metal post brackets. The post bracket will allow water to evaporate from the bottom of the column and prevent future deterioration.

The second repair technique uses traditional "scarf" patches. For solid columns, you may find that part of the base is completely rotten, while the rest of the column is in good shape. You should use the same type of wood as the column for repair or you'll get two woods that expand and contract at different rates. You'll soon have a joint or crack appearing. Common woods used for solid columns are pine, Douglas fir, and cypress.

First, cut out the rotten area carefully and square the corners. Use a rasp to take down high spots. Cut your new materials so it is a tight fit. Don't worry about the top surface. You can take that down with a chisel, rasp, or plane later on. Make sure the grain runs the same way, or you may have problems planing. Don't rely on carpenters glue and caulk to hide poor craftsmanship; use a good epoxy to secure the patch.

A third technique we use to repair rotten column bottoms or decorative railings is epoxy repair. Epoxy repairs and wood patches can be used on the same job. Both can be primed and painted with regular paint. I've been repairing exterior wood this way for many years, and I've never had a problem. Good paint prep and application are paramount. The extra effort put into a proper paint job will pay off in the long run. Don't leave the epoxy exposed to sunlight once it cures because the epoxy degrades.

Railings should be repaired or replaced as needed in the same manner. After you scrape off loose paint, you will see rotten wood. Remove or flake out rot from areas and allow the wood to dry. Fill with epoxy and prep for paint. Turned balusters with square ends beyond repair can also be saved. Cut the baluster where the turning ends and the square begins. Dowel and glue a new block of the same size to the turned end.

Ceiling. The ceiling needs to be scraped thoroughly and prepped for paint. You'll see where the problems are after you finish scraping. Falling or sagging ceiling boards or flaking paint point to a problem with the roof. Repairs to the ceiling are similar to those for the floor, because it too usually has tongue-and-groove material. You can still get "porch beading" at many lumberyards. Another option is beaded plywood that simulates tongue-and-groove paneling.

Cornices. Repairs to cornices and related moldings should be handled in much the same way as discussed previously. Paint builds up on moldings but a thorough scraping brings out the detail.

Any moldings to be replaced should be matched to that existing. To replicate a molding, we begin with a clean stripped sample to get an accurate profile. If you can't match it at your local lumberyard, you may need to go to catalogs or to a millwork shop. If you have a very small amount of molding to duplicate, you may be able to buy something close and shape it with a hand plane to conform. For small pieces, we use antique planes. For larger pieces, we use an old molding machine. It's the size of a table saw, and we can move it from job to job. We get a quick turnaround on our cutters by ordering from an independent supplier. A shaper with molding cutters will work as well.

We have touched on the basics of porch repair from bottom to top and tried to represent common problems and solutions to repair. As preservationists, we strive to repair when possible and to replace in kind with matching material and craftsmanship when necessary.

Maureen and Peter Nicolazzi run Carpenter & Smith Restorations (www.saveold.com), near Burlington, Wis.

Replacing Rotted Wood Columns

by John Leeke

You'd expect to see rotting wood in the bases of columns that are centuries old. But I was on a project in Chattanooga, Tenn., where I had to replace wood columns that were only 27 years old. Decay had started to show up only 12 years after construction. Faulty installation caused the column bases to rot prematurely.

You can slap columns in place and forget about them. But sooner or later — probably sooner — you'll be reminded that a little more care with installation would have saved lots of trouble. Here are a few of the techniques I've developed for installing wood columns that will last. These methods are good for hollow columns up to about 15 feet tall (**Figure 27**).

Preparation

Repair the porch deck and pedestal structure as well as the entablature above the porch. Then you're ready for final column installation. Keep the new or restored columns in a cool, dry place until they are installed.

The two keys to effective column installation are ventilation and even loading. Proper ventilation reduces moisture buildup — the cause of decay. Leveling the base and scribing the shaft assure even loading.

Leveling Base and Plinth

To begin installation, set the plinth in its approximate position, and see if it is level. Most porch decks

Column Elements

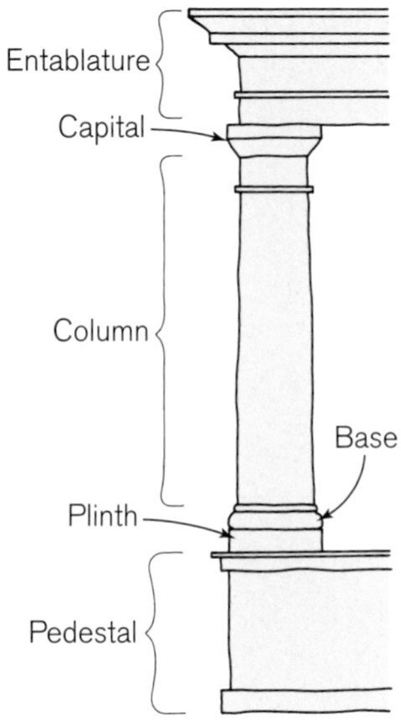

Figure 27.
Proper installation of wood columns begins with knowing the different parts of a column.

Entablature
Capital
Column
Base
Plinth
Pedestal

Level Base

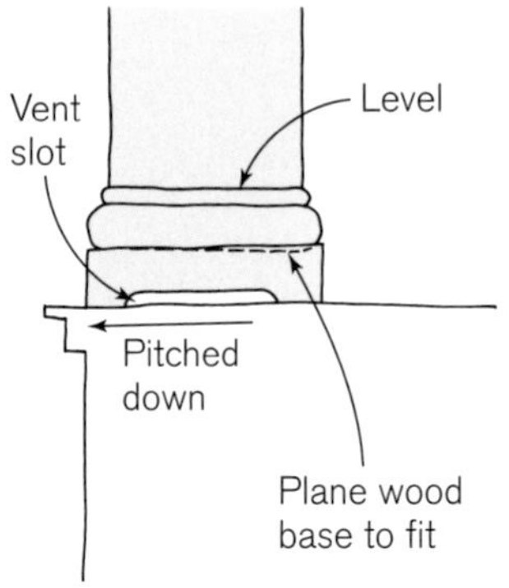

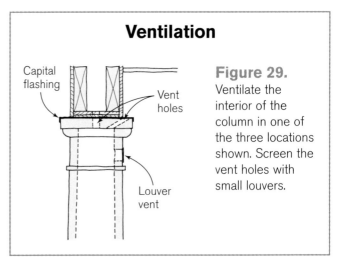

Figure 28.
Leveling the base of the column ensures that loads from the roof will be evenly distributed. Otherwise, one side of the column could be carrying most of the weight.

Vent slot
Level
Pitched down
Plane wood base to fit

Ventilation

Figure 29.
Ventilate the interior of the column in one of the three locations shown. Screen the vent holes with small louvers.

Capital flashing
Vent holes
Louver vent

slope away from the house for drainage. To make a level surface for the shaft to stand on, you must plane away part of the plinth or round base. I usually plane off the bottom side of the round base, which is less noticeable than reshaping the plinth (**Figure 28**). Never carve out a depression on the top of the base or plinth; the depression will collect water. Use a plane rather than a chisel to ensure flatness.

When the base is approximately level, cut the shaft roughly to length by trimming it at the top. The length should be one inch less than the distance from the base to the bottom of the entablature. Set the shaft in place on the base.

Even loading of the shaft around its perimeter is very important. If the shaft rocks back and forth, the base or plinth surfaces are not flat and should be trued. Trim the base until the shaft does not rock and points to its final position on the entablature above.

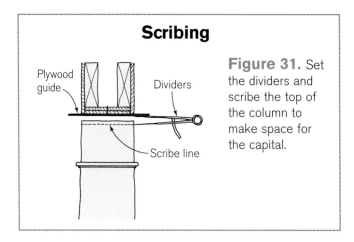

Load Transfer

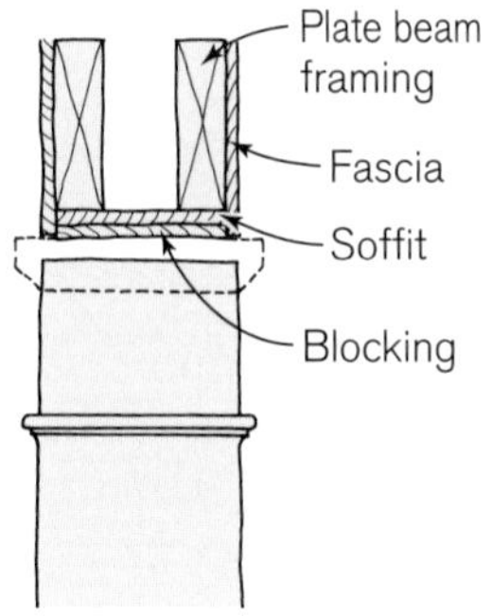

- Plate beam framing
- Fascia
- Soffit
- Blocking

Figure 30. Blocking is used to improve load transfer between the roof and the capital.

Scribing

- Plywood guide
- Dividers
- Scribe line

Figure 31. Set the dividers and scribe the top of the column to make space for the capital.

Ventilation

Ventilation from the bottom of the column to the top is very important. Without ventilation, columns rot.

Venting at the bottom is fairly straightforward. Correctly designed plinths and bases have hollow interiors. Cast aluminum plinths come with slots on all four bottom edges. You may have to cut grooves in the bottoms of wood plinths yourself.

Venting the top is more difficult. Vent straight up through the capital and soffit if the interior of the entablature is hollow and well vented. It usually isn't, but there are two alternatives. Drill a hole from the middle of the bottom of the capital through to the top, where it is protected from the weather inside the porch. Or, drill holes in the neck of the shaft on the side facing the house. This method does not look as good, but it does not interrupt the flashing over the capital. Vent holes should be screened or filled with small round louvers (**Figure 29**).

Scribing the Shaft

Scribing the shaft is a five-step process. Using this procedure assures even loading at the top of the shaft. For this example I'll assume the entablature is held 1/8 inch above its final position with temporary supports, and the capital is 2 inches thick.

First, fill the slightly recessed space at the soffit with solid wood blocking. This transfers the load from above directly to the capital and keeps the edge of the fascia boards from being crushed (**Figure 30**).

Next, screw a truly flat piece of 3/4-inch plywood to the bottom of the blocking, and set the shaft in position on top of the base and plinth.

Then, holding one leg of the dividers against the plywood, scribe a line on the neck of the shaft with dividers (**Figure 31**). Set the dividers to the thickness of the capital, plus the thickness of the plywood, plus the distance the entablature is above its final position (1 3/8 inches in this example).

Mark the relative position of the shaft, base, plinth,

and deck with reference marks. Later on, this will help you position them.

Finally, take the shaft down and cut off the neck to the scribed line. Remember there is a limit to how much the shaft can be cut off without spoiling the proportions of the column.

Flashing

The next step is to raise the column and fit the capital in place. Before doing that, you must fashion a flashing to fit over the top of the capital.

Flash capitals with copper or lead-coated copper turned down over all four edges. Don't skip this part of the work because you think copper is too expensive. The relatively small amount of metal needed doesn't cost much. I have replaced columns, at a cost of several hundred dollars each, that could have been saved if the contractor had used a few dollars worth of copper flashing in the beginning.

Earlier in the sequence, you would have flashed the bottoms of columns. Flash the bottoms of shafts, bases, or plinths resting directly on masonry with lead plates 1/4- to 3/4-inch thick. Leave gaps between the plates for ventilation slots. Space the gaps so staves are fully supported at the joints. Cut the plates slightly larger than you need, and trim them with the shaft using a woodworking gouge or chisel when installation is complete.

Painting

The main purpose of exterior paint is to prevent water from penetrating the wood. However, paint also functions as an important path for water vapor to escape from the interior of the column.

Heavy paint build-up blocks vapor from escaping and should be removed if you are reusing the original columns. This is not a popular recommendation. But, it is especially important if the paint is cracked or already peeling down to bare wood. Peeling paint may mean moisture levels in the wood are too high.

Water vapor passes more or less easily through

different types of paint. Latex paint lets vapor pass freely. Alkyd-resin paints are less permeable to moisture.

Humidity levels vary throughout the country. Columns in the South, where humidity levels are high, need a very permeable coating to allow the vapor to move out of the column. In areas with high humidity, use a latex primer with two topcoats of latex.

Areas like New England have only moderate humidity. Columns here can get adequate vapor transmission with latex paint or alkyd-resin paint specially formulated to have low permeability. Use a latex or breathable alkyd primer with two latex topcoats in areas like New England.

With careful paint selection in the beginning, you can reduce maintenance and add years to the life of your columns. The best restoration is prevention.

John Leeke, of Portland, Maine, restores and maintains historic buildings. He also consults with contractors, architects, and owners working on older structures.

Chapter 12:
Masonry Decks & Patios

- **Building a Slate-Tile Deck**
- **Paving a Deck With Stone**
- **Dry-Laying a Flagstone Terrace**
- **Brick-Paver Basics**
- **Exposed Aggregate Concrete**

Building a Slate-Tile Deck

by Cameron Habel

L ast year I got a call from a client who wanted to create more outdoor living space by building a deck along the back of her house over a part of the yard that was too steep to use. She said she wanted to use Trex, so I was picturing a conventional deck and guardrail. But when I stopped by her house — which was located in the hills above Oakland, Calif. — to look at the job, it became apparent that a conventional design was not going to work.

For one thing, the house had spectacular views of the bay and of San Francisco — views that a wood-picket guardrail would block. Therefore, I suggested using a glass or cable rail system.

Also, one end of the deck would lap onto an existing salt-finish concrete patio; in passing, the owner mentioned that she didn't like the surface of the patio and wondered if it would be possible to cover it with the same composite material we used on the deck. I suggested covering the patio with stone tile instead, and when she said she liked that idea I proposed putting the same material on the deck, too; that way, the two surfaces would match.

By the end of our meeting, the client had agreed to have my company cover the existing patio with slate tile and build a slate-covered wood-framed deck with a glass guardrail system. The deck would be accessed from the patio, the existing kitchen door, and new French doors in the dining room wall.

Deck Structure

I would have preferred to build a freestanding deck and avoid having to deal with a ledger, but there was fill along the foundation so we couldn't have installed piers there without digging deep holes. Normally we only have to excavate to undisturbed soil, because in this area the temperature almost never drops below freezing.

Our plan was to use a 4-by beam for the ledger, connect a portion of it to the house, and pick up the other end with a post on a concrete pier just beyond the end of the building. The framing at the other edges would land on posts, concrete piers, or the existing concrete patio (**Figure 1**).

Concrete piers. There were seven piers in all, each 2 feet square and about 15 inches thick, and each reinforced with four pieces of #4 rebar. Before placing the concrete, we positioned Simpson CB44HDG (hot-dip galvanized) column bases in the piers to hold the 4x4 posts. Since we were framing the deck with pressure-treated Douglas fir (ACQ) and the new chemicals are

Strong framing and a crack-isolation membrane reduce the chances of cracking.

so corrosive, we made sure all the metal connectors were hot-dip galvanized or approved for use with ACQ.

Slope. Most decks slope away from the house so that water will drain off the outboard edge. But in this case the continuous glass rail presented a barrier, so we sloped the deck toward the house and allowed it to drain through a ¾-inch space between the deck and wall. We installed a gutter below the deck to catch this water and direct it away from the foundation (**Figure 2**, page 354).

The slope presented a challenge because the structural glass-rail system needed to be in continuous contact with the perimeter beams. Sloping the end beam would have meant sloping the rail (which would look bad) or complicating the installation by requiring the glazing contractor to taper some of the

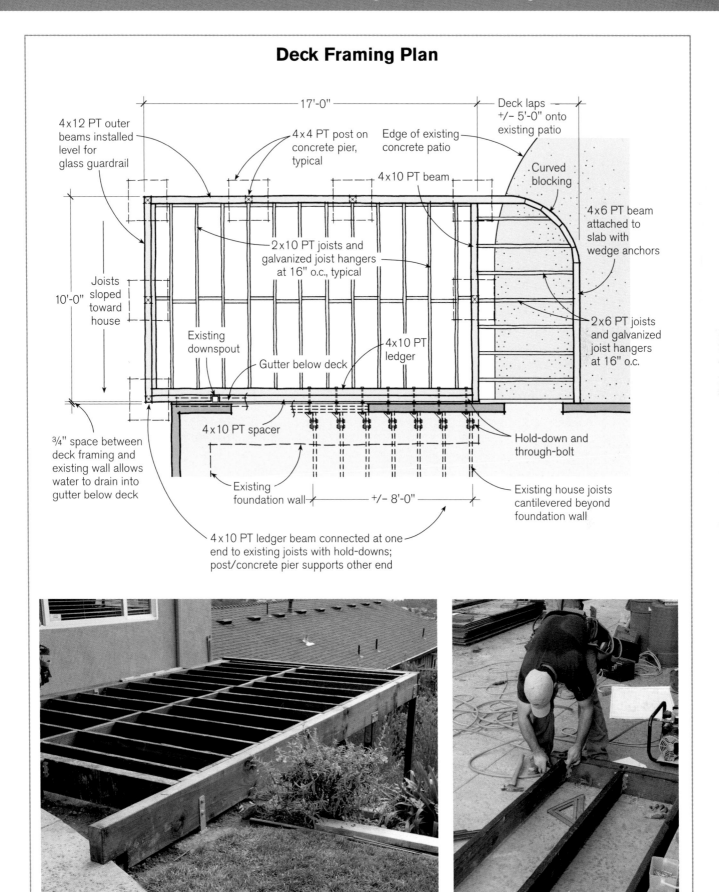

Deck Framing Plan

4x12 PT outer beams installed level for glass guardrail

4x4 PT post on concrete pier, typical

Edge of existing concrete patio

Deck laps +/- 5'-0" onto existing patio

Curved blocking

4x10 PT beam

4x6 PT beam attached to slab with wedge anchors

2x10 PT joists and galvanized joist hangers at 16" o.c., typical

17'-0"

10'-0"

Joists sloped toward house

2x6 PT joists and galvanized joist hangers at 16" o.c.

Existing downspout

Gutter below deck

4x10 PT ledger

¾" space between deck framing and existing wall allows water to drain into gutter below deck

4x10 PT spacer

Existing foundation wall

+/- 8'-0"

Hold-down and through-bolt

Existing house joists cantilevered beyond foundation wall

4x10 PT ledger beam connected at one end to existing joists with hold-downs; post/concrete pier supports other end

Figure 1. The joists run between a 4x10 ledger beam and a 4x12 outer beam carried by posts on concrete piers (left photo). One end of the deck laps about 5 feet onto an existing concrete patio (right photo and illustration above).

Figure 2. Since a continuous glass handrail will prevent water from draining off the outer edge of the deck, the author sloped the joists toward the house (left) and used stacks of 3-inch-square washers to space the ledger beam off the wall (center). Water drains through this space and is collected by a gutter below the deck (right).

glass panels. To avoid those scenarios, we installed the end beam level and allowed the joists to drop down from it at the end closest to the house. This created a small step at the bottom of one of the rails, which we later trimmed with strips of slate.

Framing Details

Since we wanted to retain an existing downspout from the roof, we blocked the 4x10 ledger beam an extra 3½ inches off the wall to allow the downspout to pass through. We used LedgerLok screws (FastenMaster, www.fastenmaster.com) to attach two lengths of 4x10 to the back of the ledger, leaving a gap for the downspout.

Wall connection detail. The usual way to fasten a deck ledger is to bolt it to the rim joist of the house. But on this house the joists cantilevered a short distance beyond the foundation wall so that we couldn't fasten to the rim, which was supported only by nails. Instead, we used Simpson HD2A hold-down hardware to attach the ledger to the floor joists beyond the rim — a connection detail similar to one an engineer had specified on an addition I'd built.

To gain access to the joists, we cut an opening through the stucco on the bottom side of the overhang; later we covered this opening with an access panel so that the connection could be inspected and maintained.

We staggered the bolts high and low through the

beam and connected it at seven locations. Each hold-down was through-bolted to a joist and tied to the beam with ⅝-inch galvanized threaded rod (**Figure 3**).

To prevent leaks, we filled the holes through the stucco and the rim with Sikaflex-1a sealant (Sika Corp., www.sikaconstruction.com) before installing the rod. And to provide drainage we spaced the deck about ¾ inch off the building by placing stacks of square 3-inch galvanized washers over the rods between the stucco and the ledger assembly.

Outboard edges. The left end of the deck lapped onto and was supported by the patio. We framed the two outboard edges of the deck with 4x12 beams, partly to support the load but also to make sure we had something solid to bolt the rail to. We provided lateral strength by cross-bracing the end of the deck with 4x6 timbers. We installed them in line with the posts and beam because that method is stronger and looks better than lapping the pieces (**Figure 4**, page 356).

Joists and sheathing. Once the perimeter framing was in place, we installed 2x10 pressure-treated Douglas fir joists 16 inches on-center, blocked mid-span and supported by Simpson ZMAX joist hangers. We then sheathed the deck with a double layer of ¾-inch T&G pressure-treated plywood glued and nailed to the framing. The added layer provides the stiffness necessary to prevent natural stone tile from cracking. Had we been using ceramic tile, a single layer over our 16-inch joist spacing would have sufficed.

Ledger Connection Detail

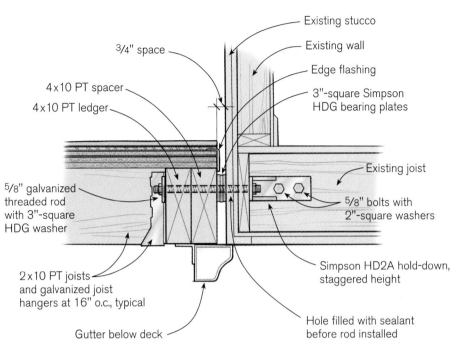

- Existing stucco
- Existing wall
- Edge flashing
- 3"-square Simpson HDG bearing plates
- 3/4" space
- 4x10 PT spacer
- 4x10 PT ledger
- 5/8" galvanized threaded rod with 3"-square HDG washer
- Existing joist
- 5/8" bolts with 2"-square washers
- 2x10 PT joists and galvanized joist hangers at 16" o.c., typical
- Gutter below deck
- Simpson HD2A hold-down, staggered height
- Hole filled with sealant before rod installed

Figure 3. The left end of the ledger beam (bottom left) is bolted to the house with 5/8-inch all-thread that runs between nuts and washers outside and Simpson HD2A hold-downs inside (bottom right). This ties the ledger to the joists instead of to the rim — which, because the joists are cantilevered, is not supported by a sill.

Crack-Isolation Membrane

An important aspect of this project was choosing a method to apply the stone that would reduce the likelihood of cracking caused by deflection or movement of the deck or slab. The proper way to do this is to install the stone (or tile) over a crack-isolation membrane. Also referred to as antifracture or uncoupling membranes, these materials are designed to reduce the amount of stress that can be transferred from the substrate to the finish. (For a list of available crack-isolation membranes, visit the Tile Council of North America Web site at www.tileusa.com.)

Some of these membranes come in liquid form and

are troweled or painted on; others are sheet membranes that are applied to the substrate with thinset mortar. After the membrane is installed, the finish material is applied over it with thinset mortar. Membranes are available for interior or exterior use over a variety of substrates, including plywood, cement board, and concrete. Many can be used to create waterproof installations suitable for use over living areas.

We used Ditra (Schluter Systems, www.schluter.com), a polyethylene sheet membrane with a distinctive grid-like surface. The indentations on the upper surface are undercut (like a dovetail joint) so that mortar will key into them. The underside of the membrane is faced with synthetic fleece, which sticks well to mortar while

Figure 4. The author cross-braced the end of the deck with 4x6 diagonals (left), which he fastened to the corner posts with the same bolts that hold the posts in the column bases (top right). The diagonals butt to a post at midspan and are bolted to it through the same Simpson CC44 column cap that connects the post to the beam above (bottom right).

preventing it from clogging the interconnected channels on the membrane's grid.

If moisture or vapor gets below the membrane it can escape horizontally through these channels. According to the manufacturer, the vertical parts of the grid further isolate the finish material from the substrate below.

Ditra is ⅛ inch thick and comes in rolls 39 inches wide by 45 or 98 feet long. Full rolls cost about $1.55 per square foot, but our supplier will sell partial rolls for an added charge.

Installation guidelines. The installation handbook for Ditra provides detailed guidelines for many different types of installations. The specs for our installation — natural stone tile over wood framing not over living space — required a substrate of two layers of plywood sheathing, a layer of ½-inch exterior-rated cement backerboard, and Ditra that's been sealed at the edges and seams.

We installed backerboard over the sheathing with modified thinset mortar and galvanized roofing nails.

Once this was done, we installed edge flashings,

and the glaziers installed the aluminum base channel for the glass-railing system.

Edge Flashings

There would be a slate-tile riser where the deck landed on the patio, but elsewhere we needed to install flashing to cover the edges of the cement board and sheathing; otherwise they'd remain exposed.

I had a sheet-metal fabricator custom-bend galvanized steel flashings for the outboard edges of the deck. For added protection we coated the flashings with Clearco's high-performance zinc spray (www. clearcoproducts.com), a cold galvanizing spray that produces a film that's 90 percent zinc.

We nailed the top edge of the flashing over the cement board so that the leg hung down and lapped onto the perimeter beam below. The drip-edge provided a clean visual transition between the framing and the base of the rail, and kept water off the edge of the sheathing material.

Edge Detail

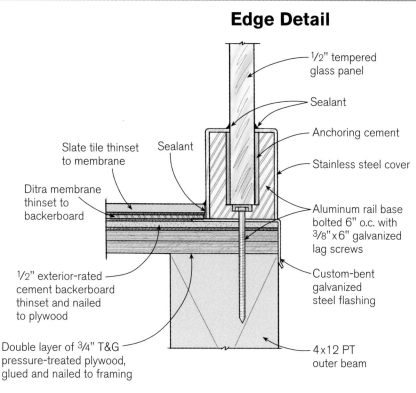

- ½" tempered glass panel
- Sealant
- Anchoring cement
- Stainless steel cover
- Aluminum rail base bolted 6" o.c. with ³/8" x 6" galvanized lag screws
- Custom-bent galvanized steel flashing
- 4 x 12 PT outer beam
- Slate tile thinset to membrane
- Sealant
- Ditra membrane thinset to backerboard
- ½" exterior-rated cement backerboard thinset and nailed to plywood
- Double layer of ¾" T&G pressure-treated plywood, glued and nailed to framing

Figure 5. After the cement board was installed, the glazing contractor bolted the aluminum base shoe (below left) over a galvanized flashing at the edge of the deck (left). Later, when the tile had been set, he cemented ½-inch tempered-glass panels into the channel, then clad the channel with a stainless steel cover (below right).

Glass Railing System

After the flashings were installed, it was time for the glazing sub to install the base shoe for the glass-railing system. There are many glass-railing systems on the market; we chose one made by C.R. Laurence (www.crlaurence.com) because it eliminated the need for posts, which would block the view.

The rail consists of a heavy aluminum base shoe, ½-inch tempered-glass panels that fit into the shoe, and a stainless steel cap railing that fits over the top edge of the panels (**Figure 5**).

Installing the base shoe. Since this rail system was designed to be installed over a steel or concrete floor assembly, we had an engineer tell us how to attach it to a wood beam. His recommendation was to bolt the base 6 inches on-center with ³/8-inch-by-6-inch galvanized lag screws. The base shoe came drilled 12 inches on-center, so we had the glaziers drill more holes. The glaziers shimmed the base level over the metal drip-edge, bolted it down, and then left while we did the tile work on the deck.

Completing the rail. After the tile on the deck was complete, the glaziers came back to install the glass and railing cap.

Figure 6. To accommodate possible movement in the slab, the tile contractor installed an isolation membrane, applying unmodified thinset to the substrate (left) and then pressing the membrane into place with a float (right).

To enhance the view through the panels we purchased glass that had been treated with TekonUS Alpha (www.tekonus.com), a chemical treatment process that reduces water spotting.

The glass panels were placed in the channel, wedged plumb with plastic wedges, and permanently secured with anchoring cement poured into the gap between glass and channel.

We purchased optional stainless steel cover pieces to hide the aluminum shoe. The stainless steel veneer is attached to the shoe with double-sided tape and sealed with silicone glazing sealant. The stainless steel cap rail has a built-in gasket that allows it to be friction-fit onto the edge of the glass.

Installing the Membrane

The tile-setter cut the membrane to length with scissors, applied it fleece-side-down on unmodified thinset mortar, and then pressed it firmly in place with a float (**Figure 6**). Unlike most sheet membranes, which lap at the seams, pieces of Ditra butt edge-to-edge. On the deck, the Ditra lapped onto edge flashings, but since there were no flashings on the slab, the membrane simply stopped at the edge.

Unmodified thinset. Schluter recommends using unmodified thinset under and over Ditra because latex-modified thinset must air-dry for the polymers in it to coalesce and harden.

Modified thinset takes much longer to cure when it's sandwiched between impermeable polyethylene

Figure 7. A seaming tape bedded in thinset prevents leaks at joints in the membrane.

Figure 8. The tile was set in unmodified thinset (top left), then grouted (top right). The completed job adds an outdoor room to the house (left).

and some other nearly impermeable material such as tile; although it will cure eventually, it could take 14 to 60 days, according to the Tile Council. And in the meantime, grouting the installation or allowing it to get rained on would be risky.

With unmodified thinset, the extended drying time is actually a plus, because the retained moisture helps it hydrate and form a stronger bond.

Waterproofing. Though the deck was built with pressure-treated lumber and was not over living space, we still wanted to prevent water from getting below the membrane; if the framing wasn't constantly going through wet/dry cycles, there would be less likelihood of the tile cracking. (Leaks would be an even greater concern in cold climates where water that gets below the membrane could freeze and break the mortar bond.)

To prevent leaks, Schluter recommends sealing the edges and seams of Ditra with unmodified thinset and a layer of its Kerdi-Band seaming tape (**Figure 7**), which is made from the same synthetic material as

the Kerdi membrane used to waterproof pans and walls in showers. The Ditra handbook contains details that allow you to create fully waterproof installations, up to and including ones suitable for use over occupied space. We didn't go that far on this job; we simply sealed the seams.

Installing the Slate

We did this job during our rainy season. To avoid having to vacuum water out of the indentations before he could set tile, the tile-setter installed the membrane and slate a section at a time, tarped his work at night, and grouted it before moving on to another section.

He set the tile with unmodified thinset and used sanded grout in the joints (**Figure 8**), leaving a movement joint of matching silicone sealant every 10 to 12 feet.

Cameron Habel is the owner of Cameron C. Habel Construction, Inc., a remodeling company in Oakland, Calif.

Paving a Deck With Stone

by Robert Viviano

Engineered framing, rubber roofing, and an inch of sand form the foundation for a high-class and low-maintenance surface.

My company builds decks, and every so often a customer wants one with stone or concrete pavers rather than the usual decking materials. A client we recently worked with wanted his deck to match a stone patio below — which he wanted to be dry, with a finished ceiling above to boot.

We made the deck above watertight and framed it stoutly enough to support a covering of the same material that would be used to pave the patio. Laying the pavers was pretty straightforward, but before we were ready to put down the stone there were a lot of details to nail down: the weight of the stone surface, the amount of support it would need, waterproofing, mounting the newel posts, drainage, and so on.

When you lay pavers — whether natural stone or cast concrete — on the ground, you typically install them on a bed of 6 inches of compacted crushed stone that's topped with a 1-inch layer of sand. The sand is used to fine-tune the elevation as the pavers are placed.

Once the pavers are set, you brush polymeric sand between the joints and water it down. It then permanently adheres to the pavers and solidifies within the crevice. Normal sand, on the other hand, washes out, dirt blows in, and then the weeds grow.

On a deck, the approach for installing pavers differs mainly in the base (**Figure 9**). Six inches of crushed stone is out of the question, of course. It's not necessary, and would add tons to the load on the deck.

Only the sand — still a 1-inch layer — is used below the pavers, to allow adjustment for variations in the thickness of the pavers. But even without the crushed stone, the framing, which includes an OSB substrate, must be beefed up to support the weight of the pavers.

Whether on the ground or on a deck, pavers must drain. Most of the water will run off the paver surface, and some will drain through the sand below. Water that gets under them and stays there can freeze and expand, which can crack the masonry.

On grade, you slope the ground and the base to provide drainage. Paved decks must slope as well, and there's an added complexity of protecting the framing from water, for which we use EPDM roofing.

Framing for Paving

Because the dead load for masonry pavers is greater than that for wood or composite decking, the span

Base for Pavers

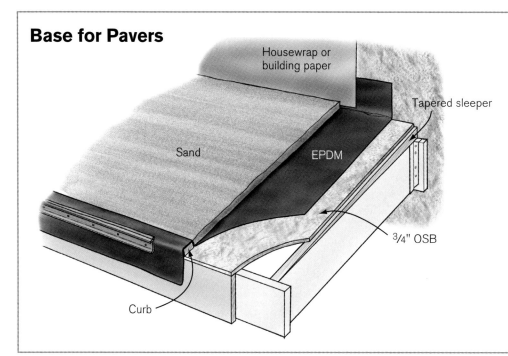

Figure 9. The details that go below the pavers count the most. They begin with a stout frame to support the additional load, followed up with an OSB floor that's topped with an EPDM waterproofing layer. One inch of sand follows to make a bed for the pavers. Tapered sleepers provide a 3/16-inch-in-12-inch pitch for drainage. The EPDM waterproofing runs up the house wall at least 6 inches and is adhered to the wall. The housewrap or building paper serves as counter-flashing.

tables in the IRC are of little use. You have to calculate the actual weight of the materials and engineer the structure and its attachment for that amount (see "Common Material Weight," below).

When designing, I start from the top down, adding in the weight of the stone, sand, framing, and so on. For example, dry sand weighs about 100 pounds per cubic foot, so the 1-inch layer of sand under the pavers adds 8.33 pounds per square foot to the dead load. The combined live and dead loads for a masonry-topped deck can run 100 pounds per sq. ft., which is double the standard load for a deck.

Most of the calculations for this deck were done on my computer using StruCalc (see "Software for Engineering," below right). The footings had to be 30 inches square and 12 inches thick and incorporate rebar. The posts were pressure-treated 6x6s. The rest of the structure was a hybrid of standard deck framing and house framing.

To provide a base for the EPDM roof membrane, we used a ¾-inch tongue-and-groove OSB subfloor over 2x12s placed 8 inches on center. An alternative that would have also satisfied the load calculations would have been to set doubled 2x12s on 16-inch centers.

I went with single joists spaced twice as close, to improve the weight distribution. Also, the tighter spacing halved the span of the OSB, minimizing deflection. I used LVLs engineered by the supplier for the beams supporting the outside of the deck.

Because the deck was going to be watertight, it wasn't necessary to use pressure-treated joists. Further, there was a good reason to use untreated lumber. Treated material can range in width by as much as ⅜-inch, which makes getting a flat deck with a uniform pitch more difficult. Untreated lumber is far more uniform.

Perfect Pitch

For water to drain off the deck, the framing has to pitch away from the house. There were two complications in this design that made it challenging to both pitch the deck surface and have the deck meet the house at a level line all the way around: The deck wrapped around a corner and it terminated against

Common Material Weight

Common brick	120 pcf
Concrete	150 pcf
Granite	168 pcf
Limestone	163 pcf
Red cedar, dry	24 pcf
Sand	100 pcf
Slate	168 pcf
Southern yellow pine, dry	45 pcf

Software for Engineering

I used StruCalc (Cascade Consulting Associates, www.strucalc.com) software to size all the structural members in this deck, except for the LVLs, which were sized by the supplier. The software costs about $500, and is well worth the money. I input the spans and loads for a project, and it prints out the engineering that inspectors in my area require for permits.

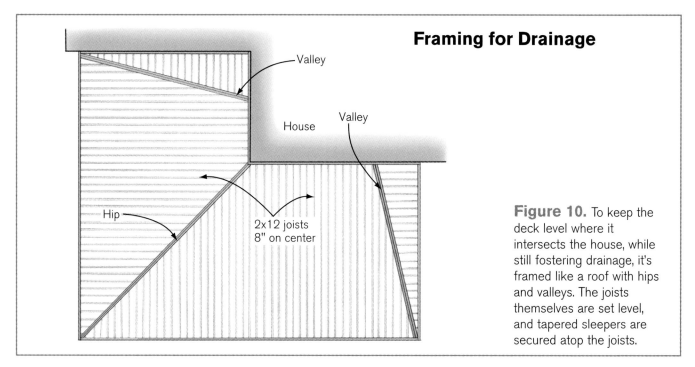

Framing for Drainage

Valley

House

Valley

Hip

2x12 joists
8" on center

Figure 10. To keep the deck level where it intersects the house, while still fostering drainage, it's framed like a roof with hips and valleys. The joists themselves are set level, and tapered sleepers are secured atop the joists.

an ell of the house (**Figure 10**). As a result, it had to be formed like a shallow hip roof at the corner, and like a roof with a valley at the ell.

So I framed the floor as I would a roof — using a beefed-up diagonal "hip joist" at the corner and a similar "valley joist" springing from the corner of the ell. However, sloping the joists themselves would have

complicated the floor framing tremendously. Instead, I ran the joists level and fastened tapered sleepers on top of them to create the pitch. This approach also kept the ceiling below flat, easing its finish work.

To determine the elevation at which the ledger would anchor to the house, I worked down from the bottom of the doorsill and deducted the stone thick-

Drain Port Details

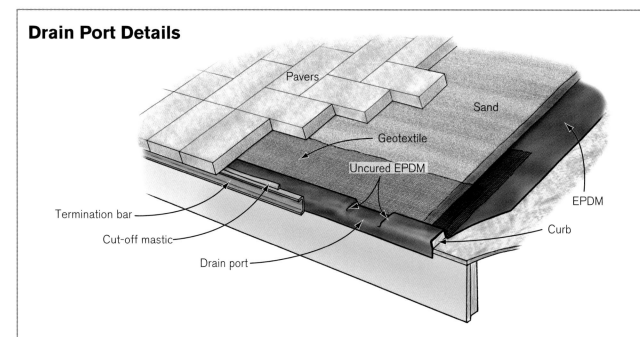

Pavers

Sand

Geotextile

Uncured EPDM

EPDM

Termination bar

Cut-off mastic

Curb

Drain port

Figure 11. One drain port is needed for about every 100 square feet of deck. A drain port is a 4-inch section where the curbing is removed. Uncured EPDM is fitted and glued to the main membrane to waterproof the interruption. Geotextile wraps the sand to hold it in place.

The EPDM termination must be watertight and — because it's visible from below — aesthetically pleasing. A U-shaped termination bar bent from 16-ounce copper is nailed to the curb, capturing the overhanging EPDM. The EPDM is trimmed flush to the bottom of the bar, and a bead of water cut-off mastic seals the top of the bar.

ness, an inch for the sand, ¾ inch for the OSB (the EPDM thickness is negligible), and the height of the sleepers at their thick ends.

To find the sleeper height, I multiplied the pitch of ³⁄₁₆ inch per foot by the length of the joists, 16 feet. That gave me a maximum sleeper height of 3 inches.

The sleepers were cut from 16-foot-long 2x4s, two from each piece. To begin, I picked a straight 2x4 and chalked a diagonal line from end to end, going from 3 inches down to nothing. This first sleeper became the pattern for marking the rest.

If the 2x4 being marked was crowned, I kept the pattern aligned with the crown as I was penciling the cut line. The crown doesn't matter, as the sleeper will lay straight when it's fastened to the top of the joist. I used PL Premium adhesive (www.stickwithpl.com) and Dec-King screws (ITW Buildex, www.itwbuildex. com) to fasten the sleepers to the joists.

I also used PL Premium and Dec-King screws to fasten the ¾-inch OSB to the sleepers. It's important not to leave oversize gaps between the sheets of OSB, and to keep adjoining sheets level with one another. This is the surface that supports the EPDM, and big irregularities can lead to leaks. Once the OSB was installed, I went over the joints with a right-angle grinder and 40-grit paper to make fast work out of smoothing out the edges.

At the outer edge, I created a 1-inch-high-by-1½-inch-wide curb to retain the sand. Since this curb would contain water as well as sand, I made one 4-inch-wide drain port for every 100 square feet of deck (**Figure 11**).

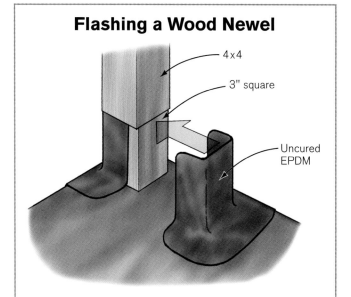

Flashing a Wood Newel

4x4

3" square

Uncured EPDM

Figure 12. Newels can be fairly traditional 4x4s let through the deck and bolted into the framing. For 6 inches above the deck, the 4x4 must be trimmed to 3 inches square so that the uncured EPDM flashing ends up flush with the upper newel's face. A sleeve dropped over the 4x4 finishes off the job.

Roofing the Deck

A good resource is the detailed online installation instructions that manufacturers of EPDM — such as GAF and Firestone — provide. If you are not confident, however, about applying EPDM roof membrane,

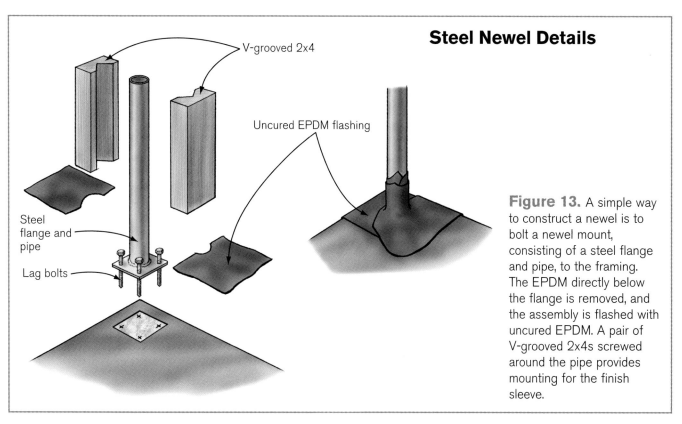

Steel Newel Details

V-grooved 2x4

Uncured EPDM flashing

Steel flange and pipe

Lag bolts

Figure 13. A simple way to construct a newel is to bolt a newel mount, consisting of a steel flange and pipe, to the framing. The EPDM directly below the flange is removed, and the assembly is flashed with uncured EPDM. A pair of V-grooved 2x4s screwed around the pipe provides mounting for the finish sleeve.

Screeding the Sand Layer

Sand

Screed board

1" PVC pipe

Figure 14. Laying a uniform layer of sand requires guides. One-inch PVC pipe laid on the deck works well to guide a screed. Once the sand in that section is leveled, the pipe is removed and the voids filled with more sand.

use a qualified roofer who can guarantee the job will be watertight. The last thing you want is a leak.

Because my company has experience installing EPDM, we placed the membrane ourselves. Without going into full detail, here are some highlights of the process.

EPDM comes in several thicknesses. For added durability, I use 60 mil rather than the lighter (and cheaper) 40 mil. It's always best to install EPDM on a sunny day, as the warmth makes it more flexible and it lays flatter. While the EPDM can be held down with just the weight of the sand and the pavers, I prefer to glue it down with EPDM mastic to prevent any shifting.

Where the EPDM meets the house, I run it up the wall at least 6 inches, adhering it directly to the house sheathing. The housewrap or building paper is then brought down over the EPDM to form the counterflashing. Inside corners are best folded to avoid cutting the EPDM, but outside corners need to be cut.

Seal the cuts with pieces of flexible, uncured EPDM. While uncured EPDM is very stretchy and adheres well with the proper glue, it's not UV stabilized, so be sure it's covered up by other materials. After the patch is on, apply a caulking bead of water cut-off mastic along the edges of the patch.

At the outside perimeter, the EPDM should roll over the curb and hang 6 inches to 8 inches over the fascia. EPDM roofs are normally fitted with an aluminum termination bar, but I don't care for the way it looks.

Instead, I bend one up from 16-ounce copper. This goes on over the EPDM and is nailed through it into the fascia and the framing. The EPDM is trimmed off even with the bottom of the termination bar, and a bead of water cut-off mastic seals the termination

bar to the EPDM, keeping water from running between them.

Newel posts can be constructed in a couple of ways. For one, you can frame pressure-treated 4x4s into the deck (**Figure 12**, previous page). The 4x4 needs to be shaved down to 3 inches square for 6 inches up from the deck to accommodate the flashing and allow it to end flush with the 4x4's face.

The flashing used in this case is uncured EPDM. Sliding a composite newel sleeve or boxed newel over the 4x4 then hides the flashing.

A simpler approach is to use a pre-made "quick-mount" galvanized pipe with flange (**Figure 13**, previous page). Solid framing needs to be installed ahead of time at newel locations. The flanges can be laid on top of the EPDM as a pattern, and the EPDM can be cut and removed. This way, the flange rests directly on the OSB and can be shimmed plumb before it's bolted to the framing.

To flash, you can use uncured EPDM or pre-made EPDM boots used for roof pipe protrusions. The newel sleeve slides over the quick-mount pipes, and manufacturer-supplied donuts fill the void between the pipe and the sleeve. If you need to make your own, just cut a "V" into the flat side of a couple of 2x4s and sandwich the pipe with one on each side.

Don't put the sleeves on until the pavers are installed.

Paving

Before installing the sand, I lay geotextile fabric along the outer perimeter at the drain ports. The geotextile allows drainage while keeping the sand in place. I extend the geotextile about 2 feet on both sides of the drain port and about 2 feet onto the deck, leaving about a foot overhanging the curb. This gets folded back on top of the sand later on.

The inch-high curb acts as one guide for laying out a uniform layer of sand. I snap a chalkline along the house 1 inch up from the EPDM for another guide.

To keep the sand consistent between these points, I lay lengths of 1-inch PVC pipe perpendicular to the wall to guide the screed (**Figure 14**). I use three lengths at a time, which allows me to screed the tops of at least two sections at a time.

I work from the house outward, lifting the pipes out as I finish each section. I just hand trowel some sand into the voids left by the pipes. In the end you should have a 1-inch layer of sand on the whole deck. To avoid uneven compaction, don't walk on the sand.

I usually start paving where the steps are, to make it easier to bring material to the deck. The pavers near the steps shouldn't overhang more than an inch so the stone doesn't flip up when it's stepped on (**Figure 15**).

Working from the step location toward the house, I lay one full paver width around the perimeter to make a border, then fill in the field with stone. The edge stone is glued down to the EPDM curb with a stone construction adhesive. The pavers are set in the sand and tapped home with a rubber mallet.

With irregular natural stone, you may need to scoop out or add in sand to make the surface even. Concrete pavers, on the other hand, are uniform in thickness, so they install much faster than stone.

Whether concrete or stone, pavers are cut using a diamond blade in a circular saw or angle grinder. You can also rent a special table saw. If you've never done this before, you should allow time for the learning curve. To finish the job, polymeric sand is swept into the joints, and wet down per the instructions on the bag.

At this point, all that's left is to install the railing. The process isn't much different from what you'd do on any other deck. If you are using base skirting at the bottom of the newel sleeves, keep the sleeves

Figure 15. Pavers should be glued to the curbing, and overhang the steps by only an inch to prevent them from being overturned.

about ¼ inch above the pavers to avoid wicking, and let the base skirt meet the pavers.

The value of this system is not only in the pavers' low maintenance and longevity, but also in the all-in-one roof system you just built for the patio below. To finish off the area below such decks, we normally install beadboard ceiling and wrap the beams with moldings.

Robert Viviano owns Deck the Yards, in Pittsburgh, Pa.

Dry-Laying a Flagstone Terrace

by Bruce Zaretsky

There's nothing wrong with brick or concrete pavers; my landscaping company uses them for walkways and patios every year. But most of our clients prefer natural stone. Several types are available in our area of upstate New York; my own favorite — by far — is bluestone.

A type of sandstone, bluestone is a sedimentary rock that naturally splits into sheets when quarried. Its color comes from the sand from which it was formed, so it exists in a range of colors besides "blue blue" (which is as uniform in hue as a natural material can possibly be), including greens, browns, burgundies, and rusts.

We generally use stone quarried in eastern Pennsylvania and southern New York, which gives our projects a regionally appropriate look and keeps shipping costs down. The patio in this article was built using irregular cleft flagstones, which are commonly referred to as "standup" because the large stones are shipped standing on edge on the pallet (**Figure 16**). Costs for flagstones start at about $3 per square foot.

Bluestone can also be cut into uniform square and rectangular pavers suitable for more formal designs and public-oriented walkways and patios. Prices for natural cleft bluestone pavers — which are split to form pieces 1 inch to 3 inches thick — start at about $5 per square foot. Prices for thermal bluestone pavers — which undergo a special heating process that imparts a rough surface and uniform appearance — run between $7 and $9 per square foot.

Paver sizes start at 12 by 12 inches and typically increase in 6-inch increments (expect to pay more per square foot for sizes exceeding 24 by 36 inches). Bluestone stair treads — ranging in thickness from 2 to 6 inches and in depth from 12 inches to over 2 feet — are also available.

In many parts of the country, stones can be mortared to a well-drained concrete slab. But here in the Northeast, where we have cold winters with significant frost action, we prefer to dry-lay the stones on a bedding course of concrete sand (an inexpensive washed sand that in coarseness falls between fine-grained mason sand and coarse-grained block sand) over a solid base of stone (**Figure 17**). In addition to being less expensive than mortaring, this technique results in paving that's easier to maintain: Dry-laid stones can be removed and reset with minimal problems and will look as good as new afterward.

Site Work and Layout

Before installing a walkway or patio, we make sure the area we're paving hasn't had more than 8 inches of fill added to it. Settling is often a problem with

For a smooth surface, cut the stones to fit and float them into place.

newly constructed homes; in some cases we've found almost 8 feet of fill within 3 or 4 feet of the house.

We can settle most soils sufficiently with soaker hoses, a process that typically takes two to three weeks. Since it invariably wets the basement walls, we always check with our client first; if the basement is finished, we avoid this approach altogether.

Another option is to delay the start of construction and return the following spring after a winter's worth of freezing and thawing has settled the site. If our client doesn't want to wait, we excavate loose fill down to undisturbed soil, then bring the grade back up with crushed stone tamped in 6-inch lifts (**Figure 18**, page 368).

Once the soil's been stabilized, we lay the proposed design out on the ground with spray paint, then set up a series of stakes at strategic points. We shoot elevations with a transit and mark the finished height of the paving on the stakes, being sure to pitch the paving slightly for drainage. In general, we slope patios or walkways about 2 inches every 8 feet (approximately a 2% grade) to keep water from collecting on the surface and to direct it away from the house foundation.

Figure 16. Less expensive than geometrically cut stone pavers, randomly sized and shaped flagstones are shipped to the job site standing up on pallets.

Next, with the strings as our guide, we excavate 8 inches (or more, depending on the soil issues described earlier) below our finish grade. We extend this excavation at least 6 inches beyond the layout on all sides to keep the edges from sloughing off. Then we tamp the excavated area with a walk-behind plate compactor.

If the site is wet — or if the soil is sandy or contains a lot of clay — we place landscape fabric over the excavated area; this helps keep the subsequent layer of base stone from mixing in with the subsoil. (Contrary to a common misconception, landscape fabric does not prevent weed growth between the pavers or stones.) Then we install the base stone to a depth of about 5 or 6 inches.

Here in western New York state, we use crusher run, a mix of crushed stone and stone dust. It comes in various sizes; for most pedestrian applications like walks and patios we use a #1 crusher run, which consists of roughly 1-inch stone mixed with dust.

Proper compaction of the base stone is critical, but most walk-behind plate compactors effectively tamp only about 3 inches of stone at a time. So we install the base stone in 3-inch lifts, with careful tamping in

Dry-Laid Flagstone Patio

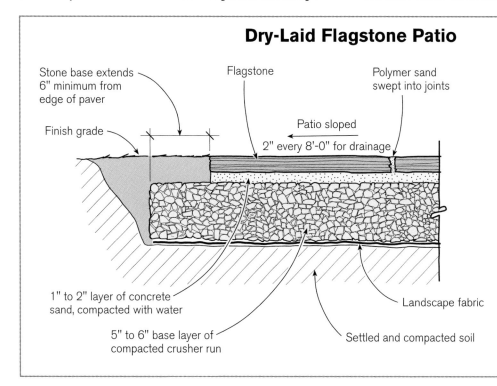

Stone base extends 6" minimum from edge of paver

Flagstone

Polymer sand swept into joints

Finish grade

Patio sloped
2" every 8'-0" for drainage

1" to 2" layer of concrete sand, compacted with water

5" to 6" base layer of compacted crusher run

Settled and compacted soil

Landscape fabric

Figure 17. Compacting the excavated area before installing the landscape fabric and stone base helps prevent uneven settling. Loose fill should be either removed and replaced with compacted crushed stone, or completely settled with soaker hoses.

Figure 18. To prepare the site and prevent settling, the author stabilizes any loose fill, excavates about 8 inches below finish grade, and then builds up a compacted, well-drained stone base (above). This patio design, which will feature a low retaining-wall border, is laid out on the stone base with spray paint (left).

between. Since our goal is 100% compaction, we run the tamper until it starts to hop. (A tamper runs fairly smoothly over uncompacted stone but begins to skim over the top with a bit of hopping as the stone approaches proper compaction.) Spraying the base stone with water keeps dust down and helps in compacting it.

Once compaction is complete, we install a 1-inch to 2-inch layer of concrete sand. We level it with a rake, using our string lines and laser levels to estimate how much is necessary to make our grades work. Because it will be flooded with water when we lay the stone, we plan on 100% compaction of this layer, too (2 inches of sand will compact down to about 1 inch when flooded with water).

Installing the Stone

My crew follows two nonnegotiable rules when installing geometric stone pavers: no lines or seams

longer than 6 feet, and no four corners together (unless it's part of the design). Otherwise, installation is simply a matter of choosing each stone to fit next to the previous one, and keeping our lines as straight as possible. With straight geometric patterns, waste is minimal. When the design has curves, I add about 10% to 15% to my square-footage estimate to allow for waste when cutting.

There are two methods of fitting flagstones together. The first, which gives the installation a more informal feel, is to find stones that have similar sides and match them up like a large jigsaw puzzle. We use this approach more often with pathways than with patios. Since all the stones are laid out and fit together before the final setting, there's virtually no waste. Sometimes we use a brick hammer to break stones into smaller, more fit-friendly pieces, or to dress up edges that don't quite fit.

We use the second method — which leaves very

Figure 19. In some projects uncut flagstones are fit together loosely like a jigsaw puzzle; in this one, the stones are cut to fit, so that joints are tighter (left). With one stone overlapping another, the author's crew cuts through both stones at once (top right), then finishes up by cleaning up the cut on the lower stone (above right).

small seams, making the paved area safer to walk on — when we're installing flagstone as a patio or more formal walkway. It entails setting one stone down and then either cutting another to fit next to it or overlapping the first stone with the second and making a cut through both (**Figure 19**). For cutting we use a Stihl gas cutoff saw equipped with a 12-inch

diamond blade. Then, to keep the Old World look of hand-cut stones, we lightly chip the edges of all stones with a brick hammer; when we're done, they appear to have been cut by hand (**Figure 20**).

This more painstaking method adds significant time (and therefore cost) to the project; also, we have to figure about 15% waste when estimating stone coverage.

Figure 20. Because cut edges can look too symmetrical and matched (left), the author's crew chips them with brick hammers to give them a more natural look (right).

Figure 21. After the flagstones have been cut and fit together (left), the author's crew floods the concrete sand base underneath with water until it achieves a quicksand-like consistency (center). Then the flagstones are set in place; a crew member wiggles each one and pushes wet sand out from between the joints to seat it fully (right).

Floating stone. The next step after fitting the stones is setting them. Over the years, I've seen people set large paving stones by banging them with dead-blow hammers and rubber mallets (bad for the stone), or by jumping up and down on them and stomping them into place (bad for the knees). But we've found that the best way to install large flagstones and pavers is to flood them into place (**Figure 21**).

Once the stones are in position, we literally flood the sand underneath with water, which accomplishes two things: First, it settles the sand completely, leaving no voids; since the sand takes the shape of the bottom of the stones, there are no hollow spots despite the irregular surfaces. Second, it creates a quicksand-like mixture that the stones hydroplane on, so one person can easily float even large heavy ones into place. As we float the stones, we wiggle them down to the proper height and pitch.

Another benefit of flooding is that we can go back and refloat stones to fine-tune the installation so

Figure 22. Once the stones are seated and the patio surface is level (left), polymer sand is swept into the joints, which locks the stones in place and minimizes weed growth (right).

there aren't any high or low spots.

To finish up, we sweep in polymeric sand, which sets up like a flexible mortar when wet. It helps keep weed growth to a minimum but doesn't get in the way if we need to remove and replace stones later (**Figure 22**).

Costs for our stone patios vary greatly, depending on such factors as access to the working area, distance from our shop, type of material chosen, and details of the installation itself, like inlays and the amount of cutting. While we never price projects by the square foot (all our work is priced by time and materials), most end up in the range of $13 to $25 per square foot installed (in 2007 dollars).

Bruce Zaretsky owns Zaretsky & Associates, a design/build landscaping firm based in Rochester, N.Y.

Brick-Paver Basics

by Brian E. Trimble

Brick paving can be installed two ways: as rigid paving or as flexible paving.

Rigid paving is commonly identified by its mortared joints. A properly designed rigid paving system consists of a well-compacted subgrade, a properly prepared base, a reinforced concrete slab, a mortar setting bed, and brick paving with mortar joints between the pavers (**Figure 23**, next page). A rigid system is often used where soil conditions are poor, where spaces between pavers are unacceptable, or where the look of mortared brick paving is desirable. Whenever mortar is used between the brick, a rigid concrete slab must be used to support the paving.

Flexible paving has a greater variety of design options. A flexible system consists of a well-compacted subgrade beneath a layer of crushed stone, a sand setting bed, and fine sand between the pavers (**Figure 24**, next page). Flexible systems can be used in applications ranging from a light-duty brick patio to a heavily traveled city street. Differing applications, however, may require different designs.

A flexible system has some advantages over a rigid system. First, a flexible system requires fewer materials and less skilled workmanship. It does not require a concrete slab or the mortar of a rigid system. The simplicity of the flexible system is reflected in its only real requirements: a base of the proper depth and a setting bed of the proper sand.

A homeowner concerned about maintenance costs might also like flexible more than mortared. His only real cost will be keeping weeds out of the sand between bricks. Most people simply apply chemicals. Mortar, on the other hand, may need periodic maintenance and, eventually, replacement long before the brick itself.

Masonry Details

Whichever system is used, decisions must be made regarding materials, design, installation, and detailing.

For most light-duty applications, a mortarless system can provide good looks and years of service.

All brick paving units should conform to ASTM C 902, Standard for Pedestrian and Light Traffic Paving Brick. For most exterior applications, a brick unit meeting or exceeding the requirements of Class SX should be used. The requirements include a minimum compressive strength of 8,000 psi, a maximum cold water absorption of 8%, and a maximum saturation coefficient of 0.78.

If you use mortar, it should be Type M, conforming to ASTM C 270. Portland cement-lime mortars provide greater durability than other cement types. Mix a Type M mortar in these proportions:
- one part Portland cement
- $1/4$ part hydrated lime (optional)
- three parts masonry sand.

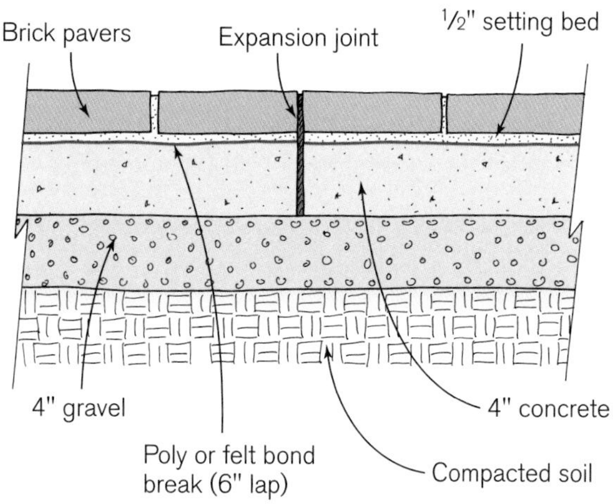

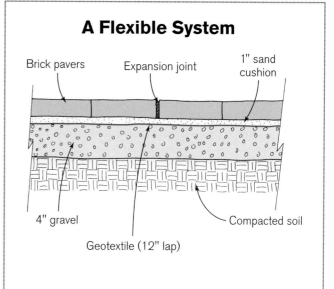

A Rigid System

Brick pavers Expansion joint ½" setting bed

4" gravel

Poly or felt bond break (6" lap)

4" concrete

Compacted soil

Figure 23. Mortared pavers lay on top of ½ inch of wet mortar, supported by 4 inches of concrete and 4 inches of gravel. Sometimes a bond break (a sheet of poly or felt) is used between the concrete and mortar bed to allow separate movement of the layers. Otherwise, expansion joints in the paver level need to align with the expansion joint in the concrete.

A Flexible System

Brick pavers Expansion joint 1" sand cushion

4" gravel

Geotextile (12" lap)

Compacted soil

Figure 24. A flexible system uses no mortar; only sand lies between pavers. Bricks rest atop a ½- to 1-inch layer of sand. To prevent the sand from filtering down into the gravel base, a geotextile is laid on top of the 4 inches of gravel. The earth should be well compacted. Expansion joints extend only to the depth of the brick.

The mortar ingredients should be mixed and laid by traditional bricklaying methods — setting the bricks in a bed of mortar and buttering the bottom and two sides. This assures proper bonding to all surfaces and retards water penetration to the base.

Building a Pavement That Lasts

When designing your brick paving job, consider the following to ensure a system that stands up under conditions at the site:

Proper base, thickness. The type of traffic you expect should determine which system to use. A driveway may require the use of a rigid base, whereas a patio can be laid on a flexible base. In a public area, although a flexible base would support pedestrian traffic, a rigid concrete slab may be necessary to allow for mortared joints, which are less of a hazard to women's heels.

The thickness of the brick depends on the type of traffic and the paving system. A rigid system may use thinner pavers, since the concrete slab resists the loads. A flexible system generally requires deeper pavers. A patio with typical light loads, however, may require only 1½-inch-deep pavers on a flexible base, while a driveway usually requires 2¼-inch pavers on either base.

Drainage. A main reason for failure in paving systems is inadequate drainage. You must design a pavement that eliminates standing water on or under the surface. Standing water that saturates the brick pav-

ing can lead to failures such as cracking or spalling during freezing.

Paving should be sloped at least ⅛ inch to ¼ inch per foot to allow proper drainage. Brick paving, even for relatively narrow walks, should slope away from the house or other structure.

A solid membrane can be placed below the brick pavers to aid in drainage. This stops grass and weed growth as well. In a rigid system, 15 pound felt will suffice, lapped 6 inches at the seams. In flexible systems, a goetextile, lapped 12 inches at seams is better. In a driveway, where cars will deliver much more weight to the surface, a heavy-duty geotextile mat is typically used.

Drainage tile is not necessarily used in all applications. Two cases do call for it: Poorly draining soils, such as clay, and large expanses of pavement, as in large patios or commercial plazas. Where tile is installed, gravel may have to extend to a depth of 8 inches. The tile should drain well away from basements and foundations.

Edge restraints. You must use a rigid edge restraint to prevent creep — the horizontal movement of pavers. Different edgings create different looks, and labor and material cost will vary as well. Edging may be a concrete curb, brick soldiers set in sand or mortar (edge-to-edge, with flat side against the edge of pavers), pressure-treated lumber supported by reinforcing rods, or rigid steel or plastic edging. Edging that requires less specialized labor or equipment —

flexible edging, timbers, or brick soldiers — generally costs less than poured concrete curbing.

All curbs or edging that could prevent drainage of surface water must be weeped 16 inches on-center (**Figure 25**, page 374). Concrete curbs should go below the frost line. Brick soldiers standing on end, however, do not have to go that deep. Edge bricks are more stable the deeper they go; therefore, set the top edge even with the paver surface so that the soldiers go deeper.

Steel and plastic edgings, which can bend to change direction, have foot-long stakes to resist shifting.

Expansion joints. Brick paving will expand due to temperature changes. Include expansion joints every 20 feet for rigid paving and every 30 feet for flexible paving. Also include them where different materials meet, where bonds change, and at walls and pillars. At the bottom of each expansion joint, use a flexible filler, such as cork or foam padding. A backer rod, which is a 3/8-inch-diameter polyethylene rope, goes

---

Paving the Way

by Gary Mayk

Bricks are typically rectangular measuring $4 \times 2^{1}/_{4} \times 8$ inches. Thinner light-duty, pedestrian-only bricks can be just $1^{1}/_{2}$ inches thick. Six-inch-square brick pavers and hexagons of 6, 8, and 12 inches also are available. Radiused bricks can be used to add variety to patterns in large paved areas – driveways and courtyards. Special shapes include ogees and bullnosed pavers for mortared stairways.

Bricks come in sizes that allow for mortared joints, such as $3^{3}/_{4} \times 7^{1}/_{2}$ inches. Patterns to be laid without mortar, such as basketweave, herringbone, and running/stack bond combinations, require bricks exactly twice as long as they are wide. Other patterns can be laid without mortar using nominal size bricks.

Concrete pavers vary in shapes and surface area but also are sized, for the most part, for laying with one hand. Light-duty concrete pavers, suitable for walks and driveways, are $2^{3}/_{8}$ inches thick. Many of the designs, since they are not rectangular, are interlocking, and some are chamfered at the edges or grooved to resemble more than one block when laid. In general, consider these factors in a design:

Pattern. This can be achieved either by arranging the bricks in a pattern or by using concrete pavers that create a pattern due to their shape. Patterns that require brick cutting will be more time-consuming. Some concrete designs offer smaller-sized end units to eliminate the need for cutting. Herringbone and running bond are less susceptible to horizontal movement.

Texture. Pavers can be as smooth as tile–often placed in entryways or around pools – or coarse for better footing.

Grade. Mortarless systems can be applied on grade. Mortared blocks or some other transition such as wood may be required between grades.

Drainage. Proper slope must be maintained, always away from buildings. Poorly draining subgrades, such as clay, and large paved areas, such as patios or a commercial plaza, may require drainage tile along the lower edge of the drained pavement.

Climate. Freeze-thaw cycles may require extra precautions against standing water, and proper footings for mortared systems.

Coordination with the home. Pavers and their borders should complement exterior and interior materials, in color, function, and formality.

Gary Mayk is a former associate editor of *The Journal of Light Construction*.

Common Brick Patterns

| Running Bond | Basket Weave | Herringbone | Herringbone | Open Herringbone |

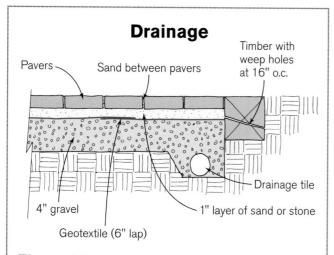

Drainage

Pavers

Sand between pavers

Timber with weep holes at 16" o.c.

Drainage tile

4" gravel

1" layer of sand or stone

Geotextile (6" lap)

Figure 25. Weep holes 16 inches on-center help drain water that may be trapped by timber or concrete edging. Drain tile can be installed along the lower edge of sloped pavement to help carry water away from large paved areas or from walks laid on top of poorly draining soils. The tile requires deepening the gravel base by about 3 inches.

next and is sandwiched in place with a top layer of urethane caulk.

Slip resistance. The coarser the texture, the better the traction. A wire-cut surface is more slip-resistant than a die-skin surface. On wire-cut brick, the surface is broken by a tiny arc-like pattern. On die-skin brick, the surface will more closely resemble indoor ceramic tile.

Installation

Shortcuts in laying brick will only shorten the life of the installation, and this is true even for aspects of the job you'll never see once the pavers are in.

Soil should be uniformly compacted to produce a stable layer. Uncompacted soil can result in differential settlement that telegraphs to the paver surface.

For More Information

For more information, contact the Brick Institute of America (www.bia.org). See Tech Notes 14 and 14a for more details on brick paver installation.

Soil can be adequately compacted with a plate compacter for larger jobs or a hand tamper for smaller jobs. For occasional jobs where a subcontractor is not used, you can rent a plate compacter.

The gravel or crushed stone base and the sand setting bed should also be compacted and should be free of salts or alkaline material. You don't want unwashed sand from near a beach area, which is likely to contain salts. Their presence will lead to efflorescence, a white discoloration that probably will last about a year. Using salt-free sand will save you from a certain callback later from a homeowner upset about the white deposit on his walkway.

You can assure the owner that efflorescence is temporary. (It is permanent only if you failed to allow for proper drainage.) Dry-brush it off and rinse it away. You may want to warn the owner before work begins that efflorescence is possible and of no great concern.

To install mortared brick, lay wet mortar on the crushed stone for use as a setting bed. A bond break between the mortar and stone is recommended, particularly where temperature swings will be great. Butter the pavers with mortar on the bottom and two sides and push them into place. This ensures that you'll fill all joints.

Not as durable, but quicker, is a dry cement/sand mixture between the bricks. You will still need a wet-mortar setting bed. But the mortar that is applied between cracks is swept in dry and then soaked with a spray for at least two hours (up to four hours in hot weather). Before dry-mortaring, you must coat the top surface of the pavers with a wax, just as you would coat unglazed ceramic tile with grout release. The wax allows you to clean excess mortar off the bricks after curing. Failure to use the wax allows mortar into pores in the brick, where it will harden and remain.

If you use this method, mix one part cement to three parts sand — not one part cement to six parts sand. But even the stronger mixture will not hold up as well as wet-mortared joints.

Flexible brick paving is installed with sand only — not a sand-cement mix — between the joints. Pavers should be spaced $1/16$ to $1/8$ inch to prohibit the pavers from bumping together and chipping the edges.

Brian Trimble is a staff engineer in the engineering and research department of the Brick Institute of America in Reston, Va.

Exposed Aggregate Concrete

by Ron Sansone

Concrete is a durable and cost-effective material for walkways, patios, and drives. While plain concrete is not particularly attractive, there are many ways to improve its looks: You can color it with pigment, texture it to look like something else, or cover it with brick or stone. One of the oldest — and best — methods for creating visually appealing concrete surfaces is to expose the aggregate.

Aggregate is present in every concrete slab, but because it's encased in a matrix of sand and cement it's not usually visible. Removing the top layer of sand and cement to expose some of the aggregate makes the surface of the concrete look a lot better, and the process is not much more expensive than plain gray flatwork (**Figure 26**).

An aggregate finish is good for walks, driveways, and stairs because it is skid-resistant and wears well. And as long as the original aggregate is still available, the surface is easier to repair or add on to than stamped or integrally colored concrete.

My company specializes in patios that are a combination of exposed aggregate concrete, brick, and stone. The masonry is set flush to the surface of the slab and forms decorative borders and bands. This is less expensive than building the entire patio from brick or stone and it creates more visual interest.

It's difficult to produce this kind of work if you have to bring in separate subs to do it. Most of the people on my crew started out as landscapers but have been trained to do masonry and concrete, which

An aggregate finish and inset masonry can dress up a humble concrete slab.

makes it easier to coordinate the work because we can do it with a single crew. Most of our jobs are in existing neighborhoods, so it helps that we can do enough landscaping to repair the yard at the end of a job.

Aggregate

The size and type of aggregate determines the look and color of the finished slab (**Figure 27**, next page). It's expensive to transport heavy material, so aggregate is usually made from locally available stone. We're located in the St. Louis area; our concrete supplier carries a few types of local stone that look good and are hard enough to be exposed. We can get a white or a slightly darker glacial rock from Illinois or we can get a brown shiny gravel that comes from the Meramec River. Different types of aggregate are available in other parts of the country.

Our local stone is cheap enough to use throughout the mix, so it's spread through the entire slab. If you expose the aggregate, this is the stone you will see. But it's also possible to throw a thin layer of aggregate onto the freshly placed concrete and float it into the surface. This is called seeding and it's the method we used when I was first starting out. Seeding allows

Figure 26. The same aggregate that is visible on top is dispersed throughout this slab. Some of it even shows through on the sides.

Figure 27. The author makes samples containing different types of aggregate for potential customers.

you to use inexpensive aggregate in the mix and put the exotic aggregate on top where it will show.

These days, no one seeds unless they're using an expensive decorative aggregate. We avoid seeding because it's hard to put the stone on evenly, it adds another step to the process, and it requires extra labor. If you can buy a reasonably priced aggregate, it's simpler and less expensive to put it in the mix.

Size. Some contractors like to use normal size (3/4-inch to 11/2-inch) stone when doing an exposed aggregate finish. I don't like doing this because if the concrete is a little too wet, you can end up with areas where there is visibly more cement than aggregate. This can happen anytime you place concrete, but it's

noticeable with an aggregate finish.

We prefer to use a smaller size stone. Our local brown river stone is available as regular size aggregate or as a smaller size called Meramec torpedo. They're the same type of stone but the torpedo has been passed through a finer screen. It's small and very consistent in size, so it produces a smooth, uniform surface.

The mix. Concrete contains water, portland cement, graded aggregate, and sand. Technically, the sand is just a finer type of aggregate. The cement, water, and sand form a paste that fills voids and binds the aggregate together. Around here, most contractors use a four- to five-sack mix (four to five 90-pound bags of cement per yard of concrete) for residential flatwork. When we do an aggregate finish, we use a six- to six-and-a-half–sack mix and a little less sand. Reducing the sand makes the pebbles stand out more on the surface, while the extra cement makes for a stronger slab.

Placing the Slab

Prepping for an exposed aggregate slab is the same as prepping for any kind of concrete. Depending on the grade, drainage, and soil conditions, we may or may not put a layer of stone under the slab. In some cases, the stone will be an added expense that does nothing to increase the quality of the job. But most of the time it's necessary to used crushed limestone to level the grade.

Formwork. Most of the patios we build have curved outer edges. We form them with 1/4-inch tempered Masonite because it's easy to bend (**Figure 28**). For straight edges, we use 1x4s. We hold the forms in

Figure 28. This walk was formed with 1/4-inch Masonite. The cedar cross members function as expansion joints but will also be left in place as a decorative element.

Figure 29. Inset masonry creates visual interest by breaking up what would otherwise be a monotonous expanse of a single material.

position by nailing them to wooden stakes. The top edge of the form functions as a screed strip, so we set its elevation with an optical level.

We used to rip our own Masonite and cut stakes from 1-by lumber, but we found it was less expensive to pay a supplier to do it. The stakes come 3,000 to a pallet and the strips of Masonite are 2⅞ inches wide. We settled on a single width because it's less complicated than keeping various sizes around. There's no chance of running out of a certain size or having someone bring the wrong size to the job. The stakes and the Masonite are cheap enough to throw away after a single use.

Most of our patios are bordered and inlayed with brick or limestone bands (**Figure 29**). Parts of the slab must be lowered to accommodate the inset material, and the 2⅞-inch strips are a good height for forming the drops (**Figure 30**). Brick is about 2⅝ inches thick, so a 2⅞-inch drop leaves room for a ¼-inch bed of mortar. The limestone is around 2¼ inches thick, so it gets a thicker bed. If the edge needs to be thicker, we either double up the hardboard Masonite strips or allow some of the concrete to ooze beneath the bottom edge. The rough edge won't be visible, because it gets buried when the yard is landscaped.

Reinforcing. Slabs are typically reinforced with 6-by-6-inch wire mesh; in some cases we will add #4 rebar. If the grade falls off badly, we dig holes for piers and cast a hidden grade beam to retain the fill below the slab. Narrow walkways don't need reinforcing.

Control joints. Unless the slab is very small, it should have control or expansion joints to prevent it from cracking. Some contractors will pour areas up to 15 feet square without using control joints. We don't like to go bigger than 10 feet square without a joint.

We avoid slabs smaller than 5 feet square because they're more likely to shift.

There are many ways to create expansion joints. Sometimes we'll break up an area by casting 1x4 cedar boards into the slab (**Figure 31**, next page). The cedar is set flush to the top of the forms, held in position with nails. It gets used as a screed strip when the concrete is placed and becomes a part of the design when the slab is finished.

Control joints can also be made by kerfing the slab when it's partially cured or by pouring the concrete around a plastic or compressed fiber joint. The plastic is not very attractive, but it's a good choice around pools because it can stand up to the constant

Figure 30. The edge of this slab was formed to accept a brick head course. There was too much concrete to pour and finish in a single day, so the crew stopped at a joint.

Figure 31. These cedar control joints divide the slab into sections that can be poured one at a time.

Figure 32. When the concrete can't be poured from the truck, it's transported in wheelbarrows and placed a section at a time.

wetting. Fiberboard, on the other hand, is ugly and rots a lot faster than wood. It's typically used for commercial work and is covered by caulking the joint.

Cedar looks the best and holds up well as long as it remains tightly wedged in place. I've seen strips that look fine after 20 years, but if the concrete shifts, the cedar can rot out in four or five years. At that point, a repair can be made by inserting a new strip, shimming it tight to one side, and filling the remaining space with cement grout.

Placing the Concrete

For maximum strength, the concrete should be as stiff as possible when it's poured. We prefer about a 4-inch slump; any stiffer and it's hard to spread. There's a limit to how much concrete you can place and finish before it starts to set. If the slab requires more than 8 or 10 yards of material, we'll pour on successive days. The cedar expansion joints provide natural stopping points when there's a need to break up the pour. The dropped areas also function as control joints and are another convenient stopping point.

Figure 33. The expansion joints are flush to the forms, so the author's crew can level the concrete by screeding across them with a strike-off board.

Figure 34. A bull float removes any unevenness produced by striking off the concrete.

Figure 35. The author uses magnesium hand floats to do the final surfacing of the concrete. This is the last thing done before the retarder is sprayed onto the slab.

Figure 36. The aggregate is exposed by washing away the top layer of cement. While most of this slab is already hard, the top layer is fresh because it was sprayed with a retarder.

We either pour directly from the truck or transport the concrete in wheelbarrows (**Figure 32**). Pumping is not usually an option, because most of our work is in existing neighborhoods and there is nowhere to dump the excess material that is left in the hoses.

The size of the pour depends on the weather: We do bigger pours in cooler weather, smaller ones when it's hot. We also take into account the weather from previous days, because it can affect the temperature of the ground and of the stored material that goes into the concrete. We can offset the impact of the temperature by putting accelerant or retarder in the mix. Neither of these additives will affect the way the aggregate finish looks.

Once the concrete is placed, we spread it with a rake and screed it level to the top of the forms (**Figure 33**). The surface will be generally flat, but we flatten it even more by bull floating from multiple directions (**Figure 34**). If we time everything properly, the concrete will begin to set shortly after it's bull floated.

The concrete is ready to finish when the bleed water has evaporated and the surface is hard enough that you can barely push your finger into it. We use a hand-held magnesium float to flatten the slab further and fill any holes in the surface (**Figure 35**). Some guys will go over the surface yet again with a steel trowel. This makes for a smoother surface on many types of concrete but it will not produce a noticeably better finish when the aggregate is exposed. We usually float the surface and leave it at that.

Exposing the Aggregate

The aggregate is exposed by removing between $1/16$ and $1/8$ inch of cement from the surface. The tops of the uppermost stones will be visible, but will remain firmly encased within the slab.

During my early years in the trade, we washed the surface with water and used brooms to scrub away the top layer of cement. This method requires careful timing. If you start too soon, it dislodges the aggregate; if you wait too long, it takes a wire brush to get the cement off.

Nowadays, finishers use a chemical retarder to slow down the rate of setting at the surface of the slab. The product we use is mixed with water and sprayed onto the freshly floated surface with a pump-up garden sprayer. Oil-based products are also available. The retarder has some color to it so you can tell if you've missed any spots, but it will not stain the concrete.

Most retarders hold the set for up to 24 hours. Many manufacturers recommend covering the surface with plastic and waiting several hours or even overnight before washing the slab. However, there is some risk to covering the slab and washing the surface the following day. If the weather is hot, the retarder might not hold the set until you get back. At that point, it may still be possible to expose the aggregate, but it will take a lot more brushing. If the plastic should blow off, the surface may dry so much that it's hard to expose the aggregate.

We prefer to wash the slab as soon as it's firm enough to stand on. In warm weather, it will be ready an hour or two after floating. All it takes to

Figure 37. The author's crew cuts stone to form an inset medallion in an aggregate finish driveway (left). A brick head course set into a patio waits to be grouted (right).

Figure 38. Here, crew members have grouted the masonry joints. They will finish them by screeding flush to the brick and sponge-cleaning the area with water.

remove the cement is a good stream of water and some light sweeping with a broom (**Figure 36**, previous page). Once the excess cement has been removed, the concrete should be allowed to cure in the normal way.

Insetting Masonry Bands

A day or two after the slab is poured, the crew comes back to install the decorative bands (**Figure 37**). Many contractors set the masonry with Type N mortar; we use Type S mortar because it forms a stronger bond.

Masons who are accustomed to building walls may be tempted to fill joints with the same mortar that's in the setting bed and strike them off with a tool. We prefer to use cement mortar and treat the joints as if they were the grout lines in a tile floor. Standard

mortar contains portland cement, sand, water, and hydrated lime. Lime makes mortar easier to work with, but it also reduces its durability. Cement mortar contains no lime, so it's more akin to concrete.

The cement mortar is mixed wet enough that it can almost be poured into the joints. After it starts to set, we scrape and sponge away the excess material (**Figure 38**). This type of joint will last much longer than a tooled joint because it's flush to the surface and won't collect water. I've seen horizontal surfaces grouted this way that are still in good shape more than 30 years later.

Ron Sansone is a second-generation concrete contractor with more than 40 years in the trade. He owns Ron Sansone Construction in Pacific, Mo.